The Eastern Front

Also by Nick Lloyd

The Western Front: A History of the Great War, 1914–1918

Passchendaele: The Lost Victory of World War I

Hundred Days: The Campaign That Ended World War I

The Amritsar Massacre: The Untold Story of One Fateful Day

Loos 1915

The Eastern Front

A History of the Great War, 1914–1918

NICK LLOYD

W. W. NORTON & COMPANY

Independent Publishers Since 1923

For information about permission to reproduce selections from this book,
write to Permissions, W. W. Norton & Company, Inc.,
500 Fifth Avenue, New York, NY 10110

For information about special discounts for bulk purchases, please contact
W. W. Norton Special Sales at specialsales@wwnorton.com or 800-233-4830

Manufacturing by Lakeside Book Company

ISBN 978-1-324-09271-1

W. W. Norton & Company, Inc.
500 Fifth Avenue, New York, N.Y. 10110
www.wwnorton.com

W. W. Norton & Company Ltd.
15 Carlisle Street, London W1D 3BS

1 2 3 4 5 6 7 8 9 0

For Isabel

Contents

Illustrations

List of Maps

Glossary

Armée d'Orient: The 'Army of the Orient' (French expeditionary force in Macedonia).

Army: Formation containing between two and seven corps, commanded by a general.

Army group or front: Two or more armies, commanded by a general.

Battalion: Unit of infantry (nominally up to 1,000 strong), commanded by a lieutenant-colonel.

Battery: Organization of artillery pieces (usually containing between four and six guns).

Bombarde: Italian heavy trench mortar.

Brigade: Major tactical formation, commanded by a brigadier-general. Each brigade usually contained two regiments.

Chief of Staff: Principal staff officer of a military organization. In the German system a chief of staff was usually a co-commander.

Comando Supremo: Italian High Command.

Corps: Collection of divisions (usually between two and five), commanded by a lieutenant-general.

Cossacks: Semi-nomadic people originating from Ukraine and southern Russia.

Counter-battery: Fire directed at an opposing side's artillery.

Division: Basic tactical unit on the battlefield, employing between 10,000 and 15,000 men with supporting medical, engineering and artillery arms, commanded by a major-general.

Dual Monarchy: Alliance of the states of Austria and Hungary into the Austro-Hungarian Empire in 1867.

Habsburg: Ruling dynasty of Austria.

Honvéd: Hungarian national guard.

Landsturm: German and Austrian reserve militia.

Landwehr: Austrian national guard.

OberOst: *Oberbefehlshabers der Gesamten Deutschen Streitkräfte im Osten.* German headquarters on the Eastern Front.

Regiment: Organization of infantry battalions (usually four, although there were three in the *Landwehr*).

Starets: Holy man or spiritual adviser.

Stavka: Russian High Command.

U-boat: German submarine. Abbreviation of *Unterseeboot.*

Voivode: Serbian rank of field marshal.

Zemstvos: Local councils.

Note on the Text

One of the first questions any historian of the Eastern Front must answer is the choice of which calendar to follow. Because two versions were in use – the Germans and Austrians kept to the western Gregorian calendar, while the Russians relied upon the Julian, which was thirteen days behind – accounts often include both versions. For the sake of consistency and ease of reading, I have used the Gregorian calendar throughout, but when sources were originally recorded in their Julian form I have added 'OS' to denote 'Old Style'. This means that the abdication of the Tsar and the Bolshevik Revolution occur in this book in March and November 1917 respectively (as opposed to February and October, which are found in most Russian histories). In February 1918, the Bolsheviks adopted the Gregorian calendar. Names of places and individuals can also appear differently across sources (place names were often changed when new occupying powers moved in), so I have tended to use the most popular or recognizable forms.

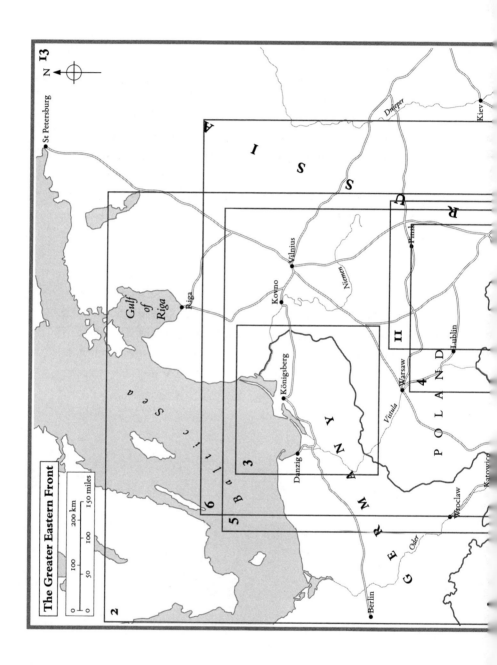

The Greater Eastern Front

100   200 km

0   50   100   150 miles

St Petersburg

Gulf of Riga

Riga

Baltic Sea

Königsberg

Danzig

Kovno

Vilnius

Niemen

Pinsk

Warsaw

Vistula

Lublin

POLAND

Wrocław

Oder

Katowice

Berlin

GERMANY

Dnieper

Kiev

RUSSIA

N

13

2

3

4

5

6

9

B

II

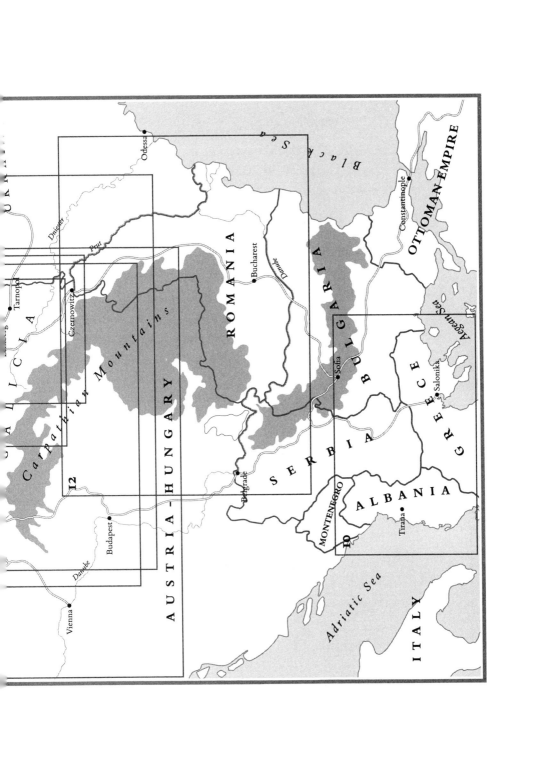

Preface

Writing in the 1920s, Winston Churchill believed that the First World War on the Eastern Front was 'incomparably the greatest war in history. In its scale, in its slaughter, in the exertions of the combatants, in its military kaleidoscope, it far surpasses by magnitude and intensity all similar human episodes'. It was, he concluded, 'the most frightful misfortune' to fall upon mankind 'since the collapse of the Roman Empire before the Barbarians'. This conflict, which pitched the Central Powers of Germany and Austria–Hungary against Imperial Russia, lies at the heart of the Great War; it was its mainspring and core, which changed the political order of Central and Eastern Europe and the Balkans for ever. This book, the second volume in a trilogy, tells the story of the 'other' First World War; where, as Churchill put it, 'the distant cannonade in France breaks only fitfully upon the ear'.[1]

Despite the immensity of Churchill's 'frightful misfortune', the Eastern Front is much less familiar to English-language audiences than the war in the west. Only a few battles, notably the Russian defeat at Tannenberg in August 1914, are widely known, with most of the other major engagements (and many of the key figures) never receiving the attention lavished on either the war in France or the campaigns in the Middle East, both of which remain highly controversial to this day. For decades the only notable study was Norman Stone's pioneering *The Eastern Front*, first published in 1975. Although an enormous amount of historical material has been produced since then, much of it remains known only to specialists, leaving our memory of the Eastern Front languishing in what the historian Sean McMeekin has called a 'deep freeze'.[2] Fortunately, in recent years scholars have started to rediscover the military history of the war in the east; transforming our understanding of the First World War and helping to bring this 'forgotten front' in from the cold.

Looking again at the Eastern Front offers a useful corrective to the preponderance of the west in many narratives of the war. While the fighting in France and Belgium was infamous for its trench stalemate, it was a more traditional affair in the east, much closer to the kind of conflict that had been expected by contemporaries. Because the front line was at least twice as long as in France, sometimes stretching to over 900 miles, the suffocating density of forces found in the west could never be achieved, meaning that breakthroughs were always possible and there continued to be space for cavalry charges and grand battles of manoeuvre throughout the war. But this did not mean that combat was any less bloody. Upwards of 2.3 million Russian soldiers were killed in their doomed struggle against the Central Powers. Their opponents, the Austro-Hungarian Empire, lost between 1.1 and 1.2 million men, only then to collapse in 1918, with the disintegration of both empires creating a human catastrophe of almost unimaginable proportions.[3]

The battlefields of the Eastern Front may have lacked the claustrophobia of France, but they witnessed a similar process of change and development in military skill and technology. The enormous power of modern rifles, machine-guns and quick-firing artillery rendered traditional battle tactics, bayonet charges and close-order drill almost suicidal. The armies of all sides had no choice but to undergo a radical transformation that required greater firepower, placed more emphasis on looser skirmish lines when making advances, and sought out new weaponry wherever it could be found. The first use of a chemical agent in the war occurred in January 1915, when thousands of lachrymatory gas shells were fired off at the village of Bolimov in Russian Poland – a full three months before chlorine was used in Belgium.[4] By 1916, the entire panoply of modern weaponry and tactics that had been pioneered in France, including extensive trench systems, creeping artillery barrages, poison gas and air power, could be found on the Eastern Front. It was at Riga in September 1917 that the first large-scale use of infiltration tactics occurred – proof of how important the Eastern Front was as a laboratory of war.[5]

Perhaps the most radical aspect of the struggle in the east was that violence was not confined to armies. In sharp contrast to the west, where brutality against civilians was (for the most part) restrained, the Eastern Front witnessed the large-scale abuse of civilian populations, particularly Jews. The inhabitants of those areas that were overrun by invading armies were routinely divided into 'reliable' or 'unreliable' ethnic groups and accused of spying or of sympathizing with the enemy. Those who were deemed problematic were rounded up and deported, their possessions looted or destroyed, and forced to undertake long and hazardous marches either into the Russian interior or back into the cities of the Habsburg Empire. This mass movement of people would bring the war to the home front in ways that were profoundly destabilizing, and it was no surprise that by as early as 1915, Russian moderates in Petrograd were complaining that 'the naked and hungry spread panic everywhere, dampening the last remnants of the enthusiasm which existed in the first months of the war . . . dragging Russia into the abyss, into revolution, and into destruction'.[6]

This book deals with what might be termed the 'greater' Eastern Front and includes the fighting in the Balkans, Italy and Macedonia. Although these campaigns usually took a back seat to the drama unfolding in Poland and Galicia (at least until 1916), they should be understood as part of one great struggle that stretched from the Baltic to the Alps, from the peaks of the Carpathians to the shores of the Aegean. This account tries to combine these theatres of war into a single narrative, showing how the battlefields were linked together and how the success – or failure – of arms in one place would impact the others. The geographical span of the book may be larger than the first volume, but its themes are broadly similar. It concerns those men who fought the war at the strategic and operational levels: the politicians and generals who raised and commanded armies. As in *The Western Front*, I wanted to present the war as it appeared to those at the highest echelons of command and leadership; to show how they tried (and often failed) to achieve their goals; and to leave any judgement to the reader.

The story that follows is based upon the letters, diary entries and reports written by these men as they passed through four years of terrible carnage. Historical accounts, biographies and collections of documents were central to the construction of my narrative, which draws from Austrian, German, Russian, Serbian, Italian, Romanian, Bulgarian and French sources, many of which have been translated for the first time. Understanding Russia's war, how she fought and subsequently collapsed, was perhaps the most challenging part; central to the story, yet curiously obscure. Historical attention has, perhaps understandably, tended to focus more on the revolution of 1917 than on the war that led up to it, which has left significant gaps in our understanding. Norman Stone's *The Eastern Front* was an essential guide, complemented by more recent research, including David Stone's *The Russian Army in the Great War. The Eastern Front, 1914– 1917*, Paul Robinson's *Grand Duke Nikolai Nikolaevich. Supreme Commander of the Russian Army*, and Oleg Airapetov's four volumes on the Russian Empire at war (published between 2014 and 2015 and richly deserving of an English translation). Several weighty collections of documents on Russian operations, compiled by the Red Army during the 1930s, were also useful in uncovering the story of the Tsar's forces between 1914 and 1916, and giving their generals – too often downplayed or ignored entirely – an authentic voice.

For the Austro-Hungarian Empire, it is impossible to overlook Manfried Rauchensteiner's *The First World War and the End of the Habsburg Monarchy*, originally written in 1993 and recently translated into English, which offers the most complete guide to the final years of the empire. Lawrence Sondhaus's *Franz Conrad von Hötzendorf. Architect of the Apocalypse* also provided a fair and reliable assessment of one of the most important, yet least understood, soldiers of the war. A special mention should go to the American historian Stan Hanna, who has single-handedly translated almost the entire seven-volume Habsburg official history, *Österreich-Ungarns Letzter Krieg* ('Austria– Hungary's Last War') into English. While the translations used in this account are my own, Hanna's achievement in making such an important source readily available to a wider audience deserves enormous respect. When looking to the other fronts, several studies were also invaluable, including John Gooch's *The Italian Army and the First World War*; David Dutton's *The Politics of Diplomacy. Britain and France in the Balkans in the First World War*; James Lyon's *Serbia and the Balkan Front,*

1914. The Outbreak of the Great War; and Glenn Torrey's extensive work on the Romanian campaign.

I have incurred various debts in the course of this project, and I would like to thank the librarians and archivists of the Hobson Library at the Joint Services Command & Staff College in Shrivenham; the National Archives of the UK, Kew; the Imperial War Museum and British Library, London; the Bodleian Library, Oxford; the Hoover Institution Archives, Stanford, California; Archivio Diaristico Nazionale, Pieve Santo Stefano; and Kriegsarchiv, Vienna. Enormous thanks go to the Defence Studies Department at King's College London, an institution that has always been supportive of my endeavours and without which this book could not have been written. Professor Niall Barr, Professor Kenneth Payne and Dr Jonathan Fennell all provided invaluable help and support when it was needed. I am also indebted to Daniel Crewe and the team at Viking; Dan Gerstle at Liveright; and my literary agent Jon Wood. Dr Vanda Wilcox was an essential guide to the Italian Front, and Professor Lothar Höbelt and Dr Susanne Bauda assisted me with Austrian sources in Vienna. Professor Sean McMeekin, Francis Flournoy Professor of European History and Culture at Bard College in upstate New York, whose books have investigated Russia's war in detail, was a welcoming and always reliable sounding board for my ideas. Much of this work is indebted to his scholarship, and his encouragement and friendship have been greatly valued.

The Eastern Front has simultaneously been the hardest and most interesting book I have written, and I hope readers who followed the travails of Generals Foch, Pétain, Haig and Pershing in France and Flanders in the first volume will be intrigued to read about what was happening elsewhere in the war. The battles that were hitherto only mentioned briefly or in passing can now be experienced in much more detail. It is a story of great tragedy and horror, cruelty and pain – as all wars are – but also of incredible courage and resilience that echoes down to our time. This book was completed under the shadow of the Russian invasion of Ukraine, and there was a sense of weary familiarity as news bulletins brought details of the fighting and shelling around Kyiv and Donetsk, L'viv and Mariupol. The weight of history still hangs over these lands, but perhaps the 'deep freeze' is now finally beginning to thaw and allow us to glimpse the Eastern Front in new and better ways.

This book is dedicated to my youngest daughter, Isabel, who brings such joy to my family. I hope that one day she reads it.

NL
Cheltenham, England
2023

Prologue

'It is nothing'

Mortally wounded, the Austro-Hungarian Archduke, Franz Ferdinand, and his wife, Sophie, lay slumped on the back seat of their car, a 1911 Gräf & Stift convertible, as they were driven back to the Konak, the governor's residence in Sarajevo. It was Sunday, 28 June 1914, and the royal visit to Bosnia had ended in disaster. Franz Ferdinand had been shot in the neck at close range, his blood spraying onto the face of his driver, while a second shot had pierced Sophie's abdomen. Major von Hüttenbrenner, the senior medical officer in the official party, attended to the royal couple as soon as they had been carried to safety. Sophie was already dead, her body limp and her white silk dress stained with a dark, seeping patch of blood. The Archduke was unconscious, his breathing shallow, with blood trickling from his neck and mouth. Count Morsey, his long-serving valet, cut open Franz Ferdinand's blue tunic to ease his chest, but it did no good. Within a matter of minutes, shortly after eleven o'clock that morning, he was dead.

The murderer was a 19-year-old Bosnian Serb, Gavrilo Princip. A sickly, thin-faced youth, Princip was a member of a secret militant organization, *Ujedinjenje ili Smrt* (Union or Death), sometimes known as the Black Hand, which was sworn to fight for a greater Serbia. After being smuggled across the border with six other conspirators, he was given a pistol and a bomb and told to position himself along the route that the Archduke would travel and strike if an opportunity presented itself. The plot had been orchestrated from Belgrade by the head of Serbian military intelligence, Colonel Dragutin Dimitrijević. When Dimitrijević heard about the royal visit to Bosnia, he was insistent that Franz Ferdinand must die. Not only was the Archduke the heir to the imperial throne, he was also a moderate and a reformer, whose stated desire to create a new kind of federal empire would have rendered the possibility of a greater Serbia far more unlikely. Franz Ferdinand believed that rising political tensions within Vienna's sprawling empire could only be dampened by more reform, by spreading power downwards. This meant revisiting the terms of the *Ausgleich* of 1867, which had created the Dual Monarchy of Austria and Hungary, and turning it into a 'trialist' structure with the addition of a South Slav kingdom – a move that might fatally weaken the appeal of an enlarged Serbia. As Princip later revealed, 'he would have prevented, as a future ruler, our union by realizing certain reforms which would evidently have been against our interests'. This was why Franz Ferdinand had to die.[1]

After spending two days out on manoeuvres in the hills surrounding Sarajevo, Franz Ferdinand had been on his way to a reception with local dignitaries at the City Hall. The first attack came as his car was passing the Ćumurija Bridge, which lay along the Appel Quay, a pleasant street running beside the Miljâcka river through the centre of the city, about 650 yards from his destination. A 'tall young man in a long black coat', a Bosnian Serb called Nedeljko Čabrinović, saw the car, lit the fuse on his bomb and hurled it. Franz Ferdinand's driver immediately spotted the assailant and slammed his foot down on the accelerator, which meant that the bomb bounced off the back hood of the car, hit the pavement and rolled under the following vehicle, detonating with a sickening explosion. Although the royal couple were unharmed, two attendants were wounded, cut by shrapnel, and their vehicle was wrecked. Čabrinović had jumped over the wall down onto the riverbed, which had sunk to a trickle in the summer months, and was chased by police officers, who seized him shortly afterwards, the bomb-thrower coughing and spluttering after taking a cyanide pill, which seared his throat but did not kill him.[2]

Within minutes the motorcade had reached the City Hall, where the royal party were ushered inside. Clutching his speaker's notes, now spattered with blood, Franz Ferdinand gave a short address before meeting with officials, including the Governor of Bosnia, General Oskar Potiorek, who was responsible for the royal family's security. The Archduke wanted to visit the wounded attendants, who were being ferried to the garrison hospital, so it was agreed that he would return by a new, quicker route, straight down the Appel Quay, instead of following the original plan, which would have had the motorcade turning right at the Latin Bridge down the narrow Franz Joseph Street. Unfortunately, no one seemed to have told the Archduke's driver, so instead of continuing along the main road, he followed the original route, slowing down and then turning right past the Moritz Schiller Spice Emporium. As he did so, Potiorek realized the mistake and turned to him:

'What is this? Stop! You are going the wrong way! We ought to go via Appel Quay.'

The Archduke's car was only motionless for a few, precious moments, but it was enough for Princip to earn his place in the pantheon of Serbian national heroes. After Čabrinović's bomb attack, Princip had drifted through the crowds, assuming that the assassination attempt had failed, and ended up in Franz Joseph Street. Suddenly realizing that his target was now right in front of him, he acted without thinking, raising his pistol and firing two shots at point-blank range. For a split second there was only a stunned stillness, broken by the sound of the shots echoing off the street walls. Then Princip was seized by the Archduke's bodyguards and hurled to the ground. Count Franz Harrach, who had been standing on the left-hand side of the car on the running board, noticed how Sophie had sunk down in her seat and Franz Ferdinand now began to dip forward, causing Harrach to ask whether His Highness was in great pain. 'His face was slightly distorted, and he repeated six or seven times, every time losing more consciousness and with a fading voice: "It is nothing."' Then the Archduke was silent, the only sound being 'a convulsive rattle in his throat' caused by blood loss. 'This ceased on arrival at the governor's residence. The two unconscious bodies were carried into the building where their death was soon established.'[3]

Austria–Hungary would react, but how exactly remained to be decided. While spontaneous anti-Serb pogroms broke out across the empire, the government was quickly recalled in Vienna. Austrian Prime Minister Karl Stürgkh, Chief of the General Staff Franz Conrad von Hötzendorf, Foreign Minister Count Leopold von

Berchtold and his deputy, Count Alexander Hoyos, were all convinced that Austria had to take a strong line, using the opportunity to strike down her foremost opponent in the Balkans. The only note of caution came from the Hungarian Prime Minister, Count István Tisza. 'We have no sufficient grounds for holding Serbia responsible', he told Emperor Franz Joseph several days after the shooting. Forcing matters 'would be a fatal mistake' for 'we should appear before the world as the disturber of the peace and would kindle the fires of a great war in the most unfavourable conditions'.[4]

Germany's position would be crucial. Despite fighting each other in 1866, the Austrian and Prussian (now German) Empires had drawn closer over subsequent decades. They were now part of the Triple Alliance – comprising Austria, Germany and Italy – which was originally signed in May 1882. This 'essentially conservative and defensive' alliance committed the signatories to mutual 'peace and friendship' and promised that none would enter into an 'alliance or engagement directed against any one of their States'. Moreover, were France to attack Italy, Germany and Austria would be 'bound to lend help and assistance with all their forces'.[5] Although Italy was decidedly nervous about taking part in a war in defence of Habsburg interests in the Balkans, and would remain neutral in July 1914, Germany had declared privately that Austria had her full support. Germany's Kaiser, Wilhelm II, regarded the assassination as an act that could not go unpunished and told his officials that it was 'high time that a clean sweep was made of the Serbs'. What is more, when Vienna's envoy, Count Hoyos, arrived in Berlin on 5 July, he was told that Germany would support Austria even in the event of a war with Russia; a prospect that did not strike the Kaiser as being particularly likely.[6]

Germany's declaration of unconditional support hardened the hearts of those in Vienna who pushed for a decisive confrontation with Belgrade. Although the Kaiser was under the impression that Austria was preparing for an immediate attack, it took weeks before she was ready. Habsburg troops from rural areas were traditionally allowed to go home during the summer months for the harvest, and with large sections of the army not due to return until 25 July, significant military action before that date was impossible. A council of war was held on 7 July, at which the Habsburg ministers repeated their demands for a firm stance. Any diplomatic manoeuvres 'should happen with a firm intention of concluding the whole affair with war'. Moreover, 'far-reaching demands should be made to Serbia, acceptance of which must be regarded as out of the question, so that a radical solution by means of military intervention can be set in motion'. Tisza again set out his objections and insisted that there must be an opportunity for Serbia to avoid hostilities. The following day, still deeply troubled at the pace of events, he wrote to Franz Joseph and warned him that a war with Serbia would 'in all conscience provoke Russian intervention and thus world war'.[7]

Tisza's refusal to be pushed into a war in the Balkans was now the chief stumbling block to Austrian action. Count Berchtold was a firm believer in a military solution and kept up the pressure on the Hungarian premier throughout the following week, assuring him of German support and muttering darkly about the disastrous consequences of disappointing the Kaiser. A week later, on 14 July, another council took place and Tisza finally gave way, agreeing that an ultimatum be sent to Belgrade after he was presented with the 'military difficulties' that might arise should action be delayed any further. Tisza had reluctantly dropped his objections, but only on the understanding that apart from making some 'small regulations' of the border, Austria would not annex Serbia (thus avoiding adding more disgruntled Slavs to the empire). 'The text of the note to be sent to Belgrade, as it was settled today,' Berchtold reported to Franz Joseph, 'is such that we must reckon with the probability of war.' The Serbs would have just forty-eight hours to respond.[8]

After being drafted and re-drafted numerous times, the ultimatum was delivered by Baron Wladimir von Giesl, Minister to Serbia, on 23 July. Preliminary investigations had revealed that the assassination of Franz Ferdinand had been planned in Belgrade, with the weapons and explosives supplied by Serbian officers belonging to the *Narodna Odbrana* (National Defence), a nationalist organization with links to *Ujedinjenje ili Smrt*. Therefore, Vienna demanded Serbia issue a proclamation condemning the 'propaganda directed against Austria–Hungary', regretting the involvement of Serbian 'officers and functionaries' in this propaganda and warning that the Royal Serbian Government should 'proceed with the utmost rigour against persons who may be guilty of such machinations'. Ten further demands were made, including the suppression of any publication that incited 'hatred and contempt' against the Austro-Hungarian monarchy, the immediate dissolution of the *Narodna Odbrana* and the acceptance of Austrian representatives into Serbia to help suppress the 'subversive movement directed against the territorial integrity of the Monarchy'.[9]

The Serbian response was, initially, one of bewilderment. The Prime Minister, Nikola Pašić, was not in Belgrade but out at Niš, in the south, campaigning for re-election, leaving one of his ministers, Dr Lazar Paču, in charge. When Pašić was found, he immediately returned to the capital and summoned his ministers. According to Paču, the demands were such 'that no Serbian government could agree to them', being inconsistent with the country's sovereignty and honour – a view echoed by Serbia's ruling monarch, Crown Prince Alexander, who sent an urgent message to the Russian Tsar, Nicholas II. Austrian demands were 'unnecessarily humiliating' and 'incompatible with her dignity as an independent State'. With only hours to go before the deadline, Alexander begged the Tsar to help. 'The much appreciated goodwill which your Majesty has so often shown towards us inspires us with the firm belief that once again our appeal to your noble Slav heart will not pass unheeded.'[10]

The mood in Belgrade grew more restive as the hours passed. There were certainly some in the Serbian Government who sympathized with Dimitrijević's pan-Slavic ideology, but the order to kill Franz Ferdinand had not come from the government or the military High Command. Moreover, Serbia was not ready for war. Her army was still recovering from the effects of the Balkan Wars (during which she had expanded south into Macedonia) and there were shortages of everything, from uniforms and ammunition to rolling stock and artillery. While Serbia hoped that the other great powers would be able to pressurize Vienna to back down, work began on drafting a response. Despite the initial tone of defiance, Pašić understood that as many of the demands as possible must be met (or at least not rejected outright). Accordingly, orders were issued for the arrest of several conspirators, and a text, messy and littered with corrections, was finally placed in a diplomatic envelope and given to the Prime Minister, who would deliver it in person to the Austro-Hungarian Legation.

Arriving just before the deadline at six o'clock on the afternoon of 25 July, Pašić handed over his government's formal response, which accepted all but one of Vienna's demands. The Royal Serbian Government was willing 'to hand over for trial any Serbian subject' if evidence was presented of their complicity in the assassination. It would also condemn all propaganda against the Dual Monarchy, dissolve the *Narodna Odbrana* and issue a public statement formally denouncing any attempt to interfere with the 'destiny' of the people of Austria–Hungary. The only point of contention was the Austrian demand to be involved in any official Serbian inquiry. The inclusion of foreign officers in such an investigation would be 'a violation of the Constitution and of the law of criminal procedure', although Belgrade would provide information on any progress to Austrian agents where necessary.[11]

Serbia had gone as far as she could, possibly as far as any independent state could go, but it quickly became clear that anything less than complete submission meant war. Within fifteen minutes of Pašić's arrival, Baron von Giesl informed his hosts that Austria–Hungary had now severed all diplomatic relations and then left, making his way to the station, where he boarded the last train out of Serbia. 'A crowd numbering many hundreds had gathered in the streets; there was no shortage of hostility towards us, but no serious threat ensued', he later remembered. 'The station was cordoned off by troops; the train ready to depart. Everything happened in great haste. A large portion of the diplomatic corps gathered on the platform; I think the Russians, French and Romanians were missing . . . We were urged to get on board. There was a long, discordant whistle, and the train rolled out of the station.' War was now just hours away.[12]

PART I

'What fighting and dying really means'

Krasnik to the Fall of Serbia (July 1914–November 1915)

1. 'A visible bloody track'

It was at noon on Tuesday, 28 July 1914, under a bright blue cloudless sky, when Austria–Hungary declared war on Serbia. Shortly afterwards, Franz Joseph, Emperor of Austria, King of Hungary and King of Bohemia, issued a manifesto to his people explaining why he must 'grasp the sword after long years of peace'. Blaming the Kingdom of Serbia for her ingratitude, 'unrestrained passion' and 'bitterest hate', the Austrian Emperor had now taken a stand against the 'incessant provocations' that had been directed against his empire. 'A series of murderous attacks, an organized, carefully prepared, and well-carried-out conspiracy, whose fruitful success wounded me and my loyal peoples to my heart, forms a visible bloody track of those secret machinations which were operated and directed in Servia [sic].' He therefore had no choice but to declare war and trust that his 'peoples', who 'throughout every storm, have always rallied in unity and loyalty round my Throne', would do so again.[1]

Now 83 years old, Emperor Franz Joseph was ailing and fragile. His face was still flanked by the thick white moustache and mutton chops that had become his trademark, but his features wore a more haggard look now, haunted by what he called the 'terrible catastrophe of Sarajevo'.[2] He had endured tragedy throughout his reign (including the suicide of his only son, Rudolf, and the assassination of his beloved wife, Elisabeth) and he took the news of Franz Ferdinand's death with surprising calm, but worries grew as the European situation deteriorated. Closeted with his chief aides at his summer residence at Bad Ischl, Franz Joseph took daily walks around the palace grounds wearing the blue-grey service uniform of a junior officer, comforting himself with the thought that war was inevitable. 'The Almighty permits no challenge!' he had said after hearing the news of Franz Ferdinand's death. 'A higher Power has restored the order that I was unhappily unable to maintain . . .'[3]

Long gone were the days when a Habsburg emperor would lead the army into war himself. That role would be played by two men: one calm and easy-going, the other hyperactive in his aggression, which seemed to sum up the contradictions of this once-great empire. Three days after Franz Ferdinand had been murdered, Archduke Friedrich, Duke of Teschen, was appointed Supreme Commander at the Austrian High Command, AOK (*Armee Oberkommando*), which was based in Vienna. Fifty-eight-year-old Friedrich was a dutiful and reliable soldier, the kind of royal courtier who could be counted upon for his discretion and loyalty, if not for any notable military expertise. He left day-to-day control of his forces to General Franz Conrad von Hötzendorf, who had been Chief of the General Staff, with one brief interval, since November 1906. Easily recognizable by his stubby grey hair and white moustache, Conrad was a forceful and confident individual who had carved out a reputation as a notable military thinker – with Friedrich happy for him to take the lead on operational planning.

Austria–Hungary's predicament – which seemed to grow more pressing every year – was that she was surrounded by enemies (Russia, Serbia and Montenegro) or states that were dubious in their intentions (Italy, Romania and Bulgaria) and might, should they get a chance, rush in to feast on her corpse. This was compounded by the growth of surging unsatisfied nationalisms within the empire, from Hungarians and Czechs to Croatians and Serbs, who saw the Dual Monarchy as a roadblock on the way to realizing their own independent national communities. Conscious of the multiple competing threats to the empire, Conrad was convinced that only an uncompromising offensive policy should be adopted, with Austria–Hungary dealing her opponents a series of powerful pre-emptive blows. He had advocated war against Italy in 1907 and Serbia in 1908, and saw the world as a stark and unrelenting struggle for dominance: either the empire destroyed its opponents or its days as a great power were over. The 'duel' against Serbia was not, as he put it, simply about gaining justice for the Archduke, 'it was more a case of the highly practical importance of upholding her status as one of the world's great powers. In fact, this "great power" had been gaining a reputation for weakness over the preceding years, due to its constant acquiescence and forbearance in the face of adversity. This had only served to further embolden its enemies – both foreign and domestic – to the extent that these enemies were taking increasingly drastic measures to bring about the collapse of the old Empire.'[4]

Given these competing threats, it was highly likely that Austria would have to divide her forces in any future conflict. Vienna's war plan, which had undergone numerous revisions since it had first been drafted in 1908, had split her army into three echelons. The largest, 'A' *Staffel*, contained 28 infantry and 10 cavalry divisions and would face the Russians along the empire's long northern border in Galicia. The second element was *Minimalgruppe Balkan* – 8 infantry divisions (plus assorted supporting brigades) that would be deployed against Serbia. The final element, 'B' *Staffel*, amounted to 12 infantry divisions and a single cavalry division – essentially the rest of the army – and was centrally located so that it could be sent either north or south as the situation demanded. Ideally, 'B' *Staffel* would reinforce the Balkan group, providing the superiority in manpower that would almost certainly be required in any campaign against Serbia. If, however, Russia entered the war quickly, then it would have to move north – but transportation experts warned Conrad that given the limitations of the railway network, it could only commence its journey on the eighteenth day after mobilization had been announced.[5]

Beginning in January 1909, Conrad and his opposite number in Berlin, Colonel-General Helmuth von Moltke, had engaged in a detailed correspondence about Austro-German cooperation in a future war. Moltke paid little attention to developments in the east and told Conrad that he should not worry because 'the fate of Austria will be decided not on the Bug, but on the Seine' – meaning that the decisive battles would all be fought in the west. Following the plans developed by Moltke's predecessor, Count Alfred von Schlieffen, Germany would mass her forces against France – Russia's main ally – and destroy her within a matter of weeks. Therefore, Austria–Hungary should not focus on Serbia, but put the bulk of her army in Galicia, mounting an offensive to draw Russian troops away from East Prussia until such time as Moltke could redeploy his own forces.

But forgoing any assault on Serbia while guarding Germany's rear held little appeal in Vienna, and Conrad warned Moltke (in a letter dated 3 March 1909) that he would only be able to take the offensive if the Germans also mounted their own attack from East Prussia – ideally driving south over the Narew river. If such an offensive was not conducted, then Conrad's armies would seek to hold the line of the Carpathians along the San and Dniester rivers.[6]

These disagreements were never satisfactorily resolved, and both Germany and Austria–Hungary entered the Great War with clear ideas about who they wanted to fight but without dealing with the perils and constraints of a two-front war that neither side wanted. Germany's war plan demanded a swift victory against France, while the Austrian High Command hoped that any conflict could be localized to the Balkans – allowing Austria to crush her troublesome neighbour Serbia without interference. But the dwindling chance that Russia would stay out of any conflict vanished on 30 July when the Tsar ordered larger mobilization, turning an Austro-Serbian squabble into a wider European war. Even so, Conrad could not bring himself to abandon the Serbian campaign, which he saw as essential to Austria's reputation and something that could be won cheaply and efficiently. On 30 July, even though Russian intervention was imminent, he met with his chief railway planner, Colonel Johann Straub, and ordered him to send 'B' *Staffel* – essentially Second Army – to the Balkans immediately. At the same time he insisted, in a note handed to Count Berchtold, the Foreign Minister, that these deployments proved Austria had no aggressive designs against Russia.[7]

The news that Conrad was still hoping to adhere to a Serbian-only campaign caused a flurry of activity in Berlin, which was still reeling from the news of Russian mobilization. Kaiser Wilhelm II fired off an urgent telegram to Franz Joseph on 31 July warning him that 'it is of utmost importance that Austria deploy her main troops against Russia and does not split them up by a simultaneous offensive against Serbia'. Moreover, 'Serbia's role in this gigantic fight, which we enter shoulder to shoulder, is completely peripheral and only requires the most basic defensive measures.'[8] Conrad still hoped that the Russians could be kept out of the war and was reluctant to mobilize his main forces in Galicia, but this position soon became untenable. When presented with evidence of Russian movements the following day, 31 July, he finally agreed to the mobilization of 'A' *Staffel* (against Russia), while also accepting that 'B' *Staffel* would have to return north as soon as space could be found on the railways and once the main deployment to Galicia had been completed.

With Germany concentrating most of her strength in the west, Austria–Hungary would have to face the opening stages of the war virtually alone. Starved of funds for decades and riven by political infighting, the Habsburg Army could only deploy 48 infantry divisions, as opposed to 80 German and 114 Russian ones, with even Serbia managing to put 11 divisions into the field despite having a population one tenth the size of Austria–Hungary's.[9] Although Austrian regiments were well equipped with modern magazine-loading rifles and with machine-guns, and some of her artillery was the best in the world (particularly the 1911 30.5 cm Škoda siege howitzers that would help Germany batter her way through Belgium's fortress network), her line infantry was critically short of artillery, both light and medium pieces. This was in part because of budget restrictions, with funding for weapons programmes being vetoed frequently by the Hungarian Parliament in the years before the war. But it was also a legacy of Austrian tactical doctrine, which remained firmly wedded to the idea that infantry was the decisive arm on the battlefield. The 1911 Infantry Regulations, which were overseen by Conrad, emphasized the spirit of the bayonet and the need for infantry to possess 'iron discipline and superior willpower'. Although recent improvements in artillery were noted, the Austro-Hungarian Army marched into the campaign of 1914 significantly outgunned by the Russians, who could boast 60 guns per division, compared to an average of 42 in Habsburg formations.[10]

Of all the armies that fought in the war, the Austro-Hungarian Army was also the most ethnically and politically fragmented. It was split into three branches, with the regular Imperial and Royal (*Kaiserlich und Königlich*) Army bolstered by the local armed forces of the two halves of the empire, the Austrian *Landwehr* and the Hungarian *Honvéd*; a structure that reflected the complex political reality of

Central Europe, but which did little for cohesion and military effectiveness. For every 100 soldiers in the regular army, there were 25 Germans, 23 Magyars, 13 Czechs, 4 Slovaks, 8 Poles, 8 Ukrainians, 2 Slovenians, 9 Serbo-Croats, 7 Romanians and 1 of Italian ethnicity.[11] The language of command remained German, but this had been the subject of growing complaint, with both Czechs and Hungarians demanding concessions over language use for their own regiments – a move that was strongly resisted by Vienna on the grounds that it would undermine the unity of the regular army.

Notwithstanding the endemic problems within the armed forces, as well as the last-minute confusion over the deployment of 'B' *Staffel*, Conrad approached the coming storm with an enormous sense of relief. The war that he had foreseen for many years had finally arrived, and with it the chance to win immortal renown and glory. He believed that whatever deficiencies there were in the army, they could be mitigated by what he called an 'active approach', aimed at seizing and maintaining the initiative. 'In this respect, swift decision-making and strength of will are characteristics crucial to a leader', he had written in 1890, in a study of tactics. 'Such an active approach is likely to surprise the enemy, causing him to dispense with his own plans and forcing him to retaliate. This puts the enemy in a situation for which he is unprepared and for which he has made no plans.' A 'passive' approach, on the contrary, 'occurs all too frequently in war, sometimes for intellectual reasons, sometimes physical, but usually for reasons of morale, and almost always results in failure'.[12]

They had once been firm allies, but by the opening decade of the twentieth century, conflicting designs in the Balkans had brought Austria–Hungary and Russia to the precipice of war. Nicholas II, Tsar of All the Russias, had long distrusted Vienna and had seen her annexation of Bosnia in 1908 as a firm indication that the Habsburgs were intent on dominating the Balkans and excluding Russian influence. When the ultimatum was delivered to Serbia, it provoked fury and disbelief in St Petersburg, as the Tsar and his chief advisers weighed the costs of intervention against the humiliation of allowing Vienna to dismember Russia's chief client state in the region. Despite an exchange of last-minute letters between the Tsar and his third cousin, the Kaiser, Nicholas saw no alternative but to order mobilization in protest at Austria's actions. 'An ignoble war has been declared upon a weak country', he telegraphed on 29 July, a day after Austria–Hungary had communicated her decision for war on Serbia. 'The indignation in Russia shared fully by me is enormous. I foresee that very soon I shall be overwhelmed by the pressure upon me, and forced to take extreme measures which will lead to war.' He therefore begged Wilhelm to do what he could to restrain the Austrians from advancing against Serbia. The German Emperor, underlining key words as he read the telegram, could only reply with an exasperated 'What?'[13]

Heavy-hearted, suffering agonies of indecision, the Tsar finally ordered full mobilization on 30 July (a partial mobilization having been ordered several days earlier). This was swiftly followed by an ultimatum from Berlin that Russia must cease all military preparations; when this was ignored, a declaration of war came on 1 August. The Russian Army had a peacetime strength of 1.4 million men, bolstered by upwards of three million reservists, so posed a potentially mortal threat to the Central Powers – provided it could concentrate its forces in time. But as with the other belligerents, Russian planners were faced with two possible fronts, north or south – Germany or Austria – and struggled to come up with a plan that would satisfactorily square this circle. Russian attention was naturally drawn to the Balkans, where her interests lay, but the pull of the French alliance, ratified in 1893, committed the Tsar to send between 700,000 and 800,000 men against Germany 'as early as possible . . . in order to force Germany to fight at the same time in the East and in the West'.[14] France kept up pressure on her ally during the frantic July days, with the French President, Raymond Poincaré, leading a three-day state visit to Russia on 20 July, which culminated in a grand military review, involving 70,000 troops drilling in long lines to the thrilling sounds of 'Sambre et Meuse' and 'Marche Lorraine'.[15] By the time the French delegation left, the two powers had coordinated their responses to the developing crisis, with Poincaré stating in his farewell speech that the visit had been 'a splendid consecration of the indissoluble alliance which unites Russia and France on all questions which arise each day before the two Governments and which demand the concerted activity of their diplomacy'.[16]

Russia's dilemma was that while she did not want to fight Germany, having a healthy respect for the prowess of the Kaiser's army, she would probably never get a better chance to do so. With the bulk of Moltke's forces set to march west, the eastern borders of Germany were largely undefended; a point that French soldiers regularly made to their Russian counterparts as they urged them on to Berlin. But Russian commanders were nervous about operating within the Polish Salient, a 230-mile-long stretch of territory west of the Bug, centred on Warsaw, which was vulnerable to counter-attacks from north and south. France had provided Russia with generous loans to fund the upgrading of existing railway lines and the construction of brand-new double tracks that would speed up Russia's mobilization on her western frontier, but Russian and French visions of what a European war entailed remained crucially out of step. By 1912, two variants of Russia's war plan had been drafted: 'A' for a major effort against Austria–Hungary and 'G' for a concentration against Germany. Despite French pressure, Plan 'G' was never Russia's preferred option and remained a largely theoretical exercise, only to come into effect in the unlikely event that Germany chose to attack Russia first. Instead, Plan 'A' would be Russia's 'automatic' deployment, concentrating her main body in Galicia, with a subsidiary force set to invade East Prussia.[17]

Matters were not helped by the factious, feud-driven nature of the Tsar's Cabinet. Nicholas II was a mild-mannered autocrat driven by love and concern for his family, particularly his 10-year-old son, Alexei (who suffered from haemophilia), but he had little experience in military or strategic affairs and relied upon an ever-shifting array of courtiers to advise him. The War Minister, General Vladimir Alexandrovich Sukhomlinov, was perhaps the most notorious of the Tsar's closest advisers. He had fought running battles with other senior officers for years over everything from the role of fortresses in the Russian war plan to the nature of infantry tactics. He ruthlessly promoted his own protégés to important positions and exiled his opponents to lesser appointments, gaining a reputation as a slippery, untrustworthy character whose only outstanding quality was his unswerving loyalty to the Romanovs and his disdain for the Duma (Russia's Parliament, which had been created in 1905). The French Ambassador, Maurice Paléologue, once remarked that he knew of 'few men' who inspired 'more distrust at first sight' than Sukhomlinov.[18]

The Tsar had originally told his ministers that he would personally lead the army, but suffering a typical spasm of uncertainty, he soon backed down, leaving Sukhomlinov searching for a replacement. Sukhomlinov was himself a decorated field commander, but was unenthusiastic about taking over, perhaps fearing early defeats and wanting to distance himself from them, so on 2 August he approached His Imperial Highness Grand Duke Nikolai Nikolaevich. A towering figure, standing at six feet six inches tall, the Grand Duke possessed a sense of authority and gravitas; of calm, silent determination. As uncle to the Tsar (who called him 'Nicolasha'), he had long been a key figure within the highest reaches of Imperial Russia and was respected for his lifetime of soldiering as well as his prowess as a hunter and as a breeder of particularly aggressive Borzoi dogs. Yet his appointment was a curious one. Although he was known as something of a modernizer within the cavalry, he was unfamiliar with Russia's recent deployment plans and had not commanded armies in the field. 'Words cannot express what I felt at that moment . . .' he later admitted. 'I possessed no right to refuse. I recognized my immense responsibility to the Fatherland, but it was my duty to point out that I felt unprepared and very unsure of what I could do but accomplish this task with confidence and a happy hand. I had no knowledge of the mobilization plan. I would have to carry out a plan I had not designed . . .'[19]

General Headquarters (*Stavka*) had been established in Baranovichi, a barren, dust-swept town about 500 miles southwest of St Petersburg. Chosen because it lay at the junction of three main railway lines (which would allow the Grand Duke's personal train to move up and down the front as required), it lacked amenities and had few buildings suitable for housing the staff required to support Russia's armies in the field. Most of the officers were accommodated in railway carriages, with General Yuri Danilov, Quartermaster-General and, by most accounts, the real driving force at *Stavka*, commandeering the biggest building in town, which housed the office of the military railway brigade, and turning it into the main planning cell. While Danilov worked dutifully on the day-to-day functioning of the army, he was handicapped by the (relatively) small number of staff available to him, just sixty officers, and what he called the 'almost complete absence' of wireless telegraphic equipment. When *Stavka* was formed, it only had a single Hughes telegraph machine to communicate with the front-line commands. This was an early form of teleprinter, first invented in 1855, with a capacity of only 600 words per hour, and it was not until the end of September 1914 that Baranovichi had direct telegraph links to the front headquarters at Rovno and Cholm.[20]

Russia's war plan was to launch two simultaneous attacks, one in East Prussia and the other in Galicia, but instead of waiting until all their forces had been mobilized, Russian commanders were under intense pressure to march hard and strike quickly, particularly while Germany's attention was elsewhere. On 10 August, *Stavka* issued a directive to General Yakov Zhilinsky, commander of the Northwest Front, who would have the task of invading East Prussia. 'According to absolutely reliable information in our possession, Germany has sent her main forces to her western frontier against France, leaving a minority of her forces against us.' It was estimated that only four corps were left in East Prussia, which meant that it was imperative for Russia to move quickly. 'Taking into consideration the fact that Germany first declared war upon us, and that France, as our ally, considered it her duty to give us immediate support and to take the field against Germany, naturally we also, constrained by the same obligations as allies, must support the French . . .' This support would take the form of the 'earliest possible offensive by us against the German forces left in East Prussia', with First Army pushing north of the Masurian Lakes, to turn the enemy's left flank, while Second Army would strike from the south, aiming to cut off the enemy's retreat across the Vistula.[21]

The situation in Galicia was much less certain and would depend upon where the Austrians deployed their main forces. Between 1907 and 1913, Colonel Alfred Redl, a highly placed Austrian intelligence officer, had passed a series of confidential documents to the Russians, giving them an invaluable insight into Habsburg strategic and operational thinking. Redl was finally caught in May 1913 after picking up a secret payment from a post office in Vienna. Special Branch officers trailed him back to his hotel room and then confronted him, handing over a revolver, which Redl used to kill himself an hour later. The Austrian military quickly closed ranks after the 'Redl Affair' became public, keen to downplay the suicide of a valued officer and the devastating effect that his treachery might have on the defence of the empire. Redl had revealed mobilization and war plans for campaigns against Russia, Serbia and Italy, as well as the layouts of key fortifications and detailed orders of battle. He had also betrayed the identities of Austrian agents within Russia, causing a collapse in the vital intelligence that was needed on the empire's adversary.[22]

Armed with this information, the four Russian armies of General Nikolai Ivanov's Southwest Front were ordered to defeat Austro-Hungarian forces and prevent any significant withdrawal of enemy troops either south towards the Dniester or west towards the city of Krakow. On the Russian left around Tarnopol, Third and Eighth Armies would march west towards Lemberg, while Fourth and Fifth Armies, concentrating around Lublin and Cholm, would come down from the north, advancing towards the great fortress of Przemyśl. Together they would crush the Austrian forces in a gigantic pincer movement, recreating the great battle of Cannae (216 BC), when the forces of Carthage crushed those of the Roman Republic in a devastating battle of envelopment.[23] 'I shall order the offensive as soon as the operation is feasible and I shall attack à fond . . .' the Grand Duke told the French Ambassador on 5 August, just hours before Austria's formal declaration of war against Russia. 'Perhaps I shan't even wait till the concentration of all my corps is complete. As soon as I feel myself strong enough I shall attack. It will probably be the 14th August.'[24]

As Russian, Austrian and German forces readied themselves for the opening skirmishes, the first shots were being fired in Serbia.

Austro-Hungarian heavy artillery had already bombarded Belgrade on the night of 28 July, firing salvos of shells into the city centre, but it would be another two weeks before the invasion took place, giving the Serbs valuable time to organize their defences while anxiously awaiting the return of their foremost soldier, *Voivode* Radomir Putnik. A national hero who had masterminded Serbia's victories in the Balkan Wars of 1912 and 1913, Putnik was now 67 years old and racked by chronic emphysema. After taking the waters at Bad Gleichenberg in Bohemia, he had been apprehended by Habsburg officials on 26 July while changing trains in Budapest, only to be released after an intervention by the Austrian Foreign Ministry. Both Franz Joseph and Conrad agreed to let him go, which allowed him to return home shortly before the campaign got under way. Often seen as a last passing act of chivalry from the old regime, the decision to release Putnik may have been inspired by more calculating reasons – after all, why not let the Serbs be commanded by an old, uneducated peasant rather than by his younger, more energetic subordinates?[25]

Short, bearded, with closely cropped white hair, Putnik was compact and stocky, seeming to personify the doughty character of Serbia, who now girded herself to receive the Austrian attack. With Putnik having to take a long, tortuous route back home (he would not be at his headquarters until the first week of August), his safe, which contained Serbia's mobilization schedules, was cracked open and orders were issued for her three armies – each about the size of an Austrian corps, about 200,000 men in total – to concentrate in a central position south of Belgrade, away from the border, where they could react quickly to any incursion before launching a counter-offensive.[26] Although battle-hardened and fighting on their own soil, Serbian forces had not yet recovered from the heavy demands of the Balkan Wars, and the army looked like a ramshackle band of scarecrows, with first-line officers and men tending to wear the 1908 pattern olive-green tunics and trousers, but second- and third-line formations having to make do with older blue uniforms or going without military outfits entirely. These 'bands of tramps', as one observer put it, 'made excellent soldiers' whose ability to withstand privation was 'marvellous'. 'At night, hundreds of them could be seen sleeping around the depot or on the hard stone pavements of the street, and yet in the morning their activity and fresh appearance would indicate perfect repose. Give the Serbian soldier bread and an onion, and he is satisfied.'[27]

There was no chance that Conrad could lead the Austro-Hungarian campaign against Russia as well as against Serbia, so General Oskar Potiorek, Governor of Bosnia and the man who had been responsible for the safety of the Archduke in Sarajevo, was appointed army group commander of the Balkans, with authority to decide if and when an incursion into the kingdom should take place. There was an urgent need to win an early victory, as much to chastise Serbia as to convince wavering states (Bulgaria and Romania) to throw in their lot with the Central Powers. On 9 August, Conrad warned Potiorek that 'under no circumstances must we suffer a setback in the Balkans' and that success 'would be of the greatest value because it would probably bring the still hesitant states of Bulgaria and Romania to our side'.[28] Three days later, on 12 August, the first Austrian troops crossed into Serbia, bridging the fast-flowing Drina river and striking east into the mountainous, heavily wooded interior in long pike-grey columns. Fifth Army provided the bulk of the invasion force, with Second Army mounting a demonstration along the northern bank of the Danube, intended to confuse enemy observers and draw their attention away from the main attack.

With three armies under his command, Potiorek had numerical superiority, but this would diminish significantly if Second Army – essentially 'B' Staffel – was ordered away to Galicia, a movement that was scheduled for 18 August. The only option, as he saw it, was to attack as soon as possible while it was still there. 'I intend to be absolutely offensive', he noted on 6 August.[29] Yet nothing seemed to go to plan. Fifth Army should have crossed the Drina in six strong columns, but bridging equipment had not turned up, which meant that only small parties were able to paddle their way across while waiting for pontoons to be hastily assembled. Almost as soon as they had reached the far bank, Potiorek's men began to be plagued by swarms of Komitadjis – Serbian partisans and irregulars who harassed Austrian troops wherever they settled, firing a few shots before disappearing into the countryside and frequently causing panic and terror as night fell. The terrain was alternately mountainous or wooded, stony and waterless; even the cornfields posed significant problems, with corn growing so high as to conceal even a mounted rider.[30]

Over the next few days, Habsburg forces advanced cautiously towards their objective of Valjevo (an important rail hub about forty miles from the Drina), skirmishing with locally raised second- and third-line Serbian units. Another bridgehead was thrown over the Sava at Sabac, but Fifth Army had to make its way inland largely unsupported by the other forces available to Potiorek. Sixth Army was deployed further south, guarding the border against Montenegro, while AOK had forbidden General Eduard von Böhm-Ermolli's Second Army from doing anything more than diversionary operations, leaving Fifth Army advancing on its own. It took days for all the invasion forces to cross into Serbia, and the leading regiments soon began to run out of water and food, while eyeing the local population with ill-disguised suspicion. 'This was yet another forced march in searing heat through a sea of dust on the shoddy Serbian roads', noted one Austrian on 15 August. 'To make matters worse, that evening a storm came down, with torrential rain soaking the troops – who were already dripping with sweat – right to the skin. The Serbian villages through which our regiment trekked were almost entirely deserted of their male and female population. The only people to be seen were old folk and children. As we marched past, they stood like sentries . . . clutching little sticks with once-white cloths and handkerchiefs tied to them; or with both hands raised.'[31]

Angered by tales of Serbian barbarity and exhausted by the constant demands of campaigning, Austrian officers and their men soon resorted to fearful atrocities against civilians. Locals would be rounded up and questioned, their houses looted or ransacked. If shots were fired or weapons found, Habsburg units would often carry out summary executions, shooting or bayoneting anyone who was suspected of aiding and abetting the Serbian Army. The informal nature of Serb forces, particularly local militia, who often went without uniform, fostered a belief that the Balkan nation was deliberately employing guerrilla tactics: dressing their men in civilian clothes to infiltrate Austrian lines and committing the worst excesses against enemy soldiers, including torture and mutilation. The commander of Fifth Army, General Liborius Ritter von Frank, even demanded that AOK 'set aside existing provisions of the Geneva Convention', and although this was denied, the campaign rapidly degenerated into a brutal contest of violence where no quarter was expected and little was given.[32]

At Serbian HQ in Kragujevac, sixty miles southeast of Belgrade, Putnik moved cautiously. Unsure whether the reports of Austrian divisions crossing the Drina indicated the main enemy offensive or just a diversion, he was reluctant to concentrate his armies until the situation became clearer. It was only in the early hours of 15 August that he decided to act, ordering his forces along the border to block the Austrians for as long as possible, while Second Army marched hard from the village of Tekeriš on the slopes of Mount Cer, a heavily forested ridge that rose up to 700 metres in height and formed a crucial objective for any army advancing on Valjevo.[33] Putnik now realized that the main Austrian attack was coming from the west and that any enemy activity in the north was most likely a demonstration, so he decided to fight a decisive battle while he still had time. His troops responded accordingly: one division making a forced march of forty kilometres in a single day to reach their jumping-off positions, the weather alternating between sapping heat and torrential rain.[34]

Habsburg troops reached the top of Mount Cer on the late afternoon of 15 August. The men were exhausted, their patience worn thin by guerrilla activity and having to operate at the end of increasingly tenuous supply lines. That night, amid a terrific thunderstorm, two crack Serbian regiments launched a series of ragged, chaotic attacks. Rushing up the hillsides through the long grass, they shouted that they were Croatians, part of the *Honvéd*, before opening fire and catching the defenders unawares. 'After a quick burst of fire, the Serbs charge . . . in dense lines with loud triumphant cries', recalled an Austrian witness. 'The attack comes too unexpectedly for the troops, for whom this is the first experience of close combat. They defend themselves valiantly in some places, but at other points some lose their nerve, retreating to the ravine 100 steps back in search of protection. Gradually, the whole battle line also moves backwards and soon the whole battalion retreats . . .'[35] The collapse on Mount Cer quickly spread through the rest of the army, shattering the already fragile morale of Potiorek's forces and causing a headlong rout towards the Drina.

The bulk of the invasion force was evacuated back into Bosnia on the evening of 19 August, and the remaining bridgehead at Sabac was abandoned several days later. In his first, abortive campaign, Potiorek had lost over 600 officers and 22,000 men killed, wounded or captured.[36] On the evening of 20 August, pacing around his headquarters in Sarajevo in a furious black mood, he telegraphed Conrad, pleading with him to sanction another try: 'I consider it my duty to report that, unless all sections of the Second and Sixth armies take immediate offensive action against Serbia in order to compensate as quickly as possible for its triumphs over the Fifth Army, we will likely have to contend with the most objectionable conditions in our Serb-inhabited territories, which would make my assignment extremely difficult.' But Conrad was not interested, forbidding the use of Second Army for further operations in the Balkans: 'The decision lies in the north, where all our strength must be gathered.'[37]

Every day, 7,000 Habsburg railway cars carried hundreds of thousands of troops north, regulars and reservists, to make up three full armies, with another corps-sized group assembling around Lemberg, to be joined by whatever units could be returned from Serbia. Conrad's original plan was for 'A' *Staffel* to deploy close to the Russian frontier and then mount an offensive northwards, but following the Redl leaks, he shifted his armies further westwards along the Krakow–Lemberg railway line, with two armies (First and Fourth) mounting an attack between the Vistula and the Bug, which would better aid the Germans, while the rest of his forces provided flanking protection. However, in the opening days of the war, Conrad suddenly wavered and elected to return to his original plan, only to be told by harassed railway staff that this was not possible, meaning that many regiments were dropped off before reaching their final destinations and had to get there on foot.[38]

So they would walk. One reserve officer noted how his battalion marched over twenty miles in the first day after getting off south of Lemberg. This was 'a very strong test of endurance' for his men who, as well as carrying a rifle and bayonet, were burdened with up to 50 lb of equipment: 'a knapsack containing emergency provisions in the form of tinned meats, coffee extract, sugar, salt, rice, and biscuits, together with various tin cooking and eating utensils', alongside another pair of shoes, a winter overcoat and part of a tent. 'Signs of fatigue soon manifested themselves more and more strongly,' he remembered, 'and slowly the men dropped out one by one, from sheer exhaustion.'[39] Ahead of them, Habsburg cavalry rode hard on long reconnaissance missions, crossing the border into Russian Poland with a cheer. There they began to pass through villages of transplanted Russian colonists, 'full of fear and suspicion', as one cavalryman put it. 'Old men with long beards, wearing baggy shirts and pantaloons with heeled, knee-high boots – Tolstoy types. Remarkably pretty, rosy-cheeked girls with long, heavily oiled plaits. The villages are pristine. Brightly painted gabled houses, built with their narrow sides facing the wide village streets, and charming onion-domed churches in the Orthodox style.'[40]

Advanced units, roaming far ahead of their toiling infantry, had already clashed on 21 August at Jaroslawice in what was one of the largest cavalry engagements of the war. Spotting the enemy, an Austrian cavalry division mounted a desperate charge, sabres drawn, in the manner that would have been familiar to their great-grandfathers at Austerlitz or Leipzig in the early nineteenth century. The result was a series of chaotic melees that left the fields covered with dead, wounded, and riderless horses 'mad with fear'. One Russian officer was amazed at the carnage:

The battle had just ended and the scene on the battlefield was awe-striking. The sun shone dimly from beyond a dark veil of smoke; pillars of restlessly curling dust, intertwined with yellow rays of light, wandered across the field like gloomy shadows. The yellow carpet of

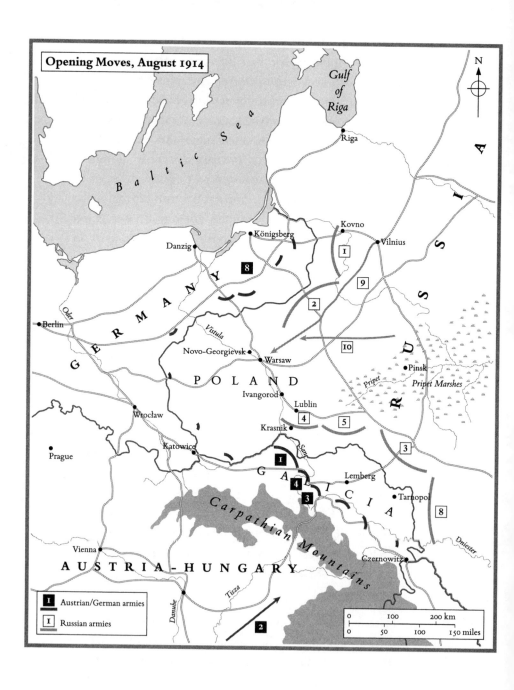

freshly harvested wheat was scattered with red and blue poppies and cornflowers – the bodies of killed and wounded Austrians. Among them, though much fewer in number, were daubs of greyish yellow – the bodies of the dead and wounded Russians. Some of the wounded men were moving; struggling to get up, their outstretched hands begging for help . . . The wounds were terrible: especially striking, with regard to the size and gruesome cruelty, were the marks on the bodies of the many dead and wounded Austrians – those were puncture wounds left by lances.[41]

Jaroslawice was an early indication that the war would present new challenges; that it would demand more than just bravery and lust for the offensive. The Habsburg cavalry, like the rest of the army, was badly outdated in its tactics and techniques, rushing into combat with an alacrity that bordered on the reckless. The Austrians had sustained up to a thousand casualties, mostly caused by enemy field guns, which showered the attacking horsemen with shrapnel as they galloped forward. The Russians, on the contrary, had suffered just 150 men killed or wounded – barely a sixth of Austrian losses – leaving them in command of the field.[42]

The struggle in the borderlands would also spring a series of nasty surprises on the Tsar's forces. As Danilov observed, 'All the border skirmishes, despite giving us certain information about the enemy, in no way gave us a definitive picture of its actual strength and grouping . . . Unfortunately, the Air Force was only in the early stages of development, so we had little support to rely upon in that department. We were still entirely dependent on the reports from our agents, as well as on rumours, which had taken various detours on their way to us and were not always reliable.'[43] Although the Russian High Command had been able to read the mobilization plan that had been leaked to them by Redl, they had not anticipated that the Austrians would greatly amend their deployments; after all, the nature of the terrain in Galicia, including the broad-backed range of the Carpathians, which curled away to the south, meant that Habsburg forces would inevitably have to focus their efforts in the northeastern corner of their empire around the city of Lemberg.

However, Conrad's unexpected shift to the left meant that the Russian right wing was badly positioned against the main body of the Habsburg Army, giving the Austrians an initial advantage in the opening battles. On 22 August, General Nikolai Yanushkevich, the Grand Duke's Chief of Staff, notified General Ivanov that they suspected something was wrong: 'It is possible that the Austrians, out of caution, have deployed most of their forces further to the west than we expected, for example in the Krakow-Przemyśl region.'[44]

Ivanov acted quickly, shifting the direction of the northern armies slightly to the west, but by the time he had reported back to *Stavka*, the two great forces had already collided at the village of Krasnik, twenty-five miles southwest of Lublin, just inside the border of Russian Poland. The twenty-third of August was a day of blazing sunshine, of heat hazes that shimmered across a parched landscape of fields and villages, farms and narrow rutted tracks. General Viktor Dankl's First Austro-Hungarian Army was drawn up in a position south of Krasnik, his men resting in woodland after days of hard marching. Dankl could deploy 230,000 men against just over 100,000 Russians, in what was the weakest of Ivanov's armies, giving him a crucial advantage in what followed.[45] Spotting columns of Russian infantry debouching to the south, he ordered his men forward, and over the course of the day, repeated attacks, often relying on sheer weight of numbers and the bayonet, resulted in what seemed like a decisive Austrian victory. 'Russians are fleeing back everywhere', Dankl wrote to his wife. 'Our troops were magnificent . . . The 76 Infantry Regiment charged three times, although half were left behind. The men are unstoppable; they charge at the enemy with unrelenting vigour.' They had captured 5,000 prisoners, three regimental flags, 28 guns and seven machine-guns, and Dankl was hopeful of reaching Lublin in several days' time. But the price of victory had been high. 'Individual battalions have suffered severe losses', he noted; 'even the cavalry has been hit fairly hard. The Russians – as long as they do not outnumber us too heavily – are no match for us.'[46]

Austrian regiments had shown an impressive willingness to go on the offensive, much as Conrad had been demanding, but the shock of battle was brutal. The troops advanced in mass formation, shoulder to shoulder, only to come under heavy bombardment as they tried to close with the enemy. In theory, Austrian divisions could deploy a similar number of field guns to Russian divisions (42 to 48 pieces), but many of these were outdated and in need of a thorough overhaul. For example, the workhorse of the army was the M.5/8 *Feldkanone*, first introduced in 1907, which had to be equipped with 'steel bronze' barrels because of a lack of funds. Not only did this make the guns much heavier, it also reduced their effective range and reliability, with the barrels tending to warp after intensive firing. The army also had severe shortages of modern heavy artillery, with only eight 150 mm howitzers per corps, leaving the Habsburg Army woefully under-gunned.[47]

Russian tactics were, in most cases, as unsubtle as Austrian ones, but there was a greater skill in Russian regiments, an earthy toughness that made them difficult to beat. The Russian Army had learnt much from its ultimately doomed war against Japan in 1904–5, when it had first experienced modern firepower: quick-firing field artillery, magazine rifles and machine-guns. Although the campaign in Manchuria had been lost, with Japanese forces seizing Port Arthur and taking control of the Korean Peninsula, it forced Russia into long-overdue military reforms. By the time war broke out in 1914, Russian infantry could boast much improved musketry, and its artillery had been trained in firing at longer ranges, including indirect fire from covered positions, a skill that most armies in the early stages of the Great War had little or no knowledge of. This quickly became a key advantage in the early battles of manoeuvre.[48]

The Battle of Krasnik was only the beginning of a mighty series of clashes right across the front. On 26 August, the Austrian Fourth Army collided with the Russian Fifth Army at Komarów, sixty miles east of Krasnik. The battle was another bloody engagement, characterized by a kind of desperate fury as both sides hurled themselves forward with all the aggression they could muster. It was as though they wanted to settle the matter quickly, one way or another. Once again Habsburg forces outnumbered their opponents and forced the Russians into a desperate scramble to hold their positions, showing a commitment to the offensive that pleased their army commander, General Moritz von Auffenberg. 'In several encounters, the regiments and battalions marched up swiftly and immediately began to advance, again with the vigour that is so characteristic of our troops, almost leaving themselves without back-up from the batteries, for which the route through the sands and marshes was slow and arduous.' Auffenberg was particularly impressed by the performance of 85 Infantry Regiment (a 'colourful mixture of Hungarians, Romanians, Ruthenians and Slovaks'), which entered battle for the first time since it had been established, 'taking three enemy positions one after the other; charging forth with bayonets and capturing 300 prisoners and four machine guns. That said, 450 men lay dead on the battlefield, and 1,000 wounded had to be brought back. In this one operation, the regiment had lost nearly fifty per cent of its strength, and it cannot be praised enough for the fact that, despite this diminishing its fighting power, its intrinsic value remained intact.'[49]

Over the next four days, Auffenberg continued to feed units into battle, sending them to his left to turn the Russian flank, conscious that time was running out for a decisive battle of envelopment. But there was never enough manpower available, and with Russian units showing a stubborn tenacity in defence – their infantry would dig in at every opportunity – Austrian regiments struggled to make progress. Russian artillery swept them away whenever they tried to close with their positions, leaving them pinned down under murderous fire. 'The unrelenting cannonade turned the battlefield . . . into a living hell', recorded one Habsburg account. 'And the events of those terrible hours exceeded all previously held expectations of the war.' It was little wonder that after being under bombardment for several hours, men would simply get up and try to leave the battlefield.[50]

Notwithstanding Russian advantages in firepower, the ferocity of the Austrian attacks meant that by the second day, the Russian line had bent and cracked, with its right flank becoming dangerously exposed. Auffenberg appealed to Conrad to send him troops from Third Army, which lay out to the east, raising the prospect that they would strike the Russian left and complete a double envelopment, but the commander of the Russian Fifth Army, General Pavel Plehve, ordered his army to break contact on 30 August. Habsburg forces tried to follow as quickly as they could, but deepening exhaustion meant that their pursuit was haphazard and slow. 'When marching through the abandoned enemy position,' recorded one regimental history, 'evidence could already be seen of heavy expansion and the skilful installation of flanking systems. Discarded rifles and huge quantities of ammunition had been left behind. The trenches of the Russian reserves were badly polluted; horse carcasses, unburied corpses, items of clothing and supplies lay scattered about. The few prisoners that had been captured were all Poles who appeared to have been taken captive voluntarily.' Losses in Plehve's army amounted to around 30,000 men – about a quarter of its entire strength.[51]

Auffenberg had won a 'half victory' at Komarów; a tantalizing glimpse of what a true battle of encirclement could have looked like in the late summer of 1914. But Plehve's decision to retreat meant that the Russians avoided the fate of being surrounded and destroyed. Auffenberg's forces had captured 20,000 prisoners and 100 guns – an impressive haul – but the cost of doing so had been extortionate. Fourth Army had lost 40,000 men, about 20 per cent of its total strength.[52] Looking back years later, Auffenberg was sanguine about what happened. 'The battle that ensued was an extremely eventful and bloody eight-day struggle. As with any real encounter battle – such as Custoza, for example – attack followed counter-attack and, with the constant arrival of new battle groups, the decision wavered back and forth until – finally – the sum of the individual victories and the compelling power of the idea forced the extremely brave enemy to evacuate the battlefield and make a general retreat.'[53] This was a fair assessment, but newspapers across the empire would soon be emblazoned with reports of the 'complete, brilliant victory' on the northern front, and Auffenberg would later be rewarded with an elevation in status to 'Baron von Komarów' in recognition of his services.[54] In the last days of August, perhaps it was still possible to think that the double-headed eagle, the legendary black and yellow symbol of the Austro-Hungarian Empire, would return with some of its old vigour, having lost nothing in the long years of sad, decaying peace.

2.   'A new and difficult task'

As Austria–Hungary grappled with the main body of the Russian Army, the German garrison of East Prussia was also faced by what seemed like dangerously lopsided odds. General Maximilian von Prittwitz, a white-haired 65-year-old veteran of the Franco-Prussian War, was responsible for the defence of this corner of Germany as commander of Eighth Army, which was deployed in an arc either side of the Masurian Lakes, from Insterburg down to Allenstein and Tannenberg. His task was not easy. With two Russian armies advancing from two different directions, east and south, a strategy of pure defence was not feasible. It was well understood that Germany would have to go onto the offensive at some point, presumably relying upon the Masurian Lakes to separate the enemy forces and strike one army before the other could intervene. But if this could not be done, then they should, as Count Schlieffen had noted as early as 1898, withdraw behind the Vistula river and abandon any attempt at holding East Prussia.[1]

Prittwitz soon began to have doubts whether any offensive plan could work. Fighting had already broken out on 20 August at the village of Gumbinnen after one of his corps had launched a spoiling attack against the advancing Russian First Army, only to be countered and driven back in confusion. 'The fire we opened on the enemy all along the line was so precise and deliberate (and the target was so big!) that the Germans, having suffered huge casualties, had to stop and drop to the ground', recorded a Russian officer. Repeated assaults all failed, 'despite the utter contempt for death displayed by the brave sons of Germany. Many of them were killed here in these open attacks, as they advanced in columns keeping tight formation!'[2] By the early afternoon, the landscape around Gumbinnen was clouded by thick smoke, the air ringing to the clatter of artillery and rifle fire as both sides dug in. Casualties had been heavier than expected: the

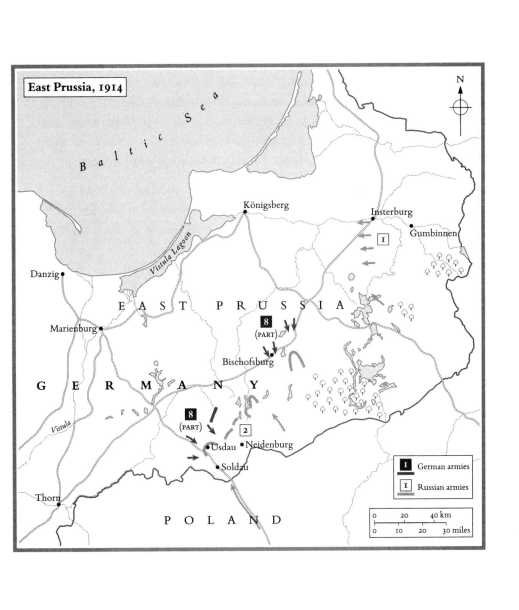

East Prussia, 1914

Russian 28th Division lost 60 per cent of its fighting strength (about 7,000 officers and men), while the German XVII Corps suffered 8,000 killed, wounded or missing including 200 officers.[3]

With the German attack having stalled, the mood in the Russian camp became increasingly bellicose. They had bested their opponent, showing that they were far from being outmatched on the modern battlefield. The following morning, as Prittwitz's forces slipped away, the commander of the Russian First Army, General Paul Rennenkampf, sent a report on tactics to *Stavka*. As in Galicia, the most noticeable aspect of the campaign so far was the power of modern artillery and its devastating effect against infantry in the open:

> In the battles on 4 and 7 August [OS], the largest number of casualties was caused by the enemy's artillery fire. As expected, it was clear that the Germans were looking to determine the fate of the battle on the flanks as they tried to swoop around them. In the lines, the enemy is deploying strong artillery, even heavy guns, in an attempt to gain an advantage in firepower. What is more, they position their heavy artillery against our flanks, which they intended to bypass. The artillery fire of the Germans is highly effective, which to some extent is explained by the precision of obviously pre-measured distances to certain lines and local objects. That said, as the outcome of the battles and the information from the interrogation of prisoners and wounded enemy soldiers revealed, the firepower of our own artillery is in no way less destructive than that of the Germans, as it inflicts heavy losses and rapidly sweeps asunder all targets in its path . . .

Rennenkampf was confident that all was proceeding to plan. 'It is not that difficult to stop the enemy on the front line', he wrote. Enemy battalions would advance and then go to ground when they came under fire, often refusing to move off again. 'The general impression is that, when the Germans manage to gain the advantage in technical equipment, they hold our troops and cause us great losses. However, I believe that – regarding the art of war and the spirit of morale – the Germans have not exhibited any advantage.'[4]

The mood at General Prittwitz's headquarters could not have been more different, and the sight of German regiments stumbling back from the front was an unnerving spectacle. 'I may now report to Your Imperial and Royal Majesty that the troops have fought with great courage and have hitherto endured all endeavours well', Prittwitz wrote to the Kaiser after Gumbinnen. He admitted that there had been some 'inadequate preparation by artillery', which had led to 'avoidable losses', and noted how Russian guns 'fire extremely well', while their infantry 'take advantage of every opportunity, even skipping rest, in order to dig new positions and trenches'. Worried about the advance of General Alexander Samsonov's Second Army, which was bypassing the Masurian Lakes to the south and threatening to cut Eighth Army off from the rest of Germany, he telephoned the Supreme Command, OHL (*Oberst Heeresleitung*), on the evening of 21 August, warning that he might be forced to abandon East Prussia if reinforcements were not rushed to him. 'The XVII Corps is as good as done', he reported. When Moltke asked what he was going to do, Prittwitz said that he wanted to break off the action. A withdrawal would be 'extremely difficult' – there were 'swarms' of Russian cavalry around – but he thought it could be done.[5]

Such a disconcerting start to the war was certainly not how the German High Command had imagined things might turn out. At almost four million men strong, with a history of victory over Denmark, Austria and France between 1864 and 1871, the German Empire had what was by common consent the strongest army in the world. It was effectively trained and well equipped, whether with its excellent 1888 Gewehr bolt-action rifle or its array of medium and heavy artillery, so much was expected from Berlin's land forces. But with most of the army sent to knock out France, the garrison in the east would have to rely on quick thinking and manoeuvre if it was not to be completely overrun. For Colonel-General Moltke, Germany's Chief of the General Staff, then struggling to coordinate the movement of seven armies in the west, this was precisely what he now feared. His uncle, Helmuth von Moltke the elder, the man who had masterminded many of these great victories, had once said that 'No plan of operations survives the first collision with the main body of the enemy.' This certainly seemed to be true in East Prussia and, accordingly, things would have to change.[6]

Sensing that Prittwitz had lost his nerve, Moltke summoned General Paul von Hindenburg and asked him to take over the defence of East Prussia. At 66 years old, Hindenburg was already retired, but was a capable and careful soldier, not likely to be panicked in a crisis and well regarded enough to have been considered as a possible replacement for Schlieffen in 1906. Moltke also ordered Erich Ludendorff, 17 years Hindenburg's junior, to act as the new Chief of Staff. Ludendorff, who had just taken part in the storming of the Belgian fortress of Liège and was known throughout the army as something of a rising star, was handed a letter on 22 August informing him of his new appointment. 'You have before you a new and difficult task', wrote Moltke. 'I know no other man in whom I have such absolute trust. You may yet be able to save the situation in the East . . . Of course, you will not be made responsible for what has already happened, but with your energy you can prevent the worst from happening.'[7]

All now hinged on the speed with which the Russian Second Army could move. On the maps at *Stavka*, the advance of General Samsonov's forces must have seemed smooth and unassailable, but the supply system it relied upon was already 'disorganized to the point of confusion'. Second Army headquarters had been hurriedly cobbled together from three different military districts, and in its rush to begin the campaign, the army went to war without its proper establishment of field bakeries and transport vehicles. Up to 60 per cent of its manpower consisted of 'newly reported reservists', and there was a disorganized feel to the invasion force as it trudged along the dirt tracks and narrow sandy roads that led towards East Prussia. Because the roads in northern Poland had been kept deliberately poor, to deter German invasion, fast movement was all but impossible. With five corps spread out over sixty miles of front, all heavily wooded and littered with lakes and ponds, Samsonov was forced to rely on wireless radio to send messages; a choice that raised the possibility of interception, but which was judged a risk worth taking in the absence of alternatives.[8]

Such frictions did not impress the commander of the Russian Northwest Front, General Zhilinsky, at his headquarters at Bialystok. Desperate for a quick victory, and assuming that the Germans were in headlong retreat towards the Vistula, he ordered Samsonov to 'execute a most energetic offensive against the front Sensburg-Allenstein' with the aim of intercepting German units fleeing from Gumbinnen. With only insignificant forces in their way, there must be no additional delays. But in General Samsonov's headquarters, there was only growing disorder and an alarming lack of intelligence. General Postovsky, Samsonov's Chief of Staff, sent a cautious report on 25 August, pointing out the difficulties they were facing. 'Though fully recognizing the necessity for advancing unceasingly and energetically . . . the Army Commander has been forced to make a halt.' He explained that they had been marching for eight days and throughout this period had struggled to provide enough bread for their men, who had to eat their iron rations and live off the land. But Zhilinsky was not interested, and when Second Army requested permission to move its line of march to the west to ward off any potential threat to its flank or rear, he refused, warning darkly that he would not permit Samsonov 'to play the coward'.[9]

Samsonov was right to be cautious. Already Hindenburg and Ludendorff were rapidly redeploying their forces, taking advantage of the dense railway network to move division after division to concentrate against Samsonov, leaving only a thin cavalry screen to ward off Rennenkampf. It was an audacious gamble – the attempt to strike a decisive blow before time ran out – but one that was thoroughly familiar to generations of staff officers who had practised such a possibility in training. It was also attempted with the certainty that little could be expected from Rennenkampf over the next few days. German intelligence had already intercepted numerous wireless messages, including a complete army order, which revealed his line of advance and showed that he would not be close enough to intervene in the forthcoming battle by 26 August.[10] The plan was simple: I Corps would be transported to attack the Russian left at Usdau, while another corps struck on the right at Bischofsburg. Meanwhile, Samsonov's two central corps would be allowed to continue marching north towards their objective of Allenstein. 'We had not merely to win a victory over Samsonoff [sic]', Hindenburg wrote years later. 'We had to annihilate him.'[11]

Battle was joined on the morning of 26 August. German regiments went straight into combat, often attacking without artillery support, with morale seemingly unimpaired by the setback at Gumbinnen. 'After the most strenuous forced march,' reported 4 Grenadier Regiment, 'under scorching heat, unbearable dust, excruciating thirst', they had reached their jumping-off point. But before they had had a chance to recuperate, orders were issued to form up immediately. With 'growling stomachs', the men got up and jogged through the 'broken terrain . . . towards the thunder of cannon fire'.[12] With the Russian left under attack, fighting broke out across the entire front, as the centre and then the right wing came under fierce pressure. Still Samsonov's forces kept moving forward, with his centre corps pushing towards Allenstein, hoping that they were driving into the German rear, only to find themselves in a bag that was rapidly being sewn up.

The plan may have been working far better than anyone dared hope, but a sense of unease still lingered over the command team at Eighth Army as the battle unfolded. On the evening of 26 August, Hindenburg and Ludendorff set up their advanced headquarters at Löbau and sifted through the reports that had come in. An intercepted message had revealed the arrival of Russian reinforcements at Soldau, which might have been part of a new corps assembling around Warsaw. Despite wearing a deep frown on his face, Hindenburg remained a stolid, unflappable presence, carefully examining the evidence before him and never overreacting. Ludendorff was more highly strung, worrying constantly about where Rennenkampf was and afraid that they would find themselves outflanked and surrounded. At some point, Ludendorff spoke to Hindenburg alone and they discussed whether they should continue their attack or break it off, with the commander of Eighth Army insisting that they must carry out their plans. The crisis was overcome.[13]

Russian troops fought with their usual stoicism and skill, but too often in a disjointed, uncoordinated manner. Each corps fought its own war, attacking where it could but frequently finding its battalions outflanked or pushed back, with little support from neighbouring units. East Prussia was not Galicia – there were no great open plains where Russian superiority could be easily brought to bear. Here, in the 'hornets' nest' (as it would soon be called), fighting was close and bitter, taking place in small hamlets, villages and dense forests, where the advantage lay with those who knew the ground. Samsonov became so disheartened by his inability to work out what was going on that on 28 August he decided to take personal control. He rode forward to the headquarters of XV Corps at the village of Nadrau, leaving his telegraph equipment behind and sending a short final note to Zhilinsky informing him that he was proceeding 'to take control of the corps in their offensive . . . I shall be temporarily without communication with you.'[14]

From this moment on, darkness rapidly began to overtake Second Army. With the Russian left flank turned at Usdau, German troops took Soldau and then began racing towards Neidenburg, while another corps came down from the north heading for Ortelsburg. Samsonov lacked the aerial reconnaissance that the Germans relied upon, leaving him flailing helplessly. Having been told that there were only the fleeing remnants of one or two corps in front of him, he was now under attack from almost every direction and could see no way out. Instead of executing a rapid withdrawal, his infantry stood their ground and fought with commendable tenacity. Soldiers fixed their bayonets and tried to flush out German positions, only to run into machine-gun fire and shrapnel that decimated their ranks. The Tsar's forces may have outgunned the Austrians, but German units possessed a marked advantage in firepower. Each division could deploy 72 guns, including eighteen powerful 105 mm howitzers. This was further enhanced by sixteen 150 mm howitzers ('the best medium guns in the world'), which were highly effective at demolishing buildings and field fortifications. Russia had planned to begin a major programme of investment in field and heavy artillery in 1915, but the war broke out before it could be implemented, leaving her first-line divisions fielding just six batteries of 76 mm field guns and two six-gun batteries of light guns (60 pieces in total).[15]

And so the net was drawn and the Russian line of retreat severed. By 30 August, three entire Russian corps had been surrounded, and however many times they tried to escape, thin German cordons were able to push them back. Thousands of increasingly desperate Russian soldiers – exhausted, hungry and thirsty – milled around the forests, seeking an escape where none existed, oblivious to the orders of their officers. And then, unit by unit, sometimes in small groups, sometimes in large pockets, they began to surrender, raising white flags and approaching the German lines to seek terms, or simply sitting on the ground, their heads on their knees, waiting for their captors to come. In total, 92,000 Russian soldiers were taken prisoner, including three corps commanders, in what became known as the Battle of Tannenberg.[16] The scale of the losses, particularly of officers, was staggering. In just a single division (1st), the Chief of Staff had been killed, two brigade commanders had died of wounds, three regimental commanders had been wounded and another three killed in action. This was the devastatingly high price paid for the Grand Duke's 'earliest possible offensive' against Germany.[17]

Hindenburg and Ludendorff had achieved what Auffenberg had failed to do at Komarów: complete the encirclement of an army and realize the dream of a modern Cannae. In the early hours of 30 August, the forests echoing to sporadic gunfire, General Samsonov realized that he was trapped. German patrols were everywhere, giving him little chance of escape. He left his personal Cossack guard behind, limped off into a quiet glade and shot himself with his revolver. The only man who could have come to his aid, General Rennenkampf, spent the day responding to a series of confused orders from Zhilinsky. At 7 a.m., a telegram arrived from army group reporting that because of the 'heavy fighting in which the Second Army is engaged', Rennenkampf was to send 'two corps to their support' and move his cavalry 'in the general direction of Allenstein'. This was followed four hours later by a second telegram: 'The Second Army having retreated, the Army Group Commander has given orders to stop the further advance of the two corps pushed forward by you.'[18]

Rennenkampf was not lacking in personal courage, but he had shown little initiative in the opening rounds, certainly not enough to overcome the lethargy inherent in the Russian command system.

Instead of ordering the ceaseless pursuit of the enemy, he let them get away. His troops did not restart their advance from Gumbinnen until 23 August, and then moved forward cautiously, scenting danger at every village and from behind every fold of land. But for days they sighted no foe. Rennenkampf reported on 25 August that he had not received any 'new information about the enemy' and that long-distance cavalry patrols had reached the town of Tilsit, with civilians fleeing into Königsberg. There were occasional shots fired at his men, with villages being burnt to the ground in retaliation, even an airship that flew overhead, but the main body of the German Eighth Army was nowhere to be found. The following morning, 26 August, the day the German offensive against Samsonov opened, Rennenkampf was still unsure, reporting that his cavalry 'has not yet discovered the direction of the enemy retreat'. It would all become clear very soon.[19]

News of the destruction of the Russian Second Army produced a wave of depression, mixed with anger, at *Stavka*. After learning of Samsonov's fate, the Grand Duke penned a lengthy telegram to the Tsar on 31 August, taking responsibility for what had happened and blaming the 'catastrophe' on a 'lack of communication' between each corps.[20] Soon afterwards, he travelled to the front headquarters at Bialystok to hear about it for himself. Peter Kondzerovskii, an aide to General Yanushkevich, observed that 'The trip was most unpleasant and the Grand Duke – along with his associates – was awfully low-spirited. Before reaching Bialystok we arrived at a small railway station, where the Grand Duke was met by General Zhilinsky, who immediately entered the Supreme Commander's carriage. The tone of the meeting was almost funereal: everyone spoke in hushed voices . . . The Grand Duke and Zhilinsky talked for an hour or an hour and a half and, after Zhilinsky left, we received the order to withdraw immediately.'[21]

A formal investigation was started, but it did not have to look far to come up with a suitable scapegoat. The army commander's suicide had saved the Grand Duke from a more searching inquiry into the reasons for the disaster: the haste with which the invasion of East Prussia had been undertaken as well as the almost total lack of reconnaissance, combined with supply shortages, which reduced Second Army to a shambolic mess. Zhilinsky's report, penned shortly after the disaster, placed the blame squarely on Samsonov's decision to move nearer the front. Because of this, he removed himself from command at a crucial time, allowing German cavalry to head for Neidenburg and cut off the Russian retreat. 'While the behaviour and orders of General Samsonov, as a commander, deserve severe condemnation, his actions as a warrior have been most valiant; putting himself in great danger, he personally directed the battle under enemy fire, and forfeited his own life out of determination not to endure defeat.'[22]

More pressing was the fact that Poland was now open to invasion. Officers at *Stavka* nervously pored over their maps and noticed that the rear areas of Fourth and Fifth Armies, then engaged in heavy fighting to the south, were vulnerable to attack. As Danilov noted, they had already been warned that as many as seventy German trains were ready to move troops between east and west. 'Given the number of trains required to transport an army corps and the length of time it would take to move an army corps from the Western Front to the Eastern Front, it was not difficult to calculate that no less than an entire army corps was en route, probably even more, and that we could therefore expect the appearance of new troops on our Eastern Front as early as the beginning of September.'[23] The need to win a decisive victory in Galicia was now paramount, with the Grand Duke looking to a new post-war settlement in this region. He had already issued a proclamation to the Poles, telling them that the 'resurrection of the Polish nation' was at hand and that the Russian armies were 'bringing you the glad message of this reconciliation', which would result in a 'reborn' Poland, 'free in her faith, language, and self-government'.[24]

If a reunified greater Poland was to be created, then the Russian Army would have to move quickly, but the advance of the Southwest Front's powerful left wing, Third and Eighth Armies, had been slower than expected, which had caused some frustration at *Stavka*. They had crossed into Galicia on 18 August – Franz Joseph's eighty-fourth birthday – with General Nikolai Ruzski, the commander of Third Army, behaving with 'almost psychotic prudence', worried that he was facing the main body of the Austrian army.[25] Impatient as ever, the Grand Duke demanded more. On 31 August, he telegraphed General Ivanov: 'In view of a great check in the 2nd Army, and of the necessity of finishing with the Austrians before the arrival from the west of German reinforcements, the Commander-in-Chief has ordered the Armies of the Southwest Front to pass to the most decisive action against the Austrians ... In those sectors where the situation renders an offensive impossible, the troops must hold their positions to the last man.'[26]

Their objective was the Austro-Hungarian right wing, the weakest part of Conrad's forces. With Böhm-Ermolli's Second Army still straggling in from Serbia, the Habsburg right flank consisted of just Third Army, with another corps, known as the Kövess Group, acting as a flank guard. Although shielded by three rivers and a series of steep valleys, they were dangerously exposed against the combined might of the Russian invaders. Habsburg officials had assessed that significant enemy forces were probably assembling somewhere east of Lemberg, but Conrad paid little attention to this. His focus remained on delivering his offensive with as few distractions as possible. When it was confirmed that Russian cavalry and at least one infantry corps had entered Habsburg territory, he ordered General Rudolf von Bruderman's Third Army to 'deliver a decisive blow' against the enemy approaching from Brody and Tarnopol, and then begin an offensive 'in a northerly direction'.[27]

Bruderman's forces made contact with the Russians along the swampy banks of the Zlota Lipa on 26 August, and it quickly became apparent that he was not dealing with an isolated force, but was now entangled with the main body of the Russian Army, eight corps strong. Urged on by AOK, he ordered his divisions forward, but whereas Dankl and Auffenberg had been able to exploit the element of surprise and make use of their superiority in numbers, Bruderman had no such advantage. Nor could he avoid the problems that had afflicted other Habsburg formations: a lack of artillery support, poor tactical coordination and a reliance on mass infantry attacks. As one regimental history noted:

Those were hard days, and now we have an idea of what fighting and dying really means. Until he has experienced all the intricacies of war with his own eyes, his own body and his own soul, no man could ever truly imagine it: marching through sand and marshland, through these fathomless swampy forests in the searing heat, with no water and often with his stomach groaning in hunger. And then suddenly, as you are plodding along, so tired and bruised and battered, the scene comes alive before you – nobody can say what is happening; the first shots are barking in your ears and the roaring and howling of the shells is getting nearer and nearer. To one side, you hear the crackling of machine-gun fire ... You taste the battle – a peculiar sour yet bland taste that settles in your mouth. And you feel it, because all your nerves and muscles contract and your brain can think of one thing and one thing only: you have to act.[28]

Habsburg officers did not lack the will to act, but they soon realized that blind courage was not enough. Leading their men into battle, they found that discipline and order broke down quickly under fire, leaving them struggling to keep attacks going. Colonel Rudolf Pfeffer, Bruderman's Chief of Staff, noted how division after division came to a halt under heavy shellfire. 'As long as the enemy artillery fire – which projected dense, explosive clouds of shrapnel onto the horizon in a thick, white line – could not be quelled to some extent by our own artillery, further action was out of the question ... But the resistance of the enemy infantry was growing greater and greater. Men also began to force their way across trenches and obstacles into the forest itself. Machine guns in trees made their presence felt. The troops were already extremely bewildered.'[29] Faced with imminent disaster, the Third Army commander had no choice but to fall back to another river line, twenty miles to the west, the Gnila Lipa, where he prepared to make another stand.

When he learnt about Bruderman's retreat, Conrad became furious, shouting at an aide that Third Army had failed because it had disobeyed his orders! He relieved Pfeffer of his duties and urgently began shifting his divisions around, plugging gaps where necessary while leaving others wide open. He ordered Auffenberg's Fourth

Army to wheel right as soon as it had completed its planned envelopment of Russian forces around Komarów, leaving only token units in
place, while marching to the relief of Third Army. The first of September was, he admitted, 'a day of serious crises': 'Will the First
Army be able to continue its attack? Will the operation of the Fourth
Army really turn out to be a great success and enable support from
the Third Army? Will they be able to hold their own at Lemberg, and
will the Second Army also be in a position to actively intervene to the
right of the Third Army? Those were the questions I was faced with.
But however they might play out, I was determined not to give up
the struggle, but to press ahead with new resolve at all times.'[30]

Conrad would find that moving armies on the map was easier than
doing it on foot. Auffenberg's troops were exhausted by the recent
hard marching and fighting, and many regiments had suffered such
heavy losses that it took days to properly re-form their companies
and reorganize their battalions. Auffenberg kept driving his men on,
trying to complete his envelopment, but he had to break off his pursuit on 2 September after receiving a direct order from Archduke
Friedrich to turn around and redeploy south as soon as possible. By
that point, Third Army had been pushed out of its positions on the
Gnila Lipa and Bruderman had ordered his men to occupy defensive
positions west of Lemberg, thus abandoning the capital of Galicia.
Aware of Conrad's growing unhappiness with his performance, Bruderman tried to remain optimistic: 'The Third and Second Army
have slowed a numerically superior enemy in his march west . . .
Now Fourth Army is turning to support us in a combined attack on
the enemy – the hour for our revenge on this overconfident foe has
come!'[31]

But revenge would have to wait. Troops from General Aleksei Brusilov's Eighth Army marched into Lemberg on 3 September, accompanied
by music and singing, while the civilian population – those who had not
fled – huddled inside their homes. A delegation from the municipal
council came out to speak to the Russian commander, who demanded
a guarantee of the safety and security of his men. Sixteen civilians were
chosen as hostages from each of the main ethnic groups in the city:
Poles, Ukrainians, Old Ruthenians and Jews.[32] The capture of such an

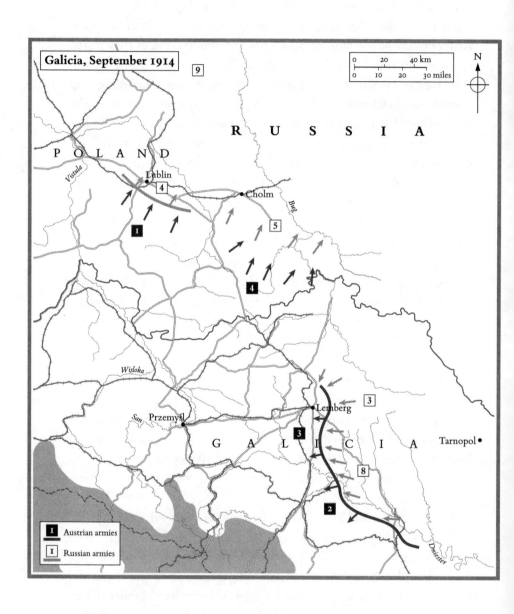

Galicia, September 1914

important centre was a triumphant moment for *Stavka*, which was still reeling in the aftermath of Tannenberg. Danilov called it 'of extreme political and psychological importance', and admitted that it gave Russia control of 'a whole series of important railway lines and roads leading to the San and Dniester' and 'compensated, to some extent, for the failures we had suffered in East Prussia'.[33] Finally, the Grand Duke had a victory to his name. He dashed off a suitably ebullient telegram to his commanders congratulating them on their 'glorious deeds' but warning them that the 'most heroic efforts' would still be required over the coming weeks.[34]

With each passing day, more Russian troops arrived in theatre. By the first week of September, their strength on the southern front had risen to thirty-six divisions (allowing the formation of a new Ninth Army) against just twenty battered Austro-Hungarian divisions. The Habsburgs were now caught in a fatal embrace with an opponent superior in almost every respect, and, even more worryingly, a dangerous gap of over thirty miles had opened up between Dankl's forces south of Krasnik and Auffenberg's Fourth Army at Rawa Ruska, raising the possibility that Conrad's armies would be defeated in detail.[35] On the day that Lemberg had fallen, General Ivanov issued new orders to his army commanders preparing them for what he hoped would be the 'final defeat' of the enemy. While Brusilov would occupy the line of the Dniester south of Lemberg, 'the armies of generals Lechitsky, Evert, Plehve, and Ruzski must relentlessly keep watch over the enemy located between the Vistula and the Bug: they must prevent them from retreating, force them to fight and inflict defeat upon them, joining up to throw the enemy back to the Vistula'.[36]

Russian forces had recovered quickly from their initial setbacks in Galicia. Although casualties had been heavy and shortages of ammunition were beginning to bite, the Russian campaign was showing a quality akin to the mythical 'steamroller' that had so haunted the pre-war European imagination. General Plehve's Fifth Army, which had been badly mauled at Komarów, had re-formed and its cavalry were beginning to probe into the yawning gap in the Hungarian line. On 6 September, Plehve fell upon Auf exposed left flank, beginning a series of desperate actions that would later be known as the Battle of Rawa Ruska. Austrian troops were able to hold on to their positions, particularly in wooded areas where shellfire was less effective, but everywhere else the superiority of Russian guns was again noticeable. 'At sunrise, artillery fire of all calibres begins on our lines', recorded a Habsburg cavalryman. 'An unearthly sound. Our battery division, close behind us on horseback, retaliates with all its might. But the Russians are far, far superior. Their heavy shells plough into the fields; the trenches burst open, loosening the soil; explosives stream through the air; the clods hit our ears, covering everything with fine dust, while the repulsive stench of the explosives takes our breath away.'[37]

By 9 September, after three days of see-sawing combat, attack followed by counter-attack, Conrad's two northern armies, First and Fourth, were teetering on the brink of collapse. Outnumbered, their flanks menaced by Russian cavalry, they had no choice but to give ground, abandoning scores of guns and leaving the field to the victors, who marched forward with ever-growing confidence. The sight of the abandoned Habsburg positions was terrible: 'piles of human and animal corpses, entire blocks of burning buildings, the crackle of bursting cartridges, the wailing of horses, wounded and abandoned in great numbers – all this along with the heavy, suffocating air, made a disheartening impression'.[38] Although *Stavka* was still concerned about the fighting around Lemberg, with Third and Eighth Armies having been under heavy attack for days, the weakening of the enemy's northern flank offered the perfect opportunity to round up Habsburg units and bring about the decisive moment of the campaign, if only Russian forces could cut off the Austrian retreat. On 10 September, General Ivanov's Chief of Staff, Alekseev, telephoned Brusilov and told him that it would be of 'great benefit to the Motherland' if Eighth Army could just hold firm, and that the fruits of its 'heroic efforts' would be reaped by the other armies.[39]

With the Austrian lines beginning to buckle, Conrad tried to get nearer the front, one of the few occasions he would do so during the war. Accompanied by Archduke Friedrich and Archduke Karl (Franz Joseph's great-nephew and the heir to the throne), he visited Third

Army's area of operations on 10 September, driving out to the town of Grodek, only to encounter a scene of chaos. 'Trains, transports of wounded soldiers, prisoner of war convoys, everything covered in thick dust, ammunition parks, camped troops. Initially muffled and incoherent, later the noise of the battlefield grew louder', he noted. 'Shelling, rifle fire, the intermittent crackling of machine guns. In the firmament, the white explosive clouds of shrapnel . . .' When they got to Grodek, they were met with grisly scenes. The town was burnt to the ground. Six bodies had been left hanging in the main square. 'Two for betraying the enemy, the others for robbing dead and wounded troops on the battlefield . . . Archduke Friedrich followed these new developments with a cold calmness; Archduke Karl with youthful interest. He was courageous and fearless, just as I always found him to be on similar occasions later on.'[40]

Conrad was taken to the highest point on the battlefield, from where he peered through his binoculars, scanning the long expanse of countryside, the ground muddied by the movement of thousands of troops, hearing the rumble of gunfire on the wind. Even though he clung to the dwindling hope that his great battle of manoeuvre and encirclement could be completed, the terrible news from his northern flank, where Dankl and Auffenberg were faced with disaster, forced his hand. At 5.30 p.m. the following day, 11 September, he finally bowed to the inevitable and ordered his armies to retreat behind the San river. 'The actions of the Second and Third Armies had not resulted in a widely effective and resounding decision', he recalled. 'On the contrary, the left wing of the Fourth Army was under serious threat and there was concern that the invasion of two Russian corps could have catastrophic consequences for the Fourth Army. This in turn would impact the Third and Second Armies and drive the main body of the Imperial and Royal forces away from Western Galicia.' He was determined to prevent this at all costs and knew that he must play for time and keep his armies intact: 'the battle would be aborted and the armies would retreat behind the San'.[41] This moment of failure, when all his plans lay in ruins, left the usually confident Chief of the General Staff bereft. It was fitting that on 12 September, as AOK left Przemyśl to take up new quarters at

Neu-Sandec, about ninety miles to the west, it rained heavily, the sky burdened by dark clouds.

The Habsburg Army would never be the same again. Of the 900,000 men who had marched north to face General Ivanov's Southwest Front, fewer than two thirds reached the San. In four weeks of campaigning, perhaps as many as 250,000 soldiers were killed or wounded and another 100,000 taken prisoner, with losses falling particularly heavily upon long-serving regular officers who could not easily be replaced. Leading their men from the front, often riding up and down the lines in plain sight of the enemy, Habsburg officers were easily spotted and easily killed.[42] While the staff at AOK congratulated themselves on such valour and courage, the long trail of shattered regiments streaming away from the line told another story: one of disorganization, hopelessness and terror. 'Train convoys of all military branches blocked the streets for miles', recorded one witness. 'The infantry had been marching along the fields next to the streets so as not to get caught up in the chaos. All the languages of the monarchy could be heard screeching in a wild cacophony of voices; the drivers struck each other with their whips, horse-mounted train commanders vented their frustration with repeated shots from their pistols. Hundreds of broken and bullet-ridden wagons lay in the trenches, alongside bloated horse carcasses and the corpses of soldiers.'[43]

AOK now began urgently to look for German support. Archduke Friedrich had written to the Kaiser as early as 2 September requesting an offensive out of Silesia, while reminding him of Germany's promise to send aid after the defeat of France. The Kaiser, unimpressed by such special pleading, dismissed it angrily, telling the Austro-Hungarian military liaison officer, Josef Stürgkh, that his 'small army' had fought off twelve enemy corps, several of which had been completely destroyed. 'You can't ask more of her than what she has achieved.'[44] Such an attitude would only become more pronounced as Austria–Hungary became even less able to mount independent operations. Stürgkh found himself an outsider at OHL, struggling to pick up information on how the war in the west was unfolding and increasingly aware of the fundamentally different perspectives on strategy held by the two allies: between Moltke's relentless focus on the Western Front and Conrad's obvious preoccupation with Russia. 'Our federal relationship was subjected to an extreme test of endurance during the first few weeks of war', he later admitted. 'It prevailed. However, there is no doubt that the relationship between the two army commanders was infused with a creeping poison, with distrust and resentment on one side, and anger at the disappointment and dismissive doubts on the other.'[45]

Moltke was not destined to stay in his post for much longer. The campaign in France had started well, but the German Army had been outflanked and counter-attacked in a series of brutal battles along the Marne river between 5 and 10 September, bringing the Schlieffen Plan to a shuddering halt. Moltke had found the burden of command too much and been relieved of his duties on 14 September, replaced by the Prussian Minister of War, Erich von Falkenhayn. Although Falkenhayn had forged a good relationship with the Kaiser, who admired his robust self-confidence, he was not well liked within the General Staff because he had no claim to the position on grounds of seniority (being only 53 years of age) and was decried as a prickly individual, too independent and difficult for such an esteemed role.[46] Despite the failure of the Schlieffen Plan, Falkenhayn was instructed to renew the assault in the west, drawing forces from his left flank and redeploying them in a major offensive towards the Belgian town of Ypres and the Channel ports, aiming to drive the Allies into the sea and then resume the advance on Paris. As for the Eastern Front, he was unsure. He knew that support had to be given to the Austrians, but how this was to be done was, in his words, 'not easy to answer'.[47]

One of Moltke's final acts as Chief of the General Staff was to authorize the deployment of two corps to East Prussia after the action at Gumbinnen. Although these units arrived too late to be of use at Tannenberg, they were a welcome reinforcement when Eighth Army turned its attention to Rennenkampf's First Army, which was now the only sizeable Russian force left on German soil. OHL informed Hindenburg of the arrival of the two new corps on 31 August, ordering him to 'clear East Prussia of Rennenkampf's army' and follow up 'in the direction of Warsaw'.[48] Hindenburg was eager to help the Austrians, but his primary focus was on how to get at Rennenkampf in the same way he had destroyed Samsonov, and it was unlikely to be as easy the second time around. On 7 September, aerial reconnaissance revealed that there was 'a wide distribution of troops behind the Russian north flank', possibly about three corps 'stretching as far back as Insterburg'. If these reports were accurate, such a distribution of forces would enable an 'overwhelming attack' against the weak Russian left.[49]

Despite the success of Tannenberg, German commanders were wary of attacking fortified positions and knew well enough how good the Russians were at constructing field defences. Therefore, Hindenburg planned to launch his forces in a long march through the Masurian Lakes to strike the Russian left flank, allowing their position to be rolled up from the south. After several days of skirmishing, the general attack opened on the morning of 8 September. Rennenkampf had been expecting an attack and had prepared his men for a stubborn defensive action. Throughout most of the day, his divisions held on, repulsing numerous attempts to push forward and counterattacking whenever they could, but the dominance of German artillery was devastating. 'The dreadful explosions of heavy shells, which sent black pillars of smoke and earth up into the air, made a horrific impression on the riflemen', recalled one Russian officer, Aleksandr Verkhovsky. 'On the very first day of the fight, I met several people who had lost their sanity right on the battlefield. An explosion of a single "suitcase" artillery shell caused buildings to collapse like houses of cards, uprooted the trees, bent gun carriages as if they were made of wax, and sent ragged shrapnel whistling through the air in all directions, tearing open flesh and inflicting the most severe wounds.'[50] On the evening of 9 September, worried about being outflanked on his left, Rennenkampf issued orders for the withdrawal of his army to the east.

Rennenkampf may have avoided total defeat, but his army had been badly mauled, sustaining 100,000 casualties, including 45,000 men taken prisoner – about a third of its strength. Losses in the German Eighth Army were about 37,000 for the whole campaign, a modest sum for the huge damage that had been inflicted upon the Russian war effort.[51] Although Russia would recover, the German Army had now seized a priceless moral advantage on the battlefield, demonstrating superior tactical and operational skills and showing the world that its leaders, at least in the east, were still possessed of the 'genius for war'. Hindenburg was now famous throughout the Central Powers, his name uncorrupted by the ensuing stalemate in France. Debate over who should take credit for the victory would go on for years, but Hindenburg (assisted by Ludendorff) was ultimately responsible for the execution of the plan, seeing it through where lesser men might have flinched and refused to roll the dice. The victory of Tannenberg, alongside its near sequel at the Masurian Lakes, sealed his glorious reputation, restoring the prowess of German arms and raising the prospect that the war could be won not in the west but in the east.

However promising Germany's situation on the Eastern Front had become, the dead weight of Austrian failure was already debilitating. On 14 September, the day that Falkenhayn had replaced Moltke, Archduke Friedrich again wrote to the Kaiser calling for more co-ordinated operations. 'With regard to the drafting in of German forces, the Austro-Hungarian Army will only strike the Eighth Army when and where union with these forces is guaranteed. Operation via the Narew is no longer in any way viable. Joining forces in Western Galicia is the only option under consideration. I therefore suggest that Your Highness may wish to provide transportation via Krakow sooner rather than later.' Despite only just having taken over from Moltke, Falkenhayn recognized that immediate support for the Austrians was 'politically necessary', so he authorized the formation of a new army with troops taken from East Prussia. They were to be transported to the Silesian border and would operate against the Russian flank. Although the Archduke was pleased by the prospect of German troops bolstering the Austrian line, his request that Ninth Army come under Habsburg control was quickly shut down when Hindenburg was appointed its commander (because he held greater seniority than Friedrich).[52]

For Russia, not even the capture of Lemberg could make amends for the terrible setbacks in East Prussia. At the Northwest Front, Zhilinsky was furious. Blaming the commander of First Army for what had happened, he sacked Rennenkampf and penned a long report to *Stavka* complaining that his 'categorical orders' had not been followed. Grand Duke Nikolai Nikolaevich looked on aghast. Although possessed of a volcanic temper when roused, Nikolai usually took a laissez-faire approach to command, letting his subordinates work through problems and only intervening when things went wrong. But now worries over the state of Rennenkampf's army proved too much for him. To lose one army in East Prussia was unfortunate; to lose two would be unforgivable. He sent his Chief of Staff, Yanushkevich, to First Army and found the situation much better than he had feared. Rennenkampf had successfully extricated his army and escaped a second Tannenberg. Recognizing that he had lost faith in Zhilinsky, Nikolai replaced him with the commander of Third Army in Galicia, General Ruzski, and also reinstated Rennenkampf. On 12 September, still mired in a deep-set gloom, he wired the Tsar: 'I openly admit that I did not understand how to carry out my orders, and so I place my guilty head at Your Majesty's feet.'[53]

3. 'Our brave army deserved a better fate'

The Habsburg retreat did not stop at the San. Because the river line was largely indefensible, Conrad had little choice but to let his armies continue their march towards the Carpathians. But this meant that the fortress of Przemyśl would have to be abandoned. With almost 50 miles of perimeter defences, drawn up in three great concentric rings, containing 19 permanent and 23 smaller forts, Przemyśl was a symbol of imperial power, guarding the passes into the mountains and forming 'the first line of defence against a Tsarist invasion of Galicia'. Knowing that he could not allow such a prize to fall into Russian hands, Conrad ordered that a garrison of six divisions (about 130,000 men) be left behind, while planning for a counter-attack as soon as possible. On the evening of 16 September, AOK issued order No. 2096: 'The Fortress Przemyśl will, for the moment, stand on its own and is to hold at all costs.'[1]

The state of the Austro-Hungarian Army was pitiful. As the long columns of pike-grey infantry trailed back along roads turned to slush by heavy rainfall, morale slumped. AOK calculated that its four main armies had now been reduced to around 400,000 men, with Third Army mustering just 70,000 effectives.[2] Such heavy wastage was particularly noticeable in the officer corps, which had been decimated in the early battles, with an alarming number of survivors breaking down or committing suicide. Conrad, never one to shy away from decisive measures, began taking action against those who were deemed to have failed. General Bruderman was dismissed a day after Lemberg had fallen, while General Auffenberg, the hero of Komarów, was asked to report sick in late September. He had once been 'a keen, critical spirit' possessed of a 'scintillating wit', but was now a 'tired, broken old man . . . with a weary voice'. By the end of 1914, four army commanders, six corps commanders, ten divisional commanders and twelve brigade commanders would be dismissed. It was a purge unprecedented in the empire's long history.[3]

The casualties of the opening campaigns even reached AOK. On 16 September, news arrived that Conrad's son, Lieutenant Herbert Freiherr von Conrad of 15 Dragoon Regiment, had been killed in action. Conrad's adjutant, Major Kundmann, visited him in his office and, with a pained expression on his face, prompted Conrad to ask if there was bad news from the front. Kundmann said that it was a personal matter concerning his son. Conrad asked if he was 'badly wounded', only for Kundmann to mutter that it was 'more than that'. He had fallen at Rawa Ruska on 8 September and was buried in a nearby churchyard. 'The force of the blow shook me deeply', remembered Conrad. 'Major Kundmann comforted me with great warmth and amity. However, I asked him to leave me alone for a short while so that I could pull myself together.' Conrad took an hour to wallow in grief and shock before washing his face, straightening his jacket and regaining his composure. 'The gravity of the war situation made it necessary to switch off any personal feelings. I made my way to the operations office, received the announcements from my officers and went about my usual work.'[4]

Conrad's mood was not improved by the situation in the Balkans. Still smarting from his repulse in August, General Potiorek had sent a stream of telegrams to the Military Chancellery in Vienna calling for a renewed invasion and insisting that the Serbs were on the verge of collapse. Although Conrad was not keen on a new offensive, a number of powerful political figures, including Tisza and Berchtold, successfully lobbied the Emperor to sanction Potiorek's plans, effectively ending Conrad's control of operations in the Balkans.[5] Fifth Army went forward in the early hours of 14 September, crossing the dark waters of the Sava as a preliminary bombardment lit up the far bank, sweeping away the defenders and allowing them to advance two miles into the northern tip of Serbia. But then movement slowed. The Serbs had dug an array of well-fortified lines and it took time and effort for Habsburg forces to fight their way through. Relying heavily upon their sappers, Austrian infantry quickly realized that specialist equipment – hand grenades, flare pistols, illumination rounds from mortars, and flame-throwers – was invaluable in this kind of fighting, even if progress remained modest.[6]

Fifth Army had come to a halt by the first week of October. Its battalions, often at half strength or less, lacking officers and NCOs, could not break the Serb lines. Potiorek ordered his men to advance 'without fear of losses', but crippling shortages of shells meant that attacks quickly broke down or could not be exploited.[7] Major General Alfred Krauss, commander of the Austro-Hungarian Combined Corps, complained that after weeks of campaigning, his force was a shadow of its former self. 'The 29th Division had only 6,500 men instead of 17,000; the lack of officers in particular would make any attack very difficult. The *Landsturm* battalions were not suited to heavy attack; four battalions would be commanded by *Landsturm* lieutenants. The artillery was too weak in terms of gun numbers, effectiveness and ammunition supplies, to adequately prepare for the attack. But it all fell on deaf ears. The idea was all wrong. It was believed that one could use human bodies to penetrate a fortified front.' This was even more dangerous given the capability of their opponents. 'I considered and do still consider their soldiers to be the strongest of our enemies', Krauss added. 'Frugal, resourceful, skilful, extraordinarily mobile, well armed, abundantly furnished with ammunition, agile in the terrain, very well led, and inflamed for battle by hatred and ardour, they presented more of a problem to our troops than the Russians, Romanians and Italians.'[8]

It was abundantly evident now, perhaps more than ever, that Austria desperately needed help from her allies. Conrad met Ludendorff for the first time on 18 September at AOK's new base at Neu-Sandec. 'The reputation of the "Stormer of Liège" preceded him,' remembered Conrad, 'his name being connected with the victories in East Prussia. We engaged openly and honestly with one another and hit it off right away. Neither of us minced our words.' Ludendorff liked Conrad, whom he found to be 'clever' and 'distinguished' with a 'genuine soldierly character', albeit having to lead an army that 'was not always strong enough to carry out his bold plans'. If Ludendorff's faint praise revealed some of Germany's misgivings about the Habsburg Army, Conrad's warm words also masked his own disillusionment about his ally, and he was not shy in blaming Austro-Hungary's reverses on Germany's refusal to mount an offensive on the Eastern Front in the opening stages of the war, leaving him to shoulder the burden alone. They had faced off against 52 Russian divisions, each of which, he noted, contained at least 3,000 more men than their own units.[9]

With a large map of the Eastern Front unrolled upon a table, they talked over their plans: where Germany should mount her offensive, and how they would cooperate. It was agreed that a new counter-offensive would be conducted by Ninth Army, moving east towards Ivangorod on the Vistula, with Dankl's First Army securing their right flank, which would mark the beginning of a broader Habsburg push towards Przemyśl.

'For Hindenburg, the stronger you are on the left wing, the better,' said Ludendorff.

'The Carpathians are occupied,' replied Conrad.

'Yet the situation as a whole is still hopeful. We shall approach it with confidence. But if the Russians do not follow up, they shall have to leave strong forces behind at Przemyśl.'

'Then we shall go to Galicia and you to Russian Poland.'[10]

The swamping, suffocating weight of Russian forces preyed heavily upon Conrad's mind, causing him to become a distracted, almost sunken figure by the last days of September. Although he still harboured dreams of martial glory, of grand counter-offensives that would restore his position, they grew fainter every day. In a letter to Arthur von Bolfras, head of the Emperor's Military Chancellery, he reported on Ludendorff's visit and outlined his hopes for a 'decisive blow' at the beginning of October, but then he slipped into a familiar self-pitying lament about the perilous state of the empire. 'Having fought . . . against an overwhelmingly superior force – perhaps not with decisive success, but certainly with great honour – our brave army deserved a better fate. Yet, abandoned by all allies, it was left to fight off a far superior enemy alone.'[11]

That 'superior enemy' was drawing closer every day. The first elements of the Russian Third Army reached Przemyśl on 16 September. Taking their time to scout the Habsburg position, noting the location of the fortresses, the long lines of trenches, recently sown minefields and newly cleared fields of fire (made by the felling of thousands of trees), it would be another ten days before the entire fortress complex was surrounded.[12] The lack of heavy artillery in the Russian inventory meant that it was not possible to recreate the tactics that Moltke had used so successfully against the Belgian and French forts (when Škoda mortars and Krupp howitzers had cracked them open in a matter of days), so General Ivanov had little choice but to wait. 'A siege of Przemyśl is not part of my plans', the Grand Duke had telegraphed on 21 September. 'I consider that you should limit yourself to screening it.' Ivanov was ordered to keep a close watch on the enemy, and if they continued to fall back behind the Carpathians, he was to 'cork up the exits' and then 'move in a north-westerly direction toward Cracow and Posen'.[13]

The Grand Duke's focus was now on Poland. On 22 September, he travelled to Cholm to meet his two front commanders, Ivanov and Ruzski, and they discussed the latest intelligence reports, which had correctly identified an enemy build-up around Krakow. The risk of a German advance towards the Vistula, potentially unhinging Russia's flank in Galicia, was obvious to all. As Danilov wrote: 'The most dangerous in our eyes was the strike prepared by the enemy marching along the left bank. There stood not only our main enemy but also our strongest: the Germans. From this point, our entire position in Galicia could be at risk.' It was agreed to redeploy Fourth Army north to Ivangorod, while sending more cavalry to western Poland to keep an eye on what the Germans were doing.[14] Nikolai Nikolaevich was not, however, satisfied with the movement of a single army and wanted to do more, dusting off an old scheme for a bold push into the heart of Germany. By 28 September, Ivanov and Ruzski had been informed that the Grand Duke now intended to mount a larger and more aggressive offensive. He proposed to mass three armies, Fourth, Ninth and Fifth, along the Vistula and the San, with a rapidly reconstructed Second Army (partially rebuilt with elite troops from Siberia) concentrated around Warsaw. Both fronts were 'to prepare to go on the offensive from the middle Vistula . . . for a deep strike into Germany'.[15] Although this required what Danilov called a 'rather

complicated regrouping', as well as a series of long marches, it promised decisive success. Ivanov was placed in charge of this 'regrouping',
with the remaining armies in Galicia coming under General Brusilov,
who had formerly commanded Eighth Army in its drive on
Lemberg.[16]

Such a massive counter-manoeuvre would certainly please the
French. On 14 September, the French Ambassador, Maurice Paléologue, received a telegram from the Foreign Minister, Théophile
Delcassé, urging Russia to conduct a 'direct offensive against Germany'. Paléologue met with Sukhomlinov that day and impressed
upon him the concern in Paris that the Russians 'may have had their
heads turned by their relatively easy successes in Galicia and may
neglect the German front in order to concentrate on forcing their
way to Vienna'. Although Germany had retreated from the Marne,
her armies had dug in along the Aisne river and showed no sign of
going anywhere, which only added to the frustrations in France that
the Russians were squandering another chance to press their advantage. Sukhomlinov pushed away Paléologue's comment and replied
that Russia had begun her offensive into Germany in early August
and had 'already sacrificed 110,000 men . . . to help the French army!'
However, he did admit that the Grand Duke was currently preparing
'an operation on a wide front in the direction of Posen and Breslau
[Wroclaw]', which pleased the Ambassador.[17]

As always with the Russian Army, squabbles between the generals
quickly surfaced. Already the two front commanders faced different
ways, with divergent priorities and competing supply needs. At the
Northwest Front, General Ruzski's characteristic caution was soon
evident as he worried about the weakness of his forces around East
Prussia. Indeed, should Germany go on to the offensive in the north,
Ruzski believed that there was little to stop her forces creating havoc,
even as far as the capital, St Petersburg (now renamed to the less
Germanic-sounding 'Petrograd'). Therefore, the Russians might
have to consider a phased withdrawal to consolidate their lines, perhaps up to the Niemen river. The Southwest Front took a different
view. Ivanov and his capable Chief of Staff, Mikhail Alekseev,
wanted to keep the Galician offensive going, pushing the Austrians

back through the mountains and then breaking into the Hungarian Plain to seize Budapest.[18]

In the absence of clear direction from *Stavka*, both commanders were left to fight it out for themselves, which only increased the rancour between them. When Ivanov heard of Ruzski's plans to retreat, he fired off an angry telegram to *Stavka* protesting in the strongest terms he could muster:

> Although it would be prudent for the Germans to proceed with caution and merely imitate real military activity, the armies of General Ruzski will not prevent the enemy from taking forceful action in the direction of Ivangorod and Lublin. The moral impact of the occupation of Warsaw must not be underestimated. The rear of the three armies is so complex and has so many supply dumps and reserves that it would take a great amount of time and tremendous effort to redeploy it. A change of location is a difficult endeavour in itself, and in the situation the southwestern armies have to face, this task becomes even harder. There are few paths south of Polesie – barely enough for two armies, and yet there are five armies that will have to use them. I need to know exactly when General Ruzski intends to withdraw his troops. It would be necessary to coincide his withdrawal with the time when the entire rear of the three armies of the Southwestern Front will be redeployed.[19]

Ruzski was unmoved. He dragged his heels on supplying troops to the Warsaw operation, haggling over units and only sending those that were not up to full strength, which provoked an angry telegram from Danilov reminding him that 'according to the Supreme Commander and with regard to the whole situation, the fate of the first stage of the campaign and perhaps of the entire war will be decided on the banks of the Vistula. Under such circumstances, as you yourself would agree, it is imperative that we make every possible effort to ensure the success of the operation. Everything must serve the main goal . . .'[20]

This lack of cooperation within the Russian High C
would seriously undermine its operations throughout the
venting Russia from bringing all her strength to bear a

her commanders to spend precious time bickering among themselves. At the centre of it all was the Grand Duke. He was still committed to assisting the French by conducting an operation into the heart of Germany (he famously kept a French flag at his headquarters), but could not bring his subordinates around to a single plan of operations and was temperamentally unsuited to bending stubborn, powerful individuals to his will. Andrei Zaionchkovski, who commanded a corps in 1914, thought that Nikolai had little idea of what he really wanted to achieve. 'The Grand Duke – who gave the impression of being a "tough man" by his conduct, but was amenable to the influence of people from his inner circle . . . could barely defend his position and, contrary to pragmatic military logic, often gave in to the selfish and narrow strategic ideas of Ruzski and Ivanov, who pushed exclusively in favour of their fronts.' The role of the Commander-in-Chief, he lamented, 'was reduced to finding compromises in an attempt to bridge the gap between the views of his two assistants. Therefore, the plan for the upcoming operation was made with great difficulty, and went through a number of compromised stages before rather belatedly taking its decisive form.'[21]

Given the difficulties of moving such a mass of men, guns and horses across ground wet from days of rain, it was something of a miracle that the Grand Duke's great march was completed at all. While thousands of troops were able to move into position via Russia's railways, most had to get there on foot. 'The road was in a dreadful state', remembered Alfred Knox, British Military Attaché, who passed along the route from Lublin to Krasnik. 'Originally a *chaussée* [a paved highway], it had been broken up by heavy artillery, pontoons, etc., and owing to the recent rains the whole was covered with several inches of liquid mud. This made it impossible to see the holes and quite dangerous to ride on the road . . . On the very outside one saw infantry struggling along the comparatively good going on the water-logged plough land.'[22] Even though Russian troops trudged on, day after day, often with little food, they were able to redeploy by the second week of October, taking up positions along a new

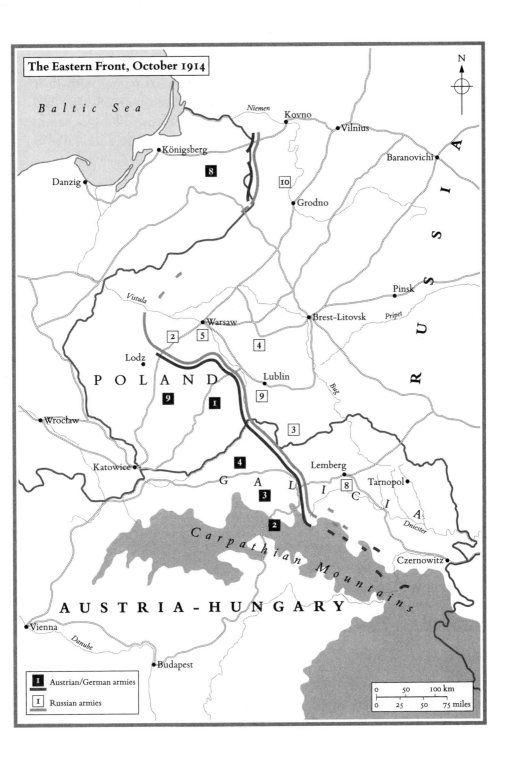

battlefront some 170 miles in length, running from Warsaw down to Sandomierz and then along the San towards Przemyśl.

The Germans were already on the move, marching with their characteristic speed and sense of purpose. Their own offensive had begun on 28 September with four German corps striking out from Katowice and making good progress despite difficult ground conditions. The main road from Krakow to Warsaw was 'knee deep' with 'a layer of mud a foot high', which made enormous demands on the labour battalions and engineering companies to keep the advance going.[23] Because the Russians had placed the bulk of their strength much further east, German divisions met with little but roaming enemy cavalry in the first few days of the offensive, and it was only when Ninth Army reached the wide expanse of the Vistula, in places up to one and a half miles across, that progress came to a halt. On their right, General Dankl's troops had only started their general advance on 1 October (after Conrad insisted on giving them a few more days of rest), but likewise found little in front of them, with wireless intercepts revealing that the Russian Ninth Army had withdrawn north several days earlier.

The first clashes were inconclusive. German artillery bombarded Russian positions along the east bank of the Vistula, and occasionally the Germans sent aircraft, even one of their Zeppelin airships, over enemy lines to spread terror. Germany had relied upon her flying service since the opening days of the war to provide long-range reconnaissance, and even though she only possessed a handful of fragile machines, they provided early warning of Russian movements, particularly any large-scale crossings of the river. On their right, the Austrian First Army was also advancing towards the confluence of the Vistula and the San to threaten the Russian flank, Conrad having scooped up every last soldier he could. 'The offensive was advancing everywhere,' he noted on 6 October, 'but the incessant rain . . . put the roads in a miserable state, which not only made the march extremely strenuous, but also seriously delayed it.'[24]

Gradually the two great hosts closed with each other, separated by the waters of the Vistula, now swollen by the autumn rains. The wet weather and surging, sucking mud gave this campaign an infamous reputation, seemingly confirming Falkenhayn's comment (upon replacing Moltke) that little could be expected from the Eastern Front. 'In view of the almost unlimited power of the Russians to evade a final decision by arms as long as they pleased,' he wrote, 'there was no hope of finishing with them before the enemies in the West had either won a decisive success or had so strengthened themselves with their almost unlimited resources as to leave little prospect of any German success over them.'[25] Victory, in Falkenhayn's opinion, could only come after a final reckoning with the Entente, and so he kept attacking in the west, trying to break the line in Flanders before the winter closed off any possibility of decisive success in 1914.

Showing their characteristic independence and single-mindedness, Hindenburg and Ludendorff were unimpressed by Falkenhayn's strategic judgement and continued with their plans anyway, determined to bend events to their will. On 9 October, Hindenburg ordered one of his most reliable field commanders, General August von Mackensen, to lead a task force north towards Warsaw, hoping that a quick seizure could be made. Although Mackensen forged ahead with his usual sense of purpose, when he stumbled upon a Russian order revealing the extent of the Grand Duke's plans, the mood changed. The Germans were faced not with a weakly defended flank, ripe for exploitation, but a solid array of four Russian armies, perhaps as many as 200 battalions against just 60 of their own. The plan was for the Russians to hold the line of the Vistula and then mount a decisive attack from Warsaw, which would either envelop German forces or push them into a precipitate retreat. If Russia's plans succeeded, 'not only our Ninth Army would be in danger, but our whole Eastern front, Silesia, and indeed the whole country, would be faced with a catastrophe'. It was, as Hindenburg later admitted, 'unquestionably a great plan . . . indeed the greatest I had known . . .'[26]

Yet the Russians struggled to launch their counter-offensive, hamstrung by command confusion and logistical bottlenecks. General Plehve's Fifth Army, which had been assigned to Ruzski's Northwest Front, had moved into position around Warsaw, only to find that supplies and ammunition were not forthcoming. Ruzski was still continuing his feud with Ivanov and was loath to provide resources for an operation that he would not command, leaving Fifth Army in a state of suspended animation. Although Russian commanders had already recognized that they could not compete with the German ability to manoeuvre and deploy quickly, the spiralling problem of feeding and supplying troops was threatening to strangle *Stavka*'s 'great plan' in its opening stages. With Ivanov wanting to wait until all his forces had come up before launching his attack, the Grand Duke was left to ponder on the vast gulf between issuing an order and seeing it carried out. Several years earlier, while on manoeuvres with the French Army, he had told the French President, Raymond Poincaré, that 'In our vast empire, having given an order, you can never be sure whether it will reach its destination.'[27]

Despite, or perhaps because of, the pressure being placed upon Hindenburg's army, promising strategic developments were soon to arise elsewhere along the front. With the redeployment of Russian troops to the north, *Stavka* had no choice but to abandon the siege of Przemyśl; a decision that was not taken lightly, but which was deemed essential in the circumstances. In a letter to Alekseev on 29 September, Yanushkevich explained that the Vistula front had now 'acquired a special importance' and it was necessary to withdraw troops from both the northern and the Galician front. 'It anguishes and embitters that your victorious advance has had to be cut short; it is painful to realise that if Lechitsky and Evert [two army commanders] had had one or two more days to act, they would have spread total panic among the Austrians, but the seriousness of the threat for you and for the common cause from Kalisz and Posen is too obvious.'[28]

The Grand Duke had wished to merely screen the fortress, but General Brusilov had no intention of letting the defenders off lightly, so he authorized heavy attacks in early October. Although Russian guns were able to seriously damage the fieldworks that surrounded the city – clearing away barbed-wire entanglements and smashing thin trenches – the main forts were largely unharmed. Lacking the super-heavy artillery that might have collapsed their thick walls and roofs, Brusilov was left hoping that his field guns would so demoralize the garrison that they would surrender. Around 45,000 shells were fired off between 5 and 8 October, causing a terrifying rolling roar to echo around the city as its citizens huddled in their homes. Sapping forward under constant fire, Russian troops closed the distance to the Austrian trenches before launching themselves in desperate frontal assaults. Perhaps as many as 10,000 Russian soldiers were killed or wounded in these attacks, their bodies lying up to a metre deep as they were caught in devastating machine-gun and artillery fire. With no chance of breaking through, Brusilov had no choice but to abandon the siege and march north. On 9 October, the day that Hindenburg had sent Mackensen towards Warsaw, the fortress was relieved by Habsburg cavalry, exhausted yet triumphant.[29]

The struggle on the crucial Vistula front was becoming increasingly bitter. Mackensen had got to within ten kilometres of Warsaw by the evening of 11 October, but was faced with Russian reinforcements streaming south from the city. 'We are currently living in a very tense situation, both tactically and operationally', he wrote. 'This has meant that my corps and I are placed on the most important flank.' He noticed the sheer variety of troops he was encountering, including Cossacks from the Urals and Turkestan, and those who had come directly from Vladivostok along the Trans-Siberian Railway. 'Russia is drafting in every last one of its men.'[30] Although they were thrown into battle in a haphazard fashion, they exhibited a stubbornness that surprised German observers. 'Heavy fighting the last three days, many attempts to force a passage on a large scale – weak as we are', recorded one of Ludendorff's staff officers, Max Hoffmann, in his diary on 12 October. 'It was indeed the hardest time of the campaign in my experience: the strain goes on day and night – endless panics and alarms.'[31]

With fighting intensifying, a sense of great pressure began to be felt in the German ranks. Wherever they marched, seemingly overwhelming masses of enemy infantry were always there, poised to close. Hindenburg and Ludendorff ordered up their heavy batteries and sent General Max von Gallwitz's Guards Reserve Corps towards Ivangorod, where Russian forces were forming a bridgehead, but the bad weather and sodden ground conditions prevented them from wiping it out. By 13 October, Gallwitz was struggling to prevent the

Russians from securing the two permanent bridges at Ivangorod and Novo-Alexandri, and in a worrying report, he admitted that despite ordering repeated attacks, his men had got nowhere. 'My subordinates claim that our failure to execute the operation is not down to the will of the officers or the morale of the troops, but merely the fact that the boggy terrain and swollen streams make it physically impossible to organise an attack strong enough to overpower the expertly equipped and well-manned position of the enemy. The infantry cannot run, only crawl; some of the artillery has already broken down, and there are no positions from which we could effectively stave off the heavy artillery of the enemy on the other side of the Vistula.'[32]

As the situation worsened, relations between the two allies began to fray. Ludendorff wanted the Austrians to take over more of Ninth Army's front, allowing it to shift northwards, but Conrad did not want to move too far left, which would stretch his line out even further than it already was. On 17 October, both Ludendorff and Hoffmann held lengthy long-distance telephone calls back to OHL in Charleville-Mézières complaining about the urgent need for unified command and the importance of putting the Habsburg First Army under German direction. Both men agreed that the 'main obstacle' was Conrad himself. 'A direct imperial telegram is urgently required in order to achieve subordination of the Austrian First Army under the Ninth Army. With Ninth Army engaged in the most arduous battle against significant superiority, one might say that everything now depends on the consistency of leadership.' When this request was eventually communicated to Emperor Franz Joseph, through Archduke Friedrich and then on to Conrad, it met with a predictably curt refusal. Conrad replied to Friedrich on 18 October admitting that although German forces were in a 'difficult situation', it was important not to subject First Army to 'a similar fate' and he considered 'its subordination under the German Ninth Army to be entirely impractical and downright dangerous. For the unified leadership of both armies, the current tried-and-tested mode of mutual agreement is perfectly adequate.'[33]

Despite seemingly endless delays, the Grand Duke had finally cornered his generals to mount their attack on 20 October. But before they could cross the Vistula in strength, their opponent had pulled back, escaping the trap that had been so carefully laid at *Stavka*. Yanushkevich urged Ruzski and Ivanov to 'take the most energetic measures' to find the direction of the German retreat and maintain contact, while 'overtaking his rearguards and forcing him to fight'.[34] But the Russians could not move quickly enough and the speed of the Germans' withdrawal was only matched by the skill of their engineers in turning parts of Poland into a ravaged wasteland. Already the rampaging armies on the Eastern Front were coming to resemble marauding bands of medieval peasants, stripping everything of value from the land they marched through, burning villages, stealing cattle and trampling crops. 'The railway stations, water towers and blockhouses were burned down; what was spared from the blaze was blown up, as were the railway lines, bridges, water pipes and viaducts – and with such skill and care that rapid restoration of the destroyed infrastructure was completely out of the question', complained Danilov. 'All in all, a horrific scene of destruction.'[35]

For commanders as ambitious as Hindenburg and Ludendorff, the withdrawal from Poland was a miserable experience. Although the operation had, from a certain perspective, achieved everything that could have been expected of it, forcing the Russians to redeploy their armies and loosening their grip on Przemyśl, the duo were not happy. 'The situation was highly critical', Ludendorff noted sourly. 'We had now to expect that very crisis – the probable invasion of Posen, Silesia and Moravia by Russian armies in superior force – which should have been prevented by our deployment in and advance from Upper Silesia at the end of September.'[36] But with all spare German reserves, including newly raised volunteers, committed to the Western Front, they were left to hope that the heavy destruction meted out to the railways and roads of western Poland would suffice to bring the Russian advance to a standstill.

On 30 October, Ludendorff was summoned to Berlin to meet Falkenhayn. The Chief of the General Staff was adamant that they must keep the bulk of the German Army in France, at least for the time being. The situation was 'very promising' and they were close to achieving decisive results in Flanders. Ludendorff understood this but asked for greater 'freedom of manoeuvre' on the Eastern Front. As long as German forces were 'chained' to the left of the Habsburg forces, there would only be limited opportunities for manoeuvre, but if they could redeploy and strike the right flank of the Russians – then deep into Poland – they could soon restore their position. Falkenhayn accepted Ludendorff's argument and signed an order that would consolidate the command structure in the east, appointing Hindenburg 'Supreme Commander, German Forces in the East of the Empire' (*Oberbefehlshaber der Gesamten Deutschen Streitkräfte im Osten* or *OberOst*) on 1 November. All German forces in both Eighth and Ninth Armies would now come under Hindenburg's authority, with Ludendorff remaining as his Chief of Staff. Mackensen, who had impressed at Warsaw, was given Ninth Army.[37]

Falkenhayn would come to realize that nothing he did would ever satisfy his generals in the east. The creation of *OberOst* merely solidified Hindenburg and Ludendorff's power base and created a rival headquarters, which spent much of its time petitioning for more manpower and questioning Falkenhayn's prioritization of the Western Front. When Ludendorff returned from Berlin, he spoke with Hindenburg and they agreed that a defensive posture, against such a numerous opponent, was unwise and they must return to the offensive. Utilizing Germany's superior railway network, they planned to redeploy Ninth Army to the north, concentrating around the towns of Posen and Thorn, before pushing off southeast towards Lodz, catching the Russian Second and Fifth Armies in the flank. Once again they petitioned Falkenhayn for reserves, emphasizing German weakness as well as the deteriorating reliability of their allies. 'Impressions of the Austrians are becoming increasingly unfavourable', Ludendorff noted in a telegram on 9 November. 'They are worryingly backward-looking. Resistance north of Krakow by the Austrian First Army is estimated at one day. The German eastern army is too weak to bring about a decision on its own. It can only count on partial success. I cannot overlook the situation in the west. If the decision is not made there soon, I would urge you to consider seeking a

decision here and freeing up three to four active corps for the east.'
He followed it up with a more detailed report several days later: 'The
Austrian officer assigned to *OberOst* was just with me and painted a
desperate picture of the situation within the Austrian army and in
Vienna. The Emperor [Franz Joseph] does not appear to have been
informed of anything so far. The Austrian officer fears hasty decisions. There is talk of the cession of Galicia as a means of making
peace. General Conrad is being heavily plotted against, but there is
no one else suitable.'[38]

The October offensive only provided a temporary reprieve for the
Habsburg Empire. As German troops headed for their own border,
the full weight of Russian power was directed against Conrad's battered armies. Conrad initially proposed that Dankl's First Army
would let the Russians cross at Ivangorod and then march north,
catching them in the flank, but the weight of enemy numbers proved
too great. By 25 October, seventeen Russian divisions were facing
just nine German and Austrian divisions, forcing Dankl's army back
in disorder. 'The shock of it shook my very soul', Dankl wrote to his
wife. 'I had to summon every ounce of reason to make the decision
to retreat. Despite all the cajoling from those around me, I remained
in situ for one day in the hope that the situation would improve, then
it was no longer viable; the Germans had already retreated, and we
had to do the same . . .' Although they had taken in the region of
12,000 prisoners – a figure that Conrad confidently reported to the
Emperor – the campaign was another costly one. First Army had lost
some 40,000–50,000 casualties and embarked upon yet another gruelling retreat.[39]

As the Austrians began to withdraw, the question of what to do
with Przemyśl returned. The man whose troops had originally
relieved the fortress, General Svetozar Boroević, wanted to order an
evacuation as soon as possible, but Conrad refused. Tales of great
heroism were already circulating across the empire, and the story of
how a valiant band of *Landsturm* men had managed to hold on to the
fortress against overwhelming odds provided a much-needed morale
boost at a time of great crisis and convinced Conrad that it could not
be abandoned. But such stirring heroism could not disguise the huge

risk that Conrad was taking. Because it had not been possible to restock the garrison's supplies (the main rail links into the city still being cut), there would need to be very careful management of its remaining food stocks if the fortress was not to be starved into submission. On 2 November, Conrad issued an order to the garrison that they must prepare for another siege: 'I have confidence that the fortress, which was heroically and successfully defended during the first siege, will not only withstand all attacks in future, but also attract considerable enemy forces.'[40]

With the retreat of German and Habsburg armies, the atmosphere at *Stavka* became increasingly positive. Although their advance gradually ground to a halt amid the autumn rains, Russian divisions were now deployed in a great arc from the borders of East Prussia to Plotsk, Lodz and then down to Tarnów, leaving them within sixty miles of the German border and just a hundred miles from Krakow. On 22 October, N. A. Kudashev, the representative of the Foreign Ministry at *Stavka*, reported on the spirit of the men, which had been 'much more optimistic than last week':

> Our success at Warsaw, Ivangorod and in fact along the entire front line encouraged headquarters. However, as with our previous successes, the first news was exaggerated: General Danilov insisted on notifying our representatives in France and England immediately. Meanwhile, it is now becoming apparent that the Germans did not suffer a crushing defeat. They only began to retreat in a hurry once they noticed superior enemy forces ahead of them. Of course, we should be grateful and thank God even for this turn of events. But we can only speak of victory over the Germans once they are hastily retreating across their own territory.[41]

The invasion of Germany was scheduled to begin on 14 November. General Yanushkevich issued new orders on 2 November: 'The ultimate goal towards which we should exert every effort is *the invasion of Germany*, and the major part of our armies should presumably be directed between the Vistula and the Sudetenland.' First, the Northwest Front was charged with 'breaking down the stubborn resistance of the Germans in East Prussia', with one army 'driving them back behind the line of the Masurian Lakes' and another 'gaining a foothold in the lower Vistula'. Second, the 'next immediate task' for the Southwest Front was 'to gain decisive advantage over the Austrians in Galicia and push them back to the west'. It would make 'powerful offensive blows' on both flanks and thus allow the main offensive to proceed.[42]

Once again, Russian plans would be undone by the speed with which Germany could act. Mackensen struck again on 11 November, having managed to re-form his forces, incorporate replacements and redeploy them all within a fortnight; what one commentator judged to be a 'masterpiece of organisation'.[43] Five corps were pushed through a narrow sector on the left of the Russian Second Army around Kutno, their left and right flanks screened by the Vistula and Warta rivers. The Germans quickly punched a hole in the line, with cavalry galloping off to spread chaos in the Russian rear and causing a flurry of confused messages to arrive at Ruzski's headquarters. Initially, Ruzski was unimpressed by the German advance and warned his army commanders not to be distracted but to continue their preparations for the invasion of Germany. So Mackensen kept going, using his artillery to batter Russian positions and then advance rapidly on Lodz – 'the Manchester of Poland', known for its mills and factories. Within two days, they had taken 20,000 prisoners and shocked the bewildered defenders with their speed and power; threatening to separate the First and Second Russian Armies and unhinge their entire position in Poland.[44]

And then something unexpected happened: the Russians moved. General Pavel Plehve, commander of Fifth Army, deployed to the south around Tomaschow, reacted quickly to the looming threat of envelopment. Refusing to be cowed by Mackensen's reputation, he ordered his men to march north, ensuring that they would not be cut off and at the same time placing the Germans in serious danger. Plehve did not look like a general. He had none of the dash and charisma of a Rennenkampf and none of the gravitas of the Grand Duke. He was 'an old man of small stature', his shoulders stooped, his mind seemingly immersed in details, a pedant. But his actions saved Russian forces from a second Tannenberg. Months later, an anecdote surfaced about how Plehve had reacted when an aide from General Sergei Scheidemann (Samsonov's replacement) had galloped up, out of breath, and told him that Second Army was surrounded and had to surrender. 'Plehve silently gazed at the young man for a couple of seconds from under his thick, furrowed eyebrows and then said: "My dear fellow, are you here to play a tragedy or to give a report? If you have a report, then you should provide it to the chief of staff, but remember, no tragedies, or else I shall put you under arrest." '[45]

Covering over forty miles in two days, Plehve's men took up a strong position southeast of Lodz, where they were able to make a defensive stand. Furious German attacks were launched against the Russian lines as Mackensen tried to get around them. He ordered General Reinhard von Scheffer-Boyadel's XXV Reserve Corps to push on to the town of Brzeziny, from where they could encircle Russian forces around Lodz, only to find Plehve's men in his way. At the same time, Ruzski finally ordered a corps from Rennenkampf's First Army to march west from Warsaw, which struck the German rear on 21 November and threatened to cut Scheffer-Boyadel's troops off from the rest of the army. For a moment, it seemed as if the Germans would themselves be threatened with a battle of encirclement. This chaotic, confusing series of manoeuvres, two great foes grappling with one another, slipping and sliding, continued for days with spiralling casualties. 'We are on a razor-edge', noted a German staff officer. 'We are standing firm on three fronts near Warsaw – but we have too few men. My nerves were worn out. Five nights' suspense is too much – one cannot keep it up.'[46]

Despite the complicated situation, enough information had got through to *Stavka* to suggest that a great victory might be possible. As Danilov noted, 'Russian hearts were beating in anxious expectation of revenge for the "Samsonov" tragedy'. On 24 November, the Russian High Command ordered seventeen trains to be sent to Warsaw to house an estimated 20,000 prisoners that were going to be captured.[47] However, Scheffer-Boyadel, a reliable and unflappable soldier who had recently come out of retirement, managed to cut his way out of the encirclement and march north to rejoin the rest of

Ninth Army, which then pulled back. The German troops, many of whom were inexperienced reservists, had shown an astonishing degree of cohesion and courage under the most terrible conditions. 'The performance of the troops exceeds anything that had hitherto been thought possible,' Mackensen wrote on 30 November, 'but the battle is tremendously gruelling and grave due to the sheer mass of the enemy, the unbelievable condition of the roads and the prevailing weather conditions. It is all very well for folks at home in the ale-house or the school yard to talk of triumph and glory. But when you are grappling for victory with a dogged and powerful enemy, entrenched to the teeth, it is a very different story.'[48]

With Scheffer-Boyadel's corps managing to fight their way out to the north, the possibility that Russia could win a late victory on the Eastern Front evaporated. Yet the Russian divisions could not have done much more. Having fired off thousands of shells, most of which could not be replaced, they found their fighting power rapidly tailing off after several days of heavy fighting, leaving their men at the mercy of the better-equipped German forces. Casualties were also correspondingly severe. Fifty-fifth Division, part of First Army, arrived in Warsaw on 20 November and was sent straight into battle. Within ten days it had almost ceased to exist, having lost three quarters of its soldiers and most of its officers, including three regimental commanders.[49]

The battlefield around Lodz had now become a bitterly contested zone of hastily dug trenches, shell holes, dead men and horses. Burning villages turned the sky red, while palls of smoke gave the landscape a hellish atmosphere. Conditions were deteriorating rapidly. Although the weather was not as wet as it had been in October, which helped prevent the worst of the mud, mornings were bitterly cold and hard frosts made it increasingly difficult to dig in. A Russian newspaper correspondent, writing for *Bourse Gazette*, found himself in the village of Lowicz soon after it had been abandoned. 'The struggle here represented the attack of an enemy at bay', he noted. 'The trenches were filled with corpses.' After dark, the roads around the town became congested with troops. 'Past us swung unit after unit, and endless artillery parks and steaming camp kitchens . . . The snow slowly fell on the black pits dug by shells and on the grey mass of soldiers, powdering the fresh corpses of men who had wandered God knows whence. In the local square of the town were burning bonfires, about which soldiers were playing like huge black shadows.'[50]

Neither side had won a decisive victory at Lodz, although the broad aim of the German attack, to stop a Russian invasion of Silesia, had been accomplished. The Germans had also demonstrated, yet again, their skills in offensive warfare, in attacking and moving quickly, which made them extremely difficult to stop. But larger strategic issues were still unresolved and the friction between OHL and *OberOst* only worsened as the Lodz operation came to an end. Hindenburg and Ludendorff's hopes that Falkenhayn could be pressurized into releasing sizeable reinforcements for the Eastern Front were dashed on the evening of 26 November when a wire informed them that five divisions were being detrained to the east, with two more to follow soon. While this might have been interpreted as a positive development, Falkenhayn poured cold water on the idea that it was a precursor to a wider realignment. 'According to the decision of His Majesty, we cannot count upon further reinforcements, since there is no value in gaining victories in the east if they come at the expense of our position in the west.' In a tense telephone conversation with Falkenhayn, Ludendorff 'had to let off some steam' and complained about what he saw as the tardy arrival of reserves and the 'lack of clarity' from OHL, which meant that they could only remain on the defensive.[51]

Falkenhayn was not yet ready to admit that Ludendorff might have a point. By mid-November, his great push in Flanders had ended in disappointment. Despite coming tantalizingly close to a breakthrough, enough French, British and Belgian troops had joined the battle to hold on to their lines at Ypres, leaving the entire Western Front deadlocked. There was now a line of trenches running from the Channel coast to the border of Switzerland and it was unclear whether such defensive positions could be broken without extortionate levels of blood (Germany had lost upwards of 80,000 men killed, wounded or missing in the Flanders fighting).[52] With this in mind, Falkenhayn pressed *OberOst* to continue its attacks. Writing to Hindenburg, he insisted that 'The success of the war now depends upon the offensive in northern Poland not petering out and becoming a war of position as it is here in the west.' Moreover, he pointed out possible mistakes in *OberOst*'s deployment of divisions and repeated his expectation that it would continue the offensive 'at all costs'.

A soldier as experienced as Hindenburg was not minded to take lessons on operations from a mere lieutenant-general. He lost no time in writing to the Kaiser complaining about what he perceived to be criticism directed against himself, and instead attempted to place the blame for any disappointments on Falkenhayn. He explained that he had told Falkenhayn that the decisive result 'would be achieved in northern Poland' and had requested urgent reinforcements, which only arrived 'gradually and with delay'. He also had to reckon with 'the constantly fluctuating decisions of the Austrian Army Command and the inferiority of the Austrian army'.[53] The Kaiser visited *OberOst*'s headquarters at Posen several days later and was in a forgiving mood. Although he still retained faith in Falkenhayn, he promoted Hindenburg to field marshal and Ludendorff to lieutenant-general, and presented Mackensen with a well-deserved *Pour le Mérite*. There were also warm words for the command team in the east, which had achieved great things and 'still enjoyed his full confidence'. Privately, the Kaiser bristled at Hindenburg's insubordination and looked in disdain at Ludendorff's rough impetuosity, which he put down to his low birth. He was a 'dubious character', thought the Kaiser; a man 'eaten away by personal ambition. What great things is he supposed to have accomplished?' Yet he could not dispense with these men, such was the power of their reputations won on the field of Tannenberg, so he was left to grumble to his courtiers in moments of quiet frustration.[54]

4. 'Not a battle but a slaughter!'

Western journalists liked to comfort their readers back home with tales of how smoothly Russia was managing the war. An American, Stanley Washburn, 'Special Correspondent with the Russian armies' for the London *Times*, was granted permission to visit *Stavka* in mid-October and was keen to highlight the great professionalism and skill he found there. Baranovichi was not particularly impressive ('one might easily imagine oneself in Western Canada'), but Washburn was struck by the importance of a location from where a 'single individual' commanded 'the largest army that has ever been mustered in the field of war'. After being taken through a grove of poplar and pine trees, he reached a siding where he was presented to the Grand Duke Nikolai Nikolaevich. 'He is a huge man of certainly 6 ft. 4 in., and impresses one greatly by his absolute lack of affectation and his simplicity . . . His dress and mien were as simple as that of any of his numerous aides. His expression was that of a serious, sober man giving his entire thought and effort to a task the importance of which he thoroughly realized.'[1]

After meeting the Grand Duke, Washburn went to the dining car to be served lunch. Once a part of the Nord Express, which ran from Berlin to St Petersburg, the carriage had now been converted to wartime use. Maps and orders plastered the walls, and three times a day headquarters staff would crowd inside to eat, 'each intent on hurrying through his meal and taking up the task that absorbs every waking hour'. Food was simple Russian fare. Orders had been issued prohibiting the drinking of spirits, particularly vodka, and the Grand Duke only permitted white wine or claret to be served at meal times. 'I think it may be taken as a positive fact that there was never a more clear-headed or more sober army in the field than that which is now facing the hordes of the Teutons at this present moment.' Such positive testimony helped to maintain Allied morale as the war went into its first winter. The great hopes that had been invested in the Russian 'steamroller' had been seriously undermined by the disaster at Tannenberg and the failure to draw more German forces east. Despite the outward appearance of efficiency and dedication that the Grand Duke was always eager to foster, the Russian war effort was already struggling by the autumn of 1914.

On 29 November, a meeting of senior generals was held at Siedlice, fifty miles east of Warsaw. 'The purpose of the meeting was to ascertain the condition of the army, which had long been a matter of great concern to headquarters', noted Danilov, who delivered a sobering report that day. After four months of uninterrupted fighting, the Russian Army was in urgent need of reinforcement and replenishment. He was particularly aggrieved by the losses of officers, with many battalions now unable to field more than a third of their full complement:

> From the very first days of the war, our officer corps has shown outstanding grit and unparalleled bravery; the consequence being that it was mowed down in droves. The order that officers should be deployed economically had unfortunately been issued far too late, and in the early days, companies entering battle had three or four officers in their ranks, and often active ones. The striking difference between the uniform and armament of the soldier and that of the officer made the latter a clearly identifiable target for enemy riflemen, who saw their primary task as being to shoot our officers down first. In order to counteract this danger, it was later decided to replace the shiny metal epaulettes with fabric ones, and to replace sabres with rifles.

A shortage of officers was not the only problem. By the end of 1914, a serious crisis was brewing across the infantry. During the fighting around Lodz, some battalions were down to a third of their normal complement of manpower, while even in Galicia – the scene of Russia's great triumphs of 1914 – Third Army was reporting regiments down to 1,200 men, barely half strength.[2]

The deficiencies that Danilov outlined were part of a series of chronic problems that affected all aspects of Russia's war effort. On the outbreak of war, Russia had 4.5 million rifles (mainly the bolt-action 7.62 mm Moisin-Nagant), but these were almost all handed out upon mobilization, leaving her depots empty. With the capability to produce just 60,000 per month, there was no chance that the growing shortfalls could be addressed. By as early as November 1914, up to 800,000 men were being held back because they could not be sent to the front without rifles. Perhaps even more critical was the shortage of shells for the field artillery (Russia had little heavy artillery to speak of). This had been noticed as early as August 1914, but by the final weeks of the year, the inability to produce enough rounds for her field guns was having a devastating effect on Russia's operations, demoralizing the infantry and contributing to a growing sense of depression among the officer corps. After the heavy fighting in Galicia in late September, General Ivanov had reported that there were only about 25 shells per gun left in his inventories. Although *Stavka* had repeatedly requested that supplies be used 'as sparingly as possible', complaints about a lack of ammunition only grew more persistent with each passing month.[3]

None of these deficiencies could be corrected in the short term. Little help could be expected from Russia's allies, who were undergoing their own supply difficulties after finding peacetime estimates of wartime consumption to be fantastically inaccurate. With London and Paris placing as many orders as possible with American arms producers, Russia found herself shut out of potential suppliers, and even though Japan promised to help, it would be months before these deliveries arrived. This isolation was compounded by the entry of the Ottoman Empire into the war on 29 October. The narrow waterway of the Dardanelles Straits, linking the Mediterranean with the Sea of Marmara, had been closed since late September, but with the war party having finally triumphed in Constantinople, Turkey launched a surprise naval raid on Odessa. Sending two requisitioned German dreadnoughts into the Black Sea to bombard the port, the Turks damaged oil storage facilities and sowed mines in the surrounding waters. The Russian response was swift and unequivocal. The following day, 1 November, the Tsar declared war, announcing that 'Turkey's reckless intervention in the present conflict' would only 'accelerate her submission to fate and open up Russia's path towards the realization of the historic task of her ancestors along the shores of the Black Sea'.[4]

At Siedlice, Danilov's report was received by the grey-faced generals in silence. When he recommended that they look to a renewed conquest of East Prussia to eliminate the danger on their right flank, there was little enthusiasm. Both Ruzski and Ivanov saw the advantages that control of this province would bring, but they struck a decidedly pessimistic attitude. Ruzski pointed to his lack of manpower and shortages of ammunition, as well as to the fact that he was having to cope with heavy counter-attacks from German units recently moved over from the Western Front. For his part, Ivanov noted that the enemy defences around Krakow were very tough – and he was already receiving reports of growing Habsburg forces at the passes through the Carpathians.[5]

The Grand Duke was never the most decisive of men, and in the face of such caution he did little to lift this counsel of despair. Writing to the Tsar on 30 November, he noted how Russian units had become 'extremely weakened' by the heavy fighting of recent weeks, even citing one division that had been reduced to barely 15 officers and 2,000 other ranks. The situation on the left bank of the Vistula was 'extremely risky', with the Germans confronting General Ruzski 'along the whole front line, while making attempts to break through our position with attacks on Lowicz and aiming to surround our left flank'. As for the Southwest Front, Ivanov had reported that 'his armies were significantly reduced in number, firearms were running out, and although we continue to achieve local successes over the Austrians, it is impossible to count upon a complete victory over them in the next few days'. Therefore, the armies of the Northwest Front would begin a short withdrawal 'to improve their strategic position'. There was not only a crisis of equipment and manpower in the Tsar's armies, but also a crisis of confidence.[6]

Another meeting was held on 13 December, when the true scale of these shortages became apparent. The shortfall in officers and men throughout the Northwest Front was already well established. On average, battalions were down to 300 men (about a third of their establishment), with a 'great shortage' of rifle cartridges and field artillery shells. *Stavka* estimated that the armies at the front needed half a million pairs of boots, but the Chief Supply Officer reported that there were only 40,000 pairs in stock. More had been ordered, but it was unclear when they would arrive. It was a similarly depressing situation along the Southwest Front. The forward battalions urgently needed more horseshoes, boots and winter clothing, while a lack of rifles meant that only half of the replacements sent to the front could be issued a weapon. Given these problems, both Ivanov and Ruzski repeated their belief that no broad offensive activity could be contemplated in the near future. There was, therefore, only one option to take: to halt all attacks and wait for resupply. There would be no further talk of invading Germany.[7]

Following up the Russian retreat, German troops marched into Lodz on 6 December, completing the push that had begun a month earlier and further enhancing the reputation of one of Germany's leading soldiers on the Eastern Front. Often photographed in the uniform of the Death's Head Hussars, with its skull and crossbones emblem on the fur busby, August von Mackensen was now a national hero, easily recognizable by his craggy face, thick eyebrows and fierce moustache. 'Today I was in Lodz', Mackensen wrote on 7 December, 'and on the hills that lie to the east . . . Lodz has suffered less than I expected. The Russians have experienced significant losses. The battlefield has not yet been cleared. The whole area has been churned up by the Russians' field fortifications; they will soon be found somewhere new. But Lodz remains a great success for us.' Since the beginning of the November offensive, his army had taken over 100,000 prisoners. 'The Russians are inexhaustible only in number', he added. 'In fact, they are growing rather than decreasing in number. But they are not getting any better, because they are bringing men with practically no training into battle. I really do have the impression now that they are starting to get worn down.'[8]

While Germany looked to the future in the east with growing confidence, Austria–Hungary limped on with painful steps. On 6 November, AOK had moved to Teschen, ninety miles to the west of

Neu-Sandec, taking up residence in a local school. The location may have been new, but familiar problems quickly arose. Przemyśl had been abandoned in early November, leaving Conrad to dream up a series of ambitious counter-offensives that would relieve the garrison, restore his fortunes and ensure his future happiness. With the loss of his son, he leant even more heavily upon Virginia ('Gina') von Reininghaus, the 35-year-old wife of a prominent Austrian businessman. He had met the young mother in 1907, two years after his first wife had passed away, and was enraptured with her, bombarding her with letters almost daily, pouring out his frustrations and telling her that she must divorce her husband and marry him. Although she had initially rebuffed his advances, by the end of 1908 they had embarked upon a public romance, with Gina's husband, Hans, content to turn a blind eye to his wife's infidelity with such a powerful, well-connected individual.[9]

Since the outbreak of the war, Conrad's reliance upon Gina for emotional support had only become more noticeable. Soon after he had left for the front, she had sent him a medallion bearing the portrait of Helmuth von Moltke, the general who had led Prussia's armies in the wars of 1866 and 1870–71, and whom Conrad idolized. Wearing the medallion around his neck, he could only contrast the victories that Moltke had won with his own struggles. 'Today is a day of worrying tension', he wrote on 29 August at the height of the fighting in Galicia. 'The two battles continue, as is the nature of today's battles, which are no longer decided in one day as they used to be, the struggle lasting instead for days on end . . .' When he received the 'exquisite medal', he asked what he had done to deserve it: 'Especially now, when we have not yet had a resounding success! You know how I feel in such cases; I was somewhat embarrassed. You can probably see from every one of my letters how much I am always with you in my thoughts, despite the grave worries of this serious time.'[10]

Conrad was cheered by the success of a counter-offensive launched on 3 December, which forced the Russian Third Army away from the important fortress city of Krakow. The Battle of Limanowa-Lapanów would, in retrospect, be his masterpiece; a bold manoeuvre that he likened to 'a masterful game of chess'.[11] After spotting a gap between two advancing Russian armies, he ordered a counter-attack into the Russian flank. It had rained heavily and the mud was knee-deep, but the Austrians hurled themselves forward with desperate courage. 'There were fierce battles fought near Krakow', remembered the squadron commander of 2 Riga Dragoon Regiment. 'The valorous Russian Army suffered very heavy losses. Every day, one could see coffins of officers being carried towards the Tarnów railway station by the relatives of the dead, so that they could be committed to the earth back in Russia.'[12]

While Conrad basked in the warm glow of Limanowa-Lapanów, news of another disaster in the Balkans came 'like a sudden clap of thunder'.[13] The brutal struggle for possession of Serbia had been going on since mid-September. Habsburg troops had gradually clawed their way into the country over the next two months, pushing forward against increasingly exhausted Serbian forces and seizing Valjevo on 15 November. Two days later, as Austrian troops reached the Kolubara river, Potiorek informed Vienna that there was no indication that the Serbs 'intended to offer resistance' along the river line, so he intended to press matters to a conclusion. After two or three days' rest, his men would move into Belgrade to help clear up the increasingly stretched supply lines. Then they would mount a general offensive to the southeast, towards Arangjelovac and then on to the Serbian base at Kragujevac. The Austrian Military Attaché in Sofia reported that there were only sparse rearguards covering the Serbian line of retreat, and it was known that the Serbian Government had despatched a report to Paris warning that the end was approaching.[14] On the day that Valjevo had fallen, Potiorek wrote to Arthur von Bolfras, informing him that 'all sections of both armies are being driven forward in immediate, unrelenting pursuit, in order to exploit the victories to the greatest possible extent, as long as troops have just enough strength to push on'.[15]

Despite Potiorek's bullishness, the campaign remained in the balance. His forces were desperately tired and at the end of long and vulnerable supply routes. Since September, the two Habsburg armies in Serbia had sustained upwards of 130,000 casualties and the survivors struggled on across a landscape that was waterlogged and deep in mud.[16] By the end of November, Austrian units along the Kolubara were in no condition to continue operations, dependent upon a single, heavily burdened road from Sabac. 'The men were in a deplorable state', recorded one account: 'no underwear, ridden with lice, their clothes tattered, their shoes – if they still had any – torn to shreds and held together with makeshift repairs of string and rags, in spite of which their feet, blue with cold, were still exposed in many places.' Men had gone weeks without bread or salt, sometimes without food for days at a time. When food did arrive, it usually consisted of boiled pork with some maize, often leaving the men still hungry and prone to growing rates of sickness.[17]

The mood in the Serbian camp was almost as bad. After the euphoria of August, when they had turned back the first invasion, the fighting throughout September and October had become a sapping, attritional struggle that the Serbian Army was ill suited for. Austrian advantages in firepower became increasingly apparent every week as more guns and heavier-calibre weapons were sent to Potiorek's army group. By September, some Serbian divisions were losing 100 men every day to shellfire, and such an unequal contest provoked a rising flood of desertions. Lacking the numbers of guns or shells to engage in long counter-battery duels, Serbian artillery could only be employed in dire emergencies, leaving their infantry, for the most part, on their own. The situation became so bad that General Stepa Stepanović, commander of Second Army, sent in his resignation on 24 October after complaining about the lack of shells. His superior, Putnik, would not countenance letting one of his most important soldiers go and ordered him to remain at his post.

'So tell me, who's going to lead?' Putnik asked.

'There will be someone,' Stepanović replied, 'but I can't do it any more.'

'Do what you can and as much as you can, and no one can blame you for anything you can't do . . . If we lack artillery, we have to resist with rifles alone, just so we don't let the damn Swabians go', Putnik added. 'Courage, my friend, courage.'

'I have never lacked courage,' Stepanović responded, 'but give me the means to fight.'[18]

Retreat was inevitable. Putnik authorized a withdrawal at the end of October, with Serbian forces pulling back to a new, shorter defensive perimeter between Mount Cer and Mišar. But even this line could not be held, and after another Austrian offensive, he had no choice but to abandon Belgrade and take up position along the eastern bank of the Kolubara. His health remained fragile, with his emphysema leaving him struggling for breath, but he had not given up hope of restoring Serbian fortunes. By late November, he had crafted a daring counter-offensive that would take advantage of Austrian disorganization and throw them back across the river. Crucially, the Serbs had managed to rush through a consignment of French ammunition from the port of Salonika, which was shuttled northwards to the town of Niš. Being of French manufacture, the shells were slightly too long for Serb artillery, which meant that they had to be individually reassembled and then dispatched to the front. In what was a feat of remarkable improvisation, by the final days of November, 11,000 shells had been brought into the Serb camp and issued to its batteries, giving Putnik's forces a priceless opportunity to go onto the offensive.[19]

Putnik put everything he had into the attack. Totalling about 215,000 men and 400 guns, the Serbian Army was outnumbered, but it had the advantage of surprise and of concentration of force.[20] It would also have the presence of Peter Karađorđević, King Peter I of Serbia. He was not a particularly imposing man, of average height with an awkward, stiff gait, owing to persistent rheumatism, but he wanted to see his men and visited the Serbian positions shortly before the attack. His face, notable for his long white moustache, was 'marked by sadness'. Walking through the Serb lines, snow falling on his cap, he looked at the anxious troops, young boys and old men, who crouched in their muddy trenches.

'My children, I have learned that some among your number tire of fighting and have decided to surrender', he said. 'Let them! But I shall stay.'

It would be victory or death. An observer noted how the Serbs had never fought with such a 'burning desire to win'. 'Each of them felt his soul gripped with a furious desire to seize victory or to die for their *Chicha* [old man or uncle], who had so graciously appeared among them, heedless of the distance and fatigue and in spite of his failing health, and who had stayed there among his soldiers – his children – in the blinding extravaganza of battle, as the cannons roared and the bullets whistled . . .'[21]

The long-awaited counter-offensive began on 3 December. Putnik's orders were clear: 'In view of the enemy's difficulties in terms of food, supplies and physical exhaustion, and to both take advantage of this moment of weakness and raise the morale and spirit of our troops, I command that tomorrow, 3 December, all three armies will attack the enemy on all fronts and force them to retreat.'[22] It was a foggy morning, the ground coated with snow, when the Serbian bombardment barked into life. Major General Franz Kalser, commander of 50th Infantry Division, which faced the brunt of the attack on the over-extended Austrian right flank, could only bemoan the terrible state of his brigades, which broke and fled under the sudden violence of the shelling: 'The decimated troops, worn down by constant fighting, with no shoes and often the artillery with little ammunition, cannot withstand the ferocious attacks of the rested Serbs, reinforced by recruits. At 1 o'clock in the morning, the retreat begins in full order . . . the troops retreating in bright moonlight over the snow-covered fields of this magnificent mountain region. With every step the men take, they stumble across yet another carcass of a fallen horse.'[23]

Potiorek still hoped to renew his own attack, but the deteriorating situation in the south soon forced him to abandon any idea of an offensive. Heavy fighting continued up and down the line, with Serb forces attacking through the darkness. 'In this surging back and forth in the pitch-black night, in the roar of the charging troops, in the overwhelming din of the rifle and machine-gun fire and the exploding hand grenades, it turned midnight', remembered one Habsburg officer. 'As the witching hour began, the regiment's losses started to peak. Field officers fell, corporals and soldiers collapsed in a record number of dead or wounded; people lost their minds and committed acts they would never normally have been capable of; machine guns gave up the ghost. To put it bluntly: "It was not a battle but a

slaughter!" '[24] Austrian morale, always fragile, now began to disintegrate. After several days of fierce fighting, Habsburg forces all along
the Kolubara started to break, streaming back along crowded roads,
while Belgrade – the crowning achievement of Potiorek's campaign –
was abandoned on 15 December, with jubilant Serb troops cheering
through the streets.

Potiorek had reached the end of the line. He crossed the Sava on 11
December, defeat etched on his face, and was presented with a telegram from Vienna ordering him to explain, in writing, the reasons
for the great reversal. In a letter to Bolfras, he admitted that the withdrawal was a 'major setback', and blamed a lack of resources:

> This tragic reversal of fate was exclusively because of the growing
> disproportion of the forces. All the higher commanders at the front
> and the troops did their duty to the fullest. But the enemy has recently
> filled its ranks, while persistent fighting and insufficient replacements
> have meant that some of ours have even dropped below peacetime
> levels. Thus, our troops finally had to yield to the overwhelming
> enemy majority and – mainly due to the poor terrain – they unfortu-
> nately lost a vast number of guns, etc. during their retreat. I say
> frankly and unreservedly that this retreat is a major setback of an
> extremely delicate nature. However, if we keep our heads held high,
> we can and will make up for it . . . This is probably the saddest letter
> I have had to write since the war began. But once again: I am con-
> vinced that everything can be made good again, but now we need
> men, guns and ammunition.[25]

Potiorek was sacked soon after his return to Austria. In the cold, bur-
eaucratic and purely functional style that he had become notorious
for, he penned a short diary entry on the day he was dismissed: 'I
shall therefore not be granted the opportunity of making good the
misfortune myself, and it will remain associated with my name.'[26]
The assassin of Sarajevo had claimed another victim.

Serbia's triumph was a disaster for Austria–Hungary, sending a great
rippling message of defeat through the Balkans. The miserable failure
to subdue Serbia left Austria's standing in great doubt, as the other

powers in the region – Romania, Bulgaria and Italy – bided their time. All had, at one moment or another, considered entering the war, and they remained wary observers, carefully weighing up the odds and judging the likelihood of victory for the Central Powers. Although the situation in Galicia had been restored somewhat following Conrad's late victory at Limanowa-Lapanów, the collapse of the campaign against Serbia had, as one authority put it, 'a devastating effect on the entire monarchy'. Of the 12,000 officers and 450,000 other ranks who had fought in the Balkans, 273,000 had become casualties by Christmas; a sobering figure that could be divided into 28,000 dead, 122,000 wounded and 74,000 missing, with the rest suffering from a range of infectious diseases including typhus, dysentery and cholera.[27]

Habsburg losses were so heavy that the size of the army had shrunk dramatically since the opening days of the war. Vienna had been able to put about one and a half million men into the field in July 1914, with another 800,000 joining the colours over the following five months, but as 1914 came to an end, the combat strength of her armed forces had dwindled. With only a million men in total, there were just over 250,000 riflemen available for operations, leaving Conrad desperately short of manpower for the crucial task of relieving Przemyśl.[28] The city had been besieged for the second time in early November and the garrison endured a gloomy, shivering existence haunted by growing hunger. Careful management of food stocks and ruthless requisitioning of supplies allowed the city commander, Lieutenant-General Hermann Kusmanek, to keep the civilian population fed until March, but their ordeal worsened each week.

The Germans looked on unimpressed. The Kaiser had travelled to Wroclaw on 2 December for a meeting with Archduke Friedrich, Archduke Karl and Conrad to discuss joint strategy. 'During a talk held in our dining car, first General von Falkenhayn, and then Conrad, present their views on operations in the East', recorded one of the Kaiser's closest aides, Hans von Plessen. 'Both agree. Eventually, full unanimity is established. The Austrians came across as decidedly lacklustre . . . I get the impression that they cannot keep up with the speed of our troops during an attack.'[29] When Falkenhayn met Conrad at the railway station at Oppeln in Silesia on 19 December, the differences in outlook were immediately apparent. Falkenhayn still had little interest in more ambitious operations on the Eastern Front and talked about the creation of a 'Chinese Wall' on the west bank of the Vistula, which would free up divisions for an offensive in France. Once again, Conrad suggested that they should attempt a major envelopment of Russian forces on both flanks, with a German thrust over the Narew towards Siedlice, only for Falkenhayn to brush the idea away. 'What about the west in the meantime?' he asked. 'If the German front were broken through there, all the victories against Russia would be of no use.'[30]

Conrad was haunted by the prospect of a separate Russo-German peace. When Captain Moritz Fleischmann, AOK's representative at *OberOst*, heard rumours that Berlin was considering making overtures to Petrograd, Conrad was aghast. 'They would conclude peace and leave us sitting in the pepper?' he asked incredulously, before sending an urgent telegram to Count Berchtold in Vienna. 'I should think that Germany, to whom we have proven so selfless an ally and whose territories we have preserved from enemy invasion for four full months under the greatest sacrifices, would not now in this difficult moment leave us in the lurch and thus unilaterally treat with our enemies to our harm.' But when Berchtold met with Germany's Foreign Minister, Gottlieb von Jagow, such concerns were waved away. Any peace would only be concluded based upon the 'complete liberation of East Prussia as well as Galicia from Russian control'. While Falkenhayn would not have been averse to a diplomatic manoeuvre that would free Germany from having to fight a war on two fronts, any attempt to make peace without significant annexations in the east would undoubtedly provoke fierce resistance from *OberOst* and the hardliners in Berlin.[31]

Falkenhayn may have been a detached observer of the Eastern Front, but the unreliability of his allies was a constant concern, threatening to drag German strength further away from the Western Front. Lieutenant-General Hugo von Freytag-Loringhoven, Germany's liaison officer at AOK, regularly updated OHL on the condition of the Habsburg Empire, and his reports did not make for pleasant reading. In a telegram to Falkenhayn on 28 December, he noted that 'The major trouble with the Austro-Hungarian Army is currently its weakness in combat. Thus, the force of its attack, which was quite weak to begin with, has diminished entirely, even against Russian forces of equal number. In addition, the Carpathian terrain makes such weak forces even more ineffective.' Freytag-Loringhoven hoped that a new recruitment drive would bring Habsburg forces back up to full strength, but worried about what he called the 'less reliable nationalities', who were already abandoning the empire. 'The two retreats have not been without consequences; our confidence in victory has been compromised.'[32]

Conrad was committed to fighting on through the winter. After hearing that Germany had raised four new corps, he wrote to Falkenhayn and suggested that they be deployed in the east. He also told Hindenburg that he might be forced to move Second Army (then occupying the left of the Habsburg line south of Lodz) and use it to cover his increasingly threadbare right flank south of the Vistula. This ill-disguised threat to force Germany's hand provoked an immediate response from Falkenhayn, who demanded that Austrian forces remain where they were. When the two men met in Berlin on New Year's Day, Conrad pointed out that 'everything was deadlocked' in France and that success could only be achieved in the east. Ludendorff, who was in attendance, said that he would not object to the deployment of three or four German divisions with the Austro-Hungarian armies for their planned operations in the Carpathians; an offer that Conrad grasped immediately, stating that he would use these troops to relieve Second Army as he concentrated his forces for a push towards Przemyśl. But Falkenhayn was unmoved. Not only was the terrain very difficult, he said in his dry, unemotional tone, but the Russians could also take advantage of their interior lines to react to any offensive quickly and efficiently. The only option was another 'frontal attack in western Poland'.[33]

Conrad left Berlin in a dark mood, with the only positive being Ludendorff's helpful offer of three or four divisions. The Chief of Staff at *OberOst* had 'stood on our side', as Conrad explained in a letter to Gina; 'a determined individual' and the 'brains' and 'will' behind

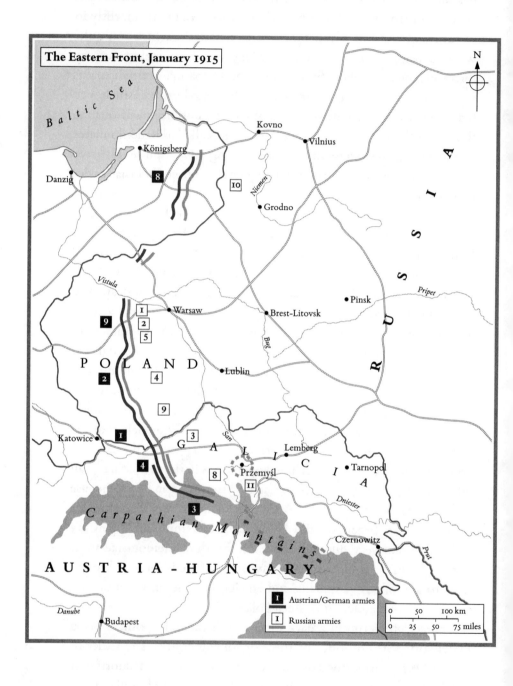

The Eastern Front, January 1915

Hindenburg, whom Conrad dismissed as an out-of-touch and ineffective old man.[34] While the duo of Hindenburg and Ludendorff were useful allies in the push to bring greater German resources onto the Eastern Front, Falkenhayn's refusal to commit more of his divisions meant that Austro-Hungary would continue to fight on in the darkest snow-bound depths of winter without a significant transfusion of German strength. By late December, Conrad had sketched out the rough outlines of a new offensive to drive north a hundred kilometres and relieve Przemyśl. It was an audacious, some would have said reckless, gamble. But Conrad saw the fate of the empire and that of his own life and career as now being indissolubly linked with the besieged fortress.

By January 1915, the Austro-Hungarian Army's long retreat had come to an end along the Carpathian Mountains, the great natural barrier that separated the Habsburg heartlands from the Galician plateau. It was a formidable obstacle, over 100 kilometres deep at its narrowest point and spanning 1,500 kilometres in a great arc that ran from the province of Moravia down to Romania. Austrian forces had retreated into this area after their early offensives had failed, fighting hard to maintain hold of the mountain passes in appalling conditions. Snow had fallen in November, and by the time Conrad returned to Teschen, his armies along the Carpathians were existing in a twilight world of swirling snowstorms, icy rain and sleet, which took its inevitable toll in the form of thousands of cases of frostbite, hypothermia and exposure.[35]

On paper, Conrad's plan had all the aggression and style he was known for, and the maps at AOK were marked up with great lines of advance in blue ink. General Boroević's Third Army would play the most important role: taking the direct northeasterly route towards Przemyśl. After breaking the Russian line, it would seize the towns of Lisko and Sanok, while forces would be sent to secure the railway junction at Ustrzyki Dolne. On its right would be the German-led *Südarmee* ('South Army'), commanded by General Alexander von Linsingen, which had been formed in early January and included three German divisions (the ones promised by Ludendorff). It would continue the attack and attempt to wheel north once it had smashed through the Russian lines. Conrad massed 175,000 men and almost 1,000 guns along the sector of attack: 35 divisions for the central thrust (against 29 enemy divisions), with another nine and a half divisions (against nine divisions) extending the attack on the right.[36]

With only a slender superiority in manpower, Conrad was relying on surprise and the elan of his attacking infantry, sweeping down from the hills, to catch the Russians off guard. But the practical difficulties of moving and resupplying thousands of troops in a frozen wilderness were overwhelming, and the Habsburg Army, now little more than a militia, was in no state to achieve Conrad's ambitious goals. The offensive began on 23 January with Third Army struggling forward towards a series of crucial passes: the Dukla, Lupków, Rostoki, Uszok and Wyszkow – gateways to the open flat land that led to Przemyśl. One Austrian officer who served with his battalion along the bare Beskid Ridge was haunted by the experience: 'We entered into battle against an enemy that was overwhelmingly superior. Armed with spades and hoes, we had to dig ourselves into the stony, frozen-solid ground in order to be able to fend off this powerful foe. Icy blizzards conspired with the Russians against us and made life difficult for everyone. In flimsy coats and torn shoes, which at times also had paper soles, old and young had to huddle tightly against the slopes of the snow-covered, icy trenches.'[37]

The Habsburg troops pushed on with remarkable tenacity. The Uszok Pass was seized on 26 January, and although not all the surrounding heights were occupied, small detachments of Russian cavalry that had been left in place showed little fight. The weather remained the most formidable opponent. When *Südarmee* went forward, three days after General Boroević's men, violent snowstorms were still blowing across the battlefield. Pushing through thick, trackless forests covered in deep snowfall, Habsburg and German battalions were able to close with the Wyszkow Pass before taking Beskid railway station on 3 February – advancing, in places, over fifteen miles. But many field guns had to be abandoned, and only specialized mountain artillery, strapped onto sledges, could be taken off the roads. Infantry toiled at clearing snowdrifts, braving sub-zero winds that left them on the verge of exposure. 'The icy wind whipped the frozen faces of our troops, covering them with a painful crust of ice and freezing the sweat that clung to their bodies from sheer exertion', recorded one account. 'The men were constantly having to step in for the faltering draft animals in order to move the sledges, which were loaded with machine-guns, mountain-guns, ammunition and military baggage.' There was no shelter, no warm food, and weapons had to be thawed out before they could be used.[38]

Both sides endured the same awful conditions in the Carpathians, but things never seemed quite so desperate for the Russians. With a better road and rail network on the northern side of the mountains, the Tsar's forces were more easily supplied and could be reinforced quickly in an emergency. Although there seemed little likelihood that the Russian hold on the Carpathians could be broken as easily as Conrad hoped, the scale of the Austrian attack was worrisome and brought into sharp focus the need for a clear Russian strategy over the coming months. On 24 January, General Ivanov telegraphed Yanushkevich at *Stavka* about the urgent need for reinforcements for the Southwest Front. The Austrian offensive had struck at 'a very sensitive and weakly occupied' sector of the line, and any success here might result in the lifting of the siege of Przemyśl. The positions occupied by his armies were 'poorly equipped to meet the enemy's blow; they are stretched; they can be easily circumvented; and they make it difficult for units to support each other'. In Ivanov's opinion, 'the most reliable course of action would be a decisive counter-attack'.[39]

Ivanov's telegram was not particularly welcome at Baranovichi. Approval had already been given for another offensive in the north with the newly formed Twelfth Army (scheduled for late February), and Danilov worried that sending more troops to Galicia would dilute Russian strength for what he regarded as their foremost operational priority – the occupation of East Prussia. He replied the following day, explaining that the situation was assessed 'somewhat differently' at the High Command and he did not think that a successful defence in the Carpathians required a counter-offensive. Yet the continuation of the Austrian attack (and the arrival of German troops) worried the Grand Duke sufficiently that he ordered General Ruzski to send an infantry corps with five or six batteries of mountain artillery to bolster Ivanov's lines. When Ivanov travelled up to *Stavka* in early February, he again pressed his case for more reinforcements, arguing that the only way they would improve their situation 'was to throw the enemy down from the mountains' and invade Hungary. The Grand Duke, amenable as ever, thought this was sound strategy and approved, in principle, the idea of an offensive in the south as well as signing off on more resources as required.[40]

When Danilov heard about this change of heart, he became visibly frustrated, complaining to his aides about the failure to prioritize one sector of the front. He had already told the Grand Duke, as clearly as he could, that they were not in a position to land a decisive blow against both their opponents and they must choose one or the other, either Vienna–Budapest or Berlin. According to Danilov, the 'existence of two competing military assignments' was 'entirely condemnable' and 'resulted in a fragmentation of force and thus compromised the success of both undertakings'. 'This conflict of interests was undoubtedly caused by the aforementioned lack of organisation within the higher army administration, which resulted in *Stavka* – in its measures and decisions – being somewhat disconnected from the fronts, which consisted of a large number of troop units, and having to remotely manage operations from a great distance.' But the Grand Duke showed little interest in making a decisive intervention either way and let his front commanders do as they pleased, only intervening strongly when the mood took him – an inconsistent style of command that reflected the muddied strategic outlook in Petrograd over whether Germany or Austria should be Russia's main focus.[41]

Fighting continued in the Carpathians into February. After receiving XXII Corps from the Northwest Front, Ivanov ordered a major counter-offensive, which concentrated on the Dukla and Uszok passes. Encountering only exhausted, apathetic Austrian troops, General Brusilov's Eighth Army was able to regain much of the ground that had been lost. The situation deteriorated so rapidly that Conrad was forced to accept the transfer of a corps from the Balkans to bolster his thin line. Within two weeks, Boroević's Third Army had lost almost 89,000 men, about half its strength, mostly from illness and injury caused by the terrible conditions. Field Marshal Lieutenant von Kralowetz, Chief of Staff at X Corps, later complained that they had been defeated by the harsh winter weather. 'The enemy had not suffered anywhere near the same level of disruption. Their main forces – which had hitherto been withheld and preserved until the inevitable moment of weakness in the attacker – now launched a counter-attack, which came up against troops who were already decimated, feeble, frozen and defenceless . . .' Such an ambitious series of operations, he concluded, could only have been successful if those troops responsible for preparing the attacks, digging the forward positions and bringing up supplies were replaced by fresh troops beforehand, but this had not been insisted upon.[42]

The plight of the besieged garrison at Przemyśl was never far from Conrad's thoughts. Almost as soon as the first Carpathian offensive had broken down, he began planning another one, replacing General Boroević with General Böhm-Ermolli and bringing in Second Army to lead the attack. But hopes were already fading. On 10 February, General Kusmanek reported (in a wireless message to AOK) that if 3,500 of the garrison's horses were slaughtered immediately, food stocks could be stretched until mid-March, although this would affect the ability of the defenders to mount breakout operations. Two days later, on 12 February, AOK informed the Emperor that it was doubtful Przemyśl could be relieved in time. Franz Joseph received this news with deep sadness, before urging his commanders to push on and prevent the fall of the city at all costs.[43]

5.   'The agony of defence'

As Conrad's armies struggled in the Carpathians, Field Marshal Hindenburg laid down his instructions for a new offensive out of East Prussia. Two German armies, Eighth and Tenth, would attempt a double envelopment of the Russian Tenth Army, which occupied a thin slice of German territory from the Niemen river down to Johannisburg. It was an ambitious goal, nothing less than the destruction of an entire army, all the more so given that Hindenburg was relying upon newly formed corps to do it. To place such importance on young recruits was not ideal, so it was agreed to assign at least 300 veterans to each battalion, with another third being made up of *Ersatz* (reserve) troops that had already seen combat. *OberOst* was confident that this would give the new corps the best chance of fighting well in what promised to be a campaign of great difficulty, but also, potentially, significant rewards.[1]

The weather would be a formidable challenge. Hindenburg and Ludendorff had moved their headquarters forward to Insterburg, where blizzards had covered the railway tracks and roads with deep layers of snow, while the streets were reduced to 'mirror-smooth' surfaces of packed ice. With the telephone and telegraph network down, there was a necessary reliance upon wireless radio to send messages, which would be of crucial importance as German units attempted to coordinate their advance.[2] Troops were equipped with winter clothing, transport was placed on runners, and officers were briefed on the need to march as far as possible. 'The experience of Tannenberg and the Battle of the Masurian Lakes had shown us that a great and rapid success in battle was only to be obtained when the enemy was attacked on two sides', noted Ludendorff. 'Both our opponent's wings were weak. We could hope to gain a lot of ground before the enemy main forces could get away from our frontal attack. Both our thrusting wings were to surround the enemy – the earlier the better.'[3]

Ludendorff was sanguine about what might be achieved. 'How the whole operation will now turn out is difficult to say', he wrote in a letter to Moltke on 27 January:

I am counting on a resounding victory in East Prussia and a slow retreat through the Carpathians. Whether or not this pressure will keep Russia east of the Vistula is questionable, but certainly possible. Only a firm push in the direction of Osowiec-Łomża could achieve more. Przemyśl can last until the end of February. And the Austrians are unlikely to arrive there either . . . I do not believe that a complete tactical overthrow of Russia is possible. The distances and sheer size of the country are too great for that. However, I do hope that we can achieve what we set out to achieve and overthrow the Russian Army.

As for Falkenhayn, Ludendorff thought that he had 'made a few slip ups' and that 'the Kaiser's confidence has been shaken'. He was hopeful that he 'will fall in the next attack'.[4]

Falkenhayn, as always, remained sceptical. The idea of fighting in the depths of winter did not appeal to the Chief of the General Staff, who entered 1915 in an ostensibly weaker position than ever before. On 16 January, the Kaiser had transferred the position of Minister of War (which Falkenhayn had held since 1913) to another Prussian officer (and court favourite), Adolph Wild von Hohenborn, while also decreeing that three recently raised corps, plus another regular corps drawn from the west, would be deployed on the Eastern Front.[5] Falkenhayn refused to let this affect his long-term strategic assessment of the importance of the war in the west. He spent most of his time at Charleville-Mézières in the Ardennes, chosen as the location of OHL because of its good links across the Western Front. The war in France and Belgium had now mutated into a new kind of conflict, a great siege of fortifications, trenches and barbed wire that grew more extensive each month. Heavy French attacks in Artois and Champagne continued through the winter, forcing a constant movement of divisions in and out of the line, which reduced Falkenhayn's ability to mass forces for any counter-offensive. On 7 January, he issued a decree to his army commanders in France stating that their aim was 'to fortify the positions in such a way that, if necessary, they could stand up to a lengthy attack by large numbers of enemy forces, even when manned by very few of our own troops'. Only after this had been achieved would it be possible 'firstly, to allow those sections of the army that have retreated to make any real recovery and, secondly, to lend those sections of the army that remain strong . . . for use in special assignments, which – for obvious reasons – is absolutely essential'.[6]

Hindenburg's attack opened on 31 January with a feint by Mackensen's Ninth Army at Bolimov, a small village thirty-five miles west of Warsaw. Intending to fix Russian attention on Poland and distract them from the movement of reinforcements to the north, German troops attacked after firing off 18,000 shells filled with a mixture of TNT and xylyl bromide (a lachrymatory agent intended to irritate the eyes and cause choking). The decision to use such an unusual weapon had been taken after a number of officers, including the heavy-artillery expert at OHL, Max Bauer, had speculated about the prospect of employing gas as a solution to the problems of trench warfare. Unfortunately, the freezing cold seems to have prevented it from working effectively and the attackers ran into large numbers of Russian soldiers still capable of defending their trenches. Max Hoffmann, who climbed up to the belfry of Bolimov church to watch the attack, was unimpressed. 'I was a little disappointed . . .' he wrote. 'I had expected much greater results from the employment of this ammunition in – as we then imagined – such large quantities . . . The tactical success, with the exception of considerable losses that the Russians sustained in killed and wounded, was only a local improvement of our position'.[7]

Hindenburg and Ludendorff were hoping for much more than a 'local improvement'. The object of their operation was nothing less than the destruction of General F. V. Sivers' Tenth Army. Sivers was a 61-year-old Baltic German, appointed to army command in September 1914 and tasked with keeping the enemy busy and covering the communications to Petrograd. He had spent the autumn of 1914 launching a series of probing attacks into German territory, which left his army strung out in a thin line; about one under-strength battalion per kilometre in a patchwork of narrow trenches and ditches. 'There were gaps in the trenches along the line and they were very weak', recalled a company commander in one of the defending divisions; 'the barbed-wire fences were in as dire a state as they could be; but most importantly, our positions also passed through open, swampy lowland areas. The passages between the trenches were so shallow that in some stretches one had to crawl so as not to be shot by the Germans, and it was very difficult to dig any deeper into the frozen ground. At the same time, the Germans occupied the strongly fortified command position across the Angerap river, and could successfully fire at us almost everywhere.'[8]

With its flanks on either side largely unguarded, little depth to the defences, and no reserves in place, the Russian Tenth Army was in a highly vulnerable position. General Sivers recognized many of these deficiencies, but had no way of ameliorating them given his shortage of manpower, lack of engineering resources, and the great length of front he had to cover – over 160 miles. On 23 January, he warned General Ruzski, 'We must not forget that no-one can guarantee Tenth Army against the possible reoccurrence of the same manoeuvre that the Germans made against the army of General Rennenkampf – that is, moving several corps against it and delivering a short but decisive blow.'[9] Yet these concerns were waved aside. Sivers was ordered to mount an offensive into East Prussia, alongside Twelfth Army on his left, on 20 February, with *Stavka* assuming that all spare German troops had been used up in their operations in Poland and that they would 'not dare to attempt anything in East Prussia'.[10]

The German Eighth Army moved off into a blinding snowstorm on the morning of 7 February, with drifts up to a metre deep. The initial clashes were confusing as Siberian troops, surprised by the sight of enemy columns moving forward, mounted a series of rear-guard actions before withdrawing in good order. By the end of the first day, the southern pincer had bent the Russian line back, reached Johannisburg and taken almost 4,000 prisoners, mostly from a single division.[11] The response from the Russian High Command was one of confusion and cross-purposes. On 9 February, Ruzski ordered Sivers to unleash a 'decisive attack' on the German forces gathering on his left flank, while another telegram, arriving shortly afterwards, to his Chief of Staff, Alexei Budberg, authorized him to begin destroying the railways to hinder any subsequent German advance.[12]

It was at this moment, when Sivers' attention was drawn to his left flank, that the main attack came on the right. Just as Hindenburg and Ludendorff had intended, the German Tenth Army arrived like a hammer blow, scattering the Russian defenders with a series of short, sharp battles preceded by powerful artillery support.

Focused on the attack in the south, General Sivers sent what few reserves he had to his left flank, and when General Yepanchin, commander of III Corps on the embattled right flank, reported on how he was being overrun, Sivers dismissed his concerns. 'There was no reason to attach any significance to the enemy forces bypassing your right flank', he wrote on 10 February, 'because the actions of the Germans are demonstrative and cannot develop into a serious threat'.[13] Compounding this was a devastating lack of intelligence on German movements. Russian cavalry, which should have provided Sivers with a sense of what the enemy was doing, had already saddled up and left the battlefield, trotting off to the east towards the town of Olita. Their commander, General Leontovich, made no attempt to establish communication with Sivers for three days, leaving him in the dark about the extent to which his right flank had been crushed. This dereliction of duty was, according to Sivers' Chief of Staff, a 'colossal' failure. Instead of writing a 'brilliant page in the history of the Russian cavalry', Leontovich took charge of Olita and began the systematic looting of local warehouses.[14]

The failure to react quickly to the northern pincer almost proved fatal to Tenth Army. With three German corps rapidly moving around its open flank, Sivers' command was in danger of being surrounded and destroyed, as Samsonov had been at Tannenberg. By 11 February, scattered groups of soldiers, leaderless and without equipment, were trudging away from the fighting eastwards towards Kovno and Mariampol. By the time Sivers authorized a general retreat, ignoring a direct order from Ruzski to hold on, it was almost too late. It then became a question of how many units could extricate themselves from the advancing German wings. Running across abandoned supply wagons, depots and stores, the attackers were able to keep themselves resupplied, pushing on each day despite mounting exhaustion. One German battalion commander remembered how the horses sank up to their stomachs in the snow. 'We can barely make out our route, all that can be seen are vast, white expanses of snow. The only signposts to guide the way are scraps of straw nailed to the trees. Then even these run out as there are no trees left in sight. What is road, trench, field? Everything is just one huge expanse of snow. Marching takes five times longer than in normal conditions. The last stretch of the march in particular, which had us wading through snow up to our hips and clambering over hills, was excruciatingly hard.'[15]

As the Russian retreat gathered momentum, XX Corps (occupying the centre of Sivers' line at Goldap) found itself threatened on both flanks. Commencing its retreat on 10 February, the corps headed for Suwalki, only to find German cavalry already ahead of it, so it changed direction and took refuge in the thick pines of the Augustów Forest – ancient woodland that had once been the property of the Polish kings. Within a matter of days, XX Corps was surrounded by an iron ring of German units. Desperate attempts were made to break out to the east, but they all failed, with German howitzers zeroing in on the Russian positions and causing carnage. 'The troops were so mixed that the senior commanders had barely any influence over the course of events in the forest', recorded one witness:

> Ammunition was running low, both for the infantry and for the artillery. The forest roads were so crowded with various carts that it became impossible to transport cartridges from ammunition park carts. As the fire ceased, the soldiers disposed of artillery equipment, gun locks, and where possible, the guns themselves, by throwing them into the river. Horses were shot with revolvers so as not to increase the enemy's trophies. The agony of defence proceeded slowly but surely. Dense lines of enemy soldiers approached closer and closer after their artillery ceased fire. Our troops, having shot all their ammunition, sold their lives dearly.[16]

Thousands of Russians would be taken prisoner in the Augustów Forest, rounded up in milling, leaderless groups and transported through the snow into captivity. With the rest of Sivers' army pushed southeast over the Niemen, there would be no grand repetition of Tannenberg, when an entire army was destroyed, which caused frustration at *OberOst*. 'However gratifying it was to have defeated the 10th Russian Army . . . we did not succeed in carrying out the operations to the desired end, nor in attaining the full strategic advantages we had looked for', wrote Hoffmann.[17] As for Hindenburg and Ludendorff, there were mixed feelings: pride at what German arms had accomplished, tempered by the disappointment that somehow Sivers' army had escaped. There was also a growing awareness of how worn out their troops had become, and after the destruction of XX Corps, *OberOst* had reluctantly withdrawn its forces back to East Prussia – fighting off heavy Russian counter-attacks as it did so.

The Grand Duke had ordered these attacks, which continued for weeks, trying to restore Russian pride and push the Germans back to their border. They changed little in a wider sense, but were a terrible ordeal for those men who found themselves advancing across open ground, often uphill, towards the enemy trenches. 'The ground was frozen, and our lines, which had to drop flat to get cover from crashing enemy fire, could not dig in and every last man was shot . . .' one participant remembered. 'The battle lasted for three days. For three days our units would rise to attack, then get shot and cling to the ground again to suffer the freezing cold. At noon, the top layer of the earth thawed and turned to mud. The Grenadiers used this opportunity and raked the mud with their hands to make some kind of cover. By the evening, the wet overcoats would freeze, turning into dirty bark. The rifles, covered with frozen mud, would not fire and were turned into clubs.'[18] By mid-March, it was over. The Grand Duke ordered a strict defensive on the Northwest Front and accepted the resignation of General Ruzski, who had asked to be relieved of his position 'for the state of his health, owing to extreme fatigue and a general weakening of the body'. He was replaced by Ivanov's Chief of Staff, General Alekseev.[19]

The kind of operational spectacular that Hindenburg and Ludendorff could seemingly pull off at will was beyond the abilities of Conrad von Hötzendorf, who continued in his quixotic attempt to relieve Przemyśl. Conrad may have told the Emperor (or indeed anyone who would listen) that Austrian suffering *enabled* German success, but this brought little comfort to an army that had known almost nothing but defeat and futility since the opening days of the war. A second offensive in the Carpathians was launched on 27 February, but it was no more successful than the first had been and produced yet more shattered regiments, shivering, frostbitten wounded, and piles of frozen bodies in the snow. General Böhm-Ermolli, brought in because he was seen as a more pliable commander than the gruff Boroević, proved unable to get his army moving in the way that Conrad wanted. Already there were signs of mounting unease across the officer corps. Almost all the corps commanders of Second Army, which would lead the new attack, reported on the exhaustion of their men, while also complaining about the lack of mountain guns, which meant that their infantry often had to attack without any artillery support whatsoever – an almost suicidal task in 1915.[20]

The lack of Austrian artillery had been bad enough in the early months of the war, but it was now a chronic problem. In October 1914, the Austrian High Command had drafted a list of its requirements for more firepower, including light and mountain guns, the production of a modern field howitzer and the greater availability of 15 cm howitzers and 10 cm cannons. This was followed in February by a further demand that each infantry division be equipped with 24 field guns, 36 light howitzers and eight assorted heavier weapons – a total of 68 guns – which would put Austrian divisions on a par with their German counterparts. But such an ambitious programme would take months, maybe even years, to implement, which left the War Ministry scrabbling around in the meantime. Guns being constructed for foreign countries in the Škoda Works (Austria's most important industrial conglomerate) were confiscated, and the empire's reserve pool of artillery was plundered, but even these desperate measures only made a small difference to an army that had been under-gunned in peacetime and was now in danger of simply being unable to fulfil even modest operational requirements.[21]

In the Carpathians, snow and ice had been replaced by mud and water as rainfall saturated the hills, with guns, men and horses sinking into slime as they endeavoured to move up to the ever-shifting front line. With storms threatening to wash away the roads and bridges that the army relied upon, there was a danger that supply routes would collapse, and with them any hopes of a breakthrough. General Böhm-Ermolli, a 59-year-old cavalryman, knew how difficult any offensive would be, but found himself wrestling with the stringent demands coming from AOK. In contrast to Conrad's first offensive in the Carpathians, this would be a relatively small-scale attack. Instead of three armies launching a coordinated offensive, there was only one weak army making a frontal assault along a narrow twelve-kilometre sector. Böhm-Ermolli would have preferred to wait and bring up more men and guns, but Conrad made it clear that such a delay could not be tolerated. The outcome was a predictably hopeless and bloody repulse. With a crippling lack of artillery support (only six guns for every kilometre of front), Austrian infantry had to fight their way forward on their own. 'It is always the same', recorded the Chief of Staff of X Corps. 'In the beginning there is an attitude of "hurray!" Then neighbouring units balk, followed by the inevitable reversals, retreats and rehabilitation . . .'[22]

Conrad pushed his armies as hard as he could, alternately bargaining with and threatening his commanders. On the evening of 6 March, he warned that the offensive must be continued: 'Across the entire battle-front, from the Vistula to Eastern Galicia, not one section of the front may limit itself to purely passive action in these crucial days.' But co-ordinating the actions of hundreds of thousands of men over such a large front and across such challenging terrain was impossible. Conrad wanted Fourth Army, out to the west, to launch a supporting attack, but this only took place on the night of 7 March after constant delays – again because of the terrible weather. Austrian infantry moved forward, made some minor gains, but stopped when they came up against entrenched Russian positions. There was little that could be done without significantly improved fire support and much better observation, both of which were unlikely in such desperate conditions. A heavy blizzard blew in on 10 March. 'All advances grind to a halt', recorded an Austrian colonel; 'any chance of evacuating the wounded is dashed; entire skirmish lines are coated with a constant blanket of deep snow. The icy ground, slippery from the storm, is completely impassable, and any digging is impossible. Without shelter and unable to move, the infantry stand before the enemy barricades, the bulk of its artillery still trailing three to four marches behind the front line.' Yet the men stuck to their task. 'Despite all the signals from their commanders, who have been steering them towards complete exhaustion for weeks; despite all the internal sedition and the espionage surrounding them: despite everything, they persevered through this hell.'[23]

In the long, expansive horror that was the Eastern Front, the campaign in the Carpathians stood out with particular intensity, demanding more of men and animals than anyone had a right to expect. One veteran from the Tyrol, writing years later, would recall:

> In a steely, dark blue sky, the stars burned, as huge as suns, as the mountain forests slept silently in the bitter cold. The scene was suffused with three colours: the ashen white of the endless fields of snow; the grave black of the endless mountain forests; the blood red of the flames of battle. The sky stretched boundlessly, mercilessly, over the death and suffering of hundreds and thousands of soldiers. Searchlights and flares bathed the landscape in a strangely magical light; often the vast horizon itself seemed to glow and burn . . . The Carpathian front consumed men at an alarming rate, draining strength from both sides. It wore them down like a hammer, day in and day out, week after week, blow after blow coming down on them with unceasing vigour.[24]

The incredible effort that had been made in the Carpathians was not enough. No matter how many times Habsburg infantry – Czechs, Croats, Magyars, Slovenes, Austrians, Ruthenes and Serbs – struggled forward across no-man's-land, traipsing through snow, ice and mud, they could not break the enemy. The Russians were simply too strong.

In Przemyśl, a last, desperate breakthrough attempt took place in the early hours of 19 March. With his relief operation unlikely to reach the city in time, Conrad told the garrison commander that the 'honour of arms' demanded that he organize a new offensive. Two assault divisions were eventually put together and ordered to break the encircling Russian lines to the east out towards Lemberg. The choice of an attack *away* from the Austrian lines was taken by General Kusmanek, who recognized that his men were too frail and exhausted to push through to the south, so they should prepare for a final, destructive raid, aimed at doing as much damage to Russian depots and infrastructure as possible. But the attacks collapsed within a matter of hours. Austrian regiments took longer than expected to get to their jumping-off points; others became lost in the snow. The Russians were then ready and waiting. When the infantry went forward, the defenders unleashed a 'hail of bullets', leaving scattered groups of *Landwehr* troops scurrying back to the main defences and clumps of dead and wounded out in no-man's-land.[25]

When word arrived of the calamitous results out beyond the wire, Kusmanek had little option but to prepare for the inevitable. Issuing his men with two days' rations, he prepared final orders for the destruction of the defences. At six o'clock on the morning of 22 March, the bridges over the San were blown, with hundreds of tons of masonry and steel collapsing into the river in great clouds of debris. At the same time, detonations ripped through the forts that had guarded the city for so long, bringing to an end the rule of the Habsburgs. 'In scenes resembling the Day of Judgement,' recorded one account, 'terrible explosions burst open huge expanses of the earth, spewing out mighty grey and yellowish clouds in which towering pillars of fire licked the sky. Stones, debris and shrapnel shot into the air, only to come back down like a shower of hail. The cloudless blue spring sky, which stretched over the fortress as dawn broke – as if to taunt the garrison, it was the first fine day in weeks – vanished behind thick billows of dense smoke.'[26]

Three hours later, Kusmanek sent his final communication, a message to the opposing commander informing him that the city was his: 'Food is exhausted. The works destroyed. I surrender the open city and await your command with no conditions.'[27] Almost four entire Austrian corps were taken captive – 120,000 men and 900 guns – with 2,500 officers and nine generals among the total. 'All the roads from Przemyśl are filled with prisoners', reported a correspondent of the *Russkiye Vedomosti* newspaper. 'The highway for dozens of miles seems blue because of the bluish Austrian uniforms. Many of the prisoners walk in huge droves under the escort of a few Cossacks, while some walk in small groups or alone. Nobody makes any attempt to escape. There are also many Austrian soldiers in the city. The evacuation of the prisoners will take about two weeks. There are a lot of Slavs among those who surrendered: Poles, Rusyns [Ruthenians] and Czechs. They do not hide their joy over the surrender.'[28]

News quickly spread across the Eastern Front and was soon picked up by German wireless. 'The Russians have just announced the surrender of Przemyśl to the world', Falkenhayn wrote to Conrad. 'Should this be true, the reminder of the heroic attitude of the garrison will only serve to reinforce – in the hearts of all Germans – the resolve to crush Austria–Hungary's enemies as well as their own at all costs.'[29] Conrad was understandably saddened by the news, but thanked Falkenhayn for his kind words. 'Yesterday, after the supply situation had rendered any further resistance impossible, Przemyśl was handed over to the Russians as a heap of rubble, without any negotiations with the enemy. It is with heartfelt, comradely thanks that I receive the sympathetic words Your Excellency addressed to me on this occasion. Please be assured that the case of Przemyśl – as deeply as it affects me – has no bearing on my conviction and the resolve of the Austro-Hungarian Army to remain loyal to the German army to the end – come what may.'[30]

Austrian casualties were staggering – far worse than Conrad had feared. Later investigations would conclude that by the time the fighting in the Carpathians had tailed off in the late spring, Conrad's armies had sustained a total of 793,000 casualties since 1 January 1915, including the garrison at Przemyśl.[31] Habsburg forces were now little more than a militia, hurriedly drafted, lacking trained officers and NCOs and held together by a fraying set of values and loyalties. That far more men were lost in the relief attempts than were contained within the garrison was a cruel and tragic irony, the Austrian High Command having convinced themselves that their prestige and authority could only be restored by retaking the city. When Emperor Franz Joseph was told of the imminent demise of the fortress, he wept, signing off a final telegram to Kusmanek:

Although it pains me most deeply that the valiant breakout from Przemyśl yesterday failed due to the superior strength of the enemy, I cannot help but look with wistful pride at the unparalleled self-sacrifice of the brave men whose efforts sadly did not come to fruition. I thank all those who fought yesterday for their heroic deeds, and I bless the glorious memory of those who died a noble death on the battlefield. Even in many years to come, history will tell of the heroic actions of the Austro-Hungarian soldiers in their dogged defence of the Przemyśl fortress; – they were steadfast and brave to the very end.[32]

★

The fall of Przemyśl marked the high point of Russia's war on the Eastern Front; a triumphant moment of victory that seemed to vindicate the great hopes that had been invested in her grand army. The London *Times* noted how the 'real marvel of the beleaguerment' was 'the astonishing tenacity of the Russians, who steadfastly clung to their intention of taking Przemysl in spite of every fluctuation of fortune elsewhere', and confidently predicted that it had come 'just at the right time, at the opening of the spring campaign'.[33] At Baranovichi, the mood was suitably ebullient. Tsar Nicholas, who was staying at *Stavka*, was brought the news by the Grand Duke at 11.30 a.m. 'Nicolasha came running into my carriage, out of breath and with tears in his eyes, and told me of the fall of Przemysl', the Tsar recorded in a letter to the Tsarina, Alexandra. 'For two days we have been waiting for this news with hope and anxiety. The fall of this fortress has an enormous moral and military significance. After several months of despondency, this news strikes as an unexpected ray of sunshine, and exactly on the first day of spring!' A *Te Deum* was sung that afternoon in the local church, with the Tsar conferring upon the Grand Duke the Second Class of the Order of St George.[34]

For a moment, it seemed that the Tsar's optimism marked a new, more decisive phase in the war. A month earlier, in February, ships of the Royal Navy had bombarded the Ottoman forts at the mouth of the Dardanelles Straits, attempting to force a passage through to Constantinople. If the straits could be secured, then the Allies would be able to enter the Black Sea, open up supply routes to Russia and knock Turkey out of the war. Although the Ottoman defences proved more stubborn than anticipated, with a major naval action on 18 March resulting in the loss of three battleships, the Allies' resolve to try again had not been impaired, and planning was under way for an amphibious landing to seize control of the Gallipoli peninsula sometime in late April.

The situation in the Mediterranean and the Adriatic would also be transformed should Italy enter the war. The kingdom had been a member of the Triple Alliance (alongside Germany and Austria) for over thirty years, but opted to remain neutral in 1914 over concerns about Austria's territorial ambitions in the Balkans. By the spring of 1915, the clamour from groups of nationalists and so-called irredentists, eager to recover what they saw as Italian soil, was becoming louder. The Prime Minister, Antonio Salandra, trod a difficult path between competing interest groups, mindful that Italy was unprepared for war but also conscious that the nation might never have a better chance of achieving a 'greater Italy' at the expense of what many Italians regarded as their 'hereditary enemy'. On 26 April, Italy signed the secret Treaty of London with Great Britain, France and Russia, committing to 'use her entire resources for the purpose of waging war' alongside the Triple Entente. In return she would 'obtain the Trentino, Cisalpine Tyrol with its geographical and natural frontier (the Brenner frontier), as well as Trieste, the counties of Gorizia and Gradisca, all Istria . . .' She would, moreover, not conclude a separate peace 'during the course of the Present European War'.[35]

Italy would not formally declare war on Austria–Hungary for another month, but she had chosen her moment well, striking when the Habsburg Empire was at its lowest ebb. Indeed, Russia was now poised to begin the invasion of Hungary. On 19 March, the Northwest Front was ordered to go onto a 'purely defensive' footing, while General Ivanov was to push his left flank forward in the direction of Budapest and, if possible, join up with Romanian forces on the Habsburg right.[36] Romania was not yet in the war, but both sides recognized that if the balance of power was tipped sufficiently, another domino would fall and, like Italy, she might take up arms. 'There was no doubt that diplomatic negotiations with these states [Romania and Bulgaria] would be much easier if we were to achieve a decisive victory in the Austro-Hungarian theatre of war', noted Danilov.[37]

Conditions remained inhospitable in the high mountains, where wind, rain and snow continued to batter the forward positions. The fighting was almost continuous throughout March; a series of Russian thrusts, parried by Austrian counter-offensives, that caused spiralling casualties. Within a week of the Russian attack, the Habsburgs had commenced a broad retreat off the main ridge, fighting hard for every mile of ground but lacking the strength to hold on to crucial positions: the railway at Mezölaborcz, and the villages of Lupków, Smolnik and Jablonki. Böhm-Ermolli's Second Army sustained 47,000 casualties in the second half of March, with some divisions losing half their strength.[38] This depressing tale of broken regiments caused increasingly fraught telegrams to be sent back to AOK on the likelihood of an imminent collapse if reserves were not rushed forward. On 30 March, Böhm-Ermolli notified Conrad that up till now he had made every effort to 'comply with the wishes of AOK', had never submitted 'pessimistic reports' and had earned the right not to be misunderstood. He had made forces available to the 'hard pressed' Third Army, but now only had 1,500 men available as a last-ditch reserve, and his other troops were 'utterly exhausted'.[39]

Fortunately for the Habsburg Empire, the curse of Russian operations, in not being able to turn a promising opening into a broad and sustained strategic victory, struck again. Despite their recent successes, the Tsar's forces barely outnumbered their opponent and were still woefully short of the guns and shells that would be required for a full-scale invasion of Hungary. By the first week of April, mutual exhaustion was settling in across the front. In Eighth Army, which had spearheaded the Russian drive south, General Brusilov complained that he only had 200 shells per gun, enough for a single battle, and was told not to expect any significant improvement until the autumn. On 9 April, he wired that his offensive had been 'progressing extremely slowly in recent days', with the enemy putting up a 'stubborn resistance'. 'Our troops have to fight with little artillery support, because the ridge to our rear has no roads, which makes it difficult for the guns to move up. The enemy, on the other hand, having roads to his rear, relies greatly on his artillery. Our units suffered heavy losses and are exhausted from a ceaseless twenty days of fighting and travelling under extremely difficult conditions.'[40]

Ivanov called a halt to his offensive the following day. 'Under these circumstances,' he wrote, 'it appears necessary to bring our advance to a temporary halt. This will allow us to get the troops in order, to organise supplies of food and ammunition, and to await the arrival of reinforcements.'[41] This was a wise and necessary precaution. For those men at the front, the conditions they encountered were some of the worst of the war. As one veteran recalled:

> It was extremely difficult to cross over the main ridge of the Carpathian Mountains. We had to follow narrow paths laid through the deep snow of a dense forest. Spring was burgeoning and the snow became loose, which made the road almost impassable. For the baggage train and artillery, it was especially hard to move forward. The horses were completely exhausted, they could not carry the heavy loads, and the soldiers had to pull out carts and guns with their own hands. In some places, we had to line the ground with felled trees so that we could tow our heavy guns through the deep snow. It took us at least five hours to ascend the Beskid mountain.[42]

They had pushed the Austro-Hungarians to the brink of collapse. National and ethnic tension had been common in the army for decades, but the terrible winter fighting produced more and more signs of political unrest and poor morale. One of the most infamous examples of this occurred at the Dukla Pass on 3 April, when 28 Infantry Regiment, composed of Czechs from the city of Prague, went over to the Russians. By the end of the day, only 150 of the 2,200 soldiers who had entered the line could be found. The rest had laid down their arms and crossed no-man's-land, preferring to take their chances in captivity rather than endure more service in the mountains. Although Boroević, the army commander, was so disgusted by the behaviour of the regiment that he had it disbanded, the collapse had less to do with political or nationalist infighting than the combined effects of exhaustion, a lack of capable officers, and a lazy, indifferent military hierarchy that treated the men like peasants. When it arrived in the frozen Carpathians, the regiment had simply had enough.[43]

Czech regiments were not the only ones suspected of disloyalty, and AOK kept a close watch on Ruthenians, Serbs, Romanians and Poles – all seen as potentially vulnerable to the siren calls of separatism. These were contrasted with Germans and Hungarians, who sat at the summit of the Habsburg 'loyalty pyramid', playing a fundamental role in the imperial state and with the most to lose should it fracture.[44] Language difficulties added another dimension to this problem. The army that had gone to war in 1914 was multilingual, with three types of language being officially recognized: 'command', 'service' and 'regimental'. The first two provided a basic set of words and instructions (in German) that the men were expected to know, helping them to understand simple drill commands or technical terms that were essential in the field. The regimental language would differ depending on where the men were from; their officers were ordered to learn this within three years.[45]

In theory, this system of recognized languages should have given the Habsburg Empire a degree of commonality across its polyglot armed forces, but exceptions abounded. Hungarian officers in the K.u.K. (*Kaiserlich und Königlich*, the Imperial and Royal Habsburg Army) were allowed to get away with not having fluency in other languages, while staff officers usually only knew German, which prevented them from communicating with large parts of the army.[46] This system was difficult enough to make work in peacetime, but in wartime it rapidly broke down. With thousands of regular officers killed or wounded in the murderous battles of 1914, decades of fluency and understanding were taken with them, helping to further loosen the bonds that held the empire together. Their replacements often did not know regimental languages and had little time or opportunity to learn them. 'The best officers and other ranks have fallen or are unfit for service', Conrad told Berchtold in late December. 'The recruits now being drafted in are either very young or old and have no basic, solid training. In other words, they are far inferior in quality to the troops with which the war was begun.'[47]

Despite these ominous portents, Conrad's mood was surprisingly positive as he looked forward to the prospect of finally making Gina his wife (they would tie the knot in October). Her husband had filed for divorce in March, but there still remained significant obstacles to overcome because of the strict marriage laws in Austria. An ingenious solution was eventually devised, whereby Gina would become a Hungarian citizen (after being adopted by one of Conrad's friends, Field Marshal Ernst Kárász) and then convert to Protestantism. Although this allowed her first marriage to be dissolved, Conrad would also have to take Hungarian citizenship and leave the Catholic Church for the new marriage to be sanctioned. But he refused to do this, and there was never any possibility that the Emperor would agree to his Chief of the General Staff becoming a Hungarian. So Conrad worked on ways to get over these hurdles throughout the spring and summer, writing regularly to Gina and petitioning the Emperor for a dispensation to marry again. 'If this woman does not eventually decide to be my wife,' he admitted, 'I do not know what is to become of me.'[48]

Outside observers confidently began to predict that the break-up of the Habsburg Empire was now only weeks away. At OHL, Falkenhayn digested the latest reports with growing concern. An Austrian collapse would have incalculable consequences for the alliance – it might even end the war – which made the latest reports from Italy even more dangerous. Although there was, as yet, no declaration of war, rumours about Italian entry were rife in diplomatic circles across Europe, and the correspondence between Vienna and Berlin had been concerned with little else for weeks. Falkenhayn had repeatedly urged the Austrians to keep Italy neutral for as long as possible, even at the cost of some territory, but there was little chance that Franz Joseph would offer the kinds of concessions that would satisfy Rome for long. Berchtold had resigned in January after admitting that he lacked 'nerves' and did not possess the 'sort of light-headedness' that was required at such times ('so that the right moment is not missed'), and was replaced by a hard-faced Hungarian diplomat, Count István Burián. Burián had been authorized by Franz Joseph to offer the Trentino (the stretch of territory in the southern Tyrol that ran along the Adige river towards Lake Garda), but this was not enough, and on 10 April, the Italian Foreign Minister, Sidney Sonnino, presented Vienna with a long list of further demands, which was summarily rejected.[49]

Falkenhayn hoped that Conrad could be persuaded to push the Emperor to grant more concessions, but this got him nowhere. Conrad knew the Austro-Italian border well. He had spent years studying the unique problems of this corner of the empire: trekking along pine-crested Alpine slopes 'to get to know the land better', clearing out Italian spies and irredentists in Trieste, and working out how the Austrian border could be defended. Although he loved the Tyrol, which contained a substantial population of Italian speakers, he had little love for the Italian people, and came to regard them as untrustworthy and contemptible. The negotiations of 1915 did nothing for his opinion of them, and he resisted Falkenhayn's pleas to support further concessions. Conrad was adamant that even if the Trentino and Tyrol were handed over to the Italians, this would not prevent war; on the contrary, it would only whet Italy's appetite for more. When Falkenhayn pressed him again, noting that any territorial losses could be restored after the Central Powers had won the war, Conrad replied, acidly, that if Germany was so interested in peace, they should give back Alsace–Lorraine to France![50]

The collapse of negotiations with Italy presented Falkenhayn with a series of hard choices. On the Western Front, France's efforts to pierce the front in Champagne had resulted in only minor adjustments to the line at the cost of over 90,000 casualties.[51] Desperately trying to meet the challenges of trench warfare, the French Commander-in-Chief, Joseph Joffre, began planning a new offensive in Artois, aiming to take the ridge at Vimy utilizing new tactics, better artillery support and more thorough preparation. Even though the French had been unable to break the lines, they ensured that the bulk of Germany's army remain fixed in the west. Together, the British and French could boast 112 divisions, which gave them a marked superiority against Germany (with 97 divisions) and made it extremely difficult for Falkenhayn to countenance a significant transfer of units eastwards. However, by removing an infantry regiment from each division and two guns from each six-gun battery, the German War Ministry was able to 'create' fourteen new reserve divisions – eight of which Falkenhayn readied to use in a new campaign.[52]

But where should they go? Looking at the map of Europe, with the Central Powers hemmed in to the west and east, Falkenhayn noticed that a way still might exist to the southeast. If they could conquer Serbia, they would remove the troublesome Balkan nation and open a route towards Turkey, which was calling for more support now that British and French ships were menacing the narrows. He had told Conrad about this, but with the Russians on the borders of Hungary, the Austrian refused to consider it, so Falkenhayn returned to his maps, strewn in piles across his desk, and talked over the matter with his aides. Soon they began to focus their efforts on what would become the decisive point on the entire Eastern Front: Gorlice, a town at the northern edge of the Carpathians, about sixty miles east of Krakow, close to where Conrad had counter-attacked in December 1914 at the Battle of Limanowa-Lapanów.

The ground was currently held by the Russian Third Army, but its lines were over-extended, and Falkenhayn sensed an opportunity. On the evening of 4 April, he wrote to August von Cramon, his liaison officer at Teschen:

> For some time now, I have been pre-occupied with the question of whether a forceful advance from the Gorlice region towards Sanok might be prudent. The execution of this depends on the general situation and provision of the necessary forces. Four divisions will not be enough, though perhaps four army corps would be feasible. The poor performance of the Austrian railways at Tarnów and over Nowy Sącz is likely to cause major difficulties. Either way, I would appreciate it if you could contact me soon to give me an idea of your thoughts on such an operation. Please also include information about the performance of the railways and the possibility of using our vehicles on local routes. It is imperative that this entire matter is kept strictly confidential, including – for the time being – from the Austrian High Command.[53]

6. 'The forerunner of a catastrophe'

Eager to see the new lands that had fallen under Russian occupation, Tsar Nicholas II paid a visit to Galicia in late April. 'It was hot and windy', he wrote of the bumpy journey by car. 'The dust we raised covered us like a white shroud. You cannot imagine what we looked like!' The Tsar found Lemberg to be 'very handsome' and 'slightly resembling Warsaw', with 'a great number of gardens and monuments, full of troops and Russians!' The following day, 23 April, he left the city and drove the short distance to Przemyśl. 'It is a small town, with narrow streets and dull grey houses, filled with troops and Orenberg Cossacks. N[ikolai]. and I stayed . . . in a fairly clean house, the owner of which had fled before the fall of the fortress. The little place is surrounded by mountains and looks very picturesque. We dined in the garrison mess, where everything has remained untouched.' He was then taken on a tour of what remained of the defences. 'They are most interesting, colossal works – terribly fortified', he wrote. 'Not an inch of ground remained undefended.' After lunch, he returned to Lemberg and then boarded a train for Brody.[1]

The Tsar's visit to Galicia may have only lasted a few days, but it was a visible demonstration of how important this region was to Russia's war aims and the dream of expanding her empire up to its 'natural' border along the Carpathians. Already Lemberg was being turned into a Russian city, and the governor, Count Bobrinsky, had ordered wholesale changes 'through the deployment of Russian symbols, the performance of Russian rituals, the establishment of Russian festivals, Russian time, and the Russian language'. Shops had to carry signs in Cyrillic and portraits of the Romanovs replaced those of the Habsburg Emperor.[2] Przemyśl was no different, and the visit of the Tsar sparked off an intensive process of 'Russification' in the city. Jews were ordered to leave; the Polish elite were deported;

Polish schools were only permitted to remain open if they provided five hours of Russian-language teaching each week; while Ukrainian-language schools found themselves being forced to teach in Russian.[3]

Most of the senior officers involved in the Tsar's visit found it a tiresome and unwelcome distraction from the war, hiding their misgivings behind masks of cold formality. General Brusilov, whose forces remained stuck in the Carpathians, thought it was 'worse than untimely; it was simply stupid', and he could not fathom why the Grand Duke had agreed to it. Galicia had only recently come under Russian occupation and Brusilov feared that the Tsar would become the focus of political protests or even assassination attempts. He also found Nicholas II to be 'a man remarkably ill-favoured by fate'. Ever since his coronation in the summer of 1896, when almost 1,400 people had been killed during a terrible stampede at Khodynka Field in Moscow, the Tsar had been seen as an unlucky monarch. 'No matter what he set his hand to throughout his reign,' Brusilov added, 'he was attended by misfortune, and I felt a sort of presentiment that this tour was the forerunner of a catastrophe.'[4]

Intelligence was coming in that the Germans were on the move. From the first week of April, the Grand Duke had noted in his regular reports to the Tsar that the enemy was regrouping and possibly looking to mount a counter-offensive. The Russians had been warned by French intelligence that at least two corps and three cavalry divisions had left the Western Front, but their destination was as yet unknown.[5] Therefore, reserves would be needed, and on 12 April, two days after Ivanov's assault in the mountains had been called off, Yanushkevich sent a telegram to the new commander of the Northwest Front, General Mikhail Alekseev, asking him to provide another corps. There were 'indications that the Germans are likely to strike the centre of Third Army, aiming to reach the right flank of your troops that have crossed over the main Carpathian Ridge; *this blow may bring them success due to the fact that the front of the named army is stretched*'. The Grand Duke was 'not inclined to exaggerate the significance of this intelligence', but was keen 'to form free reserves as soon as possible and, above all, he wants to have one corps at his disposal, and it also must remain in a state of readiness, so that he can command it, if necessary, at his own discretion'.[6]

Alekseev was a hard-working and dutiful soldier; loyal to the High Command, but not someone who would fold easily if he disagreed with his superiors. He arrived at his headquarters in Siedlice on 30 March and soon discovered that the condition of his army group left much to be desired. 'The armies were weakened by the preceding battles,' he noted, '[and] the artillery and technical supplies were in much worse condition than on the Southwest Front. The economic part of the rear was unable to satisfy the needs of the army for a variety of complex reasons, some of which were related to the activities of the central departments. The operational headquarters was in a poor state.'[7] Although he had been at one with his former chief in the belief that 'our path to Berlin lies through Vienna', he soon began to doubt the wisdom of continuing operations in the Carpathians, seeing it as an essentially secondary task and one that was potentially dangerous. Instead, they should look to an offensive on the left bank of the Vistula. With this in mind, he would not agree to the further weakening of the Northwest Front when the situation was so unclear.

The matter now rested with the Grand Duke. As Supreme Commander, it was up to him to manage the differing perspectives of the two fronts, deciding which would have priority and where the focus of effort should be. But instead of keeping a tight grip on his front commanders and ordering Alekseev to send him the corps, he did nothing. With *Stavka* preoccupied with the Tsar's trip to Galicia, it was left to Yanushkevich to try and persuade Alekseev to cooperate. He telegraphed Siedlice on 27 April confirming that it was not possible to mount an offensive in the north and that the Carpathian range 'retains its primary importance'. This was now even more vital because of the recent addition of Italy to the alliance, the Treaty of London having been signed the day before. Therefore, there might need to be further transfers of manpower from the Northwest Front.[8]

As evidence mounted about German and Austrian movements, it became increasingly clear that the Russian Army was in a poor state to repulse any serious offensive. 'The total volume of intelligence about the enemy, obtained from different fronts, indicates that the enemy is now redeploying its forces', Brusilov reported on 26 April. 'The ultimate purpose of this redeployment is yet to be identified, but it is safe to say that it has not been undertaken with the intention of passive resistance, and the enemy will do everything he can to keep the initiative.' He warned General Vladimir Dragomirov, Ivanov's Chief of Staff, that 'I nevertheless consider myself obliged to state that, in the event that the enemy develops a powerful strike in the Uzhok direction – and there are several signs to suggest this can be expected – the forces that we have here are not sufficient to form a solid resistance, let alone mount any decisive action'.[9]

These sentiments were echoed by General Radko-Dmitriev, a Bulgarian officer in Russian service who commanded Third Army. At about a hundred miles in length, from the town of Lisko on the San (one of Böhm-Ermolli's crucial objectives for his final Carpathian offensive) and then northeast past Gorlice and Tarnów until it met the broad expanses of the Vistula, the frontage occupied by Third Army lacked both strength and depth. 'The high level of ground-water did not allow digging the trenches to a full depth', recorded one account. 'The parapet was built of sandbags and had fire steps. Soldiers had to struggle constantly with the loose, soft soil, liquefied by ground water, which was prone to sliding, especially when it rained.'[10] Nor was there much confidence that the forces were ready to defend this line. Two days after Brusilov's telegram, Radko-Dmitriev inspected a newly arrived division and found 'major shortcomings', with missing battalions, serious shortages of officers, not enough transport, insufficient field kitchens and scant supplies of ammunition. At the same time, information had reached him of fresh German and Austrian divisions, equipped with heavy guns, being moved into position around Gorlice during the night, and that he would need the return of at least two regiments to 'solidify this front'.[11] But even if the Grand Duke had been minded to reinforce this sector, he had precious little time to do so.

After receiving reports back from Cramon on the viability of the railway network in this sector, Falkenhayn had acted quickly, sharing his proposal with the Kaiser – who approved it – before letting Conrad in on the secret in a telegram dated 13 April. 'An army of at least eight German divisions will be got ready with strong artillery here in the West, and entrained for Muczyn–Grybow–Bochnia, to advance from about the line Gorlice–Gromnik in the general direction of Sanok . . . This army and the 4th Austro-Hungarian Army would also be united in one command, and naturally a German one in this instance.'[12] Over the next fortnight, German and Austrian forces completed their deployments around Gorlice, massing an impressive number of men and guns into a tightly constricted thirty-kilometre section of the front: 126,000 men, 457 light and 159 heavy guns, 260 machine-guns and 96 mortars. The Russians could only field 60,000 men, 141 light guns and a handful of heavier pieces, giving the Central Powers twice the superiority in manpower, four and a half times the number of light guns and forty times as many heavy guns.[13]

The choice of ground was a sound one; indeed, Russian observers would later commend the location of the attack as being almost perfect ('very carefully chosen', in Danilov's words).[14] Falkenhayn had been insistent that German troops should not be frittered away in indecisive operations in the Carpathians, nor did he think that any attack on the Russian right from East Prussia, as Hindenburg and Ludendorff had already attempted, would work. There were only a 'few sections' of the front suitable for a breakthrough and that allowed the attackers to move forward without fear of encirclement, which was why Gorlice had been chosen. Once the attack got under way, their left flank would be covered by the Vistula in the north while the rugged Carpathian mountain range protected their right. 'We could hope with some certainty to appear at the decisive spot with undoubted superiority', he wrote.[15]

Falkenhayn's plan was simple and brutal: a massive array of artillery would smash the Russian trenches and create the conditions for a breakthrough. An Eleventh Army was created, packed with specially chosen troops, stockpiled with over 300,000 artillery shells, and Germany's best fighting general was placed in charge. Mackensen was a tough soldier, a man who came alive in the tumult of battle, but even he could not help but be awed at the scale of the operation and the heavy weight of his responsibilities, which he penned in a remarkably candid confession, dated 26 April:

A great victory is expected of me, a resounding victory, and yet, in most cases, great victories in battle come at the cost of great losses. When I order my men to attack, how many death sentences am I handing to them? It is this very thought that plagues my mind before every battle. But I am acting on orders given to me – orders given out of undeniable necessity. Like so many of the strong, fresh-faced young men who marched past me on their way to the front yesterday and today, in just a few days they will be lying on the battlefield, condemned to their final resting place or destined for the infirmary. So many of those pairs of bright eyes that have met mine will close for the last time; so many of the mouths that paraded cheerily past my window with our glorious marching songs on their lips will fall silent, never to sing again. That is the great drawback of being in a position of leadership . . .[16]

Mackensen was a romantic, beloved by his men. His chief, on the contrary, was a cold individual: a man who saw the war not in terms of courage or valour and sacrifice, but only in numbers and balance sheets, profit and loss. Falkenhayn's calculations were purely pragmatic. He recognized that the Eastern Front would, for the moment, take priority over France, so he gave it his full attention. OHL was transferred to Pless Castle in Silesia and an attack was authorized on the Ypres Salient in Flanders, this time preceded by a discharge of chlorine gas – the first mass use of an asphyxiating agent on the Western Front. The decision to employ such a novel weapon made little impact on Falkenhayn, who saw it as an ideal opportunity to test out new technology and, at the same time, distract the Allies from the movement of German units eastwards. Ignoring the doubts of numerous senior officers uneasy about the implications of using gas, Falkenhayn insisted that it did not break the terms of the Hague Convention (which had banned the use of 'poison or poisoned weapons' or 'material calculated to cause unnecessary suffering') and that, moreover, it was essential cover for their plans in the east.[17]

Mackensen's attack opened at six o'clock on the morning of 2 May with a four-hour bombardment, carefully calibrated with aerial reconnaissance, unleashing an intensity of artillery fire never seen before on the Eastern Front. General Hermann von François, commanding XXXXI Reserve Corps, remembered the violent opening of the offensive as he scanned the front line with his binoculars from a carefully concealed observation point. 'Then comes the rolling and rumbling, the crashing and pounding, as 700 guns open fire, spewing out steel and iron, which cut through the air in a frenzy of hisses and whistles. Over yonder, the shells pummel the ground, throwing chunks of earth, splinters of wood and pieces of barricade several metres into the air. Beyond the Russian lines, smoke and flames billow from the villages and homesteads. Here and there, Russians can be seen fleeing their trenches and footholds, our shrapnel flying after them in deadly pursuit.' The Russian response was unimpressive, with only a weak and intermittent counter-battery fire, which did little to stop the German bombardment, now joined by the roar of heavy mortars. 'Mortar rounds both large and small can be seen soaring in a high arc over the front line and into the enemy position. The explosions are violent and nerve-racking. The trees snap like matches, huge trunks are torn from their roots, the stone walls of the houses crumble into piles of rubble, fountains of earth spurt from the ground. The earth trembles, as though all hell has been let loose. Our soldiers lean against the parapet and watch the gruesome scene unfold, their eyes aglow.'[18]

The weight of Mackensen's forces fell on the Russian X Corps around Gorlice. German and Austrian battalions went forward into a curtain of dust and smoke and ran into a series of enemy positions, some well defended, others destroyed or abandoned. 'Most of the surviving Russians came running towards us with their hands raised, while some put up fierce resistance', remembered one junior officer. Despite being heavily outnumbered, the defenders showed the tenacity and stubbornness that their opponents had long appreciated. 'As the company proceeded towards the occupied houses, we became unpleasantly aware of enemy fire coming not only from the front, but particularly from the flanks positioned higher up.' Fortunately, excellent cooperation between the attacking infantry and artillery allowed objective after objective to be taken, 'as the German artillery fire blasted its way from one position to the next like a wildfire, advancing and spreading with unrelenting vigour'. By nightfall, Mackensen's forces had gained over two miles.[19]

Archduke Joseph Ferdinand's Habsburg Fourth Army also went into battle that day, extending the attack up to the Vistula and tasked with taking the city of Tarnów. As had been seen across the front, fighting was bitter, with Austrian troops encountering fierce enfilade machine-gun fire from a range of forested heights: 'Hill 481', the 'Sugar Lump' and 'Trigonometry Heights', to name a few. Conrad had joined Archduke Joseph Ferdinand west of Gorlice to observe the battle, and was thrilled to arrange a telephone call with his son, Erwin, who was serving with 8th Division (which Conrad had formerly commanded in the Tyrol). 'I cannot describe to you what feelings this triggered in me', he wrote to Gina. 'Ahead of us to the right were two bare hills on which the Russians were very strongly fortified. My dear old division, which I had commanded for three years in Tyrol and of which Erwin is a part, stood in battle against them . . . To the left of these hills stretched the extended Russian line. Our heaviest artillery was also in action on this part of the battlefield, firing its colossal projectiles into the Russian positions. Each shot produced towering clouds of smoke and dust.'[20]

The Russian response was one of bewilderment at first, changing to growing concern as the day wore on and their reserves were engaged. III Caucasian Corps, which had been on its way to the Carpathians, was handed over to Third Army, but it would be several days before it could reach the battlefield, leaving Radko-Dmitriev struggling to cope with a rapidly changing situation. Around midnight, he sent a telegram to General Ivanov: 'The commander of X Corps has just reported to me by telephone that the enemy, in enormous numbers, was attacking along the entire front of his corps. His lines were holding for the time being, but he doubted whether he will be able to hold until the arrival of III Caucasian Corps.' All reserves had been sent forward, but if X Corps was forced to retreat, Radko-Dmitriev would have to order a major withdrawal. Given the strength of the enemy, he was convinced that the Germans were trying to push him back to the San, relieving pressure on Hungary. He wished to place on record that his men had 'fought valiantly . . . as shown by their huge losses', but had simply been unable to withstand the 'hurricane' of artillery fire.[21]

Mackensen was determined to keep going. He moved up his artillery batteries and unleashed another series of attacks on subsequent days, breaking through what remained of the Russian defences, with the aim of getting Third Army over the Wisloka, a tributary of the Vistula. 'The troops are making good progress throughout the difficult mountainous terrain', he wrote on 4 May. 'The enemy has hold of a mountain ledge here, a ridge there, perhaps a few villages and forests, but their resistance soon crumbles once they are surrounded. The number of prisoners is growing considerably.' Advancing two to three miles per day, German and Austrian forces soon found the enemy melting away in front of them – with noticeable brown dust clouds in the distance showing how quickly the Russians were pulling out. By 6 May, Mackensen had taken 60,000 prisoners, with the battle turning into a rout. He was even impressed by the Habsburg performance. 'Austrian troops did well in the fighting', he wrote. 'It is strange how the proximity of the *pickelhaube* [the German spiked military helmet] affects their attitude in battle.'[22]

As Mackensen continued his attacks, a sense of panic began to rise among Russia's senior commanders, shocked at how quickly their divisions were being slaughtered. On 4 May, General Danilov arrived at the headquarters of the Southwest Front and spoke to Ivanov's Chief of Staff, Dragomirov, who doubted whether their armies could hold. 'According to the estimation of all the circumstances,' he said, 'we can hardly expect to withstand tough battles on these lines. We don't have enough ammunition left, the troops are greatly demoralised, 5–6 divisions have lost many men. On top of that, we have to admit that the command of Third Army is lacklustre and cannot be relied upon to succeed . . .' The only solution was to withdraw across the San. Danilov did not say much, only that it was necessary 'to take the most persistent measures and to exhaust all the means required to keep the situation as it is, avoiding any drastic changes and allowing only partial ones in accordance with the current situation'.[23]

Suggesting to the front-line commands that they limit themselves to partial changes was not exactly helpful. The Grand Duke reacted to Mackensen's offensive with his usual mixture of passivity and indecision. He had correctly anticipated the need for reserves to parry any German thrust but lacked the will to order Alekseev to provide them. And now, faced with a growing emergency, he continued to hope that the situation would eventually settle down without significant movement on either side. He wrote to the Tsar on 4 May, informing him that in Galicia the enemy was 'not displaying any energy' and that any gaps in the line had already been filled. All that was needed, he thought, was a firm and determined attitude not to fall back, and he wired Ivanov on 6 May that 'the line of the lower [W]isloka constitutes the limit of the Third Army's permissible retreat'.[24]

Radko-Dmitriev was an experienced soldier, a man 'of outstanding personal bravery' who was famous for his service in the Balkan Wars of 1912 and 1913 when he had fought against the Turks.[25] But nothing had prepared him for the disaster unfolding in front of his eyes, and he became increasingly disconsolate as he watched his men trailing back from the front, shaky from being under fire, many battalions without officers. Within ten days, X Corps had been reduced to barely 4,000–5,000 effectives, with most of its divisions little more than battalion-sized formations. In 61st Division, the Sedletsk Regiment had been reduced to five officers and 150 other ranks, and the Luvosky Regiment to barely 120 men. The divisional commander, Major-General Simansky, reported on the 'absolute valour' of his men, 'who fought for three days under the fire of the enemy's numerous heavy artillery [batteries], which caused enormous losses and inflicted severe wounds on the soldiers. The 61st Division fulfilled the order of the army commander with great honour, and only a woefully small part of it survived. The division died defending its position.' On 10 May, the day the Southwest Front was ordered to retreat to the San and Dniester rivers, Radko-Dmitriev reported to Ivanov that his army had 'literally bled to death'.[26]

The striking power of German artillery and the inability of Russian guns to make much of a reply was a defining feature of the fighting in May and June as the Russians were forced back: firstly from Gorlice and Tarnów, across the Wisloka, and then, in turn, from their advanced positions along the Carpathians. Guidance was hurriedly issued on the need 'to pay attention to the construction of trenches' as a way of slowing the enemy advance and helping Russian troops minimize the effects of heavy shellfire (they should be 'deep and narrow' with 'frequent traverses to localize the burst of shells', staggered across a considerable depth and avoiding high ground).[27] While this was sound advice, the lack of shells reaching the forward batteries had a devastating effect on the ability of Russian divisions to keep fighting, and throughout this period Third Army had only one or two rounds per gun per day.[28]

There were many stories of Russian valour during this period of trial; indeed, numerous senior officers were captured with their men after fighting on when all hope was lost. With General Brusilov's Eighth Army having to withdraw from the Carpathians after finding its flank uncovered, there was a danger that Russian forces in the mountains would be, as Brusilov put it, 'between two fires' – pinned down with frontal attacks, while having their line of retreat blocked. Brusilov sent his stores and baggage to the rear, while ordering selected units to hold the front until their retirement was complete. One of these units was 48th Division, which was surrounded and almost destroyed in the Dukla Pass on 6–7 May after mounting a desperate rearguard action. Its commanding officer was Major-General Lavr Kornilov, a tough Siberian Cossack known for his personal fearlessness, who was wounded and taken prisoner, only to escape from captivity the following year. According to Danilov, such dedicated and 'self-denying sacrifice' gave Kornilov 'a place of honour among the greatest Russian patriots of our time'.[29]

None of this could stop the German and Austrian advance, which reached the San on 14 May and was closing in on the ruined fortress complex of Przemyśl. Radko-Dmitriev was relieved of command several days later, which left General Ivanov searching for a reliable general to steady his line. He decided to trust Brusilov with the defence of the crucial fortress city, a task that the Eighth Army commander approached with great unwillingness, furious at being 'handed a mess he had not made and told to fix it'. He led his forces with his usual competence, striking back whenever he could and then withdrawing before he was overwhelmed, but he knew that the city could not be held, and that its fall would inevitably provoke a 'painful reaction throughout Russia' and 'put new heart into the enemy'. Ivanov agreed that Brusilov should abandon Przemyśl, but the Grand Duke was insistent that he fight to hold on to it, personally telegraphing Brusilov that a 'stubborn defence' of the city would 'consolidate the general state of affairs'. Brusilov noted sourly that his four corps occupied a front of over sixty miles, facing as many as 200 enemy battalions (to his 124) with a much stronger array of artillery and a 'rich supply of ammunition'. He would, however, do his best for the Tsar and Motherland. 'I will give it all I can.'[30]

The first attacks on Brusilov's line came from General Boroević's Third Army, which had followed up the Russian retreat through the Carpathian passes and had been ordered to seize Przemyśl as quickly as possible. Austrian infantry were hurled at the southwestern perimeter of the city on 15 and 16 May, but the Russians were determined to stay put, having refurbished the defences and put many of the ageing Habsburg artillery pieces to good use, which resulted in the kind of stubborn fighting that Boroević could ill afford. He was unwilling to press the matter, and it was left to the Germans to complete the liberation of the city. On 1 June, Mackensen brought up his secret weapon, a 420 mm Krupp siege howitzer that could hurl shells weighing up to 900 kilograms over 10,000 yards. After a few hours of brutal punishment, with clear skies obscured by rising dust and smoke, Russian resistance was at an end. Once again firepower had won the day. General François's corps had swung around Przemyśl and attacked from the north, finding the forts in ruins and the way open. 'Concrete blocks three metres thick lay broken, the armoured turrets smashed and overturned', he wrote. 'The sheer joy of the liberated people was indescribable. Wherever they went, German soldiers were surrounded and embraced, decorated with flowers and handed gifts. I did not see any Austrian soldiers. The houses were adorned with flags and banners. Triumphal arches were erected. All the peril of the last few months gave way to unfeigned jubilation, and the nation's hearts were filled with staunch optimism that the misery and torment of the Russian oppression was over for good.'[31]

The loss of Przemyśl, only ten weeks after it had fallen, was a bitter pill for Russia to swallow. On 6 June, the Grand Duke wrote a long memorandum to the Tsar blaming the disaster on a lack of munitions and guns, and pointing out that in such a situation no strategic approach would work:

> The military skills of the reinforcements are above any criticism, for all of them are rookies, and due to the lack of rifles, they have barely received any training in how to shoot . . . ! We cannot take the initiative into our own hands. All we can hope for now is to fend off blows. The professional quality of the troops, due to huge losses, is getting worse every day: fewer and fewer professional military personnel are left and the reinforcements are not trained; there is also a shortage of officers. Despite the fact that Italy has entered the war, the Germans have decided to increase the number of their forces on our front, probably owing to the fact that the French, who have endeavoured to advance, brought into action ten corps and *having far greater artillery and an unlimited number of shells, still failed* to break through the German front . . . It saddens and anguishes me that, due to an inadequate amount of shells, ammunition rounds and rifles, our truly heroic and valiant troops are suffering unimaginable losses and the result of their efforts does not reward those losses.[32]

Russian casualties continued to mount. On 8 June, the Grand Duke was handed reports showing that between 28 April and 28 May, the Southwest Front alone had lost 300,000 men. Even in a country of such limitless potential, this scale of bloodshed could not continue indefinitely.[33]

Shuttling between Teschen and Pless, Falkenhayn and Conrad had been considering their next move for some time. As early as 14 May, Conrad had drafted a memorandum in which he proposed that if Italy entered the war, they should abandon the offensive in Galicia after reaching the Dniester–San line and then deploy ten Austrian and ten German divisions to attack the Italians.

Falkenhayn agreed that they should keep the pressure on Russia for the time being, but thought they should then focus their efforts on the Balkans rather than on Italy. He wanted to crush Serbia, which would open a route to the south and allow the Ottoman Empire to be resupplied. Although the Allied attempt to force a passage through the Dardanelles Straits had been abandoned in late March, British and Anzac divisions had landed on Gallipoli on 25 April, supported by French troops on the Asiatic side. This caused a stream of worried telegrams from Constantinople alerting Berlin to the possibility that its armies would run out of ammunition if fighting continued at its present intensity.[34]

Conrad saw things differently. All forces made available at the current time should be 'used exclusively against Italy', and a campaign in the Balkans was 'not yet feasible', particularly without Bulgarian assistance. The problem was that Bulgaria was not yet in the war. The German Foreign Secretary, Gottlieb von Jagow, had invited Sofia to send a high-ranking officer to OHL to conclude a military alliance, but this was rebuffed, which left Falkenhayn frustrated. He would have preferred to strike quickly against the Serbs, taking advantage of a presumably laboured Italian mobilization to crush the rebellious state, but Conrad held firm. On 23 May, he warned Falkenhayn that his units along the border would face odds of at least 3:1 and might only be able to hold on for a matter of weeks. Were Italy to gain ground and cross the Drava river, her troops would be within 250 kilometres of Vienna – four weeks' march. 'If we cannot deploy strong enough forces from other theatres in time to stave off the Italian Army, then the Monarchy would be defenceless . . . To face this danger head on and with all our might is now our solemn duty.'[35]

Falkenhayn found himself temporarily outmanoeuvred and had little choice but to abandon his Serbian plans for the time being. It was agreed that Fifth Army, which had been watching the border with Serbia, would be deployed west of Zagreb, leaving only two divisions remaining in the Balkans. Furthermore, an elite German mountain division, known as the Alpine Corps, would be moved to the Tyrol, although Falkenhayn insisted that it must operate on a strictly defensive footing. 'Whatever the Italians might do,' he noted, 'the operations against the Russians were to be continued with all energy until the offensive powers of Russia were crippled for an appreciable time.' Accordingly, Mackensen was provided with another six divisions, including two taken from the Western Front, and the attacking forces were reorganized into an army group under his command with new instructions to take the city of Lemberg. Falkenhayn believed that the capture of the capital of Galicia would 'create a disastrous impression' and pile yet more misery on the embattled forces of the Tsar.[36]

Just as the shadow of Russia was beginning to lift from the Habsburg Empire, another fell across its western border. Italy declared war on 23 May, with her Prime Minister, Antonio Salandra, announcing the 'high moral and political dignity' of her cause and rejecting accusations of bad faith by the Central Powers. 'Where is, then, the treason, the iniquity, the surprise, if, after nine months of vain efforts to reach an honourable understanding which recognized in equitable measure our rights and our liberties, we resumed liberty of action?' Moreover, a 'wonderful moral union' had now been forged within Italy 'to the accomplishment of the highest destinies of the country'. The response from Vienna was short and laced with fury. 'The King of Italy has declared war on me', announced Franz Joseph in the official Austrian proclamation of war. 'Perfidy whose like history does not know was committed by the Kingdom of Italy against both allies. After an alliance of more than thirty years' duration, during which it was able to increase its territorial possessions and develop itself to an unthought of flourishing condition, Italy abandoned us in our hour of danger and went over with flying colours into the camp of our enemies.'[37]

There was, as yet, no sign of imminent danger. The Italian Army may have had months to prepare for hostilities, but it still entered the Great War in a state of shaky unreadiness that was reflective of profoundly dysfunctional political and military decision-making. Because Italy had been a member of the Triple Alliance for so long, it had been taken for granted that any future war would involve fighting *alongside* Germany and Austria. On 31 July 1914, the Chief of the General Staff, Luigi Cadorna, had even presented the King, Vittorio Emanuele III, with his war plan calling for the 'transport of the largest possible force to Germany' to join their invasion of France. When the Italian Government announced its neutrality two days later, Cadorna asked the Prime Minister what he should do, only to be told that he must 'prepare for war against Austria'.[38]

Cadorna now embarked upon an immense task: to reorient his strategy and redeploy his army while preparing for a conflict that might break out at any moment. He hailed from an aristocratic Piedmontese family and grew up in a world suffused with rich martial history and patriotism. His father, Raffaele, had served in the *Risorgimento* and marched into Rome in September 1870 in the final act of the unification of Italy. The son had inherited the father's self-determination and sense of destiny and rose through the ranks with a calm assuredness, becoming Chief of Staff in July 1914 after the death of his predecessor, Alberto Pollio. 'A short, lithe, quick-moving man' was how the British newspaper tycoon Lord Northcliffe described him, 'liked, feared, and respected by every Italian soldier or civilian with whom I conversed'.[39]

In common with many of his contemporaries, Cadorna did not accept that the advent of modern weaponry – machine-guns and quick-firing artillery, combined with the growth of entrenchments and barbed wire – had fundamentally altered the balance between attack and defence. Since the outbreak of war, he had received a stream of intelligence from his liaison officers detailing the squalid reality of trench warfare, but insisted that Italy could, indeed *must*, attack. Beginning in July 1914, he had issued six new tactical regulations as well as revising the 'Summary of Rules for Tactical Action', a document that detailed how the Italian Army would fight. Before it was published, he added an explicit statement on the importance of frontal attacks, as if he felt it necessary to remind his subordinates of what was expected of them. 'We should keep faith in the success of frontal attacks and in the effectiveness of the bayonet; for, had we ourselves no faith in this, how could we inspire our men to lead them into a storm of enemy projectiles?'[40]

Cadorna's unwavering commitment to the offensive reflected a lingering unease about his army and an undisguised distrust of his countrymen. The Italian Army of 1914 was not one that could look back confidently upon a storied history of glory and military conquest. On the contrary, it had endured numerous humiliating colonial defeats over recent decades, most notably at Adowa in March 1896, when a 17,000-man expeditionary force had been attacked and overwhelmed by the army of Emperor Menelik of Ethiopia. Italy had also struggled to control a burgeoning insurgency in North Africa after invading the Ottoman provinces of Tripolitania and Cyrenaica (modern-day Libya) in 1911. What had been intended as a swift and decisive demonstration of imperial power quickly turned into a strategic nightmare as Italian forces remained huddled in their coastal garrisons, wary of venturing out into the desert, which was controlled by bands of Turkish-led militia. The Italian Army's failure to defeat its opponents provoked a further decline in its already tattered prestige (which had never really recovered from Adowa), and led the then Prime Minister, Giovanni Giolitti, to call for the sacking of two thirds of its generals for 'intellectual inadequacy'.[41]

The problem for the Italian Army in Libya was not incompetent commanders, but that it was committed to a war that it was not trained or equipped to fight and had to execute a strategy that remained dangerously elusive. In November 1911, the Italian commander in Libya, General Caneva, telegraphed Rome that the situation his forces had encountered 'was quite different from that which we expected to find when we landed on these shores', and that they had to face not only Turks, but also 'profound and tenacious' resistance from the bulk of the local population, who remained suspicious of Italian motives. The campaign had also resulted in a steady drain of precious resources, both manpower and materiel, from the home army. By as early as 1911, almost all regular divisions had sent at least one infantry regiment to the expeditionary force, with specialist detachments, machine-gun units and sanitary companies in particularly heavy demand.[42]

Little had improved by the time war broke out in Europe. The strength of the standing army was just over 15,000 officers and 250,000 other ranks, a figure that would be swelled by the 3.1 million men liable to be called up every year. They would be formed into 25 infantry and three cavalry divisions (with an additional ten divisions manned by older reservists). While this should have enabled Italy to throw a significant force at the Austrians, the army was struggling with several alarming shortfalls, including a lack of officers, guns, equipment, uniforms and supplies. When Cadorna assumed the position of Chief of the General Staff, he sent a long memorandum to the government warning it that upon mobilization he expected to be 13,500 officers short and had neither the NCOs to make up the difference nor the facilities to train them. Perhaps as many as 200,000 sets of uniform were missing. Not all regiments could be equipped with the latest 1891 Mannlicher-Carcano rifle, with its six-round magazine, and most territorial units had to make do with the old single-shot Vetterli, which dated from the 1870s. With only 700 cartridges per weapon, there were also concerns that the army had barely enough ammunition for a few weeks' intensive campaigning.[43]

The situation with the artillery was even worse. Each corps should have had 96 guns (as against 144 in an equivalent Habsburg formation), but even this paltry figure could not be met. Of the thirty-six field regiments, ten had not yet been established, and the excellent 1911 Déport 75 mm field gun, which had been adopted from the French, had not yet arrived, so Italy had to mobilize with much of her older inventory. This included the 87B Krupp, which had been in service for thirty years, had no recoil mechanism and was incapable of indirect fire (something that would be of crucial importance on the Italian Front). Of the twenty-eight batteries of howitzers, only fourteen could be mobilized, while the rest suffered from a lack of manpower and horses. Ammunition was also in short supply. Italian arsenals were stocked with 1,200 shells per gun, but if Austrian, Russian or German experience was any guide, this would soon be fired off. With Italian factories only capable of producing 14,000 rounds of artillery ammunition per day (about seven shells per gun), it was evident that she could not afford a long, drawn-out war.[44]

Italy's military inferiority in comparison with the Habsburg Empire was well documented (she could only put about half the number of divisions into the field as Austria). It was therefore essential that she take advantage of the favourable strategic situation to strike while her enemy was engaged elsewhere, but the practical difficulties of doing so were immense. Apart from a short thirty-kilometre stretch from the mouth of the Isonzo running north, Italy's border was mountainous, and in Cadorna's words, 'the entire theatre of operations, due to the nature of the terrain and the climatic conditions, constituted an exceedingly difficult region, such as to put a strain on the endurance of the troops, their self-denial and constancy. Without doubt, there was no other theatre of war in Europe which . . . came close to ours.'[45] He located his headquarters (*Comando Supremo*) at Udine and planned his main offensive across the Friuli Plain towards Gorizia and Trieste, with the ultimate objective of reaching the Sava river at Kranj and Ljubljana. The Trentino was a crucial component of Italian war aims, but Cadorna regarded it as a 'secondary' theatre, where Italian troops would remain on the defensive.[46]

Cadorna's offensive opened on 23 June, exactly a month after Italy had declared war. He would have preferred to attack sooner, to gain a moral advantage over his opponent, but Italian divisions reached the front much later than he had anticipated, and newly strengthened Austrian positions provoked uncharacteristic caution from the Italian commander. Although there had been only a few thousand Habsburg troops manning the border in April, perhaps as many as 70,000 men were now in position, and more were arriving each day. They had the benefit of well-sited defensive lines that had been steadily improved since the outbreak of war. The road network had been upgraded, more telephone lines had been added, and miles of trenches had been dug, some protected by minefields. Artillery batteries were well concealed, often hidden away in caves, while the ground was littered with machine-guns, carefully sited to provide the most effective flanking fire.[47]

The bulk of Italian strength, Second and Third Armies, were to attack towards Gorizia, firstly crossing the Isonzo – famed for its sparkling blue waters – seizing Monfalcone, and then assaulting a series of heavily defended hilltops that barred the way to the east: Mount Sabotino, Podgora, Mount San Martino, Mount San Gabriele and Mount San Michele among others. Notwithstanding the

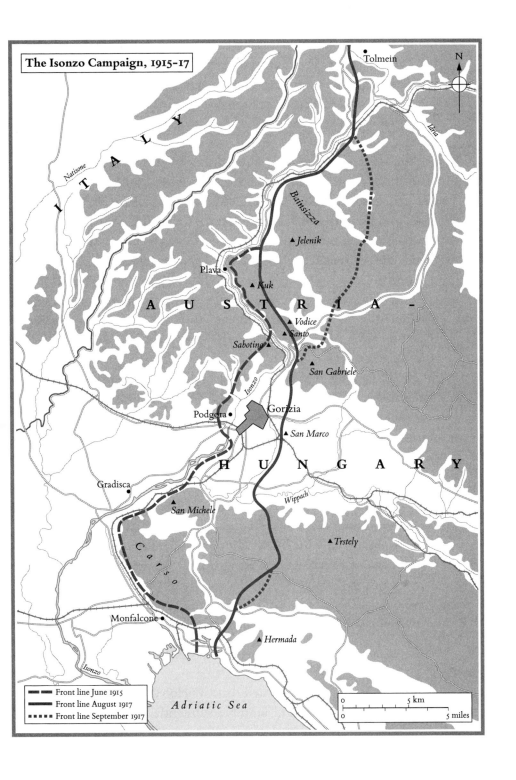

The Isonzo Campaign, 1915-17

N

• Tolmein

Natisone

I T A L Y

Bainsizza

▲ *Jelenik*

A U S T R I A -

Plava •

▲ *Kuk*

▲ *Vodice*
▲ *Santo*

Sabotino ▲

▲ *San Gabriele*

Isonzo

Podgora •   Gorizia

▲ *San Marco*

H U N G A R Y

Gradisca •

▲ *San Michele*

Wippach

▲ *Trstely*

C a r s o

Monfalcone •

▲ *Hermada*

Isonzo

Idria

— — Front line June 1915
———— Front line August 1917
▪ ▪ ▪ ▪ Front line September 1917

Adriatic Sea

0   5 km
0   5 miles

limitations of his artillery, Cadorna was hoping that it would unlock the Austrian lines, so he ordered a lengthy preliminary bombardment, which rumbled on for a week – an unheard-of spectacle at this point in the war. The gunfire looked and sounded impressive, with shellfire reverberating around the landscape, burning buildings sending thick black smoke into the air, but there was neither the weight nor the accuracy of fire to do much damage to the enemy's defences. Instead of a carefully directed bombardment that knocked out crucial strongpoints, all the Italian gunners could do was scatter their shells over the Austrian lines and hope for the best. Nor did they have much chance of finding enemy batteries hidden behind the hills, with the handful of Italian aircraft available being unable to help.

The main attack was launched on 30 June. It was a desperate, tragic episode, notorious for the slaughter of infantry caught by rifle and machine-gun fire. Cadorna's regiments rushed forward, only to find the Austrians – observing their every movement – able to concentrate their defensive fire on each attack in turn. Scenes of Italian infantry crowding together as they struggled up the steep bare slopes, frantically trying to clear away thick barbed-wire obstacles with their bare hands, were a stark demonstration of the horrors of modern warfare. An Austrian after-action report on the attack on Podgora recorded:

> The front-line companies pushed forward under artillery protection, with the sappers carrying ecrasite tubes to destroy the barbed-wire entanglements. The defenders let the attackers approach the wire, but then they subjected them to such fire that most of them sought escape in a headlong retreat. As soon as the artillery fire proved effective, a new attack was launched around 9.00 a.m. on 7th July. Strong reserves in numerous lines followed the front-line companies. Such a clear daylight attack was frightfully punished: after only thirty paces the attackers received the defenders' fire, but it was so deadly that much of the first wave was completely destroyed.[48]

A subsequent examination noted that: 'Enclosed in a triangular area of just over a kilometre and almost as substantial in height – an area containing steeply sloping ground, uncovered and pounded on all sides – the four brigades were subject to continuous losses, which shook the morale of the troops, who saw a great number of dead and wounded packed into such a small space, especially as the evacuation of the latter across the Isonzo was slow and difficult.'[49]

Cadorna finally suspended operations on 7 July, having lost 14,000 men. Austrian losses were around 10,000.[50] Italian troops had advanced towards Tolmein, and in the south, the best part of five divisions had splashed across the Isonzo, but the high ground that dominated the eastern bank had not been conquered. Nor had they been able to seize Gorizia, which had been one of Cadorna's chief objectives, and with Habsburg reinforcements moving in, any chance of a swift and sudden descent on Ljubljana had passed. Cadorna was quick to blame the failure on a lack of artillery support and resolved to try again as soon as his reserves could be brought up. Others felt that important lessons had been learnt and that the army would do better next time. General Carlo Ruelle, the commander of VI Corps, which had attempted to take Gorizia, noted that they needed 'to learn the use of the technical means that we have at our disposal, to let the conviction enter into the soul of everyone that today the enemy is not overwhelmed by a single Garibaldian impetus, but by a tenacious and uninterrupted sum of successive efforts, in which the sacrifice of the first brave men must be taken up by the last who move to the attack'.[51]

7. 'I will save Russia'

In Galicia, the high summer of 1915 was a time of great heat and dust as German and Austrian forces kept up their pursuit of General Ivanov's battered Southwest Front. 'The terrible heat persists', Mackensen wrote on 7 June. 'I was in Przemyśl yesterday afternoon and suffered terribly on the journey from the dust stirred up by the numerous convoys. But the dust not only fills the streets, it also pervades the air far off to the sides. The humidity makes any prolonged movement a wearisome effort. Added to that is the fact that one must practise great caution in this country with respect to drinking water, as isolated cases of cholera in infected towns have proven. Our doctors are extremely careful and have so far been able to nip any suspicious symptoms among our troops in the bud.'[1] Mackensen issued new orders on 10 June. Eleventh Army, joined by the Habsburg Fourth and Second Armies, would begin its joint push on 13 June, 'throwing back the enemy in front of them and advancing in an easterly direction'.[2]

Mackensen employed what was now a well-established tactical routine. 'Creeping like some huge beast, the German army would move its advanced units close to the Russian trenches, just near enough to hold the attention of its enemy and to be ready to occupy the trenches immediately after their evacuation' was how one Russian observer described the 'Mackensen steamroller'. Batteries of heavy artillery would be brought up to the sector of attack (while staying out of range of Russian field guns), before opening fire and quickly reducing the enemy trenches to a smoking ruin. Once the position had been occupied, Mackensen would either wait for wasteful counter-attacks to be launched or order his men to follow up yet another withdrawal. 'Having gained full possession of the Russian trenches the "beast" would draw up its tail again, and its heavy guns would start their methodical hammering of the next Russian line of defence.' With no prepared positions to fall back upon, the Tsar's forces had little choice but to continue their retreat, hoping that the Germans would run out of steam.[3]

As well as relying on his artillery, Mackensen's operations were heavily dependent upon aircraft. With the bulk of German air power on the Western Front, he could call upon a mere 54 machines, but they performed vital work in surveying the vast expanses of the battlefield throughout the summer. On 6 June, Eleventh Army issued detailed orders about the use of aircraft in the forthcoming attack, with air detachments conducting both close- and long-range reconnaissance – an extremely important task given Germany's lack of cavalry on the Eastern Front (at least when compared with the great clouds of Cossacks that always screened Russian movements). Russia's air capabilities were much less advanced than Germany's and she struggled to contest air dominance. At the start of the war, she could boast 244 aircraft and 14 dirigibles, but these were mostly obsolete types and Russia found that expanding her military aviation was hampered by a lack of engines and poorly trained pilots. Although she had 553 aircraft in service by the end of 1915, these were mostly French models, either Morane-Saulnier monoplanes or two-seat Voisin 'pushers' that compared poorly to the latest German models, including the Albatros C.I, which came into service in 1915.[4]

Mackensen's attack began at 4 a.m. on 13 June. 120,000 attacking infantry were readied to go forward, crouching in their trenches or peering over the top as the artillery bombardment broke over the Russian positions. Dense 'columns of smoke swirled out from the rolling fields, meadows, forest edges and villages, and thick walls of dust rose up against the blue spring sky . . .' recorded one account. 'But over yonder, for 90 minutes, hundreds of shells pounded deep holes into the sandy ground with every second that passed, hitting trenches and shelters, tearing wire barriers into shreds and throwing splinters of wood up into the smoke- and dust-laden air.'[5] When the attackers sprang forward, they faced heavy fire coming from a series of cleverly positioned machine-gun nests on the far bank of the Wisznia river, which stopped all attempts at crossing. Another artillery bombardment was fired, and this allowed the attacking infantry to try again, but fighting was hard throughout the day. Coordinating short barrages with bayonet charges, German and Austrian troops were able to forge ahead and gain several miles, breaking through the Russian second and third lines.

Such excellent infantry–artillery cooperation showed how difficult it would be for the Russians to make any kind of stand, and they began to pull out on the night of 13/14 June, with General Brusilov's Eighth Army ordered to hold Lemberg. Brusilov was frustrated, writing to his wife that 'I'm just sick. My army conquered both L'vov [Lemberg] and Przemysl', and he was now enduring defeat after defeat. 'Without guns. Without cartridges. Without shells [and] heavy artillery . . . Masses of people lost but success was not possible because to advance was not possible.'[6] Brusilov's men resisted where they could – at river crossings, along ridgelines and in towns and villages – but they could not stop their opponents for more than a day or two before being outflanked or pushed out of their trenches. 'The shortage of men in the armies of both fronts was staggering', admitted Danilov, who plotted the movement of the armies on large maps at *Stavka*. At least half a million men were required immediately, but even if they could be found, a crippling lack of rifles meant that they could not be put into the field. The training of replacements was poor, and many could hardly shoot; there was a lack of officers, telephones and field kitchens; 'everything', Danilov admitted, was 'worn out' or had been lost in the long retreat. By late June, the Russian Southwest Front barely had 40 per cent of its normal stock of ammunition left.[7]

Mackensen's troops reached the last Russian defences before Lemberg on 17 June: a line of trenches that ran north from Grodek towards Magierów. 'Bridges were destroyed everywhere, roads blocked, towns burnt to the ground', recorded General François, whose men had faced little real resistance for days. They would encounter patrols of Cossacks and come across shallow trenches whose occupants fled at the first sight of German artillery, but now the Russians had been ordered to stay put. Mackensen waited for his guns to come up before launching his attack on 19 June, preceded by another sustained and terrifying bombardment. By noon, Russian resistance had been broken. 'In the trenches, corpses, torn limb from limb, piled on top of one other; machine gun emplacements buried in earth; deep craters gouged by mortar fire; body parts scattered everywhere; the earth hacked to smithereens', François noted. 'A scene that exemplified all the many horrors of war.' While this was impressive enough, François felt that something had snapped in the enemy's morale. 'The Russian positions were still very much intact, but the morale and the physical strength of the Russian soldiers were being worn away by the constant defeats and heavy losses. This was clearly evident in the sense of contentment among their prisoners. They willingly went to the collection points they were given.'[8]

Mackensen let the Austrians take Lemberg; 'indulging them', in his words, because they had not managed to be the first into Przemyśl. 'The Russians continued to retreat almost everywhere in front of the Eleventh Army and only offered some resistance here and there', he wrote on 21 June. He was not convinced that they would mount a major defence of the city and noted how the sky was lit by the flames of burning ammunition dumps. Even railway stations had been torched in anticipation of further retreats. 'They won't give up all of Galicia yet,' he added; 'but they won't have much of it left.' On the evening of 22 June, as Austrian troops marched through the city to the sounds of cheering crowds, the Kaiser authorized Mackensen's promotion to field marshal and thanked him for his 'masterful' leadership during such a 'triumphal march'.[9]

The success of Mackensen's attacks led to the question of what to do next. On 15 June, Colonel Hans von Seeckt, Mackensen's Chief of Staff, submitted an assessment of the situation to Falkenhayn, arguing that the Second, Fourth and Eleventh Armies should swivel north once Lemberg had fallen. 'The aim of this operation', he wrote, 'would be for the Second and Eleventh Armies to approach the Brest-Litovsk line between the Bug and the Vistula, while the Fourth Army advances on both sides of the Vistula', which would 'lead to a decision'. This was also the opinion of Colonel Gerhard Tappen, Chief of Operations at OHL, who proposed the same advance between the Bug and the Vistula towards Warsaw. When Falkenhayn considered the matter, he maintained his earlier reservations about whether they

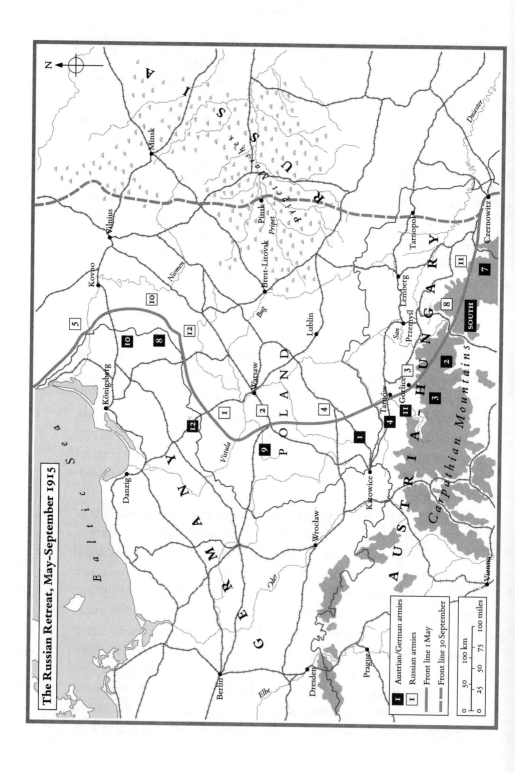

The Russian Retreat, May–September 1915

N

RUSSIA

Pripet Marshes

Minsk

Wilnius

Pinsk

Kovno

Brest-Litovsk

Tarnopol

5

Niemen

10

Lemberg

Czernowitz

II

10

8

12

Bug

Lublin

San

Przemyśl

8

7

SOUTH

Königsberg

I

2

Warsaw

4

Gorlice

II

3

2

POLAND

Tarnów

II

Danzig

12

9

4

AUSTRIA-HUNGARY

Vistula

Katowice

Carpathian Mountains

Baltic Sea

Wrocław

GERMANY

Oder

Prague

Vienna

Berlin

Elbe

Dresden

I — Austrian/German armies
I — Russian armies
—— Front line 1 May
- - - Front line 30 September

50   100 km
0   25 50 75 100 miles

could mount such a far-reaching offensive, scribbling 'a nice thought! But?' on his copy of Seeckt's report.[10]

Falkenhayn eventually agreed to a move north, to be coordinated with another offensive out of East Prussia (commanded by General Max von Gallwitz), but the aims remained strictly limited. Predictably, the duo at OberOst, Hindenburg and Ludendorff, scoffed at Seeckt's proposals and planned their own, even more ambitious strike towards Kovno, which would require fresh troops. 'Our discussions at Headquarters on this subject often became very lively', remembered Max Hoffmann. 'From the beginning I supported the opinion that we had now perhaps for the last time the possibility of dealing the Russian Army an overwhelming blow.' Mackensen's thrust would, he believed, 'gradually wear itself out', while an attack on Kovno would be the first step in a long-range offensive through to Vilnius, 'to the rear of the chief Russian Forces'. If these operations had been attempted, 'the results would have been most satisfactory, and would have led to the complete defeat of the Russian Army'.[11]

Falkenhayn had never believed that such a result was possible, citing concerns over logistics or, remembering Lodz, worrying about the dangers of being surrounded and overwhelmed. He was also wary of growing exhaustion. Certainly, German commanders had achieved a level of battlefield success in the east that had always eluded their compatriots in France, seizing huge amounts of territory and taking hundreds of thousands of demoralized prisoners, but losses among the armies of the Central Powers had begun to creep up. By the time Eleventh Army reached Lemberg, having endured scorching heat, torrential downpours and long marches on thin, rutted roads, it had lost around 87,000 men (including 12,000 dead), with German medical officers worrying about the appearance of cholera, dysentery and typhus.[12] Moreover, were German High Command to weaken Mackensen's forces in Galicia, in order to reinforce Hindenburg, they ran the risk of a local setback, which might turn the remaining Balkan states, still wavering in their allegiance, away from Berlin. At a meeting at Pless on 2 July, the Kaiser sided with Falkenhayn, dismissing Hindenburg and Ludendorff's demands for a longer flanking movement and sanctioning the more limited operation instead. Ludendorff, who never doubted that the Kaiser would support his ideas, was devastated, and telephoned Hoffmann that evening, ordering him to 'stop everything'. Hoffmann was equally frustrated, complaining that this was 'the last possibility of making a destructive attack on the Russian Army' in the summer of 1915.[13]

This had been a common refrain at *OberOst* for months: that the war could be won if only Falkenhayn would concentrate all his efforts in the east. But this downplayed the intensity of the war on the Western Front, which absorbed most of Germany's forces. There had been heavy fighting throughout May and June, with the French and British launching a series of desperate actions that forced the deployment of precious reserve divisions and depleted stocks of ammunition. Although the line held, local gains around Arras, where French troops had seized Vimy Ridge (if only for a few hours), kept Falkenhayn on his guard. He returned to Charleville-Mézières in early June and went on a tour of the front, inspecting units, handing out medals and meeting with senior officials, including OHL's principal liaison officer in the west, Fritz von Lossberg. Like many senior German officers, Lossberg found Falkenhayn to be a frustrating individual, prone to what he called 'inconsistency of operational leadership', which resulted in him 'flip-flopping' regularly between east and west. 'Even though he did listen to reasonable suggestions and recommendations,' he added, 'he mostly chose to go his own way.'[14]

The loss of Lemberg was another punishing blow to the beleaguered Russian High Command. The Tsar chaired an Extraordinary Council of Ministers on 27 June at Baranovichi and announced a number of measures to address the growing crisis. The War Minister, Sukhomlinov, was dismissed, the Tsar replacing him with his former deputy (and someone who was more acceptable to the Duma), General Aleksei Polivanov. It was also agreed to create a 'Special Council on State Defence', which would be charged with pushing forward Russia's war production. After the meeting had concluded, lunch was taken in a large tent that had been pitched alongside the Tsar's railway carriage. It was a bright summer's day and Danilov remembered the atmosphere to be remarkably positive. 'Despite the events at the front,' he wrote, 'there was an upbeat, cheerful mood. One almost had the sense that, with a wave of the sceptre, the mountains blocking the way to a bright future would part and a new sun would rise over Russia.'[15]

Remedying the lack of artillery shells was the first and most obvious priority for the Special Council. As early as September 1914, *Stavka* had requested the production of 1.5 million shells per month – three times the expenditure that had been foreseen before the war. But Russia was unable to produce the required volume of ammunition (it would take another year before her factories could produce a million shells a month), and there was little chance that the shortfall could be supplied from overseas.[16] Sukhomlinov had done what he could, but turning Russia into a major industrial power in a matter of months, able to manufacture the quantity and variety of weapons required, was a herculean task, and proved impossible. Poor relations between the War Ministry and *Stavka* meant that it took months for the urgency of the situation to be realized in Petrograd, with the War Ministry arguing that the shortages had been exaggerated by the armies in the field and that they had failed to make use of the large stocks of ammunition stored in a string of Polish fortresses from Novo-Georgievsk to Ivangorod. There was also a lamentable failure to utilize the private sector to produce munitions, with Petrograd worried about the potential for inefficiency or corruption and unwilling to provide financial incentives to Russian firms to allow them to invest in the facilities necessary to achieve mass production.[17]

It was too late. Sukhomlinov fell, the victim of an old power struggle with the Grand Duke as well as the growing clamour from Russia's liberal politicians, who used the crisis as a way of getting rid of one of the most reactionary Tsarist officials. The Tsar's faith in Sukhomlinov had survived the early crises, but even he now recognized that his War Minister was becoming a serious liability. On 24 June, Sukhomlinov was handed an official notice about his 'retirement', informing him that 'the interests of Russia and the army require your departure now'. The Tsar thanked him for his efforts and was adamant that 'Impartial history will render a verdict more generous to you than the judgment of contemporaries', which was a harsh one. Sukhomlinov was later arrested on charges of 'malfeasance', 'financial misconduct' and spying for the Central Powers – accusations that he rejected, but which were difficult to shake off – and after further investigations by the Provisional Government, he was finally convicted of treason in September 1917.[18]

Blaming Sukhomlinov for the failures of an empire was one thing; finding a way to improve the situation at the front was much more challenging. The Russian Army was now well into its 'great retreat', as it left behind its gains of earlier battles and fell back from Galicia and Poland. Such a catastrophe would be blamed upon a 'shell shortage', but for Russian soldiers and their commanders, the agony of 1915 would always be defined by what they called the 'shell hunger': an almost frantic craving for ammunition that had more in common with a famine than anything else.[19] Knowing that they were outgunned and incapable of responding effectively produced a crushing depression that affected even the most dedicated of soldiers. General Anton Denikin, commander of 4 Brigade and one of the most well-regarded fighting generals in the army, called the retreat from Galicia 'one vast tragedy' that he would never forget. 'No cartridges, no shells. Bloody fighting and difficult marches day after day. No end to weariness, physical as well as moral. Faint hopes followed by sinister dread . . . Our regiments, although completely exhausted, were beating off one attack after another by bayonet or short-range fire. Blood flowed unendingly, the ranks became thinner and thinner . . .'[20]

With each step back, the pressure grew on General Alekseev, whose Northwest Front was increasingly vulnerable as Mackensen switched his attention to the drive north into Poland. A meeting was held at Alekseev's headquarters in Siedlice on 5 July to plan for the next phase of operations, with the Grand Duke, Yanushkevich and Danilov present. The question was whether the Russians could hold on to Poland, and if not, whether they should abandon the left bank of the Vistula and the fortresses that had been built and maintained at such exorbitant cost in the decades leading up to the war. Alekseev had no illusions about the task he was facing and told the assembled officers bluntly that either they could hold Warsaw or they could keep their armies intact, but they could not do both. It was 'all about one thing now – to gain time', wrote Danilov. Alekseev's armies must hold out for three to four weeks, allowing enough time for Warsaw to be evacuated and for the construction of a series of prepared lines further to the rear.[21]

Alekseev was given operational freedom in how to manage this withdrawal. Of the 49 Russian army corps, all but 12 would now be assigned to the Northwest Front, making Alekseev the most important operational commander in the Russian Army. Although honoured by the great faith that had been placed in him at such a crucial time in Russia's history (he was the only general to whom the Grand Duke used the familiar 'ty' form of address), he was, in private, increasingly disconsolate at his inability to stem the enemy advance.[22] The day after the meeting at Siedlice, he received new intelligence, including aerial photographs, revealing another enemy build-up in the north, which always preceded an attack. That evening, he wrote to his wife:

> And there has never been such a desperate situation as the one in which I now find myself. There are two enemies torturing me. One is the external enemy of the Germans and the Austrians, who have gathered their main forces against me, withdrawing everything they could from the front of General Ivanov, against whom they seem to be merely making noise and pretending to act. It seems they may also have redeployed other forces from the West or from new army units within the state; they are coming from everywhere; their numbers are overwhelming, and they are armed with multitudinous artillery and have an unlimited supply of shells. And then there is the other enemy, the internal one, that starves me of the necessary means to pursue a war and to withstand these epic battles that we have seen in abundance in recent days.[23]

The Tsar returned to *Stavka* on 6 July, meeting the Grand Duke in his carriage, where he was given the latest reports. 'He told me that, on the whole, the situation had not changed for the worse since yesterday,' Nicholas wrote in a letter to the Tsarina, Alexandra, 'and that it would improve if the Germans ceased to press us at the same point for several days. In that case we should have to collect new (fresh) troops and try to stop them. But again there crops up this damnable question of the shortage of artillery ammunition and rifles – this puts a check on any energetic movement forward, as, after three days of hard fighting, the supply of munitions might be exhausted. Without new rifles it is impossible to make good the losses, and the army is at present only just a trifle stronger than in peace-time.' As he finished the letter, he added that he was giving this information 'only to you' and that she was not to 'speak of it' to anyone. Because the Tsarina had a habit of sharing sensitive information, even classified military intelligence, with her courtiers, particularly the Siberian *starets* Grigori Rasputin, Nicholas was keen to remind her of the importance of discretion.[24]

Rasputin was a lecher and a drunkard; a man of all-consuming sensuality who attracted fascination, flattery and hatred in equal measure. He had become a close personal friend of the royal couple in 1907 after healing the Tsarevich, Alexis, when he was suffering from a dangerous bout of bleeding brought on by his haemophilia. The Tsarina trusted him implicitly, referring to him as 'our friend' in her letters to Nicholas, seeing him both as a powerful spiritual father-figure and as a personal manifestation of the 'real' Russia: simple and homespun, intensely religious, and fanatically loyal to the imperial household. He could also have a strange, almost mesmeric effect on those around him. The Grand Duchess Olga, the youngest sister of the Tsar, was invited to meet the holy man and never forgot the strange scene. 'In Alexis's bedroom no lamps were lit; the only light came from the candles burning in front of some beautiful icons. The child stood very still by the side of the giant, whose head was bowed. I knew he was praying. It was all most impressive . . . I really cannot describe it . . .'[25]

Rasputin's influence over the royal family also spilled into political and military affairs, and he would often quiz the Tsarina on events at the front before praying with her. A point of particular interest to him was the position of the Grand Duke – someone who had been stubbornly resistant to his overtures. When Rasputin had offered to visit *Stavka* to bless an icon, the Grand Duke had invited him to come and promised that he would hang him if he did so. This was enough for Alexandra, who had long distrusted Nikolai Nikolaevich, seeing him as a potential rival for the throne, and she never lost an opportunity of reminding her husband of this. Throughout the summer of 1915, she urged the Tsar to take action; to trust his instincts and rule as a great autocrat, confident that this was what Rasputin, and by extension Russia, wanted. 'He was so much against y[ou]r. going to the *Headquarters*,' the Tsarina wrote on 29 June, 'because people get round you there & make you do things, wh[ich]. would have been better not done – here the atmosphere in your own house is a healthier one & you would see things more rightly – if only you would come back quicker. I am not speaking because of a selfish feeling, but that here I feel quieter about you & there am in a constant dread what one is concocting – you see, I have absolutely no faith in N[ikolai]. – know him to be far fr[om]. clever & having gone against a Man of God's, his work can't be blessed, nor his advice be good . . . You know N[ikolai]'s hatred for Gr[igori]. is intense.'[26]

With the Tsar spending more and more time at *Stavka*, the situation in Petrograd became increasingly tense. The Russian Parliament had been suspended on the outbreak of the war, with the Duma President, Mikhail Rodzianko, declaring that the people 'were ready to take up arms for the honour and glory of the Motherland'.[27] While the Tsar had been pleased at this display of national unity and shared resolve, pressure grew with each defeat the army suffered. Soon rumours of treason or incompetence, sometimes both, began to spread across Russia. The news of crippling shell shortages, of entire regiments being shredded by furious artillery bombardments without being able to reply in kind, sparked growing concern about the outcome of the war and, inevitably, demands for scapegoats. Anti-German riots had broken out in Moscow in late May and revealed how fragile state authority was becoming. Targeted at foreign-owned businesses or prominent citizens with German-sounding names, a protest march quickly escalated into a 'chaotic orgy of looting, arson, destruction, and violence' that left eight civilians dead, forty seriously wounded and hundreds of buildings badly damaged or razed.[28]

By June, the liberal opposition in Russia was becoming more vocal in its demands. That month, both the 'Kadet' Party (the Constitutional Democratic Party) and the All Russian Union of Zemstvos and

Towns organized conferences calling for 'a ministry of public confidence'. The Progressive Party, which represented the industrialists, was also talking about the creation of some kind of committee representing all the main parties to improve the management of the war effort. The Tsar was reluctant to involve the Duma in matters that he regarded as his prerogative, but agreed to a request from his Chairman of Ministers, the wizened figure of Ivan Longinovich Goremykin, then 76 years old, about reopening the Duma. An official announcement was made on 30 June: 'With an inviolate confidence in the inexhaustible resources of Russia', the Tsar now expected 'the administrative and public institutions, Russian industry and all the faithful sons of the Fatherland, without distinction of class or opinion, to work together with one heart and mind to supply the needs of the army'. This was 'the sole, the national problem' to which 'the thoughts of all Russia' would now be directed.[29]

Conrad von Hötzendorf had endured a frustrating summer. Sidelined by Falkenhayn, who now dominated coalition strategy, he found himself relegated to a subsidiary role, sending suggestions to Pless but being largely ignored. He had accepted (albeit reluctantly) the promotion of Mackensen to command an army group in Galicia which contained two Austrian armies, but he insisted that any expedition against Serbia must be run from AOK. Falkenhayn waved this away. Negotiations with Bulgaria (to which Conrad was not invited) had been going on at Pless since late July, and on 4 August, Falkenhayn sent Teschen a copy of a draft convention with the proviso that the campaign against Serbia would be led by Mackensen, who 'would take his orders directly from the German High Command'.[30] Conrad squirmed at this indignity and insisted that Mackensen come under Austrian control. It would 'seriously damage' the prestige of the monarchy if Austria was not leading the campaign in the Balkans, which would be 'incomprehensible' to the population. 'It will always be us', he insisted, 'who will be responsible for safeguarding the common interests of our two empires in the Balkans.'[31]

Conrad's pleas were understandable, but never likely to be acceptable given the evident military inferiority that Austria–Hungary had shown since the opening days of the war. Even the Bulgarians were concerned about whether they could rely upon the Habsburg Empire, and Lieutenant-Colonel Petur Ganchev, head of the Bulgarian Military Mission, insisted that any 'emphasis' upon the Imperial and Royal Army in the forthcoming campaign would be unacceptable to Sofia. Conrad sat back in disgust, writing to Bolfras in Vienna that there was nothing else he could do but 'hold out in a decisive and resigned manner'.[32] Relegated to a supporting role in what should have been Austria's crowning moment, when the Archduke would finally be avenged, he was left to mourn his shrinking influence on the war. There was now only a single theatre of operations, against Italy, that remained firmly under Austrian control.

Conrad was determined to hold this front at all costs, choosing one of his most respected commanders, General Svetozar Boroević, to lead the defence. Boroević, who had arrived on the Italian Front in late May, taking up residence at Fifth Army headquarters in Ljubljana, was an unusual character in the higher ranks of the Habsburg armed forces because he did not come from either a Germanic or Hungarian background. A Croat from the 'Military Frontier' of the empire – the region that had once bordered Ottoman territory – he was small of stature and lightly built, making up for his physical shortcomings with a ferocious work ethic and an almost pathological toughness. Describing himself as 'the embodiment of authority, discipline, and the freest development within the same framework', he would tolerate no weakness. 'Ruthlessly I abolish all fools!' He insisted that his men hold their lines no matter what; they must follow orders, ensure reserves were used correctly and endure whatever the cost. His first order, given to divisions reaching the front, was a statement of intent, brutal in its simplicity: 'The troops will build positions, set up barricades and stay there.'[33]

By the time the Italians launched their second attack, on 18 July, the defending garrison had risen to nine divisions (about 100,000 men and 431 guns), with the arrival of veteran Hungarian troops under the command of Archduke Joseph Ferdinand (as part of VII Corps) being a notable addition.[34] Although this was a more significant force than had been available for the first offensive, it would still be outnumbered and have to face an army that was learning quickly. Shying away from another frontal attack on the town of Gorizia, which could be enfiladed from both flanks, General Cadorna opted to concentrate on the Carso Plateau to the south. Third Army would occupy the heights at San Michele, which commanded Gorizia, while Second Army mounted a series of demonstrations further north. The artillery would also be targeted at specific locations, rather than – as in the first battle – being spread, somewhat haphazardly, over the entire sector of attack. When Cadorna spoke to Brigadier-General Sir Charles Delme-Radcliffe, head of the British Military Mission, he admitted that he had been forced to change his approach. 'He had no idea that the Austrian defensive positions were so strong and had thought at first that it would be possible to press forward along the whole front simultaneously.' Cadorna now realized that it was 'indispensable to smash a way through one section of the front with an irresistible artillery bombardment so as to gain an opening from which to extend an attack against other portions of the enemy's positions, which however were very cunningly organised for mutual defence. The enemy's ingenuity, he said, was truly astonishing.'[35]

The Carso was a terrible place to fight. The ground was dry, baked by the fierce summer heat, littered with stone fragments and broken by crevices and small caverns, which meant that there was a depressing lack of water, as any rainfall quickly drained away. Indeed, one post-war analysis would conclude that what made this sector so 'extraordinarily perilous' was that 'not only are several hundreds of thousands of men living in the most primitive conditions, alongside horses and livestock, in one of the most inhospitable territories in Europe – but all while being subjected to enemy fire of an intensity unlike anyone could previously have imagined'. With the Italian Army outnumbering the defenders, and able to fire off more ammunition, the challenge of keeping men alive and well in such circumstances was extremely difficult. 'It is safe to say, therefore, that at no other battleground has there ever been such an unrelenting accumulation of the most adverse circumstances.'[36]

The battles around San Michele were some of the fiercest of the war: a 'little Verdun' that would come to resemble the horrific struggles on the Western Front. Italian troops attacked on the morning of

18 July after a heavy bombardment had obscured the Austrian positions in rolling bursts of dust and shell splinters. 'The deafening roar of the large pieces, the thunderous crash of the field batteries scattered across the plain and mountain batteries hidden in the nearby forest give me the impression of an infernal storm', recalled one witness. 'This fury of thunder, of hisses, that rend and shake the atmosphere, this immense and dense network of bullets that pass quickly and lightly over my head, whistling, barking, howling, is something that borders on the supernatural.'[37] Clawing their way up the ridge, the Italians took Mount San Michele on 20 July, only to fall back after a fierce counter-attack by Bosnians from 12 Mountain Brigade – easily recognizable by their fezzes – who had gained a deserved reputation as aggressive fighters with a penchant for preferring close-quarter weaponry: knives, bayonets and maces. The hill would change hands several more times over the next few days, until the Austrians finally secured the summit after fierce hand-to-hand fighting.[38]

Habsburg troops seemed to fight well on the Italian Front. Whether it was the chance to face their 'hereditary enemy' or the fact that Austria was conducting a purely defensive campaign, soldiers from all over the empire fought along the Isonzo and in some of the Alpine battlefields with a skill and determination that both pleased and surprised their commanders. But the price was very high. VII Corps sustained about 25,000 casualties in its fierce defence of the Carso Plateau, particularly 20th *Honvéd* Division, which had entered the battle with 6,000 infantry and been reduced by two thirds within a matter of days.[39] 'My losses are a sensitive issue', Boroević had written, in a private letter to the Hungarian Prime Minister, Count Tisza; 'in the two battles, I lost 40,000 men, dead, wounded and taken prisoner . . . The infernal enemy artillery additionally benefits from the splintering of the shattered rock. A further problem is that the bodies cannot be buried. They contaminate the air, body parts fly around in the fire, as a result of which our people become nauseous and lose their appetite, and lose strength despite ample supplies of food . . . In the beginning, the superior enemy mass artillery fire demoralised the troops. It was pure Hell.'[40]

What later became known as the Second Battle of the Isonzo was called off in early August with the Italians having sustained another 42,000 casualties, compared with 47,000 on the Habsburg side.[41] While this could be seen as a narrow success, Cadorna's men were still short of their principal objectives and lacked the strength to launch any further large-scale operations for the rest of the summer. 'The general attack confirmed the existence of a powerful and almost uniform enemy defensive system all along the Isonzo line', Cadorna noted in a memorandum in late August. This would need to be attacked simultaneously, but the medium-calibre guns of the Second and Third Armies, along with their ammunition stocks, were 'wholly inadequate' to do this. He therefore had little choice but to continue to make progress in a 'methodical' way, keeping the consumption of ammunition as low as possible and building a line of entrenchments at the base of the Carso Plateau 'unseen from the top of the hills, and which forces the adversary wishing to attack them to descend the slopes of the plateau itself under the fire of our powerful massed artillery'.[42]

There was little respite for Russia's armies throughout July and August as they continued to buckle under repeated blows. General Max von Gallwitz, who had commanded a corps in the fighting along the Vistula in the autumn of 1914, would lead the next phase of Falkenhayn's summer campaign, striking out to the southeast of Soldau and Neidenburg – the old battlefields of Tannenberg – towards the fortress at Przasnysz, crossing the Narew and threatening Warsaw. With 500 guns stocked with over 400,000 shells, there was a similar level of artillery support as had been seen on 2 May, but this time the heavy field howitzer batteries had been given 1,000 rounds (as opposed to 600 at Gorlice), which afforded the bombardment a much greater level of destructive power. German orders were simple and to the point: 'Well-aimed, rigorous and safely observed precision fire. Heavy use of ammunition over a short period of time, but not so as to make observation impossible . . .' Barrages would be fired in order to trick the enemy into occupying their trenches (to defend them from imminent assault), and would intensify shortly before the attack. 'Artillery must provide the infantry with necessary protection from enemy fire until the breakthrough. Immediately after the last shell has landed, the first man in the assault line must be in the enemy trenches.'[43]

The Germans were facing an opponent that was already in disarray. The Russian First Army had been ordered to hold on until Warsaw could be evacuated, and its soldiers were already hard at work strengthening their lines and digging extra communication trenches, but no defence could survive in such desperate circumstances. Guns were limited to five shells per day, thousands of soldiers did not have rifles, and those that did lacked enough bullets.[44] When the Germans attacked on the morning of 13 July, marching forward through broad fields of ripening grain, a four-hour bombardment had wreaked havoc, the air spitting and cracking from the explosions. 'The enemy, shaken by the gruelling artillery preparation and the unrelenting attack of the grenadiers, fusiliers and riflemen, put up little resistance', reported 4th Guards Infantry Division. 'Other than a scuffle over a few machine-gun emplacements, in which we came out on top, little close combat was required. The enemy artillery appeared to have been completely overpowered; only a few guns were still being fired. Other than those who abandoned their weapons and hastily fled the scene, the Russians were either captured or – for those that resisted – killed. Their losses were considerable; ours were but minor.'[45]

By nightfall, German troops had penetrated up to six kilometres and taken 5,000 prisoners, with some of the defending divisions scattered in all directions. Eleventh Siberian Division, which had entered the battle 14,500 men strong, could count barely 5,000 survivors afterwards. The German pursuit was only slowed by heavy downpours of rain, combined with the heroism of a Russian cavalry brigade, which galloped forward and launched a surprise counter-attack on 16 July, losing over half its men in a series of desperate, suicidal charges. One Russian soldier, A. V. Gorbatov, witnessed the fighting in July and August and noticed that a different mood began to manifest itself among the ranks of Russia's increasingly tattered armies. 'Of course, all this affected discipline, making it weaker, and this became most noticeable in relation to defence', he wrote. 'In the Carpathians, adopting a defensive attitude by no means led to doubts or lack of belief. On the contrary, after a long and successful offensive action, the soldiers were happy to receive a well-deserved rest. However, adopting a defensive stance after such a long retreat and among such confusion is a completely different matter. The soldiers lost heart, began to think the enemy was invincible, lost their faith in the strength of the defence, and considered it only a postponement of further retreat.'[46]

Within days, Alekseev had sanctioned a withdrawal across the Narew; this was necessary, as he put it, 'to lead our troops out of the cauldron'. Russian divisions in Poland were now in a vice: attacked from the north and south and pressed from the west, with increasingly panicked telegrams coming from High Command. Orders had also been issued in Ivanov's Southwest Front for the evacuation of all men between the ages of eighteen and fifty, which was soon amended by Yanushkevich at *Stavka* to include the removal of 'all resources', including every man of military age, 'so as not to leave them in the hands of the enemy'. All livestock and food supplies were to be taken with the retreating troops. 'It will be easier', Yanushkevich noted, 'to supply the population from scratch upon our offensive than to leave material to the enemy that we could have carried away.'[47]

These orders were swiftly translated into the most destructive and desperate phase of the 'great retreat'. Villages were burnt to the ground; bridges and roads were torn up; cattle was either slaughtered or herded alongside retreating battalions, and in their wake came long columns of refugees, easily recognizable by their carts piled high with possessions, trailing across rutted roads. The staff officer Peter Kondzerovskii remembered leaving Baranovichi: 'At that time the highway, which was usually deserted, was flooded with a never-ending train of wagons: these were refugees from the western provinces, fleeing from "the Germans". Wagons, followed by cows, were loaded with household goods and equipped with makeshift tents, often sheltering a large family along with chickens and ducks. The train stretched to the east, as far as the eye could see, leaving small mounds with crosses on top here and there along the road. Those were the graves of babies that did not survive the long journey, continuing in all weather conditions.'[48]

It would never be known exactly how many people either fled or were forcibly deported, but by the end of 1915, Russian officials counted some 3.3 million displaced people, and the figure may have been significantly higher – perhaps touching six million.[49]

The fall of Warsaw on 4 August was the moment when the scale of the disaster could neither be excused nor ignored. The Polish capital had been defended by a ring of fortresses along the Vistula and the Narew, but these were not capable of holding out for long against modern heavy artillery and only contained poor-quality garrison troops without much ammunition. Alekseev finally ordered the abandonment of the city on 2 August, with the bridges over the Vistula being blown in the face of enemy cavalry patrols. One of the last western journalists still there, Stanley Washburn, watched the smoke rising from the suburbs. 'Standing on the new bridge one can see great German shells and volcanic fumes, while heavy reverberations shake the city. Across the Vistula hangs our observation balloon, while the sky is dotted with German aeroplanes, soaring hither and thither amid smoke-puffs . . . The city is deserted by all but the Poles, who intend to remain, and the evacuation, save for the last of the infantry and guns, seems to be practically completed.'[50]

Amid the chaos of the retreat, a series of important organizational changes were made in the Russian Army. The Northwest Front was split into two on 17 August, with *Stavka* hoping that an extra head-quarters would allow it to exercise greater control over what had been an increasingly unwieldy situation. Northern Front would be commanded by General Ruzski, with General Alekseev taking over a new Western Front.[51] The Tsar had also decided to make a more dramatic intervention. He wrote to the Grand Duke on 19 August, informing him of his decision to 'take supreme command of the army' and appointing him Viceroy of the Caucasus (where Russian troops faced the Turks). 'I am confident that you will accept this important appointment as visible proof that my feelings toward you have not changed in the slightest and that you will enjoy my full trust.'[52] The Grand Duke took the news stoically – there was little else he could do – departing Baranovichi the following day for *Stavka*'s new location at Mogilev, 180 miles to the northeast.

On 6 September, it was announced that the Grand Duke Nikolai Nikolaevich had been dismissed and the Emperor had assumed supreme command. When Rodzianko was told that Nicholas was placing himself 'at the head of the troops', he did not hide his dismay, and during an audience at Tsarskoe Selo, the imperial family residence outside Petrograd, he warned the Tsar about the great risks he was taking:

'Sire, against whom are you raising your hand?' he asked. 'You are the supreme arbiter, and who is to judge you in the event of failure? How can you place yourself in such a position and forsake the capital at such a time? In case of misfortune, you yourself, Sire, and the whole dynasty may be in danger.'

The Tsar shrugged. 'I know,' he replied sadly, staring out of the high windows of his office. 'I may perish, but I will save Russia.'[53]

8. 'The European war is nearing its end'

On 6 September 1915, the day the Tsar took over as Supreme Commander, Germany and Austria–Hungary signed a military convention with Bulgaria. It was formed with one purpose in mind: to coordinate the occupation and dismemberment of Serbia. Bulgaria pledged to have at least four divisions deployed along the old Serbian border within thirty-five days, ready to launch an attack five days after German and Austro-Hungarian forces had crossed the Danube. Once the campaign had been completed, she would receive her reward: a slice of Serbia east of the Morava river (which included the city of Niš) and the whole of Serbian Macedonia – lands that Sofia had long regarded as its own. Berlin and Vienna were also jointly responsible for a loan of 200 million francs, a sum that would be increased should the war last longer than another four months.[1]

The convention marked a pleasing diplomatic coup for Berlin, which had finally managed to convince King Ferdinand, Tsar of Bulgaria, to join the fray. Having listened to tempting offers from both sides, Ferdinand recognized that only the Central Powers were willing to give him everything he wanted, all at Serbia's expense. Humiliated during the Second Balkan War of 1913, when the gains that had been made from the Ottoman Empire in the First Balkan War were wiped out by coordinated Serbian, Greek and Romanian attacks, Bulgaria was eager for revenge. Ferdinand issued a 'war manifesto' the following month. All the European powers now agreed that Macedonia was largely Bulgarian, only for 'our treacherous neighbour Serbia' to refuse to accept this. 'Tired and exhausted, though undefeated, we had to furl our standards in the expectation of better days. The good days arrived much sooner than we could have expected. The European war is nearing its end . . . Our cause is just and holy!'[2]

Ferdinand of Saxe-Coburg-Gotha may have been one of the lesser sovereigns of Europe, but he more than made up for it with his colourful personality and sharp intelligence. Fifty-four years old, balding, with a noticeable paunch, a grey-white beard flaring out from beneath his chin, he was 'regarded as one of the most astute politicians in Europe'.[3] Surviving frequent assassination attempts, he took advantage of the revolt of the Young Turks in 1908 to announce Bulgaria's independence (when it had nominally been under Ottoman suzerainty), which he had defended fiercely ever since. Both the Kaiser and Emperor Franz Joseph disliked him, finding his flamboyance and rumoured homosexuality distasteful, but the war had forged new alliances and all three men were willing to overlook their individual feelings in pursuit of wartime objectives. The Central Powers were at their zenith, seemingly all-powerful on the Eastern Front, and now able to reshape the Balkans. True to his Machiavellian reputation, Ferdinand had chosen his moment well.

By the time the convention had been signed, the armies of the Central Powers had cleared Poland and advanced into the Baltic provinces and western Russia. In just six and a half weeks, two German armies (Twelfth and Eighth) had progressed 200 kilometres against a numerically superior opponent. They had crossed rivers, marched through thick forests, taken stoutly defended Russian positions and dealt with hundreds of counter-attacks. They had captured 125,000 prisoners and 350 machine-guns, with their men showing 'a willingness to sacrifice and a devotion that could not have been greater'. As well as the attack across the Narew in mid-July, Falkenhayn authorized a northern assault the following month, which allowed Hindenburg and Ludendorff to break out of East Prussia and march northeast towards Lithuania and Courland. The operation took advantage of Russia's crumbling defences and culminated in the fall of Kovno on 17 August. Kovno, which had been the strongest Russian position on the Northwest Front, surrendered after a terrifying bombardment by heavy artillery, including 1,000 of the most destructive 420 mm shells, which were reserved for the toughest targets. Twenty thousand prisoners were taken.[4]

The advance could not continue indefinitely, however, and with supply problems mounting with each mile covered, the forward

German divisions increasingly had to forage for themselves. While some areas contained a large amount of food and fodder, others had been stripped clean. Casualties were also rising. General Gallwitz's Twelfth Army had lost about 60,000 men since the attack opened in mid-July, with some divisions being reduced to just 4,000 riflemen. The war diary of one corps recorded in late August that after thirty-seven days of uninterrupted combat, the infantry and artillery were seriously under-strength, with only 'inferior' replacements arriving in small numbers. Even Gallwitz – about as aggressive as commanders came – admitted (in a diary entry on 21 August) that he was less hopeful than ever of being able to bring the campaign to a victorious conclusion: 'It would be a shame if we were to weaken our grip at this stage, since – according to statements from prisoners, letters, and the enormous losses – things are looking even bleaker for the Russians.' They were, he believed, 'ripe for the taking', and he detected a 'sense of hopelessness' in their infantry, mainly because of the strength of German artillery fire. But he lamented that it was difficult to keep going with battalions of 300 men, concluding that 'the army has done its duty'.[5]

Somewhat predictably, the growing logistical difficulties of Gall-witz's advance sparked criticism from *OberOst*. The duo had remained a sullen, argumentative presence in the German High Command for months. Ostracized for most of the summer, having been kept out of the Gorlice–Tarnów attack, they were forced to watch Gallwitz mount his assault on 13 July, being convinced that it could not lead to a truly decisive outcome. 'The strategic principles by which we are waging war are extremely unsatisfactory', Ludendorff wrote in a letter to Moltke on 15 August. 'I stressed repeatedly that the operation in Poland would end with the pushing-back of the Russian front. This is exactly what happened, and perhaps we shall still capture a few thousand men today. But the Russian has his ways about him and can do what he wants.'[6] Hindenburg went even further, writing a series of tersely worded letters to both the Kaiser and Falkenhayn complaining about the futility of frontal attacks, arguing that Gallwitz had never really turned the Russians and brought them to a decisive battle. Writing to Falkenhayn on 13 August, he insisted that the 'only possibility' of 'annihilating' the Russians lay in a series of strong attacks by their left wing against 'the enemy's communications and his rear'.[7]

Falkenhayn had heard all this before and was no more minded to consider it now than he had been a month earlier. Although Hindenburg was instructed to do as much damage to the Russians as he could during his advance towards Kovno, Falkenhayn believed there was little prospect of a truly decisive battle. 'The Russians had long realized the dangers of strategic envelopment . . .' he noted, 'and learned how to take measures against it. This was made easier for them by their superiority in numbers, the higher capacity of the railways, and the indifference with which they could, and as experience showed, did, abandon stretches of country as soon as that course seemed advisable.'[8] He had achieved what he wanted: forcing the Russians back and relieving pressure on the Habsburg Empire. Moreover, he had always taken a wider view of the war than either of the duo did – seeing German strategy in a global perspective. Instead of getting sucked deeper into Russia, they must look to the south. Falkenhayn had pushed for a campaign in the Balkans for months, and with the signing of the convention with Bulgaria, he now made it his first priority. 'It is crucial to defeat Serbia', he had told Mackensen, 'and to secure the route, via Belgrade and Sofia, to Constantinople.'[9]

Hindenburg and Ludendorff were thus left once again on the sidelines, with August von Mackensen given the green light to prepare for the next phase of the campaign. He travelled to Vienna in late September to meet Emperor Franz Joseph. 'His Royal Highness greeted me in the uniform of the Franz Regiment and was extremely cordial', Mackensen remembered. 'He has diminished in stature, his right shoulder hangs down a little and his head is stooped, but otherwise he has a fresh appearance and is unusually lively in conversation.'[10] After dinner, the two men spoke at length about the war, the qualities of their commanders, and the forthcoming operation in the Balkans. For the Habsburg Empire, this was a bittersweet moment: pleasure at the sight of its ancient opponent about to be vanquished, tinged with frustration that it would need German (and Bulgarian) help to do it. Conrad von Hötzendorf found it more difficult than most. 'You can certainly imagine that on this matter, it was no easy task for me to again call for German help,' he wrote to Bolfras in early October, 'but it weighs on me far more heavily that our war against Serbia, towards which all our traditions point and of which I dreamed in 1909, will from now on be led by the Germans. Yet this year has taught me to bear bitter disappointments . . . I hope that it will contribute to the success of our common purpose.'[11]

Conrad's armies continued to struggle without German support, and the failure of the 'Black-Yellow' offensive (so-called because of the colours of the Habsburg dynasty), which had petered out in mid-September, produced a feeling of almost total demoralization within the Austrian High Command. With Russia's armies in full retreat from Poland, Conrad had ordered a series of large encirclement battles to take advantage of a yawning gap that had opened in the Russian line between Brest-Litovsk and Kovel. It began on 25 August, when AOK directed First Army to advance towards the towns of Lutsk and then Rovno, enveloping the northern wing of General Ivanov's Southwest Front and pushing it away to the southeast, while two further armies attacked from the outskirts of Lemberg, trying to catch it in the flank. Like so many of Conrad's schemes of manoeuvre, it was brilliant on a map, bearing all the hallmarks of greatness – the ability to quickly detect the movement of armies and the possibilities for decisive battle – only to fail because of the Imperial and Royal Army's chronic weaknesses in firepower, leadership and fighting skill.

Once again Habsburg regiments, now reinforced with the latest class of replacements, went into battle with the expectation that victory was close at hand. Conrad had massed 38 infantry divisions (against just 29) and felt that this would be sufficient if only they could strike hard enough. They smashed into General Brusilov's Eighth Army on 26 August, pushing the Russians back and capturing their first major objective of Lutsk. But then the attack seemed to run into sand. The Russians quickly withdrew, taking advantage of the ground to evade their pursuers, who showed little of the initiative that would be required in any large battle of encirclement. Orders were also misunderstood or not executed properly. Instead of cascading flanking attacks from the north, Habsburg infantry were often ordered to push ahead in barren frontal assaults that caused high casualties and forced Conrad to exert a tighter grip on his subordinates. As early as 29 August, he sent a telegram to General Paul Puhallo, commander of First Army, warning him that 'The AOK expects binding orders to the corps commands to fully enforce their own will and to safely achieve the great purpose of this war. Our being significantly superior in strength, this is entirely achievable, but only if we do not waste the strength of our forces in close combat, as the enemy would have us do.'[12]

Persistent rain set in on 3 September, making it more difficult for the guns to keep up with the advance. The rivers and swamps were now swollen with floodwater, the bridges blown, while Austrian units found themselves shadowed by enemy horsemen who appeared without warning to menace their flanks. Conrad's men were soon exhausted by endless marching across the vast expanses of western Ukraine, tramping down rutted roads that had been turned to mud by the retreating Russians. Covered in dirt, with the growth of a week's beard on their faces, men would sometimes fall asleep in combat or collapse by the side of the road, unable to go another step forward no matter how hard their officers tried to rouse them. Third Infantry Division, which had been assigned to the northern section of the line because it was known as a capable, hard-fighting division, had covered almost 400 miles since Gorlice–Tarnów with only four rest days. Its men were utterly exhausted.[13]

Brusilov took advantage of the arrival of reinforcements to launch a counter-attack on 13 September, striking at the precise moment when the Austrian advance had lost all momentum: 'The 8th Army having faced 22 enemy divisions, the enemy was now down to only 14 divisions there', he wrote to Ivanov on 12 September. 'This means that we are almost equally strong and that we have Austrians before us whom we have defeated many times. I am of the opinion that we have retreated far enough; soon we will have regrouped and filled our ranks, whereupon we shall reap victory over [the Austrians] once more.' Within days they had punched a number of holes in the front, running across scores of abandoned weapons and stocks of ammunition as Habsburg units fled to the rear. Lutsk was recaptured on 23 September, with Conrad orchestrating a retreat to the Styr river, where the front lines finally began to settle down. Austrian casualties were 'unusually heavy', totalling some 230,000 men.[14]

Such adventurism did not impress OHL. Falkenhayn had already warned Conrad on 12 September, a day before Brusilov's counterattack, that he needed to wind down operations in Galicia lest they cause more damage to his forces. 'In my opinion,' he wrote, 'the only remedy for the loss of striking power that the troops have already suffered lies in refraining from further attempts to attack, instead resolutely turning to defence in a permanent position, which should be immediately expanded by all means possible.'[15] But Conrad did not take even guarded criticism well and wrote back to Falkenhayn the following day, rehearsing his reasons for the offensive and noting that 'each event should be judged solely on its development and not by sudden impressions, to which I am largely averse, since they easily lead to hasty measures, the consequences of which are apt to overestimate the unavoidable vicissitudes of military action'.[16]

Behind the bluster, Conrad was quite different: a soft, frail individual. When the full extent of the rout became apparent, he quickly sank into depression, aware that, once again, his strategic insights had not been capitalized upon. He told his adjutant, Major Kundmann, that it had been the most 'simple' and 'certain' operation that he had ever been involved in, yet it had still failed: 'with our troops one cannot plan an offensive'.[17] Once again, he had to go cap in hand to Falkenhayn, who agreed to send two divisions to the threatened sector on the understanding that the operation was abandoned, 'because no gains, but probably further losses, were to be expected from it, owing to the newly-apparent deficiency in the offensive powers of the Austro-Hungarian troops'. It was an alarming admission of just how far the Habsburg Empire had fallen after a year of war, and how little could be done to produce an improvement. It was also why the attack on Serbia would be run from Pless and not Teschen.[18]

Tsar Nicholas II had come to a momentous decision: to take direct command of Russia's armies. The Tsarina, Alexandra, had been urging him to do so for months, and was convinced that only the firm grip of imperial authority could drive Russia's peasant soldiers forward. 'Those who fear & cannot understand your actions, will be brought by events to realise your great wisdom', she wrote on 4 September. 'It is the beginning of the glory of y[ou]r. reign, He said so [meaning Rasputin] & I absolutely believe it. Your Sun is rising & to-day it shines so brightly.' The Tsar had never been the most confident and capable of men, but he took the decision in a strange, almost serene state of mind, convinced that he would be proven right in time. 'Thank God it is all over,' he replied to Alexandra on 7 September, 'and here I am with this *new* heavy responsibility on my shoulders! But God's will be fulfilled – I feel so calm – a sort of feeling after the Holy Communion!' After praying and reading his wife's letter 'over and over again', he said farewell to the Grand Duke, who was on his way to Rostov-on-Don. 'A new clean page begins, and only God Almighty knows what will be written on it!'[19]

Stavka's new location at Mogilev was certainly a more convivial place than Baranovichi had been, sitting alongside the banks of the Dnieper, with its local government buildings and numerous hotels, but it was still worlds away from the imperial capital of Petrograd. This was Russia's industrial centre and political heart: a city of factories and grand palaces buzzing with activity. It was where the political and business elites congregated and where the Duma sat, having been reconstituted on 1 August. Within weeks, a coalition had been cobbled together from both right- and left-wing parties, who temporarily set aside their differences to command a majority known as the 'Progressive Bloc'. A manifesto, published on 7 September, stated that 'only a strong, firm, and active authority can lead the fatherland to victory, and that such an authority can be only that which rests upon popular confidence and is capable of organizing the active cooperation of all citizens'. There needed to be an immediate discontinuation of cases 'of purely political and religious crimes'; the return of exiles; the end of religious persecution; the restoration of the rights of trade unions; the equalization of peasant rights; and the introduction before the Duma of all bills 'immediately concerned with national defence'.[20]

Nicholas had never found the management of the Duma easy. All his life, he continued to believe in the mystical destiny of the tsars: that he was 'the historical embodiment of the nation', who 'knew its interests better than representatives chosen from the educated classes'.[21] It was no secret that he would have preferred to spend all his time at *Stavka*, which he appreciated for its simplicity and serenity – particularly when compared to the intrigues of Petrograd, which caused him no end of despair. 'You have no idea how depressing it is to be away from the front', he told a family friend that summer. 'It seems as if everything here saps energy and enfeebles resolution.' The atmosphere at the High Command was much better: 'Out at the front men fight and die for their country. At the front there is only one thought – the determination to conquer. All else is forgotten, and, in spite of our losses and our reverses, everyone remains confident. Any man fit to bear arms should be in the army. Speaking for myself, I can never be in too much of a hurry to be with my troops.'[22]

This sense of alienation from the home front only grew stronger as the weeks passed. Although the Tsar did agree to the removal of some unpopular ministers, most notably Sukhomlinov, and the creation of special councils to examine aspects of the war effort (transport, food and fuel supply), he would not be swayed into further concessions. Many of his closest officials were worried about the growth of disorder and labour strife, and wanted to work with the Progressive Bloc, but Nicholas refused, issuing orders for the adjournment of the Duma on 16 September, barely six weeks after it had reopened. His Chairman of Ministers, Goremykin, insisted that however well-meaning, the Duma's demands meant a limitation in the powers of the Tsar, and were therefore unacceptable. 'The Government will be blamed no matter what happens', he said, after concerns were raised that prorogation might provoke civil unrest. To 'accept the whole program of the Bloc and tie our hands in war time is unthinkable . . . Talking with them will get us nowhere.'[23]

Goremykin would stand with the Tsar. Now long past retirement, this seasoned bureaucrat was a loyal servant of the Romanov family, impervious to the calls to stand up to his master. 'It is clear to every Russian that the consequences will be terrible, that the very existence of the state is in the balance', warned Sergei Sazonov, Foreign Minister, at a meeting of the Council of Ministers on 15 September. 'His Majesty sees things differently', Goremykin replied peremptorily. 'I called his attention to the dangers brought out into the Council of Ministers, but the Emperor did not change his opinion. What more is there to say?' When Alexander Krivoshein, the Minister of Agriculture, asked him what he intended to do when the 'whole machinery of Government' was opposed to him, Goremykin just shrugged. 'I shall do my duty to my Emperor to the end no matter what opposition and unpleasantness I may run up against . . . As to the future? His Majesty said that when he comes he will personally look into the whole question.' Sazonov was not persuaded. 'It may then be too late.'

Now more than ever, Nicholas needed the trusted advice of his military commanders. He chose Mikhail Alekseev to be his Chief of Staff and the replacement for Yanushkevich, who was sent to the Caucasus with the Grand Duke. Alekseev was 57 years old and was known as a man of great organizational talent, serving as General Ivanov's closest aide throughout the early battles of the war. Although Alekseev was hardly overjoyed when he was given the news by the Minister of War, Polivanov – who told him that 'he would not be a courtier' – he immediately brought a sense of order and direction to *Stavka*, which had become a somewhat slow-moving and directionless place in the final months of the Grand Duke's tenure.[24] Mikhail Lemke, a staff officer sent to Mogilev in September, could not help but be struck by the contrast between the old and the new *Stavka*. 'The former General Headquarters with Nikolai Nikolaevich and Yanushkevich in charge only registered events; the present General Headquarters, with the Tsar and Alekseev in charge, not only registers, but also controls events at the front and also in the country to some extent. Yanushkevich was completely out of place, and the person who dubbed him "Mr. Strategic Naivety" was absolutely right. The disorder of various parts of the army is significant and well known. The Tsar is very attentive to the matter; Alekseev is a very straightforward, perfectly honest person, gifted with an extraordinary memory.'[25]

Alekseev soon impressed the staff at Mogilev with his work ethic and humility, presenting lengthy reports to the Tsar and often going to find information or speak to officers himself because he did not want to bother his subordinates. The journalist Stanley Washburn thought he was the 'hardest worker' he had ever known 'in the military or any other profession', rising at seven o'clock every morning from a small camp bed and working with only an hour's break until 7.30 p.m. Quiet, reserved, with a perceptible shyness, Alekseev was known to be particularly affected by the description of the Last Judgement contained in the Gospel of Matthew (Chapter 25, Verses 41–6), in which the Lord tells his followers: 'I was hungry and you gave me no food, I was thirsty and you gave me no drink, a stranger and you gave me no welcome, naked and you gave me no clothing, ill and in prison, and you did not care for me'. Those that did not do this would 'go off to eternal punishment'.[26]

Whether Alekseev would be able to lead the Russian armies with any greater fortune than the Grand Duke remained to be seen. With the 'great retreat' gradually coming to an end in September, the Eastern Front entered a period of inactivity. The front now ran from the Gulf of Riga, along the Duna river to Jakobstadt, then directly southwards through the Pripet Marshes, past Baranovichi, Rovno and Tarnopol, and ending at the Romanian border. Casualties in recent months had been enormous, far more than could be accurately tallied, which fuelled fears that the Army had been irretrievably broken and was impossible to resurrect. Perhaps as many as 1.4 million Russians were killed or wounded during the summer campaign, with the loss of over 975,000 prisoners.[27] These misfortunes 'made a devastating impression throughout Russia', opined Danilov, who admitted that all Russia's sacrifices had been in vain. 'Our enemies raised their heads; everything we had worked for drifted silently away from us . . .'[28] The army needed to be reconstituted, re-equipped and reorganized as quickly as possible.

With the Tsar's forces perhaps fatally damaged, the Allies were also forced to rethink their strategy. On the Western Front, the French had attacked almost continuously since the winter of 1914–15, mounting offensive after offensive in Artois and Champagne, but with only limited success. Joseph Joffre, the French Commander-in-Chief – and de facto Allied Generalissimo – was not minded to accept the results of these attacks and took the opportunity of an inter-Allied council held at Chantilly on 7 July to call for the coordination of their various armies 'during the present period of the war'. 'Final victory' could only be achieved by simultaneous offensives 'against the Austro-German bloc' in all three theatres: Franco-Belgian, Italo-Serbian and Russian.[29] Joffre was determined to continue attacking and was already planning what he called a 'double action', which would begin with a preliminary operation around Arras, to fix German reserves, before a decisive strike was launched in Champagne. But there was only lukewarm enthusiasm for such an ambitious operation, and he had to work hard to enlist British support, with London being split on whether to agree to another effort in France or wait until the following year, when her 'New Armies' would be ready. Although the Italians were keen, with General Cadorna reportedly wanting a 'very vigorous offensive . . . as quickly as possible', it would be dangerous for Serbia to mount any kind of expedition across her northern border. As for the Russians, the military representative, Colonel Ignatieff, was understandably evasive. After thanking Joffre, he was unable to give any assurances on when Russia would be able to mount a counter-offensive, but was confident that further German advances would 'provide the troops on the Western Front with the opportunity of a decisive effort before the winter'.

There was only a limited amount that Britain, France or Italy could do to help their allies on the Eastern Front. Unlike Germany and Austria, which had the advantage of interior lines and could shuttle units back and forth, the Allied armies were unable to easily move manpower and equipment between the different fronts. But with Serbia about to be overrun and the Dardanelles expedition against Turkey facing the growing prospect of strategic failure, as British and Anzac troops remained deadlocked on the Gallipoli peninsula, thoughts began to focus on the Balkans. The idea of welding the Balkan states together into a great alliance was not a new one. Ever since the war had broken out, both London and Paris had fantasized about bringing these states onto their side, with potentially hundreds of thousands of bayonets able to attack the southern flank of Austria–Hungary. As early as January 1915, the British Liberal politician David Lloyd George, who was appointed Minister of Munitions in May 1915, had argued that if the Serbs, Greeks and Romanians could be persuaded to join British and French forces, landing on the Dalmatian coast or moving up from the port of Salonika in Greece, they would be able to muster 'an army of between 1,400,000 and 1,600,000 men to attack Austria on her most vulnerable frontier'.[30]

Such a scheme ultimately foundered on the unsavoury reality of power politics in the Balkans. Although the Entente still remained Serbia's greatest allies, pressure had been building on Belgrade for months to offer enough territorial concessions to keep Bulgaria from entering the war. When the Allies demanded that the Serbs give up part of Macedonia, in return for gains in Bosnia, Herzegovina, Albania and the Adriatic coast, they received a stony response: 'The Serbian government, which finds itself in a difficult position because of its high esteem for the assistance provided by the Triple Entente . . . is nonetheless compelled to state that it cannot give the Triple Entente states the authority to propose and promise territories that are within the Serbian state.' Serbia did concede, in a note dated 1 September, that she would consider giving up *some* of Macedonia, but this would have to be balanced by other territorial gains elsewhere, including Croatia and the liberation of 'Slovenian regions', which allowed Belgrade to play for time while not appearing to be needlessly obstructionist. The reality was that dreams for a 'greater Serbia', a 'Yugoslavia' that could unite the Serbs, Croats and Slovenes, remained a key war aim and one that would not be given up lightly, at least not while there were still those willing to fight and die for it.[31]

Lloyd George's interest in the Balkans was driven by his aversion to what seemed like the utter futility and waste of the Western Front, but the French also had their own reasons for looking to this region. On 22 July, an army commander, General Maurice Sarrail, had been sacked by Joffre. Although getting rid of a subordinate was hardly newsworthy – Joffre had dismissed hundreds of officers since August 1914 – Sarrail was a well-connected figure in French radical circles, with powerful political allies who were furious at the way their champion had been treated. 'Sarrail is a flag', one parliamentarian had claimed.

'Depriving him of his command would be a slap at Parliament by breaking the only republican general.' Within days, an ill-tempered row had erupted in the Chamber of Deputies that threatened to shatter the fragile political consensus in France and force the government of René Viviani to allow greater scrutiny of war policy, which had, more or less, been confined to Joffre since the outbreak of war.[32]

Recognizing the level of hostility that *l'affaire Sarrail* had aroused, the French Government acted swiftly, proposing to Sarrail that he become commander of French forces in the Dardanelles, a corps of two divisions. Joffre made it known that he would not object to the move, which would have the advantage of mollifying the Left in the Chamber and getting Sarrail out of France as quickly as possible. The general, however, objected to what he argued was an inferior appointment and stated that he would only agree if the expeditionary force was strengthened to become a full army (*l'armée d'Orient*), and that he would under no circumstances come under British command. But by the time an agreement had been hammered out, larger questions were being asked about the future of Allied operations in the Near East. Another offensive had taken place in August, but this failed to break the deadlock, leaving the Dardanelles campaign in an unhappy state of suspension. It was at this point that events in the Balkans took a surprising turn.

On 21 September, the Prime Minister of Greece, Eleftherios Venizelos, asked to see the diplomatic representatives of the Entente on urgent business. He told them that Greece would mobilize that evening and he wanted to know whether Britain and France would help. According to a military convention between Greece and Serbia that had been signed in 1913, Greece was bound to have an army of 90,000 men concentrated along her northern frontier in the event of hostilities against Bulgaria, as long as Serbia provided 150,000 troops. Now, with Serbian forces strung out across much of her northern and eastern borders, it was doubtful whether she could spare that many troops for the south, which was why Venizelos had approached the Entente. 'I must know', he pressed them, 'whether the Powers would themselves be disposed to furnish the 150,000 bayonets which, according to our Treaty, Serbia was obliged to devote to the war with Bulgaria.'[33]

The Allied response came swiftly, within just forty-eight hours. The French Ambassador was told 'to inform Mr. Venizelos that the government wishes to permit Greece the opportunity to fulfil its treaty with Serbia under the conditions envisaged by the President of the Council, and is hence prepared to supply the troops that you have requested'.[34] The French Cabinet took the opportunity of Venizelos's offer to reposition their forces quickly, with the two divisions currently at the Dardanelles being directed to redeploy to Serbia, via Salonika. At the same time, Sarrail was formally appointed head of *l'armée d'Orient* and given instructions to protect the communications between Serbia and Salonika, and, if circumstances allowed, to cooperate against the Bulgarians. Joffre, who was preoccupied with the imminent offensive on the Western Front, waved it through without a second thought. If the Allies were going to save Serbia, they needed to act quickly. Bulgaria announced general mobilization on 22 September.[35]

While Potiorek had chosen to invade Serbia from Bosnia, across the Drina, Mackensen would make his main attack in a more direct manner, via the city of Belgrade. The Third Austro-Hungarian and Eleventh German Armies would cross the Sava and Danube respectively and head south, while two Bulgarian armies waited to move eastwards into the interior. If the supply base at Kragujevac could be seized, it was confidently predicted that the Serbs would capitulate within days. German staff officers had been surveying the border for weeks, making notes on every aspect of the terrain, while squadrons of aircraft had been patrolling the skies above northern Serbia, taking oblique photographs of the landscape, which were then used to correct the often inaccurate Habsburg maps. Rail links were improved, supplies were gathered, and barges, ferries and pontoons were assembled for the crucial task of crossing the river, which in the case of the Danube, was almost a kilometre wide.[36]

Like most German commanders, Mackensen's only knowledge of the Balkans was from official reports, and he approached the forthcoming campaign with a sensible degree of caution. This would be the first and only time that he would fight with numerical superiority, but he was conscious that his allies would need careful handling.

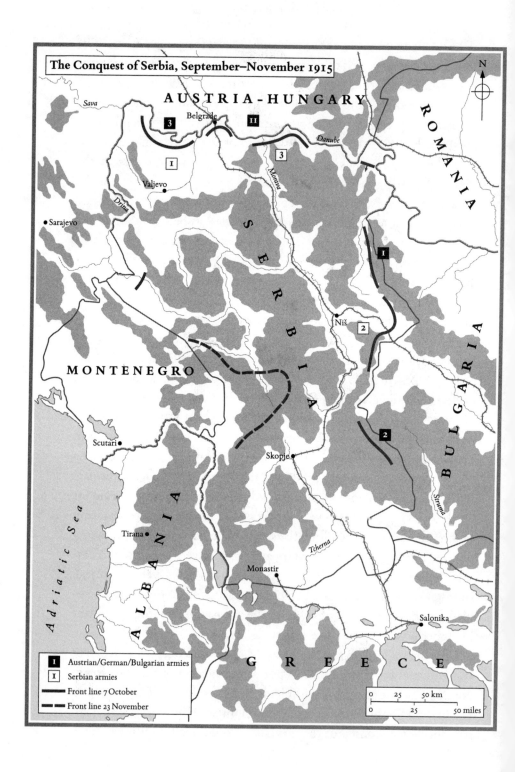

The Conquest of Serbia, September–November 1915

As well as managing the fragile Austrians, he would have to factor in the Bulgarians, who were something of an unknown quantity. Although Mackensen insisted that he respected their military prowess ('their favourite weapon was the bayonet'), he also noted that they only 'fought with enthusiasm' for goals that were 'directly tangible' to their national interests. And then there was the task that lay ahead. 'A mountain battle was to be waged in terrain with poor access to roads and shelter', he admitted. 'This posed an extraordinary challenge to German troops, especially with regard to their equipment, which was not designed for such conditions. The Serbs, however, were all too familiar with this terrain, thus strengthening their resistance. I came to know the Serbs as the best soldiers in the Balkans.'[37]

Serbian intelligence had picked up the warning signs of an invasion early: diplomatic rumours, deserters, rail movements, and the appearance of Mackensen at his headquarters at Temesvár, in Hungary. The Serbs had been outnumbered before, but there was no doubting the weight of enemy forces gathering over Serbia's frontiers. The combined Austro-German-Bulgarian army group totalled 350 battalions and 1,400 guns against 275 battalions and 654 guns, many of the latter being under-strength and short of ammunition.[38] Mackensen's plan was for Third Army to commence the attack on 5 October, opening fire with its guns against the southern bank of the Sava, demolishing trenches and engaging any Serbian batteries that disclosed themselves. The following day, General Gallwitz's Eleventh Army would begin its artillery preparation, with crossings to start on 7 October, aiming to fix Serbian forces in the north and prevent them from being able to counter the movement of Bulgarian troops from the east, which were aiming to seize the temporary capital of Niš and cut the country in half.[39] Mackensen was satisfied that everything had been prepared as well as possible. 'I do not take it lightly,' he wrote, 'but I do have confidence that it will succeed. By no means am I underestimating the military prowess of the Serbs but, together with the Bulgarians, we must overpower them even in their mountainous territories. If common sense triumphs over the hastiness of the Entente forces, Greece and Romania will remain neutral.

And if that is not the case, well, then we will try to overthrow them, too. Germany's noble cause must prevail, even if the world is full of devils. Victory is nigh.'[40]

The Serbs were understandably nervous about the Bulgarian threat, which prevented them from concentrating their strength in the north, as they had done in 1914. Most of their heavy artillery had been deployed against their eastern border, which left only a handful of batteries defending the capital. As the bombardment got under way, producing a rolling series of crashes and rumbles, the Serbs huddled in their defences and waited for the assault to begin. Most of their batteries were soon put out of action, and local militia could not prevent the enemy from securing a series of bridgeheads, despite ferocious counter-attacks. Serbs would leave their trenches and move out to meet the Austrian or German forces, crossing no-man's-land only to be lit up by the glare of searchlights. On 8 October, General Živković, commander of the Belgrade Defence Group, reported on the intense fighting and the inability of his troops to stop the enemy from crossing:

> The attack near the Danube Quay was successful at first, because the enemy, who had been occupying the embankment of the railway line for the slaughterhouse, was pushed back. Despite our troops' relentless attack, they managed to hold their own thanks to their very strong and particularly heavy artillery, which managed to completely silence all, and even disable some, of our heavy weapons. The strength of the enemy's artillery fire can best be seen from the fact that the enemy used more than 15,000 rounds of various calibres, even 30.5 cm, to prepare and support the attack in the vicinity of Belgrade. When all our heavy batteries were silenced, scouts appeared from Zemun, and began to heavily enfilade along the railroad to the slaughterhouse to stop the advance of our troops, who suffered great losses, and as a result were forced to halt their attack yesterday afternoon. They were reinforced and sent to attack again.[41]

Živković demanded a whole division be sent at once, as some of his regiments had sunk to half or even a third of their strength. He also warned that the heavy shelling, including fire from monitors on the river, had 'shaken the nerves of officers and men to breaking point'.[42]

By 9 October, the Serbs had pulled out of their capital, with German and then Austrian troops hoisting their flags on top of the royal palace and the citadel. Belgrade had not suffered particularly badly from the fighting, most of its population having fled weeks before, although the old citadel had been demolished by heavy artillery and the royal palace had sustained a direct hit, which smashed the throne room. 'So, a result!' Mackensen wrote to his wife. 'It will be even more important from a political perspective than in military terms. But in relation to the latter, it is a rare achievement as far as the transition of power is concerned. With God's help, we have the beginnings of a successful campaign!'[43] But pushing deeper into Serbia would present more difficulties, and the Košava wind that blew in on 12 October damaged pontoon bridges and caused low-lying ground to flood, which delayed the second phase of the offensive. The fields lay 'as if freshly turned', noted one account, 'torrential rain pounding down upon them, destroying the cart tracks – into which the guns sank – and tearing the pack animals from the mountain sides. It was an advance the likes of which Mackensen's troops, albeit accustomed to battle, had known neither in Galicia nor in Poland.'[44]

The other problem was waiting for the Bulgarians to join in. According to the military convention, they should have attacked five days after Mackensen (11 October), but the date came and went without any movement, which predictably annoyed OHL. It was not until 14 October that the advance finally got under way. Bulgaria would deploy two armies: First, striking east into the interior of Serbia; and Second, marching towards Macedonia to cut off the Serbs from any potential Greek or Allied intervention. Their troops quickly seized the passes over the border, but met fierce resistance the further they went. The region they had to cross was mountainous, the forested hills covered in rain and mist, even snow in places, and the few roads were unsuitable for the rapid movement of thousands of men, horses and guns. Major von Laffert, a German liaison officer attached to the Bulgarians, reported on the difficulties of the campaign. Ox-drawn wagons carrying about 400 kilograms – around half of what an infantry battalion needed in supplies – usually took about two days to move ten or twelve kilometres, a lethargic pace that meant the Serbs were never going to be overrun.[45]

It was not until 23 October that Mackensen's advance resumed. *Voivode* Putnik had little choice but to withdraw his forces, keeping his armies intact and refusing the great pitched battle that Mackensen wanted. The Serbian Commander-in-Chief was by now increasingly ailing. One visitor who saw him at this time recalled an old man whose movements were shaky, his hands trembling, his step uncertain. 'The hand grips the back of the chair, the duke straining to control his cough. "You know," the duke told me in a hoarse voice, "I haven't got out of bed for 15 days now." I, too, feel strangely excited in front of this old war veteran. On his face, the features almost destroyed by disease, all you can see are eyes made of steel, which are alive, reflecting an indomitable soul. Such a powerful mighty spirit, in such a weak and powerless body! For this wonderful old man, for whom every hour seems to be the last, this is the fifth war in four years.'[46]

The possibility of mounting a major counter-attack, as the Serbs had done before, was discussed almost daily at Putnik's ever-shifting headquarters, but there were few reserves or shells to make the attempt. The movement of the Second Bulgarian Army, which reached the Vardar river on 19 October, cutting Serbia off from its ally, Greece, meant that there would be no supplies coming from the south and it would not be possible to repeat the miracle on the Kolubara that had turned the tide of Potiorek's invasion in December 1914. Kragujevac fell on 1 November; Niš four days later, with Serbian troops pulling back with great skill, burning stores all the way.[47] By late November, the remnants of the Serbian Army were clustered around the plain of Kosovo, the 'Field of Blackbirds', the site of their infamous defeat to the Ottomans in 1389. Putnik was unable to mount a horse and had to be carried from his headquarters in a sedan chair. He signed off orders for the retreat on 25 November, admitting that they had no choice but to march through Montenegro and Albania. 'The only salvation from this grave situation lies in retreating to the Adriatic coast. There our army will be reorganised, supplied with food, weapons, ammunition, clothing and everything else necessary that is being sent by our Allies, and we shall once again be a factor for our enemies to reckon with. The state lives; it still exists, albeit on foreign land . . .'[48] With the army went a motley band of civilians and Habsburg prisoners, stumbling along in wretched columns, chased all the way by the rumbling of artillery and the occasional German aircraft droning overhead.

The conquest of Serbia brought to an end one of the most valiant and bloody defensive campaigns in modern history. Serbia's resistance had finally been broken at terrible cost. Of the 420,000 men who had nominally comprised the army in September 1915, 94,000 had been killed or wounded and another 174,000 taken prisoner or declared missing. By the time Putnik's forces had retreated through the Albanian mountains, they had shrunk to just 140,000 wasted survivors of an ordeal that would later be compared to Napoleon's doomed retreat from Moscow in 1812.[49] The ghost of Sarajevo may have been exorcized, but the war in the Balkans was far from settled, and on 5 October, a day before the invasion had begun, two Allied divisions, one French and one British, splashed ashore at the teeming port of Salonika in a late bid to aid Serbia. No sooner had the Central Powers closed down one battlefront than another one opened.

PART 2

'A deluge is approaching'

The Third Battle of the Isonzo to the Abdication
of the Tsar (October 1915–March 1917)

9. 'Even victorious wars leave wounds'

The commander of *l'armée d'Orient*, General Maurice Sarrail, arrived at Salonika on 12 October, the day the Košava played havoc with Mackensen's pontoon bridges. White-haired, with a carefully trimmed moustache, he was easily recognizable: the 'most captivating French officer' of his generation, some said. 'Tall and broad, the general's whole being conveyed an air of agile elegance', wrote a biographer. 'He looked out from a pair of astonishingly expressive, clear blue eyes.'[1] An intense and inflexible man, known for his fiercely independent spirit, Sarrail was determined to make a quick start, but found the situation in the Aegean port to be just as unpromising as he had feared. Having left Marseilles several days earlier with a rather vague set of instructions – to maintain communications between Greece and Serbia – he now found himself in a 'chaotic environment', with no further guidance on how to proceed. 'I was guided solely by my philhellenism,' he wrote, 'based entirely on my classical education and memories, my thoroughly republican ideals, and my overarching belief that, in war, one must seek an immediate result rather than being beguiled by the post-war period.'[2]

Sarrail had not been able to offer much help to the Serbs. With two French divisions ashore (the British contingent was not under his command), he ordered the first to march north to seize the railway station at Strumitsa, close to the border with Bulgaria, while also despatching a second up the single-track railway line along the Vardar river towards Krivolak, 150 kilometres away. But moving thousands of men into Serbia, alongside their supporting artillery and supplies, would take more time than he had. The trains plying the railway line along the Vardar could only carry around 250 tons of cargo each, and it was not possible to run more than six trains per day, which limited the speed with which French forces could be built up. The Bulgarians, on the contrary, knew the ground well and were moving swiftly

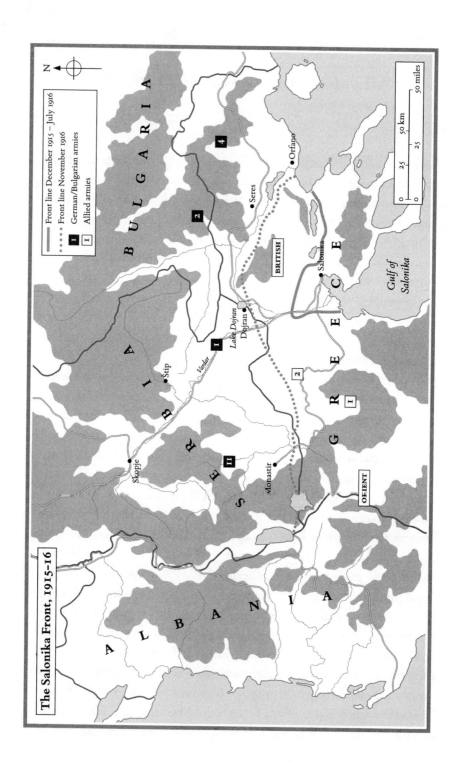

The Salonika Front, 1915-16

N

BULGARIA

SERBIA

ALBANIA

GREECE

Gulf of Salonika

Skopje
Štip
Vardar
Stip
Monastir
Lake Dojran
Dojran
Salonika
Seres
Ortane

BRITISH

ORIENT

2
4

Front line December 1915 – July 1916
Front line November 1916
German/Bulgarian armies
Allied armies

0   25   50 km
0   25   50 miles

to head off any possible Allied intervention, leaving Sarrail struggling to get his campaign under way.[3]

It was quickly becoming evident that the Allies were facing more problems than they had anticipated. On 19 October, Sarrail telegraphed Alexandre Millerand, the French Minister of War, and warned him that 'the mountainous nature of the Balkans and the almost complete lack of roads fit for vehicles, alongside the poor quality of those that do exist, excepting a few major transport arteries', meant that he needed more mountain artillery to support his troops. He recommended that a cavalry division that had been planned to arrive should be replaced with infantry, being convinced that horses were of little use in theatre; and that each unit be equipped with mule teams.[4] Those battalions that had made the winding journey north were also adjusting to the kinds of conflicts that had so scarred the Balkans, where distinctions between soldiers and civilians were often unclear. Elements of 156th Division, which had occupied the railway station at Strumitsa, soon clashed with Bulgarian troops but managed to hold their lines. However, the enemy was 'supported by bands of daring irregulars called *Komitadjis*', which would 'stop at nothing in devising tricks to surprise their foe', forcing French units to take extra precautions with security.[5]

The expedition was also becoming horribly political. Venizelos, the Greek Prime Minister, had been surprised by the speed of the Allied response, which placed him in a very delicate situation. He went to see the King of Greece, Constantine I, who told him that they must protest 'very energetically' if any British or French troops came ashore. Entente assistance would only be required if Bulgaria attacked Serbia, and until they did so, the arrival of foreign troops would be a violation of Greek neutrality. 'A grave misunderstanding threatens to develop between Greece and the Entente Powers', Venizelos wrote on 1 October in a protest letter to the legations in London, Paris, Petrograd and Rome. 'When I suggested the dispatch of 150,000 men destined to complete the Servian [sic] contingents in case of a common struggle against Bulgaria, I did not ask this succour for Greece, but for Servia in order to remove the objection raised against our Alliance, said to have become null by Servia's inability to fulfil her engagement'. Although the willingness to send such a force was to be welcomed, Venizelos wanted to specify that 'so long as Greece was neutral, the landing of international troops at Salonica could not have our official adhesion'. The Allies responded with a flurry of telegrams, openly reassuring but still roundly dismissive of Greek protests. The following day, Jean Guillemin, France's senior diplomat in Athens, confirmed the imminent arrival of the first detachment of troops, and that they fully expected that Greece, 'who has already given many evidences of her friendship', would not oppose measures designed to aid her ally.[6]

It might be thought that Bulgaria's entry into the war would have settled the matter, but it only exposed the stark divides in Greece, between those who wanted to abandon any pretence of neutrality and join the Entente and those who feared the power of Germany, Austria and Bulgaria. The Allied landings had sparked off a danger-ous political crisis between pro- and anti-Venizelist factions, with the King determined to keep Greece out of the war. Venizelos had already resigned in March 1915 over Greece's failure to support the Dardanelles expedition, but had been returned to power after the general election in June. Now he was asked to resign for a second time. King Constantine of Greece was brother-in-law to Kaiser Wil-helm II, and although not unfriendly to the Entente, he was not willing to stand by and see his country dragged into the war. 'The pitiable condition of Belgium was always before his eyes', he told a British journalist. 'Greece was only recovering from two wars, and even victorious wars leave wounds that take long to heal. At all costs, his Majesty's desire was to keep his country from sharing the perils and disasters of the great European conflagration.'[7]

A new government, led by Alexandros Zaimis, was formed on 5 October, with its chief task being the maintenance of Greek neutral-ity and the avoidance of any action towards Bulgaria. Venizelos, who had been Prime Minister when the alliance had been signed, con-tinued to argue that Greece must follow her obligations to the letter, and when Zaimis's ministry failed to secure a vote of confidence in Parliament, new elections were ordered for 19 December. Venizelos and the Liberal Party boycotted them, with the former Prime

Minister calling the exercise a 'comedy unworthy of a free people' and issuing a statement complaining that they now had 'a government system which would only have sense in a Monarchical country where the supreme organ of the State is the Monarch'.[8] When the elections were held, the Nationalist Party, led by Stefanos Skouloudis, triumphed, leaving the fate of Greece firmly in the hands of those who, like the King, wanted to remain on the sidelines. In the meantime, Skouloudis agreed to a series of demands by the Allied powers: that all Greek troops would be withdrawn from Salonika; that roads and railways between Salonika and the border would come under Entente control; and that the Allies would have freedom of the seas, including the right to inspect vessels in Greek territorial waters. 'We submit to these violations of our rights', Skouloudis wrote to Guillemin, 'without protest, trying to persuade ourselves that it is a case of an unavoidable evil.'[9]

Sarrail strode through this political and diplomatic minefield with a burning sense of frustration and injustice. By late October, three French divisions had taken up positions over the border into Serbia, with 10th (Irish) Division deploying on the right around Lake Dojran. With three Bulgarian divisions holding the heights west of the Crna river, it was not possible to link up with the beleaguered Serbs, which left Sarrail in an increasingly exposed position. He pestered Paris for reinforcements, and when none were forthcoming, he wrote to Paul Painlevé, Minister for Public Instruction and Inventions, on 21 November: 'I do not believe that anyone will be able to think that with three divisions it is possible to hold off the entire Bulgarian army and the Austro-German army in the East . . . If I have no reinforcements, it is certain that we can do nothing but get out.' A week later, he had resigned himself to withdrawing back to Greece, but still had no idea what his divisions were supposed to do next. Should they retreat in good order, he asked the Minister of War, what role would they play? For the moment, no one knew. On 3 December, Sarrail was ordered to stay put and build an 'entrenched camp' in Salonika.[10]

Allied strategy remained in a state of flux. The autumn offensive in France had failed, and decisions needed to be made about how the war effort might be intensified over the coming year. A council was held at General Joffre's headquarters at Chantilly, outside Paris, between 6 and 8 December. Joffre had already drafted a long memorandum, which called upon the Allies to 'resume the general offensive on the Franco-British, Italian and Russian fronts as soon as they are in a state to do so'. He was adamant that only 'a co-ordination of offensives' would allow 'decisive action' to take place. A joint Anglo-French offensive had been mooted for the Somme, but Joffre did not believe the two allies would be ready to undertake this for some months to come – possibly by the late spring or early summer of 1916. Therefore, in the meantime, France, the United Kingdom and Italy should 'complete their organization and equipment' and do whatever they could to supply Russia, while using 'every endeavour to wear down their opponents' until 'such time as it is possible to launch the combined offensive'.[11]

The delegates spent the next two days discussing Allied strategy, and largely accepted Joffre's recommendations. All agreed that victory would depend upon coordinated (and simultaneous) attacks, which would prevent Germany from shuttling reserves to each threatened front in turn. In the meantime, the Allied armies would wear down the enemy as much as possible ('particularly by the Powers which still have abundant reserves of men') and be ready to mount relief offensives should the Central Powers concentrate against any one of them. In what were called the 'secondary theatres', in the Middle and Near East, only the minimum number of troops consistent with the task of preventing 'German expansion' would be employed. As for Salonika, there was an urgent need for clarity. With the remnants of the Serbian Army being picked up along the Adriatic coast and taken to the island of Corfu, General Sarrail's original mission of maintaining contact with the Serbian Army had become redundant. But the Russian, Serbian, Italian and French delegates were 'unanimous' in recommending that the expeditionary force 'remain in the Salonika area' and look to its defence 'as a matter of extreme urgency'.[12]

With the exception of Lloyd George and the Colonial Secretary, Arthur Bonar Law, most of the British Government considered the expedition to Salonika with a mixture of exasperation and outright disdain. A series of ill-tempered meetings had already been held between the British and French in the first week of December, with government ministers, including the Secretary of War, Field Marshal Horatio Herbert Kitchener, making it clear how unhappy they were about the continuation of Sarrail's mission, or at least the contribution of British troops towards it. With an announcement about the evacuation of the beachheads at Gallipoli imminent, Kitchener was extremely reluctant to sanction another military operation without thorough consideration, and told the French Prime Minister, Monsieur Briand, that the position at Salonika was 'very critical'. 'As the troops had been sent to save Serbia, and that was now out of the question, His Majesty's Government wished to withdraw them for more urgent services elsewhere. The French troops had done all they possibly could, but the Allied forces were now in great danger, and were risking the whole position in the East'. When Briand outlined the unfortunate effects of any withdrawal, Kitchener countered that Great Britain could not spare the manpower, and 'In his opinion to remain in Salonica was the first step to losing the war and he refused to accept the responsibility.'[13]

The opposing positions on the Salonika campaign had now been clearly drawn. At Chantilly, the British delegation warned that there was 'no point' in maintaining a garrison of 150,000 they had no desire to reinforce, and it was already becoming difficult for the Royal Navy to maintain sea lines of communication throughout the Aegean. Joffre disagreed, and went over the familiar French complaint about the wider effects of any withdrawal. To abandon the expedition would give 'an impression of total powerlessness', undermining Allied 'prestige in the East', and leaving Germany completely free to pursue its imperial ambitions. Moreover, if they withdrew, it would almost certainly cause both Romania and Greece to cast their lot in with the Central Powers, handing control of the Adriatic and the Aegean to their enemies.[14] But no matter how frustrated th
became, they were not yet able to summon the cor
their ally. On 6 December, Lord Bertie, British An
had warned the Foreign Office that any withdra\

[the] fall of Briand's Cabinet', and Britain 'would be considered by French public opinion to have left France in the lurch'. So an unhappy middle position was adopted: Sarrail would remain in and around the port of Salonika, while awaiting a further decision on the future of *l'armée d'Orient*.[15]

With Sarrail stranded in Greece, it was up to the Italian Army to maintain pressure on the Central Powers. General Cadorna had not been able to attack in late September 1915, when Joffre had launched his great battle in Champagne, but he did order another aggressive thrust along the middle and lower Isonzo on 18 October. The frontage of the assault was almost thirty kilometres, with Cadorna hoping that such a wide offensive would stretch the Austrians to breaking point. The challenge was bringing his superiority in numbers to bear, which was difficult because of the lack of guns and ammunition and the ruggedness of the terrain. He managed to amass over 1,300 guns for the attack, including 305 medium or heavy pieces (supplied with over a million shells), but still knew that it might not be enough. It was, therefore, essential that the assault be carried out 'with irresistible impetus, unceasingly supplied, and sustained by a judicious alignment in depth', as Cadorna put it in his operation orders. 'Where one unit stops, another fresh unit must arrive to drag it forward resolutely. In all of them there must be a single and ardent will: to reach and go beyond the enemy's lines of defence as soon as possible, press him and pursue him without mercy, until complete victory.'[16]

Artillery preparation lasted for three days. 'All the battle lines and rear areas were shrouded in smoke and flames', recorded one Austrian account.[17] And then, on 21 October, the attack began:

> The Italians leap towards our most perfect defensive works with great impetus [remembered another defender]. At the first sign of attack, we see them quickly throwing down the parapets and sandbags in front of their trenches. One by one they leap over the barricade and spread out in the line of attack. Up to this point they are in no danger; but when the assault begins, when the first shouts of 'Forward Savoy!' echo, our machine-guns open fire. The assailants always advance in an

orderly fashion, without respite, as if it were only a scene in a theatre. They attack one line after another, gain a foothold behind the sharp stones, reach the parapets of our positions, and here the usual hand-to-hand fight begins.[18]

On the Carso, one Italian division attacked up the long, bloody slope towards San Martino, but found the ground littered with obstacles and swept by fire. The commander of the Catanzaro Brigade noted that without heavy artillery to break up the defences, 'nothing can be achieved by infantry action, even if conducted resolutely and with energy . . .' Italian regiments again showed a remarkable tenacity in trying to seize their objectives, sustaining horrific casualties in a series of wild charges, but nothing worked. 'Thus begins', noted a report by VII Corps, given the task of taking the southern edge of the Carso, 'an alternate and painful story of jumps forward, up to the very first lines of the enemy, up to his barbed-wire entanglements, mostly still intact, up to the first footholds consisting of dry stone walls and rocks; and of forced halts and forced retreats, under the relentless violence of enemy fire, particularly damaging due to enfilade fire.'[19]

Cadorna kept attacking throughout the rest of the month, shuttling reserves and ammunition up to the front and urging his commanders on. Renewed attacks were launched up and down the line, but no matter how many battalions were ordered against the Austrian trenches, the results were painfully similar. In a letter to the Italian Prime Minister, Antonio Salandra, on 27 October, Cadorna did not shy away from the difficulties he was facing: 'whilst being confident, I did not hide from the President of the Council that the undertaking was very challenging due to the aforementioned ground conditions and its preparation, due to the very strong imbalance of machine guns that the enemy has in great numbers while we still have very few, especially for the large quantity of enemy artillery abundantly supplied and so well hidden as to be very difficult to identify and silence, given our shortage of ammunition and aircraft'.[20] He called off the offensive on 4 November before trying again a week later, but this too – the Fourth Battle of the Isonzo – petered out in early December with only minor gains. Italian losses for the autumn offensive totalled over 116,000 dead, wounded and missing.[21]

Conditions on the Isonzo worsened with the arrival of autumn. Routes to the trenches became sunk in mud, outbreaks of disease and sickness multiplied rapidly, and the morale of the front-line garrisons continued to fall. 'We are no longer men', wrote one Italian soldier; 'we are one with the earth . . . Our clothes, our equipment are a heap of mud: likewise, our guns, rusty, soiled, no longer work; to take a few shots you have to hit the bolt with the spade; we look our companions in the face: they look like ghosts; they look at us: we look like ghosts to them.'[22] On 15 November, Lieutenant-General Luigi Capello, in charge of VI Corps, which had attacked north of Gorizia, reported to his army commander, General Pietro Frugoni, that the deteriorating conditions were having a marked impact upon the health and well-being of his men. 'The difficulties created by bad weather mean that often supplies do not reach the troops; when rations arrive in the trenches, they are cold and portions incomplete, and the soldier, who has lived for days frozen in the mud of the trenches inside collapsed shelters that no longer offer any protection, unable to restore his strength with hot and abundant rations, collapses and loses even more vigour.' Frugoni understood the complaints well enough and forwarded them on to Cadorna with a note that such troops could not possibly attack again with any hope of success unless they had been reinforced, resupplied and had the benefit of a few days' good weather.[23]

Cadorna brushed the report aside with his usual insouciance. He would continue to focus efforts on the Isonzo, and was convinced that sooner or later Boroević's lines would break. Intelligence from Austrian prisoners revealed a pathetic tale of shattered regiments being rushed back to the front line after being decimated by heavy combat. 'One might therefore believe that, by persisting in the attacks, the enemy would soon reach such a point of attrition that he would be forced to yield', Cadorna later noted. 'In addition, there was the vivid and just aspiration of Italy to reach the first major national goal represented by the nearby city of Gorizia.'[24] But this refusal to take into consideration the fragile state of his armies and the likelihood that they could break through such a heavily fortified zone began to erode confidence in him. Mario di Robilant, placed in command of Fourth Army in September 1915, called Cadorna a 'dangerous theorist' who fought his war on the basis of mathematical calculations and observations drawn from his maps at Udine:

> His whole plan of operations was conducted by this method: I go around such and such a place, this place falls, then I advance through such and such valley, I go around another such place, this too falls, and so everything always falls by force of logic and manoeuvre. But to carry out these operations, our troops would have had to throw themselves into valleys dominated by high enemy positions, live whole days without eating, carry out continuous bayonet attacks because the ammunition would not reach them in any way, die stoically without help in the snow . . . his troops could not hear his name without hatred, because he, without ever having left his headquarters . . . had stubbornly sent them to attack.[25]

Cadorna would no doubt have pointed to the terrible damage that his offensives were doing to the enemy. The Third and Fourth Battles of the Isonzo had been a brutal ordeal for the defenders, and worrying telegrams began arriving at Teschen throughout the autumn. 'Although this sector has been supplied with all the reserves that could, by necessity, be spared from elsewhere,' read one report in mid-November, 'it is not yet possible to say with any certainty for how many days our position can be held. After all, this not only depends on how outnumbered we are by the enemy, but also on their style of attack, which is getting better by the day, as well as the strength of our own troops. Since 18 October, around 60,000 men have left the army . . . It has caused great concern to the army command that, despite the efforts of all outfits, it has not yet been able to replace the divisions in the crucial area.'[26] The Habsburg Fifth Army had sustained almost 72,000 casualties between 18 October and 1 December, including over 25,000 dead. The fighting on the Italian Front had now mutated into a gigantic 'v of material', and it would later be calculated that the def fired off over 37 million bullets and 706,000 artillery shells a 76,000 hand grenades during the autumn fighting.[27]

The toll on General Boroević's army may have been appalling, but the line held. He scattered decorations on his men, toasted their success in blocking the road to Trieste, and reassured Vienna that the Italians were exhausted. He was now the 'Lion of the Isonzo' – the tough and reliable general who had saved the Habsburg Empire and bought time for Russia and Serbia to be subdued, holding off an enemy force that was two and a half times as large as his own command and possessed of plentiful ammunition. Like every natural soldier, Boroević knew brave men when he saw them, and could only admire the tenacity and courage of the Italians. Peering through his field glasses towards the battlefield with his staff, he gave an interview to a Hungarian journalist and admitted that although 'many acts of heroism' had taken place on both sides, he could not deny that the enemy had fought 'with the courage of a lion': 'Even if the regiments lose all their officers, this does not stop the soldiers from advancing to the attack with the utmost contempt for death.'[28]

For the moment at least, there would be no question of Allied troops, whether Italian or French, making deep advances into Austria–Hungary, Serbia or Bulgaria. Everywhere there was a feeling of stasis; a kind of immobility that threatened to become permanent, no matter how frantically they pressed. Nor was Russia in any position to help, and strategic coordination with the Tsar's armies remained poor. General Alekseev sent the occasional telegram to Joffre, but the belated attempt to aid Serbia revealed how difficult it was to fight a unified and coherent war. In mid-October, the Serbian Government had requested Russian assistance, either an invasion of Bulgaria via Romania; the landing of troops on the Black Sea coast; or an 'energetic offensive' from the left wing of the Southwest Front. Alekseev could only accept the last of these suggestions. Romania would not agree to the movement of foreign troops over her soil, and the mounting of an amphibious landing in the autumn was extremely risky, with Russia's transport fleet likely to be harassed by enemy submarines, so Alekseev opted for an offensive by the Southwest Front. Over the next few weeks, plans were drafted for a sudden attack, well supported by reserves and cavalry, which would throw the enemy back over the Carpathians and into the Hungarian Plain.

Although the inevitable collapse of Serbia had extinguished the original rationale behind the offensive, Alekseev let it go ahead, hopeful that good results could be achieved. It would be led by General Dmitry Shcherbachev's Seventh Army and was scheduled to begin in late December, depending upon how well the enemy's barbed-wire defences could be cleared away.[29]

Offensive operations in the winter were rarely successful in the First World War, and Alekseev's New Year offensive was no different. Two armies were to be launched against the Austro-Hungarian defences along the Strypa river, forcing them back southwest towards Stanislau, Kolomea and Czernowitz. The attack opened at 7 a.m. on 27 December, with Russian artillery firing a series of heavy bombardments, but when the infantry went forward, they were soon pinned down by terrible machine-gun fire, which scythed across no-man's-land and stopped the attacks dead. General Arthur Arz von Straussenburg, commanding the Austrian VI Corps, remembered how his own men 'did not step out of cover until the enemy lines approached the wire barriers. Targeted mass fire, reinforced by machine-gun and artillery fire from the flanks, killed whole rows of men. Countless corpses lay in front of the barriers. The soldiers' spirits were so high that they broke out of the trenches, hurling hand grenades at the enemy. The attack was defeated before the reserves were even on the scene.'[30]

The Russian Army renewed its assault two days later, managing to seize two or three lines of trenches, but the Austrians were conducting an impressive defence. Habsburg infantry would remain in their forward positions for as long as possible, with heavy guns concentrating on knocking out enemy batteries while the field artillery fired at the routes the attackers used to get to the battlefield. Special emphasis was also placed on waiting until the Russians had left their trenches and then surprising them with devastating flanking fire, a technique that had been devised on the Isonzo. Fortunately, the Russians only tended to attack in one place at a time, hoping that Seventh Army would punch a hole, which would then be followed up by the rest of the Southwest Front. This allowed the Austrians to concentrate against each penetration in turn, maximizing their firepower and causing repeated assaults to collapse, leaving no-man's-land littered with the dead.[31]

By the time Alekseev called a halt to the offensive on 6 January, Russian losses stood at over 500 officers and 46,000 other ranks. Alekseev was shocked at the failure. When he heard the news of the repulse, he showed a rare flash of anger: 'Oh these professors!' he shouted during an audience with the Tsar, referring to Shcherbachev, who had previously been Chief of the General Staff Academy.

Nicholas was visibly dismayed at Alekseev's anger and tried to calm him down. 'Well, you can't help it, losses are inevitable.'[32]

Alekseev immediately ordered an investigation, but it was not difficult to see what had gone wrong. Principally, the poor weather (ice and snow followed by a thaw) had left roads and tracks thick with mud and the infantry struggling to move forward. The main attack had also been pressed on too narrow a front and was subjected to deadly flanking fire, which choked off any early gains. There had also been a failure to cut the barbed wire, and the whole attack had suffered from a lack of reconnaissance and intelligence-gathering. Shcherbachev placed the blame on a shortage of shells, but the enemy defences had been planned with an inventiveness and creativity that baffled Russian troops. Austrian positions had been well thought out, with mutually supporting machine-gun nests, numerous dugouts and sturdy infantry shelters. They had also been protected by up to three rows of barbed wire, some of which had been painted and camouflaged, while other stretches had even been electrified.[33]

The performance of the Russian artillery had been particularly disappointing. Although the situation as regarded munitions was better than it had been in the spring and summer, there had still not been enough of them (particularly heavy guns loaded with high-explosive shells) and they had not been utilized in the correct manner. A Russian staff officer, Colonel A. A. Samoilo, reported that:

In the daytime, in order to prepare the attack, the artillery bombarded the enemy positions; at night our guns were silent, allowing the enemy to repair the damage unhindered; in the morning our army advanced and the results were, of course, unsuccessful. The offensive was carried out with a lack of shells, the battery positions were far too distant from each other, and the artillerymen could hardly track where they were firing. Seized positions could not be held, and the troops who captured them did not receive any support. The tasks were vague; the commanders were far too remote from the men; there was no communication with the rear and reports were mostly unreliable.[34]

The failure of the New Year offensive cast a pall over the Tsar's headquarters. It was another sobering reminder of how difficult it was to mount offensives and how much more complex operations had become by late 1915, requiring not only huge amounts of artillery and shells but also extensive reconnaissance and thorough planning. Nicholas II did not celebrate the New Year, only attending a church service and saying little. Mikhail Lemke, who served on Alekseev's staff, remembered watching him leave, followed by his close retinue, while the rest of the officers attended an afternoon reception. 'Wine and other refreshments were served. Alekseev made toasts to the Tsar, the Allies, the fleet and the army; the last toast, they say, was beautiful.' Alekseev himself left soon afterwards, in what seemed like a black mood. 'It was clear to see', Lemke noted, 'that Alekseev was beginning to become disappointed with the Tsar, who at first managed to charm him with his false decency and feigned interest in the life of the army and the country.'[35]

The war now seemed to be tipping decidedly in favour of the Central Powers. Even though the autumn and winter fighting had caused a steady drain of manpower, they were now masters of a vast new empire in Eastern Europe and the Balkans. Russia had not yet recovered from the horrific 'great retreat', Serbia had been conquered, and in the west France's much vaunted 'double battle' in Champagne and Artois had not achieved anything close to a decisive breakthrough. But relations between the German and Austrian High Commands were anything but harmonious, and bitter, angry exchanges were becoming commonplace as Conrad and Falkenhayn clashed over strategy. The latest spat had been caused by disagreements over what they should do in the Balkans, particularly the thorny issue of Allied intervention in Salonika. On 9 October, just days after Sarrail's forces had landed, Conrad told Falkenhayn that Greece had 'entered the ranks of our enemies'. 'A neutral party, whose neutrality obligates him to disarm troops entering his territory – by force, if necessary – but who nevertheless provides a belligerent party with his ports to disembark, his land to stay in and march through, and his railways to transport troops along, and allows all this to happen under the gaze of his mobilized army, is no longer a neutral party, but rather another enemy of the people against whom the troops in his territory are employed.'[36]

Germany's position was much less belligerent. The Kaiser had already promised Constantine that no German or Bulgarian troops would cross over into Greece, and Falkenhayn also made it clear to Conrad, in a telegram dated 10 October, that they must proceed cautiously and not force Greece into an impossible position, with the Entente able to blockade or bombard her coastal towns at will. 'We soldiers in particular – who know how to weigh up the true balance of power most plainly and correctly – have no reason to willingly attract even more enemies.'[37] Once the campaign against Serbia had been concluded, Falkenhayn acted quickly, withdrawing eight of his ten divisions from Mackensen's army group, having little desire for German troops to remain in the Balkans for any longer than absolutely necessary. The response from AOK was swift and spiteful. On 25 November, Conrad informed OHL that he no longer considered Habsburg forces in Serbia to be under Mackensen's command. Moreover, he was about to embark upon the conquest of Montenegro, which would secure Austria's southern flank, and he would do so with or without Falkenhayn's support.[38]

Falkenhayn remained in his quarters at Pless, taking regular walks around the castle grounds with his close staff, pondering his next move and cursing the stubborn independence of Conrad. It was no secret that the Austrian was pressing for a move against Italy, to be completed as soon as Montenegro had been overrun. This would take the form of an attack out of South Tyrol onto the Venetian Plain, but it would require heavy artillery, careful planning and, ideally,

German support – something that Falkenhayn would need to be persuaded to provide. A conference was held at Teschen on 10 December to try and coordinate Austro-German strategy for the forthcoming year. Conrad was insistent that the Central Powers could not fight a long-drawn-out war of attrition; they must attack and win 'on a grand scale'. No victory against Russia was likely unless Romania joined the Central Powers, and any success against the British and French in the Balkans could not be decisive. Therefore, only the French and Italian theatres of war should be considered. While seeking a decisive victory against France was the 'ideal' option, this would not be easy; a point which Falkenhayn agreed with, nodding and saying that at present the prospects were 'not good'. In such a case, Conrad continued, they must strike Italy! The fact that Germany was not at war with Italy was circumvented by Conrad's request that Falkenhayn relieve eight Austrian divisions along the Eastern Front, which would allow him to concentrate his forces for an attack out of South Tyrol.[39]

Falkenhayn had to admit that this plan was 'very inviting', but he was not interested in providing German troops to fight against what he called Austria's 'private enemy'. August von Cramon would repeatedly warn him that Conrad held a 'frenzied hatred' of Italy and would do anything to destroy her.[40] In a letter dated 16 December, Falkenhayn rebutted Conrad's claims one by one. 'Even to-day Germany would not hesitate for a moment to take part in active operations against Italy if her participation would be advantageous and if her means permitted it,' he wrote, 'having regard to the fact that she is bearing the whole burden of the war against Belgium, France and England, and by far the greater share of the burden against Russia and Serbia.' Any offensive out of the Tyrol would have to contend with difficult ground and strong defensive positions, while requiring the withdrawal of attack divisions from elsewhere along the front. In any case, Falkenhayn was not convinced that even a victory would compel Rome to sue for peace. 'She certainly cannot make peace against the wishes of the Entente, on whom she is absolutely dependent for money, food and coal.'[41]

Conrad refused to let the matter drop. He wrote to Falkenhayn on

18 December and again pressed his case. Clearly, a successful offensive against France would be of the 'greatest importance', but as Falkenhayn himself admitted, such a possibility was highly unlikely. Conrad had therefore suggested Italy. Only after the overthrow of Italy would the forces become available for a conquest of France. He was not asking this from the Austro-Hungarian point of view, he added, but because it was essential for their common cause, and because a victory against Italy was the 'necessary introduction to the final decisive combat' to take place sometime in 1916. But Falkenhayn's thoughts were already far away – on the dismal, rain-washed fortress city of Verdun, France's great citadel on the Meuse. At an audience with the Kaiser on 3 December, he had revealed plans to 'carry the war to its end' with an 'attack in the west'.[42]

Falkenhayn was seeking a new kind of battle; not in the 'grand style' that Conrad wanted, but something that followed a strategy of attrition. He had already warned the Chancellor, Theobald von Bethmann Hollweg, on 29 November that it was 'no longer a war as we previously understood it, but a fight for existence', and that any sign of weakness would be seized upon by their enemies.[43] The idea, which was gradually refined over the next month, was that Germany would attack Verdun. But instead of seeking a breakthrough in traditional fashion, the operation would be designed to fix the French Army and provoke it into making repeated, wasteful counter-attacks that would gradually 'bleed them white'. Falkenhayn shared the common prejudice of the time against his opponents ('although many French people performed brilliantly as individuals, the French, as a whole, lacked firm collective organisation') and was convinced that sooner or later they would break. It was inevitable that Germany would prevail in the long run.[44]

With Germany reorientating her strategy to the west and Austria–Hungary preparing to complete her gains in the Balkans, strategic communication between OHL and AOK was reduced to a trickle. By late December, Conrad and Falkenhayn were refusing to speak to one another, which left the Austrian unaware of the attack on Verdun and still hoping to convince Falkenhayn that they should crush Italy in one almighty blow. Indeed, the decision *not* to mount a combined attack on Italy in the spring of 1916 would retrospectively be seen as one of the greatest mistakes of the war: a lost opportunity to continue the successes of 1915, crush the weakest of their opponents and avoid the prolonged misery of Verdun. August Urbanski, one of Conrad's earliest biographers, wrote that 'The single-most disastrous military error made by the Central Powers was the division of the two army commands and the failure to carry out a unified attack in the period from December 1915 to February 1916 to overthrow Italy and destroy the Italian Army.' Even Cramon, not one of Conrad's most vocal admirers, was unable to work out why Falkenhayn had not been more open with the Austrians about his plans for 1916 and told them that he needed 'every man' and 'every gun' for an attack against France. 'If we had done this in time, then there would have been a common goal again, and in turn a sense of duty to work together to achieve that goal. But there was nothing of the sort. The armies simply parted, the sense of solidarity disintegrated, and the war was lost. The men and their energy reserves – which were already in short supply – were worn down faster than those of the enemy, who had the whole world on their side. These were the weeks and months in which the war really took a turn, with the disaster of 1916 only exacerbating matters.'[45]

Their fates may have been inexorably intertwined, but for now, at least, the German and Austrian empires would go their own way. Montenegro, the small mountain kingdom that had been a staunch ally of Serbia throughout 1914–15, was invaded on 5 January 1916. A two-pronged operation, from the northeast and west, was led by the Austro-Hungarian Third Army under the command of General Hermann von Kövess, one of the most experienced soldiers available to Conrad. Montenegro was hardly an ideal place to win a quick victory: a land of few roads, where travel was usually only possible along rivers or stream beds, defended by 'a warlike population who have never yet bowed to a foreign conqueror', as one contemporary put it.[46] It took time for Habsburg forces to get into position, particularly along her western borders, because the Bosnian and Serbian railway systems were either damaged or insufficient and new lines needed to be laid down. The road network also left much to be desired, and long columns of horse-drawn wagons, slipping over the icy paths, were a common sight as the invasion force was readied.

The Montenegrins, about 50,000 strong, were expecting the attack, but like their Serb allies they were in a terrible state, lacking munitions, uniforms and food. They had been protecting the flank of Serbian forces throughout the war, managing to hold their lines and repulse numerous Habsburg forays, but the army was starving and on the verge of mutiny by the final months of 1915. Their leader, King Nikola I, issued a proclamation on the eve of battle, announcing that his people would never surrender and would prefer death to slavery, but they were not able to prevent the swift overrunning of their country. Kövess chose to attack in two places: the north, across the Tamar and Lim rivers, where Montenegrin forces were able to fight well, repeatedly counter-attacking across the snow-covered ground; and the west, where the bulk of the Austrian assault forces were massed, heading for the capital of Cetinje. The crucial summit of Mount Lovćen, which commanded the surrounding area, was stormed by 47th Division on 11 January after a heavy bombardment, including naval gunfire support from Austrian battleships in the Bay of Kotor, which cloaked the rocky top in smoke and dust.

With the loss of Mount Lovćen, the Montenegrin Army rapidly lost hope and its men began slipping away, heading south with what remained of Serbian forces. On 16 January, a delegation arrived in the Austrian lines under a white flag, with a proposal from the Prime Minister, Lazar Mijušković, that they agree an armistice for six days to arrange negotiations. When this was relayed to Teschen, Conrad was nonplussed, wiring back that hostilities would only cease after an unconditional surrender, including all those Serbian troops that were still stationed in the country. King Nikola delayed for as long as possible, even sending a personal letter to Franz Joseph pleading for a 'just and honourable peace settlement', but it was to no avail, and the act of surrender was finally signed on the morning of 23 January. The King and most of his ministers fled into exile.[47]

The mood in Austria was one of exultation. 'The Submission of Montenegro', hailed the *Innsbrucker Nachrichten*, as news of the peace offer spread across the empire. 'A stone has fallen at a crucial point in the mighty wall that the Entente has built around the Central Powers and their allies. The solid, close relationship has now been lost. Cracks and fissures have already started to spread out from the hole, making the wall even weaker.'[48] Another state had fallen, and the realization of Austria–Hungary's war aims seemed within its grasp, sparking off detailed discussions in Vienna about how the war should be concluded. Conrad had already written to Franz Joseph in late October and warned him that the 'physical resources' of the empire ('that is men qualified for military service') would run out in June 1916. Therefore, they must 'bring our war aims into harmony with this situation'. Conrad saw Austria's future as being part of a 'Central European block' in a 'solid union' with Germany, with far-reaching territorial adjustments: a border against Russia thrown out to the River Bug; the complete incorporation of Serbia into the monarchy; a Montenegro shorn of its coastline; and a new defensive line along the Tagliamento, or ideally the Piave, against Italy.[49]

Count Tisza, the Hungarian Prime Minister, saw the chance of such an overwhelming victory as unlikely. In a letter to Count Burián, Foreign Minister, on 20 December, he had argued that for 'all the shining deeds and triumphs of our troops the situation as a whole is not of such a kind that we could speak of forcing our enemies to seek peace'. They had only really achieved 'complete victory' in the Balkans, notwithstanding the Entente presence in Salonika, and he did not think the 'annihilation of Russian war-power' could be achieved. 'We must conserve our forces', he wrote, 'and obtain a peace in a not too distant time, otherwise such an exhaustion in men and economic forces will set in, which would result, if not in our downfall in the war, at least in permanently disabling us after the war and in endangering our future.' As regarded the question of annexations, he remained cautious, warning against 'the acquisition of new and hostile elements in the south', which might have 'the most pitiful consequences'. They had to find some way to 'give Serbia a certain existence as a state', perhaps akin to the possible future relationship between Belgium and Germany.[50]

A meeting of the Joint Council of Ministers had been held on 7 January, on the eve of the invasion of Montenegro, to discuss what the changed situation in the Balkans might mean for the empire.

Serbia was high on the agenda, with the ministers debating whether it would be better to incorporate it into the monarchy outright or leave it in a much-reduced state, after the Bulgarians had taken their share: economically dependent upon the monarchy, but with the risk that it might once again become a centre of pan-Slavic agitation. As Burián noted, 'We must ask ourselves what would be more advantageous and which of the two issues is easier to solve. It would be easier to solve the Serbian issue if only 66% of all Serbs belonged to the monarchy and 34% lived in an independent state, than if 100% of all Serbs were to become our subjects.' As for Poland, much would depend upon the attitude of Germany. Burián believed that Poland should join the monarchy, but also knew that Berlin would ultimately decide her fate – particularly if it made concessions in the west over the status of Belgium and needed sufficient 'compensation' elsewhere.[51]

Familiar concerns were raised by Count Tisza. He continued to believe that full incorporation of Serbia into the monarchy was unwise, but spoke of annexing the northern part of the country, naturally to Hungary, while allowing Austria a free hand in Poland. Belgrade would become a 'provincial Hungarian town', full of imported Hungarian and German colonists, leaving the rest of Serbia nominally independent. This was a significant shift from his previous position, against any annexation of Serbia, but it still ran into opposition from several ministers, including Ernest von Koerber, Common Finance Minister. Were an independent Serbia to continue to exist, no matter how shrunken and dependent, Koerber worried that she would inevitably become a 'nursery of the Greater Serbian movement'. 'A state can be overthrown *manu militari* [by force of arms]; an idea cannot. No matter how much we restrict and repress the Serbian state, we are far from finished with its ideology. We can neither extinguish nor trample it. Our only choice is to either take control of it ourselves, or to wait for others to take control of it against us. There is no third option.'

No firm decisions were made on 7 January – the issues seemed intractable – but a resolution was adopted that 'agreed on the basic principle that those areas that could be attached to the monarchy – according to the outcome of the war in the northern theatre of war – should be unified with Austria'. All parts of Serbia, on the other hand, 'should be given over to Hungary so that, after incorporating these areas into the monarchy, the further fate of the two states would have to be decided by the legislation of Austria and Hungary, respectively'. Conrad, who had travelled from Teschen to be present, found the attitude at Vienna to be frustrating and defeatist, and he complained to Bolfras afterwards that 'only the annexation of Serbia and also Montenegro can liberate the Monarchy from the grave danger, by which it was forced into this most horrible of all wars'.[52]

10.   'Outstanding men are needed everywhere'

The Tsar entered 1916 in a pensive mood, conscious that he was now directly responsible for his armies in the field and trusting that it had been God's will for him to take command. He continued to enjoy the slower pace of life at Mogilev, a routine of morning briefings, long afternoons of walks or letter-writing, and the occasional smoke with his senior officers. Despite the terrible losses of recent months, he never wavered in his commitment to the struggle, at least never in public. 'You need have no fear', he had told the men of Fifth Army during an inspection in early January. 'As I announced at the beginning of the war, I will not make peace until we have driven the last enemy soldier beyond our frontiers, nor will I conclude a peace except by agreement with our allies, to whom we are bound not only by treaties but by sincere friendship and the blood spilt in a common cause.'[1]

The Tsarina, Alexandra, remained at Tsarskoe Selo, where she continued to keep an eye on the political situation in the capital, writing almost daily to her husband, offering advice and gently pressing him to make the political appointments that she – and Rasputin – wanted. 'Yes, truly you ought to be my eyes and ears there in the capital while I have to stay here', Nicholas had written soon after assuming command at *Stavka*. 'It rests with you to keep peace and harmony among the Ministers – thereby you do a great service to me and to our country . . . I am so happy to think that you have found at last a worthy occupation.'[2] With these instructions, the Tsarina became a great source of political power and patronage in Petrograd, which she was keen to make use of. In the seventeen months between September 1915 and February 1917, Russia went through a bewildering game of 'ministerial leapfrog', with four different Prime Ministers, five Ministers of the Interior, three Foreign Ministers, three War Ministers and four Ministers of Agriculture, alongside a host of other appointments, most of whom were chosen by the Tsarina and her 'friend'.[3]

The strange figure of Rasputin, with his lank hair, unkempt beard, and eyes 'that burned straight through you', was now infamous throughout Russia.[4] Germany had not been slow to see his potential to undermine support for the Tsarist war effort, and the rumour that the *starets* was a pro-German sympathizer, a traitor at the heart of the establishment, was a heaven-sent opportunity for destabilizing the regime. Germany had already dropped lewd drawings of Rasputin over the front lines, copies of which were widely shared by both officers and men, who needed little convincing that the holy man had intimate access to the Tsarina and her daughters, betraying the Tsar and making a mockery of their sacrifices. Alexandra's alleged corruption became 'a kind of metaphor for the diseased condition of the tsarist regime', which tested the patience of even the staunchest patriots. Although Rasputin only paid eight visits to Tsarskoe Selo in the first three months of the year, spending the rest of his time drinking, whoring, and boasting about his exploits to anyone who would listen, it was widely assumed that he was in daily contact with the imperial household, with the destiny of the regime in the palm of his hand.[5]

The idea that such a man could get so close to the royal household had been scandalous enough in peacetime, but the added strains of war made it an intolerable affront to much of the political and cultural elite in Petrograd. Plots and rumours of plots against Rasputin abounded in the winter of 1915–16, including an unsuccessful assassination attempt by Aleksei Khvostov, Minister of the Interior, who had become convinced that the *starets* was a German spy (or so he later claimed). Khvostov had originally wanted to get Rasputin out of the capital on a long pilgrimage to see Russia's great monasteries, but when this did not work, he tried to bribe the officer in charge of his security detail. When this too was unsuccessful, he contacted one of Rasputin's former associates in Norway, only for word to get out, which caused a great scandal as details of the plot were splashed across Russia's newspapers. Khvostov, who had, ironically enough, been appointed with the support of Rasputin, was now sacked, with the

Tsarina devastated that her spiritual adviser could be treated in such a manner.[6]

None of this made much of an impact upon the Tsar, who still relied implicitly upon his wife's judgement and seemed impervious to the growing complaints about Rasputin's influence. When the President of the Duma, Mikhail Rodzianko, requested an audience at Tsarskoe Selo in the early months of 1916, he was astounded by how difficult it was to convince Nicholas of how damaging his association with Rasputin had become. He spoke 'with complete frankness' about the dangerous period they were going through, with ministers intriguing and plotting, 'the continuous absence of a firm policy', and the 'orgies and debauchery of Rasputin', which shook confidence in the government.

'I find myself once again obliged to submit to your Majesty that this cannot go on much longer', Rodzianko said. 'No one tries to open your eyes with regard to the part played by this disreputable *starets*. His presence at the Imperial Court undermines the nation's confidence in the Crown; it may have fatal consequences for the fate of the dynasty, and turn the hearts of your subjects against their Sovereign.'

The Tsar, who listened to Rodzianko with an occasional flash of surprise across his face, was not interested in talking about the subject any longer. 'What, do you think, will be the end of the war?' he asked, standing up and making his way across to the window, where he peered out over the palace gardens. 'Shall we win?'[7]

Several days later, the Tsar signed off instructions for Rasputin's deportation to Tobolsk, but his heart was never in it and Alexandra soon countermanded the order anyway, insisting that she could never push 'our friend' away. All of this left the imperial family running out of allies and struggling to find suitably capable – and loyal – politicians to carry out their wishes. The Duma had reconvened on 22 February, with the Tsar making a short speech (and again rebuffing calls for a 'responsible ministry') before he departed for *Stavka*. He had recently appointed Boris Stürmer as Chairman of Ministers, replacing Goremykin, who was retired on grounds of ill-health. Stürmer was 67 years old, a former governor of Yaroslavl, and he drew a sharp reaction from Maurice Paléologue, the French Ambassador, when the news was announced. 'Neither his personal qualifications nor his administrative record and social position marked him out as fitted for the high office which has just been entrusted to him, to the astonishment of everyone', he noted in his diary. 'But his appointment becomes intelligible on the supposition that he has been selected solely as a tool; in other words, actually on account of his insignificance and servility.'[8]

For all the Tsar and Tsarina's failed political appointees, Aleksei Polivanov, Sukhomlinov's replacement as Minister of War, proved to be a more effective figure than anyone expected. Since his appointment in June 1915, he had worked tirelessly to rebuild the Russian Army: raising new manpower from classes of recruits that had previously been exempt; improving their training; and trying to strengthen the relationship between Russia's state arsenals and the private sector to produce more shells and ammunition. This would eventually reap significant benefits. Russia had produced just over 11 million 3-inch shells in 1915, but this would rise to 28 million the following year.[9] There was also increased output of supplies of all kinds, from telephones to uniforms, boots and rifles, which – when combined with orders arriving from overseas – gave hope that 1916 might be very different to the previous year and offer the Russian Army the chance to fight on equal, perhaps even superior, terms against its opponents.

General Alekseev had spent the weeks following the cessation of the New Year offensive pondering what to do. General Joffre had originally wanted to launch the main Franco-British offensive on the Somme in March, but this would now be postponed to July, to allow time for Russia to be resupplied and for the British to be ready in full strength, which meant that the Italian and Russian Armies would need to mount their own offensives later in the year, to fix German reserves before the decisive attack went in.[10] When Alekseev considered Joffre's proposals, sent from his representative in Paris, General Zhilinsky, he was unimpressed and did not consider it likely that the Germans would wait passively for the Allies to strike. Delaying until July, he thought, is 'impracticable because the enemy will forestall it'. 'We shall take the offensive', he wrote to Zhilinsky on 22 February, 'as soon as the condition of the roads allows us to, because this is the only way to confuse the plans of the Germans.

Given that the front is stretched for almost 800 miles and that we do not have enough heavy artillery, it will be easy for the enemy to discover our weak spots. As for us, passiveness will always lead to an unfavourable outcome.'[11]

The German attack at Verdun, which opened in bitterly cold weather on 21 February, confirmed Alekseev's suspicions about enemy intentions and the need to launch a relief operation as soon as possible. He delivered a report at *Stavka* on 24 February and discussed the requirement, as had been agreed with Joffre back in December, to mount a 'general offensive' no later than March. The strength of the Russian armies had now settled at 1.7 million men, and Alekseev was confident that this would increase still further when the supply of rifles was improved. Nevertheless, they now possessed a significant numerical advantage north of the Pripet Marshes, where they stood against the bulk of German strength on the Eastern Front. A victory in this sector would be of 'enormous significance', he thought, and might 'influence the whole course of the war'. They would, however, have to wait until the ground had dried up and for their divisions to receive as many weapons as possible, including the arrival of two heavy artillery brigades from Moscow. Alekseev estimated that they could mass about 400,000 troops on the crucial sector around Dvinsk and Lake Naroch, with the main attack being delivered by the left flank of Northern Front and the right flank of Western Front, striking together towards Kovno. If the line was broken, the Southwest Front would go onto the offensive towards Lutsk and Kovel. The attack was scheduled to begin on 18 March.[12]

Alekseev's proposals were soon accepted, with the Tsar asking questions and pointing to objectives on a great map that lay unfurled in the operations room. 'On the whole I am quite satisfied with the results of our long conference', he noted afterwards. 'They disputed much among themselves. I asked them all to speak out plainly, because, in these important problems, truth is of the utmost significance.' Despite the Tsar's bullishness, his generals inspired little confidence and there were lingering doubts about whether they would be able to achieve any kind of victory. Alekseev was capable and hard-working, with a level-headedness that was much admired, but his subordinates were old, infirm and haunted by the terrible fighting of the previous summer, which had destroyed faith in their men. Pavel Plehve, who had emerged from the fighting at Lodz with a reputation as a general of great skill, had replaced Ruzski as commander of the Northern Front in December 1915. He was 65 years old and had suffered from health problems for some time. At Mogilev, the Tsar had been shocked at his appearance, telling Alexandra that 'Poor Plehve looked like a dead man; he was so pale. To-day he is lying down in his sleeping carriage, unable to move – probably over-fatigued!'[13]

Neither Ivanov nor Evert, the other front commanders, were as fragile as Plehve, but both were hardly coming men. Ivanov had twice asked the Tsar for permission to resign, which had been refused, and frequently complained of how difficult it was 'to get his proper share of sleep' (probably because he 'slept the whole campaign on a broken camp-bed', which he refused to have mended). When he spoke to the British Military Attaché, Alfred Knox, he admitted that 'he belonged to a past generation' and would have to 'make way for younger men'.[14] At 58 years old, Aleksei Evert was the youngest of the front commanders. An artillery officer and veteran of both the Russo-Turkish and Russo-Japanese Wars, he had distinguished himself in the fighting in Galicia in 1914, taking over command of Fourth Army after Krasnik, before being placed in charge of the newly formed Western Front in September 1915. He tried his best, but was soon overwhelmed by the enormity of his duties, and became notorious for his struggles to communicate clearly with his staff. 'Evert's resolutions are written in terrible handwriting', remembered one staff officer. 'The letters are huge, but they all look like sticks', which caused his subordinates endless difficulties trying to decipher what had been written. Evert could even confuse himself on occasion. 'Recently, without rhyme or reason, he inserted the word "Mary" into the middle of a military report. "What happened?" he wondered. "Ah, I meant to write 'army' instead!"'[15]

After completing its ragged, desperate retreat, what remained of the Serbian Army waited for deliverance at the Albanian ports of Durazzo and Valona. It was joined by thousands of civilians and Habsburg prisoners, shuffling along in weary columns – a footsore, starving nation on the move. The journey through the Albanian mountains had been a terrible ordeal. The Serbs had no choice but to make their way along thin mountain tracks deep in snow, all the time shadowed by bandits and stalked by wolves. By the time they reached the coast, they were a sad remnant of what had once been a proud and capable army. 'We can say without any exaggeration', wrote a French observer, 'that the Serbian army is in a state of total disarray. In Shkoder [Scutari] individual soldiers wander the streets, and return to their units only during mealtimes. Order and discipline in a strict military sense no longer exist.' While many refugees went on to Italy, France or North Africa, General Joffre suggested that they transfer the army to Corfu, which was accepted by the Serbian Government-in-Exile.[16]

Moving the Serbs was easier said than done. Lieutenant-Colonel Broussaud, head of the French Military Mission, arrived on the island on 17 January and found that it was in no position to accommodate the thousands of weary Serbs due to arrive any day. 'The situation is clear: there is no scope for provisions', he reported. 'There are no supplies, no linen, no clothing, no tents, no camping or cleaning equipment, and no medicine . . . The island of Corfu boasts no supplies, wood or vehicles, and there may not even be enough food for the locals. However, it might be possible to procure a small amount of concrete and wood from Epirus and locate some rough hay on the island to replace the straw bedding.' The commander of Greek forces on the island, Lieutenant-Colonel Andreakos, did not speak French, and local officials wanted compensation to be paid to the owners of land where the Serbs would settle, insisting that this would be modest if only the soldiers did not damage the olive trees. The major Greek worry, that the Serbs would bring disease – typhus or cholera – with them, was waved away, Broussaud confirming that no cases had yet been discovered, and that all measures would be taken to reduce contact between the new arrivals and the native population.[17]

The first Serbian troops arrived in mid-January and were soon placed into makeshift camps, with the British and French working with the Greeks to provide shelter, food and water.

Heavy rainfall made the camping grounds a morass of glutinous mud. By mid-February, up to 90,000 soldiers and 5,000 civilians had arrived – numbers that climbed every week – brought on Allied ships the short distance through the Strait of Otranto. By the end of the month, there were around 135,000 evacuees on the island, including Serbia's Regent, Crown Prince Alexander.[18] It would be some time before the Serbs could be refitted and returned to full health. Already plans were being made for them to take their place alongside the other Allied forces in Salonika, which were now firmly occupied building an immense series of defensive works around the city that stretched seventy miles from the Gulf of Orfano, along Lake Beshik and Lake Langaza and then in a wide arc around the city until it reached the Vardar river.

The scale of the 'entrenched camp' was a wonder to behold; an 'Aegean Verdun' that was slowly emerging out of the rocky earth around the white city of Salonika.[19] An English journalist, George Ward Price, went to see for himself, penning a report for the London *Times*. 'Interminable strings of supply carts jog up and down behind their teams of mules or horses, Generals on horseback, motor-cycles, motor-lorries, marching detachments, and ... long caravans of Greek labourers' were some of the sights he witnessed on the bumpy drive out of the city. 'Our principal trenches lie deep and well-sandbagged, and from the front they are invisible', he wrote. 'Three hundred yards after you have passed them and look back there is nothing but the blue smoke of camp fires behind them, mingling with the mists that rise from the clayey soil to mark the line on which they lie.' North from the city centre, the ground was open – an 'unbroken treeless monotony' – gradually rising to another series of ridges about seven miles away. 'It is a most shelterless plain,' Ward Price noted, 'but its very flatness and absence of cover make it a stout stronghold to maintain on the defensive.'[20]

Following the final collapse of Serbian resistance in late 1915, Bulgarian and German divisions totalling some 350,000 men had moved towards the Greek border, launching heavy attacks on the British and French, and forcing them back to Salonika. The Central Powers had then occupied a series of rocky heights, about two kilometres from the border, from where they could observe any Allied movements. The Bulgarian Commander-in-Chief, Lieutenant-General Nikola Zhekov, urged Falkenhayn to continue the offensive, throwing the Allies back into the sea and securing Bulgaria's southern flank. '*We* have committed our entire existence to this war,' he wrote, '*we* have engaged in a bloody war and have sustained enormous losses. These circumstances entitle me to ask Your Excellency (von Falkenhayn) to keep them in mind in decisions regarding territorial and economic questions between Bulgaria and Greece.'[21]

As Hindenburg and Ludendorff had already discovered, Falkenhayn's mind was not easily changed, and he quickly shut down any question of an offensive on Salonika, which according to Mackensen's best estimates could not be undertaken before April. The roads and railways from the Serbian frontier had been badly damaged by the retreating Allies and would need to be rebuilt, which might take months. Moreover, were Bulgaria to invade Greece, this would almost certainly force King Constantine to throw in his lot with the Entente. 'It is true that the expulsion of the Entente would have had the very desirable result for the Bulgarians that they would have been free from any direct danger,' Falkenhayn admitted, 'but that was only of very doubtful advantage for the general conduct of the war.' Zhekov raised the issue again at a conference in Niš on 5 January, insisting that they strike as soon as possible and take advantage of Allied disorganization, but neither Tsar Ferdinand nor his Prime Minister, Vasil Radoslavov, would approve such an operation, or at least not yet.[22]

A curious stalemate had now been reached in the Balkans. The Bulgarians could not march on Salonika, nor could the Allies advance out of it. Sarrail spent his time at his headquarters, leafing through reports and speaking to his staff, occasionally surveying a great map of the region that had been pinned up on the wall behind his desk. On 5 January, he had been appointed commander of all Allied troops in the port city, including five British divisions, which pleased his supporters in Paris, even though the future of the expedition remained clouded in doubt. He continued to badger his government for reinforcements, pressing his case with those deputies who still saw him as a proud and unbreakable republican general, but this inevitably incurred the wrath of Joffre, who reminded him in a letter dated 17 January that he would now have around 100,000 French troops, that this was a sufficient number to accomplish his task, and that he was only to correspond with the government through him. Although the French Government agreed to despatch another division the following day, thus overruling Joffre, there was no agreement on any possible offensive action, so Sarrail was left to wait, biding his time until he received further instructions.[23]

The British remained highly sceptical of the whole affair. The Chief of the Imperial General Staff, Sir William Robertson, was a notorious opponent of the campaign and consistently advised the War Cabinet in London for a complete withdrawal of British forces. When he met Joffre on 14 February, he made it clear that they must stay the course on the Western Front and not be swayed by strategically unimportant adventures. 'We have arrived at the time of tension that is part of every war. We must grit our teeth, and not allow ourselves to be led astray from the plans required by military circumstances.' Joffre shrugged his broad shoulders and said that it was more of a political question than a military one, and that he was being advised by his government that Romania might receive an ultimatum from the Central Powers any day. It all became a question of mathematics: the Allies currently had around 225,000 troops in Salonika and could count upon the remnants of *Voivode* Putnik's Serbs (about 100,000) to bring the number somewhere close to 325,000. If they could be brought up to a strength of 400,000, this would certainly make the Bulgarians and the Germans suspect that an offensive was imminent, potentially bringing Romania into the war alongside the Entente.

Robertson was not amused. 'The Romanians!' he replied, shaking his head. 'Every day the Romanian minister in London tells us that the Germans will soon send their ultimatum to his government, and yet they never do. Were it to be sent, would the Romanians march against us, or would they merely grant passage to the Germans?' Any demonstration, even with 400,000 men, would have little effect once the enemy realized they were not serious. 'In summary, nothing will come of this', he added. 'The whole charade is not worth the effort, and this is the advice that I gave to my government.' No matter how much Joffre tried to twist Robertson's arm, asking quizzically what he would do if Romania asked for western support, the Englishman was unmoved. 'I have studied the matter of the Balkans for years, and I know it is Hell itself. One would require the greatest degree of prudence to engage there. Could our diplomats not first work to change the current situation in the Balkans?'[24]

The attack at Verdun only made these questions more pertinent. Germany had already withdrawn two divisions from the Balkans, which prompted Joffre to ask what else the expeditionary force could do to hold enemy forces on their front. Sarrail's response, dated 7 March, envisaged a number of possibilities: a large offensive, utilizing as many as 21 divisions (including the Serbs) for a massive invasion of Serbia and Bulgaria, or a much smaller series of demonstrations, perhaps even aerial bombing, that might keep the enemy guessing.[25] None of this particularly impressed Joffre, who took the opportunity of another conference at Chantilly on 12 March to press his allies for more support, including asking the British, once again, to put more manpower into the Balkans. In London, the War Cabinet had spent weeks debating the expedition, weighing the costs of pulling out and incurring the wrath of the French against the dangers of a commitment that seemed to be open-ended. After another round of feverish debate, it was agreed that *l'armée d'Orient* could not be reinforced, but it should also not suffer any depletion and must do whatever it could to threaten the enemy, marching north towards the Bulgarian lines at Lake Dojran and up the Struma Valley.[26]

Robertson was predictably unhappy, sending a note in late March demanding that 'in view of our grave deficiency in personnel and of German activity in the west it is now, more than ever, important that we should use there all men who can possibly be sent, and not keep them useless and idle in secondary theatres'. A force of 200,000 men had been 'locked up for several months without exerting any appreciable influence on the course of the war, to the amusement of neutrals and the delight of our enemy'. It was, therefore, time 'that an end was put to this ridiculous situation . . . I would remind the

[War] Committee that I have repeatedly and consistently advised them that the only sound policy is to be as strong as possible on the Western front.' Yet the British Government was not prepared to go as far as he would have liked, and recognized that complete withdrawal was, for the time being, politically unpalatable. Salonika, for all its shortfalls, 'must not be allowed to fail'.[27]

For the German High Command, the Eastern Front had now assumed a secondary importance. Falkenhayn had returned to Charleville-Mézières to oversee the attack at Verdun, concentrating on how to 'bring about the decision' in the west, as he explained in a briefing to his army commanders on 11 February. 'It is necessary to transition to the conduct of forceful strikes on the Western Front, because mere episodes are the only things we have achieved in the east, nor is there any reason to continue operations in the Balkans.' A 'decisive strike' against Italy was possible, but it 'could not result in the ending of the war'.[28] Therefore, they would turn back to the west and attack the French Army. Ideally, this operation would be conducted alongside a renewed campaign of U-boat warfare, but this ran into staunch opposition from Bethmann Hollweg, who was worried about the impact that widespread sinkings would have on American opinion and urged Falkenhayn to think carefully before chancing everything on such a largely unproven weapon, asking, 'Is our situation really so desperate that it calls for such a risky game?'[29]

With a decision on submarine warfare having been postponed until April, the Kaiser proving typically indecisive, Falkenhayn could only blame the politicians in Berlin for not giving him the tools he needed to finish the war. Hindenburg and Ludendorff would in all probability have threatened to resign on the spot when faced with such disagreement, but Falkenhayn did nothing. He had no wish to embarrass the Kaiser and shied away from issuing an ultimatum that might have decided the matter in his favour.[30] He thus found himself in a more isolated position than usual. His relations with *OberOst* remained as strained as ever, and now he had to reckon with a growing estrangement with the Imperial Chancellor. Fortunately, communication between OHL and AOK had improved markedly after the conquest of Montenegro. Conrad was in forgiving mood when he wrote to Falkenhayn on 19 January:

> Lately, a tone of disgruntlement has emerged in our hitherto trusting intercourse. I say this with regret, due to the great common cause which we are called to serve with shared strength, as well as due to the personal relationship between Your Excellency and myself, in which the unrepentant clarity and openness we have thus enjoyed would be very sorely missed. In these grave, treacherous times, as we struggle for the existence of our two kingdoms, we have gained so many connections and have so much mutual understanding for the benefit of our cause, that maintaining these relationships is extremely important to me on a personal level, too.

Conrad justified the removal of Kövess's Third Army from Mackensen's army group on the grounds of the urgent need to invade Montenegro before it could be used as a base for Serbian remnants. Moreover, he did not think it made sense to place Habsburg forces under a German general who already 'had to deal with a distant, difficult and different operation'.[31]

Falkenhayn appreciated Conrad's peace offering, writing back on 25 January that his opinion was 'not determined by what happened, but solely by how it was done', although he did admit to 'serious concerns' about the future of their association. 'For it seemed to me to make the hitherto unreserved collaboration, which is surely the only reliable way to achieve ultimate success, more difficult in the future than I am convinced it should be.' He therefore wanted to thank Conrad 'for having relieved me of this worry through your remarks, while also bestowing upon me the joyful assurance that our personal relationship of heartfelt trust has remained unchanged'.[32] This re-establishment of cordial relations between the two men did not mean that German and Austrian strategies aligned any more than they had in previous months. Conrad had not given up his dreams of a crushing attack against Italy, while as far as Falkenhayn was concerned, the war in the east was as good as finished. Although OHL continued to toy with the possibility of an attack upon Salonika, little attention was paid to the growing indications that the Russians were planning something big around Lake Naroch.

By 5 March, German intelligence had tracked the assembly of 14 enemy divisions against Tenth Army, with Russian officers, clad in their snow coats, being spotted touring the front trenches, binoculars in hand.[33] German aircrew had also seen a build-up of new artillery positions, stockpiles of ammunition, masses of cavalry, and the miles of extra communication trenches that now led to the front – all tell-tale signs of an imminent offensive. Ludendorff had been on leave in Berlin on 11 and 12 March when he received a telegram reporting these preparations, so he returned forthwith to his headquarters at Kovno. In his absence, Max Hoffmann had been placed in charge. 'It seems that the Russians have been planning an attack against us,' he wrote in his diary on 14 March, 'and I am wondering whether we should bring up our Reserves by railway or not.'[34] With the concentration of Germany's forces at Verdun, the strength of her armies on the Eastern Front had dropped perilously, and on the crucial attacking sector, Russian numerical superiority was crushing. On the day of the attack, 18 March, just 66 German battalions would face off against 368 Russian ones. Moreover, the attacks were supported by an unprecedented amount of artillery, at least for the Tsarist Army. In General Evert's army group, 5,000 field guns had been supplied with 1,250 shells per gun, and although there were only 585 field howitzers, they had almost 600 shells each – more than enough to pose a serious challenge to the German line.[35]

The mood in the Russian camp was heightened by the sense that they now had every advantage they were ever likely to possess. 'It is difficult to describe the feeling that enveloped me', remembered one regimental commander when he was told that the offensive would begin the following day. 'The riflemen received the news with delight and enthusiasm, and I thought that if they had sent us forward then, the attack would have been so bold that no German force could have withstood it.'[36] On the eve of the assault, Evert issued a stirring call to his men, reminding them of what they had gone through and calling upon them to fulfil their 'sacred duty to the homeland' by expelling the enemy from the borders of their empire.[37] Only the weather remained uncooperative. The ground was frozen, the sky low with grey clouds, and an icy wind cut across the long, featureless plain where the German and Russian armies would meet. Snow had fallen, only for a sudden thaw to set in three days before the attack was due, which turned the roads and tracks to slime and made the vital task of crossing no-man's-land even more perilous than usual.

The preliminary bombardment began at 6 a.m., with a flurry of detonations and rumbling sounds over the sector of attack. The German defences were not as extensive as they would become on the Western Front, but they were still tough, usually split into two or three separate systems, about 100 metres apart, protected by belts of barbed wire and supported by a labyrinthine network of approach trenches. The main attack had been given to General Vladimir Smirnov's Second Army, which was divided into three attacking groups and would push forward on either side of Lake Naroch before driving to the west towards Vilnius. In theory, Smirnov's men should have been able to bite deep into the German defences, but already a sense of nervousness and unease was palpable behind the scenes. Second Army did not have a particularly glorious record; after all, it had been destroyed at Tannenberg in August 1914 and had no great victories to its name. Nor did its commander have the aggression and boldness that such a large offensive required. Smirnov had been born in 1849 and was now 'old', 'soft' and 'delicate', falling ill shortly before the attack began.[38]

Orchestrating something this big, particularly against the Germans, required more than just numbers. An intricate process of meticulous organization and care, intelligence and planning would be needed if a victory was to be won. Yet the Russian operation at Lake Naroch was plagued by difficulties; some would even label it a fiasco and call for the heads of those generals involved. Repeated attacks on 18 March failed to break the German defences. A few trench systems and shattered villages were captured, occasional groups of defenders were rounded up and taken prisoner, but reserves were not on hand to exploit these gains. Moreover, there were heartbreaking scenes of slaughter that would cut deep into the psyche of the Tsarist Army. Typical was the experience of V Corps, which had been ordered to sweep through the gap along the southern shore of the lake. Two divisions were about to launch their attack when it was postponed for three hours, one of the divisions not having been able to get into position, disorientating the long lines of anxious riflemen as they readied to go forward. Although the bombardment continued, its effect began to wane, and observers scrambling along the forward trenches, binoculars in hand, soon reported that the shelling was inaccurate, not being concentrated on the most important points, and was becoming scattered over a wide area. Even more worrying was the impact of the field guns, with shells unable to penetrate the frozen ground, just pockmarking the white snow with blackened, smoking scars of dirt. When the regiments finally went 'over the top', they met with disaster, some battalions coming under their own artillery fire as they moved out, with the corps sustaining over 4,000 casualties in a series of abortive rushes, shot down by German flanking fire or becoming entangled in thickets of barbed wire.[39]

The slaughter was sickening. The attackers fell in piles, with each succeeding wave being hit by the same furious fire and collapsing into little clumps of ragged uniforms and bloodied flesh. In one sector, the Germans counted 4,000 Russian bodies, all for a cost of 200 defenders.[40] I Siberian Corps, attacking north of Lake Naroch, ran into a hurricane of fire as its men slipped over the icy, treacherous ground. In 22nd Division, there were over 5,500 killed, wounded or missing, with casualties in two of its regiments reaching 60 per cent (some battalions lost all their officers). The failure to cut the barbed wire was particularly devastating. Infantry would hurl themselves forward with a loud 'hurrah!', only to come under merciless fire and then find the barbed-wire defences intact. 'Everything is lumped together', recorded a post-war analysis; 'tasks that could be successfully performed by light artillery, such as the destruction of barbed wire entanglements, are assigned to heavy guns, whereas tasks that specifically require heavy artillery – such as fire on trenches, communication lines and enemy reserves – are assigned to light artillery, which is unable to accomplish them, not only due to its calibre but also the distance. Some tasks, such as terrain blanketing fire or making smoke screens were simply unrealistic.'[41]

Attacks continued into the following day, but there was little change to what had become a wearily familiar pattern. With the ice and snow now melting quickly, Russian infantry were left to advance through waist-deep mud and water. Battalion after battalion toiled forward, only to run up against unsuppressed machine-gun positions. 'Soldiers managed to reach the barbed wire,' one combatant recalled, 'but they couldn't get through it. Then, under dense rifle, machine-gun and artillery fire, they had to cling to the ground and dig in, waiting for night to fall so they could get a chance to cut the wire, while the wounded crawled back. It was warm during the day, but the nights were freezing. The soldiers' overcoats, wet from daytime rains and mud, froze to the ground at night, and sometimes the wounded would lie there for two to three days!'[42]

Almost everything that could go wrong had gone wrong. The decision to split the attacking divisions into groups had not worked, primarily because the generals did not know their subordinates, while group headquarters, often lacking basic communications equipment, struggled to coordinate the actions of their divisions. Reserves arrived late, or not at all, and as was common with Russian operations, when one sector attacked, its neighbours were invariably inactive, which allowed the defenders to concentrate their fire.[43] The battle soon became so chaotic that Evert launched a ferocious tirade upon the staff of Second Army, excoriating them for fighting individual actions that were not properly supported by artillery fire. 'I concentrated overwhelming masses of infantry and artillery, provided as many shells as I could', he said. All that was required was 'proper control' of the attacking groups to push the enemy out of their trenches, but this had not happened; officers had not shown enough energy and activity, which allowed the enemy to hold their positions for two days and then even launch counter-attacks![44]

Spasmodic operations continued for days: the same ineffective shellfire, followed by brave but doomed assaults that Falkenhayn later characterized as 'bloody sacrifices'.[45] After days of fighting around 'Ferdinand's Nose', a heavily defended hilltop position named after the Tsar of Bulgaria, Lieutenant-General Peter Baluev, who commanded one of the attacking groups, reported that his 'attack had bogged down'. His men were too exhausted to continue, having sustained over 30 per cent casualties, with any further assaults likely to meet with the same tragic results. When the losses from all the attacking groups were tallied up, the total reached 78,000 men. Twelve hundred prisoners had been captured, but only a few square kilometres of ground had been taken in what were later described as 'modest' results. German losses were probably around 20,000.[46]

Alekseev was never the most demonstrative individual, but he was visibly horrified by the failure of the offensive and, like Conrad before him, seemed to lose faith in his own soldiers. 'Outstanding men are needed everywhere', he wrote afterwards. 'As it was, the impossible was done in early March. We had a fivefold force superiority at the strike point, but what came of it?' There were 'no intelligent men' left to carry out his orders, which meant that 'whatever you prepare, they will botch'.[47] Others took this insight to its logical, devastating conclusion. 'Evert does not know what to do', noted Mikhail Lemke, who was well attuned to the mood of the senior officers. 'Indeed, I can now see clearly that we have lost the war – this is irrevocable . . . The havoc among the Germans, the successes of the Allies on their fronts, the rich natural resources of Russia – all of this might lead to victory, but it will not be the achievement of the Russian Army . . . It hurts, it breaks my heart to realise this, but the truth is so clear and distinct that it is almost tangible.'[48]

11. 'A moment of utmost gravity'

Nine days before Russia's doomed offensive at Lake Naroch would begin, General Luigi Cadorna launched another attack – the fifth – across the Isonzo. Cadorna had not been keen on pushing his armies forward before the arrival of warmer weather, but he had been specifically requested to do so by his allies as the full extent of the German operation in the west became clear. On 3 March, Joffre sent an urgent telegram to the head of the French Military Mission with the Italian Army, reporting that the Germans had already employed ten divisions at Verdun and, by all accounts, were looking to mount a 'decisive effort' against the fortress city. 'As concluded at the Chantilly Conference, the Italian Army must respond aggressively to any withdrawal of opposing troops. As well as minor offensives, it must prepare a large-scale offensive to be launched when weather conditions allow.' Joffre wanted to know what Cadorna planned to do and when any attack might take place.[1]

The reply, which arrived the following day, was hardly encouraging, and showed yet again how difficult it was for the Allies to coordinate their efforts. Cadorna doubted whether a 'general offensive' could be carried out before the end of May, and he remained concerned about shortages of artillery ammunition, as he had been for months. He did, however, explain to the French Military Attaché that he was 'more convinced than anyone of the need to coordinate efforts' and would do 'everything in his power to keep the forces of the Austrian Army on the Italian Front and behind the mountains where the snow precludes any action'. With the Austrian High Command 'bracing itself for an imminent attack', he would undertake 'small-scale offensives' to keep them guessing.[2] Accordingly, three days later, on 6 March, he ordered Second and Third Armies along the Isonzo to make 'a forward step towards the first gradual objective of our eastward advance, namely the conquest of the entrenched camps of Gorizia and Tolmino [Tolmein]'.[3]

A series of smaller, more progressive attacks would not be easy either. Already the Italian Front was beginning to resemble the trench deadlock found in France. Italian and Austrian positions along the Isonzo were now heavily fortified, consisting of long, mazy runs of sandbagged trenches, incessant shellfire and sniping, and a daily toll of killed and wounded. Edward Garnett, an English writer working as an orderly for the Red Cross, described the battlefield for the London press. Gorizia remained the centre of it all, the point of concentration around which everything was orientated. Before it lay the blasted hill of Podgora, barring the way to the east and often likened to an anthill. 'With a glass you can see the naked skeleton of a wood clothing its brown sides and rolling crests', wrote Garnett; 'the trees are mere dead sticks, all blasted and scarred and distorted by artillery fire. The Italian and Austrian trenches run there side by side, bisecting the hill slopes; time after time the Italians have made advances of desperate bravery, only to be held up at this segment or thrown back at that.' The great question was how to break this line. 'How to advance up that naked stony slope in the face of artillery and maxim fire against wire entanglements? It means annihilation . . .'[4]

This was a dilemma that Cadorna wrestled with day after day as he tried to forge the Italian Army into an effective fighting force. 'The whole winter of 1915–16 was spent in reorganising and strengthening the army,' he later wrote, 'in instructing officers and men, in increasing the offensive and defensive means, all in view of the operations to be resumed in the spring, and especially with regard to the resumption of the offensive planned on the Giulia front.'[5] The army was now undergoing a significant programme of expansion, from 35 divisions in 1915 to 48 by the end of the following year. In the first few months of 1916, Italy formed 24 new infantry regiments and a new 'bombardier' corps of over 200,000 men, with the total number of all ranks at the front rising from about a million in 1915 to one and a half million in 1916 (peaking at two million in 1917).[6]

Men from all over Italy were now being drawn into the army, presenting Cadorna and his generals with the enormous challenge of turning them into soldiers able to defeat Italy's enemies. Morale, and by extension discipline, thus began to assume great importance at

Comando Supremo. Cadorna had always believed in severe and exemplary punishment, and the Italian Army possessed one of the harshest disciplinary regimes of any Allied army. In total, 750 men would be executed during the war (compared to 346 in the British Army and just 48 in Germany), for a range of offences, most notably desertion, with punishments even including the summary decimation of units on a number of occasions. Although such brutal acts were not explicitly authorized by Italian military regulations, Cadorna kept his men on a tight leash, convinced that a stern disciplinary code was essential to maintain the offensive spirit of the army. As he wrote in a letter to the Prime Minister, Salandra, in January 1916, it was 'to be deplored that the current military penal code does not specify, in the case of serious collective offences, the ability to enact decimation upon the guilty units, since this is certainly the most effective method – in wartime – of keeping rebellion in check and protecting discipline'.[7]

Cadorna's willingness to employ such ruthless methods of control was a stark reminder of how much power he could now wield. Already many in the government were openly critical of their Chief of the General Staff, tired of his incessant demands for more men, guns and ammunition, and distressed at the lengthening casualty lists, but it was difficult to rein him in. Since the beginning of the war, he had steadily amassed more and more power as the army became responsible for a strip of territory that encompassed much of northern Italy, including the provinces of Brescia, Verona, Vicenza, Treviso, Udine, Padua and Venice. This 'war zone' would eventually subject about ten million Italians, a third of the entire population, to military jurisdiction, with the 'Ministry of Udine' (as it was termed) responsible for a whole range of civil functions, including the police, justice, the management of production and trade, the repression of dissent, and the general 'limitation (or annulment) of the civil and political rights of the population'.[8]

Cadorna constantly pushed back against any attempts either to limit or to curtail his powers and engaged in an ill-tempered battle against the 'internal enemy', which he claimed was just as dangerous as the Austrians. Moreover, he rejected any responsibility for the failures on the Isonzo and blamed Salandra and the government for not giving him everything he needed, which only hardened attitudes in Rome. The Foreign Secretary, Sidney Sonnino, wanted Cadorna to be sacked, but because the general only answered to the King, he was going nowhere, with Salandra lacking the nerve to press the matter much further. When rumours reached Cadorna that the mood was turning against him, he was dismissive, writing to his wife, Giovanna, that he was aware that some ministers wanted to hold 'a kind of war council' on the situation, in which the army commanders would participate. 'Just imagine if I could tolerate this pathetic Parliament whose very summoning sounds distrust of me and in which the army commanders would like to have their say, perhaps in opposition to my opinion, raising disagreements that would take us back to 1866, after all I have done to establish the authority of the command.' When the King's aide-de-camp arrived to discuss this possibility, Cadorna said that he could 'never accept such a thing' and that if the government insisted, then they must replace him. 'As you can see, my arch-enemies are not the Austrians', he added. 'But don't think that I lose any sleep. I'm fine, thank God, and I shake the dust off my shoes, always ready, after all, to pack my bags and leave immediately for Rome.'[9]

As aggressive and uncompromising as Cadorna was, he was still dependent upon results on the battlefield, and the continuous deadlock at the front provided his critics with ample ammunition to hurl in his direction. The Fifth Battle of the Isonzo began on 11 March with a forty-eight-hour bombardment that fizzled and crackled over the Austrian lines, sending fragments of rock and stone flying over the trenches but otherwise doing little damage. Along the Upper Isonzo near Tolmein, the Second Italian Army faced some of the worst terrain imaginable, with the Habsburgs occupying the Mrzli Ridge, which ran north about ten miles from Tolmein to Plezzo and included some lofty peaks, most notably Mount Krn ('Black Mountain'), which rose to 7,400 feet in height. Attacking from the valley floor, Italian troops had to struggle up to the ridgeline, the crest blasted by fire and pockmarked by shells. The defenders would then unleash a fusillade of machine-gun and rifle fire, even rolling rocks and boulders down upon the hapless attackers, which time and again produced desperate slaughter.[10]

Months of fighting in the area had resulted in only minor gains, and local Italian commanders were uneasy about pushing their men into this hellish landscape yet again. Second Army could barely mount more than a few minor patrols, with the weather conditions – snow and heavy fog – still proving unsuitable for large-scale operations. A report by 8th Division, dug in southeast of Caporetto, made for frustrating reading:

> On the nights of 9th, 10th and 11th March, patrols were sent to the Sleme, the Mrzli and the Vodil, to place explosive tubes in the [barbedwire] fences and throw bombs into the trenches. Our men, dressed in white, managed, despite the darkness, enemy fire, bad weather and snow (from two to three metres high), to approach the enemy defences and to throw numerous bombs into the trenches, but it was not possible for them to place the tubes in the barbed-wire entanglements, as these were almost completely covered with snow. Nor could the artillery, mainly due to the fog, carry out its action. The attack was suspended; however, our troops continued patrolling to keep the enemy alert, especially during the night.

Further south, another division had intended to carry out a demonstration around Plava, but when the commanding officer watched the bombardment, peering out into the murk of no-man's-land, he could not see its effects and refused to let the infantry leave their trenches. A series of patrols were later authorized, and when these crept up to the enemy wire, they were summarily repulsed.[11]

Similar scenes took place across the frontage of Third Army. A mass of artillery had been concentrated in Lieutenant-General Capello's VI Corps against Podgora and Mount Sabotino, two key objectives that remained frustratingly out of reach. Capello ordered frequent pauses in the bombardment, to make the enemy think that an attack was imminent and allow them to filter back into the trenches, while infantry in the forward positions cheered and pretended to go over the top. This worked well enough, and caused the Habsburgs some casualties, but the difficulty of observation left officers unsure what effect their guns were having. Numerous raids and heavily armed patrols were sent out over the next few days, but the

Austrian defences were largely intact and provoked furious exchanges of rifle fire, with grenades thrown back and forth, before the muddied, exhausted attackers returned to their trenches.[12] Given the relatively small scale of the Fifth Battle, losses were noticeably lighter than on previous occasions. Third Army sustained just 1,800 casualties, which inevitably caused some dismay among Italy's allies, who had been hoping for a more sizeable commitment to the offensive. At Chantilly, General Carlo Porro, the Italian military representative, emphasized the need to prolong the demonstration because of continuing heavy fighting at Verdun, but Cadorna made it clear that he was doing all he could and blamed the poor weather conditions, including frequent avalanches, for interfering with operations.[13]

Nine hundred miles to the northeast, Tsar Nicholas II was rapidly running out of capable figures – politicians or generals – that he could rely on. Aleksei Polivanov, Minister of War, was dismissed on 26 March 1916 after receiving a curt note from Nicholas telling him that the 'work of the war industry committees does not inspire me with confidence, and your supervision of them I find insufficiently authoritative'.[14] Why the Tsar had dispensed with the services of someone who had a reputation as an effective and able administrator was a complex question. Both Alexandra and Rasputin distrusted Polivanov and had been demanding his replacement for months, citing his close relationship with the prominent Duma politician and leader of the Octobrist Party, Alexander Guchkov, as proof of his unsuitability. Guchkov had been appointed chairman of the War Industries Committee in the summer of 1915, as part of the Tsar's attempts to improve the supply of war materials to the army, and his close links with a variety of industrial figures, labour unions and voluntary groups, as well as his open hostility to Rasputin, caused the Tsarina to fear that he was 'plotting against the monarchy'.[15]

Polivanov had also failed in his primary duty of supplying the shells the army desperately needed. Although the terrible 'shell hunger' of 1915 was a thing of the past, there were still huge shortfalls in projected deliveries, and the War Industries Committee struggled to fill them in time for the spring offensive. The armies at Lake

Naroch had only been able to fire off as many shells as they had because the winter lull in activity had allowed stocks to be built up. Particularly frustrating was the continuing lack of heavy shells, which were vital in demolishing trenches and clearing spaces in the thick wire entanglements that cloaked enemy positions. Much of this was not Polivanov's fault. When he had replaced Sukhomlinov, he had found that there was no 'general plan' for supplying the needs of the army and navy, and much had to be worked out from scratch. Moreover, building new factories or expanding existing ones required machine tools, which were in short supply and had to be imported from abroad.[16]

Polivanov was replaced by General Dmitry Shuvaev, 'a good and honest man', according to Rodzianko, 'but inadequately equipped to fill such a post at such a time'.[17] Shuvaev was a soldier by background, able and conscientious, and loyal to the Tsar. He had been promoted to Chief Field Quartermaster in December 1915, and thus had considerable experience in the supply side of the Russian Army. Although he worked diligently and was well regarded in the Duma, relations between the government and its assembly were 'becoming worse and more strained every day', according to Maurice Paléologue. He was unimpressed by the new Chairman of Ministers, Boris Stürmer, who 'has succeeded in making the public want Goremykin back. The whole bureaucracy is engaged in a competition in reactionary zeal', he added. 'If it was desired to provoke a violent crisis, no better course could be adopted.'[18]

The continual hiring and firing of senior ministers undermined confidence in the Tsar and contributed to the further weakening of the Russian state, which was now beset by a wave of industrial unrest and a growing food crisis. As the industrial powerhouse of Russia, Petrograd was at the centre of the campaign for better rights and working conditions. Strikes and wage disputes had been a feature of life in the Russian capital for decades, but these increased sharply in 1916. Only 2,600 workers had gone out onto the streets on 9 January 1915 – the tenth anniversary of the infamous 'Bloody Sunday' massacre, when Cossacks guarding the Winter Palace had fired on crowds of demonstrators, killing about 200 people – but the following year there were over 61,000. Unrest continued for the next two months, with thousands of workers from all over the city walking out to demand wage increases and better conditions, urged on by various radical socialist groups eager to use the discontent to bring down the monarchy. The disorder peaked in March, when 73,000 workers from 49 factories went on strike, leaving the authorities struggling to restore order and having to rely on a range of coercive measures, including firing strikers and drafting persistent offenders into the army.[19]

Semi-detached from the home front at *Stavka*, the Tsar had brought his son, Alexis, to Mogilev in the autumn of 1915 and they lived together in great happiness, the boy taking lessons every morning before playing out in the gardens around the headquarters, dressed in the uniform of a private soldier, toy gun in hand.[20] A bad bout of bleeding over Christmas had seen him return to Tsarskoe Selo to recover, which left the Tsar understandably troubled, but he never let it show. 'He is always so bright and cheerful that one cannot but be cheerful with him', remembered Major-General Sir John Hanbury-Williams, head of the British Military Mission. 'It is a wonderful temperament for a man who must have such cares and anxieties on his mind, and I am sure is a good inspiration for others.'[21]

Something was clearly missing at *Stavka*. 'Things are moving very slowly at the front; in several places we have sustained heavy losses, and many generals are making serious blunders', Nicholas wrote to Alexandra on 27 March. 'The worst of it is, that we have so few good generals. It seems to me that during the long winter rest they have forgotten all the experience which they acquired last year . . . I feel firm, and believe absolutely in our final success.'[22] Every day he spoke with Alekseev about the progress of their armies, went over the latest enemy movements, and discussed their next move. Alekseev was insistent that they must look to attack again, in line with their commitments to the Entente. In a report delivered on 6 April, he argued that it was unwise to await developments. While the French could watch for enemy attacks and then bring up reserves swiftly on their dense railway network, Russian forces were spread out over a 1,200-kilometre front and had only an 'underdeveloped' railway system to rely upon. Therefore, they must force the enemy to react to their movements. The Tsar, as he always did, agreed with Alekseev's assessment and approved an attack to take place sometime in May.[23]

There had been a notable reshuffling of senior officers after Lake Naroch, with General Plehve being replaced at Northern Front by Aleksei Kuropatkin, who had been brought out of retirement and tasked with the crucial role of defending Russia's northern flank, including the road to Petrograd. Kuropatkin was 68 years old, known for his role in the Russo-Japanese War, when he had been placed in the invidious position of commander of the 'Army of Manchuria'. Finding his men being outfought by the numerically inferior Japanese forces, he could offer little but confused direction, incessant complaints and 'near-legendary indecision'. He would later blame defeat upon an underestimation of Japanese military power and 'moral strength', their command of the sea, and Russian unpreparedness, but no one who met him ever got the sense that he had the necessary mettle to master the challenges of command. As one observer noted sadly, Kuropatkin's 'resurrection' did the army little favours. He 'had been fully tried and found wanting' in 1904, with another senior officer revealing that his 'spirit was heavy within him' when he heard who the new commander of Northern Front was.[24]

The other appointment was Aleksei Brusilov, who was put in charge of Southwest Front, replacing Ivanov, who had finally had his wish to retire approved by the Tsar. Brusilov, the former commander of Eighth Army and conqueror of Lemberg, was now 62 years old and at the peak of his powers; a lean, sprightly figure, known for his energetic and professional approach to command, which sometimes put him at odds with his fellow officers. Throughout his career, he had acquired a reputation as something of a loner; someone who did not quite fit in with the established routines and expectations of the imperial court. Unlike the vast majority of his contemporaries, he was not a graduate of the General Staff Academy, and he had always believed in the value of 'preparedness': in working hard to train his men for what they would face on the battlefield, and doing so in all conditions. Disdaining the often brutal and demeaning treatment that was meted out to soldiers by their superiors, who tended to see them as little more than peasants, Brusilov was convinced that the

Russian soldier could fight well if properly led, and did not look fondly upon those apt to judge 'the efficiency of the Army's training' from watching a handful of parades or grand reviews.[25]

Brusilov's more positive attitude immediately put him at odds with both Kuropatkin and the other front commander, Evert, when they met at *Stavka* on 14 April for a conference on the summer offensive, chaired by the Tsar. A photo was taken that day – one of the few to feature Nicholas working alongside his senior commanders – which shows them sitting at a long table, piles of documents pressed down with weights, maps pinned upon the walls. Kuropatkin is on the Tsar's right, Brusilov on his left. Ivanov, sitting at the end, stares into space. Across from Nicholas is Alekseev, looking into the camera, flanked by Shuvaev and Evert. Alekseev read out a thoughtful and carefully written document outlining the next steps they might take, while the other generals nodded along and the Tsar sat quietly, listening and smoking. Russian forces now had a superiority of approximately 670,000 men, a figure that would rise to almost 880,000 when the latest batch of recruits joined their battalions. This preponderance of manpower was particularly notable on the Northern and Western Fronts, with Alekseev believing that the Russians were twice as strong as the Austro-German forces in this sector. With this in mind, he proposed an offensive by the central bulk of Russia's armies in the direction of Vilnius, supported by as much heavy artillery and as many reserves as could be mustered.[26]

Even this impressive mass of men and materiel could not induce the Tsar's generals to offer up much enthusiasm for an offensive, and the reaction to Alekseev's proposals was muted. The true extent of the demoralization wreaked by the March fighting now became evident: a timid group of senior officers, fearful of the enemy, weighed down by the memory of past failures and haunted by the 'great retreat' of 1915. Kuropatkin talked about Lake Naroch: the poor use of artillery, the bad weather, the lack of good roads in the attacking sector, shrugging his shoulders when he considered whether such factors could be avoided in future operations. Evert was also worried. While he agreed that an attack towards Vilnius was a sound idea, he wanted at least six corps and would need as much as two months to prepare, which produced a suitably chastened mood around the conference table.[27]

There was only one general who had the ability, character and willingness to mount a new offensive. Brusilov, with his 'finely-moulded features, long, tapering fingers, steady grey eyes', spoke after Evert.[28] While he agreed that 'it would be desirable for us to have better supply of heavy guns and heavy shells', he was convinced that 'we could well attack'. He was not satisfied leaving the fighting to other fronts, and argued that they must strike the enemy every-where at the same time, 'so as to prevent him from using the advantage he has of acting along inside lines; with the result that, in spite of his numerical inferiority, he uses his railway system to move his troops from point to point as he pleases'. Therefore, he wanted permission to attack as well. 'Even supposing I obtained no success,' he added, 'I should not merely have pinned down the enemy forces opposed to me, but should also divert to myself part of the enemy reserves and thus appreciably lighten the task of Generals Kuropat-kin and Evert.'[29]

The shuffling silence that followed was palpable. Alekseev was as courteous as ever, but could not hide his surprise at such an upbeat assessment, remarking that he had no objection 'in principle' but felt bound to warn Brusilov that he would not receive any more men or guns than he already had. Brusilov shrugged. He 'asked for nothing' and would be 'satisfied with what I had'. Kuropatkin and Evert looked at each other, before suggesting that Southwest Front open the assault sometime in mid-May, with the other fronts following a fortnight later. This would mean that instead of making a relatively narrow attack along one sector, Russia would mount a series of attacks across almost the entire Eastern Front. This was agreed, and then the generals broke for dinner, with Kuropatkin coming up to Brusilov and tugging at his sleeve.

'You have only just been appointed Front Commander,' he said, 'and you are lucky enough not to be one of those picked out to take the offensive, and so aren't called upon like them to risk your military reputation . . . If I had been you, I would have done anything to be let off having to take the offensive; as things are at present, the only possible result of any such operations will be that you will break your neck, and it won't bring you any personal gain!'

Brusilov was unmoved. He did not seek personal gain, only the glory and good of Russia.[30]

The atmosphere at Mogilev was tense with speculation, whispered among some, that a conspiracy was brewing against the Tsar. He would be arrested quietly and forced to give up the throne before a dictator was appointed, possibly Alekseev, armed with the powers necessary to end the war and save Russia. But then the rumours would vanish into thin air; no one knew anything, and the Tsar continued his routines none the wiser. Mikhail Lemke, who was at *Stavka* that day, was sure it could be done, but doubted whether the conspirators would have the nerve to do so. 'At least we can say one thing for sure: it is unlikely to take place on the Northern or Western Fronts, because neither Kuropatkin nor Evert would agree to take any part in the conspiracy; it is improbable that Brusilov would do so as well, but he is smarter and more honest as a citizen, therefore, he can be convinced by others that the moment to save the country has come.' Lemke pondered on how the country would react to this. He knew that while getting rid of the Tsar was one thing, working out what would happen next and then controlling it was quite another. 'This entails an infinite series of questions and one can easily get lost in contradictions. And here we can find the weak point of the whole plan of the conspirators. For none of them could even imagine the diversity of attitudes of different classes and social groups towards everything that eventually will become the second act of the drama.' Perhaps none of this would be needed and Brusilov could take his chance on the battlefield?[31]

As Russia contemplated another push forward, Conrad was putting the finishing touches to his own attack, the biggest since the ill-fated 'Black-Yellow' offensive of the previous autumn. The first operation orders were issued as early as 6 February, with Archduke Eugen being ordered to mount an attack from South Tyrol into the enemy's rear. Eleventh Army, commanded by Viktor Dankl ('the hero of Krasnik'), would be reinforced to 14 divisions and 60 heavy batteries. Deployed between the Adige and the Sugana Valley, it would be ready to advance across the plateau from Folgaria and Lavarone to Thiene and Bassano.[32] It would be supported by Kövess's Third Army, which would then exploit the attack out of the mountains, driving on to seize Padua and in the process cutting the Italian Army in half. As ever, Conrad did not want for grand designs or ambitious manoeuvres, and he was insistent that this would be a decisive effort, a *Strafexpedition* ('punitive expedition'), aiming to knock Italy out of the war. At his headquarters in Teschen, he amended the maps to show what he meant: a straight line was drawn over the Isonzo front, a curve around South Tyrol, and then another line went directly across to the southeast, all the way to Venice.[33]

Archduke Eugen, the younger brother of Archduke Friedrich, was a popular figure in the army, a man of considerable military experience who had taken over command of the Balkans after Potiorek's disgrace in the winter of 1914. With the Italian declaration of war, he had been appointed the commander of an army group with responsibility for the Italian theatre, working alongside his Chief of Staff, Major-General Alfred Krauss. They had spent the next twelve months managing the regular movement of troops into and out of the line and dealing with the irascible General Boroević along the Isonzo. Both Eugen and Krauss were unimpressed by AOK's orders and saw reaching the Thiene–Bassano line as only a preliminary step in the operation. Moreover, they did not like the deployment of the two armies, one behind the other, and would have preferred them to operate alongside each other across a wider stretch of front, which would reduce the chance of dangerous flank attacks. Eugen warned that the rear army would 'only be able to intervene with great difficulty', and the inevitable result would be the mixing of formations and a confused chain of command.[34]

Another worry was the ebbing likelihood of gaining surprise. The date of the offensive had to be continually postponed because of the length of time it took to move men and guns into position, particularly the heavy artillery, which included enormous 42 cm siege howitzers. It snowed heavily throughout February and into March, with the Dolomites encased in deep drifts, leaving the mountain routes impassable and burdening the already creaking supply lines with hundreds of extra casualties, including those suffering from trips and falls, frostbite and exposure. On 11 March, the Chief of Artillery for Eleventh Army, Colonel Portenschlag, reported that some areas could only be reached by sled, and any sections that were shovelled clear were soon blanketed again by the falling snow. 'The snow in the trenches is over 13 feet deep', he complained. 'In these conditions, it is out of the question to think of carrying out work on constructing batteries or putting guns into position, etc. All visibility is obstructed by fog and blowing snow.'[35]

Realizing that surprise was probably already impossible, Conrad began ramping up the pressure on the Archduke, and inquired whether the army group's reluctance to set a date was solely due to the snow or perhaps to something else. The meticulous and careful Krauss, who was convinced that a premature attack would be suicidal, sent his staff officers to see the ground, and was distressed by what they told him:

> Any man who deviated from the path immediately sank up to his stomach in the snow. After a few steps, one was out of breath and unable to move. Under these conditions, any attack would certainly have become stuck in the snow and suffered heavy losses. Because all our reports were useless and fell on deaf ears, and because of the disastrous consequences if we were to have heeded one of the many orders that disregarded our reports and urged an early start to the attack, I asked the Chief of the General Staff to go himself or to send a confidant to convince them of our circumstances in person.[36]

Austria's climactic 'punishment expedition' was now plagued by ill-feeling, confusion and shifting priorities. Conrad was in no mood to haggle with Krauss and ordered him *not* to travel to Teschen, preferring instead to direct the campaign at arm's length through the two army commanders, Dankl and Kövess, whom he knew he could trust. Neither man liked Krauss, and both were only too willing to correspond directly with Conrad when they felt they needed anything. These difficulties were further aggravated by the presence of Archduke Karl, heir to the imperial throne, who had been given command of one of the assaulting corps, ostensibly to help his development as a military commander. At first Conrad refused to allow him anywhere near the battlefield, only to relent after the old Emperor insisted that he be given the appointment.[37]

Although Germany had not been informed officially of the *Straf-expedition*, it was not possible to keep word from spreading, and by early May, Falkenhayn was aware of the Austrian reinforcement of the Tyrol. Unimpressed by Conrad's willingness to go it alone, he sent August von Cramon to ask whether – in view of the poor weather and the inevitable lack of surprise – it might not be better to postpone the attack and redeploy Habsburg troops against Verdun. Conrad refused: it was too late, he replied, and it would take weeks to move his guns. Moreover, he maintained that attacking Italy was still the correct strategy and was confident that such a blow had the potential to end the war in a matter of weeks. In one of his letters to Falkenhayn, he had noted that 'There are situations in which, in the absence of anything better, an operation, even if difficult, must be carried out. On no other front can one find a position that lends itself, in the event of a successful offensive, to putting the enemy in a critical situation like South Tyrol on the Italian Front; and this precisely spurs us on to commit ourselves in this region.' It would be his final throw of the dice; his last great battle.[38]

As had been feared, the notable increase in Habsburg activity in the mountains inevitably found its way into Italian intelligence bulletins, but fortunately for Conrad, the Italian General Staff remained unconvinced that an attack was likely. General Robert Brusati, commander of First Army, which defended the bucolic, pine-crested border with Austria, grew concerned as reports landed on his desk of significant enemy concentrations. Information gleaned from deserters, foreign newspapers, rail movements and telephone intercepts began to create an alarming picture of a Habsburg build-up that might prove extremely dangerous. Brusati wrote to Cadorna on 22 March informing him that a decisive offensive from the Lavarone Plateau was to be expected within days, only for Cadorna to dismiss his concerns in his usual haughty manner. In a reply dated 6 April, he reminded Brusati that 'only a cold evaluation of events allows us to adequately deal with them, and that the same imperious calm that guides the command transfuses itself from above into the soul of everyone, engendering a great factor of success'.[39]

Notwithstanding Cadorna's belief that little was happening in the Tyrol, the intelligence picture continued to darken throughout the weeks that followed. On 26 April, a Czech deserter stumbled into Italian lines and confessed that a major assault was definitely being planned. When he was shown estimates of the number of Habsburg units that had been detected, he insisted they were too low. At least six corps were already in position, and every possible farmhouse and barn was packed with assault troops, waiting for the order to move out.[40] Still Cadorna refused to believe the Austrians were serious and dismissed the deserter's tale as disinformation. But the Czech was right. Despite the enormous challenges of operating in some of the most difficult terrain in Europe, Conrad had managed to amass 1,200 guns and 157,000 troops, including some of the best fighting divisions in the K.u.K., stripping the fronts on the Isonzo and in Galicia to give his forces a significant, if not overwhelming, advantage in the Tyrol.[41]

Beset by poor weather, it was not until 15 May that the 'punitive expedition' got under way. Habsburg guns pummelled Italian positions for four hours, the shelling increasing in intensity in the final moments before the infantry were ordered to move out. The spearhead would be delivered by Archduke Karl's XX Corps, striking southeast towards Mount Coston. The attackers, clad in their white winter cloaks, navigated the gaps in their barbed wire, and then marched – in places knee-deep in snow – towards the Italian positions. The artillery had done its work, smashing the forward trenches, splintering hundreds of pine trees that grew on the slopes, and leaving the garrison a shattered wreck. 'Italians lay huddled together, convulsing uncontrollably, weeping with nervous shock', reported 14 Infantry Regiment. 'Others hung about the necks of the storming troops, happy to have escaped this hell. Around them lay the richest loot of military paraphernalia: machine-guns, mortars, trench guns and many rifles. In the shelters, the countless types of uniform, scattered around the place in disarray, were testament to the shock and confusion that had descended upon the horrified enemy.'[42]

By the end of the day, the main Italian position had been broken.

Mount Coston fell, as did the peak at Costa d'Agra, with the Habsburgs poised to continue their advance and the defenders pulling back in disarray. Brusati had placed most of his infantry in the forward positions, in line with the offensive posture that Italian armies were encouraged to adopt, and they were soon overwhelmed, blown up by the murderous shellfire, taken prisoner in squalid huddles or shot down as they fled across the bloodied snow. It was a similar story the following day: the mass of Habsburg artillery, including 12 cm cannons and 15 cm siege howitzers, opened the way, swallowing up the Italian defences in churning clouds of dust and smoke, producing an effect that Conrad had long sought and allowing his infantry to seize more ground. The high point at Zugna Torta was reached, with two battalions climbing 'a labyrinth of rocks, ravines and crevices through the most intense enemy fire'. The men of the *Kaiserjäger* Regiment suffered only 50 casualties but took over 1,200 prisoners during their assault on Mount Maggio, a crucial objective that lay along the Italian border.[43]

At first the Habsburg advance seemed likely to fulfil Conrad's wildest dreams. By 19 May, Archduke Karl's XX Corps had taken over 6,000 prisoners and seized several crucial heights, including Mount Toraro, Mount Campomolon and Mount Melignone, which opened the way onto the Asiago Plateau below.[44] Although the attacks on the flanks had not advanced as far, lacking the powerful artillery support that had been given to the Archduke, the central punch had been delivered with a fighting spirit and commitment that had only rarely been shown in the Imperial and Royal Army since 1914. Conrad was delighted. 'Falkenhayn sent a warm telegram,' noted Cramon, 'to which Conrad replied just as warmly. Everything was bliss at Teschen.'[45] The Habsburg Chief of Staff was now poised to complete his primary task: to break the strength of Austria's last great rival and avenge the treachery of May 1915. If he could fight the Italians in the open, he was confident that he could beat them.

Conrad's opposite number, General Cadorna, now had an almighty battle on his hands. The mood at his headquarters at Udine was remarkably sanguine as news of the Austrian offensive came in. Far from panicking, he responded calmly and decisively to the enemy manoeuvre. Within just a few days, hundreds of trucks and horse-drawn wagons, accompanied by long columns of marching infantry, were flowing into the threatened sector, and a new army command (Fifth) had been established, which was mustered between Vicenza and Padua and would face Kövess's Third Army should it break out onto the Italian plain.[46] Such was the extent of the crisis that, on 24 May, Salandra, the Prime Minister, wrote to Cadorna and asked him to attend an emergency war council:

> The situation which has suddenly become so serious obliges the Government to fully acknowledge it in its causes, essential elements, and prospects. I therefore pray Your Excellency attend a meeting in which the four Army Commanders should also take part, and if Your Excellency would consider it, I would also deem appropriate His Excellency General Porro. The two military ministries and two other delegates of the Council of Ministers would deliberate with me. In this meeting, the military situation should be thoroughly examined in every aspect so that the Government can make it the basis of its other deliberations and assume the responsibility that belongs to it before Parliament and the country.[47]

Cadorna successfully held his ground. It was one of his great traits: he possessed a heart of burnished steel that could not be easily pushed around. Salandra wanted to meet in Padua (Udine was apparently too 'full of journalists'), but Cadorna refused to take part in this 'war council'. He would provide information but not get involved in any further discussions. If the King lacked confidence in him, then he should be dismissed, but Salandra recoiled in horror from this blunt ultimatum and shrank from the task of moving against his Chief of the General Staff, which would have required earnest petitions to the monarch. Instead, he sent an officer to Cadorna's headquarters to 'gather information'. Faith in Cadorna had not yet entirely been extinguished (there was, of course, the important question of who would replace him), and it seemed unwise to dispense with his services at such a time. Salandra wrote back the following day (25 May) with a not entirely convincing explanation that the Council of Ministers 'did not intend to convene a council of war' and it did not 'want to upset him in a moment of utmost gravity and urgency'.[48]

Cadorna was also fortunate that he could rely on more than the cowardice and uncertainty of Italian politicians. As was so typical of offensives during the war, the attackers found it more difficult than the defenders to bring reserves, guns and supplies forward, and the momentum that was so vital to the attack began ebbing away by late May. The high point came on 27 and 28 May, when the towns of Arsiero and Asiago fell, but by this time the battle was much more even, with Italian troops fighting hard for each scrap of ground. In what was a remarkable feat of improvisation and hard marching, by the time the Austrians were ready to push on, Fifth Army was waiting for them: 179,000 troops and over 35,000 horses, blocking the way to Padua and Venice.[49]

Back at Teschen, Conrad tried to bully his commanders, issuing the usual orders to advance without regard to cost, but his influence was already waning. The army could no longer be treated in the way it had been in 1914, and its leading commanders were notable in their determination to avoid unnecessary bloodshed, working hard to preserve the lives of their men through what had become an exhausting series of attacks over a wide, windswept expanse of mountain terrain that wore out their divisions extremely quickly. Archduke Karl, a conscientious and thoughtful man, devoted to his faith, warned his divisions against incurring excessive losses, and even Dankl, who had been given command of Eleventh Army because he knew Conrad well, was concerned about the time it was taking to move up its heavy artillery and mortars to support the second stage of the offensive. 'Despite the most intense pressure from the army command and the emphasis on the importance of as rapid an advance as possible', read one such report, 'the advance of the infantry could not be justified without adequate support in the form of several batteries pushing full steam ahead in the advance.'[50]

Waiting for the artillery to be redeployed might take weeks, and would only give the Italians more opportunity to dig in. Frustrated by the time-consuming process of fighting for every piece of high ground, which meant laboriously dragging the guns up and down, Krauss had suggested pushing the infantry as quickly as possible through the valleys, dealing with the mountain garrisons at leisure, but this was deemed too risky. With frustration boiling over, the Austrian commanders rapidly fell out with one another. Conrad thought Dankl had mismanaged the battle; Dankl blamed Krauss for not giving him enough artillery; Krauss blamed Conrad for not ordering an attack along the Isonzo to fix Italian reserves, while also excoriating Dankl for not following his idea about 'valley thrusts'. Such infighting was all the more bitter because success seemed to be there for the taking. The Austrians had lost somewhere close to 44,000 men, including 5,000 dead, in the push over the Dolomites, but had captured 47,000 prisoners and 318 guns, and were tantalizingly close to dealing Italy a potentially mortal blow.[51]

The *Strafexpedition* was in many ways a kind of early national trauma for Italy. Fighting on Austrian territory for Gorizia was one thing; seeing thousands of refugees leaving their homes and having to struggle to defend Italian soil so close to major population centres was quite another. Asiago was completely razed during the fighting, the first Italian town to suffer such a fate, which haunted all those involved and increased the pressure on Cadorna, whose reputation came under greater strain than ever before.[52] But he had survived long enough, and on 4 June the Russian Southwest Front went onto the offensive along a 250-mile front from the Pripet Marshes to the border of Romania, utilizing what seemed like overwhelming, devastating force. The 'punitive expedition' may already have been reaching its culmination, but other, larger matters would now force its swift abandonment. For Vienna, the greatest crisis of the war was about to begin.

12. 'The greatest crisis of the world war'

With Conrad's attention firmly fixed on the Trentino, the prospect of a new Russian offensive could not have come at a worse time. The warning signs had been there for weeks. Clouds of dust, movement behind the lines, the sounds of digging, Russian aircraft droning overhead – all pointed to a renewal of offensive activity in Galicia. Ever since Alekseev's New Year offensive had tailed off in January, this region had been quiet, a place where divisions came and went. The men in the trenches had got used to the wide-open skies of western Ukraine and the long, empty days of dust and work: repairing barbed wire, reinforcing parapets, bringing in supplies, all while trying to snatch precious moments of rest. In places, particularly where dense woodland meant that building material was plentiful, Habsburg troops 'devoted themselves to the beautification of their accommodation'. One officer noted that anyone who saw 'these lovely, clean wooden buildings with their small adjoining ornamental gardens could be forgiven for thinking they were in a coastal resort'. As one authority later put it, the troops had 'dug too much and exercised too little'.[1]

Ever since the conference at *Stavka*, the four armies of Brusilov's Southwest Front had been preparing for a new offensive, building shelters, narrowing the width of no-man's-land, and pushing out saps or shallow tunnels as close as possible to the Austrian lines. This was a crucial part of Brusilov's attempt to mislead and mystify his opponent, which had been confirmed in his orders to his army commanders, dated 18 April. 'The attack must be carried out on the entire Southwest Front in order to deprive the enemy of the opportunity to move all his forces towards one place and conceal the true direction of the main strike. To achieve this, each army and each corps must plan and prepare an attack on part of the enemy's fortified line . . .' The main blow would be delivered by Eighth Army towards Lutsk, the location that Brusilov deemed would be most helpful for General Evert's attack further north. The rest of his armies would concentrate on taking the positions 'currently occupied by the enemy'.[2]

Brusilov knew what he wanted to achieve and was confident that with skill and application his men could do it. In a thorough five-page order issued on 19 April, he laid down the tasks of the artillery and infantry, insisting on the closest combination of the two, which he believed would be crucial to any success.[3] With the bulk of Russian strength clustered in the Western and Northern Fronts, defending Moscow and Petrograd respectively, Southwest Front had only a narrow superiority of manpower: 40 infantry and 15 cavalry divisions faced off against 38.5 infantry and 11 cavalry divisions (mostly Austrian, with a handful of German units interspersed) – about 600,000 to 500,000 men respectively. Brusilov had an even more slender advantage in firepower: 1,770 field guns and 168 heavy against 1,301 light and 545 medium and heavier pieces in the Habsburg inventory. Given the dismal experience of both the New Year offensive and Lake Naroch, there seemed little chance that he would be able to avoid heavy losses for little gain.[4]

With both Kuropatkin and Evert requesting as much weight of fire as possible, Brusilov's plan for a wide-front attack was greeted with open scepticism at Mogilev. Torn with worry, Alekseev even telephoned Brusilov on the evening of 3 June – just hours before the attack was due to go in – and explained that he was 'rather dubious' about his plans for 'attacking the enemy simultaneously at many different points instead of delivering a single stroke with the united weight of all the men and guns'. He even suggested that it would be better to delay the offensive for a few days and redeploy his forces to 'select a single shock area'. Moreover, he had spoken to the Tsar, who also 'desired this change of plan'. But if Alekseev thought Brusilov might be tempted to abandon his preparations at such a late hour, he was mistaken. Brusilov refused, point-blank, showing the kind of self-confidence that was rare among the Tsarist officer class, which prioritized loyalty above all. He knew that his men were in their forward positions, ready to move out, and it was probable that artillery preparation was already under way, so he asked to be relieved of command. After sighing audibly down the telephone line, Alekseev

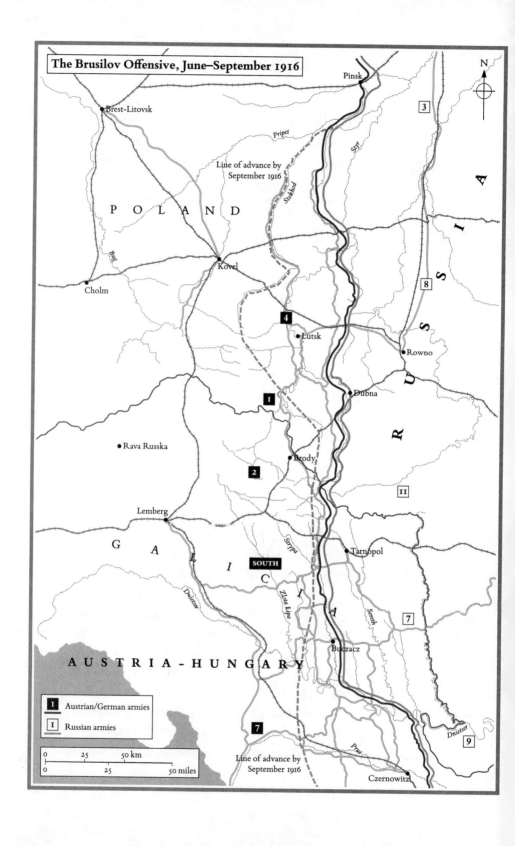

The Brusilov Offensive, June–September 1916

said that the Tsar had already gone to bed and could not be woken, only for Brusilov to snap back:

'The Commander-in-Chief's slumbers are no business of mine, and I have no intention of thinking anything over. I must ask for an immediate answer.'

'Well, God be with you!' Alekseev replied. 'Have it your own way! I will report our conversation to the Emperor to-morrow.'[5]

Brusilov would stand or fall by his decision. He issued his final orders at 1 a.m. on 4 June. Four armies, Eighth, Eleventh, Seventh and Ninth, would attack the Austrian lines from the marshy ground around Pinsk in the north to Czernowitz, close to the border with Romania. Although the assault was meant to be an 'auxiliary' operation, preventing the Central Powers from moving reserves to face Evert's main attack towards Vilnius (scheduled to take place on 10 or 11 June), there were a host of tempting objectives to aim for, including Lutsk, the transport hub of Kovel, Stanislau and even Lemberg. Brusilov eschewed any grander strategic objective for his attacks – they were merely to destroy the Austro-Hungarian forces in front of them (or so he claimed) – but he could not have been unaware of the possibilities for decisive manoeuvre should things go well. He would fight the battle from his headquarters at Berdichev, about ninety miles southwest of Kiev. There, in 'a small white-washed room, furnished only with a table and a few chairs, and the inevitable maps spread on walls and work-tables', he got to work, every so often getting up and looking out of the window at an endless sweep of wheat fields swaying gently in the breeze, 'like the expanse of the sea'.[6]

Russian artillery opened fire at 4.30 on the morning of 4 June, with field artillery opening breaches in the barbed wire while the heavier guns and howitzers concentrated on demolishing the first line of trenches and then searching out enemy batteries. This type of bombardment might not have been as intense as the furious 'drumfire' that preceded German assaults, but its power and accuracy were deeply frightening; even hardened veterans had only rarely been under such sustained shellfire. 'The Russian artillery fire continued all morning with increasing intensity', recorded one Habsburg account. 'At times it sounded like heavy railroad trains crashing into each other at roaring speed. There was a wild raging, rumbling, crashing and splintering that shook you to your very soul. Towards noon, the terrible fire subsided a little, only to swell again to the greatest intensity in the afternoon, and especially towards the evening.'[7] As the day wore on, a series of patrols were sent in to test the strength of the defences, with the artillery continuing to fire for most of the afternoon, slackening every now and again, and inevitably provoking counter-bombardments, before numerous battalion-sized attacks were launched. Most of these were beaten off by machine-gun fire, but the damage had been extensive. Across long sections of the front, telephone connections had been severed, front trenches blown in and buried in sand and dirt, with sections of barbed wire tossed aside. Moreover, reports brought in by aerial reconnaissance of columns of reserves moving up to the front from multiple directions hinted at further attacks over the coming days and provoked a scramble to repair the damage overnight. But this made little impact at AOK, where nothing was allowed to interfere with the sixtieth-birthday celebrations of the Commander-in-Chief, Archduke Friedrich, which included a torchlight procession and many toasts to the health of the Emperor.[8]

The events of the following week would kill off any lingering complacency in Vienna about how precarious the situation was. Brusilov's main assault, delivered by Eighth Army towards Lutsk, came on the second day, 5 June. In the line was the Austrian Fourth Army, commanded by Archduke Joseph Ferdinand, the 44-year-old son of the last Grand Duke of Tuscany, who had replaced Auffenberg as army commander in September 1914. Nothing had prepared him for the violence and power that would be unleashed against his forces. Harassing fire had been falling all night, but the shelling began to increase in volume shortly before 9 a.m., with the explosions raising a great curtain of debris and smoke over the trenches and causing the air to howl and shriek as shells passed overhead. Seeing the effects of the bombardment and knowing that they were facing the Austrians buoyed the mood of the Russian attackers. As one company commander noted, a sigh of relief went around the trenches when they saw the 'familiar pink haze' that Austrian shells tended to give off.[9]

Up and down the front, Habsburg regiments quickly found

themselves isolated and disoriented, fighting against an enemy that seemed to be upon them as soon as the barrage lifted. In the line at Olyka, a village twenty miles east of Lutsk, 2nd Infantry Division was swamped by an entire Russian corps, which took advantage of the dust and smoke to take most of the garrison prisoner. In the forward trenches was 82 Infantry Regiment, which was almost destroyed in a matter of minutes, with only 718 survivors out of a full strength of 5,330 men. The first news of its fate came from an out-of-breath runner, who told a supporting battalion that the enemy had broken through the first position. 'We climbed out of the parapet and actually saw the earth-coloured hats of the Russians by the trench in front of us', remembered one witness. 'To our shock and bewilderment, there was nothing left of 82 Infantry Regiment. It had suddenly disappeared, as though the gaping ground had swallowed it up with a single gulp. There was not a cap to be seen.'[10]

Disaster now began to spread across the front like a seeping, spreading oil stain. Regiment after regiment crumbled under the pressure of Brusilov's multiple, divergent thrusts. At the southern edge of the attacking zone, General Platon Lechitsky's Ninth Army threw everything it had at the Habsburg Seventh Army. Carefully observed artillery fire demolished the Austrian positions during the morning, and then cylinders of gas were transported up to the front and let off, further contributing to the sense of disorder and panic in the sand-blown trenches. That day, Ninth Army penetrated south of the Dniester and gained about five kilometres of ground. It quickly became evident that once the first position had been taken, there were few well-prepared defensive lines for the Austrians to fall back on. Germany had already learnt on the Western Front that no matter how strong the first line, it could always be breached, so what was required was a deeper defensive zone, consisting of two or more lines sprinkled with mutually supporting strongpoints that would exhaust an attacker the further they advanced. Conventional wisdom in the Imperial and Royal Army was that the first line must be as strong as possible – and it usually was, consisting of three rows of heavily fortified trenches and shelters, protected by thick belts of barbed wire staked deeply into the ground. But once this was taken, the rearward positions were much less well prepared. As one of the leading artillery commanders in the Russian Southwest Front told his men, 'Once you have broken through, the front will roll on and on!'[11]

With the main Austrian position broken, the Russian attack surged forward, continuing to take vast numbers of prisoners and exploit the yawning gaps that began to open up right across the front. The city of Lutsk was captured on 7 June, with the Austrians in headlong retreat, crossing the Strypa river in long, disordered columns. Major-General Nikolai Stogov, Quartermaster-General of Eighth Army, was astonished by what he found. 'A crowd of unarmed Austrian soldiers from various units fled in panic through Lutsk, leaving everything behind. Many prisoners testified that they were ordered to drop everything except their weapons to ease the retreat, but in fact they often got rid of weapons first of all ... Officers of the defeated Austrian regiments were also greatly demoralised: many prisoners reported that their officers were among the first ones to flee to the rear, leaving NCOs to take care of the soldiers.'[12]

Within just six days of fighting, the Austrian Fourth Army had collapsed, losing 82,000 men out of a total strength of 110,000, at least half of whom were prisoners. The army commander, Joseph Ferdinand, was relieved on 7 June, an inevitable scapegoat whom not even the Emperor would save. A huge gap of fifteen kilometres had opened up between Fourth Army and the forces on its right, with General Aleksei Kaledin's Eighth Army poised to continue its drive westwards, exploiting this opening with as much cavalry as could be mustered. Local counter-attacks were thrown in, but they did little to stem the advance, with Habsburg forces suffering from what seemed like a terminal decline in morale. They simply did not believe they could fight and win any more, with officers finding it increasingly difficult to corral their men forward into what seemed like a dangerous vortex. Unless something changed, the Habsburg Empire would be on the brink of total and irredeemable collapse.[13]

Faced with what he called 'the greatest crisis of the world war', Conrad blamed everyone but himself.[14] When his wife, Gina (they had finally married in October 1915), returned to Teschen from

Vienna on the day Lutsk fell, she found him 'in the deepest depression': sunk in his chair, staring blankly at the wall. He cited a 'fateful combination' of factors against him: Russia had learnt much from the attack at Gorlice–Tarnów in May 1915; Archduke Joseph Ferdinand had spent too much time hunting; and he had been misled by the Germans on the strength of their defences. 'Above all,' she wrote, 'he complained that Stolzmann, the Chief of Staff of Linsingen's [South] Army, had repeatedly assured him in response to his constant inquiries about the situation on the front: "Your Excellency, we have an impenetrable wall up there." The long silence on this field of battle had led us into a false sense of security, for which Archduke Joseph Ferdinand was also to blame.' There was only one thing to do. 'I have to go to Falkenhayn right away', he said. 'I have to ask for troops.'[15]

A meeting was arranged in Berlin on 8 June. Much as it pained him to go, Conrad had no choice but to make the long rail journey north to meet Falkenhayn, who he knew would be determined to drive a hard bargain. Major Kundmann, who accompanied him, remembered how the 'boss doesn't have it in him to speak forcibly with Falkenhayn, always like the naughty schoolboy towards the teacher upbraiding him'. At one point, Kundmann came into the meeting to see Conrad with 'his head between hands . . . staring at the map'.[16] Falkenhayn agreed that support must be given, and signed off on the deployment of five divisions to Linsingen's army group, including three taken from the Western Front, which would be employed in a counter-offensive around Kovel. In return, he insisted that the *Strafexpedition* be wound down and all available Austrian reserves and heavy artillery ('the importance of which for unreliable troops is well known') be withdrawn from the Tyrol as soon as possible. Moreover, he moved swiftly to assert control of key positions within the Habsburg armed forces. Hans von Seeckt, who had formerly served with Mackensen, was appointed Chief of Staff at Seventh Army, a crucial position that would effectively hand over command of one of Conrad's armies to OHL. Falkenhayn would have liked to go further, but Conrad's pleas as to the sensitivity of such matters in Vienna prevailed, albeit with a sour warning that there 'must be no repetition of these occurrences'.[17]

The situation at the front seemed to worsen every day. General Pflanzer-Baltin's Seventh Army had little choice but to make a full-scale retreat on 10 June, with its scattered forces falling back south of the Dniester towards the Carpathian passes, while Conrad desperately tried to prevent them from losing touch with the rest of his forces, ordering them to retreat to the west instead. But diverting the troops in the 'right' direction was simply not possible. Supply routes were choked with guns and horse-drawn wagons; men were streaming away from the front in a haze, lacking officers, looking balefully at the eastern horizon obscured by plumes of dark smoke. In two weeks of heavy fighting, Seventh Army lost a total of 133,600 men – more than half its strength. The Russians had now punched a hole through the Habsburg lines in places up to sixty kilometres deep (along a front of around ninety kilometres) as they closed on Czernowitz, which would be an ideal springboard to cross Bukhovina, and then through the mountain passes onto the Hungarian Plain.[18]

Discussions over unified command went on. On 12 June, Falkenhayn suggested placing Mackensen – a man 'whose name meant something' – in charge of the entire Austrian half of the Eastern Front, from the Pripet Marshes to the Dniester, but Conrad refused. This would impose severe limitations upon AOK, which had to fight in other theatres, and in any case providing 'the greatest possible number of troops' was the most important thing, not the name of the commander. Mackensen might, Conrad responded, take charge of a new army group at the southernmost point of the Eastern Front, including the battered Seventh Army, but this was summarily rejected by Falkenhayn. 'Only if Mackensen commands the entire front, in which the really powerful parts are predominantly German, does he have sufficient freedom to determine the deferral and use of power in such a serious situation, putting an end to the dragging dispute between His Excellency von Conrad and myself . . .'[19]

The full extent of Austrian demoralization became apparent as soon as Seeckt arrived at Seventh Army headquarters. He wired an assessment of the situation on 15 June, warning Falkenhayn that holding on to their positions would not be easy. 'The first impression of the situation of Seventh Army is that their task of covering and blocking the area between the Prut and Dniester, including Czernowitz's access to Hungary, is extremely difficult with the forces available. There have been very heavy losses. Above all, however, the position of a great number of units seems unreliable. The artillery is far inferior to that of the Russians. We will try everything to hold on to the positions now occupied, but since all the leaders in the rear have already been given positions and all commands are already expecting a further retreat, success is doubtful.' Falkenhayn read the note with growing alarm. 'The situation with Seventh Army is certainly difficult', he replied. 'If that were not the case, you would not have been called there.' The main problem was a failure of leadership. 'Your most important role', he told Seeckt, 'will be to intervene in this matter with ruthless vigour, and to force Teschen to transfer sufficient artillery from the Tyrol front. Not one foot of the ground should be abandoned without direct orders.'[20]

The counter-attack around Kovel went in on 16 June. It was a difficult engagement. German divisions had only just arrived, and in many cases went into action without all their artillery. Both sides had little idea where their opponents were: the front was obscured by dust and smoke, aerial reconnaissance could not help, and thunderstorms and heavy downpours inundated the battlefield, causing rivers to rise and muddy tracks to become treacherous or disappear entirely.[21] Regiments blundered into each other, engaging in a series of swirling battles that were extremely difficult to control. 'I am in the midst of a battle . . .' reported General Georg von der Marwitz, whose corps was designated as the spearhead on 16 June. 'The roads are destroyed, unusable by car, and the distances are so great that it would take all day to travel on horseback, so one would have no effect whatsoever. So there is nothing left to do but to stay on the telephone line at headquarters.'[22]

Instead of smashing into an enemy ripe for a counter-offensive, German and Austrian units had become stuck in fierce positional warfare, with nine Russian corps, strung out in a half-circle around Lutsk, defending stoutly. The Habsburg First Army, which had attacked along the southern rim of the Russian positions, had been driven back to its starting lines; Fourth Army had even struggled to hold its own trenches; and General Marwitz's forces, in the centre, had not progressed far at all. Yet the intensity of the fighting was a powerful reminder that time was running out for the Southwest Front. With German divisions arriving in increasing numbers, Brusilov was no longer facing a demoralized and scattered opponent. He was also struggling for ammunition, particularly rifle cartridges, which were being expended at an astronomical rate. His forces were firing off 3.5 million rounds per day, but only 3 million were arriving from their depots, and this would reduce significantly in late June.[23]

At Berdichev, the general looked anxiously to the north, urging *Stavka* to make its main assault as soon as possible, but General Evert, whose Western Front was primed to attack towards Vilnius, was not going to be rushed. He had spent weeks accumulating as much artillery and ammunition as possible, haggling with Mogilev over more supplies because he did not like the ground. Nor did he rate his chances without a truly punishing preliminary bombardment. He told Alekseev that any attack would likely only make 'very slow progress with the greatest of difficulty', such was the strength of the defences he was facing. By early June, he had amassed about two thirds of the entire inventory of Russia's heavy guns, but still he vacillated, pondering on which sector to attack and whether his projected offensive towards Vilnius should be switched further south. As a Soviet analyst later noted, 'Evert made use of telegraph more than any other front commander. He prepared all operations in the most thorough manner, interfering with the work of army and corps commanders and scrutinising all the details, yet he did not dare attack.'[24]

Communicating with his front commanders via the Hughes telegraph machine at *Stavka*, Alekseev fought a strange, disconnected war. Already he was having second thoughts about unleashing the main assault so far north, and he had been sending reserves south as quickly as he could, shifting forces from his right to his left while all the time trying to keep the Germans guessing. On 9 June, he ordered Brusilov to concentrate on his right flank, trying to cut the Austrians off from the San river, while sanctioning a delay in Evert's main attack. Every day he would pore over reports from the front, and on 16 June – the day of Marwitz's counter-attack – he cancelled the

Vilnius operation, ordering a new attack that would shield Brusilov's right flank around Pinsk. But with more cold weather blowing in, causing water to rise in the Pripet Marshes, the attack was switched back seventy miles north to *Stavka*'s old home at Baranovichi, where the ground was drier, and which was defended by an Austrian corps – an obvious weak spot – even if it did provoke howls of protest from Brusilov.[25]

With his own armies forced into a temporary halt, the commander of Southwest Front wrote to Alekseev on 18 June, imploring him to order Evert to attack on schedule:

> The refusal of the Commander-in-Chief of the Western Front to attack the enemy on 4 June puts the front entrusted to me in an extremely dangerous position, and it may turn out that the battle we had won will become a defeat. We shall leave no stone unturned, but there is a limit to human capabilities. The losses are significant, and the reinforcements made up of young, unseasoned soldiers, as well as the loss of experienced combat officers, inevitably reduces the quality of the troops. I am an optimist rather than a pessimist by nature, but I must admit that the situation is difficult to say the least. The troops cannot understand – and, of course, it is impossible to explain the situation to them – why the other fronts remain inactive, and I have already received two anonymous letters with a warning that General Evert is supposedly a German and a traitor, and that we will be abandoned in order for the war to be lost.

Brusilov warned that most of his shells and ammunition had already been expended, and that it was essential his forces were either supported in a timely fashion or resupplied with everything they needed. 'I repeat that I shall not complain, nor shall I lose heart, and I know for certain that the troops will fight selflessly, but there are certain limits that cannot be crossed, and I consider it a duty of my conscience, and the oath of allegiance I have pledged to His Majesty the Emperor, to explain to you the situation we are in through no fault of our own.'[26]

Alekseev tried to soothe his fears, writing to him on 22 June and noting that 'Of course, the delay in taking the offensive on the

Western Front is disadvantageous in the overall course of our affairs . . . The reason the Germans pay such exceptional attention to you is your decisive success, which turned the general state of affairs in our favour, and the movement of part of your forces towards the weakest and most vital direction for the enemy. It does not matter if the Western Front would have carried out an attack or not; the enemy is forced to throw his forces against you, otherwise he puts himself at great risk.'[27] His defensiveness was understandable. Brusilov would later claim that Alekseev had not felt able to handle Evert and Kuropatkin more firmly because he had served under them in Manchuria, 'so he always did what he could to cover up their lack of initiative'. The truth was that both men had been tormented by the slaughter at Lake Naroch and saw no reason to rush into another dangerous engagement without doing everything they could to ensure success. Alekseev understood this, so tried to make the best of things, sending reserves to Brusilov while at the same time nudging Evert on.[28]

The danger of attacking without thorough preparation became evident on 2 July, when Evert's attack finally took place. A powerful artillery bombardment had rained shells on a narrow sector of the front north of Baranovichi for most of the day. Then massed infantry assaults went in like waves washing against the shore, with Russian troops showing their usual willingness to advance into the deadly fire-swept zone. This time, however, the artillery had not been able to destroy, or even seriously damage, the trenches, and Evert's worst fears – that the slaughter of Lake Naroch would be repeated – were realized. 'Russian infantrymen crept carefully and cautiously here and there', recorded a German account. 'Drumfire had been rattling our positions since 1:40 in the morning. Then, at least one division . . . advanced in vast numbers to attack. They surged forward in great dense waves, shoulder to shoulder. But the attacks shattered and splintered in the defensive fire in front of the barriers'.[29]

Whatever numerical superiority the Russians possessed was soon squandered in close-order attacks that achieved nothing. Aerial observation was poor, the artillery was unable to silence the machine-guns that commanded the front, and communication broke down, leaving senior officers in the dark about the extent of the disaster.

Casualties were horrific. In one sector, the defenders counted over 2,600 dead, the bodies strewn in front of the trenches, their brown cloth uniforms bleached almost white in the sunshine. Yet again, a Russian commander had overseen a heartrending slaughter and been unable to achieve more than a few temporary, localized break-throughs. General Alexander Ragoza, whose Fourth Army had made the attack, was unsurprised at the failure, later telling the British Military Attaché, Alfred Knox, that he blamed *Stavka* for the 'lack of a properly-thought-out plan, and for lack of character to stick to a plan whether good or bad'. Deeply opposed to changing objectives at such short notice, he had written to Evert on 16 June and complained about the 'colossal physical and moral stress' of months of tireless effort, warning him that he needed at least one month to prepare for a new attack, 'otherwise the operation is doomed to failure'. But he was ignored.[30]

The main Russian offensive may have been blunted, but the magnitude of events in Galicia inevitably affected the strategic independence of the Dual Monarchy. The *Strafexpedition* was the first casualty. As early as 10 June, Conrad had ordered two divisions to be withdrawn from the Tyrol, alongside their heavy artillery, and informed Archduke Eugen that he must look to what long-term defensive line they should occupy. This was followed a week later by a final order from AOK confirming that two more divisions were to leave and all remaining forces would go onto the defensive. Eugen issued a suitably solemn order of the day to his troops: 'Just as, after a short period of preparation, you were about to strike a new blow that would destroy the last enemy positions in the mountains and completely clear the way into the plain – I had to tell you, with a heavy heart, to cease. The many troops that the enemy had hastily drafted against you from across the globe would not have hindered your course of victory. However, greater consideration demanded this sacrifice from us, so that the borders of our great Fatherland could be better defended elsewhere.'[31]

Protecting that Fatherland was now the overriding priority as the Austro-Hungarian Empire faced the prospect of collapse and defeat, or at least ignominious subordination to Berlin. On 23 June, Count Burián demanded 'a full and clear insight' into the military situation, sending Conrad a barrage of questions on likely Russian movements and the state of Habsburg forces. At the same time, the Austrian Prime Minister, Karl Stürgkh, and his counterpart in Budapest, Count Tisza, joined Burián in complaining to the Emperor about the lack of information they received from the military command. Franz Joseph agreed that they should be given anything they wanted and informed Archduke Friedrich that Conrad must comply with their wishes. More demeaning still was having to read through sharply worded telegrams from Burián. 'At the present moment when the war has reached its high point, or at least appears to be reaching it,' the Foreign Minister wrote on 7 July, 'and the development of military events can possibly lead to a decision, the directors of foreign policy need a continual and detailed orientation on the war situation more urgently than before.' Conrad was now to send 'full appraisals' to Vienna and Budapest.[32]

Despite his obvious ascendancy over Conrad, Falkenhayn also trod a delicate path, only too aware of the growing opposition to his command. Like Conrad, he was weakened by his previous strategic choices, particularly the blood-soaked Battle of Verdun, which had become indelibly associated with his name. Originally intended to 'bleed white' the French Army, Verdun had mutated into a quagmire, where blood was being shed on both sides in gargantuan quantities. Moreover, the Anglo-French attack on the Somme, which began on 1 July, would cause another 429,000 German casualties by the time it was called off in late November.[33] Although the Entente sustained heavy losses in both these engagements, which would strain its armies almost to breaking point, it at least had the benefit of superior numbers, and could afford to fight a 'material battle' (*Materialschlacht*), employing increasing numbers of guns, shells and (from September) armoured vehicles in the form of 'tanks'.

Falkenhayn had always been a secretive individual, keen to keep crucial intelligence within a very small circle of trusted acolytes, but the reality of Germany's position could no longer be denied. The numerical superiority of the Entente on the Western Front was clear.

Combined, the British, French and Belgian armies could deploy 150 divisions against 125 German ones. On the Eastern Front, where the enemy's manpower superiority was even more marked, Germany's 48 divisions and Austria's 42 were faced by some 141 Russian divisions. Most Russian units were also big, consisting of 16 battalions, which comfortably outnumbered their counterparts (Austrian divisions contained 12 battalions and German divisions now only possessed 9). Although Austria had another 35 divisions on the Italian Front, they were also outnumbered (against 53). It was, therefore, becoming clear that the Central Powers had to coordinate their actions more effectively, using resources in a more efficient manner without the distractions or adventures of the kind to which Conrad was prone.[34]

The subject of unified command bubbled away throughout the summer, gaining in urgency with every Russian advance. It was now part of a complex and ever-moving political game played out between Berlin, Pless, Teschen and Vienna. From Pless's perspective, the dangerous unreliability and independence of the Habsburg Empire needed to be curbed and brought into closer alignment with Germany's war effort. But Falkenhayn (and the Kaiser) realized that the creation of a new, strengthened position on the Eastern Front would probably reduce OHL's authority, with Hindenburg and Ludendorff being the likely beneficiaries. As for Conrad, he resisted the encroachment of German influence over Habsburg armies as much as he could, but found himself bypassed by politicians at home, who increasingly saw German control as not only inevitable, but also necessary for the survival of the empire in any recognizable form. On 23 July, Julius Andrássy, opposition leader in Hungary, travelled to Berlin to speak to Bethmann Hollweg, and told him bluntly that Hindenburg must be appointed Supreme Commander on the Eastern Front 'otherwise the Danube Monarchy would lose the war'.[35]

A meeting was held at Pless on 27 July, with most of the leading figures from both empires present. They sat around a large table, trying to resolve the competing interests and frustrations of a war that was forcing the two powers closer together. The Kaiser was 'visibly nervous and impatient', wanting to push for a solution but loath to place more power in Hindenburg's hands. Falkenhayn, who should have been in attendance, cried off, blaming toothache, leaving a decision to be taken without him. After tortuous negotiations, a compromise was hammered out that extended German control but was not too destructive of Austrian independence. Hindenburg would take charge of all forces on the Eastern Front from the Baltic down to Lemberg, leaving a 200-mile section of the front under Austro-Hungarian control. This would be overseen by a new army group commanded by Archduke Karl. Furthermore, Hindenburg would be subordinate to the German High Command and would only issue orders to those forces south of the Pripet Marshes after they had been agreed with Teschen. The reorganization would come into effect from 1 August.[36]

The meeting at Pless had an unsatisfactory, unfinished air about it, as if it was only a precursor to wider, more substantive changes. Those who had pressed for a single command across the entire front – Bethmann Hollweg and Ludendorff primarily – were left disappointed. Max Hoffmann noted that the agreements made at Pless were 'half-measures', albeit an improvement on the current situation.[37] Conrad must have been expecting the worst, but came away from the meeting with some scrap of pride left. Archduke Karl's army group and the forces in Italy and the Balkans would remain under AOK's orders, albeit with one significant caveat: the Germans had insisted on appointing Hans von Seeckt as Karl's Chief of Staff, again ensuring that Austria's main army group would be under the de facto command of a reliable German officer. As for Hindenburg, the old soldier (he was now 68 years of age) took things in his stride. He said little at the meeting, with Ludendorff doing most of the talking, emphasizing the urgent need for a Supreme Commander in the east and more reinforcements to ward off what was coming. 'It was clear that the Russians were gathering strength for another mighty blow', remembered Ludendorff. 'Storms were threatening, and our nerves were strung to the highest pitch.'[38]

Throughout July, as the Central Powers struggled to work out new command arrangements, Brusilov's armies continued to advance. In the south, Ninth Army had punched a great hole in the Austrian lines, driving over the Dniester, taking Czernowitz and Kolomea and pushing the scattered forces back to the approaches of the Carpathians. Despite these successes, Brusilov's focus remained on his right flank, and the operation in the south would now be consigned to a secondary importance, much to AOK's relief. He was convinced that if he could take the city of Kovel, with its crucial rail and road junctions, the enemy line could be rolled up, making another sizeable retreat almost inevitable and allowing the main attack along the Western Front to be resumed. After halting his armies in mid-July, Brusilov prepared to launch this assault before the end of the month, using the time to resupply and incorporate reinforcements in the form of the so-called 'Special Army', which consisted of the pride of the Russian military, I and II Corps of the Imperial Guard. Their commander, Lieutenant-General Vladimir Bezobrazov, was an old favourite of the Tsar and knew how much depended upon his men. 'Our goal is to open by fire and bayonet a road to Kovel and thus liberate, since immemorial times, Russian soil from an invasion of aliens', read an order of the day issued shortly before the attack. 'Your ancient flags and standards, bearers of the glory of your ancestors, will watch proudly your acts of heroism . . . Forward for the Tsar and Motherland.'[39]

Kovel was now a heavily defended fortress, swarming with reinforcements. Already sizeable reserves were beginning to arrive from the Western Front, including the veteran German X Corps, which was charged with defending the southeastern approaches to the city. Any attack would also have to cross the Stokhod river, which ran parallel to the front lines about twenty-five miles east of Kovel. German and Austrian forces had blown the bridges over the river and settled down into a series of strong defensive positions along the far bank, where they waited for the inevitable assault. The Stokhod was not a particularly wide body of water, but it was surrounded by marshes, swamps and tangled undergrowth, which made manoeuvring difficult and reduced the ability of Russian forces to bring their artillery to bear. When a Guards officer arrived at the front, he was dismayed by what he found. 'It was with sadness and bewilderment', he recalled, 'that we observed the terrain over which we would have to move during the forthcoming attack. First, we had to cross the strip of the Sukhodol marshes, open and flat, like the palm of a hand, then cut across the river, beyond which were wooded and swampy passages of land that stretched all the way to Kovel and could be easily defended by small forces with a sufficient number of machine guns and artillery.'[40]

As if mimicking the shifting fortunes of war, the weather became changeable in late July, with sweltering sunshine replaced by heavy downpours and thunderstorms that rolled over the plains. After weeks of skirmishing, Brusilov launched his offensive on 28 July. Third Army struck from the north, Special Army from the centre and Eighth Army from the south. Despite the numerical superiority of Russian forces (about 250,000 to 115,000), they would be fighting blind. A tethered balloon was sent up, but it was soon shot down, and when a biplane undertook a reconnaissance sortie over the river valley, it was immediately attacked by three German aircraft, which sent it hurtling to the ground. Without the ability to see behind enemy lines, the artillery bombardment was scattered, with the dugouts that dotted the German and Austrian positions coming as a terrible surprise when the Russian infantry attacked. In places, usually when they came up against Austrian divisions, they got through; but elsewhere, German machine-gun teams and their supporting artillery proved highly effective at destroying crossing points, interfering with the movement of reserves and shattering the attacks in no-man's-land.[41]

The Special Army fought as well as could have been expected. Bezobrazov watched through his field glasses as his beloved divisions went forward, the men splashing through the water, often knee-deep, before disappearing across the Stokhod with the sky pockmarked by smoke and shell bursts. 'The 1st Guards Infantry Corps ran into heavy resistance at the village of Raimesto', he recalled. 'The 2nd Guards Infantry Corps began advancing successfully and the Imperial Rifles captured by surprise an entire enemy headquarters.' Eight thousand prisoners were taken, alongside scores of machine-guns, with Bezobrazov ordering his local reserves forward while petitioning Brusilov to give him another corps to exploit the attack. The main reserve unit, the Siberian Corps, had already been assigned to a neighbouring army, and Brusilov could only shrug his shoulders at Bezobrazov's increasingly frantic requests. By 30 July, the Guards had come to a standstill. 'Around Vitonezh cruel fighting lasted all night', noted the general; 'the village changed hands several times, bayonet fighting went on in the streets, but we could not hold the place because enemy reserves constantly came in from the Kovel railroad junction.'[42]

The Special Army continued to mount attacks into August, but it could not take Kovel. The familiar picture of increasing losses, supply difficulties and faltering morale left Brusilov disconsolate and irritable. He blamed Evert and Kuropatkin for leaving him isolated, and Alekseev for failing to provide direction to their efforts. 'We had no real Supreme Commander-in-Chief,' he complained, 'and his Chief of Staff, in spite of his intelligence and knowledge, had no real personality.' He was also furious with Bezobrazov and would demand his removal within weeks, complaining that his staff work had not been good enough and the attacks had failed 'owing to the bad artillery direction'. He was particularly unimpressed by the officers who had commanded the guns in the Special Army. 'War is different work from living in a hotel', he told Knox, who was visiting Berdichev. 'The artillery was directed as it might have been after two days of war instead of after two years.' When Knox remarked that it was unfortunate that the Guards had been sent through a marsh, Brusilov replied sharply, his eyes bearing down on him, 'There are marshes everywhere.'[43]

Brusilov's anger was understandable. A battle that had started out so well was now descending into recriminations and all too predictable ill-feeling. Bezobrazov was dismissed in late August after being told that the troops had 'lost trust' in him; a claim that he rejected, blaming instead Alekseev and Brusilov for not giving him enough reserves and for allowing his attack to go unexploited.[44] It was an all too familiar story for the Russian Army: making a breach and then being unable to press its advantage, leaving the men more disheartened than ever. There was something desperately poignant about the efforts of the Imperial Guard in the swamps of the Stokhod. The dead were everywhere: lined up in rows, often when hit by a stream of machine-gun fire; bodies blown to pieces and tumbled into shell holes; or floating bloated and white in a river that ran red with blood. Even worse was the sight at night, as Russian scouts crawled through the undergrowth searching for survivors. 'Many abandoned corpses, covered with tall marsh grass, lay scattered throughout the swampy valley', reported one regimental history. 'They spread a sour, sweet-ish smell of decay, which was especially distinctive in the evenings. On dark nights, wandering phosphorescent lights often appeared over the swamp, making the soldiers feel superstitious.'[45] It was an omen of ill fortune. Tsarist Russia had made its last great charge.

13. 'This means the end of the war!'

The battered city of Gorizia fell on 9 August 1916. That day squadrons of Italian cavalry trotted through its dusty streets, now littered with fallen masonry and abandoned pieces of equipment, giving General Cadorna a first tangible victory. He had not been slow to profit from the Russian offensive, and with the noticeable slackening of pressure in the Trentino in early June, he dissolved Fifth Army and redeployed thousands of troops and guns back to the Isonzo, determined to strike while Vienna's attention was elsewhere. They would go when the weather was fine, with the Duke of Aosta's Third Army mounting attacks against the three great bastions that defended Gorizia: Mount Sabotino, Podgora, and Mount San Michele. To allay suspicions, Cadorna did not return to his headquarters at Udine, but remained on the Alpine front, touring the ground, inspecting units and meeting with the Prime Minister, which he made sure was well covered in the press. At the same time, rumours were spread that preparations along the Isonzo were a ruse and that the main operation would be conducted on the Asiago, towards Val Sugana.[1]

Cadorna's critics would always decry him as an out-of-date warrior, a headstrong opponent of tactical innovation, but the Italian general worked hard to forge his army into a better fighting instrument. Tactical regulations were regularly updated with the latest information from the front as well as best practice taken from other armies, particularly the French, with Cadorna keen to profit from the experience of previous offensives.[2] In July 1916, he issued 'Criteria for the Use of Infantry in Trench Warfare', a new document that provided the framework for how offensives should be conducted in future. 'Infantry must not be sent into the attack without sufficient preparation.' Attacks required 'scrupulous reconnaissance of the territory and enemy lines, and a complete, detailed plan which assigns specific responsibilities and objectives to each unit engaged in the action'. Cadorna recommended that battalions organize their companies into a series of 'waves', which would advance onto successive objectives, mounting new attacks only after the guns had been brought forward and the barbed wire and trenches destroyed. 'The final objective is the destruction of the enemy; the conquest of his positions is not an end in itself.'[3]

Cadorna's new doctrine, based on meticulous preparation and overwhelming firepower, would be tested in what became the Sixth Battle of the Isonzo. The preliminary bombardment began on the morning of 6 August, and carefully coordinated shelling by 1,188 guns, thickened up by the fire of 774 trench mortars, known as *bombardes*, lasted all day, leaving Gorizia obscured by 'a huge greyish brown wall of smoke, from which there came a constant thunderous rumbling and lightning flashes from the impact and explosions of countless grenades and mines'.[4] It was not until four o'clock in the afternoon that the infantry stepped out of their trenches. Extensive efforts had been made to narrow the distance of no-man's-land, and in places the attackers had as little as fifty metres to cross. Moving forward in waves, wearing a modified version of the Adrian steel helmet that had been introduced in the French Army the previous year, alongside white cloth discs stitched onto their backs so they could be spotted by artillery observers, the Italians were well prepared and confident of success. With a fourfold advantage in battalions, and up to six times as many guns, they were upon the defenders before they had much chance to respond, and swamped their objectives in a matter of minutes. The attack was led by Colonel Pietro Badoglio, who charged up Mount Sabotino in just thirty-eight minutes, securing the battle-scarred summit and earning a reputation as a coming man of action. Podgora fell that evening, with Mount San Michele being seized the following day. With these bastions gone, there was no chance that Gorizia could hold.[5]

The victory was toasted eagerly in Allied capitals, with diplomats and politicians vying with one another to celebrate Italian success. 'The more the Italian offensive on the Isonzo is studied, the greater does its significance appear, and the clearer is manifest the ability of the strategic conception on which it was based', wrote the newspaper baron Lord Northcliffe, who visited the battlefield a few days after the attack had taken place.[6] Although the Italian Army had not been able to exploit the disorganization in the Austrian lines, advancing about six kilometres, Cadorna had not intended to do much more than secure the Gorizia bridgehead and was well satisfied. 'Regardless of the lack of intended follow-up, the conquest of Gorizia deserves to be counted among the most important military enterprises of our country', he wrote. 'In just three days, the most important of the enemy fortresses on the Isonzo Front fell into our possession as a result of a strong attack, one of the most powerful and violent attacks on fortresses that the history of the European War can remember.'[7]

The fall of Gorizia may not have been as seismic as Lemberg or Przemyśl, but its loss was deeply felt at General Boroević's headquarters in Ljubljana. Such was the state of his men that Boroević had little choice but to abandon the bridgehead on 8 August, evacuating the Carso and pulling back to another defensive line further east. That evening he reported to Teschen: 'With the combat value of the Gorizia garrison now at 66 percent and that of 20th Division now at 50 percent, these divisions now barely count at all. Enemy troops were able to cross the Isonzo with two battalions south of Gorizia today – and the Isonzo is hardly an obstacle.' The retreat would be completed by 10 August, but in the meantime, he asked whether he could be given significant reinforcements, as Italian transfers from the Tyrol (he had so far counted seven brigades) were making his position increasingly precarious. 'As difficult as this decision was for me, I believed it was necessary if we were to continue the battle with any prospect of success.'[8]

Significant reinforcements were simply not available. Throughout August, Conrad wrestled with the effects of multiple offensives, with fighting around Kovel and Bukhovina sucking in any spare manpower that became available. The Habsburg Empire had lost 10,756 officers and 464,382 other ranks in just two months – a staggering cost that left the army on life support, kept in line by an increasingly strict disciplinary code and propped up by more and more German troops.[9] By mid-July, eighteen German divisions had been deployed in the Austrian sector south of the Pripet Marshes, as part of a strategy known as *Korsettstangen* ('corset stays'), with the Germans having a steadying effect on the units around them. Yet there were never enough Germans to go around, and Habsburg forces remained noticeably fragile – 'like a mouth full of sensitive teeth', as one observer put it, crumbling under pressure and struggling to hold on to any position for long. When the city of Brody fell on 27 July, the local army commander, General Böhm-Ermolli, issued orders to prepare for the evacuation of Lemberg, about thirty kilometres further west, only to have these swiftly countermanded by Conrad, who would not countenance the possibility of losing such an important city.[10]

Already the influence of the new command team in the east was being felt, with Hindenburg and Ludendorff moving quickly to exert their control. Leaving their former headquarters at Kovno, the duo travelled 200 miles south to the town of Brest-Litovsk, which was a much more central location and a better place to manage the movement of divisions up and down the front. As soon as they were settled in, they made a number of dramatic decisions. No longer would Germany stand by while Habsburg units crumbled. Instead, the Austro-Hungarian Army would be rebuilt, or at least thoroughly reorganized, on German lines. Its men would undergo more training, attend joint courses, and work with German staff allocated to their units. The experience of the Western Front would also be adopted, particularly relating to the need for more artillery, with German guns being redistributed to Austrian divisions, which were notoriously light on firepower. This was combined with other changes. By late 1916, the pre-war pike-grey uniform of the Imperial and Royal Army was being phased out, replaced by Prussian field grey (*Feldgrau*), with battalions also being equipped with the new German steel helmet (*Stahlhelm*), meaning that they would increasingly look indistinguishable from their German allies. The old royal army was no more.[11]

Hindenburg and Ludendorff's newly strengthened position did not ease relations with OHL. They squabbled over transfers to the Eastern Front, with tense telegrams wired back and forth between Pless and Brest-Litovsk, always demanding more than Falkenhayn would give. The 'comical thing about the whole business', thought

Max Hoffmann, was that OHL 'do everything that we telegraph them to do, but it must look as if they had done it on their own. One needs nerves like ropes.'[12] Ludendorff raged against what he thought was the profound, naked selfishness of Falkenhayn and talked of little else but resigning in case his latest demands were not met. 'He [Ludendorff] waged war in the east as if the other fronts did not exist', remarked one critic, completely failing to appreciate that Falkenhayn's war was a high-wire balancing act, holding on to the Western Front while scraping up as much manpower as possible to send elsewhere. Hindenburg showed the same propensity, sending direct telegrams to the Kaiser imploring him to transfer further reserves eastwards, which understandably provoked yet more frustration at OHL.[13]

Falkenhayn could probably sense that his time was running out, that nothing he did would ever satisfy the command team in the east. Persistent toothache frayed his nerves, which were already strained by the pressure of overwork. On 21 August, he wrote a short memorandum to the Chancellor on why it was not possible to decisively defeat Russia – at least not when the Entente remained so strong on the Western Front. 'With the tremendous pressure that rests upon us, we have no surplus of strength. Any shift in one direction inevitably leads to a dangerous weakening of strength elsewhere, which means that even the slightest oversight in weighing up the actions expected of our enemy could result in our annihilation.' He had also made it clear that the war would be lost if the Western Front crumbled. 'For him, it all depends on whether he draws one man too many from the west, rather than sending one man too few to the east.'[14]

August 1916 was a traumatic month for the Central Powers. At almost every point along their extended battle line the enemy were on the offensive. In Galicia and across the Isonzo, at Verdun and the Somme, German and Austrian armies encountered a new kind of warfare, frightening in its intensity and seemingly endless in its duration. Even in Macedonia, which had become something of a strategic backwater, there was no lessening of Allied efforts. By the summer of 1916, Salonika – a city of bell towers and minarets, its bay crowded with ships and its streets loud with traders and hawkers – was home to a sprawling multinational army. General Sarrail's expeditionary force had now grown to fifteen divisions, about 325,000 men (opposed by around 260,000 Bulgarians), and included French and British, as well as Russians (sent to keep an eye on the Greeks), Italians (there to carve out new possessions in Albania) and Serbs (after being transported from Corfu).[15] Salonika would be the only place where all the main powers of the Entente would fight side by side, which made for a chaotic and strange theatre of operations, not helped by chronic Greek infighting, and political strife that threatened either to end the Entente's involvement in the region or to drag it in even deeper.

Greece remained in a highly delicate position: formally neutral, yet having to accept that parts of her country were occupied, and effectively run, by foreign troops. In late May, a combined German and Bulgarian force had occupied Fort Roupel, a key defensive position overlooking the Struma river, about two miles from the Bulgarian border. The fact that the Greeks had been ordered to abandon the fortress by the King sparked outrage and provoked a series of diplomatic spats between Paris and Athens. The Prime Minister, Skouloudis, maintained that there was nothing else they could do without precipitating war with the Central Powers, while protesting about what he saw as the continued violation of Greek sovereignty by the Entente. Unconvinced, the French Prime Minister, Monsieur Briand, ordered Sarrail to 'take all measures that you deem appropriate to guarantee the security of *l'armée d'Orient*', including taking control of the railway, telegraph and postal networks within Salonika.[16]

France was determined to deal with King Constantine, whom it regarded as a dangerous opponent, just waiting for a suitable opportunity to deliver Greece to the Central Powers. British objections were overcome, and a squadron was ordered to steam for Athens, ready to bombard the city, while a formal note, dated 21 June, warned the Greek Government that 'The entry of Bulgarian forces into Greece, the occupation of Fort Roupel and other points of strategic value, with the connivance of the Hellenic Cabinet, constitute a new menace to the Allied troops, and one which imposes on the three powers the obligation of demanding immediate guarantees and measures.' The Allies wanted the 'absolute and total demobilisation of the Greek Army', the replacement of the current ministry by a 'non-political Cabinet', which would guarantee a state of 'benevolent neutrality', the dissolution of the Chamber of Deputies and the holding of new elections. Suitably chastened, King Constantine agreed to the terms and replaced Skouloudis with Alexandros Zaimis, who was seen as a more pro-Entente figure.[17]

The simmering tension between Greece and the Allies did not make General Sarrail's task any easier. He bided his time, trying to maintain a sense of purpose and progress, but frustrated by the limitations placed upon him. He had spent the spring and early summer consolidating his forces and extending his deployment area. They had marched out of the 'entrenched camp' in April, spreading out to occupy a nearly 300-kilometre front, from the Gulf of Orfano in the east, along the Struma to Lake Dojran, then southwest to cross the Monastir–Salonika railway line, past Florina and on to the Albanian border. The British held the right flank, with the rest of the front being split between the French, an Italian division, six Serbian divisions and two Russian brigades. Sarrail's relationship with these forces was always a delicate and somewhat unorthodox affair. He had not been given any instructions as to what to do with the Russians, but he would set broad objectives for the Italians and Serbs, including start dates, with each commander responsible for carrying them out. 'It is not difficult to comprehend the difficulties arising from these varied approaches to command', he later admitted. 'Add to this the fact that the Russians had neither artillery nor a supply line, that the Italians only had mountain artillery and their service corps depended on ours for certain foodstuffs, that a lack of resources made it impossible to even begin to provide the Serbs with a supply line, that the Greeks had nothing, and that there was only one single supply line by rail, which had to meet the needs of all allies, including the English.'[18]

The Serbs would be Sarrail's most pressing concern. The first contingent had left Corfu in early April and taken the winding passage around Greece, carefully avoiding enemy submarines that were known to lurk in that part of the Mediterranean. Given the shortages of shipping and the need for secrecy and extreme caution, it was not until late May that the entire army – about 112,000 men – had been transported, without incident, to Salonika, from where they would be refitted and returned to the fight.[19] Many Allied officers were unimpressed when they saw the Serbs, unfavourably comparing the relaxed ways of the new arrivals with their own discipline. Lieutenant-Colonel Garsia, head of the British Military Mission, reported that 'there appears to be a feeling of self-satisfaction and complacency' among the Serbian officer corps, 'which is not justified by the state of efficiency of the troops'. 'The impression has been gained', he noted, 'that (with a few exceptions) they [the officers] let the show run itself and it does not occur to them that their duties go beyond giving general orders.' Nor did Serbian High Command seem to care, apparently taking little interest in training and leaving most of it up to the French, though Garsia did admit that perhaps the Serbs could be forgiven for such nonchalance. 'It may be pointed out', he added, 'that the Serbian Army has been more or less continuously at war since 1912, and has its own method of warfare which (however ill-suited to France) has had at times, some success in the Balkans.'[20]

The British remained Sarrail's most powerful ally but were no nearer to offering him the kind of unconditional support he wanted. A new commander, Lieutenant-General George Milne, had been appointed in May because of the need for a man 'of altogether exceptional firmness and strength of will' to stand up to Sarrail. This was followed up by a formal statement from the War Council in London rejecting any offensive unless Romania joined the war. This possibility, which had flickered and guttered before Allied diplomats for months, now seemed more certain, and by late July, an agreement had been reached between the British and French commands for just such an eventuality. Milne would give Sarrail 'support and co-operation proportionate to the numbers and equipment of the troops under his orders', with the broad objectives to be set by the Frenchman. Their mission would be to 'cover the mobilization of the Rumanian [sic] Army, as well as its action against Austria–Hungary, from an enemy offensive on its southern front . . . with a view to containing the maximum number of Bulgarian troops'. The date was set for 1 August.[21]

Yet the date came and went without any attack. An agreement would not be signed with Romania until 17 August, and Sarrail found himself having to bide his time. At a meeting with his senior officers on 20 August, he put the final touches to his operational plan. Instead of driving up either side of the Vardar, as had originally been intended, they would now outflank the Bulgarian right, with French, Russian and Serbian troops advancing towards Florina before crossing into Serbia and seizing Monastir. If all went well, they would sever the railway line at Veles, thus collapsing the entire Bulgarian position. This attack would take place on 12 September, by which time Romania would have completed her mobilization and begun the full-scale invasion of Transylvania.[22] Sarrail was sanguine about what they might achieve, but Milne was unconvinced. 'The enemy have held for one year the rim of the saucer – a perfect defensive position – during which time they have perfected their defences and communications', he wrote to Robertson. 'The enemy's communications converge on the front – ours diverge from one base. I allow this is against the enemy once his line is broken, but even then the natural strength of each line assists the defence nearly to the walls of Sofia.'[23]

Romania had been the sole power in the Balkans to remain neutral thus far, joining neither the Central Powers nor the Allies, but negotiations with both sides had been ongoing since the death of King Carol I in October 1914. Carol had been a Germanophile who was proud of Romania's long-standing membership of the Triple Alliance, but his death left the Prime Minister, Ionel Bratianu, with his pro-Entente sympathies, as the dominant figure in Romanian foreign policy. Carol's successor, his nephew King Ferdinand, had been born in Prussia and educated at Kassel and Leipzig, but he agreed to act in accordance with the wishes of the government and let the Prime Minister follow a policy of 'watching and waiting', conscious that this might be the only opportunity to realize the goal of national unification.[24] Still Bratianu did not commit himself and constantly calculated the odds of victory for the Entente, which seemed to oscillate wildly throughout 1915 and 1916. But with Allied diplomats running out of patience, he finally opted for intervention, knowing that if Romania were to join, she must do so now, taking advantage of the devastation that had been wreaked by Brusilov's offensive in Galicia as well as the sizeable force now at General Sarrail's disposal in the south.

Bratianu hoped that he had chosen his moment well. Under the terms of the agreement with Britain, France, Russia and Italy, Romania would declare war against Austria–Hungary no later than 28 August in exchange for the right of Romanians in Transylvania, Bukhovina and Banat to join a 'greater' Romania after the war. When a Crown Council was held in Bucharest on 27 August, he tried to dispel any doubts and argued that they 'must take the long view of history and not be diverted from their *preordained path* by thoughts of failure . . . There were times in the lives of nations', he went on, 'when the failure to seize the moment and act, however high the stakes and risky the outcome, was an abdication of responsibility by its leaders, a *moral betrayal.*' He therefore took full responsibility for what would happen, and the King, keeping his promise, stood by him.[25]

Entente politicians had been casting covetous glances towards Romania since August 1914 and dreamed that her military power might topple the Habsburg Empire, causing a rapid collapse of the entire Eastern Front. Romania would mobilize about 800,000 men, divided into twenty-three infantry divisions and two cavalry divisions, with 329 batteries of artillery – a potent force that would strike at the most vulnerable flank of Austria–Hungary. Her war plan, known as 'Hypothesis Z', sketched out the immediate invasion of Hungary by three armies, about 370,000 men. They would move quickly through the mountain passes along the border and then occupy Transylvania, taking advantage of the lack of strong enemy forces to present Budapest with a fait accompli. From there they would push on northwest to the Maros river, before continuing on to Cluj and up to the city of Oradea in the Hungarian Plain. If all went smoothly, the Habsburg Empire would be dealt a potentially mortal blow.[26]

Russia remained the most important ally for Romania, but also the prickliest. In the long series of discussions over Romanian entry, Sergei Sazonov, Russia's Foreign Minister, had baulked at Bratianu's long list of demands, only to find his position weakening with every reverse the Russian Army suffered. General Alekseev had been even

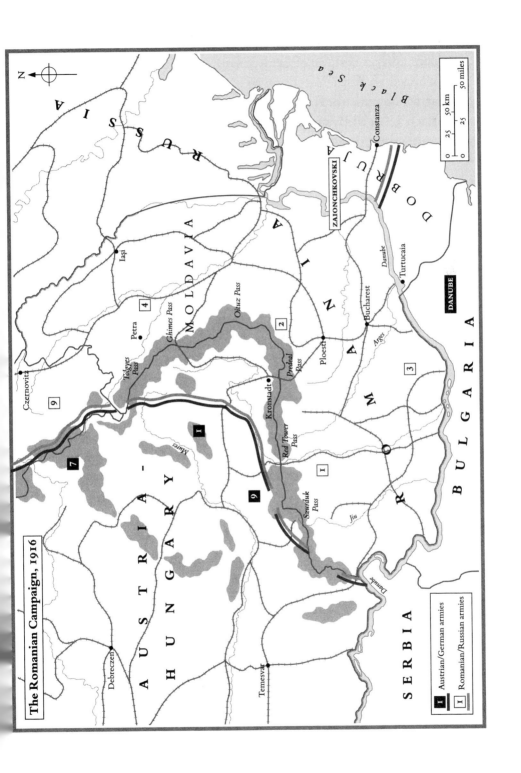

The Romanian Campaign, 1916

more sceptical of Romania's entry and would have preferred her to maintain her position of 'armed neutrality' for as long as possible. He worried about the extension to his front it would inevitably entail and feared that the Romanians would soon become a liability. When Bucharest called for half a million soldiers to guard the country's southern border with Bulgaria in exchange for joining the Allies, Alekseev flatly refused, eventually sending 'an undermanned Cossack cavalry division, an exhausted Russian infantry division, and an untried Serb division recruited from among Austro-Hungarian prisoners of war'. Indeed, General Andrei Zaionchkovski, who was appointed to command them, complained about the weakness of his corps, only to find Alekseev uninterested. 'I have always been against Romania's entry into the war,' Alekseev said, 'but I was forced to agree under pressure from France and England. Now the main decisions have been made, and if the Emperor were to order me to send 15 Russian wounded men there, I would never send 16.'[27]

Notwithstanding these difficulties, Romania's war plan moved swiftly into action. On the day war was declared, King Ferdinand issued a call to his countrymen, urging them to 'bear manfully all the sacrifices inseparable from an arduous war' and to work towards the 'union of all branches of our nation . . . namely, a Rumanian [*sic*] union on both slopes of the Carpathians'.[28] Already three armies were on the move, marching in long, heavily laden columns through the forested passes towards Transylvania and routing the small numbers of border guards they encountered. By 30 August, the frontier towns of Sibiu and Brasov had been captured, and General Constantin Prezan's North Army, which protected the right flank, had reported that the enemy was 'fragmented in isolated and disorganized units, beaten all along the front, in retreat followed by our columns'.[29]

Defending Transylvania was First Army, commanded by General Arz von Straussenburg, a 59-year-old Hungarian officer who had a reputation as a sound, if not spectacular, commander. Recalled from his corps along the Russian sector in mid-August, he had been sent to take charge of the disparate forces that defended this part of the empire as rumours grew about Romanian belligerence. With only fifteen 'very weakened' infantry battalions and four *Honvéd* cavalry regiments, he could muster just 34,000 men and 76 guns, which was dwarfed by the tenfold superiority of the Romanian invasion force. Arz was not minded to worry too much; he was not a nervous man and tended to his duties with an assuredness and efficiency that would soon be noticed in the Austrian High Command. Border fortifications were hastily repaired, supplies gathered, troops assigned to their defensive positions, and slowly but surely the Habsburg defenders readied themselves to fight on home soil and for ground that was integral to the empire and the Dual Monarchy.[30]

A lack of Habsburg resistance was to be expected at this stage of the campaign, but already a note of caution had crept into the Romanian High Command. At a Crown Council meeting on 2 September, General Alexandru Averescu, commanding Second Army, argued that they must not rush the invasion. 'Hypothesis Z' had called for the main advance to begin after twelve days, when it was estimated that all the attacking divisions would have crossed the mountains, and Averescu warned that any forcing of the pace might cause supply difficulties and confusion. His fellow army commanders disagreed, and persuaded the King to let the advance continue. Averescu, however, showed none of the furious intent that would be needed if the Romanian Army was to drive deep into the Hungarian Plain, spending the following week consolidating his position and gradually expanding his bridgehead. By the time the three armies were ready to move on again, the situation had changed dramatically for the worse.[31]

As the Romanians seemed to hesitate, the response from the Central Powers was swift and decisive. In Pless, the Kaiser had been stunned by news of the invasion, lapsing into a deep depression and declaring that 'This means the end of the war!' His advisers tried to cheer him up, but a sense of hopelessness gripped the Supreme Warlord as he agonized over the prospect of an imminent Austrian collapse.[32] He summoned Falkenhayn, and the two men circled around a large pair of maps laid out in the operations room. Falkenhayn had not been expecting Romanian intervention – as late as 13 August, he had told Conrad that any declaration of war would likely come in October, once the harvest had been gathered – and the Kaiser grew concerned that the public mood would turn against them.[33] Falkenhayn had few supporters within the High Command, and even fewer people were willing to defend him publicly, which left the Kaiser unable to muster the strength to stand up to the growing chorus calling for a change at OHL. When he consulted Hindenburg on the prospects for a Romanian campaign, Falkenhayn sent in a half-hearted protest and offered his resignation, which was accepted. On 29 August, Paul von Hindenburg was appointed Chief of the General Staff, with Ludendorff becoming First Quartermaster-General, a title he chose himself after being 'assured that I should have joint responsibility in all decisions and measures that might be taken'.[34]

The Kaiser had been anxious to still the endless wrangling between his commanders, but could raise little enthusiasm for the new appointments, only now reluctantly accepting what many of his staff had long regarded as an inevitability. 'In contrast, His Majesty', as an aide noted in his diary, 'holds a long account of the services of Falkenhayn and the great disadvantage of the change.'[35] While Falkenhayn had become notorious for his reluctance to concentrate forces in the east, Hindenburg and Ludendorff had no such doubts. As soon as they had arrived in Pless, they announced that everything must go to Romania. Every spare division must be scooped up and sent immediately to mount a counter-offensive, ideally before the autumn weather closed off the passes. In contrast to the sullen Falkenhayn, the duo brought a welcome dose of bullish confidence to OHL. When he was told of the Romanian declaration of war, Hindenburg said that they should 'rejoice' because finally they had 'an adversary that is not mired down in trench warfare. I do not know today where and how we will defeat him. But I assure you that we will defeat him.'[36]

While the Brusilov Offensive had forced Germany and Austria–Hungary to pool resources more effectively across the Russian front, the Romanian declaration of war prompted further centralization that included all the Central Powers. On 6 September, an agreement ('Regulations for the Unified Supreme Command of the Central Powers and Their Allies') was signed that formally transferred 'supreme command' of all military forces to Kaiser Wilhelm II. 'The Army Commanders (Generals) of the Allied armed forces and their

Chiefs of Staff are at the German Emperor's disposal and shall exercise supreme leadership on His behalf . . .' This control would consist of the 'implementation of operations' on 'a large scale' and would include 'the basic objectives of the operations to be carried out in the various war zones', 'the forces to be used for this' and the management of 'the relationship between commanders and subordinates in situations where troops of several allies are to cooperate'. Each commander would be required to send regular reports to OHL, and although their agreement would be sought on all relevant matters, the Kaiser's word would be final.[37]

Now heavily indebted to Germany, both militarily and financially, Vienna had little choice but to limp along and hope that Berlin's domination would not prove too uncomfortable. Predictably, Conrad refused to support the agreement and warned Franz Joseph that he could not possibly take responsibility for the conduct of the war should it be ratified. Both the Emperor and Count Burián understood Conrad's concerns, but conscious as they were of Austria's deteriorating position within the alliance, they felt they had little choice but to accept, although they were able to insert a special clause ensuring that the Kaiser would be guided by a consideration for 'the protection and integrity of the territories of the Austro-Hungarian equal to those of the German Empire'. In a telegram to the Kaiser on 13 September, Franz Joseph gave his consent for the new arrangements, signing away another slice of his sovereignty and independence while describing them as a 'valuable guarantee for the success of our great common task'.[38]

By the time the agreement had formally come into effect, the mood had lightened somewhat because of an early success for Field Marshal Mackensen, whose mixed German and Bulgarian force had captured the town of Turtucaia on 6 September. Having spent the last ten months in the Balkans with his army group, Mackensen reacted to news of Romania's declaration of war with undisguised concern, spending a sleepless night worrying about the vulnerability of his men and the reliability of his allies. Yet Bulgaria proved more effective than he had anticipated, and her troops were eager to avenge the Second Balkan War of 1913, when Romania had seized southern

Dobrogea. The Bulgarian Third Army crossed the Romanian border on 2 September, having been ordered to mount a series of demonstrations to tie down as many enemy divisions as possible and distract them from Transylvania. Key to the Romanian position was the fortress of Turtucaia, which lay on the southern bank of the Danube and was garrisoned by a reinforced infantry division, occupying fortified entrenchments along a range of hills outside the town.

The main assault began on 5 September, with Bulgarian troops launching furious bayonet charges. The defenders fought hard for every piece of ground but found the accuracy and lethality of Bulgarian machine-gun and artillery fire, often directed by German advisers, to be devastating. One by one the Romanian forts fell, surrounded by heaps of Bulgarian corpses, until morale began to break. At 4.30 the following morning, the final attack went in with a heavy bombardment, which sparked a headlong rush for the riverbank. Because there was no bridge over this part of the Danube, the garrison had been left without a line of retreat, and although some were able to get on the few remaining boats, others tried to swim across the 800 metres of river and were drowned. 'A few capsized vessels floating on the water, propelled by the current, colliding now and then with the bodies of drowned soldiers', recalled one survivor. 'In the meantime, the enemy had advanced and, with their machine guns placed on the shore, mowed down the fleeing soldiers without mercy.' When the Bulgarians stormed through the town, they found a scene of chaos: dead horses, heaps of bodies, and the sky choked by columns of smoke from burning supply dumps. Twenty-eight thousand prisoners were taken, including three generals.[39]

The fall of Turtucaia was a disaster for Romania, stripping away any confidence her leaders may have had and provoking a knee-jerk movement of units back to defend the homeland. Bratianu was crestfallen. One of his colleagues remembered how he fell into a 'veritable mental decline':

> For about 15 days he wasn't himself – he was unrecognisable, wandering from room to room all day long, seeing almost no-one, and when you spoke he didn't hear you; it was hard even to get him to answer

questions that were directly in his remit. He was physically defeated, almost elderly, he was carrying a horrible despair inside him. It wasn't because of Turtucaia; like the King he considered Turtucaia a very painful incident, but nothing more. The outcome of the war could not be linked to him, something else was the cause of his crippling psychological turmoil: the Allies had betrayed him, and he could not come to terms with this idea. He could not forgive them and nor could he forgive himself.[40]

At a sombre Crown Council on 15 September, General Averescu, who had been transferred to command Romanian troops in the south, argued that they could not fight on two fronts at the same time and must concentrate their resources. He recommended holding fast in the north, where the ground was more suitable for a defensive campaign, and switching to fight Mackensen in the south.[41]

Romania was rapidly finding out that making war against the Central Powers was no half-hearted affair. German divisions were already assembling in Transylvania with frightening speed. In what was a remarkably impressive feat, twenty-two trains per day were steaming into Hungary to form the German Ninth Army, which would be led by Falkenhayn. Although he had been offered a position at Constantinople as Ambassador to the Ottoman Empire, Falkenhayn told the Kaiser that he would prefer to remain a soldier. It was not unprecedented, but it was certainly a strange turn of events for a former Chief of the General Staff to accept a field command under those who had previously been his subordinates, but Falkenhayn cared little for what others thought of him and saw the Romanian campaign as an opportunity to restore his reputation; to show that he still possessed the ability to lead as a Prussian general.[42]

After leaving Berlin on 15 September, he boarded a train, packed with troops, bound for the Carpathians, and went through the latest intelligence reports, which revealed that the Romanian push had stalled. Their advance was 'evidently very cautious and hesitant', which could only be explained by either 'supply difficulties in the mountains' or 'bad news from the Dobrogea'. After arriving in Transylvania, he sketched out a plan with his staff for a swift counter-offensive, emphasizing that they must be prepared to move quickly and to conduct the most ruthless form of attack, no matter the odds against them.[43] His target would be the Romanian First Army, which occupied the westernmost sector of the front, with three corps strung out in a long and vulnerable defensive cordon. He concentrated his efforts on I Corps around Sibiu, intending to drive them back through the mountains, while sending the Alpine Corps, an elite division trained in mountain warfare, on a flanking march to attack the rear, seize the Red Tower Pass and block the enemy's retreat. He knew that the situation was finely balanced: Romanian divisions were usually big, sometimes consisting of twenty or more battalions, over twice what a German division could deploy, but Germany had the edge in artillery, training and experience. As for the Alpine Corps, they would have to climb up to 2,000 metres, making their way along stony mule tracks in icy winds, across dangerous ravines and through dense woodland, all without alerting the enemy.[44]

It took some time for Falkenhayn to gather his forces, and it was not until 26 September that the offensive began. The first day's fighting was inconclusive, with the Romanians launching repeated counter-attacks. This left Falkenhayn restless and uneasy, anxious about the vulnerability of his left flank, where another Romanian army, the Second, was deployed, and frustrated at the failure to break through the enemy positions, which were defended stubbornly. The Alpine Corps had managed to intercept the movement of reinforcements north and south along the winding Red Tower Pass, but came under fierce attack and could not completely block the road because of a lack of artillery.[45] When the battle resumed the following day, the Romanians 'stood bravely in a large semicircle around the entrance to the pass', noted Falkenhayn. 'The situation of the Alpine Corps was beginning to cause concern'. With reinforcements 'constantly rolling in from the south', he worried about how long they could hold their positions. Unless more forces could be freed up, 'there would be very little prospect of success' against Second Army, which was moving closer.[46]

Falkenhayn's worries were premature. Early on the morning of 28 September, the German commander, wearing his grey coat, field glasses around his neck, clambered up to the top of the Protestant church in Sibiu to observe the battle. Once again the defenders fought with what one authority described as 'great tenacity', launching frequent counter-attacks, but as the day wore on, German experience, firepower and fighting skill began to tell. Romanian units may have looked impressive at a distance, but the army could only equip its regiments with four to six machine-guns (compared with up to 24 in a German regiment); they had no automatic rifles or mountain artillery, and only 180 batteries of modern field guns, which left them at a real disadvantage. They continued to fight well, as most German or Habsburg officers would have admitted, but struggled to withstand the heavy bombardments that their opponents relied on, constantly finding themselves outgunned or outmanoeuvred, sometimes coming under air attack, which left their men impatient and demoralized. On the evening of 28 September, with German troops continuing to attack, the commander of the Romanian I Corps, General Popovici, ordered his men to fall back through the pass. An aeroplane had been sent with a message from High Command urging him to stand and fight for a little longer, but it never arrived, leaving him with no choice but to brave the perils of the withdrawal and try to get as many of his men as possible to safety.[47]

Falkenhayn spent no time savouring his triumph. Without waiting for his men to recover, he ordered them to sweep east along the Olt river to face Second Army, which was dug in at Brasov. Once again he took a calculated risk, knowing that he was outnumbered and would have to march hard and strike with all the ferocity he could muster, but heavy rain began falling on 1 October, leaving the hills wreathed in mist and preventing the aerial observation that was so vital to German operational planning. A series of bloody actions were fought over succeeding days: short, intensive bombardments followed by bayonet charges, exchanges of rifle and machine-gun fire, even cavalry charges. The defenders fought hard but gave ground, having few experienced NCOs and officers who could have helped steady their lines. As one post-war analysis noted, the fighting had required swift, accurate decision-making. 'But fear of initiative paralyses the majority of Romanian leaders' actions; this was the peace-time, passive school of discipline, which endured into wartime with fatal effects, and, moreover, by over-diluting the army and multiplying the units, they had to resort to officers who were known to be mediocre even in peacetime, deploying those who had never had any contact with the troops (the war-training school *par excellence*), and the consequences were felt immediately.'[48]

Everywhere a sense of fear and inferiority was spreading among Romanian officers, who were horrified at German battlefield prowess. General Grighore Crainiceanu, who had replaced Averescu at Second Army, ordered his troops to abandon Brasov on the night of 8 October, with division after division marching back through the mountains in a state of shock and despair. When Averescu returned to his headquarters the following morning, he was appalled at what he found; men were milling around and there was total incomprehension when he asked what routes their divisions were taking. 'The ugliest of situations', he wrote. 'The commanders are literally dominated by fear. Ready to retreat at the tiniest pressure from the enemy. It seems they imagine that going to war does not involve fighting.'[49] The invasion of Transylvania was over, and with it a war plan that had become redundant in less than six weeks. With the Russians proving unwilling to help, Romania's only hope of substantial assistance lay with General Sarrail's expeditionary force, which was slowly but surely proving its detractors wrong.

14.   'Falkenhayn is here!'

Russian attacks around Kovel were finally abandoned in early October. A renewed offensive had been undertaken in September, but it hardly progressed against German and Austrian positions that seemed to be made of iron. Poor artillery support and bad ground condemned division after division, including some of the best units in the Russian Army, to heavy losses and left the trenches covered with piles of the dead and dying. Brusilov blamed a combination of enemy reinforcements and their aerial superiority, which prevented him from accurately surveying the battlefield. 'I did not know the exact location of the enemy guns,' he complained, 'and the fire of our heavy artillery could not be directed in that flat, heavily wooded country. Consequently our gunners, whose firing was very accurate, could not demonstrate their quality, carry out proper preparation for infantry attacks, or silence the enemy artillery, which, apart from anything else, was numerically superior to ours.'[1]

Russian casualties were harrowing. The two Guards corps thrown across the Stokhod had lost 54,000 men, but this was only a fraction of the total casualties that had been incurred in the summer offensives, which some authorities thought could be as a high as two million, including the wounded and missing.[2] Depressed by such a heavy bloodletting, the Tsar recognized that there was little point in continuing to press when the focus of the war was shifting towards Romania. On 5 October, he wrote to Alekseev and explained that he was 'decisively against further development of the operations of the Eighth and Special Armies, operations promising us minimal success and huge losses'.[3] Even in the Carpathians, which had seemed one of the more promising avenues for Russian activity, the advance had ground to a halt by the first week of October. General Lechitsky, commander of Ninth Army, at the southern end of the front, did everything he could to keep his men moving, but lacked the strength to mount an invasion of Hungary with a shortage of supplies strangling the momentum of his forward units. 'Most of the army is operating without roads, on extremely difficult terrain, which inevitably affects the supply of my men', he admitted. 'The troops become utterly exhausted and their offensive urge is weakening. Meanwhile, the situation imperiously demands that we should persist with the offensive in order to cross the Carpathians and reach the Tisza Valley before winter comes.'[4]

It was not just a shortage of supplies, ammunition and food that the Russian Army was suffering from. Observers began to notice that something had gone from the troops who had fought so bravely all summer, and the sense of promise and purpose that Brusilov had brought to the army in May and June had all but evaporated. Major-General Boris Gerua, Quartermaster-General of the Special Army, reported that his men were more lethargic and indifferent to their orders than at any time he could remember. 'From October onwards, the troops in the trenches began to receive revolutionary leaflets. These mostly contained anti-war propaganda that gradually formed the basis for the Bolshevik slogan: "A world without annexations and indemnities".' Although officers did what they could to stop this 'seeping poison' of propaganda, they noticed that cases of insubordination soon began to rise. Even when units received reinforcements, their strength did not increase: 'the soldiers were no longer the same as they used to be; training and education in the rear were far from perfect; the officers gradually degenerated into an army of "warrant officers" and among their ranks were those who would become demagogues of the first and second revolutions that would take place the following year'.[5]

For the time being, niggling worries over the morale of the army were shelved. This was inevitable, officers would say, and to be expected from bored, homesick men, exhausted after months of heavy combat. Once their units had been returned to full strength, their fighting spirit would surely return. But no matter how many times senior officers insisted that all was well, an uneasy sense of foreboding was becoming pervasive. On 15 August, the politician Alexander Guchkov had sent an unusually candid letter to Alekseev imploring him to 'do something' about what he called the 'disintegration' in the 'rear'. 'No matter how good the conditions now may be at the front, the rotting rear is once more threatening, just as it did a year ago, to drag your gallant front and your clever strategy, nay, the whole country, into that impassable swamp . . .' Guchkov complained about the railways and food supplies, lamented the unsuitability of the Chairman of Ministers, Stürmer ('a man who, if not a traitor, is ready to commit treason'), and warned that 'a deluge is approaching'.[6]

Alekseev knew that such talk was highly dangerous. The Tsar had already been handed a copy of the letter via his secret police, the *Okhrana*, and summoned Alekseev to see him. No action was taken; Nicholas II evidently still trusted his Chief of Staff, and he showed a serene, almost impassive attitude to the growing crisis in Petrograd.[7] The Tsar continued to rule in the authoritarian style he had always preferred, trusting an ever-shrinking circle of advisers and only issuing instructions after taking the advice of the Tsarina and Rasputin. Although this ministerial carousel did not spin as fast as it once had, his chief ministers came and went with alarming frequency. Alexander Protopopov was appointed Minister of the Interior in September, after the Tsarina's incessant pleas. As a member of the Progressive Bloc and former deputy chairman, he had been well regarded in the Duma, but his willingness to do the Tsar's bidding soon alienated his former colleagues. The 'deputies did not trust him', recorded Rodzianko, who found his eccentricity off-putting – Protopopov would sometimes appear wearing the uniform of the Chief of the Gendarmerie – and who roundly condemned his decision to release Sukhomlinov, who had been imprisoned on charges of treason. The Tsar had been unsure whether to press ahead with the trial of his former War Minister, but when Rasputin warned that *'he should not die in jail'*, it was agreed to place him under house arrest.[8]

Protopopov may not have been the worst of the Tsar's ministers, but his appointment only stoked feelings of betrayal and helplessness in liberal circles. The monarchy, or at least the current Tsar, was deemed incapable of reform and totally unable to pull the country out of what looked like a death spiral, leaving Russia's political class increasingly bereft: afraid of what a revolution might bring, but knowing that it was probably inevitable. Indeed, for some, a violent reckoning with the old regime might be just what was needed to revitalize the war effort. On 14 November, Pavel Miliukov, a founder of the Kadet Party and a distinguished historian, addressed the Duma and poured out his frustrations, asking whether the government's decisions were the product of 'stupidity or treason' and insinuating that it was run by a pro-German clique who were not fully committed to the war. 'All the Allied Powers have summoned to the support of the Government the best men of all parties, all the confidence, and all those organizing elements present in their countries, which are better organized than our own country. What has our own Government accomplished?' There was no answer. Boris Stürmer, the embattled Chairman, walked out to loud jeers.[9]

The growing turmoil on the home front did not make General Alekseev's job any easier. He was not a natural politician and shied away from engaging too much with those who looked to him for a solution to Russia's woes. Although sympathetic to the complaints that were regularly made about the Tsar and his government, he remained indecisive and unsure of himself. On a number of occasions, senior figures had come to Mogilev and urged him to do something about Rasputin, to make the Tsar see how damaging the *starets* was becoming, but Alekseev never made a decisive move. Whenever the question was raised about whether Rasputin should come to *Stavka*, Alekseev had always refused to allow it, or at least politely made excuses as to why it could not happen, but even this coolness was quickly picked up by the Tsarina, who could not hide her growing suspicion of him. When she heard about the letter that Guchkov had sent to Alekseev, she wrote to Nicholas warning him about it. 'Now a correspondence between *Alexeiev* [*sic*] & that brute *Gutchkov* [*sic*] is going on & he fills him with vile things', she wrote on 1 October; 'warn him, he is such a clever brute & *Alexeiev* will certainly, alas, listen to things against our Friend too – & that won't bring him luck.'[10]

Alekseev was also beginning to suffer from ill-health. The first indications of what would later be diagnosed as uraemia (kidney disease) occurred in September, and the painful attacks grew in severity until he had to be sent to the Crimea to recuperate in November. When Father George Shavelsky, Chaplain-General of the Army and Navy and a regular visitor to *Stavka*, saw him in mid-October he noticed how weak and distressed the general had become:

> I found General Alekseev terribly exhausted, gaunt-looking and aged. He used to be attentive to my reports, but now he listened to me listlessly, apathetically, almost indifferently, and then all of a sudden interrupted me: 'You know, Father George, I want to leave the office! There is no point in serving: nothing can be done, nothing can help the cause. What can we do with this childish person? He is dancing over the abyss . . . and he doesn't care. While the state is ruled by an insane woman along with a tangled ball of filthy worms: Rasputin . . . Stürmer . . . I spoke to him the other day and told him everything.'[11]

Alekseev was not a natural dictator, and his stern sense of duty always tempered his interactions with the Tsar. With Nicholas largely indifferent to his advice, he lacked the stomach to really press the matter and demand action. He was also increasingly preoccupied with the changing situation at the front. As he had feared, Romania's entry into the war had shifted the focus of Russian efforts further south, siphoning off precious reserves and forcing Lechitsky's Ninth Army to extend its front down through the Carpathians. King Ferdinand had already petitioned the Tsar for more help, calling for at least twenty divisions, Romanian and Russian, to be rushed to Transylvania, but this received a predictably curt response from *Stavka*, which recognized the 'difficulties faced by the Romanian High Command' but did not believe that the situation 'should have raised any particular concerns' because the number of enemy divisions was still 'relatively small'. Although two corps were ordered from Brusilov's front and some heavy artillery was sent to General Zaionchkovski's corps in the Dobrogea, the poor railway connections meant that it might take weeks for more significant reinforcements to arrive.[12]

The campaign was rapidly becoming a fiasco. The port of Constanza fell on 22 October, including its precious stores of grain and oil, with Russian and Romanian troops retreating north in demoralized columns. Zaionchkovski was furious at his erstwhile allies, complaining bitterly to Alekseev that his forces were 'only the bone thrown to the Romanians to get them into this war' and he could not understand why he had been placed in such a difficult situation – having to labour under a Romanian commander whom he despised, and ordered to send some of his best units to buttress the lines in the north. Although outnumbering his opponent, his forces were deployed across a sizeable front, with their supply lines thoroughly mixed up. Moreover, the Romanians showed an 'utter misunderstanding of modern war' and had an 'appalling inclination to panic'. Alekseev was furious: 'You were given everything that could be given under the circumstances', he wrote on 28 October; 'so it is very difficult for me to comprehend the disorder, the chaotic administration, and breaking contact with the enemy . . .' Zaionchkovski was relieved of command two days later.[13]

The Zaionchkovski affair revealed in vivid colours the extent of the Allied problem in Romania. There was no proper coordination of manpower and strategy, with the Romanian High Command becoming nervous and panicky, struggling to stick to a clear plan and prone to moving units back and forth between Transylvania and the Dobrogea. By now the Prime Minister, Bratianu, had no confidence in any of his generals and looked desperately for outside help. On 16 October, General Henri Berthelot, one of Joffre's closest advisers, arrived in Bucharest to take charge of the French Military Mission, and both the King and Bratianu immediately sought his advice. 'The King welcomes me very warmly,' Berthelot recalled, 'without much fanfare, but the decidedly negative military circumstances create an anxious atmosphere that hangs over the dinner and the anxious diners. The Prime Minister Mr Bratianu makes no secret of his disappointment, roundly blaming General Sarrail for doing nothing to support Romania's entry into the war, despite the promised large-scale offensive in Macedonia.' Berthelot tried to mollify his hosts, talking of the extraordinary sacrifices that would be required, the surprise that most armies had felt at the power of modern weaponry, and the need to raise morale so that the army could recover. 'My conclusion from this first day is that we must act, and act fast. We seem to be losing ground all across the front. We need to dispense entirely with the idea of retreat, and doggedly defend the border itself, our home soil. This will provide time to create a thoroughly considered plan of operations!'[14]

The other Allied powers did what they could to support Romania. Britain and France launched new attacks on the Somme, including rushing forward the deployment of the first tanks, and the Italians continued to press on from Gorizia. The Seventh Battle of the Isonzo opened on 14 September with a heavy nine-hour bombardment and a coordinated attack on the Carso. Despite being outnumbered two to one, the defenders held firm. Interlocking machine-gun and rifle fire, combined with effective artillery barrages, did enough to force a suspension of the offensive after just three days. Cadorna blamed the 'modest' results on a combination of tactical failings: not cutting wide enough breaches in the barbed wire; not crossing no-man's-land quickly enough, before the Austrians had been able to man their defences; and expending too many shells on the second line without ensuring that the first line had been totally demolished. He also pointed to the poor weather, which prevented observation and reduced the effectiveness of the preliminary bombardment. The following month he ordered that no major offensive should go ahead unless the atmospheric conditions allowed unimpeded observation of the fall of shell.[15]

This was certainly a sensible and necessary precaution, but Cadorna needed battlefield success. He tried again twice before the end of the year. The Eighth Battle opened on 10 October with another push on the Carso, which was once again called off after a few days. He made another attempt in November (the Ninth Battle), but somehow the thin and battered line of Habsburg defenders maintained their positions in what would become a minor miracle of resistance. In the first five days of October, Austrian divisions sustained 700 dead and 3,000 wounded from what seemed like an incessant rain of artillery and mortar fire. When a colonel from the engineering staff was sent to report on the situation, he had to admit that:

> The only thing really covering the lines to be held are the bodies of our heroic defenders. The reason for the inadequacy of the

fortifications lies in the extraordinary difficulties presented by the terrain, which is in no way accounted for by the workforce. Despite the extreme efforts of the combat troops to work their way into the hard rock, the trenches on the front line are only partially sunk into the ground . . . [T]he enemy's heavy guns are able to dominate the entire Karst [Carso] Plateau as far as the area to the rear of Comen and Gorjansko – that is 13 to 14 kilometres behind the front. As a result, any fortification to be carried out within the specified zone must be done under the constant threat of heavy shellfire.[16]

The weather would be their saviour. By November, persistent rainfall, snowstorms on higher ground and lingering fog all helped to avert a crisis that many Habsburg officers felt was coming. Given Cadorna's growing superiority, it was surely inevitable that sooner or later their lines would break and their men would fail. In the meantime, all that was left was the daily struggle for survival and the occasional minor action: a raid or sortie out into no-man's-land to recover a lost position, gain intelligence, or maintain the kind of moral ascendancy that so many officers prized.

With Italy engaged in bloody trench warfare, Romania's hopes centred upon General Sarrail's *armée d'Orient*. But any offensive into Serbia or Bulgaria would have to get through some of the most formidable natural defensive positions found anywhere in Europe, perhaps even more challenging than the Isonzo. The bulk of the Bulgarians' strength, including the crack 9th (Pleven) Division, lay on their left, around Lake Dojran, which guarded the quickest and most direct route into Bulgaria. Here the hilly terrain had been turned into what was widely considered to be an impregnable fortress, with trenches and machine-gun posts blasted out of solid rock and hidden among a series of imposing heights that would become infamous: the Petit Couronné, Hill 340, Teton Hill, Hill 380 and the Grand Couronné. Out to the west, where the French, Serbs and Russians were deployed, the ground was even more unfavourable for the attacker. The Bulgarian line rested upon the Nidže mountain range, 'a great chain of hills' crowned by the snow-covered peak at Kajmakcalan, which rose to 2,500 metres in height.[17]

Sarrail's offensive was launched on 12 September, with the Serbs

1. General Franz Conrad von Hötzendorf, Austro-Hungarian Chief of the General Staff. Irascible and delusional, if occasionally brilliant, Conrad was unable to line up Austria's limited military power with its sizeable strategic objectives.

Austro-Hungarian horsemen in Galicia in 1914. Badly outdated in tactics and equipment, the bsburg cavalry were soon exhausted by the demands of modern campaigning.

3. Tsar Nicholas II (*second from left*) and Grand Duke Nikolai Nikolaevich (*centre*), Commander-in-Chief of the Russian Army, confer at Baranovichi in September 1914. Nikolaevich was an experienced soldier, but was unfamiliar with Russia's mobilization plans and admitted that 'I would have to carry out a plan I had not designed'.

4. The entry of Russian cavalry into Lemberg, September 1914. The capture of the Galician capital was 'of extreme political and psychological importance', and was followed by an intensive programme of 'Russification'.

General Paul von Hindenburg with his staff at the headquarters of Eighth Army in East Prussia, ugust 1914. Ludendorff is to his right; Max Hoffman to his left. The generals in the east soon came to conflict with higher command as they demanded greater manpower and resources for the war ainst Russia.

German infantry advance under fire during the Battle of Tannenberg, August 1914. The extent of rmany's victory in East Prussia established a moral supremacy over Russian forces that would last oughout the war.

7. Radomir Putnik led Serbia's armies during the campaigns of 1914 and 1915, successfully repulsing numerous Habsburg invasions and becoming a symbol of Serbian resistance.

8. Serbian troops advance during the Battle of Kolubara, December 1914. This devastating counter-attack pushed the Austro-Hungarian Army back across the Sava and ensured Serbia's survival for another year.

German and Austro-Hungarian columns pass alongside each other somewhere on the Eastern
ont. Austrian units were seriously under-gunned and proved tactically weak throughout the war,
quently needing 'stiffening' by German forces in a process known as *Korsettstangen* ('corset stays').

The Habsburg command team at dinner. Archduke Friedrich (Commander-in-Chief) is in the
tre, with Conrad von Hötzendorf to his right (with the white moustache) and General Eduard
hm-Ermolli (Second Army commander) sitting on his left.

11. General Luigi Cadorna, Italian Chief of the General Staff. Aggressive and uncompromising, Cadorna demanded more of his men than many thought possible. 'His troops could not bear his name without hatred,' recorded one senior commander, 'because he, without ever having left his headquarters . . had stubbornly sent them to attack.'

12. Italian troops in the trenches at Mount Sabotino. After the early assaults had failed with terrible losses, General Cadorna admitted that 'he had no idea that the Austrian defensive positions were so strong . . .'

. General August von Mackensen became one of the most decorated soldiers of the war. He led the
tacks on Russia in the spring and summer of 1915, and masterminded the invasion of Serbia.
Germany's noble cause must prevail,' he wrote, 'even if the world is full of devils.'

. Austro-Hungarian troops march through Serbia, October 1915. The combined weight of the
erman, Habsburg and Bulgarian armies was enough to finally overrun the country and give the
entral Powers control of the Balkans.

15. Serbian infantry marching to camp near Salonika, April 1916. Incorporated into the Allied Expeditionary Force after being reorganized at Corfu, the Serbs played a key role in the offensives of 1917 and 1918.

16. Men of 9th (Pleven) Division of the Bulgarian Army digging trenches in the hills around the town of Dojran in the spring of 1916. The defences in this sector were some of the most formidable on any front in the entire war.

. General Maurice Sarrail, commander of the *l'armée d'Orient* with Lieutenant-General George
ilne, in charge of the British Salonika Force, in May 1916. Both men struggled to deal with the
nstraints placed upon them in Greece, but they forged a good working relationship.

18. Russian dead at Lake Naroch, March 1916. The inability of Russian forces to break the enemy lines provoked widespread disillusionment. Even Mikhail Alekseev, Chief of Staff, asked incredulously 'We had a fivefold force superiority at the strike point, but what came of it?'

19. The Tsar (*centre*) chairs a conference at *Stavka* on the summer offensive, 14 April 1916. Brusilov i to his left and Alekseev is sitting opposite, staring at the camera. This photo captures the mood of despondency that affected senior Russian commanders after Lake Naroch, with only Brusilov urging an attack.

. Grigori Rasputin, the Tsarina Alexandra and her five children with their governess. Rasputin's
luence on the imperial household became a running sore in Russian politics, and contributed to a
owing feeling of alienation towards the Tsar.

21. A German sentry occupies a flooded trench, June 1916.

22. Russian troops resting in captured trenches during the summer of 1916. The initial phase of the Brusilov Offensive was devastating for the Habsburg Army and forced the Austrian High Command to ask for yet more German support.

. General Svetozar Boroević at his headquarters in Ljubljana. Appointed commander of the
ustro-Hungarian Fifth Army in May 1915, he masterminded a stubborn and tenacious defence of the
onzo.

. Dead bodies litter the slopes of Podgora, 8 August 1916. Often likened to an anthill, Podgora
red the way to Gorizia. 'The trees are mere dead sticks,' wrote one witness, 'all blasted and scarred
artillery fire.'

25. General Erich von Falkenhayn at his headquarters in Romania during the autumn of 1916. Col[
calculating, but thoroughly modern in his understanding of operations, Falkenhayn oversaw the mo[
successful period of the war for Germany.

. Dead horses on the banks of the Danube at Turtucaia, August 1916. The fall of this fortress town
used despair in the Romanian High Command and sparked a belated reinforcement of its southern
nk.

A column of French infantry crossing the Monastir Plain during the final advance on the town in
vember 1916. The capture of Monastir was a moment of rare triumph for the *l'armée d'Orient*.

28. Alexander Kerensky, Minister President of the Provisional Government. A lawyer and Socialist Revolutionary by background, Kerensky struggled to hold Russia together and was deposed by the Bolsheviks in November 1917. He had 'the air of a very unassuming bourgeois man . . . His p face is clean-shaven, his eyes are shades of blue and black, and do not give the impression of an hone man.'

29. A Siberian regiment waits to go 'over the top' during the Kerensky Offensive. The failure of the attacks marked a crucial moment in the final dissolution of the Russian Army. 'Most of the military units are in a state of complete disorganization, their enthusiasm for an offensive has rapidly disappeared . . .' reported local commissars.

General Lavr Kornilov, ...ussian Commander-in-Chief : a brief period in the late ...mmer of 1917. Pugnacious ...d determined, Kornilov ...s accused of trying to ...erthrow the Provisional ...overnment and went on to ...n the Volunteer movement ...the south.

31. Italian infantry attacking Austrian positions on the Carso. The fighting on the Italian Front in the spring and summer of 1917 was ferocious. One officer remembered the 'indescribable confusion of the front . . . In some places the trenches were in good condition, but most are shattered, collapsed, sometimes completely obliterated.'

32. Emperor Karl visiting wounded troops during the Eleventh Battle of the Isonzo, August 1917. B this point, Karl had become convinced that Austria could no longer remain on the defensive and m attack. 'A triumphant thrust against Italy may quickly bring about the end of the war.'

. A group of Italian soldiers, taken prisoner somewhere in the hills and forests above Caporetto, are oved on by their captors. The Austro-German attack in October 1917 was the most successful mbined operation of the war and brought the Italian Army to the brink of defeat.

34. Heavy equipment lies abandoned on the road towards the Tagliamento in the days after the Battl of Caporetto, November 1917.

35. General Armando Diaz (*centre with a walking stick*) visiting the trenches soon after replacing Cadorna as Italian Chief of the General Staff in November 1917. The urgency of restoring Italian morale was paramount. 'The weapon which I am summoned to grasp has been blunted', he said. 'It must be re-tempered without delay.'

. The Bolshevik delegation arrives at Brest-Litovsk, December 1917. The discussions over ending e war on the Eastern Front were a strange and disorientating experience for the German command am, who soon grew exasperated by their guests' novel methods.

. An anxious-looking Emperor Karl faces Kaiser Wilhelm II at the railway station in Spa, Belgium, May 1918. With his German allies furious that he had entertained peace negotiations with the tente, Karl was presented with renewed demands to agree to 'a close, long-term political alliance' th Germany.

38. General Mikhail Alekseev, commander of the Volunteer Army, near Ekaterinodar, shortly before his death in October 1918. Alekseev 'gave his last bit of energy to the Volunteer Army he created wi his own hands . . . he walked alongside his creation down the thorny path to the cherished goal of t salvation of his Homeland'.

. A panorama of the Dojran front, October 1918. The town of Dojran lies on the right with the
ulgarian positions dug into the hills on the left. 'No map, no aeroplane photograph, could have
ven any idea of the desperate strength of the place . . .'

General Franchet d'Espèrey signs the armistice agreement at his headquarters in Salonika,
September 1918.

41. Italian infantry crossing the Piave on a pontoon bridge, November 1918. The Battle of Vittorio Veneto marked the end of the war on the Italian Front and was a triumph for the Chief of the General Staff, Armando Diaz.

42. The Italian delegation, led by Pietro Badoglio (*standing right, feet together*), awaits the arrival of the Austro-Hungarians at Villa Giusti, November 1918.

striking northwest towards Kajmakcalan, while the French and Russians would operate on their left, 'constantly striving to outflank the enemy'.[18] Many Allied officers worried about whether the Serbs had retained their legendary offensive spirit, but they went forward with a stoic cheerfulness, seizing part of the Bulgarian forward positions after fierce hand-to-hand fighting. On the left, where the French and Russians moved through the valley floor towards Monastir, the Bulgarians fell back steadily, even if this was not quick enough for Sarrail, who had envisaged a much swifter, more decisive attack. 'Advance rapidly towards Florina with the railway on your right, and march at least as quickly as the Serbian left flank, remaining in constant liaison with them if you are unable to catch up', he wired on 15 September, reminding General Victor Cordonnier, who had been sent out by Joffre to command the four French divisions, that he was responsible for the safety of the left flank. 'Avoid complicated manoeuvres . . . and so forth. I repeat that you are to make a vigorous, prolonged and rapid effort, the results of which can contribute – and should already have contributed – enormously towards turning the enemy's retreat into a rout. Advance your heavy artillery rapidly in order to vigorously attack the enemy in their main defensive line before they have a chance to regroup. March, march, march.'[19]

The village of Florina, an important waystation on the route to Monastir, fell on 17 September. This was an encouraging start, but the Allied advance remained sluggish. The Bulgarians moved in reinforcements taken from Lake Dojran and the Struma Valley and unleashed frequent counter-attacks. The Russians and French had to move through a largely uninhabited countryside, without detailed maps, in the heat of early autumn. Their progress was also hampered by the pace at which supplies of food and ammunition could reach the forward lines. The Eksisu railway viaduct, part of the main line between Salonika and Monastir, had been demolished by the retreating enemy, which left Cordonnier relying upon a patchy supply network until it could be repaired. As he later noted, 'An army is an unwieldy thing to move when not only its munitions, but all its supplies are drawn from the rear.' *L'armée d'Orient* had, in his words, had 'its wings clipped'.[20]

Up on the Nidže heights, the Serbs continued to advance steadily.

'Little entrenching was possible on the stonebound mountain-side', noted a British journalist who scrambled up after them. 'In clefts and gullies, behind outcrops of rock or under shelter of individual heaps of stones collected under cover of dark, the soldiers of these two Balkan armies . . . fought each other with savage and bitter hatred, under the fiercest weather conditions of cold and exposure.'[21] By 30 September, they had managed to seize the crest of Kajmakcalan, with the Bulgarians withdrawing to the north. General von Winckler, commander of the German Eleventh Army, which mostly comprised Bulgarian troops, ordered an immediate counter-attack, but his men refused, citing their exhaustion and heavy losses. When the news was relayed to Tsar Ferdinand in Sofia, he was visibly disturbed, sending a telegram to OHL warning that the loss of 'Bitola (Monastir) and Ohrid – and perhaps other Macedonian positions besides – will result in irrevocable disappointment within the army and the discrediting of the government'. More support was needed or 'the foundations of our common alliance will suffer irreparable damage'.[22]

The Bulgarians pulled out soon afterwards, withdrawing to a prepared position near Kenali along the Serbian border, about nine miles south of Monastir, from where they prepared to make a stand. When Cordonnier saw the Bulgarian lines, well sited and heavily wired, he knew that any attack would be costly and require extensive artillery preparation, as well as a division of colonial troops that he had been promised, but Sarrail was not interested. Dismissing the idea of a flanking manoeuvre through the hills, he demanded a frontal assault by 3 October, insisting that it be 'pushed home with vigour'; if not, Cordonnier should resign. Cordonnier replied anxiously on 29 September, stating that he had not intended to attack for another week. He had ridden up to the front and come under fire, but 'I do not fear battle. We will go to die when you wish, but we will not defeat the enemy until the Russians are able to lend their aid and until we have the support of the colonial division. I owe you this candour, regardless of what it may mean for me.'[23]

The spat between Sarrail and Cordonnier was not unusual during the war. Plenty of senior officers clashed with their subordinates who were nearer the front and who saw the dangers that over-hasty action might entail. Cordonnier knew that his men were tired and in need of reinforcement, but Sarrail had been instructed to advance and would see that his orders were followed. A massive assault took place all along the line on 14 October. The Bulgarian trenches had been bombarded all morning, but with only mixed success; the barbed wire had not been breached and the attackers, led by two French colonial brigades, suffered heavy losses trying to cross no-man's-land. Cordonnier, who watched the attack take place, saw the colonel of 4 Russian Regiment, on horseback, galloping in front of his men urging them on, bullets zipping through the air. 'With a single bound, his regiment leapt into the enemy trenches. Within a moment it was forced back, with 600 men left on the ground.' In total, around 50 officers and 1,600 men were killed, wounded or missing on 14 October. As Cordonnier put it bluntly, 'Our soldiers gave generously of their blood.'[24]

As it was on the Isonzo, so it would be in Macedonia. It took six weeks of hard fighting to break the Kenali line. Each day the artillery on both sides shelled the opposing trenches, while the hours of darkness were frequently broken by the glow of flares fired off by nervous sentries. French, Russian and Serbian troops spent their time digging trenches and narrowing the width of no-man's-land, while enduring heavy thunderstorms that left the ground inundated with rain and the roads and tracks thick with mud. As one British observer sadly noted, 'Flanders mud is bad, but Macedonian mud beats it completely.'[25] Activity was also intense on the other side of the line, with the Bulgarians busily reinforcing their defences. When a French liaison officer inspected them the following month, he was impressed by their complexity and strength ('bearing the hallmarks of the Germans'), noting that the Bulgarians were planning on spending the winter there. 'There is a first defensive line made up of a deep, sheltered trench, then a support line and a second defensive line, two networks and partitions, small passages, a number of shelters for reserves, batteries with bunkers and flanking batteries within the village itself, and sheltered pits dug for machine guns.'[26]

The defences were strong for a reason. Neither Bulgaria nor Germany could spare any more men for a prolonged campaign in the Balkans. There was only a single German division in Macedonia, the surviving remnant of the army that had conquered Serbia in the autumn of 1915, although some support elements were still in place: telephone operators, air force squadrons, machine-gun units and artillery batteries, all of which helped to 'stiffen' the Bulgarians.[27] Outnumbered and outgunned, the Bulgarian Army would lose around 40,000 men in its defence of Monastir, which led to an increasingly fractious relationship with Bulgaria's German protectors. From Sofia's perspective, the reappearance of Serbian troops among the Allied forces meant that she was still entitled to the level of support that had been agreed in the military convention of 6 September 1915 (six divisions each from Berlin and Vienna) and that she could not be expected to hold on to the southern front indefinitely against what seemed like inexhaustible Allied manpower.[28]

The Bulgarians had a point, but Hindenburg and Ludendorff held firm and insisted that reinforcements would not be sent until Romania had been dealt with. 'We could not do everything with German troops', complained Ludendorff, who knew that the ground was difficult and the poor state of the roads and railways meant they could barely supply the small number of men that were already in Macedonia. 'To send more troops there', he added, 'would have been bad policy.'[29] It was decided to appoint General Otto von Below, a capable officer with experience of both Western and Eastern Fronts, as commander of a new army group in the Balkans, comprising Eleventh Army and the First and Second Bulgarian Armies. He was able to bring in two German battalions and several more machine-gun teams, but otherwise could only repeat OHL's mantra that they must hang on for as long as possible without further support. General Zhekov, the Bulgarian Commander-in-Chief, continued to insist that more resources were necessary if they were to hold on to Monastir, which had 'special political and moral importance', but Below could only shrug his shoulders. Realizing that there was little they could do, the Bulgarians relented. Writing to Hindenburg in mid-October, Prime Minister Radoslavov looked forward to the overthrow of Romania, when the 'Balkan problem' would be solved: 'Then the Bulgarian troops will easily be able to finish off Sarrail.'[30]

Sarrail's difficulties seemed to multiply each week. General

Cordonnier was sent home on 20 October, a casualty of Sarrail's vindictiveness, and was replaced by Major-General Leblois, who had commanded one of the French divisions. This change certainly pleased Sarrail, even if it did little to address the serious manpower deficiencies that were now threatening to bring the expeditionary force's progress to a premature halt. By November, the French contingent in Macedonia was 28,000 men under-strength, having been worn down by battlefield losses and the ever-present scourge of malaria.[31] Worsening weather was another concern. If Monastir was going to fall, they needed to move quickly, but the mountains were covered in snow and ice, the plain was a 'quagmire', and as one authority later explained, 'all movement was slow, painful, and sometimes dangerous'.[32] With the main route to Monastir blocked, Sarrail had little choice but to shift his efforts to the flanks, and he authorized thrusts on both right and left, with the Serbs pushing across the Crna river and threatening to outflank the main Bulgarian defences, while French and Italian troops attacked along the shores of Lake Prespa. He was fortunate in being able to rely upon *Voivode* Mišić, the commander of the Serbian First Army, who had led his men throughout the campaign with great elan. A liaison officer sent by Joffre to report on the situation enthused that this seasoned fighter, a veteran of the Balkan Wars, was 'the soul of the offensive'. By 13 November, the Serbs had seized more high ground east of Monastir and forced a further withdrawal of Bulgarian forces, with even some German battalions, thrown into action, being unable to stop Mišić's army.[33]

Combined with pressure in the centre, it was enough to break the enemy's resistance. A heavy assault, with the attackers and defenders almost indistinguishable because of 'teeming rain' and the 'worst mud conceivable', finally cracked the Bulgarian lines on 14 November. Kenali fell that day and with it the last hope of holding on through the winter. Four days later, the Allies realized something was happening at Monastir. Columns of smoke were rising, obscuring the famous white minarets, while explosions rocked the air. Bulgarian prisoners, now dribbling into the French lines, revealed that they were intending to pull out during the night. Allied troops dragged themselves forward, cavalry trotting on ahead, and found the enemy trenches abandoned and the last limbers leaving. On the morning of 19 November, as Sarrail's men entered the town, 'the most perfect triple rainbow' appeared in the sky.[34] Sarrail issued a gushing order of the day, saluting the various forces under his command and the role they had played in what he called the first victory since the German invasion of France had been turned back at the Battle of the Marne in September 1914. 'Monastir is in the hands of the allies', he wrote, offering 'warmest congratulations' to his men:

> Serbs, you were the first to open the way and the first to finally see our enemies flee; your tenacity allowed us to capture Monastir. Russians, whether in the mountains of Greece or the plains of Serbia, your legendary courage never wavered. The British Army, to this day you have had one of the most thankless tasks. You have had to fight on a front that has to this point remained defensive, yet you have not been sparing with your blood, sweat and tears. You have fulfilled the role entrusted to you with honour, ready to push forward whenever the order might come. Italians, in all areas where your colours have flown, you have remembered the mighty deeds that you have previously done in the Alps. Frenchmen, I am proud to have led you here in the Orient. May today's success be no more than a prelude to greater successes to come.

Sarrail would have liked to push on – he always did – but even he admitted that they did not have the forces to do so: 'The Serbs, Russians, French were out of breath.'[35]

The fall of Monastir was the crowning moment of Sarrail's war, but it came too late to save Romania. A week earlier, on 11 November, General Falkenhayn's Ninth Army had begun to force the passes through the Carpathians as part of a concerted effort to finish off the campaign before winter. The conditions were already far from ideal. Heavy storms had left the mountains thick with ice and snow and the lowland passes treacherous underfoot. Falkenhayn had massed his forces out to the west, at the Szurduk Pass, and his divisions began moving into position at five o'clock that morning; about 60,000 men and 30,000 horses, plus their artillery and an enormous baggage train, marching south in heavy fog. Proceeding along a path that was, as Falkenhayn put it, 'not half as wide as the Friedrichstrasse in Berlin' was a colossal undertaking:

> The sheer rock faces on one side and on the other the raging Jiu river, to which the slope from the roadside fell just as suddenly, prevented any deviation from the narrow path. In many cases, this was narrowed even further by the breaking off of individual pieces, by rocks falling down . . . Our columns surged out of the narrow pass in unrelenting waves, building up to the right and left and continuing their march south. Not once did I see even the slightest hesitation or incertitude, despite the fact that on multiple occasions the Romanian counter-attacks were getting alarmingly close to the entrance of the pass. The whole crowd was willed on by a single common objective: to make it through the mountains and towards the enemy![36]

The Romanians were well aware of how important it was to keep Falkenhayn bottled up on the far side of the Carpathians. Fighting had been ongoing since the retreats from Sibiu and Brasov, with First and Second Armies successfully defending the routes into Romania, albeit at heavy cost. With over 700 kilometres of frontier and up to 15 passes to cover, Romania would need to concentrate her forces as soon as Falkenhayn's hand was revealed. But this might take a week or more, and would depend upon good liaison and communication. Falken-hayn ordered a series of demonstrations up and down the front, while massing 40 battalions and 52 cavalry squadrons at Szurduk. They faced just 18 enemy battalions, and many of these were exhausted, under-strength and demoralized by the fighting of recent weeks.[37] He knew that time was running out, but he gambled anyway, deciding to punch through at Szurduk, which was one of the narrowest points in the mountains. His corps commander, Lieutenant-General Kühne, was ordered to 'open and keep open the routes from the mountains around Targu Jiu, so that Schmettov's cavalry corps could be driven south into the Romanian hills'.[38]

As soon as the Romanian High Command realized what was hap-pening, it launched waves of infantry across the rain-swept ground, but outnumbered and without the fire support they needed, they were soon coming back, demoralized and shaken. 'In spite of all our efforts, it was not possible to push back the enemy, due to their much stronger infantry, cavalry and artillery', reported Major-General Cocorascu, commanding 1st Division. 'The enemy's superior forces can be deduced not only from the communications of the battalion, regiment, and brigade commanders, but also from the number of enemy columns and the expansive front on which they operated, which was at least 40 kilometres. I can't say with precision what forces the enemy had. However, I had the sense that they had had, did have, and would soon have, some very great forces, and that that would make our situation most critical.'[39] Falkenhayn's forces occupied the city of Targu Jiu, at the southern edge of the Szurduk Pass, on 15 November. The door was now open to Wallachia – the westernmost province of Romania.

Falkenhayn was determined to press his advantage and ordered Lieutenant-General Eberhard Graf von Schmettow's Cavalry Corps to exploit out to the south. For so long condemned to inactivity on other fronts, mounted troops found Romania to be an ideal place to fight. Once they had cleared the mountain passes, the Cavalry Corps galloped off, skirmishing with enemy troops and spreading chaos in the Romanian rear. The second city of Craiova was occupied on 21 November, with Romanian forces falling back to the line of the Olt river, which formed a major obstacle to any invader coming from the west. The Romanian High Command hoped to hold the river line against any enemy incursion, but Schmettow's horsemen seized several bridges and passed over onto the far bank. In the south, Mackensen was also on the move. His forces crossed the Danube on 23 November, making use of pontoon bridges, ferry boats and barges to conquer this vast water obstacle – the second time he had done so. After carefully choosing their site (at Sistov, about sixty-five miles southwest of Bucharest), they were able to get five divisions, with all their horses, wagons and artillery, over to the Romanian side in less than three days and to do so with almost no interference. 'The troops were in high spirits', wrote Mackensen. The Bulgarians were taken across on large barges to the sound of their regimental musicians. From there they moved into the interior, marching or riding north to join Falkenhayn's army for the assault on Bucharest.[40]

The Romanian Army had not yet given up hope, although a sense of depression was spreading rapidly among its senior commanders, overwhelmed at how quickly the Germans were moving. Second Army commander General Averescu struggled to raise his spirits. 'Events in Oltenia are becoming more and more catastrophic', he wrote in his diary on 19 November. 'Our troops are retreating in a disorderly fashion and the enemy is advancing rapidly. While we make war in complete disarray, they are doing it as shrewdly as can be! . . . It makes my heart bleed and ache as I am convinced that all this misfortune could have been avoided. It might not have been an illustrious war, due to our unpreparedness, but we might still have made it an honourable one!' He resented Berthelot's presence and scoffed at his plans for a 'mass of manoeuvre' that, it was hoped, would reproduce the Battle of the Marne along the Arges river, which ran to the southeast in front of Bucharest. Berthelot did not 'inspire much confidence' in Averescu. 'He might have been a very good corps commander, as a subordinate executive officer. I have not, as yet, had the sense that he is as gifted at discerning the strategic future, in order for him to rise to the level of army command.'[41]

Berthelot was not interested in listening to such defeatism and did what he could to reorganize the Romanian forces, trying his best to keep up morale and urge them to continue fighting, even if their notorious inconsistency tried his patience. 'One day they fight ably', he grumbled; 'the next they panic, and it is unclear why.'[42] Already three separate columns were converging on Bucharest: Mackensen from the south, Falkenhayn's main body from the west, and the Alpine Corps, which was moving through the Red Tower Pass in the north. On 25 November, General Constantin Prezan was placed in charge of all troops defending the capital. Working alongside Berthelot, he sketched out a simple plan to concentrate against Mackensen, crushing him before he could combine with Falkenhayn. First and Second Armies would hold the line in the north and west, giving Prezan enough manpower to sweep the enemy back into the Danube: 'I intend to go on the offensive and beat the enemy forces wherever we encounter them.'[43]

Prezan's plan was daring, some would have said reckless, but it offered the only chance of staving off the coming storm. The difficulty was getting his divisions into place and ready to attack at the right moment. A staff car carrying two officers and a copy of his operation orders fell into German hands late on the afternoon of 1 December, which alerted Falkenhayn to the danger on his right flank and gave him precious time to send reinforcements. The other problem was that employing a 'mass of manoeuvre', as Berthelot wanted, could only work against an enemy that was fixed in place. The Germans presented Prezan with a moving target that was not easy to strike, at least not without overwhelming numbers. Prezan only managed to scrape together two amalgamated divisions for his counter-attack and pushed them out of the capital defences on 1 December. They were to drive into the gap between Falkenhayn's main force and Mackensen's 'Danube Army', which was moving up from the town of Draganesti to the southwest. 'The future of our people hangs on the operation begun today . . .' Prezan stated in his final orders. 'Save our beloved land from the hordes of the grim barbarians.'[44]

For a few precious hours, it seemed like Prezan's plan was going to work. His strike force ran into one of Mackensen's divisions and almost surrounded it, fighting hard to turn both its flanks during two days of savage combat. By 3 December, the Germans were struggling to hold on, with some regiments down to just 300 men and ammunition beginning to run out. Fortunately, at noon, 'great white clouds of shrapnel' could be seen in the rear and the sound of artillery fire 'from the west and north-west' was 'becoming noticeably heavier'. Soon the cry of 'Falkenhayn is here!' could be heard, and the Romanians fell back in confusion. 'In wild flight, the enemy is still trying to reach the safe passage on the Arges', recorded one account. 'Only a few succeed!' In the 'burning village of Epuresti – white cloths billow and flutter, while entire battalions march to surrender'. Just in time, a relief force (11th Bavarian Division) had come down from the northwest, breaking the ring and causing an immediate panic, which spread through Prezan's forces like a shock wave.[45]

It was over very quickly. Once Mackensen and Falkenhayn had joined forces, there was little Prezan or Berthelot could do to prevent their men from being defeated. The great counter-attack had devolved into a series of isolated battles, with some Romanian regiments surrendering while others kept fighting. In the first week of December, Falkenhayn's Ninth Army captured 60,000 men and 83 guns (with Mackensen bagging another 5,000 prisoners) as the Romanian forces rapidly fell apart. 'This is the very picture of a battlefield the evening after a defeat, exactly as we would have seen in the illustrated books of war we read as children', recorded one witness as he rode through the flame-licked village of Gorneni, southwest of Bucharest. 'Supply wagons with broken wheels, their draught beams raised like hands to the sky in prayer, abandoned cannons, infantrymen face down in the dirt, and mess kits, bullets and bags strewn everywhere, the sorry debris of men defeated and put to flight.'[46]

Bucharest was declared an 'open city' – to spare its destruction – and the Romanian Army was ordered to withdraw back to the east. The capital fell on 6 December, with German and Bulgarian units urged to pursue their foe as quickly as they could. But even Mackensen recognized that the conditions were becoming insurmountable. 'The persistent rain', he later wrote, 'caused such poor conditions on the generally unkempt roads in the Wallachian lowlands that every step of the way was a great strain for both people and animals, even on what was supposedly a highway. In fact, the oxen progressed almost more quickly – or at least more safely – than the best motor vehicle. The verge was also turned into a muddy swamp. Many waterways had burst their banks and flooded the roads. The few road crossings were mostly destroyed. The only thing that kept the leaders and troops pushing ahead was sheer willpower.'[47] The Romanian Army was now making its way to a new line along the Sereth river, 100 miles to the northeast. Strung out in long columns, troops splashed through the mud and sleet, starving and demoralized, heading into an uncertain future. 'We have put roadblocks all over to stop the fleeing soldiers,' noted Averescu. 'It appears that the disintegration is progressing. Those who prepared for war can congratulate themselves.'[48]

15. 'Born for misfortune'

On 30 December 1916, during a frozen, impossibly cold night in Petrograd, Grigori Rasputin was murdered. A group of conspirators centred on the Grand Duke Dmitry Pavlovich, the Tsar's cousin, Prince Felix Yusupov, reportedly the wealthiest man in Russia, and Vladimir Purishkevich, an outspoken rightist member of the Duma, had been planning the assassination for weeks, each convinced that only radical action could save the monarchy and, by extension, Russia. On 2 December, Purishkevich had spoken in the Duma, delivering a sustained attack on the 'chaos prevailing among our rulers' and 'those corrupting influences which reach the organs of the Government and undermine the will of its highest representative'. They had no choice, he told the assembled members, but to 'go to Headquarters and plead with the Sovereign . . . to deliver Russia from Rasputin'.[1]

Everyone knew that the Tsar was unlikely to dispense with Rasputin's services, so deliverance would have to come from elsewhere. A plan was hatched that saw Yusupov befriend the *starets* and invite him to dinner at the Moika Palace, where he would be poisoned and his body disposed of. When Rasputin arrived on the night of 29 December, he was shown into a basement room and offered cream cakes, washed down with wine, which had been laced with enough cyanide, so it was said, to kill several men. But according to those present, he proved curiously immune to the effects of the poison, eating, drinking and chatting with his hosts with all the conviviality he was known for. At some point in the early hours, Yusupov tired of this, and after excusing himself for a few moments, he returned to the basement armed with a revolver and shot the *starets* in the chest. But once again Rasputin refused to die, and suddenly lurched at Yusupov, staggering out of the house in a furious rage. At that moment, Purishkevich ran down the stairs, saw their victim hobbling away into the snow and shot him twice, once in the back and the second time in his forehead. Rasputin's body was bundled into a waiting car and then dumped in the Lower Neva.[2]

The reaction across Russia was mixed. Crowds gathered at the Cathedral of Our Lady of Kazan, lighting candles and singing hymns, and the streets were full of citizens cheering and dancing, but the mood in Siberia was muted. There, the *starets* was regarded as a powerful prophet who had spoken truth to the highest power on earth and been killed for it. When the Tsarina heard rumours that something had happened, she wrote a bitter, tear-stained letter to Nicholas reporting that their 'friend' had disappeared. 'This night [there was a] big scandal at *Yussupov's* house – big meeting, Dmitri, *Purishkevich* etc. all drunk, Police heard shots, *Purishkevich* ran out screaming to the Police that our Friend was killed . . . I cannot & won't believe He has been killed. God have mercy. Such utter anguish (am calm & can't believe it).'[3] It was not until the body was found several days later that Nicholas left *Stavka* and returned home to comfort his wife. While the Tsar was shaken by the murder, his over-riding feeling was one of disgust. 'Before all Russia,' he said, 'I am filled with shame that the hands of my kinsmen are stained with the blood of a simple peasant.'[4] But he refused to wreak vengeance on the conspirators. Pavlovich was ordered to join the Russian armies in Persia, Yusupov was exiled to his estate, while Purishkevich was simply left alone.

The response to Rasputin's murder in London and Paris was generally positive: there was a sense of relief that a possible German agent had been eliminated and of hope that this would strengthen the war effort. 'The End of a Nightmare', reported *The Times* on 4 January. 'It is no exaggeration to say that the whole of Russia breathes more freely for the removal of a most baleful influence, recognized as one of the pivots of the Germanophil[e] forces . . . His unlimited sway over certain personalities is generally ascribed to hypnotic powers.'[5] Others were not so sure that it was a good omen. When the French Ambassador, Maurice Paléologue, spoke to the Grand Duke Paul, whose son, Dmitry, had been involved in the plot, he was struck by the sense of fatalism that was spreading among even the Tsar's most devoted servants. 'The Emperor is more under the Empress's thumb than ever', he said. 'She has succeeded in persuading him that the hostile movement against her – and it's beginning to be against *him*, unfortunately – is nothing but a conspiracy of the Grand Dukes and a drawing-room revolt. All this can only end with a tragedy . . .'[6]

The winter of 1916–17 was a strange, unsettling time. A mood of restlessness and impatience seemed to hang in the air, which was unsurprising given the fortunes of the Entente: everywhere outnumbering and outmuscling its opponents, yet unable to land a decisive blow. An inter-Allied meeting had been held in Paris on 15–16 November that outlined the stark problem. As the French Prime Minister, Monsieur Briand, noted, 'When studying the situation using the documents provided by the military authorities and carefully checked by GQG, the first thing that strikes the observer is that the Allies have at their disposal superior manpower of at least 50% more than can be employed against them by the Germans, the Austrians, the Bulgarians and the Turks combined.' The heavy fighting throughout 1916 had forced their opponents onto the defensive but done little else. Therefore, it was agreed to fight on through the winter wherever possible and prepare for a coordinated general offensive on all fronts in the first half of February 1917.[7]

As the year came to an end, the Entente underwent a period of marked turmoil. New leaders came in, old ones were jettisoned, and questions that had already been settled were reopened in earnest. Marshal Joffre, the man who had led France's armies since 1911, was moved aside in December as Briand tried to answer growing criticism of his ministry. War-weariness and frustration at two years of indecisive fighting, combined with the Romanian disaster, had sapped public confidence. Joffre was appointed 'general-in-chief' and technical adviser to the government – a nominal promotion – while operational control of the French armies was transferred to General Robert Nivelle; a charismatic artillery officer who claimed to have the 'formula' for success. Nivelle quickly scrapped Joffre's plans for a renewal of the Somme offensive and explained that France could not sustain another year of indecisive attrition. Instead, they must 'strive to destroy the main body of the enemy's Armies on the Western Front'. This would require a preliminary attack by the British to pin down enemy forces before an '*attaque brusquée*' was carried out along the French sector that would 'bring about the break-through'.[8]

Nivelle's plan was impressive in scope and highly ambitious – and it would need sizeable support from the British. In London, Herbert Asquith, Prime Minister since 1908, was ousted in December by David Lloyd George, the energetic Liberal politician who promised to revitalize the British war effort. In his first speech to Parliament as Prime Minster, Lloyd George made it clear that the alliance had to find 'some means of arriving at quicker and readier decisions, and of carrying them out'. Contrasting the Central Powers, where 'Austrian guns are helping German infantry, and German infantry are stiffening Austrian arms', he called for 'more consultation, more real consultation between the men who matter in the direction of affairs' and stated that there needed to 'be less of the feeling that each country has got its own front to look after'.[9] This was an important and necessary observation, but the practical difficulties of binding together a disparate coalition and fighting a war across multiple theatres proved extremely challenging. Indeed, Lloyd George had enough trouble persuading his own generals, including the Chief of the Imperial General Staff, Sir William Robertson, to agree to his plan to send additional batteries of heavy artillery to the Italian Front to enable General Cadorna to push on to Trieste and Pola.

Working assiduously to have his voice heard, Lloyd George proposed another conference, this time in Rome, 'to have a frank discussion on the whole military and political situation'.[10] When he arrived in the Italian capital on 5 January, he circulated a memorandum that laid out, in his typically direct style, the failures of the Entente and the urgent need for better coordination. 'The efforts of the British and French armies on the Western Front; of the Italian army on the Southern Front; and of the Russians in the East, though latterly co-ordinated in point of time, have not been sufficient to prevent an inferior enemy from overrunning first Serbia, and latterly Roumania [*sic*]. This is a serious reflection on our common efforts, and it behoves each Government to do its utmost to rectify this fundamental error.' Given the difficulties of shipping extra troops to Salonika, and the onerous task of keeping them supplied across long and vulnerable sea lines of communication, Lloyd George suggested that Italians should be sent instead. Furthermore, they should transport heavy guns, with plenty of ammunition, to allow Cadorna to take the offensive. 'Would it not be possible', he asked, 'to make a great and sudden stroke against the enemy by a concentration of British and French artillery on the Isonzo front, so as not only to ensure the safety of Italy against any enemy concentration, but what is more important, to shatter the enemy's forces, to inflict a decisive defeat on him, and to press forward to Trieste and to get astride the Istrian Peninsula?'[11]

Lloyd George had certainly made a compelling case, his eyes darting around the room and his hands pointing and switching with every gesture, but his audience remained unmoved. Briand asked 'how great was the organisation needed, under modern conditions, for an offensive' (possibly three or four months). Preparations for Nivelle's spring offensive were already under way, and it would be unwise to change them now. The matter came down to the practicalities of moving the guns, which would have to be sent from France. When Cadorna, who attended the conference, was asked for his thoughts, he pointed to myriad issues that would need to be solved. How long would the guns be at his disposal? He had heard that they would have to be returned by May, but this would be difficult:

> He reminded the Conference [recorded the secretary] that to be useful for offensive operations the material must be back [in France] some eight or ten days before the offensive began. Then an allowance had to be made for the time necessary for the transport to and from France. Time also had to be allowed for loading and unloading off the railways. Then there were the different methods of the various nations to be considered in regard to technical matters, such as fire control, the use of metres instead of yards, fire observation, &c.; some time would be required to accustom the British and French artillery to the Italian methods. After you had made allowance for all these things, he asked how much time remained?

Lloyd George shrugged and said that this 'might apply to the French guns', but he was not averse to allowing British guns to remain for longer. Albert Thomas, the French Minister of Munitions, visibly baulked at this remark and said that Lloyd George 'talked as though his resources were unlimited'. He had already spoken of sending guns to both Italy and Russia, but how could this be done 'without altering the whole equilibrium of the position on the Western Front?'[12]

That perennial source of inter-Allied friction, Salonika, remained as tortuous as ever. In Rome, Briand announced that two French divisions would sail for Greece, and argued that with a few more divisions 'victory on this front was certain', but if the British refused to provide them then a 'catastrophe' might occur. This was a familiar line of argument, rehearsed at previous conferences, and it did not make any difference this time. The British were concerned about how much shipping was available and how costly it would be to find the tonnage necessary to bring coal and food to France and Italy as well as supporting the expeditionary force at Salonika. Robertson, who watched Lloyd George's efforts with a mixture of weariness and fascination, sent him a short note the following evening warning him not to be distracted by French promises. 'I don't know what effect M. Briand's oratory may have upon you in regard to the wretched Salonika business, but it seems only right and fair to you that I should tell you now that I could never bring myself to sign an order for the despatch of further British divisions to Salonika.'[13]

The fate of Romania hung over the Entente powers as a vivid indication of their impotence. With no way to provide immediate assistance, they could only look upon her ruin from afar, urging Russia to do more but otherwise unable to prevent Germany from seizing considerable agricultural and industrial resources, which would prove essential in the coming winter, a time plagued by food shortages and domestic unrest. All they were able to do was send a small team of engineers and demolition experts led by Lieutenant-Colonel John Norton-Griffiths, who was charged with making sure that Romania's valuable oil and grain reserves did not fall into enemy hands. He arrived in Bucharest on 17 November and visited as many sites as he could before the Germans arrived. Machinery was smashed with sledgehammers, oil stocks were fired, wells were plugged by throwing in iron bars, tools and wrenches, with Norton-Griffiths estimating that he had destroyed 210 million gallons of oil and vast stores of grain, only regretting that there had not been the time or manpower to accomplish more. He was also disappointed at the lack of cooperation from Romanian officials, who were sceptical of his ideas and insistent that the situation surely did not require such a total and devastating response. 'It certainly has been a revelation . . .' he admitted, 'that our conception of obstructing the enemy means sacrificing the individual and the fruits of the earth, at no matter what cost to either, to accomplish our ends.'[14]

The loss of these resources was unfortunate for the Central Powers, but it could not distract from what had been a brilliant display of military skill and endurance. As the man whose forces had marched into the Romanian capital, Field Marshal Mackensen added further plaudits to an already stellar reputation. The Kaiser wrote to him on 11 January confirming that he would receive the Grand Cross of the Iron Cross for his 'masterly' performance – one of only a handful to be awarded during the war. 'You knew just how to unite the armies for joint action – which were initially so widely separated – in an exemplary manner. The demands on the troops were extraordinary. But the German, Austro-Hungarian, Ottoman and Bulgarian armies withstood the trials and tribulations with the most laudable zeal, and achieved victory everywhere.' Mackensen was delighted: 'How am I to thank God for such grace? How should I thank my troops, or those who supported me on my staff, or those who shed their own blood in the name of victory? I will try to find the words to thank the Emperor.'[15]

As for Falkenhayn, whose Ninth Army had done so much to break through into Wallachia, he ended the year in a frustrated mood. His men were heading towards the Sereth river, but a combination of exhaustion, lack of supplies and heavy rainfall slowed them down. 'The weather, which had been a little better in recent days, had worsened again', he wrote on 31 December. 'It pelted down incessantly. Every time we veered from the path, we were met with the most monstrous difficulties. It is indicative of the condition of the roads that even on the Râmnicu Sârat–Focşani national highway, riding and draught animals drowning or sinking in the mud were not the exception but the daily reality.' He was also smarting from persistent disagreements with OHL, which had left him convinced that his achievements were being downplayed or even ignored. While Hindenburg was awarded the same honour as Mackensen, Falkenhayn received nothing.[16]

Hindenburg and Ludendorff looked upon the Romanian campaign with an understandable degree of satisfaction, but perhaps for the first time in the war, their attention was not on Galicia or the Balkans, East Prussia or the Carpathians. Now the Western Front loomed foremost in their minds. They moved OHL from Pless, where it had been since the days of Gorlice–Tarnów, to the resort town of Bad Kreuznach, forty miles from Frankfurt, which was a firm indication that the centre of gravity had switched back to the west. The weight of British and French resources massed against them was suffocating, with most observers convinced that new attacks would be launched in the spring. Now more than ever, the Central Powers resembled a besieged fortress, with the fighting at the front mirrored at sea by an ever-tightening naval blockade. As early as October 1916, Hindenburg had written to Bethmann Hollweg and told him that the coming months would 'decide the existence and non-existence of the German people', and they would only avoid succumbing 'if we exert all our strengths'.[17]

Something had to be done to break this stranglehold. The duo had already called for a total and ruthless remobilization of German and Austrian societies for the next phase of the war, and demanded significant increases in armament production, particularly machine-guns, artillery pieces, shells and aircraft – the so-called 'Hindenburg Programme'. At the same time, they pressed for an intensification of U-boat activity, which had only been employed sporadically since 1914. Bethmann Hollweg was the chief opponent of such a move, fearing that it would bring the United States of America into the war, and he sought to take advantage of Germany's recent victories with an overture to the Entente. On 12 December, he issued a note to the Allied powers offering to enter negotiations 'for the restoration of a lasting peace', but nothing came of it. The Allies were bound together not to accept a separate settlement and refused to

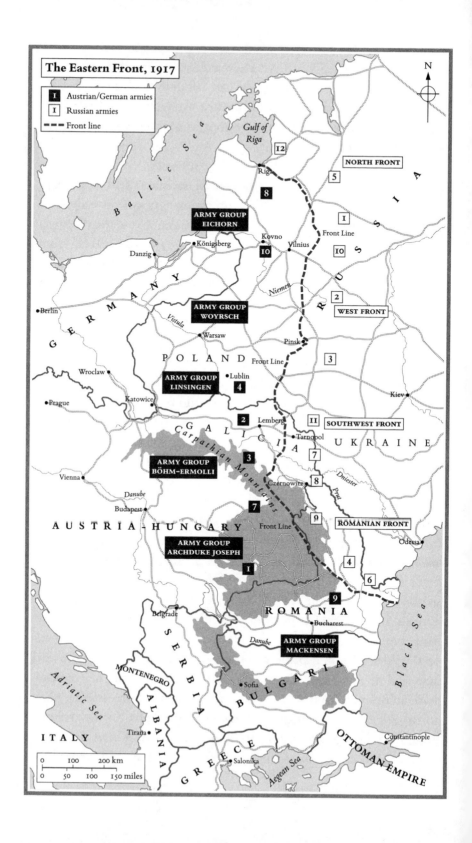

countenance discussions at this time, which left the matter still to be decided on the battlefield.[18]

The failure of the December peace note placed the initiative firmly back in the hands of OHL, which had viewed Bethmann Hollweg's plans with little enthusiasm. On 23 December, Hindenburg reminded the Chancellor that 'in view of the military situation', they 'must lose no time in adopting the measure of torpedoing armed enemy merchantmen without notice'. In a reply the following day, Bethmann Hollweg noted that the advantages of conducting this method of warfare had to 'outweigh the disadvantages of the entry of America into the ranks of our enemies'.[19] During a meeting on 9 January, Wilhelm II agreed to begin unrestricted submarine warfare on 1 February, having been persuaded that it was essential for morale and would possibly force Britain to her knees within six months. Bethmann Hollweg registered his usual half-hearted protest. 'If the submarine war does not succeed,' he warned, 'we are exposed to complete defeat, for we can be certain of America's entry into the war, as well as the impossibility of ending the war by any other means than merely deciding on weapons.' Having said that, the Entente's rejection of the December peace offer 'shows that it has no interest in peace negotiations', and in these circumstances 'he could not advise His Majesty to make a decision that would contradict the vote of the army and naval command'.[20]

None of these decisions had been made with much reference to Austria–Hungary, which limped into 1917 with a sense of deepening gloom, dragged along in Germany's wake, unwilling and helpless. Food shortages were now becoming desperate, and the term 'Vienna sickness' had been coined to describe the sufferings of the poor shivering wretches, racked by tuberculosis, who haunted the capital's streets. The potato harvest had been particularly disappointing. Just 50 million quintals had been produced in 1916 (the last peacetime figure had been over 120 million), and because the amount of cereal crops almost halved between 1914 and 1916, the empire's citizens were faced with a bleak winter. Things were not so bad in Hungary, which remained the agricultural heart of the Dual Monarchy, but Budapest was not above using the 'food question' to further her own interests.

She sold surpluses to Germany while at the same time reducing imports to Austria, which strengthened the already dangerous centrifugal forces that were threatening to tear the empire apart.[21]

The man who had spent his life trying to keep it all together was no more. On 21 November, Emperor Franz Joseph died in Vienna. He had spent his final years in quiet solitude, rarely leaving the grounds of the Schönbrunn Palace and hardly interfering in the war effort. His successor, Karl, could not have been more different and was determined to take a more active role in Austrian affairs. At just 29 years old, he was widely considered to be too young and inexperienced for such a heavy burden, and was briefed extensively in the days after the old emperor died, with what seemed like mixed results. Visitors would often complain that he was too impressionable, often saying 'yes, yes' and nodding whenever he was listening to someone, but this did not mean that he lacked his own ideas. On the contrary, he possessed a strong sense of purpose combined with a modesty that was surprising. 'One must always look for the good in people', he would tell his wife, the Empress Zita. He wanted to be a ruler who was close to his people. He had been to the front and seen its horror. He spoke to his ministers and told them that he had one overriding priority: 'to bring peace as quickly as possible'. He was certain that 'just as they served the most gracious gentleman now sadly deceased', they would also support him. 'I count on your help', he told them. 'There are great challenges ahead of us.'[22]

Securing a favourable peace would depend upon having the complete trust of his commanders. Karl had always recognized Conrad's strengths, but knew that meaningful change would require total control of an increasingly aloof AOK. Conrad was promoted to field marshal soon after the old emperor had died, but this was not the prelude to a new and expanded authority, only a coda to a long and distinguished career. Karl personally assumed supreme command of the empire's armed forces on 2 December, with Archduke Friedrich becoming his new 'assistant'. This left Conrad in a subordinate and, inevitably, uncomfortable position. He disapproved of Karl's decision to transfer AOK from Teschen to Baden, a short drive south of Vienna, and quarrelled with the young emperor as often as he dared.

When he was informed that his wife would not be able to stay at the new headquarters, he was dismayed, writing to her of his loneliness. Gina was convinced that Karl's wife, Zita, was to blame. 'The Empress, who was extremely pious, could not bear the fact that the field marshal had married a divorced woman without having the union blessed by a Catholic priest, and that he also had a reputation for being a free spirit.'[23]

This arrangement was not destined to last long, and after further rows, Archduke Friedrich came to Baden on 27 February and told Conrad that he was being relieved of command. After much cajoling, Conrad agreed to take charge of an army group in the Tyrol, with the Emperor having to make a personal appeal, removing the Grand Cross of the Order of Maria Theresa from his own breast and pinning it on the general as a sign of his esteem: 'I firmly believe that your proven strength and the very sound of your name, which is so highly regarded among my army and so greatly feared among our enemies, will be an essential factor in achieving further victories in the Tyrolean theatre of war.'[24] Conrad's replacement as Chief of the General Staff was General Arthur Arz von Straussenburg, who had been commanding First Army in Romania. Arz was a surprise choice. He had an unmilitary appearance, with pince-nez always perched on his nose, but he possessed the kind of genial and easy-going nature that was essential in such a sensitive role, particularly when Austria's position was so tenuous. He approached his task with a degree of caution and humility that would have been alien to Conrad. He understood the fragility of the army and the need for careful handling if it was to be nursed to the finishing line. 'The longer the war went on,' he admitted, 'the greater the danger of adverse influences, which could penetrate more easily within such a complex organism as the Austro-Hungarian Army than with nationally unified armies.' Were these influences to grow, a weakening in the army was almost inevitable.[25]

Moving Conrad aside was a significantly easier task than wresting Austria's independence back from Germany. Upon ascending the throne, Karl had been informed of the existence of the 'unified supreme command', which meant that he would be subordinate to the Kaiser. He tried to renegotiate the agreement, but Berlin had no intention of relinquishing its power over its allies, and although a slight modification was made to the wording, the Kaiser retained ultimate authority over all decisions and would not listen to Karl's entreaties.[26] Unrestricted submarine warfare followed a similar pattern. At a high-level meeting in Vienna on 20 January, the Prime Ministers of both Austria (Count Heinrich Clam-Martinic) and Hungary (Count Tisza), alongside the Foreign Minister, Count Ottokar Czernin, whom Karl had appointed in December, warned the German delegation of 'what disastrous consequences would ensue from America's intervention, in a military, moral, agricultural and financial sense'. Doubts were also expressed about the 'very vague and by no means convincing data' that the Imperial German Navy was relying upon. Although Austria only possessed a handful of submarines, Germany was insistent that the campaign had to be carried out in the Mediterranean, and would therefore require the use of Habsburg naval bases along the Adriatic coast. Once again it was up to Vienna to decide how far to push its disapproval and risk the complete breakdown of the alliance. As Czernin noted sadly, 'This was again one of those instances that prove that when a strong and a weak nation concert in war, the weak one cannot desist unless it changes sides entirely and enters into war with its former ally.'[27]

It was almost as if the Germans were trying to humiliate Karl. He arranged a private audience with Henning von Holtzendorff, Chief of the Admiralty Staff, but was told that 'the issue of the submarine war could no longer be the subject of debate'. The matter had been decided on 9 January, and in any case, the submarine fleet had already set sail and it would be impossible to countermand the order and bring it home.[28] Karl was now faced with a dismal predicament, trapped in a war that he'd had no part in starting and with no obvious way out. The Entente's reply to Bethmann Hollweg's note was published on 29 December and affirmed that 'no peace is possible as long as the reparation of violated rights and liberties, the acknowledgement of the principle of nationalities and of the free existence of small States shall not be assured', which could only be interpreted as a mortal threat to the survival of the empire and its polyglot existence.[29]

Karl acquiesced in the submarine campaign – he could do little else – but retained few illusions about the nature of German power. The survival of the monarchy and the empire had been bound up with Germany for so long, but it was becoming increasingly evident that Austria might have to ditch her erstwhile ally if she was to have any hope of survival. On 29 January, just days after Karl's meeting with Holtzendorff, the first part of a complex and risky diplomatic manoeuvre took place in Switzerland. Acting on Karl's request, his mother-in-law, the Duchess of Parma, had contacted her two sons, Princes Sixtus and Xavier, who were serving in the Belgian Army, and asked to see them on urgent business. After procuring the relevant papers, both men travelled to Neuchâtel, where they were handed a letter from their sister, the Empress Zita, which implored them to act as intermediaries between Austria–Hungary and the Entente, and to 'assist her in realising the ideal of peace which the Emperor had formulated on his accession'.[30]

Karl had to tread carefully. Germany must not suspect that he was negotiating behind her back – a clear betrayal of their alliance – but every effort must be made to see if an agreement was possible. Sixtus believed that four conditions needed to be met if the Entente were to make peace: the return of Alsace–Lorraine to France, the restoration of Belgium, the restoration of Serbia, and Russia's annexation of Constantinople. Karl quickly drafted a letter explaining that he was willing to consider an armistice with Russia and would not object to Constantinople coming under Tsarist occupation. He also agreed to the restoration of Alsace–Lorraine and Belgium. As for Serbia, this was an obvious difficulty for the Dual Monarchy, but it might be possible to form a 'Southern Slav Monarchy', albeit still under Habsburg authority, which would include Bosnia, Serbia, Albania and Montenegro. This was communicated to the brothers by Count Tamás Erdödy, Karl's personal representative, at Neuchâtel on 13 February. Sixtus understood Karl's reticence about granting Serbian independence, but stressed the need to present Germany with a fait accompli: to publicly announce that he was making peace with the Entente and to do so before relations between Germany and the United States were fractured beyond repair.[31]

Karl knew that he would need the support of his ministers if he was to drive through a peace treaty. This meant that the Foreign Minister, Count Czernin, would have to be brought in. As a seasoned diplomat, Czernin understood the intricacies of international politics and assumed that the French had approached the Emperor rather than the other way around.[32] With this in mind, he insisted, in a formal note he dictated on 20 February, that Austria–Hungary's treaties with Germany, Turkey and Bulgaria were 'absolutely indissoluble' and there could be no 'separate peace' by any one of these states. The Dual Monarchy had 'never contemplated the destruction of Serbia', only acted against the 'political activities' that had led to the assassination of the Archduke. He agreed that Belgium should 'be restored', and Austria would, of course, make no complaint were Germany to 'relinquish Alsace-Lorraine', but this was as far as he would go. When this document was handed back to Erdödy, for transfer on to the princes, Karl added a second note explaining his own position. 'We will support France and use all the means in our Power to bring pressure to bear upon Germany', he wrote. His 'sole aim', he reiterated, was to 'maintain the Monarchy within its existing frontiers'.[33]

When the French President, Raymond Poincaré, was handed these documents, during an interview with Sixtus on 5 March, he was unimpressed. 'This note is wholly inadequate', he said, referring to Czernin's paper with obvious disdain. When Sixtus urged him to look at the Emperor's additional letter, handwritten and sent without Czernin's knowledge, Poincaré agreed that it did 'provide some basis for negotiation', but he would need to consult France's allies. 'I shall not dwell upon the tedious and difficult manoeuvres I have had to make in Paris', Sixtus wrote to Karl afterwards. 'The tenor of the [Czernin] Note nearly ruined everything by its reserve and lack of precision, and by the evasiveness of its phrasing. Your commentary was partly successful in removing this unfortunate impression; but I had to expound and re-expound it with all the persuasive skill imaginable; which was not easy.' He added that a formal statement was required from the Emperor that gave his 'definite and unambiguous assent' to the four matters that had been raised, which he hoped would be 'the starting-point towards a possible agreement'.[34]

★

Trouble had been brewing in Russia for months, and as the murder of Rasputin had shown, it was creeping closer to the imperial household. Food shortages had been seen periodically throughout the war, but the situation in Petrograd had become particularly acute as the winter dragged on. The city was swollen by hundreds of thousands of wartime workers and refugees, creating what one *Okhrana* report called 'stockpiles of flammable material, needing only a spark to set them afire'. A sudden and devastating food supply crisis brought matters to a head. Raging blizzards had left the capital blanketed under deep snowfall, the temperatures falling to an average of minus 14.5 degrees Celsius. With many railway carriages and freight cars unable to move, food and fuel began to run out. Between December 1916 and February 1917, prices skyrocketed, increasing by 50 per cent for sausages, 25 per cent for potatoes and 40 per cent for milk, with reserves of flour dropping to perilously low levels.[35]

The authorities could do little. They tried price controls and requisitions, but infighting between different organizations within the city meant there was no concerted and urgent response to the crisis. And then the weather cleared. On the morning of 8 March, warm sunshine flooded the snowy streets of the capital, and by noon, thousands of people, including many protesters, were out on the streets. This was only the beginning of a vast movement; a swelling series of demonstrations, strikes and gatherings that would engulf Petrograd over the following week and cause the complete collapse of Tsarist authority across the capital. The first instances of violence took place on Saturday, 10 March, when huge crowds – possibly as large as 200,000 – came together, carrying red flags, singing the *Marseillaise* and shouting 'down with the government' and 'down with the war'. The Cossacks deployed at strategic locations displayed an alarming lack of interest in stamping out the disorder. Although fighting broke out in places, there was no decisive crackdown, only a surly mood of aggression, confusion and unease. As one authority later put it, the atmosphere 'was thick with that peculiar Russian air of generalized, unfocused violence' that everyone suspected was only a precursor to something much worse.[36]

A show of strength was ordered for Sunday, 11 March. Up to

10,000 soldiers and police officers had been called out, intending to bring the trouble to a swift conclusion. Scattered outbreaks of firing occurred during the day, most notably at Znamenskaia Square, where two training detachments from the Volynsky Regiment fired on crowds, killing about forty people. While hopes were raised that this would settle things down, the fragile loyalty of the troops garrisoned in and around the city began to dissolve. A company of the Pavlovsky Regiment broke out of their barracks, ransacked their arsenal, and marched onto the streets determined to prevent any further violence against the crowds. At this point, members of the Duma began to sense that the situation was slipping out of control. That evening, Rodzianko despatched a telegram to Mogilev calling for the formation of a 'responsible ministry'. 'The situation is serious', he wrote. 'The Capital is in a state of anarchy. The Government is paralysed; the transport service is broken down; the food and fuel supplies are completely disorganized. Discontent is general and on the increase. There is wild shooting on the streets; troops are firing at each other. It is urgent that some one enjoying the confidence of the country be entrusted with the formation of a new Government. There must be no delay. Hesitation is fatal. I pray God at this hour the responsibility may not fall upon the monarch.' When he received no reply, he sent another telegram the following day. 'The situation is growing worse . . . The last hour has struck, when the fate of the country and dynasty is being decided.'[37]

The Tsar reacted to Rodzianko's telegrams with a mixture of disdain and exasperation. 'That fat Rodzianko has sent me some nonsense,' he told Alekseev on the evening of 11 March, 'which I shall not bother to answer.'[38] After receiving the second telegram, he summoned General Ivanov and told him that he was being appointed commander of the Petrograd Military District, with instructions to restore order. Alekseev then announced that Ivanov was being given four of the most reliable regiments from the Northern Front, alongside several machine-gun detachments. It was difficult to know exactly what was going on in the capital, but firm leadership was urgently required. Alekseev ordered Ivanov to get reliable soldiers into the city as quickly as possible. 'This is a menacing moment and we must do everything to ensure the early arrival of strong troops. Our future depends on it.'[39]

Whatever authority the imperial regime still possessed in Petrograd dissolved for ever on 12 March. That day most of the garrison joined the uprising, including the Pavlovsky, Volynsky and Lithuanian Regiments, 6 Sapper Battalion, and even the elite Preobrazhensky Regiment. Encouraged by socialist agitators and driven on by long-pent-up grievances, soldiers murdered their officers, spilled out into the streets and attacked a host of key buildings, including the Kresty Prison, the telephone exchange and the main artillery administration and arsenal, with its 40,000 rifles and 30,000 revolvers.[40] Faced with such alarming news, the Tsar decided that he must return to the capital. Alekseev tried to dissuade him from doing so, claiming that conditions were too disturbed to allow him to proceed in safety, but the Tsar would not listen. 'After yesterday's news from the town I saw many frightened faces here', he wrote to Alexandra. 'Fortunately, Alexeiev [sic] is calm, but he thinks it necessary to appoint a very energetic man, so as to compel the Ministers to work out the solution of the problems – supplies, railways, coal, etc.'[41] He boarded the imperial train at five o'clock on the morning of 13 March. Owing to the movement of Ivanov's troops, it had to take a diversion, and he ended up at Pskov, the headquarters of the Northern Front, about 160 miles south of Petrograd. There he met General Ruzski, one of his oldest and most experienced generals (who had been persuaded to come out of retirement after resigning in December 1915), who updated him on the latest reports that had been received from *Stavka*. It was perhaps only at this moment that Nicholas realized the depth of his predicament.

The Tsar trusted his Chief of Staff perhaps more than any other senior commander, relying upon his great work ethic and endless application to duty, but Alekseev was already re-evaluating his loyalty to the imperial throne and seeing it as only part of a broader duty to Russia and her people. His overwhelming priority was maintaining the stability of the army and keeping the war effort going. As the imperial train had been steaming to Pskov, news had been received of the formation of a Duma Committee, led by Rodzianko, which had been created to restore order in the capital. With this in mind, Alekseev cabled Ivanov on the evening of 13 March and ordered him to stand down: 'your course of action should be altered: negotiations will lead to pacification, so that the shameful civil strife for which our enemy longs will be avoided, institutions and factories will remain intact, and work will be resumed'. This was followed by a telegram to the Tsar warning him that any revolution would lead to the loss of the war. 'It is impossible to ask the army calmly to wage war while a revolution is in progress in the rear.' Therefore, it was imperative 'to appoint a ministry responsible to the representatives of the people, and to entrust the President of the Duma, Rodzianko, to form it with the help of persons possessing the confidence of all Russia'.[42]

It was sometime after ten o'clock on the evening of 14 March that the Tsar conceded the formation of a 'responsible ministry'. This had not been an easy decision. He continued to believe that a monarch must be absolute or nothing; that he was 'accountable to God and Russia for all that has happened and will happen', and must wield supreme power as his ancestors had before him.[43] But the forces arrayed against him were growing stronger, and he lacked the determination to fight against them. By the morning of 15 March, after a torrid, sleepless night, he was faced with another round of demands. Ruzski had managed to communicate with Rodzianko via the Hughes telegraph machine at his headquarters, and when he was told about the Tsar's concessions, he could only cry with exasperation. 'Unfortunately . . .' he said, 'the people's passions have become so inflamed that it will hardly be possible to restrain them; the troops are completely demoralised; not only do they refuse to obey orders, but they are murdering their officers; hatred of the Empress has reached the utmost limits.' Therefore, he felt it his duty to state that 'the dynastic question demands an immediate decision'; 'everywhere troops are siding with the Duma and the people, and the threatening demands for an abdication in favour of the son, with Mikhail Alexandrovich [Nicholas's brother] as regent, are becoming quite definite'.[44]

When Rodzianko's words were relayed to Mogilev, Alekseev was distraught. He had assumed that the formation of a 'responsible ministry' would quickly quell the disorder and, moreover, that Rodzianko had the matter in hand. Now it seemed that he had been mistaken. He decided to take the initiative himself, and wrote a telegram to his front commanders (plus the admirals in charge of the Baltic and Black Sea Fleets), asking for their views:

> A decision on the dynastic question is now demanded, and the war can be continued to a victorious end only if requests for the Emperor's abdication in his son's favour, with Mikhail Aleksandrovich [*sic*] acting as regent, are satisfied . . . The army in the field must be saved from disintegration. We must carry on the struggle with the external enemy; we must safeguard Russia's independence and the future of the dynasty. We must give this the highest priority even at the cost of considerable sacrifice. I regret that every minute lost can be fatal to Russia, and that we must establish unity of thought and purpose among the highest commanders of the armies in the field, so that the army can be saved from instability and perhaps treason.[45]

The responses, received an hour or two later, all favoured abdication. From the Caucasus, Grand Duke Nikolai Nikolaevich urged the Tsar 'on my knees to save Russia and your heir, knowing as I do the feelings of sacred love you bear towards Russia and him'. At Western Front, General Evert implored Nicholas to 'save the Fatherland and the dynasty' by acting 'in accordance with the declaration of the President of the State Duma'. Likewise, Brusilov, at Southwest Front, was equally forthright. 'Please submit to the Emperor my loyal petition . . . that he renounce the throne in favour of His Highness the heir'.[46]

The loss of his generals' confidence was devastating for the Tsar. He read the telegrams shortly before three o'clock that afternoon. Smoking continuously and occasionally getting up to look out of the window at the snowy ground outside, he told Ruzski that he had been 'born for misfortune'.[47] He then signed the abdication manifesto, his hands shaking slightly, all the energy and vigour drained out of his face. 'In the midst of the great struggle against a foreign foe, who has been striving for three years to enslave our country, it has pleased God to lay on Russia a new and painful trial.' What Nicholas called 'newly arisen popular disturbances' now threatened the successful prosecution of the war, and to 'help our people to draw together and unite all their forces', he had agreed to 'lay down the Supreme Power'. In direct contravention of the Law of Succession, which specified that the throne would pass automatically to the next male heir, he had decided that he could not be parted from his son, Alexis, and that he would hand it to his brother, the Grand Duke Mikhail Alexandrovich. But the Grand Duke reacted with horror when he was told the news and quickly divested himself of the responsibility, hurriedly issuing a statement confirming that he would only accept the 'supreme power' 'if that be the desire of our great people' expressed at a general election. In the meantime, he urged his fellow countrymen to 'subject themselves to the Provisional Government, which is created by and invested with full power by the State Duma'.[48]

It was done. What had started as a series of demonstrations about bread had turned into a raging torrent of anger and violence that had overturned one of the most enduring royal dynasties in the world. The Tsar had always struggled in his role, despising the idea of a constitutional monarchy, yet lacking the fierce and brutal determination of an autocrat (at least when compared with those that came after him). Nicholas de Basily, director of the Imperial Chancellery at *Stavka*, was astonished at his demeanour throughout the crisis. 'He accepted fate without the least revolt, without the least show of anger or ill humor, without the least reproach to anyone', he remembered. 'This man, who on so many occasions had seemed to us to lack will, had made his decision with great courage and dignity, without hesitation . . . According to the English expression, he knew how to lose.'[49] As for Alekseev – the man who had driven the knife into Nicholas II – he would soon come to bitterly regret his actions. His understanding that the abdication of the Tsar would assist Rodzianko and the Duma in the restoration of order; that it would strengthen their position and allow for the war effort to proceed on a smoother basis than before, was nothing but a tragic delusion. Far from dousing the flames of revolution, the abdication had poured kerosene on them. Things could never go back to the way they had been.

PART 3

'A new enemy'

The First Battle of Dojran to Vittorio Veneto (March 1917–November 1918)

16. 'Neither peace nor war'

Colonel Nicholas Romanov left *Stavka* on 21 March. It was a cold, wintry day and snow was lying on the ground. Wearing a black uniform and sword belt, he gave a short farewell address to his staff in which he thanked them for their service, and said that he had abdicated for the good of the country and still had confidence Russia would win the war. His brother-in-law, Grand Duke Alexander Mikhailovich, was present. 'By eleven a.m. the hall is packed', he recalled. 'Generals, officers, and persons in attendance on the Emperor are present. Nicky enters – calm, reserved, bearing the semblance of a smile on his lips . . . He invites them to forget all feuds, to serve Russia and lead our army to victory . . . His modesty made a tremendous impression.' They then cheered a loud 'hurrah!'. Some of the generals wept. That evening, the former emperor left for the station. Only Alekseev accompanied him. Both men were emotional; tears filled their eyes as they parted outside the railway carriage that would carry Nicholas to Tsarskoe Selo and the long-awaited reunion with his family. Alekseev's final words were to tell him that he was under arrest.[1]

The abdication of the Tsar left Russia in a bewildering new world of confusion and disorientation. As Tsarist authority in Petrograd collapsed, a Temporary Committee was formed from the leading members of the State Duma, led by Rodzianko. At the same time, the Soviet of Workers' and Soldiers' Deputies had been established by a loose coalition of socialist parties and soldiers' and workers' groups, which had elected around 600 representatives during a series of raucous meetings in the Tauride Palace. The two sides viewed each other warily. Though they shared an interest in defending the revolution and defeating any attempt to undermine it, they represented radically different constituencies. The Temporary Committee was formed of Russia's liberal opposition, including many landowners and businessmen, while the Soviet was led by an eclectic mix of socialists and communists, including members of the Bolshevik, Menshevik and Socialist Revolutionary Parties. For the Temporary Committee, the events of March 1917 were merely a transfer of power and a bloodless political revolution; for the Soviet, they symbolized something far more radical.

Negotiations between these two groups resulted in the formation of the Provisional Government on 15 March, which was to rule Russia until a Constituent Assembly could be elected. It was headed up not by Rodzianko – who was widely reviled – but by Prince Georgii Lvov, who had run the Union of Zemstvos during the war and was known as a man of honour; someone the moderates could trust. He was joined by an array of familiar names, including Miliukov (Minister of Foreign Affairs) and Guchkov (Minister of War), with a single Socialist Revolutionary, Alexander Kerensky, appointed Minister of Justice. It was established with eight founding principles, which included an amnesty for political and religious offences; freedom of speech and of the press; the abolition of all religious or national restrictions; the preparation of a Constituent Assembly to be elected 'on the basis of universal, direct, equal, and secret suffrage'; the organization of a 'national militia' to replace the police; and a guarantee that those troops that had 'taken part in the revolutionary movement' would not be disarmed. The Soviet agreed to support the Provisional Government 'in so far as it carries out its announced political programme', and welcomed the appointment of Kerensky, whom it regarded 'as the defender of the people's interests and freedom'.[2]

The Provisional Government thus rested upon unstable foundations from the very beginning of its existence, lacking the natural legitimacy and authority of an elected government and painfully aware that the weight of numbers in the streets belonged to the Soviet, which could withdraw its support at any moment. On 22 March, just a week after the abdication, Guchkov was forced to admit to Alekseev that the 'Provisional Government does not wield any real power and its orders are carried [out] only to the extent allowed by the Soviet ... the troops, railroads, postal service, and the

telegraph are in its hands. I can say directly that the Provisional Government only exists so long as the Soviet allows it to.'[3] It was also
unfortunate that Prince Lvov was soon overwhelmed by his responsibilities. A gentleman, known for preferring compromise and
agreement, he was 'not distinguished by political strength', according
to Vladimir Nabokov, who served as the head of the Chancellery of
the Provisional Government. It was necessary to act quickly – to take
advantage of the political turmoil and forge a new path for Russia –
but Lvov was the 'very embodiment of passivity' and Nabokov
wondered whether this was 'conscious policy or the result of his
awareness of his own powerlessness'.[4]

One of the last acts of the Tsar had been to appoint Grand Duke
Nikolai Nikolaevich as Commander-in-Chief, but this order was
quickly rescinded by the Provisional Government under pressure
from the Soviet. The Grand Duke had left his position in the Caucasus on 20 March, and it took him three days to make his way to *Stavka*,
with the long journey being broken by frequent stops to receive
deputations from local groups, soldiers and Cossacks who wanted to
pledge their loyalty to his standard. When he eventually arrived at
Mogilev, he was handed a letter from Prince Lvov informing him
that the 'national feeling' was 'decidedly and insistently against the
employment of any members of the house of Romanov in any official position' and it was necessary for him to resign. Doing as he was
told, the Grand Duke signed an oath of allegiance to the Provisional
Government, announced that according to paragraph 47 of the Field
Manual, authority automatically passed to Alekseev as Chief of Staff,
and then retired to the Crimea. Many in the Soviet did not trust
Alekseev, but Lvov made it clear that there was simply no one else
who could replace the general.[5]

Chaos was already spreading out of Petrograd. The great fear at
Stavka, that the revolution would rapidly infect the rest of the army,
was beginning to come true; sparked off, at least in part, by Army
Order No. 1, which had been issued by the Soviet on 14 March. All
companies, battalions, regiments and batteries were to have 'elected
representatives of the lower ranks', and only instructions from the
Duma that did not 'conflict' with the 'orders and resolutions of the

Soviet of Workers' and Soldiers' Deputies' were to be acted upon. Furthermore, all titles formerly applied to officers, such as 'Your Excellency' and 'Your Honour', were to be abolished.[6] Although this order was only to have applied to those units in and around Petrograd, word of it quickly spread and began to have a corrosive effect on discipline right across the army. On 22 March, Alekseev replied to Guchkov's letter, lamenting that:

> Recent events have changed the strategic situation and the picture of the whole war dramatically . . . Agitators spread from Petrograd in all directions, reaching every part of the army. They call for disobedience to the authorities and appeal to the soldiers to establish an elective principle for officer and command positions; officers and commanders are being arrested, thus undermining their authority. The rear of the armies is degrading at a rapid pace and in some places this wave of decay has already reached the trenches. In such a situation it may well be that the fateful hour, when individual parts of the armies will become completely unfit for battle, has almost come.[7]

Were they to lose Petrograd, Russia would lose the war. 'In this regard, it is necessary to take urgent and decisive measures without any further delay. Otherwise, if the army perishes, Russia shall meet its doom.'

The revolution was having a terribly disorienting effect on the army, turning its world of long-established routines and precedents upside down. Almost as soon as the Provisional Government had been established, political commissars and representatives of various socialist and workers' groups began turning up at the front, and even *Stavka* was not immune from this disruption. Several of its buildings, including the Tsar's former apartments, were commandeered and used for meetings or rallies, much to the General Staff's annoyance. Desertions also increased fivefold. Released from their oath of allegiance to the Emperor, rising numbers of soldiers saw little point in continuing the war and took the chance to go home. Between the outbreak of war and the abdication of the Tsar, there had been just under 200,000 desertions, or about 6,000 per month, but in the three months that followed the revolution, over 85,000 men would go missing. Something had changed dramatically in the Russian soldiers' attitude to the war, and unless a sense of purpose and loyalty could be re-established quickly, the army was at risk of disintegration.[8]

Alekseev sent repeated warnings to Petrograd about the deterioration in the ranks and the urgent need to restore discipline and order. On 27 March, he gave Lvov a lengthy summary of the communications he had received from the front commanders, which made for sobering reading. News of the abdication of the Tsar had been met with 'calm and composure', although many soldiers could not 'as yet find their way among the events that have occurred'. Alekseev was anxious to warn Lvov of the concern that had been expressed about the role of the Soviet, particularly amongst the officer class. There were 'clear signs of discontent, indignation, and apprehension at the fact that a self-appointed group of politicians, presenting itself as the Soviet of Workers' and Soldiers' Deputies, delegated neither by the people nor by the armies, acts as a usurper in [sic] behalf of the country, interferes with the orders of the Provisional Government, and even acts and issues orders against the wishes of the latter'. Nevertheless, Alekseev felt that the morale of the men was 'good'. 'There prevails a sense of the necessity of bringing the war to a victorious conclusion, making it essential to maintain complete calm at the front and to work intensively in the rear.'[9]

Things were unravelling at frightening speed. On 1 April, the Soviet issued orders, rubber-stamped by the Provisional Government, for political commissars to be attached to military units, 'in order to achieve quick and systematic solution of problems arising in the internal and political life of the army and to expedite the transmission of directives, as well as for the purpose of preventing any wrong steps on the part of the organs now in charge of army life'. Commissars would be attached to the Ministry of War, *Stavka* and each front command. No instructions, orders or proclamations 'relating to the internal or political life of the army', or the local population under its jurisdiction, could be issued without the consent of the commissar and the Soviet.[10] This was followed later in the month by an order on 'Elective Military Organizations and Disciplinary Courts', which introduced a system of committees designed to 'guarantee every soldier the exercise of his civil and political rights'. When

Alekseev was given this order to sign by a representative of the War Ministry, Lieutenant-Colonel Verkhovsky, he could not hide his sadness, convinced that any loosening of the disciplinary framework in the army would have a devastating effect on its ability to fight. 'Alekseev did not resist', remembered Verkhovsky, 'and the regulation on the committees was carried out by army order. But the old man bowed his head low while signing the document, and his eyes blurred with tears. He felt he had put his hand to the death of the army.'[11]

Alekseev, now a virtual prisoner of the Provisional Government, sensed that something had to give. He continued to operate as he had always done, albeit at a slower pace owing to his chronic illness, devising plans for new offensives and reading reports late into the night, but the realization that each day took the new army further away from the old one left him doubtful and struggling to sleep. He tried his best to enter into the spirit of the new age, on one occasion even meeting some of the soldiers' delegates who were staying at a barracks close to *Stavka*. Sitting among them, he explained the strategic situation and urged upon them the importance of fighting on, telling them that 'one good victory, one good push forward', would bring peace. 'What times these are when the Supreme Commander has to entreat and implore everyone to do their duty! But we are sick, and it is because of this sickness I am doing this – I am doing all I can to waken in you your dormant love of your motherland.' He then took off his cap and bowed.[12]

While Alekseev tried his best to keep the Russian Army together, his opponents were doing their best to prise it apart. News of the unrest in Petrograd sparked off frantic deliberations at OHL. 'I felt as though a weight had been removed from my chest', recalled Ludendorff, who greeted reports of the abdication of the Tsar with unrestrained delight.[13] Hindenburg was more cautious. When he briefed the Kaiser on 14 March, onlookers noticed how he looked 'very careworn'. There were rumours that Britain was the prime mover behind events in the capital, aiming at intensifying the Russian war effort through a palace coup. 'His Majesty is convinced that this will prolong the war', recorded one of the Kaiser's staff, 'because

it has been engineered by the Entente and by England in particular.'
With the situation so obscure, Bethmann Hollweg suggested that
they should do nothing to disturb Russia, which OHL agreed to,
citing the need to 'shut down the Eastern Front' and use the opportunity to allow for a 'necessary and welcome' reinforcement of the
Western Front 'in view of the impending onslaught of the Western
powers'.[14]

Germany's strategic situation was now curiously balanced, both
encouraging and concerning. The entry of the United States into the
war on 6 April added another great power to the ranks of her enemies,
but America was still months, maybe years away from being able to
raise an army big enough to tilt the balance on the Western Front. In
the meantime, Ludendorff was determined to exploit every resource
available to Germany as she prepared to hold the line in France,
giving time for the U-boat campaign to complete its deadly work.
By instituting a thorough audit of manpower, he was able to pull
4,500 officers from rear echelons or administrative posts and gather
another 124,000 men from the home front. The 1899 class was also
brought in earlier than expected, which added another 310,000 men
to the colours for what would clearly be a demanding season of fighting. The British would launch the first phase of General Nivelle's
spring offensive on 9 April, with the main attack coming a week
later.[15]

With German forces massed in the west, the Eastern Front entered
'a condition of neither peace nor war', as Ludendorff put it.[16] Since
General Brusilov's ill-fated attacks at Kovel had tailed off in October,
large stretches of the front had become quiet, with fighting shifting to
Romania before being halted by the December snows. Romania's
remaining armies were dug in behind the Sereth river in Moldavia and
showed little signs of being able to restore their fortunes. A great thaw
began on 10 March, melting the ice on the Danube, Sereth and Prut
rivers, which caused flooding in low-lying areas and made campaigning in their vicinity almost impossible. Further south, in Macedonia,
General Sarrail's drive through Serbia may have stalled after Monastir,
but the Bulgarians were growing more impatient. Having been at war
almost continuously since 1912, Bulgaria was exhausted. Apart from

Monastir and (possibly) the island of Thasos, she was only interested in securing the gains she already possessed.[17]

Propaganda would now become a key weapon for Germany on the Eastern Front. The Chief of Staff at *OberOst*, Max Hoffmann, had a leaflet printed, which would be dropped over enemy lines, 'to explain the cause of the troubles to the Russian soldiers in the trenches. Otherwise the poor fellows would know nothing about it, which', he added mischievously, 'would be a pity.'[18] As well as trying to undermine the morale of the Russian front-line soldiers, Germany also utilized more unorthodox methods. On 25 March, OHL gave its approval to a plan drawn up by the Political Section of the General Staff to arrange for a number of Russian émigrés, currently in Switzerland, to return home. Chief among these was Vladimir Ilich Ulyanov, known by his sobriquet, 'Lenin', a 47-year-old professional revolutionary from Simbirsk on the Volga. He had founded a radical Marxist party, the Bolsheviks, in 1903, and had dedicated his life to bringing down Tsarism, driven on by a burning sense of injustice. His older brother, Sasha, had been executed for his involvement in an assassination attempt against Tsar Alexander III, which gave Lenin more reason than most to hate the Romanovs. He had spent years in exile, moving between Switzerland, France, England and Sweden, writing books, editing newspapers and painstakingly (and often fruitlessly) building up networks of like-minded agitators across Europe. The outbreak of the war found him in Austria Hungary, and after being briefly detained by the authorities, he was allowed to return to Switzerland, with the Interior Minister agreeing that he was as fervent an enemy of the Tsar as they could possibly hope to find. When news of the revolution arrived in Zurich, Lenin was desperate to go home. At a local café full of Russian exiles, he rushed in 'like a bundle of nervous energy', repeating over and over a single phrase, 'We must go at all costs, even if we go through hell.'[19]

Lenin's party, thirty-two in all, boarded what became known as the 'sealed train' at Zurich on 9 April. It would take them a week to complete an exhausting 2,000-mile journey to Petrograd via Germany, Sweden and Finland. When the train pulled into the Finland Station late on 16 April – an event that would live long in Soviet mythology – a great crowd had turned up, eager to welcome the returning hero. 'Banners hung across the platform at every step', remembered a member of the Soviet, Nikolai Sukhanov; 'triumphal arches had been set up, adorned with red and gold; one's eyes were dazzled by every possible welcoming inscription and revolutionary slogan, while at the end of the platform, where the carriage was expected to stop, there was a band, and a group of representatives of the central Bolshevik organizations stood holding flowers.' After stepping down from his carriage, Lenin clambered on top of a nearby armoured car and gave a short speech, most of which was incomprehensible to his audience, before being driven off to Bolshevik Party headquarters, located at the suitably imposing Kshesinskaya mansion, home of a former mistress of the Tsar.[20]

Lenin arrived in Petrograd at a moment of great tension. On 9 April, the day he had left Zurich, Prince Lvov had issued a statement on war aims that attempted to reassure the Allies that Russia was still a reliable partner. The 'foremost and most urgent task' of the people was to defend their 'inheritance at any price' and seek the 'liberation of our country from the invading enemy'. Lvov was keen to emphasize that the aim of a 'free Russia' was 'not domination over other nations, or seizure of their national possessions, or forcible occupation of foreign territories', but a peace based upon 'the self-determination of peoples'. Therefore, the Provisional Government would 'execute the will of the people' and 'defend the rights of the fatherland', while at the same time 'fully observing . . . all obligations assumed towards our Allies'.[21] Lenin was predictably unimpressed by this declaration, and penned what became known as his 'April Theses' on the journey to Petrograd. It was as stark and uncompromising as the man himself. Under Lvov, Russia continued to wage 'a predatory imperialist war'. There should be no support for the Provisional Government, only the exposure of 'the utter falsity of all its promises' until the transfer of 'the entire state power to the Soviets of Workers' Deputies'. Only then could justice be served, which included the confiscation and nationalization of all private land and the abolition of the police, army and bureaucracy.[22]

Lenin's 'April Theses' were wildly unpopular, even among fellow

Bolsheviks, but he was now strategically placed to take advantage of any missteps by the new regime. Although he never had any direct contact with German agents, either in Switzerland or elsewhere, various intermediaries operated a lucrative credit line from Berlin through neutral Sweden that magnified his power greatly. Wire transfers and the laundering of roubles through a Swedish import business allowed Germany to provide him with considerable sums of money, perhaps as much as 50 million gold marks (over $1 billion in current valuations).[23] This gave him the firepower he needed to wage an unrelenting propaganda war against the Provisional Government. A printing press was purchased for 250,000 roubles, and within days it was churning out regular issues of the workers' newspaper *Pravda* ('Truth'), with special editions being produced for soldiers and sailors. Print runs often reached 100,000 per day, about one per company, with the stated purpose to 'understand and explain to all soldiers for what purpose this war was begun, *who* began the war, who needs the war'.[24]

This was just the kind of return that Germany had hoped for when she had invested in Lenin. As Richard von Kühlmann, Germany's Foreign Minister, later explained, her most important diplomatic aim during 1917 was the 'disruption of the Entente and the subsequent creation of political combinations agreeable to us', which focused on Russia because it was 'the weakest link in the enemy chain'.[25] But supporting revolutionaries with dangerous ideas was a high-stakes gamble, and not all of Germany's allies approved. The attitude in Vienna was much more cautious. Emperor Karl sent Kaiser Wilhelm a wide-ranging report on 14 April, which, he said, had been prepared for him by Count Czernin. The document was a sobering assessment of the current situation and the extreme danger that faced the Central Powers. It was 'quite obvious that our military strength is coming to an end', and although they would certainly hold out 'during the next few months . . . another winter campaign would be absolutely out of the question'. Revolution in Russia had 'opened a new era in the history of the world', and they must consider the possibility that such an event could occur in either Berlin or Vienna. In his covering letter, Karl said that he 'fully identified' with Czernin's arguments and urged the German Emperor to take them seriously. 'I hasten to send you the document, dear friend, and beg you most sincerely not to shut yourself off from these reflections. We are fighting against a new enemy; one that is more dangerous even than the Entente. We are contending with the international revolution, whose strongest ally lies in the general famine.' He implored the Kaiser 'not to overlook this fateful side of the question and to consider that a speedy end to the war − possibly with heavy casualties − would give us the opportunity to successfully counteract the subversive movements that are being prepared'.[26]

Count Czernin's signature may have been on the document, but it was all Karl's work. Fearing that his well-known pessimism would prevent his assessment from being considered, the Emperor had asked his Foreign Minister to sign the report, believing that it would count for more in Berlin.[27] But it did him little good. The Kaiser did not reply for several weeks, having asked Bethmann Hollweg to prepare a response to the points that had been raised. Agreeing that Czernin's argument was largely correct, Wilhelm was still outwardly confident of victory and urged the Emperor to hold fast to their alliance and trust that matters were now moving firmly in their direction. 'I am not ignoring the growing difficulties of the long duration of the war and my eyes are not closed to the possible repercussions of the Russian Revolution. However, I do believe that − in this respect, too − the situation within the Central Powers, who were attacked by their enemies and came out victorious on the battlefields, is different from that in Russia, whose government, which has now been abolished, started the war in August 1914 and whose armies suffered heavy and painful defeats.'[28]

Karl took little comfort from these bland reassurances and remained desperate to strike a compromise peace with the Entente. As he told Zita after one frustrating visit to see the Kaiser, 'There is terrible trouble with the Germans because they simply will not see reason. In the end we may have to go our own way, even at the risk of being taken over by them. But first we must try everything in our power. Perhaps it will work out after all.'[29] Princes Sixtus and Xavier had travelled, at some personal risk, to Karl and Zita's residence at

Laxenburg on 24 March, where they were handed a letter, signed by the Emperor, to be given to the French President. 'All the peoples of my Empire are united more firmly than ever in the determination to preserve the integrity of the Monarchy, even at the cost of the greatest sacrifices', wrote Karl. He wanted the princes to convey to Poincaré that he would use all his 'personal influence' with Germany to recognize France's 'just claims' in Alsace–Lorraine. Moreover, he agreed that Belgium 'must be restored in her entirety as a Sovereign State', as should Serbia. He was even prepared to offer the Balkan nation 'a just and natural approach to the Adriatic', as well as economic concessions, in return for the suppression of all political groups that worked towards the 'disintegration of the Monarchy'.[30]

Within days, Sixtus had shuttled back to Paris for the first of an exhausting series of meetings with the major politicians of the Entente, including the new French Prime Minister, Alexandre Ribot, who had replaced Briand in March, and the British Prime Minister, David Lloyd George. Both men were keen on grasping the opportunity of peace with Austria but knew that Italy would have to be consulted first. On 19 April, they met with their Italian counterpart, Prime Minister Paolo Boselli, and his Foreign Secretary, Baron Sidney Sonnino, at the Alpine village of Saint-Jean-de-Maurienne, close to the Italian border. Although they did not reveal the contents of Karl's letter (Sixtus had sworn them to secrecy), they talked broadly about what Italy might want to achieve and what she might be willing to forgo in any future peace settlement. But this went nowhere. 'Baron Sonnino did not like the idea of any separate peace with Austria', remembered Lloyd George. 'He conceived that the Central Powers were endeavouring to entangle the Allies in peace negotiations. It would, he said, be very difficult to induce public opinion in Italy to carry on the War if peace were once made with Austria . . .' Whether the British and French should have shown Karl's letter to Sonnino remained an open question. Lloyd George thought not. 'The reading of the Emperor's letter, in which Italy was not even mentioned, would have exasperated him', he thought. 'He was a hot-tempered man and once irritated he was not easily soothed. A few hours in a snow-laden valley would not have chilled his anger.'[31]

Lloyd George met Sixtus at the Hotel Crillon the following day.

'It is essential that Austria give up something to Italy', he said. 'Italy is our Ally, and we cannot make peace without her.'

'In that case,' replied Sixtus, 'why does not Italy take the territory she covets by force of arms?'

Lloyd George smiled. 'So far as we are concerned, we ask nothing more than to make Peace with Austria. We have no feeling of hatred towards her, any more than you have in France. If she really wants Peace, she must make these concessions . . .'

It was becoming clear that Karl had to agree to more than the French position on Alsace–Lorraine if he was to secure a lasting peace with the Entente. On 22 April, a formal rejection of the Emperor's offer was handed to Sixtus, who once again acted as go-between. Returning to Switzerland, he met with Count Erdödy, and they discussed the need for Karl to 'make a definite statement of his views' on Italy. This was followed up by a further visit to Laxenburg and more discussions with Czernin. While Karl was hopeful that Italian demands could be confined to the Italian-speaking area of the Tyrol, Czernin was more reserved, claiming that there could be no 'unilateral cession of territory' and they would require a guarantee on the 'integrity of the Monarchy'.[32]

The negotiations now began to grow stale. Sixtus and Xavier continued to shuttle between Switzerland, France and England, deploying all their wit and energy, but the Entente was becoming less interested in parleying with Vienna, or at least putting sustained pressure on the Italians to moderate their demands. When Sixtus met Poincaré and Ribot in Paris on 20 May, several objections were raised to the Emperor's letter. There was no mention of Romania; it would be very difficult to row back upon Italian claims, which had been promised to her by the Entente; arranging suitable compensation between Austria and the western powers would not be simple; and a separate peace between Italy and Austria would 'deprive ourselves of an Ally' against Germany. Ribot was always 'taking off and putting on his tinted spectacles', Sixtus noted, obsessing over 'the difficulties of the undertaking' and lacking the drive to push for peace. In London, Lloyd George had also lost his earlier urgency and went over the Emperor's letter with a quizzical eye, complaining that finding somewhere the Italians could 'compensate' the Austrians for the loss of the Tyrol was a great riddle. 'Perhaps we could manage it with some of the German colonies', he said.[33]

With Russia in turmoil and a separate peace with Austria looking less likely, the Allies entered a dangerous phase of the war. The abdication of the Tsar had been greeted with a mixture of bewilderment and undue optimism in Allied capitals, with hopes raised that this might produce a renewed determination to win the war. But as the chaos in Russia grew worse, observers reluctantly began to accept that a period of extended uncertainty was more likely. Sir George Buchanan, British Ambassador in Petrograd, wrote to Lord Milner, Minister Without Portfolio, in April, complaining about the 'transformation' in the Russian scene since they had both attended a conference on war materiel in the Russian capital shortly before the revolution. 'The military outlook is most discouraging,' he wrote, 'and I, personally, have abandoned all hope of a successful Russian offensive in the spring. Nor do I take an optimistic view of the immediate future of this country. Russia is not ripe for a purely democratic form of government, and for the next few years we shall probably see a series of revolutions and counter-revolutions, as in the "troublesome times" nearly five hundred years ago.'[34]

The situation on the Western Front offered little cause for encouragement. General Nivelle had launched a massive attack on the Chemin des Dames on 16 April, but his army had struggled to break through because of a combination of stubborn enemy resistance, poor planning, bad weather and wildly ambitious objectives. The morale of the French Army had been battered by the failure to win a decisive victory as Nivelle had promised, and division after division began to show alarming signs of indiscipline and disorder, inspired, in part, by events in Russia. In public the leaders of the Entente insisted that all was well, but behind closed doors a different attitude was apparent. Even the good news of American entry was clouded by the devastating effect of unrestricted submarine warfare, which had sunk 1.9 million tons of Allied shipping between February and April

1917, threatening to starve Britain out of the war.[35] At an Anglo-French summit in Paris on 5 May, Sir William Robertson had explained, in his usual blunt way, that they had 'reached a very critical stage of the war', and they must avoid 'making any mistake in the conduct of the war, more especially so because of the collapse of Russia'.[36]

Political volatility was on the rise almost everywhere. The winter had seen unprecedented turmoil in Greece as civil war threatened to break out between royalist forces loyal to King Constantine and those who backed the former Prime Minister, Eleftherios Venizelos, who had arrived in Salonika in October, determined to lead a rival government that would raise an army and join the Entente. Whether the Allies should recognize this 'Provisional Government' was the subject of much rumour and discussion. Sarrail had already greeted Venizelos in person, an act that seemed to convey quasi-official recognition upon him. Wearing 'full uniform, with gold-laced cap', Sarrail strode through the crowd, shook Venizelos's hand, and said some words to the watching public, who were cheering '*Vive la France!*' and '*Vivent les Alliés!*' Such an act alienated the British, who were cautious about further involvement in Greek affairs, and infuriated both the Russians and the Italians, who were wary of recognizing someone who might prove unsympathetic to their ambitions in the Near East and the Adriatic. It was no coincidence that soon afterwards, the British, Italian and Russian Governments began to press the French to relieve Sarrail of command.[37]

Undisturbed by these rumours, Sarrail had spent the winter busily preparing for a new offensive, which the British had agreed to support, even if there was little enthusiasm in London. On 8 February, he had outlined plans for a combined attack by the Serbs, French, Italians and Russians advancing from Monastir towards the Vardar, with the British seizing Seres on the right. When he was asked to be more specific and lay down an actual objective, he replied that the 'end goal' would be Sofia, the Bulgarian capital. Lieutenant-General Milne then objected to the choice of Seres, citing the high incidence of malaria in the Struma Valley during the summer, so the British sector was switched to Lake Dojran. This made eminent sense, but the odds were still stacked against Allied forces in Macedonia. With 274 battalions, Sarrail only held a slender superiority against the enemy, who had 255 battalions, mostly Bulgarian. Moreover, they would have to advance uphill against a series of heavily fortified defences, some of which could lay claim to being the most formidable on any front in the war.[38]

An early indication of these difficulties took place on the night of 24 April, when the British attacked at Dojran. Scrambling up the rocky heights west of the lake, the sky lit by Bulgarian searchlights, they failed in almost every attempt to move forward. Artillery fire and uncut barbed wire condemned one British division to what the official historian described as 'one of those complete and costly failures which recur so frequently in the grim annals of trench warfare, and which are as depressing to read about as they are to study and record'.[39] 'When the sun rose in the morning there were 800 English bodies left on the battlefield', recorded a Bulgarian officer, Major Nedeff, who served with 9th (Pleven) Division. He was particularly proud of the fighting spirit of his men, who had endured intensive bombardment yet still repulsed the enemy. 'The British soldiers were fighting splendidly when at a distance from us', he wrote. 'They used their machine-guns perfectly, and also their automatic rifles and bombs, and are even good marksmen, but they could not withstand our bayonets, and if our counter-attack[s] were conducted before they had time to organize themselves in our trenches, they were invariably forced to abandon them.'[40]

This latest failure, combined with the ongoing strategic uncertainty, resulted in a sudden hardening of Britain's position towards the whole idea of a Macedonian campaign. In a fraught meeting at the Hotel Crillon on 5 May, Lloyd George threatened to pull the plug on the British Salonika Force, arguing that it would be better employed on the Palestine Front against the Turks. Current difficulties with shipping meant that 'the essential needs of the civil populations of the Allies can only be met by a reduction of the force at Salonica to that required to hold an entrenched camp surrounding the harbour'. Therefore, one infantry division and two cavalry brigades would be withdrawn from Macedonia after the completion of Sarrail's spring offensive. Clearly, if his operations 'should be attended by such measure of success as to render it reasonably certain, not later than the end of May, that Bulgaria would come to terms', then this would be reconsidered.[41]

The response from the French delegation was predictably spiky, and familiar arguments in favour of the expedition were repeated once again. Any British withdrawal would place the French Government in an 'impossible position'. It would deliver Greece over to Germany and encourage both Bulgaria and Turkey 'beyond their wildest hopes'. 'It was really a question', Ribot said, 'of the fate of the whole of Eastern Europe', but Lloyd George was insistent, and for once, Robertson came away from an Allied conference in a good mood: 'On the whole I think it is about the best Conference we have had', he told a friend. 'The Prime Minister did his part well and I feel that we have once more pulled the French together and got them going. Of course the Greece business is very complicated and will cause a great deal of trouble in the French Chamber. But anyway the Prime Minister made it quite clear that we shall begin to bring away one division and two cavalry brigades on the 1st June unless Bulgaria has before been made to contemplate suing for peace, a most unlikely contingency . . .'[42]

When Sarrail's attack finally took place, on 9 May, after repeated postponements owing to wet weather, it confirmed all of Robertson's misgivings. Instead of being a coherent, combined offensive, it was another disjointed, short-lived affair. Sarrail's orders had emphasized the importance of surprise and of attacking simultaneously all along the line. The infantry should possess a single thought: to 'go straight ahead and do not let up'. The attacking waves would cross no-man's-land 'without noise or shouts, bypass the defenders in an instant and (immediately) proceed beyond'. But instilling an irresistible elan in the infantry could not compensate for a chronic lack of fire support. A preliminary bombardment had opened on 5 May, occasionally ceasing so that patrols could check the state of the defences, but these remained largely intact and the Bulgarian garrisons extremely vigilant. Despite extensive efforts to locate and destroy enemy gun batteries, Bulgarian and German artillery was 'still just as intense, better and better adjusted' than before, with the shellfire 'of increasing intensity after each feint attack'. So disappointing were the effects of the bombardment that on 8 May the decision was taken to delay the offensive for twenty-four hours.[43]

The extra day made little difference. Only 2 Russian Brigade was able to reach its objective on 9 May, going more than a mile to reach the village of Orle, but this could not be held because of the widespread failure of units on either flank. Attack after attack came under heavy fire, from both flanking machine-guns and artillery barrages, before being pushed back by fresh forces coming from the rear. Subsequent investigations placed the failure firmly on the difficulties of artillery support. Counter-battery fire was difficult because of the problems of visibility and insufficient aerial reconnaissance. There were too many enemy batteries and not enough long-range howitzers that could be used for this kind of mission. The preliminary bombardment was also disappointing. French guns struggled to obliterate trenches or those shelters hewn out of solid rock, leaving the infantry exposed to heavy fire as they made the long march up bare slopes towards the enemy positions. By the time Sarrail closed down the offensive twelve days later, he had lost 12,950 men and 450 officers.[44]

The losses were hardly catastrophic, particularly when compared to the rivers of blood spilled on other fronts, but this latest setback left *l'armée d'Orient* facing new questions about its long-term future. Concern about the reliability of the British was only one of Sarrail's problems, and he grew worried about the morale of his other contingents, particularly the Serbs, who had become increasingly disaffected. Having sustained over 30,000 casualties in the Monastir offensive, they were growing reluctant to accept any more losses. The Serbs had gone forward on 9 May and captured Hill 1824, but their Chief of Staff, General Petar Bojović, who had replaced the ailing Putnik, had already warned Sarrail that they would only be able to take part in an offensive that was 'well-planned and capable of gaining decisive results'. It was evident, much to Sarrail's chagrin, that Bojović did not want to press his men too hard while also worrying about the effects of political agitation among the ranks. By the time the army had been re-formed in Macedonia, rivalry between Crown Prince

Alexander, Prime Minister Nikola Pašić and Colonel Dragutin Dimitrijević, who headed up the secretive Black Hand organization that had murdered the Archduke, was having a destabilizing effect on morale.[45]

Serbian infighting culminated in what became known as the 'Salonika Trial', which opened in late April and continued until June. After visiting troops near the front in August 1916, the Serbian Crown Prince heard the crack of gunshots close by, an incident that quickly became the pretext for the wholesale repression of the Black Hand. Dimitrijević was arrested, alongside scores of other officers with ties to the organization, accused of conspiring to murder both the Crown Prince and the Prime Minister, seize the reins of government, suspend the constitution and then institute a military dictatorship.[46] Dimitrijević was no friend of his accusers and had long felt that they were not pursuing the dream of a 'greater Serbia' with sufficient zeal, but there was no conspiracy to murder anyone. After a rushed trial that involved 'gross violations of Serbian military law and accepted judicial practice', and despite appeals for clemency from the Allies, he was taken to a ravine outside Salonika on 26 June and executed.[47]

What effect this bloody settling of scores would have on the Serbian Army, and the campaign more generally, remained to be seen. The Allies issued a half-hearted protest, but had little interest in getting involved in what seemed like a private Balkan quarrel, particularly when there was no alternative to the current Serbian leadership. The overwhelming priority was keeping the Serbian Army in as effective a state as possible, which was not easy. Sarrail had called off his offensive on 21 May, aware that he now had a serious problem with the morale of his expeditionary force. 'After beginning the offensive with artillery on 8th May, the Serbs faced problems with weather and the challenging terrain, and in the end they only attacked with two of their six divisions. Given their losses – they say 1,000 men, I say fewer – they asked me to halt the attack', he wrote to Paul Painlevé, Minister of War, on 23 May. 'I struggled in vain for eight days to push them forward, using every method at my disposal. I believe that the cause of this inexplicable halt is desertions among the Serbian ranks, new Russian pessimists, and their vexed expectations of what results our attacks on the Crna and Dojran would yield.'[48] Sarrail knew that he needed the Serbs' fighting strength and determination if he was to reconquer their homeland and take the war to Bulgaria, but for the time being there was nothing else to do but bring out the wounded, improve their defensive positions, and wait.

17.   'Days of imperishable glory'

With Russian pressure having relaxed significantly since the revolution, Italy had now become the Habsburg Empire's foremost opponent. But the place of Italy within Allied strategy was somewhat unclear – an afterthought rather than a central component – the subject of long periods of inactivity punctuated by occasional flurries of interest. General Cadorna had originally promised to support General Nivelle's spring offensive on the Western Front with another attack across the Isonzo, bolstered by Lloyd George's offer of 300 heavy guns, but thought he needed considerably more help, at least eight extra divisions, if his forces were to reach Trieste. In a letter to Sonnino in late March, he had explained that no other front in the western theatre of war was as sensitive to the enemy as the Isonzo and that 'a violent and powerful action there would provoke the enemy into such an energetic reaction as to distract him from other offensive purposes, and to make the simultaneous action of the allies on the Anglo-French front more effective'.[1]

Cadorna had been unimpressed with Allied leadership for some time, and felt that the British and the French did not appreciate either the possibilities of the Italian Front or the dangers his army faced. Intelligence had been accumulating for weeks about a possible enemy build-up in the Trentino, which provoked unease at Italian General Headquarters. The *Strafexpedition* still cast a long shadow, and Cadorna fretted about what a combined Austro-German assault against Italy could do. Nivelle had travelled to Udine in February, and though the two men had got on well, the Frenchman was unmoved by Cadorna's concerns about the vulnerability of his front. Impressed by the scale of the Italian defences, and convinced that his attack in France would work, he reassured Cadorna that 'You are therefore in a position to oppose an [enemy] offensive, even a powerful one, for long enough to allow the Allied offensives taking place in other theatres to extricate you or, if the circumstances allow, for forces to be sent to you in direct support.'[2]

Cadorna was not entirely mollified by Nivelle's confident tone and remained worried about the Trentino, which forced him to keep back significant forces in case of enemy activity. He replied in late February: 'These considerations are of particular importance on our front given that, because of its relative isolation from other theatres and the arrangement of our armies in an arc, if an enemy were to attack with significant superiority in artillery, it would put us in a critical situation.'[3] He was also unimpressed by Sir William Robertson, who came to Udine on 23 March and again dismissed Cadorna's pleas. The Italians outnumbered their opponents, and with their 'considerable superiority in artillery', Robertson hoped they would conduct 'a vigorous offensive action as soon as possible' to support Nivelle's main offensive. Cadorna was furious. 'I talked myself hoarse for hours', he wrote to his son, Raffaele, 'to make them understand that if the Austrians and Germans mass against us and we don't do the same we'll be beaten one at a time. They are infatuated with their offensive in France, which will achieve nothing very much.'[4]

Cadorna held more positive discussions with another senior French general, Ferdinand Foch, in April. Nivelle had appointed Foch to undertake a series of 'special studies' over the winter and spring, one of which was to look at how support could be provided to Italy in the event of a major enemy attack. Foch had only fought on the Western Front, but he clearly understood the dangers of leaving Italy isolated and insisted that these concerns were 'not a chimera'. On the contrary, Paris and London needed to come to an agreement to send a Franco-British corps in the event of enemy action. 'By flying all the Allied flags in Italy, we can show the enemy the strong solidarity and effective assistance that the Allies are providing to the Italian struggle', he wrote. 'The enemy can expect to come up against vast Allied forces that are closely united and well organised.' Foch travelled to Udine to meet Cadorna, and the two men sketched out a schedule for transporting up to ten divisions to Italy, plus their accompanying artillery, within twenty-five days, which was exactly the kind of support Cadorna wanted.[5]

Encouraging though this was, the events of late spring and early summer cast doubt on whether the French could be relied upon. With large numbers of their divisions raising the red flag and daring to mutiny, the French Army was plunged into its greatest crisis since the opening months of the war. Nivelle was relieved of command in mid-May and replaced by the more cautious General Philippe Pétain, who vowed that no more wildly ambitious attacks would be conducted, at least not until the Americans could take to the field in strength. In the meantime, Cadorna was left to fight it out along the battle-scarred Isonzo, mounting yet more attacks over ground where so many battalions had already failed, if for no other reason than that he could not stop without admitting the war might already be lost.

New orders were issued on 19 April. Cadorna would concentrate 220,000 men, against just under 150,000 Austrians, to make a sustained advance in what he termed the 'area of greatest sensitivity to the enemy'. The offensive would take place in three stages. First, a heavy bombardment would be fired for three or four days right across the front, masking Italian preparations and interfering with the movement of reserves between the Carso and the north. Second, an attack would then be launched by Lieutenant-General Luigi Capello's group of corps (known as *Zona di Gorizia*) towards a series of imposing heights around the Gorizia basin. Three attacks would be mounted: the first out from Plava towards Hill 383, Mount Kuk and Mount Vodice; the second across the Isonzo to take Mount Santo and Mount San Gabriele; while another corps moved out of Gorizia heading for Mount San Marco. The Duke of Aosta's Third Army would then strike from the south, driving through the Carso to seize the line Trstely–Hermada. With artillery again proving to be a decisive factor, Cadorna arranged that 100 guns from Third Army would be made available to Capello for his opening assault. After he had achieved his objectives, perhaps after one or two days, these weapons would be transferred, along with 100 of Capello's own guns, to Third Army for the main assault.[6]

Cadorna's 'artillery manoeuvre' was a bold plan, depending upon teamwork, cooperation and timing. It was also a sad reflection of the constraints the Italian Army was still operating under in its second year of war. In total, he managed to bring up 2,300 guns, but supplies of ammunition were always tightly controlled. Capello thought he needed about 1.4 million shells, but received just over half that figure, with particular shortfalls in the shells used for counter-battery fire. When the preliminary bombardment opened on 12 May, there was none of the furious 'drumfire' that could be found on other fronts, only a more methodical type of bombardment that flashed and rumbled across the front from Tolmein down to the sea. With the Austrian lines still shrouded in thick fog, the shelling paused every now and again to allow observers the chance to see what damage had been done. And then it continued, gradually increasing in intensity, with *bombardes* smashing the front trenches and clearing away the barbed wire, while the heaviest guns searched out enemy rear positions for headquarters or command posts.[7]

Capello's infantry went forward at noon on 14 May, picking their way across the smoke-filled battlefield under strict orders not to fire but to close with the enemy and use the bayonet. The bombardment had done significant damage, breaking open trenches and splintering barbed wire, even if it did not have the weight or power to destroy many of the caves, or deep dugouts constructed out of solid rock, that the enemy sheltered in. Capello entrusted the opening attack to II Corps, commanded by Pietro Badoglio. The hero of Mount Sabotino was now a lieutenant-general and one of the few officers Capello knew who would throw everything into the assault.[8] To take the first objective, the imposing Hill 383, Badoglio ordered five regiments to rush up its fire-swept slopes, crushing the Hungarian defenders without mercy. They were met almost immediately with heavy machine-gun fire and flurries of hand grenades that caused grievous losses, with one battalion having five different commanding officers within the first half-hour. As well as facing fierce resistance, the Italians had to advance uphill across an 'extraordinarily chaotic' landscape, strewn with debris and broken coils of wire. Queues would form under the shattered ledges, men handing their rifles on to those who had already scrambled up, before the lines re-formed and continued on to the summit. By the afternoon, Hill 383 had been taken, and several hours later, Mount Santo, another one of Capello's main objectives, was also reached, causing elation at *Comando Supremo*. For Cadorna, this was proof of the effectiveness of his methods and of Italian valour. 'These were days . . .' he wrote, 'of imperishable glory for our troops.'[9]

Unfortunately, such early successes were not the precursor to a wider breakthrough, only to continued heavy fighting. A counter-attack soon wrested back the summit of Mount Santo, with AOK determined to hold on to the Vodice Ridge, which commanded wide views over the entire Isonzo Valley. With the bridges and walkways across the river under intermittent shellfire, still the Italians went forward, swarming up the heights in great numbers. Mount Kuk fell on 17 May, but already *Zona di Gorizia* was reaching its limits. Capello wrote to Cadorna that evening to report on the critical ammunition situation. He estimated that if he just concentrated on taking the Vodice Ridge, abandoning any flanking operations, he would still only have enough shells for another three days of fighting. He was at pains to explain that his gunners had been very careful with their shooting, firing off just 100 shells per artillery piece. 'With this relatively limited consumption of ammunition, results have been obtained that may affirm that each shot was a precision shot. The gunners knew the value of each shot well; they did not allow themselves to be intoxicated by the noise; they fired well; and thus they opened all the gates to the infantry, whose advance they effectively and constantly supported.' It was, therefore, with 'great regret' that Capello would not be able to assist the action of Third Army, further south, by sending the 200 medium and heavy guns, which were still needed on his front.[10]

Fighting along the Mount Santo–Vodice Ridge continued for days, with heavy shelling by both sides covering the rocky slopes in clouds of dust and smoke. 'The artillery shook the whole mountain: and the echoes captured in the Isonzo gorge screamed like stormy waves', recalled one Italian soldier, awestruck at the 'mournful roars' that echoed around the battlefield.[11] On 18 May, the men of 53rd Division managed to reach the summit, but they were exhausted, low on ammunition and severely reduced in number. Yet they held on, only to face repeated counter-attacks from an enemy desperate to push them off. Soon the entire hill reeked of blood and death, and clusters of stretcher bearers and walking wounded began to trickle down from the heights, eyes vacant with horror. 'Up there it was hell', remembered one survivor; 'enormous losses, infectious diseases creeping around, laborious work to dig the trenches. Under the bombardment, the notes of national and martial anthems played by divisional music rang out. Only with a steel fist could Vodice be held.'[12]

There was certainly much horror along the Isonzo that spring, but also what seemed like tantalizing progress. The head of the British Military Mission, Brigadier-General Delme-Radcliffe, struck a positive note in a series of reports to London. He was impressed with Badoglio ('a commander of resource and energy . . . who knows the ground') and wanted to make the British Government realize just how formidable the Austrian positions were. He included a series of panoramic photographs that 'give some idea of the difficulty of the ground over which the attack on the Mount Kuk–Mount Santo Ridge took place, but, like all photographs, give little idea of the steepness and roughness of the ground'. He would never forget witnessing 'rocks as big as cottages, disturbed by heavy shells, crashing 2,000 feet down the hill sides, carrying away trees and gradually breaking up as they went down, showering splinters in all directions and ending up with a mighty plunge into the river . . .' The hilltops were 'honeycombed with galleries, tunnels, [and] machine-gun emplacements which make progress on the open slopes extremely difficult. The slopes themselves are also swept by artillery fire from the Bainsizza Plateau, over the top of the hills, from batteries in the hills' and beyond.[13]

The Duke of Aosta's main attack on the Carso opened on 23 May. Lacking the 200 guns that should have been made available to him, he attacked anyway, launching a sustained bombardment that hurled perhaps as many as half a million shells into the enemy positions. With Austrian reserves concentrated to the north, Aosta's divisions advanced up to four kilometres, taking 9,000 prisoners and finally coming to a halt some way short of their main objective (the line Trstely–Hermada). The Austrian High Command was already scouring every available corner for spare troops to throw into a battle that was reaching an intensity 'that the Isonzo Front had never thus far experienced', according to General Boroević.[14] Eventually two divisions were taken from the Russian front and sent to the Carso, where they entered a battlefield that almost defied description: furious exchanges of shell and machine-gun fire; low-flying aircraft bombing and strafing; while the infantry of both sides, bent over, scurried across the torn ground. An Italian engineer officer, scrambling up to the forward lines, remembered the 'indescribable confusion' of the front. 'In some places the trenches were in good condition, but most are shattered, collapsed, sometimes completely obliterated. Our shelling was frightening and it was frighteningly precise. At every few steps the trench was clogged with corpses and you had to manoeuvre to avoid the terrible stench.' But once you had ascended one of the innumerable heights on the Carso, you entered a different world. There it was not hard to spot the glittering blue waters of the Adriatic, and then, skirting the coast, the large houses of Trieste, just eleven miles away.[15]

For the time being, Trieste would remain a pipe dream. With ammunition stocks almost exhausted and casualties rising, Cadorna suspended operations on 28 May. In total, the Italian effort had cost 36,000 dead, 96,000 wounded and 25,000 prisoners.[16] Once again Cadorna had rattled the cage, pushing the Austrians as hard as he could, only to see his efforts tail off over subsequent days. Delme-Radcliffe was insistent that more needed to be done. 'General Cadorna has been obliged to cut his coat according to his cloth', he noted; 'the amount of cloth available has not been in proportion to the figure to be clothed. The cloth, in this instance, is heavy artillery ammunition, which is a ruling factor in the plans of operations for the Italian Army.' He urged London to send more support, not only ammunition, but enough raw materials to allow the Italians to manufacture more heavy shells, ideally up to 40,000 per day, which would make all the difference. 'In view of the great importance on political and military grounds of a really crushing defeat of the Austrians and as the prospect of inflicting this defeat can almost be mathematically calculated in terms of expenditure of heavy gun ammunition,' he wrote, 'it appears all the more clear that heavy gun ammunition before all else must be provided in quantities sufficient for the purpose.'[17]

The prospect of 'really crushing' the Austrians seemed to recede further into the distance as the battle wound down. Yet again the Italian Army had fallen just short of what was required to mount and sustain a decisive offensive, and it was now struggling with widespread exhaustion. Russian inactivity had allowed the Austrians to move in reinforcements, and on 4 June – a day of shimmering heat hazes and thick, choking dust – they launched a counter-offensive on the Carso, taking back much of the ground that had been lost over the past fortnight. When Cadorna was told that three Sicilian regiments had surrendered, he flew into a rage and threatened to write directly to Boroević asking for the men to be shot. Once his anger had passed, he began to realize that morale was becoming harder to maintain as more and more of his divisions were sinking into a dangerous state of lassitude and fatigue. On 6 June, he wrote to the Prime Minister and noted that the number of men being taken prisoner, particularly on 4 June, was 'very worrying', more so than any loss of ground.[18]

Yet another attack across the Isonzo had been brought to a halt. This battle, the Tenth, was a heavy ordeal for the Imperial and Royal Army, but it remained unbroken, showing a remarkable determination to keep the enemy at bay, albeit at terrible cost. Of the 165,000 riflemen of the Army of the Isonzo (as Fifth Army had been renamed) who had entered the battle, almost half had become casualties, mostly from the fierce artillery fire that swept the battlefield. In total, they had lost 7,300 dead, 45,000 wounded and 23,400 taken prisoner.[19] General Boroević continued to work wonders in marshalling his resources, holding his army together and barring the way to Trieste, earning the Commander's Cross of the Military Order of Maria Theresa, which was presented to him by the Emperor on a visit to the front in early June. Thanking 'from the bottom of my heart' all those who had served, Karl wanted his men to know that Boroević's award 'symbolises not only my utmost appreciation of the army commander, but also represents the heartfelt gratitude and proud satisfaction I have towards all of you, leaders and fighters alike. God's blessings have been with us, and we pray to the Almighty that he may continue to find us worthy of his gracious protection and shield. This shall grant us our final victory!'[20]

The political struggle in Petrograd had only worsened since Lenin's arrival. Street protests had broken out in early May, orchestrated by the Bolsheviks and mutinous sailors at the naval base in Kronstadt who objected to the Provisional Government's continued support for what they regarded as a nakedly imperialist war. The Foreign Minister, Pavel Miliukov, had already tried to reassure Russia's allies that she would honour her commitments, and in a press interview on 5 April had directly addressed the question of her war aims, which had been posed by the American President, Woodrow Wilson, at the beginning of the year. Her task was the 'reorganization of Austro-Hungary with the liberation of the nationalities she oppresses, and the liquidation of European Turkey', which would include the 'transfer' of Constantinople and the Straits (the waterway between the Black Sea and the Mediterranean) to Russia. 'Up to the present day', Miliukov added, 'Turks remain an alien element there, resting exclusively on the right of the conqueror, the right of the strongest', and giving the area to Russia 'would in no way contradict the principles advanced by Woodrow Wilson . . .'[21]

None of this was particularly convincing, and as the clamour for a 'peace without annexations' grew, Miliukov was forced to issue a revised declaration several days later. The 'aim of free Russia is not domination over other nations, or seizure of their national possession, or forcible occupation of foreign territories,' he stated, 'but the establishment of a stable peace on the basis of the self-determination of peoples'. This struggle over Russia's war aims, or whether Russia should even remain in the war, now threatened to tear apart the fragile ad hoc arrangements between the Provisional Government and the Soviet. With Miliukov still insisting that Russia would 'fully observe the obligations taken with respect to our Allies', violent clashes took place in Petrograd on 3–4 May between loyal those who, like the Bolsheviks, wanted peace at any c ever eager to stoke the fires of discontent, was committed to opposing the government in all circumstances. 'No class-conscious worker, no class-conscious soldier will further support the policy of "confidence" in the Provisional Government', he thundered in *Pravda*. 'The policy of confidence is bankrupt.'[23]

Prince Lvov was able to ride out the storm with the help of the Soviet, which had been spooked by the prospect of civil war and answered his call to enter into a coalition. It took six Cabinet positions, including Minister of War and Navy (taken over by Kerensky) and Minister of Agriculture (which was handed to the founder of the Socialist Revolutionaries, Viktor Chernov). Two of the Soviet's foremost opponents, Guchkov and Miliukov, resigned in protest, leaving Prince Lvov's authority hanging by a thread – and the future of Russian participation in the war highly doubtful. Nikolai Sukhanov, whose position in the Soviet gave him a ringside seat to chronicle the revolution, thought that the formation of a coalition was an essential, albeit awkward, step for the liberals. 'They could not remain suspended. They could not be so flatly ignored by the populace. They could not tolerate being recognized simply out of loyalty to the Soviet. They could not exist with their castrated administrative machine. It was vital to acquire all the attributes of power – even at the price of a compromise, even at a very high price.' This was, he added, a kind of marriage without love. 'And as a dowry the Soviet would bring the army, the real power, immediate confidence and support, and all the technical means of administration.'[24]

Alexander Kerensky, who had been the sole representative of the Soviet within the original Provisional Government, had now become one of the most powerful men in Russia. Thirty-six years old in 1917, he hailed, ironically enough, from Lenin's home town of Simbirsk and had trained as a lawyer before being elected to the Duma in 1912. Possessing a supreme self-confidence, he quickly gained a devoted following as the 'man of the hour' and as a tribune of the people who would speak up on behalf of the oppressed. He was 'thin, of medium height, clean shaven; with his bristling hair, waxen complexion, and half-closed eyes (through which he darted sharp and uneasy glances)'.

He struck Maurice Paléologue as 'the most original figure of the Provisional Government', who 'seems bound to become its main spring'. As Minister of War and Navy, he was now responsible for Russia's vast war effort and charged with restoring 'by all means at hand . . . the fighting capacity of the army'.[25]

Kerensky was convinced that Russia had to continue the war to defend the revolution. 'The fate of our freedom depends on whether the army and the navy fulfil to the end their duty towards their country', he said upon taking office. 'Let the freest army and navy in the world demonstrate that freedom is strength, not weakness, let them forge a new ironclad discipline of duty, raise the fighting might of the country, and convey to the popular will that authority of strength which will bring nearer the realization of the people's hopes. Forward to liberty, land, and freedom.'[26] In January 1917, Russia had promised 'to attack the enemy resolutely not later than three weeks following the beginning of the Allies' offensive', but this had been pushed back to May because of the organizational chaos in the rear. Alekseev had already warned the Provisional Government that it would be necessary to tell the Entente that 'they cannot count upon us before July' and this 'shirking' would have serious consequences for the war effort. 'We depend so much on our allies,' he wrote, 'both with regard to materials and financing, that a refusal of the Allies to assist us would place us in a still more difficult situation than the present one.'[27]

Kerensky set off on an extensive tour of the front, earning the nickname 'persuader-in-chief' as he tried to galvanize the spirit of the army. It was on these inspections that he got to know General Brusilov, who remained the most active field commander. Driving for hours in an open-top car, often getting soaked when rainstorms passed overhead, the two men discussed the war and revolution, and Kerensky decided that Brusilov must replace Alekseev. Unlike Alekseev, he was a man of action, and someone who shared a desire 'to bring the Russian army back to life'. Together they would speak to as many soldiers as possible and try to wean them away from the lure of the Bolsheviks and the temptation, understandable though it was, to ignore their officers, desert the army and demand peace at any price.

The mode of inspection was always the same [Kerensky wrote]: We walked down the line, swinging around into the heart of the ranks to an improvised platform. On our mounting the platform, came the word of command and from all sides thousands of troops would rush towards us, surrounding the platform in a huge circle. The commanders spoke first, followed by committee delegates. Then I came, and then the discontented, hesitating mass of armed human beings in gray, confused in mind and weary in body and spirit, would become animated by a kind of new life. Their souls would become aglow with enthusiasm which at times reached the peaks of mad ecstasy. It was not always easy to escape from this raging sea of human beings to our automobile and speed away to the next inspection.[28]

Kerensky could be an outstanding orator. He had a remarkable ability to transform the mood of his audience and transport them on a torrent of words and feelings, but this effect wore off almost as quickly as it had arrived. 'Kerensky was the incarnation of scurrying back and forth' was the verdict of Leon Trotsky, the flamboyant revolutionary who would become a key player in the Bolshevik movement over the summer.[29]

For Alekseev, the events of May 1917 were a shattering blow to his hopes that the abdication of the Tsar would allow the war to be prosecuted in a spirit of greater national cooperation and harmony. 'Russia is perishing', he told a congress of officers on 20 May in Mogilev; 'she is on the brink of the abyss; another push or two, and she will go over completely.' The army was now 'fallen', he added with a look of grave concern. 'Only yesterday it was mighty and threatening; today, it stands a pitiful weakling before the enemy.'[30] A secretive, shy man, almost shrew-like in his mannerisms, Alekseev knew that these words would be quickly relayed to Petrograd, but he did not care. He was relieved of command the following day, thus breaking the last link with the old *Stavka* that had taken Imperial Russia to war under the Grand Duke and the Tsar. 'He fought to the end,' recalled the head of the British Military Mission, Sir John Hanbury-Williams, 'ashamed no doubt that the Russia he loved should give cause for the idea that she had failed her Allies, and to us as well as to his own land I assert that he was loyal to the end.'[31]

There was a certain inevitability about the choice of Alekseev's successor. General Aleksei Brusilov was the best-known general in the army, famous throughout the world as the mastermind of Russia's most successful offensive, and someone who had embraced the revolution in a way that most of his fellow officers had not. Shedding his reputation as a strict disciplinarian, he had quickly become known for his willingness to speak to soldiers' committees, addressing them in person, taking off his hat and jacket, and promising that their grievances would be looked into.[32] On his first day at Mogilev on 4 June 1917 – a year to the day since he had opened his great offensive in Galicia – he authorized the creation of 'Battalions of Death', something that Alekseev had categorically refused to do. These battalions, made up of female volunteers, would 'arouse in the army the offensive spirit of the Revolution'.[33] Whether Brusilov had any faith in these units is difficult to say. He had greeted the abdication of the Tsar and the establishment of the Provisional Government with a fatalistic shrug of his shoulders, claiming that Nicholas II's failings had produced the inevitable reaction and that there was no point in opposing it. Therefore, one must accept the new reality and hope that a triumphant spirit of democracy and freedom would surge through the army and restore its fortunes. The Battalions of Death were a key test of this assumption.

Mounting an offensive with an army in such a delicate position was a dangerous gamble. General Anton Denikin, one of Brusilov's hard-fighting generals, who had been promoted to command Western Front (among a slew of senior appointments that had been made since the revolution), warned on 24 June that there were grave problems wherever he looked. In Third Army, disciplinary courts were not being held and morale in the infantry 'varied'. Tenth Army was little better. 'The best morale is to be found in the artillery . . .' he reported. 'The II Caucasian Corps feels the transition from the old to the new regime with especial acuteness; according to the opinion of the army commander, the 2nd Caucasian Grenadier Division, the

51st Division, and the 134th Division are not battle-fit as far as their morale is concerned . . . The attitude of the soldiers of the Tenth Army toward the offensive is in general rather negative.' Again, in Second Army, the morale of the artillery was 'quite good', but the infantry was 'much worse than in the other armies'. There was also a serious shortage of manpower 'developing in a threatening manner', and by 1 June, Tenth Army was 63,000 men below establishment. When Brusilov read Denikin's report, he could only shake his head in wonder. 'Is it worth while to prepare a blow there with such morale?' he scribbled on the document.[34]

Brusilov struck a more optimistic note in his dealings with Kerensky, and was determined to justify the confidence shown in him. He telegraphed on 15 June: 'The impression of the situation on the Northern Front is contradictory. On the Western Front the picture is similar, but somewhat better. I propose to launch an attack on the South-Western Front on 25 June. It is impossible to start earlier. In general, I think that there are opportunities for success, but the scale of these is impossible to determine.'[35] The attack was entrusted to General Aleksei Gutor, who had served under Brusilov and been promoted when his former chief had moved to Mogilev. He would have four armies under his command, with Eleventh and Seventh making the main assault towards Lemberg. Gutor could call upon 52 infantry and 8 cavalry divisions and over 1,100 guns deployed across a 100-kilometre front. This was an impressive mass of military power, at least in theory. They outnumbered the enemy three times over in manpower and twice in guns, and had the benefit of improved organization, centralized control of artillery, aerial reconnaissance, and large stocks of shells, which should have given them a strong chance of replicating the early success of the great attack of the previous summer.[36]

By the last days of June, after repeated delays to allow the Minister of War more time to tour the front and fill the men with his 'revolutionary ecstasy', the Russian armies had been given their objectives, and final movements were being made behind the lines.[37] Morale remained extremely fragile, and a sinking malaise was detectable in almost every corner of the army. In one case, two regiments had

refused to move up to the front and then almost killed their divisional commander when he came to find out what was going on.
Other regiments had to be disbanded, and even those that were more
reliable were often awash with drunkenness, rowdyism and rampant
indiscipline. One senior officer, General Tsykhovich, reported in late
June that his division had 'ceased to exist as a fighting unit', being
infiltrated by 'German agents who cover themselves with a veneer of
Bolshevism' and who appealed to 'the most sensitive feelings of
exhaustion with the war'.[38]

There was little that could be done. Brusilov pleaded with his men
to understand the need to defend the revolution, but he struggled to
be heard. Because the death penalty had been abolished, officers
lacked the coercive power that might have steadied their men, and
many were understandably reluctant to openly call for an offensive
lest they anger the other ranks. *Stavka* was left hoping that enough
fighting spirit remained at the front, and looked to the special 'shock
battalions' that were being trained in the latest trench-clearing techniques to lead the way. Kerensky rose to the occasion, issuing a
stirring appeal on the eve of the offensive: 'Russia, having thrown off
the chains of slavery, has firmly resolved to defend, at all costs, its
rights, honour, and freedom . . . *Warriors, our country is in danger!* Liberty and revolution are threatened. The time has come for the army
to do its duty. Your Supreme Commander, beloved through victory,
is convinced that each day of delay merely helps the enemy, and that
only by an immediate and determined blow can we disrupt his
plans . . . Forward!'[39]

This was a different Russian Army. Now carrying the red banners
of revolution, its men fought not for Tsar and Motherland, but for
the Provisional Government and the Soviet, for 'peace without
annexations or reparations'. But the commitment to these new gods
was only ever skin deep – 'not potent enough' was Brusilov's verdict
on the new slogans – and *Stavka* soon realized that the most reliable
troops in the army did not come from those areas rife with revolutionary spirit. On the contrary, Brusilov made sure that most of the
attacking divisions were Finnish or Siberian – seen as more aggressive
than regular Russian regiments – while the Southwest Front also

deployed a Czech rifle brigade and a Polish division, which had been formed from deserters and prisoners of war who had agreed to fight against their former masters. While this was encouraging, the plan of attack was also dependent upon as much artillery as possible, on the assumption that an impressive display of firepower was essential to get the men to advance.[40]

The preliminary bombardment opened on 29 June. For the first time, Russia could deploy complete heavy artillery brigades, with 8- and 12-inch howitzer batteries, to finally give them the firepower to break into strongly fortified trench systems.[41] Shells smashed into the enemy lines for two days, raising a vast, almost volcanic curtain of dust, and pulverizing the defenders in what was possibly the most intensive and destructive artillery bombardment ever seen on the Eastern Front. At nine in the morning of 1 July – a day of bright sunshine and stifling heat – the infantry went forward, led by the Battalions of Death. They were able to smash a hole between General Böhm-Ermolli's Second Army and the German-led South Army, which held the front east of Lemberg. In what seemed like a miraculous precursor to final victory, the attackers advanced to a depth of two miles on a forty-mile front, capturing over 18,000 soldiers. For a moment it seemed that the Imperial and Royal Army had finally reached its nadir, worn down by years of fighting and its discipline rotted away by internal subversion. In one celebrated example, two Bohemian infantry regiments, dug in around the village of Pomo rzany, lost over 4,500 men, most of whom were taken prisoner. Although they had fought well, when they were fired on by other Czech soldiers they lost heart and gave up, surrendering en masse. For the first time in the war, Habsburg troops had been attacked by their fellow citizens and former comrades-in-arms.[42]

This was an impressive start, but a crucial component of fighting strength – morale and the offensive spirit – was missing from the Russian Army. Attacking divisions had shown enthusiasm in the early stages of the operation, when the guns had razed the enemy's forward positions and shattered their counter-attacks, but within a few days all momentum had drained away, and battalion after battalion shouldered arms and either refused to move on from their objectives or simply returned to their old trenches. One officer, part of I Imperial Guard Corps, recorded his frustration as a succession of units refused to fight on the second day of battle. 'Everything seemed to be in order,' he wrote, 'except the most important element: a dependable infantry. After 7.00 our artillery began to pound the enemy's defences. The Germans did not reply; only their aeroplanes burned two of our balloons, one after another.' By noon the shelling had become intensive: 'the horizon was filled with smoke and dust from the bursts of fire'. However, when the Germans began to bombard the Russian front trenches, the men could not be persuaded to move out. 'Immediately after that both our divisional commanders reported that our infantrymen refused to go over the top.' Soon columns of disorderly men were returning from the front, deaf to the appeals of even the most senior commanders. General Ivan Erdeli, the commander of Eleventh Army, went to see some of them, shaking hands and pleading with them to go back, but without success. 'An amusing way to conduct a battle' was the verdict of one staff officer, who watched as Erdeli returned to his command post, a resigned look on his face, spitting on the ground in disgust.[43]

Kerensky and Brusilov issued a succession of urgent telegrams pleading with commanding officers to get their units moving again, but a fatal paralysis seemed to have infected the armies under their command. Hope was briefly rekindled by General Lavr Kornilov, a Siberian Cossack with a reputation as one of the most courageous officers in Russia. He had escaped from captivity in 1916 and returned to the front, taking charge of Eighth Army south of the Dniester. He drove his men on with sheer force of will, demanding that they go forward with all the fury they could muster. When his attack was launched on 6 July, the Austrian defenders again showed little fight, dissolving into sheepish clusters of ragged men, resigned to their capture. By 11 July, he was closing on the town of Kalusz, an advance of roughly fifteen miles, which threatened to turn the flank of the defenders to the north and unhinge their trench system. As a Soviet analyst later put it, this was like a 'brilliant firework . . . the last victorious glow of a dying army'.[44]

With the Habsburg line undergoing what seemed like an all too familiar collapse, it was left to Germany to restore the situation. At OHL, staff officers were preoccupied with the impending British offensive in Flanders (which would open on 31 July and continue until early November), but still kept a close eye on the Eastern Front. Deserters had been coming in for weeks with news of Russian operations, which gave them enough time to assemble a group of six divisions for a counter-attack. The basic idea, as communicated to *OberOst*, was to break through the Russian line, using the Sereth river as flank protection, and advance to the southeast 'in order to open up the Russian Front as far as possible'. The operation, codenamed 'Summer Journey', opened like a thunderclap on 19 July.[45] It should have taken place on 12 July, but unexpected difficulties in getting the guns deployed and registered meant that the date was delayed by a week. Fortunately, what had been lost in speed had been gained in efficiency, and the opening of a seven-hour preliminary bombardment at 3 a.m. was a brutal demonstration of German technical prowess. Russian gun batteries were smothered in shellfire and their forward positions torn to pieces, while their artillery could only respond with a few stray shots. Then the infantry moved out. It was an oppressively hot day. Shimmering heat hazes obscured the thick air and left men panting, desperate for water after a few hours' marching. It was fortunate that there was little fighting. German divisions overran the first and second Russian positions and took around 6,000 prisoners in just a few hours. It was said later that two Finnish divisions fled at the sight of just three German companies.[46]

This was all it took to break Kerensky's offensive and then push it back into a headlong, chaotic retreat. The weather changed the following day, with torrential downpours soaking the ground, but not before German aircraft had spotted the signs of a sudden withdrawal: lines of marching infantry, heavy rail traffic heading towards Tarnopol, and the black smoke of burning supply dumps.[47] On 22 July, a group of commissars on the Southwest Front jointly authored a telegram to Kerensky warning him that they were now amidst 'a fatal crisis' in morale. 'Most of the military units are in a state of complete disorganisation, their enthusiasm for an offensive has rapidly disappeared, and they no longer listen to the orders of their leaders and neglect all the exhortations of their comrades, even replying to them with threats and shots.' Deserters were now streaming away from the front, grouping together in ever larger bands, and 'men who are in good health and robust, who have lost all shame and feel that they can act altogether with impunity' were heading to the rear. Sometimes entire units disappeared in this way. The commissars urged Kerensky to act. 'Let the country know the truth, let it act without mercy, and let it find enough courage to strike those who by their cowardice are destroying and selling Russia and the revolution.'[48]

Large swathes of the Russian Army were now simply unwilling to fight on, ignoring what few officers they had left and prone to panicking at the slightest thing. Soon the entire front was on the move, breaking and shifting like great tectonic plates. For Denikin, who as commander of Western Front had only played a supporting role so far, the reality of what they were now facing was difficult to appreciate. One of his corps commanders had come to see him, distraught at what had happened. 'Everything was ready for the advance: the plan had been worked out in detail', he said; 'we had a powerful and efficient artillery; the weather was favourable . . . we had superior numbers, our Reserves were drawn up in time, we had plenty of ammunition, and the sector was well chosen for the advance'. He told Denikin that they had taken three successive lines of trenches and silenced the enemy's artillery, only for night to fall. 'Immediately I began to receive anxious reports from officers commanding sectors at the Front to the effect that the men were abandoning the unattacked [sic] Front Line en masse, entire companies deserting.' In just a single day they had 'lived through the joy of victory . . . as well as the horror of seeing the fruits of victory deliberately cast away by the soldiery'.[49]

Not even the chance of fighting alongside the women's Battalion of Death, an all-female unit made up of about 300 volunteers and led by a decorated and patriotic peasant, Maria Bochkareva, could shame the men into action. The women's battalion went into battle on 22 July near Smorgon. 'We swept forward and overwhelmed the first German line, and then the second', Bochkareva wrote proudly. 'Our regiment alone captured two thousand prisoners.' Then their difficulties multiplied. Finding stocks of vodka and beer 'in abundance', half the regiment began to indulge, 'throwing themselves ravenously on the alcohol', while their officers stumbled up and down the trenches shouting at them to move on. Bochkareva managed to round up enough of her soldiers to occupy the third line, only to be counter-attacked in force. 'We were met with such a violent and effective fire that our soldiers lost heart and took to their heels by the hundred . . .' She appealed desperately for reinforcements, only to be told that the rest of the corps were 'holding a meeting' to debate whether to advance. When another bombardment opened on their lines, the rem-nants of the battalion, 'bespattered with mud and blood', returned to their original trenches angry and demoralized. Bochkareva had been wounded by a shell and was carried back on a stretcher. 'The offensive had all been to no purpose.'[50]

In Mogilev, Kerensky had greeted the initial successes of the attack with wild glee, issuing a communiqué in which he lauded 'the great triumph of the revolution' and stated, with his usual turn of phrase, that the Russian soldiers had shown 'by their offensive the new dis-cipline based on the feeling of civic duty'.[51] But this did little to calm the situation in Petrograd, which remained deeply unstable through-out the summer months. 'The appearance of the city changed quickly', remembered Vladimir Nabokov, who was still working for the Provisional Government. 'Automobiles of private citizens van-ished, armoured cars and vehicles darted through the streets, packed with armed workers and soldiers. Every now and again shooting would break out from various places, and the crackle of shots would start up from various directions.'[52] Rioting broke out again in mid-July, with Lenin orchestrating what looked like an attempted *coup d'état*, trying to flood the streets with supporters, only for loyal troops to arrive and drive them off. But this was all too much for Prince Lvov, the genteel Prime Minister, who resigned on 16 July, putting forward Kerensky as his successor 'in the profound conviction that it was precisely he who was needed at this, perhaps the moment of the revolution, in the post of Minister President'.[53]

Kerensky had more authority than ever, but it seemed to dissolve outside the confines of his office. He could only issue a barrage of powerfully worded telegrams demanding obedience and sacrifice. On 21 July, he called for the restoration of military discipline, 'implementing the full force of revolutionary power, including recourse to force of arms, in order to save the army'. All those who were guilty of disobedience would be arrested for high treason and he urged unity 'against traitors who are consciously leading the army into defeat'. He dismissed General Gutor and replaced him with Kornilov, the only general who seemed up for a fight, but it made little difference. Career Tsarist officers, men who had been on the battlefields of Lemberg and Lake Naroch, could only watch in horror as their army disintegrated around them, dissolving into indifferent masses of men, throwing away their weapons, or huddling in groups of squabbling 'delegates' discussing the latest rumours. By the final days of July, the Southwest Front was in full retreat. 'In general the army is on the run', reported the commander of Eleventh Army, General Erdeli, on 25 July, the day that Tarnopol fell.[54]

18.   'Time is running out'

Tsar Nicholas II was not the only monarch to lose his throne in 1917. At an inter-Allied council held in late May, the British and French had agreed to depose King Constantine of Greece. This step had not been an easy one to take. The British regarded French machinations in Greece with understandable suspicion, only to struggle to formulate a cohesive set of alternative policies. Worries for French domestic harmony should they not get their way usually prevented the British from risking a major breach in the Entente, leaving them following the French, sheepishly at first and then racing to catch up. The new government of Monsieur Ribot wanted to take a much harder line with Constantine, whom they regarded as a dangerous saboteur, and because the British were still intent on withdrawing forces from Macedonia, the French insisted that they must be allowed 'to carry out the measures which we consider necessary'. With plans well advanced for a military occupation of Thessaly, London finally acquiesced in French demands that 'it was essential to the security of the Allied forces in Salonica that King Constantine ceases to reign'.[1]

A reinforced French division left Salonika on 8 June and sailed for Piraeus, while an ultimatum was despatched to the King warning him that 'the Allies could tolerate neither his continued violation of the Greek Constitution in governing the country as an absolute Monarch, nor the prolonged division of Greece into two factions; that they must, therefore, insist on his abdication in favour of one of his sons, who would have to bind himself to rule as a Constitutional Monarch with M. Venizelos, or a nominee of M. Venizelos as his Prime Minister'.[2] Constantine left Greece on 14 June, moving aside in favour of his 23-year-old son, Prince Alexander. Venizelos was escorted into Athens by French troops and publicly called for Greece to shed her neutrality and join the Allies. 'In taking part in this World War,' he said, 'we shall not only regain the national territories we have lost, we shall not only re-establish our honour as a nation, we shall not only effectively defend our national interests at the Peace Conference and secure our national future, but we shall also be a worthy member of the family of free nations which that Conference will organize'.[3] Greece formally severed relations with the Central Powers on 30 June, with Venizelos being sworn in as Prime Minister several days later.

The question of Sarrail was never far from the surface of discussions about Salonika. At a meeting of the War Cabinet on 5 June, Robertson reported that 'General Sarrail's handling of the recent offensive at Salonica had not been good, and that the consensus of opinion was that he concerned himself more with the political aspect of the campaign than with the actual conduct of military operations'. With the Serbs, Italians and Russians also unhappy, Lloyd George wrote to Ribot and demanded that Sarrail be replaced.[4] There were many in the French Government who would have liked to dispense with Sarrail's services, but War Minister Paul Painlevé argued that it would be unwise to move him on while Greece remained unsettled. Painlevé also told the British that the outbreak of mutiny in parts of the French Army meant that the recall of Sarrail might cause an outcry and bring down the government, which was enough to scare the British off, at least for the time being.[5]

These political machinations meant that there would be no major military operations undertaken on the Macedonian Front for the remainder of 1917. With *l'armée d'Orient* in a curious state of limbo, unsure whether it was to attack or defend, Sarrail and Milne spent their time reporting back to their national capitals, arranging and rearranging reliefs and dealing with interminable questions of supply. A year earlier, Milne had warned London that 'another summer of comparative inaction would ruin this army even if it escaped the ravages of disease', because 'all ranks from Corps Commanders downwards live in tents or bivouacs under trying climatic conditions without any of the rest periods they had in France and none of the glamour surrounding a main army'.[6] Although things had improved somewhat in the intervening period, the men of the expeditionary force could not escape another long season of waiting and working in the shimmering all-enveloping summer heat, pestered by mosquitoes and lice and wondering what was to become of them. '[T]he fact remains that, after three full years of war, we don't seem to be getting anywhere and we can see not the slightest sign of it ever ending' was the depressing verdict of one British NCO.[7]

Fortunately, there were signs of life elsewhere in southeastern Europe that summer. The French mission to Romania, headed by Henri Berthelot, had managed to oversee an almost miraculous resurrection of the Romanian Army, which had been nearly destroyed during the 1916 campaign. Of the half a million men who had mobilized with Romania's declaration of war, barely 40 per cent had retreated behind the Sereth river four months later, abandoning 80 per cent of their rifles, half their artillery, and most of their machine-guns. Working with a small team of determined officers, Berthelot put new hope into the army by orchestrating the delivery of thousands of tons of supplies and weaponry from France, via the long journey through Russia from the Arctic port of Archangel. By June 1917, ten divisions had been reconstituted, with another five in the pipeline, now equipped with a much better, more modern array of weaponry, including 200 aircraft, 220,000 rifles, 2,700 machine-guns, 85 120 mm howitzers, 1.9 million artillery shells, 1.4 million grenades, 101 million rifle cartridges and 600,000 gas masks.[8]

This sudden abundance of equipment could only be used properly with detailed instruction and training. French teams had spent months working with Romanian officers and their men, taking them through tactical drills and battle plans, and explaining the latest lessons from the Western Front. Although relations between the French and the Romanians were not always easy – the French could sometimes be overbearing or impatient, the Romanians overly sensitive to accusations of laziness or disinterest – Berthelot did his best to encourage a spirit of cooperation between his officers and their students, who had been given six months to prepare for a new offensive. 'Fervent activity reigns within the regiments', recorded one French officer. 'New weapons, which they were not previously aware of, have been distributed to our troops: grenades, machine-guns and trench artillery. These give rise to new combat techniques, which we

off after the first or second day as troops became exhausted and moved further away from their supply lines. Moreover, OHL had already ordered a counter-attack around Averescu's left flank. This would have 'far-reaching operational effects', rolling up the Romanian front line and advancing towards Iaşi between the Prut and the Sereth rivers, which would give the Central Powers possession of Moldavia, the last remaining Romanian province not under their control.[13]

The counter-offensive – the Battle of Mărăşeşti – opened in the early hours of 6 August. German gun batteries unleashed their usual ferocious bombardment, high explosive interspersed with poison gas. With the darkness lit up by the pounding gunfire, German troops moved out, wading across the Putna and chasing off the Russian defenders, who occupied thin trenches and showed little fight. They managed to drive about seven miles, taking 1,200 prisoners, only for resistance to stiffen as Romanian troops joined the battle. Numerous artillery batteries, situated on high ground on the east bank of the Sereth, enfiladed the line of advance, while a series of counter-attacks, often led by Romanian or French officers, were launched throughout the day. Moreover, the scorching August heat, which rose to dangerously high temperatures, quickly wore out men and left them exhausted (some even passed out by the side of the road). It was quickly becoming clear that this would not be an easy battle. This time the Romanian Army would stand and fight.[14]

Field Marshal Mackensen, who had spent the year overseeing the military administration of Romania from a hotel in Bucharest, left the capital to set up a command post on the Magura Odobesti. This was a hilltop peak about fifteen miles northwest of Focşani, from where he could overlook the entire battlefield. He was impressed by the tenacity of the Romanians, both in the attack and now in defence. 'The Russians and Romanians are doing better than we might have expected based on their recent performance', he admitted. After a week of fighting, Mackensen's divisions had taken 15,000 prisoners and 29 guns, but Romanian spirit remained intact and there was a growing acceptance that more reserves or extra gun batteries would be needed to help them 'eat their way through', as Ludendorff put it.

'Advancing in this terrain, which is very confusing for the individual rifleman, is made very difficult by numerous steep slopes, but particularly by the type of viticulture', opined Mackensen. 'All the vines in each row are connected by tensioned wire. They are impossible to get past without wire cutters. The corn is at head height and planted in dense rows. The forests usually have dense undergrowth and many thorn bushes. Yesterday almost 4,000 prisoners were taken again. But the enemy does not decrease in number. New divisions were constantly being brought in . . .'[15]

As the Battle of Mărăşeşti continued, fighting flared up again on the Isonzo. After waiting for his ammunition to be restocked, General Cadorna launched another offensive (the eleventh) on 19 August. He was insistent that the Italians had no choice but to keep going. The May fighting had achieved important, albeit incomplete, results. Were they to advance across the Bainsizza Plateau north of Gorizia, they would occupy good defensive positions while also depriving the enemy of the crucial supply route through the mist-wreathed Chiapovano Valley. Cadorna had thinned out his line as much as he dared, massing 600 of his 887 battalions and 5,200 guns (including *bombardes*) from Tolmein to the sea to make the 'supreme effort'. They outnumbered their opponents almost 3:1 in infantry and 4:1 in weight of shell, with General Boroević now facing one of the largest offensives of the war. The Croat took the news of the impending attack with his characteristically granite stoicism. 'We do not retreat a single step', he told a journalist. A triumphal procession to Trieste would only take place 'over their dead bodies'.[16]

Cadorna's emphasis upon sheer brute strength was well known, but there were encouraging signs of development elsewhere in the army. Lieutenant-General Capello, commanding Second Army, had formed the first 'shock troops', the *Arditi*, in June 1917. These men, mostly volunteers, were known for their black or dark green jerseys and special badges, which were meant to distinguish them from regular infantry. They were given extra pay, equipped with grenades and new light machine-guns and underwent enhanced training in close combat. Army doctrine was also beginning to reflect the increasing firepower available to infantry battalions, including more machine-guns, as well as rifle grenades and trench mortars. Rules for the deployment of infantry, issued in June 1917, ordered rifle companies to make their attacks in three waves. The first would press ahead, ignoring their flanks; the second was tasked with 'mopping up' captured trenches; while the third would push both waves onwards. Yet these encouraging developments were only rarely applied in the field, and the poor level of training of many junior officers, mainly reservists, meant that too often Italian attacks were conducted en masse – often whole brigades – which made them irresistible targets for the defenders.[17]

Artillery and mortar fire opened on 17 August and continued for two days, a rain of destruction that reduced the Habsburg defences to a churned, smoky ruin and set large fires burning in the rear areas. At dawn on 19 August, the air still reverberating to thunderous shellfire, two Italian armies went forward. At Second Army, General Capello's main attack opened with a series of thrusts that began north of Tolmein and spread down to the hills around Gorizia. Italian troops were able to cross the Isonzo at numerous places, stumbling over perilous pontoon bridges or splashing across on boats, often under shell and mortar fire, before advancing up to the Bainsizza Plateau. To the south, along the Vodice Ridge, which had been gained at such cost in the Tenth Battle, progress was slow and bitterly fought. Moving forward behind a heavy barrage, Italian regiments ran into thick belts of barbed wire, which had to be cut by hand – a fruitless task when under heavy fire from machine-gun nests, which were always positioned to provide the deadliest crossfire.[18]

Battle was also joined on the Carso that day. Four reinforced corps went forward, only to be repulsed by terrible fire from the Habsburg defenders, enough of whom had managed to survive the preliminary bombardment. Only the under-strength 12th Division, containing mostly Polish troops, broke, falling back from the village of Selo to their second position. Counter-attacks were thrown in, but reserve units could not move forward because of the 'murderous mass fire' on the rear zones.[19] Austrian battalions died where they stood, ground down by murderous barrages, which even included shells from 15-inch naval guns. Originally intended for battleships, these enormous weapons had been repurposed and placed on barges, from where they could provide direct gunfire support to ground operations. Emperor Karl visited the Carso the following day and was horrified by the scenes unfolding in his field glasses. 'An impenetrable wall of smoke and dust hung over the heights, which for several minutes made it impossible to recognise the tactical situation', recorded a journalist from *Neue Freie Press*. 'Our own artillery pinned down the enemy infantry in their trenches, long-range guns sent their shells beyond the Isonzo, whose glittering reflection shone in all directions. Then the Italian wall of fire pushed itself behind our trenches, the enemy charged and laid a barrage of fire in front of our reserves. At that moment, hundreds of muzzle flashes were aimed at the advancing Italian infantry.'[20]

Fortunately for the Austrians, General Cadorna was becoming increasingly nervous about sustaining heavy losses for little gain and cancelled Third Army's operations on the evening of 21 August, transferring as many guns as he could to support the main assault further north. The following day, 22 August, renewed attacks finally broke through the defences on the Bainsizza Plateau. Situated to the northeast of Gorizia, the Bainsizza was a vast, undulating and largely featureless wilderness, waterless and without roads, rising to some 600–700 metres in height. The defences here had been under heavy pressure for days, and when another Italian offensive opened that morning, behind the usual crushing bombardment, the line broke. One Austrian regimental commander scribbled a short note for his superiors ('the losses are enormous!') before falling back, leaving his entrenchments piled with dead and dying men. Italian columns were able to reach the Jelenik Heights, the lynchpin of the Austrian defensive system, and force Boroević to authorize the evacuation of the plateau, concerned that his divisions would cease to exist if they held on any longer.[21]

The Austrian line had finally cracked, at great cost, but it remained to be seen whether it was only the beginning of a wider breakthrough. General Capello followed up as quickly as he could, but moving guns across such broken terrain was extremely difficult, and it took weeks before his troops were ready to push on again, by which time

Boroević's men had occupied a new line on the eastern side of the Bainsizza, having retreated ten kilometres and abandoned a hundred square miles of territory. For the time being, Capello concentrated on widening the breach, attacking the 'mountain of death', Mount San Gabriele, a key position about three miles northeast of Gorizia. At 646 metres in height, it commanded the surrounding area and had been fought over repeatedly. Its summit had been cleared of vegetation, its topsoil blown off, leaving a landscape that was almost impassable: 'numerous shell holes, scattered boulders, and wire barricades all shot to pieces . . . countless pieces of discarded equipment and the bodies of the many men killed in previous battles'.[22] The Italians gradually surrounded the mountain, shelling it with every gun they could bring up, before wave after wave of infantry clambered up its slopes, only to meet deadly fire from the defenders, who seemed to cling on no matter how many tons of shells were directed at them. 'If any peak deserves to bear a monument to heroism, it is Mount San Gabriele', wrote the Austrian official historian. 'It shall remain synonymous with the heroism of the glorious Austro-Hungarian Army; but even the enemy of that time can remember the battles that raged around the mountain without shame.'[23]

By mid-September, mutual exhaustion had settled on both sides. Cadorna could only blame his usual bugbears for his inability to achieve more decisive results – particularly a lack of ammunition – but he called it a victory anyway, pointing to the gains on the Bainsizza as proof that his methods were as sound as ever. Italian losses were high, at 143,000, with morale dipping as yet more attacks withered in the face of stubborn enemy resistance.[24] The atmosphere in the opposite camp was similarly depressed. The Army of the Isonzo may have prevented a decisive breakthrough on the Carso, but the loss of Bainsizza and the sheer scale of Italian resources left Boroević in a subdued, anxious mood. By the time the battle tailed off, Austrian casualties may have been as high as 110,000, a figure that was simply unsustainable with no more reserves of manpower to tap into (other than those who had already been wounded). Ammunition was also being expended in previously unimaginable quantities. Austrian artillery had fired over 1.5 million shells, with almost 40 per cent of their guns breaking down because of such heavy wear and tear, leading AOK to conclude that Eleventh Isonzo may well have been the last defensive victory they were capable of.[25]

No one felt this more deeply than Emperor Karl. On 26 August, just days after he had returned from the Isonzo, he wrote to the Kaiser and told him of his growing desperation: 'With the experiences we had in the Eleventh Battle of Isonzo, there grows in me the conviction that we will occupy an extremely difficult position should there be a twelfth Isonzo battle, as expected.' His commanders, he wrote, had become convinced that they must launch an offensive lest they be overwhelmed, but in order to do so they would need reinforcements taken from the Eastern Front:

> I therefore ask you, dear friend, to implore your leading generals to free up Austro-Hungarian divisions in the east by detaching German troops. I am sure you will understand my emphasis on conducting the offensive against Italy with only my troops. My whole army is calling the war against Italy 'our war'. From their youth onwards, every officer has inherited from his father the deep sense of longing in his breast to fight against his hereditary enemy. If German troops were to help us, it would have a dampening effect on morale, crippling our enthusiasm. Only German artillery, especially heavy artillery, would be welcomed by me and my army as much sought-after help in the Italian theatre of war. Time is running out. A triumphant thrust against Italy may quickly bring about the end of the war.[26]

The Kaiser responded on 1 September, explaining that because all available reserves were already committed to operations around Riga, he could not relieve any Habsburg troops. However, as soon as these were completed, it might be possible to revisit the idea of an offensive across the Isonzo, which would be undertaken 'by troops from our two armies'.[27]

The idea of an Austro-German offensive against Italy was not new. Conrad had been pleading for one since 1915, but the urgency of doing something to relieve the Austrians was now more pressing than ever. It was not until German troops had marched into Riga on 5 September that OHL could spare more than a passing thought to an Italian expedition. The attack at Riga may have only been relatively minor by the standards of some Eastern Front operations, but it showcased a range of new tactics that could be employed if Germany was to go back onto the offensive, whether against Italy or France. General Oskar von Hutier's Eighth Army was chosen for the attack, ordered to cross the Dvina river and outflank the city from the southeast. It opened on 1 September with a devastating five-hour bombardment, which had been devised by one of the most innovative artillery officers in the German Army, Lieutenant-Colonel Georg Bruchmüller. 615 guns and 544 trench mortars were brought up to the front in the strictest secrecy and stocked with 407,000 rounds of high explosive, 154,000 gas shells, 3,000 smoke shells and 82,000 mortar bombs.[28]

The guns opened fire at 4 a.m., and for two hours they concentrated on counter-battery tasks, firing thousands of gas shells at Russian artillery positions, blanketing them in choking fumes, before switching onto the front trenches. After another three hours of punishment, German infantry moved out, crossing the Dvina on pontoon bridges covered by a creeping barrage that forced the defenders to keep their heads down. The attackers were soon on the far bank, where they began to spread out into the Russian lines, infiltrating through any weak spots, bombing dugouts and rounding up prisoners, many of whom were too shocked or demoralized to resist. By nightfall, Hutier had six divisions across the river, outflanking Riga and making the city impossible to hold. Aircraft circling high over the battlefield spotted long columns of retreating units streaming away to the north in leaderless packs, only stopping to pull up and eat the turnips that could be found in nearby fields. They were no longer an army, reported a commissar sent to investigate; 'they were a crowd, incapable of even the slightest resistance'.[29]

Despite the success of the Riga attack, Ludendorff had no choice but to bring it to a halt within a few days. He shifted divisions around, sending two to France so they would relieve other units bound for the Italian Front. He also wrote to Conrad on 12 September, updating the former Chief of the General Staff on his hopes for the new offensive. He did not conceal his concerns that they lacked the strength for a truly crushing attack. 'The forces are largely not as I would have them', he admitted. 'But in war things are not always as one would like them to be, Your Excellency, and I know that. I have therefore pushed all doubts aside and shall undergo this deployment with the conviction that success will ensue.'[30] Ludendorff was not being entirely honest. While Conrad had long seen Italy as the primary front and the theatre in which he wanted to strike a decisive blow, the First Quartermaster-General regarded any operation against Italy as a minor, and strictly limited, affair. 'The attack on Italy might no doubt have a great effect and immediately relieve the Western Front', he mused, 'but whether it would, in conjunction with the shortage of coal, produce a crisis in Italy could not be foretold.' He thought not.[31]

Germany could only spare six to eight divisions for any projected attack, so it was evident that the location would have to be carefully chosen – somewhere that would allow for quick and decisive penetration. OHL had already ruled out attacking from the Tyrol, which only left a small number of other possible avenues. With the lower Isonzo too full of Italian troops, Major-General Alfred von Waldstätten, Arz's deputy at Baden, highlighted the prospects of an attack from Tolmein to Caporetto. If they could cross the Isonzo in a south-westerly direction and take the heights of the Kolovrat range (up to 1,100 metres), where the main Italian defences were situated, they could then push on to Cividale, unhinging the entire Isonzo line and perhaps even forcing the enemy back behind the Tagliamento river. OHL had sent the commander of the Alpine Corps (and expert in mountain warfare), General Krafft von Dellmensingen, to the Isonzo, and he soon confirmed that the attack could be carried out if certain difficulties were overcome. Soon afterwards, Ludendorff agreed to go ahead, and gave it the codename *Waffentreue* ('Loyalty to Arms').[32]

Throughout August 1917, with its alternating burning heat and heavy downpours, the Russian Army continued to dissolve. In sector after sector, units crumbled and fell away, opening up huge swathes of the front to the Central Powers, who gorged themselves on thousands of square miles of conquered territory in Galicia and Bukhovina.

Desperate to master the situation, Kerensky removed Brusilov as Commander-in-Chief on 1 August, replacing him with the 46-year-old General Kornilov, whose short period in charge of Eighth Army and then Southwest Front had confirmed his credentials as perhaps the only man who might be able to restore the army's fortunes. A great patriot, hardened by service throughout the Russian Empire, Kornilov was known for his personal courage and ramrod-like discipline. He was escorted everywhere by a bodyguard of devoted Tekintzy tribesmen, which only added to his mystique. 'The physique of the man harmonizes with his intellectual and moral qualities', recorded an admiring journalist. 'Of middle height, spare and erect, he is hardy and untiring like his Cossack ancestors. His brows and head are well shaped, his features rugged and swarthy, his eyes small and piercing, and his manner calm and collected. He impressed you as a man who has infinite control over himself, kindly but adamant.'[33]

Whereas Brusilov had worked alongside Kerensky relatively smoothly, Kornilov was much less amenable to the ways of the Provisional Government. Upon being informed of his appointment, he telegraphed Petrograd that he would only agree if there would be no interference in his 'operational orders', or in the appointment of senior officers, and that the death penalty would be applied 'behind the lines where the reserve troops were stationed'. He would also, crucially, 'consider himself responsible only to his conscience and the nation as a whole'.[34] Kerensky was not minded to be dictated to in this manner, which he saw as an affront both to himself and to the sovereignty of the Provisional Government. He threatened to rescind Kornilov's appointment, only for his ministers to demur, insisting that he ignore the telegram (being 'unworthy of notice'). Kerensky thus decided to treat Kornilov's terms as 'mere *literature*', either dictated to him by 'chance persons' or the product of a mind absent 'of even an elementary knowledge of statesmanship', and he simply folded the telegram and placed it in his desk drawer under lock and key. They were 'such terrible times', he insisted years later, 'there was such sore need of a strong personality at the front'.[35]

Kerensky was increasingly besieged, torn left and right, with his support base crumbling away with every reverse at the front. The

Bolshevik leadership had been scattered, either imprisoned or on the run, after the coup had been defeated in July (Lenin was in hiding in Finland), but their influence on the Soviet in Petrograd was growing. Kerensky had formed a second coalition government in early August, but he was dependent upon the support of the right, particularly the Kadets, who had offered to join his government on the condition that he would take whatever steps were necessary 'to develop a mighty army by restoring strict military discipline' and ending all 'interference by soldier committees in questions of war tactics and strategy'.[36] Eager to entrench his position, he organized an All-Russia State Conference in Moscow on 26 August, intending to outline the programme of the new government and lay before the country the truth of what it was facing. The Bolsheviks boycotted the event, with some trade unions attempting to hold a general strike in the city, but over 2,000 delegates, including former members of the Duma, representatives from the Soviet, key industrial and financial figures and senior officers (among them Alekseev and Brusilov) made their way to the Bolshoi Theatre for three days of speeches that had been billed as the opportunity for 'all live forces of the State' to 'rally around the Provisional Government'.[37]

Kerensky intended that he should be the centre of attention, but it was Kornilov, the newly appointed Commander-in-Chief, who quickly became the figure everyone wanted to see, carried aloft into the theatre like some conquering hero. His speech on the second day (27 August) may have lacked the charismatic power that Kerensky could usually bring to the rostrum, but it was no less effective for that. With his sober, matter-of-fact delivery, Kornilov presented the delegates with the horrifying truth about the collapse of their once proud army. It is 'with deep sorrow that I have to add and declare openly that I do not have the confidence that the Russian army will staunchly perform its duty to the country'. He had tried to improve discipline with the restoration of the death penalty, but this was not enough in the face of continuous 'destructive propaganda'. The men 'have become like animals', he lamented, looking around the room, before going on to list some of the officers who had been killed by their own troops. 'All these murders were committed by soldiers in a nightmarish atmosphere of irrational, hideous club law, of interminable ignorance and abominable hooliganism.' They had lost Galicia. They had lost Bukhovina. They had lost 'all of the fruits of our victories of the past and present years', and now the road to Petrograd was open. The only way to restore the army was to reaffirm discipline, enhance the prestige of the officer corps and limit the activities of any council or soviet strictly to economic issues. 'I believe in the genius of the Russian people . . .' he added finally. 'But I declare that there is no time to lose.'[38]

Half of the audience, primarily those sitting on the right-hand side, rose to applaud the general, cheering and even throwing flowers in his direction, while those on the left – the soviets and groups of workers with some soldiers – sat stony-faced. Despite Kerensky's earnest appeals for unity and understanding, for all sides to recognize the great difficulties they faced together, the only outcome of the state conference was – in the words of Pavel Miliukov – the realization 'that the country was divided into two camps between which there could be no essential reconciliation or agreement'.[39] And now the army and the bourgeoisie had a new champion. *Novoe Vremia*, chief mouthpiece of the liberal, anti-Bolshevik classes, was clear that Kornilov had been the star of the conference. 'He was the first to put a finger boldly into the wound', its editorial declared. 'Owing to the abolition of military discipline, the heretofore valiant army has degenerated in places into a mob of robbers.' Only Kornilov had set out practical measures by which the army could be restored to health, and he would either be allowed to carry them out or the army would undergo 'its final disintegration, with the unavoidable ruin of Russia and all of her freedoms'.[40]

Kerensky could not ride two horses at the same time. He knew that it was not possible to support all of Kornilov's demands without fatally compromising his own radical credentials and ruining any relationship he still had with the Soviet. But without giving Kornilov what he wanted, he risked the collapse of his government, and in any case, he doubted whether military morale could be restored.[41] From this moment on, he became increasingly fixated on the possibility of a counter-revolution, and one that would be led by his own

Commander-in-Chief. Kornilov's new-found position as the darling of the right, as a man of authority who would rally the country and restore the army, gnawed away at Kerensky, who came to suspect the worst. Under 'the thunder of oratorical speeches in the main hall of the Bolshoy [*sic*] Theatre,' he wrote, 'in the lobbies and behind the scenes, was being born . . . the mad idea of a dictatorship', with Kornilov 'the bearer of the dictatorial robe'.[42] When news arrived a week later that the German Army had captured Riga, thus proving the accuracy of Kornilov's warnings about the danger to Petrograd, the Provisional Government was plunged into a new crisis.

On 7 September, just days after Riga had fallen, Vladimir Lvov, a member of the State Duma, arrived at Mogilev to speak with Kornilov. He had come as a 'delegate' of Kerensky, whom he had met several days earlier, and wanted to discuss the best ways of creating 'a strong authority'. He suggested a number of possibilities: Kerensky becoming dictator; a government of three or four ministers, including Kornilov, invested with 'unlimited powers'; or the general acting as dictator. Kornilov, who believed that Lvov was 'a perfect gentleman' and an honest interlocutor, said that he would, of course, prefer the last, and assumed that Kerensky was open to the possibility. However, because he believed that the government was in grave peril from an imminent Bolshevik uprising, Kerensky should come straight away to *Stavka*, where they could discuss these matters.[43] Lvov then returned to Petrograd, where he presented Kerensky with what he said were Kornilov's proposals to take over 'all civil and military power'. Here was proof that Kornilov was making his move, and that he must be stopped. Kerensky demanded to speak to Kornilov immediately. He was able to contact *Stavka* via the Hughes telegraph machine, and held a brief and awkward conversation in which he posed as Lvov and asked the general to confirm that he did indeed wish him to speak to the Prime Minister about his proposals and the need to come to Mogilev immediately.

Kornilov was happy to approve these requests and confirm that he did want Kerensky to come to *Stavka*. The conversation then ended, leaving the Prime Minister convinced (or at least that was what he would subsequently claim) that a counter-revolution was about to begin. On 9 September, he issued a proclamation warning the people about the attempts 'to establish a regime opposed to the conquests of the revolution' and ordering Kornilov to resign.[44] Kornilov, who had been under the impression that there was complete agreement between Mogilev and Petrograd and that they were merely discussing ways to strengthen the power of the government, reacted with fury. The entire telegraph, he proclaimed in a despatch published in *Novoe Vremia* on 11 September, was 'a lie from beginning to end'. 'It is not I who sent Vl. N. Lvov, member of the Duma, to the Provisional Government, but it was the Prime Minister who sent him to me as his emissary.' This was, he added, 'a great provocation which threatens the fate of the country'. He desired nothing for himself, 'other than the salvation of our Great Russia, and vow to lead the people, through victory over our enemies, to the Constituent Assembly, where it can determine its future destiny and the forms of its future political life'. Kornilov thus refused to resign and, convinced that Kerensky was now in thrall to the Bolsheviks, vowed to march on Petrograd.[45]

The bewildering series of accusations and counter-accusations between Kerensky, Lvov and Kornilov were devastating for the stability of the Provisional Government. At no point had either Kerensky or Kornilov sought to question the motives or credibility of Vladimir Lvov, the man who had provoked the affair. He had been Procurator of the Holy Synod in the first coalition government, a nobleman of little significance who drifted in various right-wing circles, becoming convinced that he needed to save Russia from its looming collapse. What exactly he thought he was doing acting as an intermediary between the two men remains unclear. He would later write a florid memoir of his mission to caution Kerensky about Kornilov, who had 'an evil glint' in his eyes and who wanted to become dictator. 'I was bringing a warning to Kerensky that his life was in danger', he wrote. 'Kerensky did not believe in bloodshed. If during the revolution the blood of the Ministers in the Tauride Palace was spared – this was only thanks to Kerensky; if no tsarist blood was shed in Tsarskoe Selo, it was only thanks to Kerensky. It was my duty to repay him with the same, i.e., to save his life . . .'[46]

Perhaps none of this mattered to Kerensky anyway. Lvov's strange and sudden appearance on the scene was a heaven-sent opportunity to outflank Kornilov and pose as the true defender of the revolution. With this in mind, Kerensky made no effort to reach a compromise or even call for further investigations into whether it was all a misunderstanding. Everything became visible, he later admitted; 'all instantly shone clear in a very brilliant light and merged into one clear picture. The double game was manifest.'[47] He called an urgent meeting of the Cabinet on 10 September and demanded emergency powers to defend the revolution. He also enlisted the support of both the Soviet and the Bolsheviks to defeat Kornilov's 'revolt'. The following day, the Central Executive Committee of the Soviet issued an appeal to 'Comrade Soldiers and Comrade Officers', alerting them to 'stand up, as one man, in defence of land and freedom'. Working alongside the Bolsheviks to form a 'Committee for the People's Struggle Against Counterrevolution', they undertook to organize groups of workers and send them to defend key locations within Petrograd. Kerensky also took the decisive step of handing out up to 40,000 firearms, many of which ended up in Bolshevik hands, while signing off on the release of most of those who had been detained for their role in the July coup, including Trotsky.[48]

Kornilov now had little choice but to act. He ordered Lieutenant-General A. M. Krymov to lead III Cavalry Corps into Petrograd and occupy the city, releasing the Provisional Government from its (presumably) Bolshevik captors. This unit, which had been sent to Velikiye Luki, almost equidistant between Petrograd and Moscow, to act as a strategic reserve should the capital need reinforcing, was now at the centre of a grave crisis of trust between Kerensky and Kornilov. By 10 September, Krymov had concentrated his forces at Luga, about eighty miles south of the capital, but then things began to go wrong. As General Ivanov had found back in March, when he was ordered by the Tsar to quell the disturbances in Petrograd, problems on the railways, disinformation and poor morale all combined to frustrate any move north. Telegraph officers and railway signallers were quick to alert the Soviet, which acted with great haste, sending messengers to contact Krymov's troops. There had been no rising in Petrograd, they said; the city was not under the control of the Bolsheviks, and there was no need for them to come. At the same time, the local soviet had also scraped together a makeshift garrison, mined the bridges over the Luga river, north of the city, and vowed to prevent any troops from crossing.[49]

With his divisions stuck on the other side of the river, Krymov needed to force his way through, but he was not sure this could be done. Battalions that had formerly been known for their loyalty and discipline were suddenly uneasy, beginning to question the motives of their officers and worried that they were being used to overturn the revolution. Committees were formed and discussions opened with the Soviet, which arrested Krymov on 12 September. He was taken to see Kerensky, who accused him of betrayal and deception. The general, grim-faced, said that he wanted to hang every politician in the capital. Kerensky, who was becoming worked up, told him to write down what he had just said, but Krymov refused. When Kerensky threatened to rip his epaulettes off him, the general retorted: 'They were not awarded to me by you, boy, and it's not for you to tear them off my shoulders!' Krymov was allowed to go to an apartment owned by his former orderly and was given a pen and some paper. He drafted a short note for his wife ('I decided to die because I love my homeland too much'), then took out his personal revolver and shot himself. His single bullet to the chest was the first shot of the Russian Civil War.[50]

Kerensky had won. Flushed with a sense of victory, he appointed himself Commander-in-Chief and managed to persuade General Alekseev to become his Chief of Staff, tasked with travelling to Mogilev to arrest Kornilov and his fellow 'plotters'. Alekseev had no love for Kerensky, but his sense of duty and loyalty to the Motherland meant that he agreed to go, as long as there would be no threat to the accused. As news spread of Kornilov's dismissal, officers rallied to his side. At Mogilev, his Chief of Staff, General Lukomsky, refused to take over interim command, despatching a telegram to Petrograd warning that this would 'bring upon Russia as yet unheard-of horrors'. At Southwest Front, General Denikin also announced that he could not follow the Provisional Government in its decision to dismiss Kornilov, which was 'a return to the planned destruction of the

Army, having as its consequence the downfall of our country'.[51] Yet Kornilov himself had little appetite to precipitate violence with the civil power, at least not yet, so he agreed to go quietly, convinced of his innocence. He and many of his loyal followers, including Denikin, were taken to a prison in Bykhov, twenty-five miles south of Mogilev, where they languished in small cells, seven feet by seven, at the mercy of Kerensky's revolutionary government.

Kerensky's victory was pyrrhic, won at great cost for only questionable benefit. In the aftermath of what would be known as the 'Kornilov Affair', he became a more isolated figure than ever before. He was now a man with few friends. He had alienated most of the officer corps, and those on the right who had put their faith in Kornilov, while winning little credit from either the Soviet, which still distrusted him, or the Bolsheviks, who were growing in confidence, strength and power. He tried to appear master of the situation and the dynamic man of action at all times, but in quieter moments the mask slipped. His private secretary, Pitirim Sorokin, remembered watching him one day 'sitting alone in the corner of the Military Staff Headquarters, bowed with chagrin and disappointment. He looked like nothing but a deserted child, helpless and homeless. Yesterday a ruler, today a forsaken idol, he sat face to face with ruin and despair.' He had taken up residence in Alexander III's suite in the Winter Palace and would sometimes walk the corridors at night, often the only person in the building, his skin 'white, like paper'; a fading ghost surrounded by the trappings of a fallen empire. The Provisional Government had entered its last days.[52]

19. 'The troops do not fight'

Plans for Operation *Waffentreue* were put together with breathless speed. A new command, Fourteenth Army, was created, with General Otto von Below moved from his position in Macedonia to take charge, and six German divisions were brought in, including the Alpine Corps. On 18 September, just days after the decision to mount a combined Austro-German offensive had been made, Fourteenth Army was ordered to break the front west of Tolmein and 'then take the line of the heights north of Cividale'. With this in mind, General Below wanted the main focus to be on his right wing to push on to where the Tagliamento emerged from the mountains, outflanking the Isonzo line from the north. 'From the outset the army must constantly focus its efforts on the right wing . . .'[1]

Achieving such an ambitious attack so late in the year would not be easy. Both General Below and Emperor Karl made well-publicized trips to the Tyrol, hoping to draw attention away from the Isonzo, while orchestrating an enormous rail effort to bring up the men, guns and supplies that would be needed. In the month prior to the attack, 2,400 trains carried 100,000 wagons, about a third of the rolling stock devoted to wartime use within the Dual Monarchy.[2] Heavy batteries were withdrawn from Romania and Galicia, and then transported on Austria's creaking railway network towards the border. Once they had reached the railheads, they then had to undergo a daunting journey of at least thirty kilometres up to the front around hairpin bends and through high mountain passes where it was already snowing heavily. By the eve of the attack, Fourteenth Army could boast 1,720 guns and plentiful ammunition, with Habsburg forces supplied with a million shells, a tenth of which contained gas for the counter-battery effort. As one of the Austrian corps commanders, Alfred Krauss, noted proudly, 'The artillery, so laboriously assembled and dragged into the rocks, paved the way to victory in an exemplary manner when our heroic infantry attacked.'[3]

Assault divisions were moved up at night, spending the day under cover to avoid detection before continuing their long marches after dark. The skies were laden with thick clouds and frequent flurries of sleet and snow, while the presence of German fighter squadrons was enough to ward off any Italian aircraft that ventured too close. The Central Powers would not possess much numerical superiority – estimates of opposing forces were roughly equal – but on the crucial sector around Tolmein they had a 3:1 advantage, which was bolstered by the weight of artillery and mortar fire that would be employed.[4] Should the shelling not work, the attacking troops could rely upon mountain guns and light machine-guns, such as the Model 08/15 Maxim, a modified and lightened version of the famous heavy machine-gun, first introduced in 1916. This gave them a significant edge in fire support, which was extremely useful when operating in small teams across difficult terrain.[5]

The Italians suspected that an attack was coming, but used to long-drawn-out offensives with modest gains, they anticipated it in a leisurely, unhurried state of mind. Assuming that any offensive would be focused on recovering all or part of the Bainsizza Plateau, they could not see that their northern flank remained extremely vulnerable. As early as 19 September, Cadorna had written to General Capello, upon whose sector the main attack would fall, and noted that should he face an enemy onslaught on the Bainsizza, he was to adopt *difesa ad oltranza* ('defence to the bitter end'), albeit holding his front line with small numbers of troops, with the bulk of his strength being deployed in the second and third lines. Long known as one of Italy's finest fighting generals, Capello brushed off Cadorna's uncharacteristic caution and insisted that he would mount a swift counter-offensive if the enemy made any movement. Moreover, he continued, even though Italian defensive positions had to be improved, they must be constructed with the idea of the offensive. 'In addition to the defensive works, we must strive to organise the advanced line of the infantry as a starting line for offensive action, therefore, we must build offensive caverns capable of keeping the attacking troops under cover.'[6]

Second Army's defensive arrangements were further hampered by the condition of General Capello, who had been hospitalized in early October with an acute form of nephritis. Because he was confined to his bed for most of the month, he was not able to oversee with any sense of purpose the work that needed to be done. Of Second Army's 353 infantry battalions, 231 were still in the front line, poised for the next offensive, which meant that their defences had little depth. Capello was also slow to redeploy his artillery to the rear in line with direct instructions from *Comando Supremo*, and by the eve of the offensive, only 120 medium and heavy pieces had been moved back across the Isonzo, out of a total of 730, leaving many of Capello's best guns 'prey' to a sudden Austro-German advance.[7] It was only on 19 October, just days before the Central Powers would strike, that Cadorna realized what was going on. Suddenly sensing the danger that Second Army was in, he flew into a furious rage and, in what was described as a 'direct' conversation, told Capello in no uncertain terms that his arrangements must conform with his instructions. The following day, in a slightly calmer mood, Cadorna confirmed that the 'very serious' shortages of reserves meant that any idea for a counter-attack 'in a grand style' must now be given up. This was a necessary restatement of the need for caution in the face of the enemy, but it was already too late.[8]

By the night of 23–24 October, the assaulting divisions were ready. It had been a bleak night, dark and foggy, with a fine rain beginning to fall around midnight. At 2 a.m., the preliminary bombardment opened and a sea of fire began to explode on the Italian positions between Plezzo and Tolmein, with heavy doses of gas fired against gun batteries and concentrations of troops in the low ground. The artillery preparation lasted for seven hours, with large clouds of smoke gathering in the valleys, obscuring much of what was happening and giving the first day of battle a strange, almost dreamlike quality. Although the Italian response was initially strong, with searchlights probing the darkness and guns firing back on pre-arranged locations, within an hour the artillery began to fall silent, their crews rendered incapable by the terrible clouds of phosgene (a toxic colourless gas which causes respiratory failure) that surrounded each battery. And then, at 8 a.m., the infantry went forward in small teams through the dank fog, their haversacks full of grenades as they swept along the valley floors. This kind of approach, which bypassed the main defensive positions, spreading chaos and confusion, was exactly what some Austro-Hungarian officers had called for during the *Strafexpedition*, and now they had the chance to see if it might work. 'Your attack contradicts all basic tactical rules', was the verdict of one Italian officer as he was bundled along after being taken prisoner. 'Such a thing simply cannot be accepted!'[9]

The twenty-fourth of October 1917 was the day the Italian Army broke, shattering into a thousand pieces as the combined weight of years of savage combat suddenly became too heavy to bear. Morale sagged when word spread that the Germans were in the line, and men just gave up, either fleeing in all directions or staying put, waiting to surrender. The commander of 155 Brigade, dug in around Mount Krn on the east bank of the Isonzo, later admitted that they had little idea of what was happening until it was too late:

> The thick fog cleared somewhat around 8 o'clock; at this time, a column of several hundred men who looked like ours was spotted on the Volzana road, on the right of the Isonzo, about a kilometre from the Yolarje footbridge, who marched in four ranks, orderly, without safety measures. No artillery shells were directed at them [and there was] no evidence of combat in the valley floor. Among all of us in the regimental command it was thought that we could not deal with enemies at that time and in that place, and we tried to distinguish whether the column were ours who retreated or enemy prisoners.[10]

This was a common experience, as the enemy moved too quickly for the defenders to respond. With communication all but extinguished, the Italians were left on their own, unsupported and wondering what was happening up and down the front. This led to the strange phenomenon of entire units, with all their officers, surrendering together once they realized they were surrounded. At least six generals and fifty colonels were taken prisoner in this way.[11]

Very quickly Second Army's left flank began to cave in. By the evening of the first day, the attackers had crossed the Isonzo, reached the small town of Caporetto (from where the battle would take its name) and were closing in on the Kolovrat Ridge, which Cadorna had identified as a crucial defensive bastion. Some German units marched twenty-three kilometres that day, showing what one senior officer called an 'unparalleled spirit of aggression', the kind that General Cadorna could only wonder at.[12] On the contrary, too many Italian units showed that fatal mixture of indecision and paralysis that left them dangerously vulnerable to being outflanked and overwhelmed as soon as they ran out of ammunition. Major-General Giovanni Villani, commander of 19th Division around Tolmein, signed off his final report at eight o'clock that evening: 'After putting up all possible resistance, the troops of 19th Division were overwhelmed at around 5 p.m. along the whole extent of the front. The remains of the Spezia Brigade, with its commander, was reduced to very few forces in Lombaj. The remains of the Taro Brigade are in Clabuzzaro . . . Overall, it is a matter of a few hundred men. The artillery, for the most part dismantled and having lost almost all of its personnel, is entirely destroyed.' Distraught at what had happened to his division, Villani killed himself the following day.[13]

There would be no respite for the Italian Army as the battle continued. Orders were issued to renew the attack and to complete the victory that had been won on the first day. Once again Fourteenth Army moved forward, this time in bright sunshine as the leading columns raced on towards Cividale. That day, elements of the Alpine Corps, steel-helmeted veterans led by the future field marshal, Erwin Rommel, seized the crest of Mount Matajur, three miles southwest of Caporetto, and made any serious Italian stand almost impossible. With the roads behind the line already choked with men, guns and horses, Italian reserves could not get to where they were needed, which left their officers struggling forward, consumed by a growing feeling of hopelessness. It was only at this moment that Cadorna began to realize the seriousness of the situation. Although he still hoped that the offensive would bog down, enough alarming information had arrived at *Comando Supremo* to indicate that unless action was taken immediately, there might be a catastrophe from which Italy would not recover. 'Events hurry on, the troops do not fight.

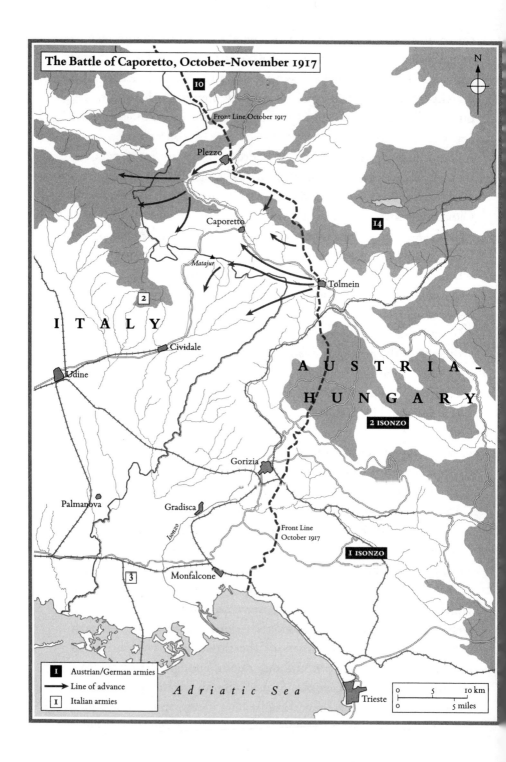

The Battle of Caporetto, October–November 1917

Front Line October 1917

Plezzo

Caporetto

Matajur

Tolmein

2

I T A L Y

Cividale

Udine

A U S T R I A –
H U N G A R Y

2 ISONZO

Gorizia

Palmanova

Gradisca

Isonzo

Front Line
October 1917

I ISONZO

3

Monfalcone

N

10

14

Austrian/German armies

Line of advance

Italian armies

A d r i a t i c   S e a

Trieste

0   5   10 km
0   5 miles

This being the case, an imminent disaster is evident', he wrote to his son on the afternoon of 25 October.[14]

That evening, after a visit from General Capello, who was still suffering from his illness and evidently in pain, Cadorna pondered whether to order a retreat to save what was left of the army, if necessary as far back as the Tagliamento. Capello was insistent that a decision needed to be made as soon as possible, given the difficulties of arranging such a vast movement of men and supplies, a point that Cadorna accepted, albeit not without some personal agony. The decision to let go of what had been gained, at such cost, over two years of hard campaigning was a bitter pill to swallow. Angelo Gatti, a historian attached to *Comando Supremo* who knew Cadorna well, remembered watching the general pace up and down his office, becoming angrier as he railed against all those who had betrayed him. This was worse, much worse, than the *Strafexpedition*:

> At first glance, this disaster may seem like that of Trentino. But it is not. This is much more serious. No Napoleon could do anything under these conditions. Does it not seem so? You tell me. My personal influence cannot extend to 2,000,000 men. Even Napoleon, in the Russian campaign, could not make it felt. Troops surrendered, commanded by General Badoglio, among the most daringly commanded . . . Now the sign of the disaster in Trentino was, that an unstoppable panic, in the first days, had seized the troops: shortage of men on the front line, bad command, etc., had produced this. But it was a panic; and after only one year of war, it could be repaired, because the body was good. But the sign of this disaster is fatigue. The army, polluted by propaganda from within, against which I have always fought in vain, is broken in its soul. Anything but fighting. This is the terrible thing about this situation.[15]

Cadorna's rage was understandable, if misplaced. Caporetto was more than just a moral collapse, important though that was; it was a complete breakdown in defensive organization and tactics, a second Adowa, only this time much closer to home and with ramifications that were immediate and devastating. A whole range of causes were identified during the subsequent inquiry, including the 'power of the enemy' and a sense of inferiority towards it; the mishandling of reserves; poor commanders; draconian punishments and an 'inconsistent disciplinary regime'; all heightened by the 'widespread conviction . . . of the sterility of the blood sacrifices made and the uselessness of the further sacrifices that might be required'.[16] Much but not all of this was Cadorna's fault.

Italy was now undergoing the greatest crisis in her modern history. With the remnants of Second Army streaming away from the front, its regiments haemorrhaging men and guns with every mile it covered, the Duke of Aosta's Third Army was also forced to withdraw from the Carso, managing to do so in good order despite a mood of panic that threatened to sweep everything away. 'On the night of 26–27 October, we no longer understood anything about our situation', remembered one soldier; 'entire regiments retreating; brigades that went to shore up the lines; ammunition depots exploding with a hellish roar; batteries pulling their pieces towards more solid positions, to protect the retreat of the infantry. The sky of Gorizia had been brightly lit until dawn by the fire of the enemy guns, which spewed out shells of all calibres on the lines and rear positions, while our artillery had begun to be silent . . .'[17]

The swiftness of the disaster was hard to comprehend for those who had experienced fighting on the Isonzo or the Carso, where advances and retreats could often be counted in metres or feet. Within days, German and Austrian columns had penetrated deep into northern Italy and were showing no signs of stopping, General Below ordering that the pursuit be continued 'until the Italian Army is destroyed'.[18] Udine fell on 29 October, with the *Comando Supremo* moving to Treviso without bothering to leave an advanced headquarters near the front, and within another five days the Central Powers had reached the Tagliamento – over thirty-five miles from their starting positions. Yet even this did not mark the limit of the advance, and Cadorna had no choice but to let his armies carry on retreating, all the time shedding men and guns. In total, some 280,000 Italian soldiers were captured, alongside enormous amounts of war supplies, munitions and weaponry, including 3,150 pieces of artillery, 1,700 heavy mortars and 3,000 machine-guns. In one great sweeping disaster, the Italian Army had lost two thirds of its heavy guns, half of its medium calibres and two fifths of its light guns. By the second week of November, what was left of a once proud army was on the far side of the Piave river, frantically digging in.[19]

The scale of the victory had been astounding – proof, it seemed, that Italian morale was as fragile as had been hoped. But the wider context was still troubling, demanding clear decisions about where German and Austrian effort should be concentrated, and already Ludendorff was looking elsewhere. As early as 29 October, he had asked Arz about the future of the offensive, with the Austrian Chief of Staff recommending that the Piave should be the 'preliminary aim of the joint operation'. Several days later, Arz added that no forces should be withdrawn from Italy because the aim was to make the attack as successful as possible. But this was never likely to be acceptable to the German command team, who had their sights firmly on the Western Front. On 3 November, a meeting was held in Berlin between the combined staffs, where it was agreed that the operation should be continued until the Piave was reached, but then German troops would have to pull out. OHL was seeking a decision in the west in the spring of 1918 and would need every division that could be spared.[20]

There had always been tension between German and Austrian leadership, and this showed no signs of easing in the weeks after Caporetto. Karl made no attempt to hide his distrust of his allies as he sought to distance the Dual Monarchy from its erstwhile protectors. He directed Arz to draft an order congratulating their men on the results of the battle which pointedly made no mention of the Germans, only for it to be subtly rewritten to avoid alienating their partners. There was also an unfortunate squabble over decorations, which helped to sow further mistrust between the two armies. Karl awarded the Military Order of Maria Theresa – the highest decoration in the K.u.K. – only three times, none of them to a German officer. This caused so much disquiet at OHL that henceforth it 'refrained from decorating Austrian officers with high awards'. It was a sad and unnecessary ending to what had been one of the most successful combined operations of the war, bringing chaos, confusion and demoralization to their opponents.[21]

On 7 November, just thirteen days after the Austro-German attack had begun, General Luigi Cadorna was notified of his dismissal. His superiors, long suspicious of their fractious soldier, found their patience exhausted and, under French and British pressure, the King took the only possible decision: to dispense with his services. He was appointed Italian representative at the Supreme War Council, a new consultative body that had been set up by the Allied powers as part of a desperate attempt to provide support to Italy, but he would not hide his disgust, and during the subsequent inquiry into the disaster, he was insistent that blame should not lie at his door:

> I will never accept it. Those who have had an office like mine cannot limit themselves to being a consultant . . . of people whom I highly despise and to whom I have always shouted my contempt in their face . . . I don't care if others bring me down: I know what I'm worth. I, with my will, with my fist, have created and held in my hand this organism of an army, of three million men, until yesterday. If I hadn't been there, we would never have had a voice in Europe. They come forward and deny me this merit . . . the strength of Italy strikes at me . . . But I believe that they are internal enemies. And not just the socialists.[22]

Cadorna's replacement was a corps commander in Third Army named Armando Diaz, who had gained a reputation as a capable and reliable soldier, and someone moreover who was untainted by the disaster at Caporetto. He had served as Director of Operations at *Comando Supremo* and won praise for his handling of firstly a division, and then a corps, on the Carso. His appointment had been championed by Italy's new Prime Minister, Vittorio Orlando, who had been asked to form a government by the King on 28 October as news of Caporetto began to spread. The most senior army commander, the Duke of Aosta, was considered for the role, only to be turned down because of his royal connections, with Orlando preferring the more malleable and personable Diaz.[23] At 55 years old, Diaz was young for the position and without the stern, demanding countenance of a Cadorna, but Orlando was determined to break the power of the *Comando Supremo* and restore civilian primacy to the war effort, and he thought

Diaz would be the ideal man to help him. Often seen leaning back slightly, his hands thrust into the pockets of his jacket, the general possessed a relaxed charisma, which always put subordinates at ease. But this informality did not mean that he lacked seriousness. Upon first receiving news of his promotion, his face took on a grey pallor as he contemplated the enormous task of rebuilding the army. 'The weapon which I am summoned to grasp has been blunted', he said. 'It must be re-tempered without delay. This will be done.'[24]

On 7 November, the day that Cadorna was replaced, Vladimir Lenin's Bolsheviks stormed the Winter Palace in Petrograd and deposed the Provisional Government. This marked the final, climactic moment in months of skirmishing between Kerensky and Lenin, and paved the way for Russia's exit from the war. Ever since the Kornilov 'rebellion' had fizzled out in September, an atmosphere of drift and lethargy had taken hold of the government and its increasingly fragile army. Kerensky had tried to strike a positive note of authority, ordering that all officers suspected of involvement with Kornilov be replaced by those 'who are devoted to the Republic', but morale continued to slump. A report on the condition of VI Siberian Corps, part of the Northern Front, which had been badly affected by Bolshevik subversion, noted that 'morale has worsened in almost all the divisions of the Corps' in recent weeks, with men refusing to attack and asking why they should fight when they had abandoned Riga 'without bloodshed'. Officers were regularly beaten, dragged through the streets and lynched, while others fled or tore off their epaulettes and joined the ranks. The report concluded that only 'a definite consolidation of the Government's authority can put an end to this phenomenon'.[25]

The Bolsheviks had only profited from this chaos. During a series of municipal elections in September, they had increased their share of the vote even as the number of voters fell away. In Petrograd, they had secured a third of the ballots, a significant increase on the 20 per cent they had won in May. Likewise, in Moscow, they had won almost half of the electorate, with support for the less radical socialist parties entering into a steep decline.[26] Electoral success was certainly encouraging, but Lenin had little interest in a route to power through democratic means. Even though he was still in hiding, he was quick to see the advantages in the current political situation. 'Kornilov's revolt is an extremely unexpected . . . and a downright unbelievably sharp turn in the course of events', he wrote in a letter to the Bolshevik Central Committee in late August.[27] Over the following fortnight he wrestled with what strategy to adopt, when and how to begin an uprising, and became convinced that he must act soon or lose the chance of power for ever. 'We must at once begin to plan the practical details of a second revolution', he wrote on 12 September. While many of his fellow Bolsheviks wanted to wait until the great conference of soviets due to be held on 7 November, or even work with the government to arrange elections to the Constituent Assembly, Lenin grew impatient. 'It would be naïve to wait for a formal majority for the Bolsheviks . . . History will never forgive us if we do not take power now.'[28]

Lenin won out in the end. He was smuggled back into Petrograd on 20 October and held a series of meetings with his chief conspirators at the apartment of Nikolai Sukhanov, persuading them that they could not tolerate any further delays. A vote was taken, and it was agreed to seize power on the day of the soviet conference. In the early hours of 7 November, as citizens slept, groups of armed Bolshevik volunteers, known as the Red Guards, secured key sites in the capital, most of which fell without bloodshed, showing only a supine indifference to the latest disorder to sweep the city. No resistance was encountered, noted Sukhanov, writing with a sense of amazement. 'Beginning at 2 in the morning the stations, bridges, lighting installations, telegraphs, and telegraphic agency were gradually occupied by small forces brought from the barracks. The little groups of cadets could not resist and didn't think of it. In general the military operations in the politically important centres of the city rather resembled a changing of the guard . . . Both the centre and the suburbs were sunk in a deep sleep, not suspecting what was going on in the quiet of the cold autumn night.'[29]

Kerensky had been confident of his ability to suppress any new rising, which he expected to be a repeat of July, but much had changed since the summer. With telephone lines down and wild rumours spreading around the streets, the authorities urgently needed to call upon reliable troops. But no plans had been made to organize pro-government forces, leaving the Winter Palace – about the only important building still in government hands – garrisoned by a make-shift force of officer cadets and 140 volunteers from a women's Battalion of Death. Kerensky decided to rally support at Northern Front head-quarters in Pskov. At eleven o'clock that morning, he left the General Staff building and was driven south out of Petrograd, but when he reached his destination, he found a distressing mood of lassitude and resignation. The only troops immediately available belonged to III Cavalry Corps, which had been commanded by the unfortunate Lieutenant-General Krymov, and the officers had little interest in risk-ing their lives for someone they roundly despised. Some Cossack detachments eventually saddled up and rode off towards Tsarskoe Selo, but they would go no further, worried that they were being directed against the revolution and unwilling to push on through a Bolshevik picket line that had been hurriedly sent from the capital. The few men who would have had the nerve and courage to retake Petrograd – men like Kornilov – were nowhere to be found.[30]

The green and white Winter Palace, official residence of the tsars and symbol of Imperial Russia's greatness, fell shortly after 2 a.m. on 8 November as the garrison, demoralized and hungry, dwindled away until there was almost no one left. When the Bolsheviks finally entered the building, looting and firing as they went, they arrested the remain-ing members of the Provisional Government and bundled them outside to jeering crowds. There would be no deliverance from the south. The third and final attempt to march into the capital had fal-tered in the same way that the previous ones had, leaving Kerensky powerless. 'A face with traces of heavy, sleepless nights' was how Gen-eral Krasnov, commander of III Cavalry Corps, described the Prime Minister. 'Pale, unhealthy, with an ill-looking skin and swollen red eyes. Clean-shaven like an actor. His head too large for his trunk. Military jacket, breeches, boots with gaiters – all this made him look like a civilian who had got himself up for a Sunday ride.' Fearing that he would soon be betrayed by the Cossacks, who were discussing whether to exchange him for Lenin, Kerensky slipped away and went into hiding, leaving Petrograd at the mercy of the newly installed Bolshevik regime.[31]

Lenin moved quickly to cement his power and declare to the world that a new age had arrived. He gave a speech to the Petrograd Soviet on the evening of 8 November and announced that this was 'the beginning of a new period in the history of Russia'. His first task would be ending the war as soon as possible.[32] A decree was issued that called for 'an immediate peace without annexation . . . and without indemnity'. The new government 'proposes that this kind of peace be concluded immediately between all the warring nations'. Moreover, any attempt to prolong the war 'because the rich and strong nations cannot agree how to divide the small and weak nationalities which they had seized is, in the opinion of the Government, a most criminal act against humanity, and it solemnly announces its decision to sign at once terms of peace bringing this war to an end on the indicated conditions, which are equally just to all nationalities without exception'. This was combined with another decree that called for the abolition of private property and the transfer of all lands to the state.[33]

As Petrograd fell to the red wave, the atmosphere at *Stavka* was one of paralysing uncertainty. General Alekseev had resigned as Chief of Staff soon after Kornilov's arrest, leaving the position vacant until Kerensky could fill it with General Nikolai Dukhonin, who had been serving as Chief of Staff at Western Front. A 40-year-old who had commanded a regiment in 1914, Dukhonin had come to the notice of Alekseev and was well thought of by Kerensky, who had been impressed by his willingness to work on restructuring the army. On 21 November, he received a telegram from Lenin instructing him to 'contact the enemy military authorities with an offer of the immediate cessation of hostilities for the purpose of opening up peace negotiations'. Dukhonin did not know what to do – whether to recognize the new masters in Petrograd and betray all Russia had fought for, or find some other way out. He claimed that he could not act on the instructions because he did not know what the Allied response would be, nor was he sure whether the peace offer included Romania, or whether it referred just to Germany or all of the Central Powers. His objections were swiftly rejected, and Lenin ordered him 'immediately and without further obstruction to undertake formal negotiations for an armistice between all the belligerent powers'. Still Dukhonin would not move; only the 'authoritative central government of all Russia' was entitled to take such a decision.[34]

Lenin had no patience for such distractions. The following day, he issued a proclamation, published in the Bolshevik newspaper *Izvestiya*, which announced Dukhonin's dismissal for 'disobeying the orders of the government and for acting in the manner that was bound to lead to great calamities for the toiling masses of all countries'. He also authorized front-line units to elect representatives and 'open formal truce negotiations with the enemy'.[35] Ensign Nikolai Krylenko, an experienced revolutionary and people's commissar, was sent to Mogilev to relieve Dukhonin of command. Dukhonin sent troops to block the railway line north of the city, which held Krylenko up for a week, but like the cadets in the Winter Palace, there was little willingness to fight on, and the men either drifted away or agreed to join the Bolsheviks. Dukhonin knew that he would soon be arrested, but in his remaining few hours of liberty he took what steps he could to assist his friends and allies, who were now girding themselves for a civil war. He released Kornilov from Bykhov, and had much of the technical and signalling equipment at *Stavka* loaded up and sent to the south, while letting his officers and men slip away if they wanted to.[36]

Krylenko arrived in Mogilev on 3 December. Dukhonin was seized and taken to the railway station, followed by an angry, spitting crowd of Bolshevik militia. George Hall, a British spy and member of the Allied Military Mission, happened to be passing through *Stavka* and saw what happened next. As Dukhonin was being taken away, he either slipped or was pushed over on the platform, and was suddenly surrounded by the surging, angry mob. 'It was like watching a pack of wild wolves', Hall remembered. 'There was a scuffle. It ended. There was a pause. A circle was being formed in the middle of the crowd and then, as a man is tossed in a blanket, Dukhonin was thrown into the air. Round the circle came a crackle of musketry, and as his body fell it was caught on the waiting bayonets . . . The sadistic lust of the mob was satisfied and it started to disperse. A few curious persons pressed forward to look at the poor mangled body as it lay oozing in its pool of blood.'[37] *Stavka*, the brain and nerve centre of the Russian war effort, had ceased to exist.

The devastating events on what had been the Eastern and Italian Fronts produced a quick and far-reaching response from the Allies. On 5–6 November, as the remnants of General Cadorna's army were streaming back across the few bridges still standing over the Piave, a series of urgent meetings were held between the British and French at the city of Rapallo. Four British and six French divisions were already on their way to Italy, and they would filter into the line before the end of the month, but in the meantime, it was essential to formulate a common strategy and ensure that Rome did not sue for peace. General Foch, who had already worked out schedules for the arrival of reinforcements, gave a blunt assessment of what had happened. '[O]n the 24th, 25th, and part of the 26th October, the Italian army had been attacked but not very heavily. The result had been that the line has been broken and the troops on either side of the breach had had to give way. There had followed a disaster, which had resulted in the virtual destruction of the Second Army, which was the most important of the four armies . . .'[38]

When Italy's new Prime Minister, Vittorio Orlando, and the Foreign Minister, Sonnino, joined the British and French delegations the following day, 6 November, the mood was sombre, yet purposeful. Lloyd George began by insisting that they would do all that was necessary to help Italy. 'This was no time for bargaining with Italy as to the question of one division or one battery . . . It was a situation in which to save the Alliance from a far greater disaster than had yet befallen it, and this was the spirit in which we approached the problem.' The French Prime Minister, Monsieur Painlevé, added only a few well-chosen words to what Lloyd George had said. 'In the name of the French Government he declared that it is in brotherly feeling and in a complete fusion of arms that we were coming to the assistance of our Ally in its peril.' Orlando nodded, with tears in his eyes, saying that he could find 'no words' to express himself. 'Italy had made so great a military effort,' he replied after composing himself, 'perhaps she had erred in relation to her sentiments. If her means corresponded to her sentiments, we should by this time have victory.'[39]

The following day, the Allies agreed to form a Supreme War Council. It would be comprised of the Prime Minister of each of the major Allied powers, joined by a member of their government, and charged with watching over the conduct of the war, preparing recommendations and scrutinizing plans. The offices of three Permanent Military Representatives, one each from Britain, France and Italy (America would join later), were opened at Versailles, tasked with preparing 'Joint Notes' on strategy that would be presented to the council. It was not a fully unified command on the lines of the arrangements within the Central Powers, and it had no executive power, but it was a start. For Lloyd George, the 'fundamental defect in Allied war organisation' had been the failure to see 'the whole front as one and indivisible'. They had no choice but to try and replicate the kind of coordination that their enemies had pioneered. 'Unity – not sham unity, but real unity – is the only sure pathway to victory', he told an audience in Paris shortly after returning from Rapallo. 'All personal, all sectional, considerations should be relentlessly suppressed. This is one of the greatest hours in the history of mankind. Let us not dishonour greatness with pettiness . . .'[40]

A fierce wind was now blowing through the Entente, clearing out the dead wood and forcing the pace of change. This attitude was epitomized by the new French Prime Minister, Georges Clemenceau, who had been appointed on 16 November, just after the Rapallo conference. He promised to end waste and muddle, and to redouble French efforts at a time of growing war-weariness. At the second session of the Supreme War Council on 1 December, Clemenceau had insisted that the first task of the council was 'to consider the nature of the military campaigns to be undertaken in 1918'. There were three new factors that must be addressed by the Permanent Military Representatives: Russian impotence, the situation on the Italian Front, and the 'gradual maturing' of American strength on the Western Front. The war had 'become largely one of exhaustion', he noted. 'It may be that victory will be achieved by endurance rather than by military decision. Russia has already collapsed, at any rate, for the present, but it must be remembered that Turkey and Austria are neither of them very far from collapse.' They must find out how to overthrow 'Prussian militarism' – and he urged the military advisers to work as one and see these questions 'not from a national standpoint, but from that of the Allies as a whole'.[41]

Inevitably, there were objections. Sir William Robertson, the increasingly disgruntled Chief of the Imperial General Staff, had long been wary of schemes for unified command, and was similarly unimpressed by the prospect of sending military aid to Italy. 'The Italian debacle was unpardonable and was brought about purely by the refusal of the troops to fight', he wrote to General Milne in Salonika on 23 November. 'I fear that Italy will be a burden to us to some extent for the remainder of the war. I cannot quite see that we shall be able to leave her alone ever again. I need hardly say that this is a most unwelcomed addition to our task.'[42] He was similarly unenthusiastic when briefing General Sir Herbert Plumer, the newly appointed commander of British forces in Italy. 'You know my views on the general policy, namely to fight the Germans on the West front, nearest to our own base, and where Germans can be killed.' Any offensive in Italy would be 'unsound', and he trusted that Plumer would not send any communication 'tending to imply that you think that the war can easily and properly be won by sending more troops from the West front to Italy'.[43]

It was commonly assumed, at least in Paris and London, that the Italian Army was a lost cause. There were fears that it would need to be propped up for as long as the war lasted, becoming yet another drain on precious resources. Although it now occupied a much shorter line than it had along the Isonzo (just 400 kilometres, a reduction of more than 200 kilometres), the loss of much of its medium and heavy artillery meant that it was highly vulnerable to renewed attacks. General Diaz could call upon just twenty-nine divisions of varying quality to hold the line, which now ran from Stelvio on the border with Switzerland, south to Lake Garda, then eastwards to Asiago and Mount Grappa, before finally down the Piave to the sea. Diaz set up his headquarters in Padua and got to work on restoring the army's fortunes. He took to his duties with little fanfare, only a serious and methodical work ethic that was soon noticed. Observers were quick to spot the 'calm and unruffled' atmosphere at the new *Comando Supremo*, which was a marked departure from the feelings of fear and suspicion that had haunted its old home at Udine.[44]

The arrival of almost a quarter of a million French and British troops was received with mixed feelings across Italy. It was certainly appreciated as a kind and noble gesture of solidarity for a country that had never truly felt part of the alliance, even if their presence was a daily reminder of the shame of Caporetto. The Allied contingents were deployed in two of the most sensitive sectors of the front: the French at Mount Tomba, and the British on their right at Montello, along the upper Piave, about eleven miles north of the city of Treviso. This marked the key central zone and 'hinge' of the new front line, which protected Italian positions along the Piave and ensured that they could not be outflanked from the north. There had been heavy fighting along this sector throughout November as Arz had tried to complete the victory at Caporetto with a concerted thrust towards Vicenza and Padua. But strength was fading from Austria's armies and the Italians were able to hold on; still prone to the occasional lapse in discipline, but possessed of enough fighting spirit to give hopes of a more sustained recovery over the winter. In late December, with the Allied divisions busily improving their defences, General Émile Fayolle, commander of the French contingent, was impressed enough to write to Foch, telling him that 'the Italian armies are full of confidence and wish to fight. If the Austrians and the Hun wish to continue their offensive, even into winter, we are sure to stop them. If they wish to begin their campaign in Spring of 1918 by putting Italy out of the picture, it will be too late, and they will fail.'[45]

As gratifying as this was, Diaz knew that he could not rely too heavily on Allied troops and would have to restore the morale and fighting spirit of his own forces as soon as possible. He was determined to improve conditions for his soldiers and signed off on an ambitious series of changes that would be much welcomed. Leave was increased, rations were brought back up to 3,580 calories (they had been reduced earlier in the war), periods in the front line were shortened, efforts were made to find better accommodation for battalions when out of the line, and free life insurance was granted to everyone who served.[46] On 20 November, he issued a circular that drew a line under the draconian and what had often seemed like increasingly arbitrary disciplinary measures that Cadorna had become infamous for, promising that men would not be punished for honest mistakes, nor would they be sacked unless they had consistently failed to adopt correct behaviour. 'These constant dismissals and severe indiscriminate punishments for mistakes, however caused, destroy all peace of mind – a very necessary attribute in the present difficult situation.' Officers would also no longer be subjected to 'torpedoes' from *Comando Supremo*, when Cadorna had telephoned subordinates and dressed them down, with Diaz insisting that he wanted a more productive, supportive relationship with all ranks.[47]

This attitude was combined with an acknowledgement that the army would need to be rebuilt, with improved training and armaments. Diaz appointed Lieutenant-General Pietro Badoglio as one of his Sub-Chiefs of Staff, with responsibility for reorganizing the army and for incorporating the new weaponry that would be supplied over the winter. Allied governments had agreed to provide Rome with large amounts of equipment, including 300,000 rifles, 600 field guns, 400 medium howitzers, 40 heavy guns and as many as 100 Nieuport biplanes.[48] This would certainly help to replace the losses of the autumn, but Caporetto signified something more important than a military defeat, with its mangled dead, wounded and missing. The twenty-fourth of October 1917 was a watershed; a moment that revealed perhaps what had always been there, the weaknesses and vulnerabilities of a new nation at war. On 15 December, Signor Gambarotta, a liberal politician and deputy for Novara in Lombardy, spoke to a secret session of the Chamber of Deputies about the sense of shock he felt towards what had happened. 'We thought we had a great general and a great army.' Exorcizing these demons would take an unprecedented effort. If the Italian Army was to recover, the whole country, its people and politicians, would need to work together with a much greater degree of cohesion and efficiency than ever before.[49]

20. 'We are going out of the war'

Those two events – Caporetto and the Bolshevik seizure of power – transformed the strategic situation in Europe, giving Germany a priceless opportunity to win the war and secure for herself the kind of world position that the Kaiser had long dreamed of. Hindenburg and Ludendorff met with senior officers at Mons on 11 November to discuss the western offensive, an idea that had often been mooted, but which had now become their foremost operational priority. There were still 74 divisions on the Eastern Front – about a third of the entire German Army – and if peace could be secured with Russia, then a significant number of these could be brought to France for a decisive showdown with the Allied powers.[1] It all depended upon how quickly an agreement could be signed and whether Lenin would be able to maintain his position for long enough to make it count. When OHL received a wireless message from the newly installed Bolshevik Commander-in-Chief, Krylenko, on 26 November, asking whether it would be interested in concluding an armistice, Ludendorff telephoned Major-General Max Hoffmann at *OberOst*.

'Is it possible to negotiate with these people?' he asked.

'Yes,' Hoffmann replied, 'it is possible.'[2]

At Baden, Emperor Karl was desperate to come to terms with Russia. He had Count Czernin write to the German Chancellor, Georg von Hertling, urging him to seize the opportunity. 'The revolution in Petrograd, which has at least temporarily placed the power into the hands of Lenin and his followers, has come sooner than we had thought possible.' Whether the Bolsheviks would be able to stay in power for much longer was a question that could not be answered, but Czernin felt that if Lenin was able to do so, they would 'be forced to carry out with the utmost vigour the governmental programme which they have formulated'. An armistice would mean 'we should have won almost a complete victory on the Russian sector, for, if it achieved an armistice, the Russian army, in its present state, would surely pour back into the hinterland in order to be on the spot when the estates are distributed'. Therefore, Czernin added, 'we should not allow this moment to pass unexploited, nor miss any opportunity of bringing the war in the East to an end'.[3]

They would not have to wait long. News of the Bolshevik proposal had a shattering effect across the front, releasing months of pent-up frustration and breaking the deadlock that had endured for so long. Romania was the first casualty. After she had gallantly held her lines since the battles of the summer, the realization of what Lenin was proposing was a terrible, crushing moment for King Ferdinand and his generals. Even though her fighting capacity was gradually being restored, there would be no possibility of continuing the war if Russia reached an accord with the Central Powers. The local Russian commander, General Dmitry Shcherbachev, wanted to carry on fighting, and had initially rejected Lenin's call for an armistice, but his soldiers, restless and yearning for home, were slipping from his control. Shrugging his shoulders with a mixture of despair and hopelessness, he sent emissaries to Field Marshal Mackensen on 4 December.[4]

Romania found herself in a terrible bind. During a series of fraught war councils in Iaşi, Berthelot had tried to convince the Romanians to fight on. The new French Prime Minister, Clemenceau, had warned that any decision to disband Romania's army, which France had supported at great cost, would 'sacrifice her future', but Prime Minister Bratianu could only plead that his country was faced with an impossible situation. Accordingly, the same day, the Romanian Chief of Staff, General Prezan, was authorized to open discussions for a ceasefire, which was signed at Focşani on 5 December. 'The Russian command having proposed an armistice to the enemy and to the Roumanian [sic] troops forming part of this front, it was decided that the Roumanian troops should associate themselves with his proposition', read a formal announcement. 'As a consequence hostilities were suspended at 8 o'clock on the whole of the front.'[5] The Allies could only look on in despair. In London, *The Times*'s 'special correspondent' was sanguine, insisting that the armistice was 'merely a military measure dictated by circumstances'. 'The Rumanian [sic] Army is like an island in an ocean', he added. 'It is surrounded by utterly disorganized Russian troops, who obey nobody but their own instincts. None of the belligerent countries has yet had to pass through so terrible an ordeal.'[6]

Russia's ordeal was only just beginning. The Bolshevik negotiating team, led by one of Lenin's most trusted acolytes, Adolph Joffe, arrived in Brest-Litovsk on 3 December. They were greeted by their German counterparts in their distinctive *feldgrau* greatcoats and *Pickelhauben* and ushered into the citadel where the discussions would take place. Hoping to gain as much publicity as possible, Lenin insisted that a single representative from each of the main classes that had taken part in the revolution would make their way to Brest-Litovsk. There was Nicholas Bieliakov, a gruff, weather-beaten soldier; Fedor Olich, a sailor; Obukhov, a worker; and Roman Stashkov, a somewhat bewildered old peasant who had been picked up on the way to the railway station at Petrograd. They made for a highly unusual and colourful addition to the party, not entirely sure why they were there, and were a source of endless amusement for those who sat on the other side of the table. Max Hoffmann, the man who had been put in charge of the negotiations, would never forget their first dinner with the Russians: Obukhov using his fork as a toothpick; and Stashkov, 'a typical Russian figure with ... an enormous, untrimmed beard', causing eyebrows to raise after he was asked whether he would prefer the claret or the hock, and replying that he would take whichever was the stronger.[7]

The Bolsheviks came to Brest-Litovsk with an entirely new set of ideas about how diplomacy should be conducted. They insisted on publishing the proceedings of the conference, with a bulletin being released to the press each day, and saw it as another step in the inevitable process of world revolution. Opening with a call for 'a truce on all the fronts', Joffe suggested that an invitation should be extended to all belligerents to take part in the negotiations. When Hoffmann asked whether Joffe was 'empowered to speak in the name of Russia's Allies', he could only shake his head and admit that he was not. The Russian delegation, he said, 'regarded the question of the armistice much more broadly' and looked to strike a 'general peace', only for Hoffmann to insist that they must only discuss 'purely military questions regarding the armistice'. This tussle between Hoffmann, who wanted to narrow the subjects under discussion, and Joffe, who was constantly trying to expand them, would be a continual feature of the negotiations, giving them a curious, unsettling atmosphere. The Central Powers were now dealing with 'strange creatures, these Bolsheviks', wrote Czernin. 'They talk of freedom and the reconciliation of the peoples of the world, of peace and unity, and withal they are said to be the most cruel tyrants history has ever known.'[8]

The following day, 4 December, the Bolsheviks made their main proposal: an armistice for six months during which no military unit could be moved 'from one front to another, from the front to the rear, or from the rear to the front'. They also insisted upon the withdrawal of German forces from the islands in the Gulf of Riga, which had been occupied shortly before the seizure of power. Understandably, the Russians were eager to see these evacuated lest they be a springboard for a descent upon Petrograd. Hoffmann, with a bullish shaven head, brown eyes peering through pince-nez, was almost lost for words. His reaction, recorded by an observer, was akin to a 'physical blow' as he 'bristled' from what had been said. He began by 'expressing his astonishment' that such terms could have been raised. He countered with his own proposal for a rolling armistice of fourteen days, and categorically refused to sanction any movement of troops or vessels from the vicinity of Riga ('absolutely beyond discussion'). As to the proposal to ban troop movements, he replied that this was a 'one-sided obligation' upon Germany, which had 'two main battle fronts', although they would certainly agree 'not to move across any troops for the purpose of making an attack on the Russian troops' if this was a mutual obligation.[9]

At this point the Bolsheviks requested a ten-day extension to the current ceasefire so that they could travel back to Petrograd for further instructions. When negotiations resumed on 12 December, Joffe accepted that he was unlikely to get the evacuation of the Gulf of Riga, so that demand was dropped, which paved the way for a settlement. The armistice was finally signed on 15 December and would be in force for a month. It applied to 'all the military and air forces . . . between the Black Sea and the Baltic'. There would be no increase in the number of units at the front, nor would the agreement permit any 'regrouping on these fronts with a view to preparing an offensive'. Peace negotiations would commence a week later.[10] Even though a larger and more comprehensive settlement might take months to reach, the agreement at Brest-Litovsk was a moment of enormous significance, bringing the curtain down on what had been one of the most bloody and dangerous conflicts in human history. Local ceasefires and fraternization had been happening up and down the front for weeks, but news of the armistice, which flashed across the now frozen, snow-bound wastes of western Russia, caused a flurry of activity, celebration and disorder.

The Bolsheviks wasted no time in publicizing their achievement and squeezing every possible advantage from it. Within days, Trotsky was urging the 'working class in all lands' to overthrow their masters, 'seize state power' and join proletarians across the world 'under the flag of peace and social revolution'. Lenin was equally triumphant, crowing that 'in a matter of weeks the undemocratic institutions in the army, the countryside and industry have been almost completely destroyed. There is no other way – there can be no other way – to socialism save through such destruction . . . [Bolshevism's critics] refuse to see that in a few weeks, the lying imperialist foreign policy, which dragged out the war and covered up plunder and seizure through secret treaties, has been replaced by a truly revolutionary-democratic policy working for a really democratic peace, a policy which has already produced such great practical success as the armistice and has increased the propaganda power of our revolution a hundredfold.'[11]

The duo at OHL were unconcerned with Lenin's theatrics. During an interview with Vienna's *Neue Freie Press*, the two men had struck a calm and satisfied air. 'Hindenburg recently turned 70', the reporter noted. 'But there is not a trace of senility in his appearance. His build is tall and powerful, his blue eyes bright and vivid. He shakes his guest's hand with his mighty right hand (a lion's paw) and greets him with the heart-warming kindness that has become his hallmark.' If

Ludendorff was not quite as imposing as the Field Marshal, his appearance was perhaps 'the same as it was a year ago, two years ago, three years ago. Perhaps his character has become even more expressive, even more energetic, even more intellectual . . .' Both men were confident that events were now moving firmly in their direction.

'All is well', said Hindenburg. 'Of course, we must get through the winter and we will probably still have to make some efforts, both ourselves and our allies. The closer we come to the end of the war, the less we must allow our strength to sink. Just stand firm and be strong – then peace will naturally follow!'

When the subject turned to the revolution in Russia, Ludendorff was at pains to stress that it was not a stroke of luck but a direct consequence of German strategy. Modern conflict had changed, he said; now whole societies went to war:

> It used to be a war between armies, now it is a war of the people. War used to end by defeating the enemy's army, now war ends by defeating the enemy's people. None of us knew that before this war and we had to learn it for the first time. The decisive battles of earlier campaigns no longer exist, or rather, as the Battle of Tannenberg has shown, they are decided not directly but indirectly. The military defeats shake the people's confidence in their government, the opposition strengthens and gains power, the government falls. And then when, as in Russia, the whole system is rotten and ripe for decay, general collapse ensues. No, the Russian revolution is not a happy coincidence, it is the result of our victories.[12]

★

As the New Year arrived, the looming shadow of Germany's offensive fell across the Allied powers, the only bright spot being the promise of American support, which helped to keep morale afloat throughout the long winter months, even if the US build-up was always too slow and hesitant to really satisfy either London or Paris. In Italy, General Diaz worried that the Allied contingents would soon return to the Western Front. In a letter to Orlando on 19 January, he asked for further guidance on whether Italy should look to an offensive in the spring. Did the other Allies intend to wait until the 'full arrival' of the Americans before attacking? 'In this case it seems clear to me that we should continue to give impetus to defensive works and limit ourselves to resistance until the arrival of the Americans is completed, only conducting those limited offensive actions imposed on us by the need to improve our situation here and there.' Could he also rely on the British and French keeping their divisions in Italy? If not, then any offensive action must be either strictly limited or given up entirely.[13]

Everywhere there seemed to be a curious lull as the warring powers took stock of the global situation and tried to conserve their dwindling strength for the coming campaign. Nowhere was this more evident than in Macedonia. Even though Greece had entered the war in the summer, the front lines had barely moved and the stalemate seemed permanent and immovable. But one thing had changed: General Sarrail, the divisive commander of l'armée d'Orient, was finally relieved of command on 9 December, leaving Salonika two weeks later. His twenty-seven months in charge had left a mixed legacy, the high point being the capture of Monastir. He was insistent that more could have been achieved, but that he was undermined by those who should have supported him, blaming the English ('who wish to leave Constantine in Athens and evacuate Salonika'), the Italians ('who have come only to occupy Albania and take their place at the negotiating table for the peace treaty'), the Greeks ('who frequently only wish for the triumph of one party, and constantly seek maximum benefits with a minimum of risk and effort'), and even some Frenchmen back home ('who do not wish the efforts in the Orient to be successful').[14]

Sarrail was certainly correct in acknowledging the disparate motives of those involved in Macedonia, but he always brought with him intrigue and rumour, spending as much time on political and economic questions as he did on operational matters.[15] His successor was General Adolphe Guillaumat, a hard-fighting soldier with extensive combat experience, whose main directive was simply 'to prevent the enemy from conquering Greece'. He was to maintain the integrity of his current position, but if 'obliged to yield ground', he was to 'deny the enemy all access to Greece, particularly to the region east of the Pindus, while keeping possession, as long as possible, of the entrenched camp at Salonika, and combining his action with the Italian forces at Valona'.[16] These orders were a striking indication of how far Allied war aims in the Balkans had shrunk. He was there to hold the line and ensure that Greek forces were able to contribute to the war effort, and only then could he think about resuming the offensive. Much would depend, as it always had done, on the attitude in Paris, which was now becoming more sceptical of the Macedonian campaign than ever before.

Clemenceau had never been particularly enamoured of the Salonika expedition, seeing it as a flagrant waste of resources at a time of national crisis. He regularly reminded the readers of his newspaper, *L'homme Enchaîné*, that the enemy was in Noyon, a mere sixty miles from Paris, and he saw no reason why France should pour resources into the Balkans when the danger was so close to home. During a meeting of the Supreme War Council on 1 December, he had broached the topic of Salonika, 'about which we only know that we knew nothing, or at any rate what little we knew, was not very favourable'. He feared a German attack and wanted to know 'what the Greek army could do' and what it required in terms of munitions or weaponry. Venizelos, who had travelled to Paris, was eager to enlist Clemenceau's support and reminded him that he had offered to mobilize twelve divisions in the summer but the Allies had not been able to equip more than nine. He was also worried about the food situation in the country, which was suffering from the recent blockade and required urgent financial and economic assistance.[17]

Whether the Allies liked it or not, they were now responsible for the Greeks and must ensure that they could be sustained over the winter. Venizelos toured the Allied capitals, drank the health of his new partners, and pressed his country's claims whenever he could. He knew that if Greece was to profit from the war, she needed to materially assist the Entente – and for that he required an army. By the beginning of 1918, the strength of the Hellenic Army had risen to 116,000 men, including 37,000 stationed in Macedonia. The latter were part of the Army of National Defence that had joined Venizelos in his attempt to form a rival government in the north. In December, the Entente had promised to send a military mission to Athens, tasked with turning this into a modern force able to take to the field against the Central Powers. Venizelos was hopeful that much could be achieved, but the mood in the army was febrile, split down the middle between his supporters and those who remained loyal to the former king. The country was perched uneasily close to civil war.[18]

The winter passed slowly in Macedonia. The troops continued to move up and down the line, but there was little activity other than the occasional aerial sortie or trench raid. General Guillaumat was keen to give the forces under his command a sense of purpose and energy. He toured the front, read reports of small-scale operations and artillery bombardments, and kept an eye on any indications of an enemy build-up, which fortunately never seemed to amount to much. It did not take him long to realize the extent of the challenge facing the expeditionary force. As he wrote in a report to the War Ministry in mid-February, 'Upon arriving in Macedonia, one comes to realise the difficulties that all of the Allied armies have had to overcome and the efforts that have had to be made in order to achieve the current situation.' Considering the chronic lack of manpower and a general insufficiency of resources of all kinds, the construction of the 'entrenched camp' and the creation of nearly 1,200 kilometres of roads was an impressive achievement, particularly 'in a country of low swampy plains that are flooded in winter and burned by the sun in summer', with 'high, steep and desolate mountains often without the slightest vegetation, where rocky outcrops make for gruelling work . . .'[19]

Inevitably, the maintenance of the coalition took up much of Guillaumat's time. He came to the conclusion that a single headquarters, with a common staff, was absolutely necessary to help curb the independence of the national contingents and ensure that they worked together more harmoniously. He pressed for an artillery reserve, which could be moved up and down the front as required, and also outlined a series of administrative reforms to prevent duplication of effort. But the most pressing problem was manpower, and he asked urgently for reinforcements, partly to take the place of the Russian division, which had been withdrawn from the front in mid-January. 'The relief has not involved any serious incidents, but the troops are disorganised, and many of their officers have left them', he reported on 15 January. 'They cannot be kept here since they are no longer doing their duty; no further delusions must be cherished with regard to the possibility of making use of these misguided people responsible or not . . . The relief of the Russians has cost me four regiments.'[20]

Guillaumat's steady leadership soon settled nerves among the other commanders in Salonika. 'He appears to be essentially a soldier and to regard the situation from a military point of view' was the verdict of General Milne in a report to the War Office on 17 January. 'At present he is visiting all the fronts consulting with the Commanders and endeavouring to appreciate the situation as regards both its strategical and tactical aspects. He appears to be a firm believer in thorough organization and is willing to listen to the opinion of others, though at the same time he has very clear views of his own.' Guillaumat had told Milne that 'he has not the means for achieving any success and that at present the general military situation is not suitable' for an offensive, although he would plan for one when the time came. His thoughts would eventually coalesce on an operation west of Lake Dojran in the Vardar Valley, but this could not be undertaken before the summer, so it would have to take place in the autumn, when the weather was cooler. So once again the prospect of a decisive attack in Salonika receded into the distance as the war passed Macedonia by and left the expeditionary force in a frustrating state of limbo – its moment of redemption and triumph forever postponed.[21]

For their opponents, this sense of boredom and frustration would have been all too familiar. Bulgarian troops continued to garrison the long Salonika front with only token assistance from their allies. Of the 292 battalions in theatre, almost 85 per cent were Bulgarian, which had become a steady drain on the state's finances.[22] The effect of the Allied naval blockade was even felt in this corner of the Balkans, squeezing supplies of food, clothing and fuel, and making life miserable for the men in the trenches. By the end of 1917, rear-echelon Bulgarian soldiers were surviving on just 600 grams of bread per day. Those in the front lines received a more generous 800 grams, although this was still some way off what was needed to maintain a healthy weight.[23] Clothing was also in short supply, and Bulgarian battalions had become notorious for their unkempt appearance. Men often wore a mixture of items, old uniforms or ones patched up or hastily mended, and no matter how many times their commanders complained, little ever seemed to change.

Morale was not helped by what was seen as Bulgaria's abandonment by her allies. By March 1918, Germany had withdrawn six infantry battalions and six batteries of heavy artillery from Macedonia, and a month later, Hindenburg asked the Bulgarian High Command to agree to the removal of all German infantry and artillery units. The Commander-in-Chief, General Zhekov, protested, arguing that this would have an effect 'the consequences of which cannot be foreseen'. Once again the Bulgarians returned to the agreement that had been signed in 1915 that obliged Germany and Austria to keep six divisions each in the Balkans, but to no avail.[24] Nor was OHL particularly interested in allaying Bulgaria's concerns about the peace negotiations at Brest-Litovsk, where the Bolshevik plea for 'no annexations' was being considered. Sofia was highly sensitive to any manoeuvring that might result in her losing out on Dobrogea or those parts of Macedonia she had overrun, which were regarded as essential to her mission of national unification. But when Germany, Austria and Turkey declared themselves in favour of a general peace 'without annexations and indemnities', Bulgaria found herself isolated. She protested vigorously and was unimpressed by Berlin's insistence that this declaration changed nothing and that their secret treaties were still in force. It was abundantly clear that any deal with the Bolsheviks would favour German interests and not necessarily those of the weakest member of the Central Powers.[25]

The Bolsheviks returned to Brest-Litovsk on 22 December armed with a series of six proposals, including the evacuation of all occupied territories, the political independence of those peoples who had been deprived of it 'during the course of the present war', the protection of minorities, and an agreement that no indemnities would be paid. Max Hoffmann had taken the lead in the first stage of proceedings, but the negotiation of a peace treaty required more diplomatic involvement, and Berlin had sent the Foreign Secretary, Richard von Kühlmann, to oversee matters, assisted by Vienna's representative, Count Czernin. After looking over the Bolsheviks' proposals, Czernin read out a prepared statement that acknowledged the desire of Germany, Austria–Hungary, Bulgaria and Turkey to conclude matters as soon as possible 'without forcible acquisitions of territory and without war indemnities'. However, this binding commitment must be made by *all* the powers involved in the war, 'for it would not do for the Powers of the Quadruple Alliance negotiating with Russia one-sidedly to tie themselves to these conditions without a guaranty [*sic*] that Russia's Allies will recognise and will carry out these conditions honestly and without reserve . . .'[26]

There may not have been much chance that the Allies would agree to these terms, but the public statement that Germany was not seeking to annex any territory immediately ruffled feathers at OHL. 'Furious wire from Hindenburg about "renunciation" of everything', recorded Czernin on 27 December. 'Ludendorff telephoning every minute; more furious outbursts, Hoffmann very excited, Kühlmann true to his name and "cool" as ever.'[27] Such an excited reaction to Czernin's declaration was an indication of a growing split within the German camp over the kind of treaty that needed to be signed. The generals at OHL were firmly of the opinion that only a harsh expansionist peace would secure the empire. Ludendorff had telegraphed instructions to *OberOst* on 16 December, outlining the need for the annexation of Lithuania and Courland ('since we need more land in order to feed the nation'), with Poland being 'associated' with the Central Powers. He also wanted the Russian evacuation of Finland, Estonia, Eastern Galicia, Moldavia and Armenia.[28] Hindenburg even wrote to the Kaiser on 7 January warning him that the representatives at Brest-Litovsk 'appeared to be more diplomatic than resolute', and that their performance was 'very likely to produce an unfavourable opinion of the Supreme Command, which is held responsible for all this in the army'.[29]

The Kaiser's opinion shifted with an almost predictable regularity, between dreams of a vast empire in the east and more sober assessments of political and military reality. He was certainly aware of how Hindenburg and Ludendorff viewed his negotiating team, but he dismissed this thinly veiled threat of resignation and maintained that he still had trust in his Chancellor and Foreign Secretary. Georg von Hertling, who had been appointed Imperial Chancellor in November 1917, insisted that they must strike a balance in how they approached negotiations and that they had to think about more than just military considerations. 'As regards Russia we have to solve the amazingly difficult problem of establishing good economic and political relations with the new Russia, completely freeing our rear in the military sense and at the same time separating large areas from the old Russian state and converting them into effective bulwarks on our frontiers.' They could certainly compel the Bolsheviks 'to bow to our will by military pressure', but this would 'have made tolerable relations with Russia impossible, certainly for some time to come, and we should have met with such strong opposition in our own country that it would not have been feasible to carry through the annexations, as it is constitutionally impossible without the consent of Parliament'.[30]

Misunderstandings, either intentional or otherwise, soon marred the discussions at Brest-Litovsk. When it became clear that the Allies were not going to respond to an invitation to take part in the talks, Kühlmann admitted that any previous statements on a general peace 'without annexations' were no longer valid. While initially jubilant that the Central Powers had agreed to their proposals, the Russian delegation were corrected in this misapprehension by Hoffmann, who told Joffe that this would not apply to those states such as Poland, Lithuania or Courland that had voluntarily withdrawn from the Russian Empire (and were now firmly under German military control). Their fate would be decided between their representatives and the Central Powers alone. 'Joffe looked as if he had received a blow on the head', remembered Hoffmann. The Bolshevik delegation spent the afternoon giving 'free vent to their disappointment and indignation'.[31] Nor were they able to get the negotiations moved to a neutral venue, ideally Stockholm, with the Central Powers fearing enemy interference and concerned that this would prolong the talks even further. 'The transfer of the negotiations to neutral territory would give the Entente the desired opportunity to interfere in a disturbing manner', noted Czernin. 'We refuse to give the Western powers this opportunity . . .'[32]

With no chance of securing a peace 'without annexations', the Bolsheviks needed to change tactics. Leon Trotsky, the People's Commissar for Foreign Affairs, arrived in Brest-Litovsk on 9 January, replacing Joffe as the lead negotiator, and lost no time in berating his hosts for their refusal to shift the location of the talks. Trotsky had in many ways become the face of the revolution: he was an indefatigable speaker, possessed of a supreme memory, who had become the chief propagandist for the Bolsheviks while Lenin was in hiding. Recognizable by his thick wavy hair, moustache and trademark pince-nez, he made a profound impression upon the conference, announcing that:

> The Russian delegation knows perfectly well what it is losing by conducting peace pourparlers [*sic*] at Brest-Litovsk, a capital of the German conqueror, but it also knows what greater loss it would suffer in breaking off the pourparlers over the question of locality. The peoples are thirsting for peace, and for this the Russian Delegation can frankly admit that it has submitted to the ultimatum. You are the stronger from the military point of view, but you are forced to hide the motives of your policy from the masses. We are the weaker, but our strength increases in proportion as we unmask your policy, and that is why we are staying.[33]

The Germans and Austrians could only look upon Trotsky with a mixture of intrigue, fascination and outright contempt. 'Trotski [*sic*] is undoubtedly an interesting, clever fellow, and a very dangerous adversary' was the verdict of Count Czernin.[34]

This diplomatic fencing went on for weeks, broken by frequent interruptions as the Bolsheviks tried to play for time, convinced that revolution was either already breaking out in Germany and Austria or would do so imminently. Lenin was now desperately trying to consolidate his power at home. Elections had been held for the Constituent Assembly in late November, with the Socialist Revolutionaries winning almost 40 per cent of the vote, forcing the Bolsheviks into second place.[35] But Lenin was never going to transfer power, and argued that the elections were not a real representation of the will of the people and could therefore be safely ignored. The Constituent Assembly must accept Bolshevik rule and 'proclaim that it unreservedly recognises Soviet Power'. Anything less 'would be tantamount to aiding counter-revolution'.[36] Although the Socialist Revolutionaries and their allies dismissed Lenin's arguments and tried to form a new government, Red Guards closed down the assembly on 19 January, with its members being bundled outside and the doors of the Tauride Palace firmly locked. The following day the Bolsheviks declared that the Constituent Assembly had been dissolved. Democracy in Russia, which had lasted for just eleven months, had been extinguished. There was now only the stark reality of Bolshevik power.

Not everyone was resigned to the continuation of Lenin's regime. With rival forces gathering at Novocherkassk in the Don, where hundreds of ex-Tsarist officers had formed a 'Volunteer Army', Bolshevik writ only ran across a limited part of the country — a central belt between Petrograd, Moscow and the Caspian Sea. Finland had already declared independence in December, and shortly afterwards, in late January, the Ukrainian national assembly, known as the Rada, which had been formed in Kiev, announced their formal separation from Russia. This chaotic situation confirmed in Lenin's mind the need for peace as quickly as possible. On 20 January, he issued his 'Theses on the Question of the Immediate Conclusion of a Separate and Annexationist Peace', which considered whether Russia should carry on fighting. The negotiations, he wrote, had 'made it perfectly clear that the war party has undoubtedly gained the upper hand in the German Government', and Russia would soon be faced with a deadly choice: either accept an unfavourable peace or 'wage a revolutionary war'. He was insistent that they must have peace at any cost. 'In concluding a separate peace we free ourselves *as much as is possible at the present moment* from both hostile imperialist groups, we take advantage of their mutual enmity and warfare which hamper concerted action on their part against us, and for a certain period have our hands free to advance and consolidate the socialist revolution.' He was pleased at the out-break of strikes and food riots in Vienna and Berlin, and was confident that this would soon transform the situation. 'This fact offers us the opportunity,' he concluded, 'for the time being, of further delaying and dragging out the peace negotiations.'[37]

Trotsky played his part to perfection. Day after day he debated with Kühlmann, arguing over the meaning of self-determination and questioning points of procedure. When Kühlmann tired of these games, he gave the floor to Hoffmann, who stood up and told the Russian delegation that it talked 'as if it stood victorious on our soil'. The Bolsheviks wanted self-determination to be applied to the occu-pied territories in such a way that it did not apply to their own land. 'Its government is based purely on violence', he said; 'ruthlessly sup-pressing all who think differently. Anyone with different ideas is regarded as a counter-revolutionary and bourgeois and is declared outside the law.' There would be no interference in the life of these occupied territories, nor would they evacuate the lands they had conquered. Trotsky could only reply in his usual hectoring tone. 'The position of our opponents . . .' he declared, 'is now absolutely clear . . . Germany and Austria wish to cut off from the possessions of the former Russian Empire a territory comprising over 150,000 square versts [160,500 square kilometres]. That territory includes the former Kingdom of Poland, Lithuania, and large areas inhabited by Ukrainians and White Russians . . .'[38]

Talks continued throughout January and into February. With unrest spreading through Austria and into Hungary, the mood in Vienna was grim. 'The entire fate of the Monarchy and the dynasty depends upon the earliest possible conclusion of peace at Brest-Litovsk', Karl wrote to Czernin on 17 January. 'If the peace at Brest does not become a reality, then there will be revolution here no matter how much there is to eat.'[39] Czernin reiterated to his German counterparts that they must secure a peace now, even threatening to sign a separate agreement with Russia or Ukraine if things dragged on any longer. But this was never taken seriously, either by Vienna or by Berlin, which left the Austrians with little to do but go along with whatever the Germans decided. There was simply no way that Karl or Czernin could square the circle of competing interests between Germany, Austria, Ukraine, Poland and Russia; between the ideas of self-determination and the realities of conquest; between bread and peace.

Trotsky walked out of the conference on 18 January, requesting a ten-day break, so it was not until late January that discussions recommenced. In the meantime, Kühlmann and Czernin focused their efforts on wooing the Ukrainian delegation, who had come to Brest-Litovsk with hopes of a new birth for their country. In exchange for promising to deliver one million tons of grain to the Central Powers by the end of July 1918, the Ukrainians secured peace, recognition, and a number of territorial concessions. They were granted the area around Cholm, with its mixed Polish–Ruthenian population, and also won reforms to Habsburg governance in Eastern Galicia. Agreeing to these demands had not been easy for Karl, who was aware of how this would cut across Poles' hopes for their own state, but the urgency of the food situation forced his hand. The 'bread peace' was signed with the Rada in the early hours of 9 February.[40]

The Bolshevik response was a mixture of fury and petulance. The following day, Trotsky stated in his usual florid manner that Russia would refuse to sign any 'peace of annexation' and declared that the state of war with the Central Powers was ended. 'We are going out of the war', he said. 'We inform all peoples and their Governments of this fact. We are giving the order for a general demobilization of all armies opposed at the present to the troops of Germany, Austria–Hungary, Turkey, and Bulgaria.' Their opponents were 'determined to possess lands and peoples by might', which they could not condone. 'We are going out of the war, but we feel ourselves compelled to refuse to sign the peace treaty.' This novel approach, what Trotsky called 'no war, no peace', stunned the representatives at Brest-Litovsk, horrifying the Austrians and causing a bemused 'unheard of!' to escape from Hoffmann's lips. Trotsky then led the Bolsheviks out, boarding their train for Petrograd and leaving the remaining delegates unsure what to do. It did not take long for Hindenburg and Ludendorff to insist upon a resumption of hostilities. On 17 February, an official communiqué from Berlin announced that Russia had thereby given seven days' notice of the termination of the armistice, and accordingly, the German Government would now 'reserve a free hand in every direction'.[41]

The German Army in the east may not have been as strong as it once was, having lost its best officers and men to the Western Front, along-side stores of all kinds and thousands of horses, but its opponents were in a state of acute disintegration. Operation *Faustschlag* ('Fist Punch') opened on 18 February with mounted columns pushing off from Riga and striking eastwards towards Minsk. It was a strange kind of war, fought more on the railways than in the trenches; a semi-mobile expedition into the vast interior of what was now Soviet Russia. The attackers advanced across land deep in snow, its lakes and ponds covered over with thick sheets of ice; the skies leaden grey as far as the eye could see. There was no organized resistance to speak of. The defenders either threw down their arms and fled, or surren-dered after firing a few stray shots. Minsk was reached within three days, with 3,000 officers and 10,000 men being captured, including the entire staff of a front headquarters.[42]

The German terms were wired to Petrograd on 21 February. A map had been handed to the Bolsheviks before they left Brest-Litovsk, with a thick line drawn upon it that started at Narva, then headed down to Pskov, before going directly south, east of Minsk, and bending eastwards past Homel towards the Ukrainian border. Everything to the west of this line would 'no longer be under a Rus-sian protectorate'. Livonia, Estonia, Ukraine and Finland would be immediately cleared of all Russian troops; Russia's army would be fully demobilized; all her warships in the Black Sea, Baltic Sea and Arctic Ocean would sail home and be interned; and she would stop all 'agitation and propaganda' against any member of the Central Powers. The Bolsheviks had forty-eight hours to sign.[43] When Krylenko was summoned to Bolshevik General Headquarters and asked for his opinion, he could only repeat what he had already said: that resistance was impossible. The enemy were advancing rapidly with cavalry, supported by small detachments of infantry carried on trucks or armoured cars. Lenin insisted that 'special commanders' be

The Treaty of Brest-Litovsk, March 1918

N

NORWAY

SWEDEN

FINLAND

Helsinki
Petrograd

Christiana

Stockholm

ESTONIA

North
Sea

LIVONIA

RUSSIA

DENMARK

Copenhagen

Baltic Sea

Approximate Front Line
November 1918

UNITED
KINGDOM

NETH.

Berlin

POLAND

Brest-Litovsk

London

Amsterdam

Brussels

BEL.

GERMAN EMPIRE

UKRAINE

Paris

Prague

Vienna

FRANCE

Bern

SWITZ.

Budapest

AUSTRIA-HUNGARY

Black Sea

ROMANIA

Bucharest

ITALY

Adriatic Sea

SERBIA

BULGARIA

MONT.

Sofia

Constantinople

SPAIN

Rome

ALBANIA

OTTOMAN EMPIRE

GREECE

Athens

Areas annexed by Germany

Areas given self-determination

Western, Italian and Salonika
front lines

Mediterranean Sea

0   200   400 km
0   100   200   300   400 miles

sent to the front to stop the troops from falling back, but Krylenko could only shake his head in disbelief. Soldiers were told every day that their officers were landowners or counter-revolutionaries, he said, and there was little chance that they would listen to anyone coming from Petrograd.[44]

The Bolsheviks were on the brink of losing everything. With the Germans only 150 miles from the capital, an emergency proclamation was published ('The Socialist Fatherland is in Danger!'), which tried to rally support. In order 'to save our exhausted and depleted country from the miseries of a new war', the Bolsheviks had 'made the supreme sacrifice' and told Germany that they were willing to accept any terms she cared to offer. While they waited for the German proletariat to rise up, they had a 'sacred duty' to defend the republic from its enemies. But the mood of lassitude and depression that had been evident in the Petrograd garrison for months made it almost impossible to form up enough units. Most regiments pledged to defend the capital, but they rarely left their barracks and would only agree to go to the front if they received more food and pay. Even the factory workers, those men who had formed the backbone of the Soviet, proved unwilling to join the new Red Army en masse, preferring instead to spend their time digging trenches or preparing to evacuate the city. 'We have no army', Krylenko told the Central Executive Committee of leading Bolsheviks on 23 February; 'our demoralized soldiers fly panic-stricken before the German bayonets, leaving behind them artillery, transport, and ammunition. The divisions of the Red Guard are swept away like flies. Only the immediate signing of the peace can save us from ruin.'[45]

Opinion among the Executive Committee was split, between those like Lenin who argued that they had no choice and must have peace, and the others who urged resistance. But with Lenin threatening to resign and Trotsky, though he vacillated and struggled to accept such ruinous terms, eventually siding with his chief, there was only one outcome. The Treaty of Brest-Litovsk was signed at five o'clock on the afternoon of 3 March, four hours after hostilities had ceased across the Eastern Front. The Russian delegation was not led by Trotsky, who could not bring himself to sign the treaty and resigned in protest, but by another leading Bolshevik, Grigori Sokol-nikov, who was ordered to go by Lenin. This was no 'peace by agreement', read an official Bolshevik statement, but 'a peace dictated at the point of the gun' that left them with no choice but to sign. 'We have no doubt that the triumph of imperialism and militarism over the international proletarian revolution will prove to be temporary and ephemeral. Meanwhile the Soviet Government . . . is forced to accept the peace terms so as to save revolutionary Russia.'[46]

The price of peace had been extortionate. Russia lost almost 1.3 million square miles of territory, containing 62 million people. The settlement deprived her of about a quarter of the entire land mass of what had once been Imperial Russia, 44 per cent of her population, a third of her crops, and almost three quarters of her iron and coal. But an agreement had been reached, with Article 1 of the treaty committing Russia and the four Central Powers 'to live in peace and amity henceforth'.[47] Lenin had now secured invaluable breathing space in which to consolidate his revolution and take the war south, where his greatest enemies now lay. For the Central Powers, Brest-Litovsk was a stunning vindication of their military supremacy, opening up a vast arena of influence, even if there would not be the time or resources to properly consolidate their position or exploit these new gains, at least until matters were settled on the Western Front. On 21 March 1918, just eighteen days after Brest-Litovsk, the German Army went on the offensive in one last, supreme effort for glory. The war in the east had ended in a resounding victory for Germany. She would now attempt to repeat this in the west.

21.   'Gambler's throw'

With the issue of the war being decided in France, the Allies were left desperately trying to resurrect the Eastern Front, or at least part of it. Knowledge of what was going on inside Russia was extremely poor; half-truths and rumours left the decision-makers in London and Paris floundering in the dark. Discussions over recognition for the Bolsheviks had got nowhere, and with no agreement on common objectives or strategy, there was only a series of half-hearted, uncoordinated proposals that took up much time and effort with little result. The problem of a post-Brest-Litovsk world, with Germany penetrating deep into Russia and Ukraine, gaining access to potentially limitless supplies of wheat and barley, horrified Allied planners, as did the presence of thousands of tons of supplies and equipment sitting idly at the ports of Murmansk, Archangel and Vladivostok. At a meeting of the War Council in London on 7 December, the stark dilemma was apparent. Either the Allies should 'recognise the Bolsheviks and make the best arrangements possible with them; or . . . refuse to recognise them, and take open and energetic steps against them'.[1]

The need to continue the war against Germany was the Allies' overriding strategic priority, but the chaos within Russia meant that they had to look for novel ways to do this. As early as November 1917, General Foch, who had been appointed French Army Chief of Staff, argued that they must re-establish control of the Trans-Siberian Railway. This could only be done by the Japanese or the Americans, who could secure Vladivostok and then move west into the interior. There had also been discussions over the winter between the British and the French, who had agreed to divide their responsibilities in southern Russia, with the French taking Romania and Ukraine and the British the Caucasus.[2] Contact had already been made with General Aleksei Kaledin, the *Ataman* (leader) of the Don Cossacks, who had emerged as the foremost anti-Bolshevik figure in Russia, with many ex-Tsarist officers, including former generals Alekseev, Kornilov and Denikin, making their way to Novocherkassk to raise a new army. On 9 January, Kornilov and Alekseev had issued a joint statement on the aims of what became known as the 'Volunteer' movement (or 'Whites' to their enemies): 'to resist an armed invasion of South and South-East Russia'; to 'defend to the last drop of its blood the autonomy of the territories which give it sanctuary and which are the last bastion of Russian independence, the last hope for the restoration of a Free, Great Russia'; and to see the election of a Constituent Assembly.[3]

The fate of the Volunteer Army was a tragic one. By February 1918, it was just 4,000 men strong and lacked arms, with only a few rifles and little ammunition. Forced to retreat in the face of a Bolshevik expedition towards Rostov, it had no choice but to head towards the Kuban, on the northeastern shore of the Black Sea, in what became known as the 'ice march'. It was here where General Kornilov's leadership came into its own. He led the Volunteers south, fighting against what seemed like overwhelming odds, only to die a soldier's death on 13 April during an assault on the Red-held city of Ekaterinodar. According to those who were with him in those days, Kornilov had suspected that an attack on the city would be extremely hazardous. 'Of course, we may all fall here,' he told a friend, 'but in my opinion it is better to die with honour. To retreat now would bring certain destruction, because we have no supplies and no munitions. It would be a slow agony.' He was killed when an enemy shell hit his headquarters, which was located in a farmhouse close to the front. General Denikin took over command of the army and vowed to continue the war, ordering a march north back to the Don.[4]

Dreams of a miraculous resurrection of the Eastern Front were always illusory. Even if there had been a force strong enough to dislodge the Bolsheviks from Petrograd, it was highly unlikely that this would mean a renewal of the war against Germany. Russia was too far gone; too broken and fragmented by infighting to return to what it had been. Even Kaledin, who for a brief moment had seemed to be a unifying figure, was always more concerned with Cossack autonomy than anything else, and realized that the Volunteers' wish to restore 'Great Russia' conflicted with his own more parochial goals. As early as November 1917, a British liaison officer had managed to interview Kaledin, but came away unconvinced that he could be relied upon. 'I had four interviews with him in three days and he gave me the impression of being very tired, very afraid of the Bolsheviks, and very uncertain of his power over his troops.' When the Reds finally arrived in the Don in February, most of the Cossack regiments mutinied, leaving the *Ataman* with just a handful of reliable soldiers. On 11 February, the day Kornilov left for the Kuban, Kaledin retired to his room, took out his revolver and shot himself.[5]

The Volunteer Army was evidently too small and ill-equipped to pose much of a threat to Lenin's Red Army, at least for the time being, which left the Allies still searching for a reliable partner in Russia. The French had pinned their hopes on the 'Czech Legion': two divisions of Czech and Slovak troops that had been serving with the Tsar, their numbers bolstered by those who had either deserted or been taken prisoner. By February 1918, the Czechs were stranded around Kiev, but had pledged their service to the Allies and were trying to find a way home to fight for an independent state. The French had already recognized the legion as an intrinsic part of a Czech national army, and were keen for it to be deployed on the Western Front, but getting it to France, via Vladivostok and the Pacific, was an enormously complicated task that would take months. The British would need to be persuaded to provide the shipping, and with much of their fleet concentrated in home waters and the Mediterranean, as well as helping to bring the Americans across the Atlantic, it was not clear that reallocating precious resources to the Czechs would be a worthwhile endeavour, particularly when the balance of the war was so delicately poised.

The difficulty of moving the Czechs meant that alternative plans were quickly drawn up for what role they might play *within* Russia, either guarding Allied supplies at Murmansk and Archangel or perhaps forming the nucleus of a Bolshevik army against the Germans. But none of these schemes was particularly feasible. It was highly doubtful that Lenin or Trotsky – who already viewed the legion with suspicion – would allow them to go to the northern ports, which was why they had promised them free passage along the Trans-Siberian Railway if they agreed to three terms: an immediate evacuation; the removal of any Russian non-communist ('counter-revolutionary') officers; and that the legion would move 'not as fighting units but as a group of free citizens', with only enough weaponry for self-defence.[6] The Czechs refused to part with all their rifles and machine-guns, but surrendered enough of their arsenal to mollify the Soviet Government and get the wagons rolling on their long journey eastwards. 'The Russian railways were in an incredible state of muddle', remembered one Czech veteran. 'Every town, almost every station, had set up its own small republic, and every local soviet, and each petty Bolshevik commander, issued orders which not infrequently directly conflicted with each other.'[7]

Paris and London would have to strike a delicate balance, keeping lines of communication open with all sides while avoiding the appearance of favouring one group or the other. 'We were not concerned to overthrow the Bolshevik Government in Moscow', Lloyd George admitted years later. 'But we were concerned to keep them, so long as the war with Germany was afoot, from overthrowing those non-Bolshevik administrations and movements outside Moscow which were prepared to work with us against the enemy.'[8] Their relationship with Russia's new rulers was particularly turbulent, switching from outright hostility to a curious attitude of neutrality, even cooperation, and back again. Lenin had always taken a pragmatic approach to diplomacy. While he never stopped calling for the destruction of capitalism and seeking to overthrow the imperialist powers, he would work with them while his young regime remained fragile. On 6 March, 130 Royal Marines landed at the Arctic port of Murmansk, home to perhaps 450,000 tons of stores.[9] This unexpected move, which had been specifically requested by the local soviet, fearing that the newly independent Finns were about to march on the town, saw the first British troops step onto Russian soil. Trotsky, who had been unsure of how likely a Finnish attack was, authorized the move anyway, sending a telegram to the soviet ordering them to 'accept any and all assistance from the Allied missions and use every means to obstruct the advance of the plunderers'.[10]

The landing of small naval detachments was the limit of what Britain could do in Russia in the spring of 1918, which was why the possibility of Japanese intervention was treated with growing seriousness. The US Government had already rejected the idea in February, but Washington would warm to it as the extent of the German triumph at Brest-Litovsk became apparent.[11] The matter was discussed at a meeting of the Supreme War Council on 15 March. The French were keenest on the idea, hopefully with US support, with Monsieur Stephen Pichon, Foreign Minister, arguing that it was 'the only means of preventing the penetration of Germany into Asia'. According to Clemenceau, who had become an uncompromising advocate of total, unrestrained war, they simply did not have the luxury of time. 'Russia was rapidly falling to pieces . . .' he said. 'We are at war with Germany, and Russia's collapse is becoming ever more complete. Siberia was one of the most interesting Provinces of Russia, and one from which the Germans could draw much in the way of food and supplies. We ought to try and stop Germany from utilising these resources while we could.'[12]

The British were not convinced. Urging a note of caution, Arthur Balfour, Foreign Secretary, said that there was 'a good deal of evidence to show that, although the Russians could not resist, German penetration would be very slow. There was no immediate fear that Germany would satisfy her needs from Siberia, nor penetrate into the country.' Therefore, they had time 'to endeavour to bring Russia to our point of view, that Japanese assistance could save her'. He urged a 'period of waiting' to see what happened before they took what he called Pichon's 'gambler's throw'. Moreover, there would inevitably be delays before they could consult with President Wilson and the Japanese. Lloyd George said that two points needed to be made clear in any discussions with Tokyo. Firstly, 'that Japan must not stop at the point which suited her in Siberia, but must go to the point which suited the Allies; and second, we must treat Japan as an Ally, and not ask for all sorts of guarantees; in fact, we must not treat Japan as though she belonged to an inferior race'. With this in mind, the conference agreed to send a despatch to Washington 'advocating Japanese intervention in Siberia'.

Before President Wilson could respond, the Japanese had already landed at Vladivostok. In a surprising unilateral move, Japanese troops marched into the city on 4 April, ordered by their government to protect their citizens, several of whom had been murdered by marauding Russian soldiers. The British swiftly followed, sending a landing party ashore to protect their consulate and watch over what the Japanese were doing. Although foreign troops would not remain in the Russian port for long (they would be evacuated before the end of the month), the sudden Japanese intervention concentrated minds on whether it would be better to wait for a Bolshevik request before supporting any large-scale intervention, as the British were proposing, while also adding urgency to the Czech question. At a meeting of the Supreme War Council the following month, Clemenceau said that it was 'clearly to the interest of the Allies to bring them [the Czech Legion] as rapidly as possible to the Western front', only for Lloyd George to pour cold water on the idea. Shipping could only be provided by the United States or Japan, and so they should either request Japanese assistance or urge the Soviet Government to allow the legion to move to Archangel or Murmansk, from where it would be easier to transport them to France.[13]

The arguments over intervention in Russia and what to do about the Czechs consumed significant amounts of time and energy as the war entered its most decisive phase. The Allies had many strategies for reconstituting the Eastern Front, and played them out on large maps in their council chambers, but the tyrannies of distance and lack of resources, poor intelligence and an ever-shifting situation combined to thwart their best efforts. Even the reappearance of Alexander Kerensky, who had managed to flee to London, had little effect on Allied strategy. The former Russian leader turned up at Downing Street in late June, presenting himself as an envoy of the Constituent Assembly and asking for 'intervention to oust the Germans and the Bolsheviks'. He insisted that the strength of Lenin's forces had been wildly overestimated, and tried hard to convince the British Prime Minister of his enduring popularity within Russia, only to encounter a hardened scepticism. 'Resolutions on paper are of little value against machine-guns', said Lloyd George; 'and in the heart of Russia it was the Bolsheviks who had the machine-guns.' Kerensky was 'vague as to how many of his friends and Committees had been left at large in Soviet Russia' and 'I could get no clear assurance that he represented any organised force, apart from resolutions passed in secret by disgruntled Socialists'.[14]

Kerensky's problem was all too familiar to those exiles who had fled Russia as she slipped into revolution and civil war. Unless they could demonstrate that they had strong forces at their disposal, they were unlikely to be of much interest or use to the Entente. Kerensky was still a striking individual – his pale, almost ghost-like skin and piercing eyes were often commented upon by contemporaries – but his famed rhetorical skills made little impression now. When Raymond Poincaré granted him an audience during the summer, he saw a curious and sadly unconvincing figure. 'I found him to be less thin, less frail and less sickly than he is generally reported to be. However, he has the air of a very unassuming bourgeois man. His pale face is clean-shaven, his eyes are shades of blue and black, and do not give the impression of an honest man. His voice is full, loud and musical, with accents that bring to mind Briand's voice. He speaks poor French, often looking for words that he does not find. He seems to be emotional and with poor self-control.' When a friend later asked him what he thought of Kerensky, the French President was unimpressed, echoing Lloyd George. 'I fear, I tell him, that he has a mistaken impression of his forces.'[15]

The possibilities of intervention in Russia paled into insignificance when compared to the great battle unfolding on the Western Front. There were now three and a half million German soldiers in France and Belgium, leaving a million in the east, as OHL launched its biggest offensive since the opening weeks of the war. Hindenburg and Ludendorff had gambled everything on a crushing blow in the west, and in the heady days of late March and early April 1918, it looked like they had succeeded. Operation *Michael* began in spectacular fashion. Advancing through thick fog, utilizing the assault tactics that had been honed at Riga and Caporetto, three German armies broke against the British line on the morning of 21 March. Within five days, the British Expeditionary Force had suffered almost 75,000 casualties and was falling back from the Somme, sparking alarm in Allied capitals that they would lose the war before the Americans could intervene in strength. Such was the speed and violence of the assault, which threatened to separate the British and French armies, that the Allies were forced to work more closely together, and on 3 April, General Ferdinand Foch was appointed Generalissimo, charged with the 'strategic direction of military operations' on the Western Front.[16]

Ludendorff was unconcerned about this sudden spasm of Allied cooperation and continued his offensive throughout April, trying to drag Allied reserves out of position before he delivered the *coup de grâce*. More than 90,000 prisoners and 1,300 guns had been taken, with the leading divisions having advanced more than sixty kilometres from their starting positions, but the British and French refused to surrender, showing a fierce unwillingness to give up any more ground. Within two weeks the German armies in the west had sustained 230,000 casualties and were beginning to slow down, struggling to cross the battle-scarred ground and showing a disturbing lack of aggression, with most of the elite storm divisions that had opened the attack worn down and replaced with those of lesser calibre. And with every week that passed, the Allies got closer to full-scale US participation, while the Germans could only call upon weak states that were incapable of providing much assistance.[17]

Germany desperately needed a fresh injection of manpower to carry things forward and exploit her gains. As Hindenburg noted, in a telegram to Arz, 'Great things have already been achieved, but the job must be thoroughly finished.'[18] Although four Habsburg divisions would eventually serve on the Western Front, Austria–Hungary went into the 1918 campaign in a state of almost total exhaustion. The armed forces were still over four million men strong, but replacements were becoming much harder to find. More than 70 per cent of all men eligible for the draft had already been called up. At least 780,000 men had been killed in action or died of wounds, 1.6 million more were prisoners of war, and half a million had been discharged because of debilitating wounds or disability. Former captives were beginning to return from Russia, but they would need to be quarantined, given leave, and then re-trained before they could be drafted into the ranks, which would undoubtedly be unpopular and was not likely to happen before the late summer. Moreover, their return was balanced out by the release of those who went back to Russia, most of whom had been performing invaluable work across the empire in industry and agriculture.[19]

With Germany focused on the Western Front, AOK at Baden considered its own strategy for the coming year. Thoughts inevitably turned towards Italy, and the desire to finish off its last remaining opponent. Conrad von Hötzendorf, whose army group held the Tyrol, had been calling for a major offensive in this sector for months. He wanted to advance between the Astico and Piave rivers, thrusting southeast towards the coast in what was in many ways a repeat of the *Strafexpedition* of 1916, but with the added combination of a supporting attack across the Piave towards Treviso.[20] This pincer movement, which he hoped would crush Italian forces in a vice, was certainly noteworthy, bearing all the hallmarks of the former Chief of the General Staff's notorious ambition, but there were several problems with it. The first was logistics. Behind Conrad's front lay only one railway, which ran through the Val Sugana, and there were few roads that could take the artillery that Austrian troops relied upon. The second problem was a lack of manpower to conduct two simultaneous attacks, which was pointed out by Boroević, now promoted to field marshal, whose two armies would have to cross the Piave. He was doubtful of the whole exercise and was not convinced that they could, or indeed should, mount an offensive. Peace would come, he insisted, and when it did, Austria must be in the best position with the strongest possible army.[21]

The condition of that army was already a source of great concern. Unrest and disorder were becoming more common; a mutiny had even broken out at the naval base at Cattaro, in Montenegro, with sailors raising the red flag of Bolshevism and calling for bread and peace. Boroević's men were already struggling to survive in Italy, and the lack of food in the newly conquered territories was a source of great disappointment. In a telegram to Arz on 17 February, Boroević had made it clear that the 'food situation' in his armies was 'extremely critical', with the growing likelihood of unrest and what he called 'a loosening of discipline'. A week later, he wired another gloomy summary. 'The troops are no longer being reassured by the constant promises that the rear is starving and that we have to hold out. Even more so since it is known that there are still vast areas within the monarchy with inexhaustible means of subsistence, and because the men know perfectly well that the supply for German troops is far better. The troops do not tolerate experiments; they must be properly cared for in order to be able to live and fight . . .'[22]

These concerns were certainly valid ones, but pressure on Baden to make an offensive was becoming stronger. Shortly before Operation *Michael* had begun, Hindenburg had asked for Austria–Hungary's support in the form of an offensive against Italy, which might help to shift Allied troops away from the Western Front. Arz agreed to do something by the end of May and told Hindenburg that he was consulting with both Conrad and Boroević on an attack that would reach the Adige river. This would entail the capture of Vicenza, Padua and Venice, resulting in the 'military collapse of Italy', which was just what the German Chief of Staff was hoping for.[23] In private, however, Arz was far from sanguine that much could be achieved. 'Although the enemy was not significantly superior in number, I was of the opinion – perhaps erroneously – that the imperial powers' forces were not sufficient to allow us to hope for the complete defeat of the enemy simultaneously in the western and south-western theatres of war. I therefore thought that, in fulfilling our task of tying down the enemy, I should content myself with defeating the enemy in the Grappa area and on the Piave and taking possession of the territory up to the Brenta river.'[24]

Arz may have doubted the likelihood of outright success, but he opted for Conrad's plan anyway; an acknowledgement of how much the old Field Marshal still shaped AOK's thinking. On 23 March, he announced what he called Operation *Radetzky*, a large-scale attack towards the southwest. 'The main thrust, strongly supported by artillery and mortars (mainly gas ammunition), will have to be made on both sides of the Brenta in order to . . . dismantle the Piave front. The aim of the operation is to reach the Bacchiglione [a river that ran through Padua].' Accordingly, Conrad finalized his operational plan and sent it off to Baden on 1 April. He would need thirty-one infantry and three cavalry divisions, which would almost double the current size of his army group. He understood that this might seem excessive, but the troops could be taken from the armies along the Piave, which would allow him to overwhelm his opponent and bring about the decisive battle.[25]

Arguments over who would get which divisions, and how many, continued throughout the spring, with AOK blanching at Conrad's enormous appetite. At the same time, Arz was beginning to reconsider whether the main assault should actually be conducted across the Piave rather than from the mountains. Boroević had remained a doughty opponent of Conrad's grand scheme for weeks, but he had finally agreed to draft his own plan, and argued that the most important attack had to come from his army group. 'Either one wishes to stage an attack from two fronts . . . in which case the necessary forces must not only be available, but also grouped accordingly. Or, if one lacks the strength, one must forgo the operation, since no one can be responsible for the defeat that would surely result from pursuing an attack with insufficient forces.' By late May, he was becoming even more explicit, warning that 'no one can take responsibility for starting an operation with insufficient material supplies and with undernourished and, for this reason, inefficient troops. If one does not wish to embark on a mission whose consequences could have an incalculable impact on the morale of the troops – the only possible outcome of the supply conditions already described to AOK – then the only option is to delay the start of operations until the troops are at least provisionally equipped and have sufficient nourishment to enable them to withstand the efforts required of them.'[26]

With both Conrad and Boroević claiming that they should undertake the main offensive – and, accordingly, be given the bulk of the reserves and artillery – a decision needed to be made. But none was. Neither Emperor Karl nor Arz could summon the character to make this choice, evidently thinking that if the attack was conducted along a wide enough front, it would break through somewhere and, with strategically placed reserves ready to move forward, could achieve something substantial. There would, therefore, be no decisive concentration either in the north or along the Piave. Conrad had twenty-three divisions, almost exactly what Boroević had, with no great superiority over the enemy anywhere, leaving both men dissatisfied.[27] Alfred Krauss, who had been involved in the plans for the attack, could only speak of what he called the 'certain peacetime ease' with which the operation was designed, 'with no acknowledgement of the terrible gravity of the situation'. The problem was that there was no uniformly accepted plan; 'instead each group of the army got its own way and led its own attack. Thus, there were serious attacks at Asiago, on the lower Piave and by Sixth Army against Montello, with inadequate means and without internal coherence.'[28]

Emperor Karl, Austria's beleaguered monarch, who should have been able to provide this coherence, found himself distracted by other pressing matters. He had become increasingly at odds with his Foreign Minister, Count Czernin, who had always trod a more cautious path in their search for peace, viewing Karl's impatience as something that needed careful management. But Czernin's own missteps were as much to blame for their deteriorating relationship. On 2 April, he had given a speech at the city council in Vienna, in which he discussed Brest-Litovsk and the failure to secure peace with the western powers. 'A little while before the offensive in the West was started,' he said, 'Clemenceau enquired of me whether I was prepared for negotiations and, if so, on what basis.' According to Czernin, he informed Clemenceau that the obstacle to an agreement was 'France's desire for Alsace-Lorraine', only to be told that 'no negotiations were possible on this basis. After that we had no further choice and the mighty battle broke out.'[29]

The French were quick to spot Czernin's admission. On 12 April, Clemenceau published the full text of Karl's letter that had been handed to Prince Sixtus on 24 March 1917, in which the Emperor acknowledged France's 'just claims' to Alsace–Lorraine. This diplomatic spat, which was followed several days later by Czernin's resignation, proved highly embarrassing for Karl, who could now be

accused of betraying the Central Powers. He wrote immediately to
Kaiser Wilhelm, insisting that he was loyal to the alliance and the war
effort, but this was received with cold formality and an invitation to
a conference at the Belgian resort town of Spa, the current location
of OHL, where he would have the opportunity of demonstrating his
commitment to their shared cause. He arrived on 12 May. 'The reception at Spa was fairly cold to begin with', he remembered. 'Kaiser
Wilhelm even wanted to give me a moral lesson at first, but that did
not go well for him . . .' The Kaiser made pointed remarks about the
two princes who had been involved in the affair. 'What an impression
it would make on his soldiers to learn that the brothers-in-law of the
Austrian Emperor, his ally, were fighting on the opposing side', he
said, suggesting that Karl bring the princes to a neutral country. Karl
responded that 'the two were by no means princes of my house and
that I therefore had no desire to interfere in their actions . . .'[30]

Germany's patience with her ally had run out. After the formalities
were over, Karl was presented with a draft agreement for the further
integration of the two empires. Austria was now being asked to shed
whatever remaining independence she still had, becoming a satellite
of a greater German Reich that would be completely under the control of the generals at OHL. There would be 'a close, long-term
political alliance to defend and secure the two empires', including a
'league of arms', the 'conclusion of a customs and economic alliance',
'uniformity in organisation, regulations and armament' in the armed
forces, and joint command and planning.[31] Karl agreed to the terms;
it was the only way, as he put it, 'to moderate the "furor teutonicus"
a little bit'.[32] He did, however, insist that the provisions would only
come into force once an agreement on the future status of Poland had
been reached – something that might never happen given the differing designs that Germany and Austria had in this region. This was a
clever move, effectively kicking the agreement into the long grass,
but it could not disguise the depressing reality of what Karl was up
against. Whatever transpired in the war, whether Germany broke the
Allies or not, Austria's position would be very different to what it
had been in 1914.

The domestic situation remained worrisome. Since becoming

Emperor, Karl had tried to implement various reforms to shore up the monarchy, but had only run into deadlock. Powerful groups in both halves of the empire were unhappy about any move towards 'constitutional democracy' and made it impossible for him to push through the policies he believed would be necessary in any future peace settlement with Britain and France.[33] Nor did he have any hope of returning the genie of self-determination to its bottle. The President of the United States, Woodrow Wilson, had already outlined his 'Fourteen Points' for a post-war settlement, including the evacuation of Romania, Serbia and Montenegro; the creation of an independent Polish state; and Point 10 – 'the freest opportunity for autonomous development' for the 'peoples of Austria–Hungary'.[34] This marked a dangerous moment in the Allied attitude towards the Habsburg Empire. At a meeting of the Supreme War Council on 28 May, Monsieur Pichon had been forthright. '[A]ll thought of a separate peace with Austria was over. We need trouble no more to "ménager" the Austrians, and President Wilson had apparently come to the same conclusion. Therefore the Allies should use every means to make difficulties for the Austrian Government. They should support the Slavs and non-Austrian or non-Magyar elements in the Empire.' Vienna was left in an unenviable bind. Either the monarchy would be broken up and splintered into a collection of independent states, or it would be subsumed within a larger conglomeration run from Berlin.[35]

The reorganization of the Italian Army, which Diaz and Badoglio had overseen, was complete by the spring of 1918. In a lengthy report to London on 11 April, the head of the British Military Mission, Brigadier-General Delme-Radcliffe, noted how food had been improved, leave had been increased, and extensive efforts were being made to produce 'a better quality of regimental officer', with more effective staff work. Although most senior commanders were satisfied that the men 'would fight well on the defensive', there were still questions over how they would behave in the attack, with an acknowledgement that more time was needed to intensify training and what Delme-Radcliffe called 'patriotic propaganda'. Nevertheless, he was impressed. 'The Italian Army, now, has gone a long way towards regaining confidence in itself. The broken units have been re-organised, re-equipped and re-armed; their material conditions as regards rations, etc., are better than before', he added. 'The rapidity with which the reorganisation has taken place and the heavy losses in materiel, etc., made good, is a legitimate source of pride to the country . . .'[36]

Whereas General Cadorna had utilized four armies, including Capello's enormous Second Army, which had been overwhelmed at Caporetto, General Diaz split his forces into seven commands, designed to be smaller and more flexible. These armies may have been weaker in numbers, but they were better prepared and now had access to significantly improved equipment. In 1915, an Italian regiment comprised 3,000 infantrymen and just two machine-guns. Three years later, regiments contained around 2,600 men and 81 officers, but had vastly upgraded firepower, with three machine-gun companies (a total of 36 weapons), three sections of 76 mm mortars, a flamethrower section, a 37 mm mountain gun detachment, and an assault platoon armed with large numbers of pistols, automatic rifles, bombs and grenades. Three million British gas masks, which offered excellent protection, were also distributed among front-line divisions.[37]

The infantry was not the only arm to undergo an impressive programme of investment. Significant attention was paid to both artillery and aviation. By May, there were 6,548 guns of all calibres in service. Admittedly, this was not as many as Cadorna had commanded at Caporetto (7,138), but these were all of recent construction, many were brand new, and when the reduction in the length of the front line was taken into consideration, it meant a noticeable increase in firepower. At the same time, the number of aircraft in service rose from 450 in March to 608 in April, and by June to 736, split into 15 fighter squadrons, a number bolstered by the presence of 100 Allied fighters. The Italian Army was now reaping the benefit of the vast industrial expansion that had taken place since May 1915, as Italy's munitions factories and industrial firms finally began to provide the quantities of weaponry, trench supplies and war machines that would allow it to enter 1918 with something approaching confidence and skill.[38]

This reorganization was completed not a moment too soon. With the fighting in France consuming ever larger numbers of divisions, it was inevitable that the Italian Front would be affected. Soon after Operation *Michael* had begun, Foch had withdrawn half of the British and French contingent, along with two Italian divisions (whose transfer had been agreed beforehand), which left Diaz more committed than ever to a cautious, defensive strategy. At a meeting of the Supreme War Council at Abbeville on 2 May, the question of extending Foch's authority over the Italian Front was discussed. Both Orlando and Diaz were wary about submitting to Paris and London, fearful of the consequences of losing their strategic independence at a crucial moment in the war, but they were so dependent on Allied support, including credit and regular deliveries of coal, wheat and steel, that it was difficult to refuse. It was agreed that Foch's 'powers of coordination' would now include Italy, and that the Western Front would extend 'from the North Sea to the Adriatic'.[39]

Diaz soon felt the pressure from these new arrangements. Writing on 7 May, Foch brought up the numerical inferiority of the Austro-Hungarian forces on the Italian Front and their hesitation, which he assessed as being evidence of poor morale, 'the internal situation with the monarchy, and doubts over the likely outcome of the German offensive'. He wanted Diaz to launch an attack towards enemy lines of communication in the Sugana Valley, possibly before the end of May or the beginning of June, but Diaz was evasive. 'I agree with you that the decision must naturally depend not only on having a clear and reciprocal benefit with respect to the general war situation,' he replied, 'but also on the possibility of an unexpected change in circumstances that could, at any given moment, transform an idea that currently seems to be opportune and beneficial into one that is less advisable.' By late May, Italian intelligence had come to a much less favourable estimate about Habsburg manpower and reported that there were as many as sixty-one enemy divisions in theatre, which clearly meant they still held a numerical advantage, with indications that AOK was preparing a major offensive along the Asiago sector. Accordingly, on 28 May, *Comando Supremo* requested two additional Allied divisions.[40]

Foch was a soldier as fierce and uncompromising as they came,

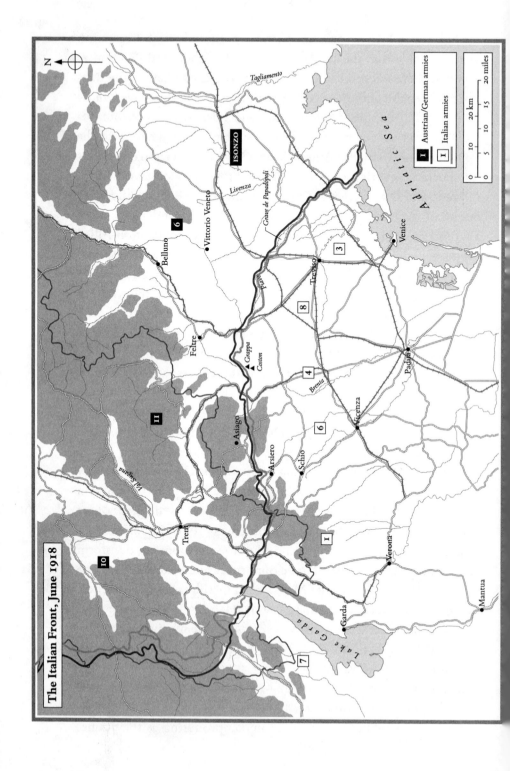

The Italian Front, June 1918

N

Tagliamento

ISONZO

Livenza

Grave de Papadopoli

Vittorio Veneto

Belluno

6

Feltre

Piave

▲ Grappa
Coston

8

Treviso

3

Venice

Adriatic Sea

II

Asiago

Arsiero

Schio

Brenta

4

6

Vicenza

Padua

Val Sugana

Trent

10

I

Verona

7

Lake Garda

Garda

Mantua

Austrian/German armies

Italian armies

0   5   10   15   20 miles
0   10   20 km

but he showed an unusual degree of diplomacy and tact when dealing with the Italian commander. He understood Diaz's concerns and tried to reassure him of his complete support. A renewed German offensive on the Chemin des Dames on 27 May had caused panic in the French capital, which only sharpened Foch's keenness to bring Diaz's armies into battle as soon as possible. In a letter on 12 June, he pondered on why there had been no Austrian attack, and whether this was connected to low morale, or maybe another reason. Perhaps it had all been part of a campaign of deception intended to keep the Allies guessing or even to make them send reinforcements from France? In any case, he believed that the best thing to do was to attack the Austrians now. 'We must act rapidly to take advantage of these hesitations and the moment when the Germans, having concentrated their reserves for a decisive effort in France, are unable to reinforce the Austro-Hungarian Army in Italy.'[41]

Still Diaz refused to move. He knew his army was a fragile creation, only now beginning to recover, and he did not want to risk it unnecessarily. He would not waste the lives of his men in sporadic, small-scale offensives, and wanted to build up enough reserves in a strong, centrally positioned body, furnished with sufficient motor vehicles and trucks to seal off any penetrations and then counter-attack. He had also prepared a sophisticated system of defence-in-depth, with extensive artillery support, that would allow his men to absorb any enemy thrust without collapsing, ensuring that there could never be a repeat of Caporetto. With that in mind, he held his nerve, believing that an offensive was imminent, and on the following day, 13 June, Austrian units attacked the Tonale Pass, about thirty miles northwest of Lake Garda. This was a diversionary operation launched by Conrad to pull Diaz's attention away from crucial sectors further east. It failed; one of the attacking *Kaiserjäger* battalions, composed mostly of Czechs, deserted, which left the Italians completely untroubled, their lines firmly held.[42]

Much more was expected from Conrad's main attack, on the Asiago Plateau, which began in the early hours of 15 June with a four-hour bombardment, interspersed with gas shelling. Conrad's army group had been given over 3,000 guns, about 40 per cent of the entire inventory, which meant there was one gun for every 11 metres of front – an unheard-of concentration of fire for a Habsburg offensive.[43] Unfortunately, the Italians had gained good intelligence on what was going to happen and commenced a programme of 'counter-preparation' shortly before the bombardment was due to begin. With Italian guns firing into the Austrian lines, forcing troops there to keep their heads down, severing telephone connections and hitting ammunition dumps, Habsburg officers had little choice but to carry on with their own programme and hope that it would still work. This soon produced an almighty artillery duel, with salvos being fired back and forth in the pre-dawn skies; an impressive enough spectacle, but one that left the Austrians wondering whether they were about to be attacked themselves. 'I still have a vivid memory of that day's duel between opposing artillery; soon the Italians had the upper hand, and one wondered who was actually preparing an attack', wrote an eyewitness, Colonel Maximilian Lauer.[44]

Spurred on by a typically Conrad-*esque* announcement urging them to push forward to the 'sunny plains of Italy', eight Habsburg divisions launched their attack at 7 a.m.[45] The air was thick with mist and choked with high explosive, gas and dust, which hindered aerial observation and left most battalions struggling to maintain direction in what rapidly became a confusing melee. Most of the attacks quickly went awry, either stopped in no-man's-land by long bursts of machine-gun fire, or quickly counter-attacked whenever they achieved a breakthrough. Two corps of Eleventh Army, which attacked south of Asiago, managed to take some trenches in the British sector, aided by the thick woodland, but soon found their offensive momentum draining away. 'Later, when the sun broke through the layer of fog, the artillery spotters were able to capture an almost devastating sight in their binoculars', recorded the historian of one of the attacking regiments. 'The infantry had been stopped without reaching their objectives. The enemy's machine-gun fire swept over the infantry, deprived of the help of their own artillery, and pinned them to the hard-won ground.' A counter-attack that afternoon restored most of the line and left the Austrian troops back in their own trenches, thoroughly demoralized. That evening Eleventh Army headquarters ordered its men to maintain their old positions and any gains they still held.[46]

With Eleventh Army's attack having failed, Austrian hopes now rested upon Boroević's offensive over the Piave. The general had gone to the village of Oderzo, about five miles from the river, and clambered up the church tower, field glasses in hand, to observe the attack. Covered by a huge wall of smoke and gas, the Army of the Isonzo had started crossing at 6 a.m., managing to secure a sizeable foothold on the lower Piave, at the furthest point going about four kilometres along an eight-kilometre front.[47] This was regarded at army headquarters as a significant achievement. The Piave was about 250 metres wide at its narrowest, strewn with obstacles and its waters surging with recent rainfall, with the attackers having to cope with long-range artillery fire and, once the skies cleared, persistent enemy aircraft. Little could be done about this aerial menace, which grew more pronounced as the battle continued. AOK had massed 'all available aerial forces' for the June offensive (395 fighters and almost 200 reconnaissance and ground-attack aircraft), but their machines were outnumbered and almost entirely outclassed by their opponents, who could rely upon state-of-the-art aircraft from overseas, including Sopwith Camels and SPADS, which were powerful and effective killing machines.[48]

As night fell, the Austrian High Command knew that the first day had gone against them. The preliminary bombardment had been an undoubtedly powerful spectacle, but its effect on deeply layered defences was disappointing. Moreover, Italian 'counter-preparation' had been demoralizing to infantry about to go over the top. 'During the crossing,' remembered one Habsburg soldier, 'the Italians aimed heavy artillery fire against us; this being directed by Italians from trenches which we thought would be deserted. The Italians had tricked us; their manoeuvre was, after the betrayal of our intentions by some Czech deserters, moving back into their trenches after the bombardment; thus avoiding heavy casualties . . . the water of the Piave was coloured pink with blood. It was only due to our strong reserves that we reached the other side of the river.'[49] Yet they had still gone forward, as one post-war account admitted, possessing the 'elan of 1914', with combat engineers and sappers working miracles to get their men over the river. One Austrian veteran remembered observing the construction of a pontoon bridge and how it continued despite heavy shellfire. 'We watch the spectacle with bated breath . . . shrapnel shells burst by the dozen over the river, erupting in foaming fountains. But the bridge grows and grows as more and more iron barges are pushed out by the foolhardy. Now and then there is a direct hit to one of the densely occupied pontoons; people plunge into the water, disappear with waving arms, reappear, desperately fight for their lives, and are pulled mercilessly into the depths by the weight of their equipment.'[50]

The challenges of crossing the Piave were magnified by the angry response of an opponent growing in strength and confidence, no longer cowed by the ghosts of Caporetto. General Diaz was pleased with the first day's fighting. He wrote to his wife, Sarah, the following day:

> Yesterday was one of those that count in the life of a man, such was the violence of the enemy attack, which for a moment, for lack of precise news, kept us in great uncertainty, while everything made one believe that we had to resist well to regain the upper hand. But the fragmentary news, which we received at the beginning and did not allow for a correct evaluation, was a torment for several hours. Things are clearing up well, the troops, even the most exhausted, are of high morale, our arrangements have been timely and opportune and now everything is stabilising. The enemy seems to be wearing down; certainly he will make new attacks and there will be further arduous tests, but we can see clearly that the first impetus has been broken and held back, very different from what happened in France.[51]

Holding on to the bridgeheads was now Boroević's primary concern. On the second day, after receiving news of Eleventh Army's lack of progress, he warned AOK that victory could only be won on the Piave, but that his army group was too weak to do so. 'The operation therefore must be renewed. I have instructed my armies that their main task is now to hold on to what they have already gained, even against the strongest counter-attacks, in order to avoid unnecessary casualties from trying to force the Piave.' The Austrian High Command was not willing to accept all of Boroević's conclusions, at least not yet, and during a long conversation with Alfred von Waldstätten, Deputy Chief of Staff, Karl ordered army reserves to be sent to Boroević, who would then renew the offensive towards Treviso. But this received a blunt response from the Croat. When he was told to push on, Boroević insisted that he must wait before trying again. He lacked medium artillery, trucks and bridging material. He could only secure his objectives if his requests for more equipment were met, and he cautioned AOK against ordering attacks prematurely with insufficient forces.[52]

Heavy rain fell on 16 and 17 June, causing the Piave to rise still further and imperil the hold on the western bank. Austrian divisions tried to make progress, but found their enemy reinforced and fresh, while their own units were being rapidly exhausted. Telephone lines were severed, bridges came under intensive shellfire, and pontoons were swamped by columns of rising water. 'It was hard to believe what could be seen there', noted one Czech soldier as he approached the assembly points from where troops would cross. 'Dismembered, mutilated bodies of men and animals, torn limbs hanging from tree stumps, crushed skulls, open bloody stomachs with intestines flowing out – the horror was beyond the worst nightmare . . . The place was hell. The men found it difficult to navigate their carts through the sea of corpses and limbs. Getting into position . . . was a bloody eternity.'[53]

On the morning of 18 June, it was found that all the bridges had been washed away in the night, leaving Habsburg troops without hope of food or relief. With the Austrian attack stalled, Diaz moved quickly to counter-attack, realizing that now was the moment to strike. Reinforcements were already entering the lines and the weather was beginning to clear. Italian troops went forward on the morning of 19 June, their morale electrified by the knowledge that the Austrian challenge was fading. Fighting was stubborn up and down the front. Habsburg forces, with their backs to the raging river, fought with a kind of desperate fury, as if they knew that this might be their last battle. Losses were catastrophic. In just eleven days of fighting, Austrian units sustained 142,500 casualties, including over 11,000 killed in action; a total that was even greater than comparable figures for the hellish Eleventh Battle of the Isonzo, which had lasted twice as long. An Austrian veteran, summarizing their terrible experience, could only list the devastation caused: 'Endless columns of wounded . . . 40% casualties, 160th Infantry annihilated, colonel wounded, six majors captured, 2nd *Feldjäger* destroyed, 7th Infantry massacred, 19th Infantry partly lost and the Italians back on the embankment. We are retreating to the reserve lines.'[54]

On 19 June, the day of Diaz's counter-attack, the Emperor, accompanied by a stony-faced General Arz, arrived at Spilimbergo for an audience with Boroević. The nature of the problem was swiftly diagnosed. Getting ammunition and reinforcements over the river under fire was 'slow and laborious', while the enemy could bring up reserves much quicker.[55] Boroević was unrepentant, arguing that they should have never attempted it and Conrad had got it wrong.

'Did I defend myself against this operation with all my might, jeopardising my position by saying that they would not want to take the bull by the horns? It was all in vain!'

'But Conrad wanted it' was all Karl could say.

Boroević then asked for authorization to evacuate the bridgehead and retreat across the Piave. The Emperor did not want to do it, thinking of all the men who had been killed or wounded trying to cross the river, but he eventually gave in with a nod of his head. Boroević then went further. The Emperor *must* go back to Vienna, he pleaded, and convene a Council of Ministers. He *must* place before them the 'bleak material situation' facing the empire: the food shortages, the lack of reserves and weaponry, the problems with industrial production. 'The governments of the two halves of the empire could no longer ignore these mounting dangers.' Karl just shook his head. He could not do it.[56]

22.   'The off-chance of something good'

On 23 June, as news began to spread of Italy's great victory on the Piave, the French Prime Minister, Georges Clemenceau, despatched sealed instructions to the new commander of *l'armée d'Orient*, General Louis Franchet d'Espèrey. With the fighting on the Western Front still delicately balanced, a soldier of General Guillaumat's calibre could not be left in what was considered an inconsequential backwater, and so he was recalled to France, leaving a vacancy in Salonika. Clemenceau had already lined up the perfect replacement. Although he had recently been removed from his position as head of France's Northern Army Group, Franchet d'Espèrey was an experienced general, straightforward and industrious, willing to take risks where necessary and drive his men on without mercy if he thought there might be an advantage worth pursuing. 'A soldier at heart,' his biographer wrote, 'Franchet d'Espèrey became known both for his appearance and his physique, and those who met him saw a strong and driven man. He was of average height and well built, with a wide and lively head. His gaze was sharp and direct, and he had a ruddy complexion with a moustache trimmed close to his upper lip and hair flat on the top. He stood straight, his legs planted firmly on the ground.'[1]

Clemenceau had always been sceptical of the value of France's efforts in Salonika. As Franchet d'Espèrey later noted, the Prime Minister 'never liked the east', but 'as a great Frenchman', he appreciated the important interests that were at stake.[2] With the battle in France showing no signs of dying down, Clemenceau was naturally keen to maintain as much pressure on the enemy as possible and informed his new commander that it 'behoves the Allied Armies in the outer theatres and especially on the Eastern Front to assume a definitely aggressive attitude'. The current situation in Macedonia was 'particularly favourable' for such activity. Morale within the

Bulgarian Army was known to be poor and had only worsened as Germany had pulled out her forces for the great offensive in the west, which meant that the Allies now had the freedom to act and must do so without delay. But Clemenceau remained cautious, explaining that they should mount a series of 'local offensives . . . spread out over a period of time', which would gradually increase in scope until the enemy's defences were dislocated enough to trigger a 'general offensive' before the autumn. 'The object to be aimed at in the offensive action of the Allied Armies of the East must be to break through the Bulgarian system of defence, in order to force the enemy to make an important withdrawal, such as will open to the Serbian and Greek Armies access to their lost territories.'[3]

As Clemenceau's directive was making its way to Salonika, Franchet d'Espèrey had the chance to familiarize himself with the Macedonian Front, taking long horse rides up to the forward zones, along stony tracks, across scrubland and down forest tracks, where he met the officers and men of his disparate expeditionary force. The total strength of the Allied contingent, including the Greeks, had now risen to 543,000 men, plus 113,000 in the rear services, with 1,068 field guns and 472 heavy pieces. They were faced by around 385,000 soldiers, mostly Bulgarian, but they were occupying strong defensive positions that helped to mask this numerical inferiority.[4] Moreover, as Guillaumat had done before him, Franchet d'Espèrey soon realized that this nominal superiority was deceptive. General Milne was 'very correct and very well-mannered', but his four divisions were 'eaten away by malaria' and lacked rest and reinforcement. Although he was impressed by those volunteers who had joined Venizelos's Army of National Defence (the Archipelago, Crete and Seres Divisions), he was less keen on the other newly formed Greek units, which contained 'many undesirables' and were of only 'questionable' value.[5]

The general would not receive Clemenceau's note until 2 July, by which time he had come to a different set of conclusions about what needed to be done. 'In France, the importance of the east is not understood', he told a friend soon after his arrival. He instinctively felt that the war could not be won on the Western Front, at least in the foreseeable future, but in the Balkans 'there was no second line'.

'The Austrians are far from excellent, the Bulgarians are disgruntled. It is here that we could quickly have the Austrians on the back foot. A minimum level of resources is still required.'[6] He had already taken note of the attack on the Skra di Legen, a heavily defended hillock that jutted out of the Bulgarian lines about twenty miles west of Lake Dojran. On 30 May, men of the Archipelago and Crete Divisions had gone over the top, taking advantage of a heavy artillery bombardment to seize the position and capture almost 2,000 prisoners. The attack made the newspapers in Athens and caused Venizelos's reputation to soar, showing that under the right circumstances, with well-prepared and motivated infantry, supported by enough artillery, the Bulgarian trench lines could be broken.[7]

Detailed plans had already been drawn up for a combined Franco-Serbian attack on Dobro Pole, part of the chain of hills that included the peak at Kajmakcalan and which divided the Bulgarian lines between the Crna and Vardar rivers. At 1,800 metres, Dobro Pole was a significant obstacle, but because it was not as formidable as the peaks on either side (at Sokol and Veternik), it might offer a way through if its defences could be captured. 'The first enemy position follows the military crest and is made up of multiple lines of trenches located 50, 100 and 200 metres away, with criss-crossing barbed wire, rallying points, machine-gun nests and passive shelters for reserves, all connected by small passageways. A significant proportion of this arrangement is well concealed and cannot be seen from the ground at a long-distance, particularly in the area of Kravica and Veternik, because of how the wooded terrain is broken up.' But were the attackers to break the line here, they 'would push any enemy danger away from this part of the front' and provide a 'favourable base for a potentially larger scale offensive' out to the north, moving on to Skopje and crossing the Vardar.[8]

Franchet d'Espèrey quickly made up his mind to attack in this sector. On 30 June, he travelled to the Serbian headquarters at Yelak, a 5,500-foot-high 'clearing in a forest of fir-trees', eighty-five miles northwest of Salonika.[9] There he had a long conversation with Crown Prince Alexander and the Chief of the General Staff, *Voivode* Mišić, revealing that an offensive would be launched by the French and Serbs along the line Dobro Pole–Veternik, with supporting operations by the Greeks and the British further east. It would not be a local action, but a decisive attack to break the front and threaten the enemy's lines of communication. Estimating that it would take two months to get everything ready, he wanted the attack to take place no later than 15 September, otherwise they ran the risk of not being able to get going before the arrival of cold weather. Preparations would have to begin immediately. He needed the Serbs to spearhead the assault, which was why he was putting two French divisions under their control for the forthcoming operation. When he said this, the Crown Prince got up without a word, shook his hand and smiled warmly. 'The agreement was complete.'[10]

No sooner had Franchet d'Espèrey left Yelak than he was handed the directive from Clemenceau that instructed him to mount nothing more than 'local offensives'. Determined not to be swayed from his vision, the general only reported back to the War Ministry on 13 July, by which time a predictable row had erupted at Versailles over Clemenceau's plans for Macedonia. At a meeting of the Supreme War Council on 3 July, Lloyd George had scolded Clemenceau for appointing Franchet d'Espèrey without consultation and for ignoring the Allied governments on the orders he had been issued with, which seemed to indicate that their strategy had changed. 'He quite agreed', said Lloyd George, 'that great freedom of action must be given to the local commanders, and it was quite impossible to decide at Versailles on the execution of any operations. But the orders in question indicated a complete change in the Allied attitude in the Balkans. They had decided on a defensive attitude, whereas these instructions now laid down that a great offensive must be undertaken.' While Lloyd George was not prepared to say what should be done instead, he insisted that before he could accept this change of plan, they must consider the question further and 'have the advice of the military representatives'.[11]

These frustrations were nothing new. With fighting on the Western Front absorbing most of their energies, Allied leaders found their tempers frayed and their patience exhausted, and it did not take much for old suspicions to resurface. Matters would be papered over, reports written and consultations made, while Clemenceau promised that Allied governments would be included in any future decisions on command appointments. These gestures were enough to restore harmony, at least for the time being, even if the British remained to be convinced that an offensive policy should be adopted. On 15 July, the British representative on the Supreme War Council, Major-General Charles Sackville-West, posed a series of eleven questions about the forthcoming operation, including what the frontage of the attack would be, what its objectives were, how many forces would be employed, what works would need to be completed beforehand (such as the construction of railways or roads), what was the plan of attack, what were the expected losses, and what reasons they had to believe that the Bulgarian Army would suffer a catastrophic defeat.[12]

General Guillaumat, who had now arrived back in France, was able to fill in some of these blanks, albeit without any certainty on the exact location of the attack or how it would be conducted, those matters being the responsibility of the Commander-in-Chief. He was, nevertheless, confident that the front line could be broken relatively easily. 'It can also be observed that operations in Macedonia are different from those on the Western Front. The enemy emplacements are spread out without much depth (generally two defensive lines separated by two or three kilometres). The terrain has largely not been bombarded. Once the enemy's defensive front is breached, primarily through the support of the British and French forces, it can be expected that the operations will take on the typical nature of war in the Balkans.' The Serbian and Greek Armies, he added, were 'well suited' to this kind of mountain warfare and could be relied upon to exploit any success with great skill. With the qualitative and numerical superiority of the Allied forces, 'the question of the likelihood of an offensive succeeding does not even need to be asked'.[13]

Guillaumat's positive assessment was mirrored by the commander of the British contingent in Salonika, General Milne, who wrote to the War Office on 22 July. He noted that the assumptions previously guiding Allied strategy in Macedonia – that wide-ranging offensive operations were impossible until the situation in France changed – no longer applied. 'Now that the Bulgarians are beginning to get war weary, the Austrians are in difficulties in Italy and the Germans more than held up in France, it appears that the time may be approaching when this army should be able to take action in this theatre possibly with far reaching results, and that we should stand ready to do so when the necessity arises.' Milne did not think that any major operation should be launched around Lake Dojran, where the enemy positions were 'naturally strong, well fortified, and well supplied with artillery', but along the Serbian positions out to the west. If they were able to attack in this sector, 'it must be carried out with determination and sufficient means to achieve a strategical result as I am fairly certain that once [the] Bulgarian line is turned or broken their army would begin to disintegrate . . .'[14]

By late July, Franchet d'Espèrey had still not received any further word from Paris, which left him unhappy, more convinced than ever that a decisive opportunity was there to be taken. Impatient, he decided to pre-empt any forthcoming instructions by writing to Milne on 24 July and confirming that an assault would likely take place 'at the beginning of the last fortnight in September', and that Milne's task would be to attack the Bulgarian First Army and deprive it of 'all freedom of manoeuvre'.[15] The following day, Milne wrote again to the War Office, warning them that he would need reinforcements and more ammunition, and 'I should be glad to know how I stand as regards this'. The Chief of the Imperial General Staff in London, Sir Henry Wilson, who had replaced Robertson in February, could only offer the usual equivocation. 'I cannot hold out any hope that reinforcements and ammunition in excess of the usual allotment will be available in existing circumstances', and Milne should guard against any failure that would 'encourage [the] Bulgarians and relieve [the] Germans of a considerable source of anxiety'. Any offensive, he believed, should only take place 'when Germany cannot safely detach troops from the Western front', which would not happen in September, and possibly not before the spring of 1919.[16]

Wilson's scepticism was certainly not unique. Years of false starts and frustration had produced a caustic, cynical attitude among many senior British officers towards anything connected with the Balkans. But with the situation in France improving and the imminent danger of a German breakthrough receding, opposition to Franchet d'Espèrey's plans began to diminish. The matter was considered at a meeting of military representatives of the Supreme War Council on 3 August, where, after the usual tussles, it was agreed to 'push on with all speed the preparations for an offensive in Macedonia on the basis contemplated', with Franchet d'Espèrey free to decide upon its exact timing. Sackville-West, who had attended on behalf of the British Government, had only signed the resolution (which would be sent off to London for approval) on the understanding that an offensive was necessary to sustain the morale of the Greeks and that it would not require any greater resources than were currently available.[17]

It would be another month before full agreement was secured to mount the offensive. It took an appearance by Guillaumat, who briefed the War Cabinet in person and impressed the British members with his lucidity and grasp of detail; 'a French General who was thoroughly acquainted with the facts' was Lloyd George's verdict. After discussion with his chief aides, the British Prime Minister decided that they must go ahead and approve what their military representatives had already recommended. So, after more than fifteen months of inactivity, the Salonika force would once again go into action with an attack all along the line; the French and Serbs mounting the main assault at Dobro Pole, with the British and Greeks in support. Even Wilson, who remained doubtful, admitted that the proposal was enticing for three main reasons: 'to give the Bulgars a good tap', to 'put the Greek Army on its feet', and 'thereby to release a certain number of French and English troops, all with the off-chance of something good'.[18]

Coming to an agreement on a new offensive in Macedonia had been a tortuous process, and so it would prove in Italy. There had been loud cheers in Parliament after the Battle of the Piave, when the Prime Minister, Orlando, had saluted the army and its chief, 'who with unforgettably heroic work, had ensured the great fortune of the country'. The realization that their army had fought and won sent a sudden, joyous thrill of relief around the country, even if General

Diaz was quick to temper expectations of a swift collapse in enemy resistance. His armies had sustained almost 85,000 casualties, markedly fewer than their opponents, but even so a heavy burden on an Army and a nation that were still recovering from the near-death experience of Caporetto. In a letter to the Prime Minister, he had warned about advancing beyond the Piave, which would be a 'grave error', involving 'an injurious extension of our front with the serious obstacle of the river at our back'.[19]

Crossing the Piave without adequate preparation was one thing, staying put for the remainder of the year was quite another – and victory did not ease the pressure on Diaz. As early as 27 June, Foch had urged him to take advantage of enemy disorganization and mount an offensive, noting that even a limited push forward might yield significant results, particularly on the Asiago. This would become a familiar refrain as Foch continued to badger the Italian Chief of Staff throughout the summer, imploring him to do *something* while the enemy was unlikely to get much help from the German Army in the west. On 17 July, Foch sent another letter, in which he thanked Diaz for lending him thousands of Italian labourers (who proved extremely valuable behind the lines) and asked whether they might remain in France for longer. Moreover, this should not prevent the Italian commander from 'pursuing your offensive plans, in particular between the Piave and Astico'. With the current situation becoming more favourable by the day, Foch strongly recommended attacking.[20]

Diaz's caution, so noticeable when compared with his predecessor, was again evident in a long letter to Foch on 30 July. While he fully agreed on the kinds of operations the Italians should mount, including a 'strong push' on the Asiago, which would help to consolidate their recent gains, he would need at least twenty days to prepare. He then included a long list of requirements – tons of gas, thousands of artillery shells, even tanks – while complaining about his lack of reinforcements ('barely sufficient for two to three months'), which had forced him to look everywhere for spare manpower. 'As I have told you in the general interest of all allies and of the common cause, nothing would pain me more than having to renounce or limit an offensive programme that you yourself recognised as appropriate and on which you rightly insist in your last letter of the 17th of the current month, by telling me that current conditions imperiously command an attack. This I recognise as perfectly right; but precisely for this reason, it would be very serious not to maintain the efficiency of the Army which has the specific task of operating.'[21]

Plans for an offensive were gradually refined over the summer, albeit without a great sense of urgency. The Italian Government was itself split over what policy to adopt. There were those who found Diaz's caution disappointing – such as Baron Sonnino, who always emphasized Italy's dependence on her allies and the need for battlefield success to underwrite any post-war gains – but the Cabinet also included more pessimistic voices, such as the Interior Minister, Francesco Nitti, who was acutely conscious of the state of fatigue and weariness within the country and was opposed to further offensives.[22] As for the Prime Minister, he was a frequent visitor to Diaz at *Comando Supremo*, where the two men spent hours discussing Italy's situation. Both knew that whatever path they took, much would depend upon the decisions made at the Supreme War Council. Italy had now outsourced much of her strategy to Versailles and would have to fit into plans she had little or no part in making. Orlando understood this more than most. He had never forgotten the first meetings with his Allied counterparts at Rapallo in the dark days after Caporetto, where he had been forced to wait outside 'like a servant', as he put it, while others decided his fate.[23]

There was a settled belief within the Italian High Command, which was also shared at the Supreme War Council, that the final offensive would take place on the Western Front during the spring of 1919. On 16 August, Diaz's Sub-Chief of Staff, Badoglio, completed a memorandum on future plans, which concluded that the enemy was 'not so shaken, nor of such poor quality', as was believed in French circles, including in Foch's headquarters. Given the possibility of a sudden enemy attack, with German reinforcements pouring into Italy and then executing a second Caporetto, they should remain vigilant and continue to plan for an offensive, but he also believed that this should only be launched if three conditions were fulfilled:

the gathering of sufficient forces, the transfer of at least ten Allied divisions from France to Italy ('in the likely event of a powerful Austro-German reaction'), and the simultaneous execution of a 'vigorous' attack on the Western Front.[24]

Diaz shared Badoglio's reservations, and in late August authored his own paper, which emphasized how Austria's armies were not yet on the verge of disintegration. 'The Austrian military body has a solid backbone that neither defeats, deprivations, nor nationality struggles have yet significantly weakened; the morale of the troops is high, the nutrition, although not abundant, is however sufficient to replenish the physical energies of the soldier, the clothing and footwear are excellent . . . And besides, I repeat, the rumour of the Austrian Army in dissolution has been circulating more than three years, and the Austrian soldier continues, nevertheless, to fight stubbornly, as the allies who fight in Italy on our side know . . .' Diaz estimated that the enemy now had a superiority of at least 140 battalions, and he was not minded to risk his own forces unless he faced a dramatic change in the situation, such as a notable reduction in Austrian manpower or a catastrophic defeat of the German Army in France. Even though he had previously talked about an offensive on the Asiago, he had now cooled on this and believed that it would only produce costly and attritional Carso-like fighting, preferring instead an attack across the Piave. He was, nevertheless, insistent that given the limitations of his reserves, the Italian Army should only be committed to battle when decisive results, such as the complete destruction of the Habsburg Army, could be confidently expected.[25]

Frustration with Diaz only increased as the summer wore on and the Allied position on the Western Front continued to improve. Sir Henry Wilson paid a visit to the Italian Front and quickly detected the lack of confidence at *Comando Supremo*. 'Diaz wanted to know what I would do if the Boches sent a number of divisions down to attack him', recalled Wilson, who shrugged his shoulders and said that the Allies could probably send three or four divisions from France, but it was, of course, not up to him to decide. 'He then spoke quite frankly about Foch', Wilson added. 'He appeared to be afraid of Foch and wanted me to back him up in his request for reinforcements, coal, tanks, gas shells, etc . . . It is quite clear that neither he nor Badoglio like nor admire Foch.'[26] Diaz would surely have baulked at Wilson's unflattering portrait and said, in his calm and measured way, that he had good reasons for prudence. 'Diaz, with a rational evaluation of problems and objectives very rare in the Italian ruling class since the proclamation of the Kingdom of Italy, always worried about the congruence between objectives and available power, between ambitions and possibilities', noted one of his biographers. He also avoided – 'as was the Italian habit – irrational solutions to rational problems and therefore he was prudent after June 1918, and would still be there when the war was over . . .'[27]

Peace may have been signed with the Bolsheviks, but German troops continued to advance deep into what had once been the Eastern Front, intent on securing the glittering prizes that lay before them: foodstuffs, oil, iron ore, manganese and coal. But with the bulk of Germany's armies deployed on the Western Front, any large-scale expropriation of these resources would have to wait. OHL's garrison in the east, amounting to about a million men after Brest-Litovsk, was not of the best quality. It was mainly composed of 'older reservists and Home Guardsmen', with even reluctant Poles and Alsatians being pressed into service, and they lacked the aggression and drive of Germany's best soldiers, often becoming susceptible to the Bolshevik propaganda that was directed at them.[28] Ludendorff had already addressed this point in a letter to the Chancellor, Georg von Hertling, on 9 June, in which he admitted that OHL needed assistance, whether from Finland, Ukraine or Georgia, to achieve its aims in the east:

> In view of our shortage of man-power we shall have to make further calls on our divisions there. They are strong enough to perform their function of an army of occupation, but they will not be adequate if the position in the east gets worse. The ambiguous attitude of the Soviet Government compels us in any case to look round for additional allies . . . The Ukraine has not yet succeeded in forming an army. We need the Ukraine, both for supplies of food and raw

material. We are thus justified from the military point of view in using troops there. Otherwise it would be a mistake. As in Finland, Georgia offers us a chance of multiplying our resources with weak forces. We must organise the Georgian army there.

Ludendorff was also furious at the 'dishonest agitation' from the Bolsheviks, who refused to be cowed by German military prowess. 'As soon as it is in a position to do so the Soviet Government begins to adopt the same attitude towards us as it did at the time of the first negotiations at Brest. It procrastinates in all matters which are important to us and works against us wherever it can.' This had become so frustrating that he even considered getting in touch with 'the more monarchist groups of the right' – presumably Alekseev's Volunteers – and helping them to fight Lenin.[29]

Ludendorff was not the only one thinking of toppling the Bolsheviks. Max Hoffmann had long been of the opinion that they must 'form another Russian Government', which would then be offered better terms than Brest-Litovsk in order for a new alliance to be struck.[30] Germany's Ambassador to the Bolsheviks, Count von Mirbach, thought this would not be necessary and was already prophesying the imminent end of Lenin's rule. 'Quite apart from the fact that Bolshevism would definitely soon, of its own accord, fall a victim to the process of internal disintegration which is devouring it, there are all too many elements working tirelessly to hurry its end as much as possible', he reported in late June. If the Germans accepted that Russia's new regime would soon collapse, then they should 'ensure that we are in a position to fill the vacuum which will result from its disappearance with a regime which would be favourable to *our* designs and interests', possibly from 'monarchists' or those so-called 'moderates from the right wing, Octobrists and Kadets', with support from influential industrial and banking figures.[31]

Lenin had no intention of going anywhere. Having shifted the seat of government to Moscow, which was far less vulnerable to any German advance, the Bolshevik leader was prepared to do whatever it took to safeguard the revolution, and ordered a ferocious round of bloodletting, including the murder of the imperial family. The former Tsar had been transported, with his wife and children, firstly to Tobolsk in western Siberia, and then, in April 1918, to Ekaterinburg in the Urals, an industrial city and Bolshevik stronghold where they were placed under guard in the house of a local engineer named Nicholas Ipatiev. Here there would be no communication with the outside world, no letters and few comforts. The family remained close, the girls sewing clothes, playing games or looking after their brother, who remained sickly, with Nicholas and Alexandra drawing strength from their faith and the dwindling hope that they would be allowed to seek refuge abroad. But the Bolsheviks had no intention of letting the Romanovs escape. Trotsky had suggested that Nicholas should be tried for his crimes, but Lenin was not so keen. No direct orders for the liquidation of the imperial family were ever found, but his visceral hatred for the Romanovs, whom he called 'monarchist filth', was well known. It was only in mid-July, when anti-Bolshevik forces were advancing on Ekaterinburg, that a final decision was made. The family were woken before dawn on 18 July, led down into the cellar, and then murdered in a volley of rifle and pistol fire.[32]

The Romanovs were certainly the most notorious victims of the Bolsheviks, but thousands of other families would be swept up in the orgy of violence and retribution that was unleashed in the summer of 1918. Upwards of 15,000 people would be killed in July and August alone, with many more dispossessed, in what became known as the 'Red Terror'.[33] With the Volunteer Army under General Denikin re-forming to mount another campaign in the Kuban, and the Czech Legion turning against the Bolsheviks as tensions mounted along the Trans-Siberian Railway, opposition to the new regime in Moscow was hardening. The city of Samara in the Volga had been occupied by White forces, and a rival government ('The Committee of Members of the Constituent Assembly') was founded that threatened to become a focal point for resistance. Lenin reacted in the only way he knew how. When several districts in Penza, 300 miles southeast of Moscow, dared to revolt, he ordered his local henchmen to 'pitilessly suppress' and make an example of the insurrectionists. They were to hang *no fewer than one hundred* known kulaks [peasant landowners], rich men, bloodsuckers'. Their grain was to be seized and hostages taken. 'Do it in such a fashion that for hundreds of kilometres around the people might see, tremble, know, shout: *they are strangling* and will strangle to death the bloodsucking kulaks.'[34]

The chaos that reigned across most of central Russia, as well as the newly independent state of Ukraine, threatened to derail OHL's dreams for a great empire in the east, 'a vast parade ground' that would, as Hindenburg put it, allow him enough space to manoeuvre in any future war.[35] The Ukrainian Rada had been overthrown on 27 April after OHL had become frustrated with the lack of cooperation it was receiving from the government. The installation of a former adjutant to the Tsar, General Pavlo Skoropadsky, as leader or *Hetman* of Ukraine had been intended to restore a measure of stability, but it did little good. By the end of June, only 130,000 tons of grain had been delivered to the Central Powers (mostly to Vienna), a fraction of the million tons that had been promised during the negotiations at Brest-Litovsk. Even more galling was the urgent need for Germany to send coal to Ukraine to keep the railways running, as well as the ongoing financial burden of propping up the Ukrainian state, which amounted to around 125 million Reichsmarks per month, plus over a billion Reichsmarks in loans that would never be repaid.[36]

With Ukraine ravaged by war, hunger and despair, OHL was forced to resort to increasingly desperate measures to draw resources from the land, which began to turn the sullen cooperation of the peasantry into outright hostility. Field Marshal Hermann von Eichhorn, commander of German forces in Ukraine, was murdered in Kiev on 30 July, just three weeks after Count von Mirbach had also been killed. Both men died at the hands of Socialist Revolutionaries who were opposed to the Treaty of Brest-Litovsk and wanted to throw off the German occupation at all costs. These killings were a clear indication of the dangers Germany was facing if she continued to occupy large parts of the former Tsarist empire without either broad popular support or the number of troops that permanent occupation would require. But the alternative, packing up and leaving, was hardly encouraging either, and Count Johann Forgách, the Austro-Hungarian Ambassador in Kiev, would soon warn Vienna that 'the same conditions would prevail in Ukraine as prevail in the rest of Russia' were the Austrians to go home. 'The first explosion of the powder keg we are sitting on would likely be very violent and bloody as the anarchistic elements, painstakingly disciplined by our troops, would gain the upper hand . . . As soon as our troops leave the country, any economic exploitation of Ukraine will become completely impossible.'[37]

Everyone knew that the future of these lands would depend upon the result of Germany's campaign on the Western Front. It had all seemed so promising in late May and early June, with German troops just forty miles from Paris, but further attempts to push on gradually ran out of steam over the following six weeks, flaring out with a last, dying gasp at the Second Battle of the Marne in mid-July. The defenders were now able to predict Ludendorff's moves with startling accuracy, having broken OHL's wireless codes and adapted to the tactics that had been so successfully employed since Riga and Caporetto. Another push had been launched over the Marne river on 15 July, only for a massive Franco-American counter-offensive to break through the German defences and snatch the initiative away from OHL three days later. Ludendorff had been comprehensively outfought, and lapsed into alternating states of depression and confidence, inertia and hyperactivity. He was 'much shattered, very sad', wrote a staff officer in late July. 'Five times I have had to move troops back during the war,' Ludendorff told Hertling, 'but in the end I beat the enemy. Why shouldn't this happen a sixth time?' A week later, he was in a 'completely inert mood', sunk in his chair, staring into the distance, before regaining his composure and telephoning his subordinates to order the movement of even the smallest units.[38]

Austrian High Command in Baden knew little of this, preoccupied as it was with the increasingly hopeless task of keeping its own armies in the field. A fortnight before the counter-attack on the Marne, a meeting of senior officials had taken place to mull over a possible new offensive against Italy. Of Austria–Hungary's 82 divisions, 60 were now on the Italian Front, with the rest either in Galicia, Romania or Albania. With some shuffling of units, it might be possible to concentrate around 30 divisions for a new offensive, but this depended upon their condition, how many guns and mortars they possessed, what their food situation was like, and so on. As for the likelihood of an enemy attack, Boroević accurately assessed the feelings of hesitation, doubt even, that settled in General Diaz's mind after the Battle of the Piave. In a detailed report that reached Baden on 20 July, he estimated that even though his army group was outnumbered (he was facing 39 divisions to his 25 infantry and four cavalry divisions, many of which were at half-strength), Diaz would not make any rash moves forward, at least for the time being, firstly because of the need to wait until the situation in the west became clearer, and secondly because the fighting spirit of the Habsburg troops remained strong. Diaz knew that he was not yet facing a 'defeated opponent'.[39]

The Imperial and Royal Army may have fought with stubbornness on the Piave, but its condition steadily deteriorated throughout the summer. More and more men were taking the chance to desert, while the twin dangers of malnutrition and disease caused ever-growing numbers to join the sick roll, which often reached 800 men per day. Even Conrad von Hötzendorf, who was dismissed in mid-July as part of the inevitable reckoning following the battle, realized the end was near, telling Karl that 'the troops will hold their positions, but an offensive is no longer possible'.[40] An assessment compiled by the Army of the Isonzo also warned about the stark dangers of national disintegration. While instances of poor feeling between the nationalities of the empire were not particularly unusual, the army was less able to keep a lid on the simmering discontent than ever before. 'The firm cohesion of the army, the good active officer corps is no more', it read. 'All the reserve officers and also the crew have become politicised. All the destructive actions at the front, betrayal, defection from hunger or national incitement are consequences of the situation within the state. The army is still doing its duty. But things are bound to get worse and worse if order is not brought about in every direction within the state.'[41]

The moment for achieving 'sound order' within the Habsburg Empire had now passed. Karl's efforts to secure peace, either a separate agreement with the Entente or a general settlement across all the belligerents, had got nowhere, and events were now moving too quickly to apply the brakes. In late June, the French Government had formally recognized the Czechoslovak National Council 'as a supreme organ representing all interests of the nation and as a foundation of the future Czecho-Slovak government', in a move that appalled Vienna.[42] This council had been founded in Paris in 1916 as a government-in-exile that agitated for an independent Czech and Slovak state, something that now looked to be an inevitability. Karl fared no better with his attempts to restructure the empire; with every move, he encountered obstruction or more radical demands for reform that could not be granted. He lacked the authoritarian impulse that came so easily to the other crowned heads of Europe, and having already rejected the idea that he should rule by decree, he could only propose policies, not compel their adoption by the parliaments in Vienna and Budapest.[43]

Resistance to political reform could be found in most parts of the Dual Monarchy, but it was in Hungary where its most fervent opponents resided. Count Tisza, the formidable Prime Minister, had resigned in May 1917 over a disagreement about the introduction of greater voting rights in the Hungarian half of the empire, to match those in Austria, which Karl had seen as an important first step in his reform programme. Having been crowned King of Hungary in Budapest, where he had taken a solemn coronation oath to maintain the integrity of St Stephen's lands, Karl could not push through constitutional change without the agreement of the Hungarian Parliament, which was dominated by Magyar landowners, loath to give up any of the privileges that had been codified in the *Ausgleich* of 1867. Karl had hoped that greater democratic pressure from below would help to concentrate minds in Budapest on the need for reform, but it was never implemented. Even with Tisza gone, there was still determined opposition to constitutional change, and the Emperor could not force matters without breaking the promise he had made. 'I have taken my coronation oath', he told one of his closest advisers, 'and I will keep it as long as I live.'[44]

As the situation darkened, Karl found himself and his family the target of bitter accusations and hatred. When the Austrian Parliament, the Reichsrat, opened on 16 July, debate immediately began on the 'foolishness and irresponsibility' of the June offensive, with rumours spreading that the Empress Zita ('the Frenchwoman') had betrayed the attack to the Allies – a highly damaging accusation that played on her family's connections to France and Italy and echoed the way in which the reputation of the Tsarina had been discredited in the months before the March Revolution in Russia.[45] Even Karl, who led as austere and disciplined a life as any monarch in Europe, was accused of drinking too much and of being a womanizer, both without foundation; nor would he countenance the idea that Zita 'henpecked' him, with too much influence over imperial policies. It was true that the Empress would usually be present each evening, after the children had gone to bed, when Karl received the final reports of the day, but she never interfered. 'Her assistance was purely passive', recalled the Emperor's Chief Private Secretary, Arthur Polzer-Hoditz. 'She sat apart as a rule, reading or writing letters . . . Occasionally she would ask me to tell her about the position of this or that affair, never anything of importance.'[46]

Karl trod his own path, working towards peace in whatever way he could, but knowing that his fate, like that of his crumbling empire, lay in other hands. A Crown Council was held at OHL in Spa on 14 August, just days after renewed British and French attacks on the Western Front had broken the line east of Amiens. The Emperor arrived that day, accompanied by General Arz and Count Burián, Czernin's replacement as Foreign Secretary, to find a mood of suppressed anxiety. 'German Headquarters did not present the usual picture of the central organ of the war machine working with quiet confidence', noted Burián. 'The atmosphere was distinctly depressed. Grave concern was depicted upon the faces of the German High Command and suite, with all their soldierly bearing. Conversation was carried on in more hushed tones than usual.'[47] But stubborn to the end, still believing that their armies would achieve another breakthrough that would shatter the Entente, Hindenburg and Ludendorff insisted that it was not the right moment to approach the Allies, at least not until the front lines had stabilized. Arz took the duo aside and tried to explain just how serious things were in the Dual Monarchy. 'It was my own conviction that the Central Powers were no longer in a position to defeat the enemy decisively enough that peace could be dictated to them.' He admitted that he was in no condition to judge how long Germany could continue the war, but asserted 'with confidence' that Austria–Hungary could only keep going until December. 'I also drew special attention to the fact that the battle must not proceed to the point of complete exhaustion, because the army will likely be needed in order to settle internal and external political questions and to maintain order even after peace has been concluded.'[48]

Karl was pleased at the somewhat vague promise that peace talks would begin at some future point, and accepted the Kaiser's request that he would not make any 'unilateral demand for peace' over the coming months, but his unease was obvious to spot. Colonel Alfred Niemann, a liaison officer to the Kaiser, could not hide his disdain for the young Habsburg. 'His youthful, soft face showed traces of deep exhaustion; his unsteady gaze, poor posture and the nervous, unclear way in which he expressed himself revealed the inner turmoil that placed the monarch at the mercy of ever-changing influences.'[49] Karl's Chief of Staff, Arz, who had stood by His Majesty's side throughout, could not help but be struck by the different attitudes of the two emperors. 'Trusting in the strength of the German people, Kaiser Wilhelm believed unshakeably that the Germans would be victorious; Emperor Karl, no longer counting on his opponent being defeated by force of arms, was carried away by the longing to give peace to his people.' The two men would never meet again.[50]

23.   'The honour of the army'

Writing to a friend on 11 September 1918, Franchet d'Espèrey was in a buoyant mood about the readiness of the expeditionary force. 'It is still very hot, particularly in Salonika,' he noted. 'I do not understand why Sarrail has not created a base in the mountains as the English and Serbs did. I created one for my troops, whom I sent out of Salonika. I also monitored the effects on their health conditions, which were utterly transformed. My reserve divisions, rather than being in disgusting dugouts located close to all of the bistros and whorehouses of Salonika, were based at a height of 1,000 metres in the oak and chestnut forests. I also have very few cases of malaria . . . a total of only 75 across the whole army over the last few months. These are the facts.'[1] The general was convinced that the men were in the best condition possible, ready to take their objectives in the looming offensive. He had only received authorization a few days earlier, but everything had already been prepared: roads and tracks had been improved, supplies and ammunition had been stockpiled, heavy guns had been towed up into the Allied lines opposite Dobro Pole, and the attacking infantry had been told what was expected of them. On the eve of the assault, the Serbian High Command informed its officers and men that 'the success of the entire offensive depends upon rapid penetration . . . It is necessary to violently penetrate without resting to the final limits possible of human and equine ability.'[2]

The determination of the Allied armies in Macedonia contrasted sharply with the lassitude that was spreading through the defenders. Increasingly destitute, struggling with worn-out equipment and poor food, Bulgarian soldiers looked to the future with foreboding. 'There is no doubt that the mood in the Bulgarian Army is very low and is leading to serious misgivings', German advisers had reported in June. 'The main reasons for the dissatisfaction are the bad food, the inadequate clothing, the officers' lack of care for their men, and

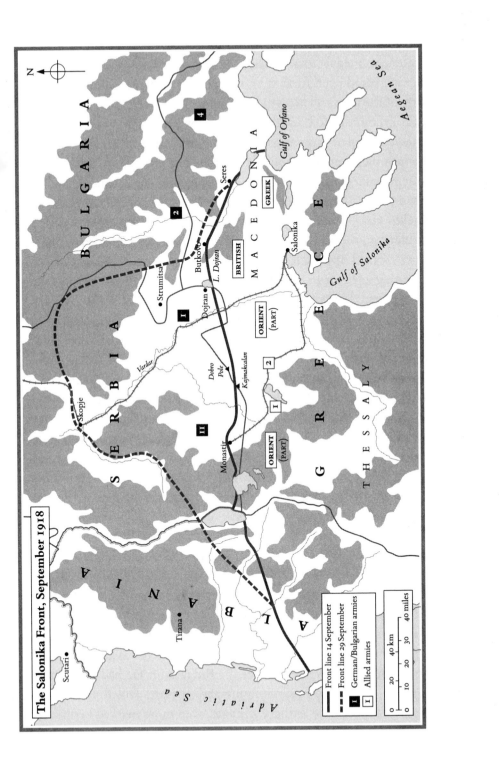

The Salonika Front, September 1918

N

BULGARIA

SERBIA

MACEDONIA

GREECE

THESSALY

ALBANIA

4

2

Seres

Butkovo

L. Dojran

Strumitsa

BRITISH

Dojran

I

Vardar

Dobro Pole

Kajmakalan

ORIENT (PART)

2

I

Skopje

III

Monastir

ORIENT (PART)

GREEK

Gulf of Orfano

Salonika

Gulf of Salonika

Aegean Sea

Tirana

Scutari

Adriatic Sea

Front line 14 September
Front line 29 September
German/Bulgarian armies **I**
Allied armies **I**

0   10   20   30   40 miles
0   20   40 km

severe fatigue among both officers and troops, brought about by the aforementioned factors and the long duration of the war. Low morale is exacerbated even further by unfavourable reports about the situation of the men's relatives in the larger towns at home.'[3] The German team recommended an immediate reorganization of staff and a renewed emphasis upon 'political activity', but were unimpressed by the lack of urgency in Sofia, lamenting that there were not enough younger officers, decisions took too long, and 'If General Zhekov is absent, the machine stands almost completely still.' Unfortunately, Zhekov retired to a care home in Vienna in early September, leaving his deputy, General Georgi Todorov, in charge. Todorov took a more relaxed approach to his duties than his predecessor and was attending a parade in Sofia when news of the Allied attacks came in.[4]

The first shots of the preliminary bombardment were fired at 8 a.m. on 14 September. The sky was overcast and soon disrupted by rising clouds of yellow-grey dust and smoke. As the guns thundered overhead, French and Serbian patrols slid out into no-man's-land and began to cut breaches in the barbed wire, opening a way for the main attack, which would begin at five o'clock the following morning. The artillery did what it could, but there was little chance of total devastation: the rocky outcrops and deep dugouts that the defenders sheltered in were almost impossible to destroy, even with a direct hit, but it was certainly possible to cause casualties, clear away barbed wire, and further demoralize the already fragile morale of the garrison. The Bulgarian position was not a bad one – the army had fought on this line throughout 1916 and 1917 with success – but it lacked depth. Were it to be attacked, strong and highly mobile reserves would need to be brought forward quickly, but these were stationed in small groups right across the front and could only reach Dobro Pole after twenty-four hours' hard marching.[5]

Franchet d'Espèrey concentrated almost the entire Serbian Army, with supporting French divisions, against the sector of attack, achieving a 'crushing superiority' over the Bulgarians. He had three times as many battalions, machine-guns and aircraft, and four times as many guns, with the artillery strength even more marked because of the larger-calibre weapons that were being employed.[6] Even these advantages did not mean that the attack was easy; the assault on Sokol almost failed, with the Drina Division encountering formidable resistance. 'Murderous rifle and machine-gun fire, as well as the enemy's trench weapons, fearfully sprayed over the ground where they attacked so bravely', recorded the official Serbian account. 'The waves of units made yet another superhuman effort, disregarding the danger to their lives, as they climbed the steep terrain and jagged rocks. The French left wing (148 French Regiment) managed to partially reach their objective, but faltered, surprised by the enemy's counter-attack, which caused them to retreat to their starting trenches.' Sokol would only be taken with a renewed assault during the night.[7]

The attack at Dobro Pole was no easier. The attackers had to clamber up a 200-metre-long slope under fire. Scampering forward when they could, taking cover behind rocky outcrops and boulders, the French and Serbs had to work together to advance. Enemy machine-gun positions – those that had survived the preliminary bombardment – took a fearful toll of attackers' lives and had to be taken out, one after the other, with specially equipped flamethrower teams helping to secure the summit by mid-morning. The 17th Colonial Division, which had attacked up the eastern flank, sustained over 1,200 casualties, with the Serbs, advancing from the west, losing about 700 men, although they had made the first breach in the Bulgarian position.[8]

Within days, the capture of Dobro Pole had been converted into a wider and more dangerous bulge in the Bulgarian line. Along a front of twenty-five kilometres, French and Serbian troops moved forward, their morale rising with every step they took and every prisoner they rounded up. Elated at the realization that they had broken through, Franchet d'Espèrey ordered that the attacks be continued without respite and shuttled reserves forward as quickly as he could. 'The Franco-Serbian troops fought alongside each other, competing in terms of their endurance, courage and spirit of sacrifice', he reported enthusiastically back to Paris. 'Their morale is splendid.' Bulgarian will to fight, so strong on the first day of battle, now began to dissolve into apathy and disorder. On the evening of 17 September, *Voivode* Mišić reported that they had already taken 3,000 prisoners and 18 large-calibre guns. Although the enemy defended the peaks 'tenaciously', the Serbian advance was now unstoppable. 'The enemy made a disordered retreat, leaving behind them a significant amount of equipment and injured men.'[9]

The front line may have been broken, with the Bulgarians retreating towards the Vardar, but they remained firmly in place at Dojran. General Milne's part in the offensive was launched shortly after five o'clock on the morning of 18 September. Under the warm glare of the rising sun, which bathed the hillsides in a shade of deep red, a British division, supported by Greek soldiers of the Seres Division, went forward against the Bulgarian positions west of Lake Dojran. The Greeks were able to overrun the first set of enemy trenches before quickly moving on to seize Hill 340 and Teton Hill, making an advance of over a mile. This was an encouraging start, but the British, on their left, could not break through. Heavy artillery and mortar fire – the Bulgarians being unusually well stocked with ammunition in this sector – proved highly effective, and the difficult ground forced the infantry to approach along predictable lines of advance that were covered by machine-guns. 'No map, no aeroplane photograph, could have given any idea of the desperate strength of the place; he himself, who had spent the best part of two years staring at it through telescopes, had no idea', remembered one survivor. 'All formation had been lost; the narrowness of the footing had destroyed the carefully rehearsed battle order, and like a cup-tie the attackers herded towards the slowly sinking cloud of dust which covered the next objective . . .' The result was a bloody and predictable repulse. One British battalion sustained 65 per cent casualties, including the loss of its commanding officer and adjutant, both killed in action as they tried to rally the men.[10]

Milne was frustrated, if not surprised, greeting the reverses of the day with the same stoicism he would show when Bulgarian resistance collapsed just days later. He had been requesting extra artillery for months and had specifically warned London that stocks of 18-pounder ammunition (his most important field gun) were just over half of what they should have been. He was also keen to have some more 8-inch howitzers, which were essential for long-range counter-battery work, being convinced that the inability to silence the enemy's guns had been largely to blame for the failure of the offensives in the spring of 1917. The War Office sent what it could, but Milne's resources were so scarce that even Franchet d'Espèrey felt it necessary to contact Clemenceau and urge him to protest to the British Government about the lack of priority it was placing on operations in Macedonia. A renewal of the attack was ordered for the following day, 19 September, but this just resulted in another series of fruitless assaults over open ground. After a telephone conversation with his two corps commanders, Milne agreed to suspend further operations for the time being. His forces had sustained about 7,000 casualties in two days. Bulgarian losses were much lower, around 3,000 killed, wounded or missing.[11]

The Bulgarian position was holding around Lake Dojran, but for how long? Reinforcements had been requested from OHL as early as 16 September, but Hindenburg would only agree to send a brigade from Sevastopol and one Habsburg division, rather than the six German divisions that had been asked for. In a telegram to General Todorov on 19 September, he admitted that his forces were now 'engaged in a most terrific struggle on the Western Front', where 'doubtless the issue of the Great War will be decided'. He was sympathetic to his ally's plight, but powerless to do anything more to help. 'I am extremely sorry that I am unable to do more to satisfy Your Excellency's request', he added. 'In the present highly critical military situation the Bulgarian High Command must try to deal with the situation with the forces now at its disposal which are not less numerous than those of the enemy and must reconcile itself to a possible loss of territory.'[12] Todorov read the telegram with a mixture of frustration and resignation. Making a withdrawal to a more defensible rear line – if one could be found – was not a welcome prospect, and he worried that once his divisions were on the move, they would simply dissolve. But the breakthrough at Dobro Pole could not be ignored, so on 20 September he ordered a retreat north, abandoning positions that had been held since 1915.[13]

News of the retreat was quickly relayed to Milne, who ordered his exhausted divisions forward. When they moved off during the night of 21 September, they found the enemy posts either deserted or occupied by only a handful of nervous rearguards. Milne urged advanced patrols to push on, but the real work would be done from the air. Allied aircraft, which had busied themselves over the front throughout the battle, quickly spotted the signs of the evacuation: camps packed up and removed, store dumps set on fire, and hundreds of trucks and wagons making their way up the Vardar Valley towards Kosturino, just inside the Bulgarian border. Such a vulnerable target was too tempting to ignore, and soon single-engined DH.9s from the Royal Air Force were swooping low, bombing and strafing and turning an orderly retreat into a desperate, murderous stampede. By the time British and Greek forces arrived several days later, they were greeted by the devastating sight of burned-out trucks, carcasses of mules and oxen, tumbled-down field guns, and small mountains of abandoned supplies. 'The whole of the country . . . was strewn with dead horses and men, and the smell was awful', recalled a British officer. 'I looked at several Bulgars and they were hardly recognizable as men; absolutely black, swollen and distorted . . .' Here was defeat in all its shocking brutality; something you could touch and see.[14]

The Macedonian Front had been immobile and indecisive for so long that the end, when it came, was sudden and unexpected. Rumours about the Allied offensive provoked chaos in Sofia, where Bolshevik sympathizers flooded the streets, agitating for bread and peace, followed by news that armed soldiers had cast off their loyalty to Tsar Ferdinand and were marching on the capital, intent on deposing him. Ferdinand acted with his usual adroitness, sending an armistice request to the Allies on 24 September. 'In view of the conjunction of circumstances which have recently arisen . . .' the document read, as if discussing anything other than a devastating battlefield defeat, 'the Bulgarian Government, desiring to put an end to the bloodshed, authorized the Commander-in-Chief of the army to propose to the Generalissimo of the armies of the Entente at Saloniki [*sic*], a cessation of hostilities and the beginning of negotiations for obtaining an armistice and peace.' Franchet d'Espèrey's reply was blunt and to the point. He would not countenance a suspension of hostilities until he had received the Bulgarian delegation, which he directed to 'present themselves at the British lines accompanied by an interpreter'.[15]

Three men – Andrei Lyapchev (Minister of Finance), General Ivan Lukov (commander of Second Army), and a technical adviser, Simon Radev – arrived in Salonika on 28 September. They were taken to Allied Headquarters, which was located, ironically enough, in the former Bulgarian Consulate, with its wide views of the bay and the unmistakeable white peaks of Mount Olympus.[16] They were exhausted, having endured a long drive over rutted roads packed with troops, horses and guns, but Franchet d'Espèrey was in no mood to extend them any pleasantries. 'You marched against us for no reason, and for that you must pay', he said in a cold and purely functional way. 'I do not wish for revolution, and so I will not involve your government, but I seek to finish this war quickly and properly, and you will provide me everything I need for this.' The following morning, the two parties got to work, thrashing out a settlement that would see Bulgaria agree to seven conditions, most notably the 'immediate evacuation of the territories still occupied by Bulgarians in Greece and Serbia', the 'immediate demobilization of the entire Bulgarian Army', the surrender of arms, munitions, military vehicles and horses, and the withdrawal of German and Austrian forces from their borders within four weeks. Tsar Ferdinand abdicated on 3 October, renouncing the throne in favour of his son, Crown Prince Boris.[17]

It was all the Allies had wanted and more; indeed, Franchet d'Espèrey was determined to use the Balkans as a springboard for an invasion of Germany from the south. It was only this way, he thought, that the Western Front could be outflanked and the war brought home to the enemy. But this would not be necessary. The position of Germany's armies in France had steadily worsened since the Crown Council at Spa, and far from witnessing an improvement in the situation and a stabilization of the front, the last days of September had seen a full-blown crisis at OHL. On 28 September, as news arrived of Bulgaria's armistice request, Ludendorff went to meet Hindenburg and admitted that the war had to be ended as soon as possible. This sparked off an ill-tempered discussion between the

German High Command and the government in Berlin, which eventually resulted in a note addressed to President Wilson asking him to 'take steps for the restoration of peace', based upon his Fourteen Points, and requesting the 'immediate conclusion of a general armistice on land, on water, and in the air'.[18]

The sudden breaking of the front, both at Salonika and in France, was devastating for Hindenburg and Ludendorff, the two men who had gambled on the western offensive alongside a set of maximalist war aims. They could only bemoan their luck and mutter darkly about betrayal, hoping against hope that some reserves could be mustered for a decisive counter-offensive. But their armies were now plagued by desertion and influenza, their men giving themselves up in larger and larger numbers. A new Cabinet had been formed, led by Prince Maximilian of Baden, who promised liberal reforms in the hope that this would satisfy the Allies. Wilson's first response, dated 8 October, blankly refused to consider any armistice as long as the Central Powers were on 'invaded territory', and pointedly asked whether the new Imperial Chancellor was empowered to speak on behalf of those 'constituted authorities of the Empire who have so far conducted the war' – a clear indication that the Allies would require genuine democratic reform if they were to entertain serious discussions with Germany.[19]

In Vienna, Emperor Karl could only watch the unfolding disaster with a feeling of great weariness. Having been ignored during the Crown Council in August, when he had insisted upon the urgent need for peace, he was now racing to catch up with events. In its desperate panic, Berlin had demanded 'parallel notes' be sent by its allies asking Wilson for an armistice, which Karl did on 7 October. He reminded the US President that Austria–Hungary had 'waged war always and solely as a defensive war, and repeatedly given documentary evidence of its readiness to stop the shedding of blood and to arrive at a just and honourable peace'.[20] He hoped to receive a softer response than that given to Berlin and was determined to provide proof of his willingness to meet Allied concerns over the self-determination of his peoples. On 16 October, he published his *Völkermanifest* ('People's Manifesto'), a last attempt to keep the shell of the empire and the monarchy intact. 'Austria must, in accordance with the will of its people, become a federal state, in which every nationality shall form its own national territory in its own settlement zone . . . This reorganization, which will in no way affect the integrity of the countries of the Holy Crown of Hungary, will guarantee the independence of each individual national state . . .'[21]

Karl had done his best, keeping his coronation oath to Hungary while at the same time creating a federalized Austrian half of the empire. He realized that this would not be acceptable to those national groupings who were determined, come what may, to seek their own destiny outside the empire, but hoped that something good might come from it and that enough loyalty to the monarchy remained intact. The American response, dated 18 October, made matters brutally clear. Things had changed, Wilson wrote, and the attitude of his government had been 'necessarily altered' by the course of events. Washington was now committed to the creation of a 'Yugoslavia' in the Balkans, while also recognizing 'that a state of belligerency exists between the Czecho-Slovaks and the German and Austro-Hungarian Empires and that the Czecho-Slovak National Council is a *de facto* belligerent government clothed with proper authority to direct the military and political affairs of the Czecho-Slovaks'. He was, therefore, 'no longer at liberty to accept the mere "autonomy" of these peoples as a basis for peace' and must inevitably go further.[22]

No concession that Karl might now offer – and his manifesto was certainly a sizeable one – was going to dissuade the Allies from dismembering the empire and letting new nations rise in its place. According to Count Burián, the rejection of Karl's proposals 'burst like a bomb upon the final efforts of the Austrian and Hungarian governments to get control of the disruptive forces', with a series of independence declarations ringing out across the Dual Monarchy over the next fortnight: in Prague and Zagreb as well as in Vienna and Budapest.[23] AOK had already ordered the evacuation of Albania, Serbia and Montenegro, Ukraine and Poland, and with Franchet d'Espèrey's forces driving north, there was a growing fear that the heart of the monarchy would soon be reached by enemy columns. Hungarian politicians now began to demand that 'their' soldiers return home to 'defend the Fatherland'. 'We have lost the war', Count Tisza told the Hungarian Parliament on 17 October. He was murdered by a group of disgruntled deserters a fortnight later.[24]

Only the Italian Front remained deadlocked, as if preserved in aspic. The Italian Army, slowly but surely rebuilt by General Diaz, was still dug into its sandbagged positions along the Piave and the Asiago, having held its line in June, but without a great victory to its name. For the Italian High Command, the summer and autumn of 1918 were dominated by one subject above all else: when, where, how and even *if* an offensive should be attempted. General Foch had been urging Diaz to attack for months, but the circumstances never seemed to align; there was always more that could be done and too many doubts to silence completely. In late August, Diaz had travelled to Foch's headquarters, where he explained that he fully agreed as to 'the necessity of being ready to act decisively', but that he would not 'push our operations this year to the point of compromising the efficiency of our Army', particularly now that they could no longer count upon any more reinforcements from the Western Front for the remainder of 1918. In the meantime, he would mount an 'aggressive contact' defence, holding his forces ready to 'profit by any favourable opportunity which may occur'. Neither Foch nor Poincaré, who met with Diaz when he was in France, were convinced by what they saw as tired excuses. 'They always want somebody to do their fighting for them' was Foch's downbeat verdict, while Poincaré was even less impressed with the Italian general. 'General Diaz came to see me', he observed. 'He was a small, dark-haired man who appeared shrewd.'[25]

Relations between Paris and Rome remained tense. On 28 September, with news of the Bulgarian armistice ringing in his ears, Foch finally ran out of patience. He wrote to Orlando, going over Diaz's head to reaffirm the urgent need to attack as soon as possible. Since May, he had regularly reminded Diaz about 'the importance of an offensive in Italy', while at the same time removing 'the difficulties that this presented by providing him with all of the materials required'. Still Diaz had not moved. 'In fact,' he added, 'the season demands that we launch an offensive . . . without delay.' Diaz had been pleading for Allied divisions for weeks; he had even called on General John Pershing, the commander of the American Expeditionary Force in France, and asked for twenty divisions to be sent to the Italian Front, an audacious move that was immediately waved away by the American. Foch was insistent that Diaz act. 'War does not come without risks', he wrote. 'The question now is whether, given the wavering morale and disorganisation of the Austrian army, the Italian command is prepared to accept them.'[26]

Irritated by Foch's tone, Orlando could only issue a bland reply in which he repeated his enthusiasm for an offensive and assured him that Diaz was planning to mount one as soon as possible.[27] Whenever the subject was raised in the Italian Cabinet, the same few questions were pondered time and again. Could troops break through the heavily fortified positions along the Piave, and how would they avoid encountering the difficulties that had faced the Austrians in June? Would they be able to scrape up enough manpower to continue the war into 1919 if they suffered heavy losses? Why even bother conquering ground that might fall into their hands within a week or two without a shot being fired? But how long could they ignore the blandishments of their allies, which might, as Baron Sonnino regularly warned, imperil their gains at a future peace conference? Orlando would not move without the full agreement of his military authorities, who remained adamant throughout September and into October that the time was not right. When the Prime Minister turned up at army headquarters one day insisting that an offensive be mounted, Diaz's deputy, the formidable Pietro Badoglio, lost his patience and slammed his fist on the desk, shouting, 'then give the order!'[28]

But no order came. The Prime Minister could not offer much clarity and vacillated between wanting an attack and warning his commanders of the terrible consequences if it went wrong. In a rambling letter to Diaz, dated 14 October, he had struggled to reconcile these two positions, eventually proposing an operation that would be a 'natural development' of normal activities, rather than one in 'great style', which provoked yet more fury from Badoglio, who annotated the note with a set of caustic comments: 'don't attack', 'attack', 'attack in half'. Diaz simply got on with his job, ensuring that everything was in place and that he could attack decisively when it mattered. 'As you know,' he wrote in a reply to the Prime Minister, 'my programme involves cautious procedures so as not to run the risk of failure, and I have done this by arranging for an action that may have a gradual development and also be stopped without serious inconveniences, but a certain initial vastness is always needed, without which it might turn into sterile attempts, which is to be absolutely avoided.'[29]

With rising water levels in the Piave predicted to peak in the last week of October, Diaz knew that any crossing would be fraught with difficulty, but he also knew that if he did not act soon, it might be too late to do anything before the war ended. It was not until 12 October that *Comando Supremo* issued its first operation orders. The main assault would be delivered by Eighth and Tenth Armies across the Piave, assisted by subsidiary attacks on the right and left, by Fourth Army at Mount Grappa and Third Army towards the Livenza river. Diaz's armies could call upon 7,700 guns (against just over 6,000 Austrian pieces), two million shells, and an impressive array of bridging material, including 5,000 yards of footbridges and hundreds of barges and boats, which were concentrated behind the front in the weeks before the attack. The concept was to separate the two Austrian armies by slicing through the point at which they joined, cutting their communications, throwing them back against the Piave, and then exploiting out to the east. This was nothing less than a devastating blow that would end the war and liberate the entire Venetian Plain.[30]

The opposing sides may have had approximate parity in numbers, even if the Allies had an advantage in guns and aircraft, but the crucial factor would be the fighting spirit of the defenders. The condition of the Habsburg infantry was pitiful. Painful, racking hunger was the chief complaint. There would be little meat or fat for days, and the men subsisted on a diet of unsweetened coffee, dried greens, some cheese, and perhaps a slice of pumpkin or black bread if they were fortunate. In 20th *Honvéd* Division, the average weight of the men had dropped to just 50 kilograms, which meant that they could rarely summon the strength to complete their regular duties. There was a widespread shortage of coats and shoes, and they wore old uniforms, ragged and torn, having been mended too many times. Malaria, influenza and desertion thinned the ranks to dangerously low levels, with seven of the fifteen divisions in the Army of the Isonzo down to less than a third of their full complement. When a liaison officer was sent by AOK to report on the state of the forces in Italy, his conclusion was stark. 'The food and clothing conditions are unbearable for any length of time. They are the focus of all dissatisfaction and threaten to become the catalyst for the failure of military discipline, just as they are at present – albeit on a small scale – the cause for all the lack of discipline that has already found its way from the rear into the army training areas.'[31]

Given these complaints, it was something of a miracle that the Habsburg troops resisted for as long and as fiercely as they did. Diaz had originally wanted all his attacks to go in on the same day, but the weather was still uncooperative, as it had been for most of the month, and with heavy rain still falling, he sanctioned Fourth Army's attack in the Mount Grappa sector to go ahead as planned on 24 October – a year to the day since Caporetto. The preliminary bombardment opened at 5 a.m., and although it thundered and echoed around the mountains, still wreathed in rain and mist, it was ragged and inconsistent. Bad weather prevented aerial reconnaissance, and only a third of the guns had been able to deploy correctly, which left the infantry under fire almost as soon as they left their jumping-off positions. Battalion-sized columns made their way towards a number of high points, including the Col Caprile and Mount Asolone, but faced fierce resistance, and only small lodgements were made in the Habsburg positions. The sole unequivocal triumph was at Mount Valderoa, which was taken in a brilliant action by 50th Division, whose troops had climbed the scree-lined slopes under cover of darkness and sprang forward into the enemy trenches at Zero Hour.[32]

However disappointing the attacks around Mount Grappa had been, Diaz had not pinned his hopes on much success in the north. That would come along the Piave, between the Grave di Papadopoli and Montello, a 25-mile sector of river line that he believed offered the best chance of breaking through and then advancing northeast towards the town of Vittorio (later renamed 'Vittorio Veneto' in commemoration of the victory). The decisive point would be at the Grave di Papadopoli, where the Piave split into two separate channels, creating an island about four miles long and a mile wide. This was the first objective for Tenth Army, now commanded by an Englishman, General Lord Cavan, who had succeeded Sir Herbert Plumer as commander of British forces in Italy in March. The decision to give Cavan an Italian army, albeit one that included a British corps, was certainly made with his seniority as a full general in mind, so that he would not come under the orders of a lower-ranking Italian officer, but Diaz wanted to include British troops for alliance reasons, giving them a tangible stake in the forthcoming offensive.[33]

The Grave, a flat, drab island of scrub and sandy gravel, was being held as an outpost line, with the main Austrian position situated behind the eastern bank. After consultation with his corps and divisional commanders, Cavan accepted that they must seize the island first, otherwise they ran the risk of outrunning their artillery support. British troops began crossing the 'inky black' waters of the Piave in flat-bottomed boats ('the shape of a Venetian gondola only of a sturdy build and rough wood'), rowed by Italian *pontieri*, shortly after eight o'clock on the evening of 23 October. It was a delicate affair. 'The boat would start off and push hard up stream and the current would in a minute swing it right across the first ship, at the lower end', remembered one British private; 'a file of figures could then be seen towing the ship across the moonshine and embark in a second ship at the top end. This proceeding was repeated and the second ship reached from whence the men waded ashore.' It did not take long for the Austrians to realize something was happening, and they periodically shelled the island while sweeping the ground with a powerful searchlight. 'It was hell lying there without practically any cover and expecting every minute to be blown to bits, but nevertheless, the embarkation went steadily on without mishap and eventually we all crossed.'[34]

With the Grave di Papadopoli in Allied hands, the next phase of Diaz's plans could go ahead. Even though the Piave remained turbulent, with water levels higher than anyone would have liked, a break in the weather on 25 October was enough for him to order the main attack to go ahead at 6.45 on the morning of the 27th, with a preliminary bombardment beginning seven hours earlier. British artillery had moved into position that night, only disclosing their presence to the enemy when they opened fire, which added to the sense of shock and surprise in the Austrian trenches as the shelling broke over their lines, clearing away barbed wire and isolating the forward positions. The eastern channel of the Piave was easier to cross than its western counterpart, being narrower and shallower, but it still presented a significant obstacle to infantry, fast-flowing and waist-deep. Carrying heavy equipment and extra ammunition, some men slipped and were washed away in the current, but most were able to make their way across and run the gauntlet of machine-gun fire that soon erupted from the Austrian lines.

Up and down the stretch of tortured river, in the half-light of morning, British, French and Italian divisions fought their way forward. It was said that the men of two Italian brigades, crossing the Piave under fire, placed their hands in the water and made the sign of the cross, 'as if consecrating themselves to Italy and victory'.[35] The defenders contested their progress, but lacked the strength to isolate and crush the attackers as had been done in June. Some Habsburg regiments were now beginning to fail, either mutinying outright and refusing to enter battle or fleeing to the rear at the first sight of the enemy. Hungarian troops had already ceased fighting in the Tyrol, demanding to be sent home as they no longer recognized their duty to defend Austria, a spirit that began to spread rapidly across almost the entire Imperial and Royal Army and its *Landwehr* and *Honvéd* contingents, beginning in the rear areas and then infecting those units closer to the front. Most of 7th Division, facing the British, collapsed into mass panic, and to the north, 32 Infantry Regiment, hailing from Budapest, disintegrated into loose groups of fleeing men when it came under attack by a French unit. Similarly, the men of 11th *Honvéd* Cavalry Division, stationed south of Moriago, either fell back or were taken prisoner in their hundreds when Italian assault troops overran their trenches.[36]

There was little that Boroević could do as he considered the situation at his headquarters in Udine. He telephoned his subordinates and tried to inject some of the ferocity and stubbornness that had been the hallmark of his armies during their long defence of the Isonzo. He brought up all available air units and ordered them to concentrate on bombing the footbridges and pontoons, while his artillery shelled the crossing points. He tried to counter-attack, but only a handful of units were still reliable. On the morning of 28 October, with the situation deteriorating by the hour, he despatched an urgent telegram to AOK: 'The strength of our troops' resistance is noticeably weakening; all the more so as the number of units refusing to obey the Manifesto is increasing, along with the independence of Poland, Hungary and the Czech, Slovak and South Slavic states, and the means are lacking to enforce their obedience. If we are to avoid all-out anarchy – which would be catastrophic to the monarchy – then it is of the utmost importance to be clear about what is to come and to bring about resolutions for political change.'[37]

Emperor Karl had already taken this fateful step. Twenty-four hours earlier, he had written a short telegram to the Kaiser that read like an epitaph for their brief, unhappy acquaintance. 'My dear friend,' it began, 'it is my duty, however difficult it may be for me, to let you know that my people are neither able nor willing to continue the war . . . The internal order and the monarchical principle are in the gravest danger if we do not stop fighting immediately. Even the deepest fraternal and friendly feelings must take second place to the consideration that I am saving the existence of those states whose fate has been entrusted to me by divine providence.' He added that he would sue for peace within twenty-four hours. 'I cannot help it, my conscience as ruler commands me to act.' When the Kaiser read the note, he replied immediately, urging Karl not to do anything, but to hold fast to their joint appeals to the Allied powers. 'The more united we stand, even at such a distance, the greater the chance that our adversaries, who are also suffering greatly from the burdens and horrors of war, will agree to terms of peace that are in harmony with the honour and interests of our peoples.'[38]

True to his word, Karl waited a day and then ordered that an approach be made to the Italians. A single officer, Captain Camillo

Ruggera, crossed the lines under a white flag on the morning of 29 October, only to find that his captors were in no hurry to conclude an armistice. It took hours for his letter to be transferred to Diaz's staff, who doubted its veracity, and it was only when AOK sent out an open wireless message requesting the beginning of negotiations that the Italians agreed to meet with a formal Austrian delegation, chaired by General Viktor Weber, the former Governor-General of Montenegro.[39] In Baden, General Arz wrote a belated report to Hindenburg, trying to offer a justification for why AOK had no choice but to approach the enemy. Troops from 'over 30 divisions, without distinction of nationality, refuse to continue fighting!' he wrote. 'Parts of individual regiments autonomously leave their positions; a reserve regiment has marched off. March formations cannot be induced to line up. Hungarian troops declare that they will not continue fighting under any circumstances [and] demand to be transported home because their homeland is endangered and the enemy is at the gates of their fatherland. Commanders are powerless . . . Under these circumstances, we must save whatever possible. Since it is a matter of hours, we must act quickly. Wilson's route is too long.'[40] By this point, Hindenburg was almost beyond caring. Ludendorff had been dismissed on 26 October, replaced by Lieutenant-General Wilhelm Groener, who began orchestrating the retreat of German forces from France and Belgium. The 'unified supreme command', which had once seemed all-powerful, was now broken beyond repair.

Fighting continued along the Piave throughout 28 and 29 October as the Italians fed men and supplies into the battle. The defenders continued to shell the crossing points and keep the attackers under fire, but could not stop the flow of men and materials onto the far bank. One Italian journalist, who went up to the front that day, remembered how:

> The battle burns all around, very bitter and victorious. On the reconquered shore there is a convulsion of cannon fire that digs muddy fountains in the ground soaked by recent rains. Thousands of Austrian bullets are hissing and plunging into the river, behind us, between island and island, they raise foaming columns that fall with a

roar. It is the enemy artillery that looks for our bridges and walkways to smash, to cut our communication routes. Some bridges are hit; transit stops; but teams of magnificent bridge builders, naked in the cold and very fast water, unperturbed under the firestorm, work continuously to rebuild, to repair.[41]

This was the spirit that General Diaz had called for when he had taken charge of the Italian Army in November 1917: a force able to deal with setbacks, to work around them, and to show the initiative and strength of character that victory demanded. At eight o'clock on the evening of 29 October, Boroević received orders from AOK that he was to immediately relay on to his army commanders. They were to leave the Veneto at once, only offering resistance if it became absolutely necessary. The Habsburg Army would evacuate its positions that night, abandoning whatever supplies and stores it must, and then start on its long journey home, leaving the field to the victors.[42]

When he was told that the Austrians were suing for peace, Diaz sat down at his desk and wrote a short, emotional letter to his wife. '[T]hings are proceeding remarkably well. We hope to enter Vittorio this evening; it is advancing energetically . . . The hopes and forecasts have largely worked out, and I see in this not only the fruit of our forecasts and our work, but also the hand of Providence that helps our country in this decisive moment for our future . . . Badoglio tells you that we have kept our promise, and I add: largely.'[43] Critics would complain that he had waited too long; that his offensive had been a 'non-battle' against an opponent on the verge of disintegration, and that had he attacked earlier, perhaps in September, the war could have been ended sooner and lives saved. But such arguments were easy to make in hindsight. Diaz had seen the army at Caporetto, watched in dismay as the wet, bedraggled columns came home, and the fragility of Italian arms had been burnt deep into his psyche. He did what he thought was best; he attacked when he was ready, and he kept the risks as low as they could possibly be. The delay, caused by the rising floodwater, was frustrating, forcing a postponement of the offensive by a month, but it was also necessary. Perhaps the crossing of the Piave was not as impressive as some operations during the war, but it hardly mattered. Diaz had done all that was expected of him: he had won.[44]

The Austro-Hungarian armistice delegation was escorted through Italian lines on the evening of 30 October, being driven to the Villa Giusti, a handsome private residence on the outskirts of Padua. General Badoglio, whom Diaz had appointed President of the Italian Armistice Commission, made a suitably grand entrance on the morning of 1 November, driving through the main gates as forty carabinieri lined up outside to salute. The armistice terms – hammered out between Orlando and the other Allied leaders – were predictably harsh. Hostilities would end; the Austro-Hungarian Army would demobilize; half of all its equipment and artillery would be surrendered; all occupied territories, as well as parts of the Tyrol, the Isonzo Valley and Trieste, would be evacuated; and the Allies would have 'right of free movement' across the lands of the Dual Monarchy.[45] When the head of the Austrian delegation, General Weber, read the terms, which included several more pages of military and naval conditions, he stood up, put the document down and said that he could not sign because they were 'incompatible with the honour of the army and navy'. Two officers were sent by car to Trento, from where they would communicate the terms to Baden with a request for specific orders. 'It must be left to the AOK to decide whether the conditions are not so severe that they force us to continue our resistance.'[46]

Badoglio made it clear that there would be no cessation of hostilities until an agreement could be reached, so Weber and his staff had to wait, knowing that Diaz's armies would continue their advance. When the terms reached Emperor Karl, he summoned five representatives from the Austrian Parliament, presented them with the document and asked their opinion. He was determined to prevent any attempt by the Allies to attack Germany from Austria, but he also knew that his armies were incapable of continued resistance; indeed, Hungary had already severed its relations with the Austrian half of the empire and ordered its soldiers to lay down their arms. The politicians refused to get involved and would not state whether they should accept or reject the terms, only that it was up to Karl to make the decision. Victor Adler, the newly appointed Foreign Minister, put it bluntly: 'The Emperor started the war; it is up to the Emperor to end it.' Karl could do little more. He telegraphed his authorization to General Weber at midnight on 3 November, adding a futile, almost pathetic protest at the insistence of free passage for Allied troops.[47]

Final agreement was reached on the evening of 3 November, with the terms of the armistice coming into force at three o'clock the following afternoon. In the final few hours, Italian patrols were ordered to seize as much ground as possible, so they pushed across the Venetian Plain, rounding up hundreds of thousands of Habsburg soldiers and reaching the places they had known so well in earlier times: Udine and Cividale, even Gorizia and the Isonzo. Those men of the Imperial and Royal Army who managed to escape had no choice but to embark upon the long march home, an experience that was 'painful and interminable', as one veteran remembered, 'up and down the mountains without contact with or news of other bodies of troops, wedged in between masses of men, horses and lorries all striving northwards and apparently having no other object than to hinder one another from getting away'.[48] Diaz published a short victory bulletin on 4 November announcing the 'annihilation' of the Austro-Hungarian Army: 'it has suffered very heavy losses in the stubborn resistance on the first few days and during the pursuit; it has lost very considerable quantities of material of all sorts and almost entire its magazines and depots. The remains of what was one of the most powerful armies in the world are going back, in disorder and hopeless, up the valleys they had descended with proud surety.' Austria–Hungary was finally out of the war. Germany followed a week later.[49]

Epilogue

The Habsburg Empire, founded by a dynasty that had survived for a thousand years, ceased to exist on 11 November 1918. It splintered into four successor states: German-Austria, Hungary, Czechoslovakia, and the Kingdom of Serbs, Croats and Slovenes (what would become Yugoslavia); with parts of the old empire being sliced off by Italy, the new states of Poland and Czechoslovakia, and a resurgent greater Romania. Emperor Karl formally renounced 'all participation in the affairs of state' in an announcement at noon that day. 'Ever since my accession I have tried to lead my peoples out of the horrors of a war for whose inception I bear no trace of blame. I have not hesitated to restore constitutional life and I have opened up for the peoples the path of their development as independent states. Filled, now as ever, with unwavering devotion to all my peoples, I do not wish to oppose their free growth with my own person.' He then left the palace at Schönbrunn and departed for his hunting lodge at Erkartsau, about twenty miles east of Vienna, not entirely sure what was to become of him and his family. The Republic of German-Austria was proclaimed the following day.[1]

Karl's announcement brought the curtain down on the Austro-Hungarian Empire, but because he had refused to abdicate, the imperial throne was still technically in existence, albeit without power; a constitutional absurdity that would not last long. The new socialist government in Vienna was understandably nervous about his presence on Austrian soil and managed to persuade him to go into exile in Switzerland, but still Karl would not countenance any thought of abdication. 'I went into retirement on November 4th, 1918, pending the restoration of order', he said. 'I am still Emperor.'[2] He eventually settled into a villa on the shores of Lake Geneva, from where he toyed with the idea of forming a new 'Catholic Empire', with the southern German state of Bavaria joining Upper Austria and the Tyrol, but nothing ever came of it – the world had already moved on. On 18 January 1919, the Allies and Associated Powers met in Paris to open a great peace conference that would take the first steps in remaking the world in the aftermath of war. In the opening address, Clemenceau called for a 'new order of things' that would 'seek nothing but justice', including 'the punishment of the guilty' and the creation of 'effective guarantees against an active return of the spirit by which they were tempted'.[3]

The settlement with Germany inevitably took up most of the time in Paris, but the victorious powers were soon faced with intractable questions concerning Central and Eastern Europe, which remained in turmoil. The doctrine of self-determination, brandished so confidently by President Wilson, would be applied inconsistently, given to some states but not others, and providing fertile soil for grievances to take root, particularly in the lands of the former Austro-Hungarian Empire. Because they had thrown off the shackles of the Dual Monarchy, there was cautious hope in Vienna and Budapest that they would be treated in a lenient manner, but other, more strategic interests prevailed. A draft treaty was presented to Dr Karl Renner, the Chancellor of German-Austria, on 2 June 1919. The republic was forbidden from unifying with Germany, in stark contrast to the rhetoric of Wilsonian 'self-determination' that suffused much of the discussions in Paris, and would cede South Tyrol, with its German-speaking population, to Italy. While it was recognized that Austria could not make 'complete reparation' for the damage caused by the war, she would commit to pay suitable compensation to the Allied powers, to be determined by a reparations committee.[4]

The shock in Vienna was deep and profound, with days of protests and calls for flags of mourning to be draped from every window. Renner tried to convince the Allies that the republic could not be held responsible for the sins of the former empire. The 'Danubian Monarchy, with which the Allied and Associated Powers were at war and with which they concluded the Armistice, has ceased to exist', he said. 'The 12th November, 1918 may be regarded as the date of its disappearance. From that day onwards there was no longer a monarch, nor any Great Power for him to rule . . . Our young Republic has been constituted in the same way as all the other States: it is, therefore, in no greater degree than they are the successor of the former Monarchy.'[5] But Renner's pleas would get him nowhere and he had little choice but to sign the treaty on 10 September, leaving the Republic of German-Austria a shrunken remnant of what had once been half of the empire.

Nor was the situation any better in Hungary. A republic had been proclaimed on 16 November, led by Count Mihály Károlyi, but he struggled to hold the country together. Facing invasion from the armies of the neighbouring powers (Czechoslovakia, Romania and Serbia), and beset by industrial unrest and violence in the countryside, Károlyi's government resigned in March 1919 and was replaced by a Soviet republic, led by a committed Bolshevik, Béla Kun. The prospect of another major European state coming under communist rule was sufficiently alarming that the western powers were forced to intervene, authorizing a Romanian invasion that reached the capital in August and deposed Kun. It was not until the Romanians pulled out and nationalist forces, led by a former admiral, Miklós Horthy, were able to march back in that some form of stability returned. Horthy was a 'link' and 'compromise' between different groups within Hungarian society: a decorated war hero who had served the monarchy loyally; an apolitical figure who was acceptable to the great powers; a Protestant who got along smoothly with Catholics; and someone who was popular with landowners, keen to banish Bolshevism. He was elected Regent in March 1920, with Hungary remaining a monarchy, albeit one without its king.[6]

Hungary's troubles were not yet over. The Treaty of Trianon was signed on 4 June 1920. It was perhaps the most punishing of all the post-war agreements, even eclipsing Brest-Litovsk, and destined to be long remembered because it codified the dismemberment of what had been the old Hungary. Transylvania and most of Banat would go to Romania; Slovakia, Ruthenia and Bratislava to Czechoslovakia; and Croatia-Slovenia to the Kingdom of Serbs, Croats and Slovenes. Hungary would be allowed to have an army no larger than 35,000 men and, like German-Austria, would sign a clause on war guilt and be responsible for reparations. In all, it lost two thirds of its land mass (145,000 square miles) and ten million citizens. In his letter of address to the Allies, Count Apponyi, president of the Hungarian delegation, accused them of failing to apply their own principles: 'namely the imprescriptible right of the people of disposing of themselves'. From that day forth, all flags in Hungary would be flown at half-mast, and they would remain so for another eighteen years, until the world was on the verge of another great war.[7]

Nor did the treaty mark the end of the infighting. Emperor Karl had never given up hope of restoring his throne, and made two attempts to return, in March and October 1921, travelling incognito to Hungary, where he met with loyalist forces and prepared to lead them into the capital. Horthy was in no mood to bargain, and despite repeated protestations of loyalty claimed that it was not the right time for a restoration of the monarchy, begging Karl to give up the idea. The 'Little Entente' of Romania, Czechoslovakia and the Kingdom of Serbs, Croats and Slovenes would never allow him to take the throne again, and if he proceeded towards Budapest, 'our fate is certain and within a few days our country would be under foreign domination'.[8] Though skirmishes broke out in the suburbs of Budapest between Karl's troops and government forces still loyal to Horthy, the Emperor lacked the ruthlessness to see it through. He was loath to let the fighting escalate and stood his men down. The Hungarian Parliament subsequently declared that Karl's 'sovereign rights' had 'expired' and placed him under the protection of the British Government, which agreed to escort him into exile on the island of Madeira. Heartbroken, but still trusting that all would be well, he died in April 1922, having caught bronchitis that quickly turned to pneumonia. He was just 34 years of age.[9]

Political volatility and regular crises of legitimacy would remain a recurring problem across Europe as a new continent began to emerge from the ruins of war. For Germany, the tragedy of 1918, when the army in the west crumbled against the combined might of Britain, France and America, was almost impossible to accept. How could the country that had dismantled Tsarist Russia and overrun the Balkans, creating a vast new empire in the process, have lost the war? The German High Command's inability to square the circle of competing priorities and create a viable strategy that might have balanced victories in the east with a stalemate in the west, perhaps renouncing

Belgium and returning to the borders of 1914, meant that defeat was total and devastating. Whether it was the decision not to attack Italy in 1916 and go for France instead, or not to chase the Entente out of Salonika, or the dismissal of any thought of a compromise peace, the tantalizing possibilities of the Eastern Front, its myriad missed opportunities, would long haunt Germany. But this did not produce a belated recognition of the need for clear thinking, or of the importance of making sensible strategic choices. Instead, it all boiled down to a simple and seductive conclusion: the war had been won in the east and it was not hard to believe that it could be done again.

This unsatisfying end to the war did not only affect the losers, and even the victors were not immune to the siren calls of strong men who sought new ways to challenge the verdict of 1918. Italy had paid a heavy price for her participation – over half a million dead – and struggled to recover from the war's enormous costs. Vittorio Orlando went to Paris intent on claiming his country's just rewards, but returned home angry that Italy was not being treated with the respect he thought she deserved. Frustration centred around the city of Fiume, the Adriatic port that she now coveted, claiming that because half the population was Italian-speaking, it would naturally belong to Italy on the grounds of self-determination.[10] The British and French had baulked at this demand and had instead agreed to include the city in the new Kingdom of Serbs, Croats and Slovenes, which prompted Orlando to walk out of the conference in late April 1919, complaining that 'Italy had made Fiume a national question'.[11]

He would return to Paris, but the matter of Fiume quickly became a lightning rod for Italian nationalists dissatisfied with the peace conference. Discussions over the status of the city continued all summer, with neither side – Italy or the Kingdom of Serbs, Croats and Slovenes – able to find a way forward, much to the disquiet of the Allied powers, who found themselves being sucked into lengthy discussions over the status of a relatively unimportant Croatian port. With no resolution in sight, the flamboyant novelist and poet Gabriele D'Annunzio led a ragged band of followers and disgruntled veterans into the city and occupied it as its *duce* (dictator). In his first speech, which he delivered in dramatic fashion from the balcony of the town hall, he announced that 'In the mad and cowardly world, Fiume today is the symbol of liberty. In the mad and cowardly world there is a single pure element: Fiume. There is a single truth: and this is Fiume. There is a single love: and this is Fiume! Fiume is like a blazing searchlight that radiates in the midst of an ocean of abjection.'[12]

D'Annunzio could be written off as an eccentric and harmless poseur, but the events at Fiume provided a perfect dress rehearsal for the far more dangerous 'march on Rome' that radical journalist Benito Mussolini would conduct three years later, mounting a *coup d'état* that deposed the Italian Government and ushered in the first fascist dictatorship in Europe. Like many on the far right, Mussolini rejected the Treaty of Rapallo, which had been signed in November 1920 and established Fiume as an independent free state. In a speech in June 1923, he called for a 'progressive revaluation of our diplomatic and political position in Europe and in the world', and complained that Italy had been 'excluded in the Peace of Versailles and other successive treaties from all other benefits of an economic and colonial nature. Solemn pacts signed during the war have lapsed and have not been replaced. The position of inferiority assigned to Italy has weighed and still weighs heavily on the economic life of our people. It is useless to dwell upon recriminations of the past. We must rather seek to regain the ground and time lost.' He promptly tore up Rapallo and formally annexed the city in 1924.[13]

The need to revise the post-war treaties and 'regain the ground lost' would remain a consistent theme in European politics until the outbreak of the Second World War in September 1939. In that sense, the treaties that dealt with Central and Eastern Europe settled little, only opening great wounds that often required even more radical surgery to heal. Instead of multinational empires, a new region of nation states, ethnically homogeneous and suspicious of minorities, would be constructed that proved highly vulnerable to the two great powers that would eventually seek their revenge: Germany and the Soviet Union. For this reason, the guns never really fell silent on the Eastern Front. The war just changed its form and mutated into another series of rolling conflicts that continued to ravage lands that had known nothing but suffering and strife for years. Because Germany had been required to abrogate the Treaty of Brest-Litovsk, the future of those areas that had been under *OberOst*'s military control was suddenly thrown into chaos in November 1918, with Lenin being the chief beneficiary. He wasted no time in trying to reabsorb those states that had broken away from Russia, establishing Soviet republics in Estonia, Latvia, Lithuania and Ukraine.[14]

There was a growing danger that all of Eastern Europe would fall under the red flag of Bolshevism. In a triumphant speech before the Second Communist International in Petrograd on 19 July 1920, Lenin called for further efforts to overturn international order. 'A proletarian army exists everywhere, although sometimes it is poorly organised and needs reorganising. If our comrades in all lands help us now to organise a united army, no shortcomings will prevent us from accomplishing our task. That task is the world proletarian revolution, the creation of a world Soviet republic.'[15] His armies were only stopped outside Warsaw, in what became known as the 'Miracle on the Vistula', when a Polish counter-attack threw the Bolsheviks back in disorder. This ensured the survival of the new Polish state and prevented communism from spreading even further west. The architect of the operation, Józef Piłsudski, noted that it had been 'an unreal war, a half-war, a quarter-war even, a sort of childish tussle, a brawl from which grand military theory was contemptuously excluded . . . a brawl, nonetheless, which launched the destinies of two states and of 150 million people, and which all but shook the fate of the entire civilized world'.[16]

Lenin's forces may have overreached at Warsaw, but the Bolsheviks were able to steadily consolidate their power in the months that followed. The Russian Civil War finally burnt itself out in November 1920, with the defeat of the Volunteer Army on the shores of the Crimea. In a departing address, as his forces embarked upon Allied ships to take them to Constantinople, the last White general, Baron Petr Wrangel, announced that the army, 'which has shed its blood in great torrents in fighting, not only for the Russian cause, but for the whole world, is now leaving its native shores, abandoned by everybody. We are going into exile; we are not going as beggars with outstretched hands, but with our heads held high, conscious of having done our duty to the end.' They left a land that was ravaged by war, its peoples subjected to spiralling levels of brutality and coercion. The execution of civilians had become commonplace, anti-Jewish pogroms flared up (and were conducted by both sides), while disease and famine had caused the deaths of perhaps two million people, possibly exceeding the number of those killed in action in the Russian Army between 1914 and 1917.[17]

The Tsar's old generals, the men who had tried to conquer Galicia and East Prussia, were mostly gone; either in exile, like Grand Duke Nikolai, or dead. Scores of Russian commanders were murdered by their new class enemies in the years after the revolution, including Generals Ruzski, Yanushkevich, Radko-Dmitriev and Zhilinsky. General Rennenkampf was arrested by the Bolsheviks in March 1918 and executed after refusing to join the Red Army. One of the few who avoided this fate was Aleksei Brusilov, who had returned to his home in Moscow in August 1917, opting to work alongside Russia's new government after a brief period of incarceration. He served on an advisory body on military reform, the Special Military Council, and called for officers to come back to Russia to help her defeat her foreign enemies, a stance that won him some personal safety, but which soured his reputation among the old officer class, who considered him a traitor and a turncoat. For better or worse, Brusilov felt that Russia had chosen her new leaders and they must make the best of it. He was a soldier after all. 'My husband served Russia under the tsarist government,' his wife later said, '[he] served also under the Bolsheviks, but he served not the government but his *country*'.[18]

These were difficult choices, something that Brusilov's old chief, Alekseev, had known all too well. Alekseev had died in October 1918 while leading the Volunteer Army, still trying to rescue Russia from the oblivion into which she had fallen. His decision to break his loyalty to the Tsar in March 1917 and to press for abdication had set off a terrible chain reaction that had made a bad situation even worse, ushering in a new age of barbarity and darkness. In Alekseev's funeral oration in Ekaterinodar, General Denikin had called him a great patriot who had died in the service of his country and not lived to see its resurrection: 'When the army ceased to exist and Russia was on the brink of doom, he was the first to raise his voice, crying out to Russian officers and the Russian people. He gave his last bit of energy to the Volunteer Army he created with his own hands: having endured the persecution, misunderstanding and hardships of a terrible campaign that broke him physically, he walked alongside his creation down the thorny path to the cherished goal of the salvation of his Homeland. By the will of God, he was not destined to see the dawn.'[19] That dawn would not come until the collapse of communism in 1991.

The long and unsatisfactory end of the First World War on the Eastern Front showed how dangerous the push for war had been in 1914. Those men who had called for action, and urged their states to mobilize, had been proved catastrophically wrong. Kaiser Wilhelm II, Tsar Nicholas II and Emperor Franz Joseph, alongside crucial advisers such as Count Berchtold and Conrad von Hötzendorf, would all find that war had been nothing like their preconceptions. They could not control it in the ways they had imagined. It slipped its bounds too easily, was hard to pursue and direct, and it spread far more widely than they had anticipated. All had believed that war was manageable, even desirable; that it offered a better way of settling disputes, allowing them to achieve their strategic goals more easily than in peacetime, and without having to make any painful political compromises. For these men, the fear of looking weak took an almost pathological hold and was something they would go to great lengths to avoid – only to bring about the very thing they feared most of all: the collapse of their empires and the destruction of an entire social order.

Nor would there be much remorse. The Kaiser was in exile, Nicholas II and Franz Joseph were dead, and Conrad lived in obscurity in Vienna. In a piece he submitted to (but that was never published by) *Neues Wiener Tagblatt* in November 1918, Conrad framed the war as Austria–Hungary's final struggle, at once defensive and glorious, sadly defeated by treachery at home. It had also been, in his opinion, inevitable. Individuals '*had almost no voice*' in the 'catastrophe', which had been brought upon the Central Powers by the 'aggressive goals' of the enemy.[20] He tried to distance himself from all that had happened and claimed that he had warned about the fatal combination of opponents ranged against them, but his responsibility ran deep. He had called for war and then proved unable to line up Austria's military capabilities with her goals; to craft a strategy that took account of the limitations of her armed forces and used them in a way that worked. Other commanders did not make these mistakes, or at least not as many. There were those who looked the war straight in the eye; who knew its dangers and directed their armies with a sense of realism and skill. Generals like Mikhail Alekseev and Aleksei Brusilov, Svetozar Boroević and Armando Diaz tried their best with what they had been given, and in some cases achieved what had seemed impossible. There were others who commanded their men with more elan – August von Mackensen stands out as a soldier of remarkable talent – but it was those individuals who had to formulate strategy under the greatest pressure, often with conflicting goals, who would face the toughest test of leadership.

Despite Germany winning victories over Serbia, Russia and Romania, and gaining the right to determine the fate of Eastern Europe and the Balkans, her defeat on the Western Front condemned her to defeat elsewhere. As soon as the German armistice delegation arrived at Foch's headquarters at Compiègne, these great triumphs, which had made the reputations of Hindenburg and Ludendorff, began to dissolve. That Germany and the Central Powers were unable to hold on to their gains on the Eastern Front was a strategic disaster of almost unparalleled proportions. Blame for the failure to convert these conquests into a viable strategy to end the war and come to terms with the Allies (and America) must fall squarely on the duo, who refused to make the necessary compromises; going for total victory in 1918 – a last desperate game of *va banque* – only to see it fail. Perhaps it was just Emperor Karl, so often derided as a naïve boy, dangerously out of his depth, who saw clearly how devastating the war was becoming and understood the absolute necessity of ending it as quickly as possible. He may not have succeeded, but his pursuit of peace won him a reputation for holiness and sanctity that continues to grow. In 2004, Pope John Paul II announced that the last Habsburg Emperor would be beatified and put on the path to sainthood.

Cast of Characters

ALBRECHT, Archduke Friedrich Maria (1856–1936): Appointed Austro-Hungarian Commander-in-Chief in July 1914 and served until his retirement in February 1917.

ALEKSEEV, General Mikhail Vasilyevich (1857–1918): Russian officer who served as Chief of Staff to Southwest Front (1914) and commander of Northwest Front (1915). Became Chief of Staff to the Tsar in August 1915 and held the position until the formation of the Provisional Government. One of the founders of the Volunteer Army.

ARZ VON STRAUSSENBURG, General Arthur (1857–1935): Austro-Hungarian army officer who was appointed Chief of the General Staff in March 1917.

AUFFENBERG, General Moritz (1852–1928): Austro-Hungarian army officer who was appointed commander of Fourth Army on the outbreak of war. Arrested in April 1915.

AVERESCU, General Alexandru (1859–1938): Romanian army commander who served in a variety of positions before his appointment as Prime Minister in February 1918.

BADOGLIO, General Pietro (1871–1956): Italian army officer who was appointed Deputy Chief of the General Staff in 1917. Led the Italian Armistice Commission.

BELOW, General Otto Ernst Vinzent Leo von (1857–1944): German army officer who commanded I Reserve Corps before taking charge of Eighth Army in November 1914. Promoted to army group command in 1916. Commanded Fourteenth Army at the Battle of Caporetto.

BERCHTOLD, Count Leopold von (1863–1942): Austro-Hungarian Foreign Minister (1912–15).

BERTHELOT, General Henri Matthais (1861–1931): head of the French Military Mission to Romania (1916–18).

BETHMANN HOLLWEG, Theobald von (1856–1921): German Imperial Chancellor (1909–17).

BÖHM-ERMOLLI, General Eduard von (1856–1941): Commander of the Austro-Hungarian Second Army (1914–15). Promoted to army group command in October 1915.

BOLFRAS, Arthur von (1838–1922): Austro-Hungarian army officer who was head of the Emperor's Military Chancellery (1889–1917).

BOROEVIĆ, Field Marshal Svetozar (1856–1920): Austro-Hungarian army officer who served in a variety of positions before taking charge of Fifth (later Isonzo) Army in May 1915. Promoted to army group command in 1917.

BOURBON-PARMA, Prince Sixtus Ferdinand von (1886–1934): Brother-in-law of Emperor Karl of Austria who served as an officer in the Belgian Army. Acted as a go-between in the negotiations over a compromise peace in the spring of 1917.

BRATIANU, Ionel (1864–1927): Romanian statesman who became leader of the National Liberal Party and served twice as Prime Minister (1909–10 and 1914–18).

BRIAND, Aristide (1862–1932): French Prime Minister (1915–17).

BRUSILOV, General Aleksei (1853–1926): Russian army officer who commanded Eighth Army (1914–16) and Southwest Front (1916–17). Promoted to Commander-in-Chief in the summer of 1917.

Arrested by the Bolsheviks in August 1918, but all charges were subsequently dropped.

BURIÁN, Count István (1851–1922): Diplomat who served twice as Austro-Hungarian Foreign Minister (in 1915–16 and again in 1918).

CADORNA, General Luigi (1850–1928): Italian Chief of the General Staff between July 1914 and November 1917.

CAPELLO, General Luigi (1859–1941): Italian army officer who was appointed Second Army commander in June 1917. Dismissed in February 1918.

CLEMENCEAU, Georges (1841–1929): French senator who served as Prime Minister between November 1917 and January 1920.

CONRAD VON HÖTZENDORF, Field Marshal Franz (1852–1925): Chief of the General Staff of the Austro-Hungarian Army and Navy (1906–17).

CZERNIN, Count Ottokar (1872–1932): Austro-Hungarian Foreign Minister (1916–18).

DANILOV, General Yuri (1866–1937): Russian army officer who was appointed Quartermaster-General at *Stavka* in August 1914. Served as Chief of Staff at Northern Front (1915–17).

DANKL, General Viktor (1854–1941): Commander of the Austro-Hungarian First Army (1914–15). Later served as an army commander on the Italian Front.

DENIKIN, General Anton Ivanovich (1872–1947): Russian army officer who rose to command the Western and Southwest Fronts in 1917. Took command of the Volunteer Army in the wake of General Kornilov's death.

DIAZ, General Armando (1861–1928): Succeeded General Cadorna as Italian Chief of the General Staff in November 1917.

EVERT, General Aleksei Ermolaevich (1857–1926): Commanded the Russian Tenth and Fourth Armies in 1914 before taking charge of Western Front (1915–17). Dismissed in March 1917.

FALKENHAYN, General Erich (1861–1922): Prussian Minister of War (1913–15) and Chief of the General Staff (1914–16). Commanded Ninth Army during the Romanian campaign (1916).

FILIBERTO, Prince Emanuele (1869–1931): Duke of Aosta. Commander of the Italian Third Army.

FOCH, Marshal Ferdinand (1851–1929): French Army Chief of Staff (May 1917–April 1918) who was appointed Allied Generalissimo in April 1918.

FRANCHET D'ESPÈREY, General Louis Félix Marie François (1856–1942): Experienced French army officer who served on the Western Front before being appointed commander of *l'armée d'Orient* in June 1918.

GALLWITZ, General Max Karl Wilhelm von (1852–1937): German army officer who commanded Twelfth Army and later Eleventh Army during the campaign of 1915. Transferred to the Western Front in 1916.

GUCHKOV, Alexander Ivanovich (1862–1936): Russian liberal politician and member of the Octobrist Party who became chairman of the War Industries Committee. Served as Minister of War in the Provisional Government (March–April 1917).

GUILLAUMAT, General Marie Louis Adolphe (1863–1940): Commander of *l'armée d'Orient* between December 1917 and June 1918.

HABSBURG-LORRAINE, Franz Joseph (1830–1916): Emperor of Austria and King of Hungary ('Franz Joseph I') who became the longest-serving Habsburg monarch (reigning from 1848 to 1916).

HABSBURG-LORRAINE, Karl Franz Joseph von (1887–1922): Last Emperor of Austria ('Charles I') and King of Hungary ('Károly IV'), who reigned between November 1916 and November 1918. Died in exile in Madeira. Beatified by Pope John Paul II in 2004.

HINDENBURG, Paul Ludwig Hans Anton von Beneckendorff und von (1847–1934): Brought out of retirement in August 1914 to take charge of the German Eighth Army in East Prussia. Replaced Falkenhayn as Chief of the General Staff in August 1916.

HOFFMANN, Major-General Carl Adolf Maximilian (1869–1927): Deputy Chief of Staff of the German Eighth Army during the Battle of Tannenberg. Served as Chief of Staff at *OberOst* (1916–18).

HOHENZOLLERN, Kaiser Friedrich Wilhelm Viktor Albert ('Wilhelm II') (1859–1941): German Emperor, King of Prussia, who reigned from 1888 to 1918. Abdicated on 9 November 1918.

IVANOV, General Nikolai (1851–1919): Distinguished Russian officer who commanded Southwest Front (1914–16) and later joined the Volunteer Army. Died of typhus in November 1918.

JOFFRE, Marshal Joseph Jacques Césaire (1852–1931): Appointed Chief of the French General Staff in 1911 and Commander-in-Chief on the outbreak of war. Commanded France's armies on the Western Front until December 1916.

KARAĐORĐEVIĆ, Crown Prince Alexander (1888–1934): Serbian Prince Regent and nominal Commander-in-Chief. King of Yugoslavia ('Alexander I') between 1921 and 1934. Assassinated during a state visit to France.

KERENSKY, Alexander Fyodorovich (1881–1970): Lawyer and Socialist Revolutionary who became Minister of Justice and later Minister of War in the Provisional Government. Appointed Prime Minister in July 1917. Deposed in the Bolshevik seizure of power.

KNOX, Major-General Sir Alfred William Fortescue (1870–1964): British Military Attaché in Russia (1911–17).

KORNILOV General Lavr Georgyevich (1870–1918): Russian army officer who rose to command the armies of the Provisional Government in August 1917. After the Bolshevik Revolution he led the Volunteer Army and was killed in action at Ekaterinodar in April 1918.

KRYLENKO, Ensign Nikolai Vasilyevich (1885–1938): Bolshevik revolutionary who was appointed Commander-in-Chief in November 1917. Executed during the 'Great Terror'.

KÜHLMANN, Richard von (1873–1948): German Foreign Secretary who took part in the negotiations at Brest-Litovsk.

KUROPATKIN, General Aleksei Nikolaevich (1848–1925): Senior Russian commander who had served in the Russo-Turkish War (1877–8) and commanded troops in Manchuria (1904–5). Recalled from retirement to take charge of Northern Front in 1916.

LENIN, Vladimir Ilich (born Vladimir Ilich Ulyanov) (1870–1924): Leader of the Bolshevik Party and Chairman of the Council of People's Commissars of the Soviet Union (1918–24).

LLOYD GEORGE, David (1863–1945): Liberal politician who was put in charge of the Ministry of Munitions in May 1915. Replaced Herbert Asquith as British Prime Minister in December 1916.

LUDENDORFF, General Erich (1865–1937): Formed a long-standing partnership with Hindenburg, firstly as Chief of Staff of Eighth Army and then as First Quartermaster-General. Ludendorff was Germany's foremost operational commander between August 1916 and October 1918.

MACKENSEN, Field Marshal August von (1849–1945): Commanded a corps and then an army in 1914 before being promoted to army group in 1915. Led the invasion of Serbia. Appointed head of the occupying forces in Romania (1916–18). One of the most decorated soldiers of the First World War.

MILIUKOV, Pavel Nikolaevich (1859–1943): One of the founders of the 'Kadet' Party who became leader of the Progressive Bloc. Served as Foreign Minister in the Provisional Government.

MILNE, General George Francis (1866–1948): Commander of the British Salonika Force (1916–18).

MIŠIĆ, *Voivode* Živojin (1855–1921): Serbian army officer who was appointed commander of First Army in 1914. Became Chief of the General Staff in 1918.

MOLTKE, Colonel-General Helmuth Johannes Ludwig von (1848–1916): Chief of the General Staff (1906–14) and one of the architects of the German war plan of 1914. Replaced on 14 September 1914 by Falkenhayn.

NIVELLE, General Robert Georges (1856–1924): French artillery officer who served as Chief of the General Staff between December 1916 and May 1917.

ORLANDO, Vittorio Emanuele (1860–1952): Professor of Constitutional Law who entered politics in 1897 and served as Italian Prime Minister (1917–19).

ÖSTERREICH-ESTE, Archduke Franz Ferdinand Carl Ludwig Joseph Maria von (1863–1914): Nephew of Emperor Franz Joseph and heir to the Habsburg throne. Murdered in Sarajevo in June 1914.

PALÉOLOGUE, Maurice (1859–1944): French Ambassador to Russia (1914–17).

PAŠIĆ, Nikola (1845–1926): Serbian politician who served numerous terms as Prime Minister.

PLEHVE, General Pavel Adamovich (1850–1916): Commander of the Russian Fifth Army (1914–15) and Twelfth Army (1915), and Commander-in-Chief of Northern Front (1915–16).

POINCARÉ, Raymond Nicolas Landry (1860–1934): President of the French Republic (1913–20).

POTIOREK, General Oskar (1853–1933): Governor of Bosnia and Herzegovina (1911–14) and commander of the Balkan Army Group. Resigned in disgrace in December 1914.

PREZAN, General Constantin (1861–1943): Romanian officer who commanded North Army in the campaign of 1916. Took charge of an army group before the fall of Bucharest. Promoted to Army Chief of Staff in December 1916.

PUTNIK, *Voivode* Radomir (1847–1917): Legendary Serbian soldier who was appointed Chief of the General Staff in 1903 and served as Serbia's field commander during the campaigns of 1914–15. Evacuated to France after the fall of Serbia, he was dismissed in January 1916, and died the following year.

RADKO-DMITRIEV, General R. D. (1859–1918): Bulgarian officer who joined the Russian Army in 1914 and rose to command Third Army. Dismissed after the Gorlice–Tarnów offensive, but returned to active service in the spring of 1916. Murdered by the Bolsheviks in October 1918.

RASPUTIN, Grigori (1871–1916): Russian peasant healer and holy man who possessed extraordinary influence over the family of Tsar Nicholas II. Murdered in December 1916.

RENNENKAMPF, General Paul George Edler von (1858–1918): Commanded the Russian First Army in 1914. A commission of inquiry exonerated him for his performance at Tannenberg, but he was dismissed from service the following year. Arrested by the Bolsheviks in March 1918 and executed after refusing to join the Red Army.

RIBOT, Alexandre Félix Joseph (1842–1923): French Finance Minister who formed a short-lived government between March and September 1917.

ROBERTSON, General Sir William Robert (1860–1933): British army officer who served as Chief of the Imperial General Staff (1915–18).

RODZIANKO, Mikhail Vladimirovich (1859–1924): Russian statesman who was one of the leaders of the Progressive Bloc. Served as Chairman of the Provisional Committee of the State Duma until the Bolsheviks seized power in November 1917.

ROMANOV, Nikolai Alexandrovich (1868–1918): Last Tsar of Russia ('Nicholas II'), who reigned between 1894 and 1917. Murdered with his family in Ekaterinburg in July 1918.

ROMANOV, Grand Duke Nikolai Nikolaevich (1856–1929): Russian Commander-in-Chief (1914–15). Left *Stavka* in September 1915 and was appointed Viceroy of the Caucasus.

RUZSKI, General Nikolai Vladimirovich (1854–1918): Commander of the Russian Third Army (August–September 1914) and Northwest Front (1914–15). Resigned in March 1915, but returned to take charge of Northern Front several months later. Murdered by the Bolsheviks in September 1918.

SACHSEN-COBURG UND GOTHA, Ferdinand Maximilian (1861–1948): Tsar of Bulgaria ('Ferdinand I') between 1887 and 1918.

SALANDRA, Antonio (1853–1931): Italian Prime Minister (1914–16).

SAMSONOV, General Alexander Vasilyevich (1859–1914): Cavalryman who was appointed commander of the Russian Second Army in July 1914. Committed suicide at the Battle of Tannenberg.

SARRAIL, General Maurice (1858–1929): French army officer known for his republican and left-wing sympathies. Served as commander of *l'armée d'Orient* between 1915 and 1917.

SCHLESWIG-HOLSTEIN-SONDERBURG-GLÜCKSBURG, Constantine (1868–1923): King of Greece ('Constantine I') between 1913 and 1917.

SEECKT, General Johannes Friedrich Leopold Hans von (1866–1936): Highly regarded staff officer who worked as Mackensen's Chief of Staff throughout 1915–16. Served as Chief of Staff to Archduke Karl.

SONNINO, Sidney (1847–1922): Italian Minister of Foreign Affairs (1914–19).

SUKHOMLINOV, Vladimir Alexandrovich (1848–1926): Cavalry officer who served as Russian Minister of War (1909–15).

TISZA, Count István (1861–1918): Statesman who served as Hungarian Prime Minister in 1903–5 and 1913–17. Murdered in October 1918.

TROTSKY, Leon (born Lev Davidovich Bronstein) (1879–1940): Russian revolutionary who joined the Bolshevik Party in 1917 and served as People's Commissar for Foreign Affairs during the negotiations at Brest-Litovsk.

VENIZELOS, Eleftherios (1864–1936): Greek statesman who founded the Liberal Party and struck a pro-Entente position throughout his career. Served as Prime Minister seven times.

WILSON, Lieutenant-General Sir Henry Hughes (1864–1922): British army officer who was appointed Chief of the Imperial General Staff in February 1918.

WILSON, Thomas Woodrow (1856–1924): 28th President of the United States (1913–21).

YANUSHKEVICH, General Nikolai Nikolaevich (1868–1918): Chief of Staff to Grand Duke Nikolai Nikolaevich between August 1914 and September 1915. Arrested at Mogilev and murdered by his guards on the way to Petrograd in 1918.

ZAIMIS, Alexandros (1855–1936): Greek politician who served as Prime Minister six times.

ZHEKOV, General Nikola (1865–1949): Bulgarian army officer who was appointed Commander-in-Chief in October 1915. Retired because of ill-health shortly before the beginning of the final Allied offensive in September 1918.

ZHILINSKY, General Yakov Grigorievich (1853–1918): Russian cavalry officer who commanded Northwest Front in 1914. Went on to serve as *Stavka*'s military representative to the Entente (1915–16). Killed while trying to flee Russia after the Bolshevik Revolution.

Abbreviations

ADN: Archivio Diaristico Nazionale, Pieve Santo Stefano

AFGG: *Les Armées Françaises dans la Grande Guerre*

AOK: *Armee Oberkommando* (Austro-Hungarian High Command)

BA-MA: Bundesarchiv-Militärarchiv, Freiburg

CAB: Cabinet Office files

GQG: *Grand Quartier Général* (French High Command)

HIA: Hoover Institution Archives, Stanford

IWM: Imperial War Museum, London

KA: Kriegsarchiv, Vienna

K.u.K.: *Kaiserlich und Königlich* (Imperial and Royal Habsburg Army)

NCO: Non-commissioned officer

OHL: *Oberste Heeresleitung* (German Supreme Command)

OS: Old Style (the Julian calendar was used in Russia prior to February 1918, and was thirteen days behind the western Gregorian calendar)

TNA: The National Archives, Kew

WO: War Office files

References

Preface

1 W. S. Churchill, *The World Crisis. The Eastern Front* (London: Thornton Butterworth, 1931), pp. 7, 17, 82.

2 S. McMeekin, *The Russian Origins of the First World War* (Cambridge, MA: Harvard University Press, 2011), pp. 1–5.

3 H. H. Herwig, *The First World War. Germany and Austria–Hungary 1914–1918* (London: Arnold, 1997), p. 446; and A. Watson, *Ring of Steel. Germany and Austria–Hungary at War, 1914–1918* (London: Allen Lane, 2015; first publ. 2014), p. 565.

4 S. J. Main, 'Gas on the Eastern Front during the First World War (1915–1917)', *Journal of Slavic Military Studies*, Vol. 28, No. 1 (2015), p. 102.

5 D. T. Zabecki, *The German 1918 Offensives. A Case Study in the Operational Level of War* (London and New York: Routledge, 2006), p. 69.

6 J. A. Sanborn, *Imperial Apocalypse. The Great War and the Destruction of the Russian Empire* (Oxford: Oxford University Press, 2015; first publ. 2014), p. 91.

Prologue: 'It is nothing'

1 T. G. Otte, *July Crisis. The World's Descent into War, Summer 1914* (Cambridge: Cambridge University Press, 2014), p. 18.

2 V. Dedijer, *The Road to Sarajevo* (London: MacGibbon & Kee, 1966), p. 12; and C. Clark, *The Sleepwalkers. How Europe Went to War in 1914* (London: Penguin, 2013; first publ. 2012), pp. 370–71.

3 Dedijer, *The Road to Sarajevo*, pp. 15–16.

4 Cited in S. McMeekin, *July 1914. Countdown to War* (London: Icon Books, 2013), p. 32.

5 J. A. S. Grenville and B. Wasserstein (eds.), *The Major International Treaties of the Twentieth Century. A History and Guide with Texts* (2 vols., London: Routledge, 2001), I, p. 38.

6 L. Cecil, *Wilhelm II. Volume 2. Emperor and Exile, 1900–1941* (Chapel Hill, NC: University of North Carolina Press, 1996), p. 200.

7 N. Stone, 'Hungary and the Crisis of July 1914', *Journal of Contemporary History*, Vol. 1, No. 3 (July 1966), pp. 164–5.

8 Berchtold to Franz Joseph, 14 July 1914, in A. Mombauer (ed. and trans.), *The Origins of the First World War. Diplomatic and Military Documents* (Manchester: Manchester University Press, 2013), pp. 246–7.

9 *Austro-Hungarian Red Book. Official English Edition with an Introduction* (New York: J. C. Rankin, 1915), pp. 6–9.

10 A. Mitrović, *Serbia's Great War 1914–1918* (London: Hurst, 2007), p. 45; and Prince Regent of Serbia to Tsar Nicholas II, 24 July 1914, in *Collected Diplomatic Documents Relating to the Outbreak of the European War* (London: HMSO, 1915), p. 268.

11 'Serbia's Reply to the Austro-Hungarian Ultimatum', in Mombauer (ed. and trans.), *The Origins of the First World War*, pp. 352–6.

12 M. Rauchensteiner, *The First World War and the End of the Habsburg Monarchy, 1914–1918*, trans. A. J. Kay and A. Güttel-Bellert (Vienna: Böhlau Verlag, 2014; first publ. 1993), p. 119; and W. Giesl, *Zwei Jahrzehnte im Nahen Orient*, ed. R. von Steinitz (Berlin: Verlag für Kulturpolitik, 1927), p. 271.

1. *'A visible bloody track'*

1 'Austrian Emperor to His People', *The Times*, 30 July 1914.

2 Emperor Franz Joseph to Kaiser Wilhelm II, 2 July 1914, in *Austrian Red Book. Official Files Pertaining to Pre-War History. Part 1. 28 June to 23 July 1914* (London: George Allen & Unwin, 1920), p. 1.

3 J. Redlich, *Emperor Francis Joseph of Austria. A Biography* (London: Macmillan & Co., 1929), p. 524. Original emphasis.

4 F. Conrad von Hötzendorf, *Aus Meiner Dienstzeit 1906–1918* (5 vols., Vienna: Rikola Verlag, 1921–5), IV, p. 31.

5 E. Glaise-Horstenau, *Österreich-Ungarns Letzter Krieg 1914–1918*, I, *Das Kriegsjahr 1914* (Vienna: Verlag der Militärwissenschaftlichen Mitteilungen, 1931), pp. 6–7.

6 N. Stone, 'Moltke–Conrad: Relations Between the Austro-Hungarian and German General Staffs, 1909–14', *The Historical Journal*, Vol. IX, No. 2 (1966), pp. 210, 213.

7 G. Wawro, *A Mad Catastrophe. The Outbreak of World War I and the Collapse of the Habsburg Empire* (New York: Basic Books, 2015; first publ. 2014), p. 127; and Conrad von Hötzendorf, *Aus Meiner Dienstzeit*, III, p. 147.

8 William II to Franz Joseph, 31 July 1914, in A. Mombauer (ed. and trans.), *The Origins of the First World War. Diplomatic and Military Documents* (Manchester and New York: Manchester University Press, 2013), pp. 497–8.

9 J. M. B. Lyon, ' "A Peasant Mob": The Serbian Army on the Eve of the Great War', *The Journal of Military History*, Vol. 61, No. 3 (July 1997), pp. 481, 488; G. E. Rothenberg, *The Army of Francis Joseph* (West Lafayette, IN: Purdue University Press, 1976), p. 173; and N. N. Golovine, *The Russian Campaign of 1914. The Beginning of the War and Operations in East Prussia*, trans. A. G. S. Muntz (Fort Leavenworth, KS: Command & General Staff School Press, 1933), p. 26.

10 J. R. Schindler, *Fall of the Double Eagle. The Battle for Galicia and the Demise of Austria–Hungary* (Lincoln, NE: Potomac Books, 2015), pp. 74–5, 79.

11 Glaise-Horstenau, *Österreich-Ungarns Letzter Krieg 1914-1918*, I, p. 44, n. 1.

12 Conrad von Hötzendorf, *Aus Meiner Dienstzeit*, IV, pp. 290, 291.

13 Nicholas II to Wilhelm II, 29 July 1914, in Mombauer (ed. and trans.), *The Origins of the First World War*, p. 418.

14 Golovine, *The Russian Campaign of 1914*, pp. 25, 45.

15 C. Clark, *The Sleepwalkers. How Europe Went to War in 1914* (London: Penguin, 2013; first publ. 2012), p. 447.

16 'President Poincaré's Visit to Russia', *The Times*, 25 July 1914.

17 B. W. Menning, 'War Planning and Initial Operations in the Russian Context', in R. F. Hamilton and H. H. Herwig (eds.), *War Planning 1914* (Cambridge: Cambridge University Press, 2013; first publ. 2010),

pp. 121–2; and S. McMeekin, *The Russian Origins of the First World War* (Cambridge, MA: Harvard University Press, 2011), pp. 19, 79–80.

18 M. Paléologue, *An Ambassador's Memoirs*, trans. F. A. Holt (3 vols., London: Hutchinson & Co., 1925), I, p. 83.

19 N. Stone, *The Eastern Front 1914–1917* (London: Penguin, 1998; first publ. 1975), pp. 51–2; and P. Robinson, *Grand Duke Nikolai Nikolaevich. Supreme Commander of the Russian Army* (DeKalb, IL: Northern Illinois University Press, 2014), pp. 29, 134.

20 Robinson, *Grand Duke Nikolai Nikolaevich*, pp. 143–4; J. N. Danilov, *Rußland im Weltkriege 1914–1915*, trans. R. Freiherr von Campenhausen (Jena: Walter Biedermann, 1925), pp. 277–8; and O. R. Airapetov, *Uchastie Rossiiskoi imperii v Pervoi mirovoi voine (1914–1917). 1914 god* (Moscow: Kuchkovo Pole, 2014), p. 133.

21 Golovine, *The Russian Campaign of 1914*, pp. 90–92.

22 J. R. Schindler, 'Redl – Spy of the Century?', *International Journal of Intelligence and Counterintelligence*, Vol. 18, No. 3 (2005), pp. 498–9.

23 Menning, 'War Planning and Initial Operations in the Russian Context', p. 136.

24 Paléologue, *An Ambassador's Memoirs*, I, p. 62.

25 Lyon, '"A Peasant Mob": The Serbian Army on the Eve of the Great War', p. 486.

26 J. Lyon, *Serbia and the Balkan Front, 1914. The Outbreak of the Great War* (London: Bloomsbury, 2015), pp. 110, 113.

27 C. J. Vopicka, *Secrets of the Balkans. Seven Years of a Diplomatist's Life in the Storm Centre of Europe* (Chicago: Rand McNally & Company, 1921), pp. 34, 38–9.

28 Conrad von Hötzendorf, *Aus Meiner Dienstzeit*, IV, p. 358.

29 R. Jeřábek, *Potiorek. General im Schatten von Sarajevo* (Vienna: Verlag Styria, 1991), p. 111.

30 Glaise-Horstenau, *Österreich-Ungarns Letzter Krieg 1914–1918*, I, pp. 100, 111.

31 *Regiments-Geschichte des Infanterie-Regimentes Nr. 42 1674–1918* (Leitzmeritz and Böhm. Leipa: Unterstützungsverband gedienter Infanteristen des Ergänzungsbezirkes, 1933), p. 164.

32 J. E. Gumz, *The Resurrection and Collapse of Empire in Habsburg Serbia, 1914–1918* (Cambridge: Cambridge University Press, 2013; first publ. 2009), pp. 47–9.

33 Lyon, *Serbia and the Balkan Front, 1914*, p. 130.

34 *Veliki rat Srbije za oslobođenje i ujedinjenje Srba, Hrvata i Slovenaca* (28 vols., Belgrade: Glavni đeneralštab, 1924–37), I, p. 95.

35 R. Wagner, *Geschichte des ehemaligen Schützenregimentes Nr. 6* (Karlsbad: Der Heimat Söhne im Weltkrieg, 1932), p. 77.

36 M. Rauchensteiner, *The First World War and the End of the Habsburg Monarchy, 1914–1918*, trans. A. J. Kay and A. Güttel-Bellert (Vienna: Böhlau Verlag, 2014; first publ. 1993), p. 188.

37 Conrad von Hötzendorf, *Aus Meiner Dienstzeit*, IV, p. 440.

38 Glaise-Horstenau, *Österreich-Ungarns Letzter Krieg 1914–1918*, I, p. 163; Conrad von Hötzendorf, *Aus Meiner Dienstzeit*, III, pp. 606–7; and L. Sondhaus, *Franz Conrad von Hötzendorf. Architect of the Apocalypse* (Boston: Humanities Press, 2000), p. 150.

39 F. Kreisler, *Four Weeks in the Trenches. The War Story of a Violinist* (Boston and New York: Houghton Mifflin Company, 1915), pp. 13–14.

40 F. F. Schramm-Schliessl von Perstorff, *Die Geschichte des K.u.K. Mährischen Dragoner-Regimentes Friedrich Franz IV. Grossherzog von Mecklenburg-Schwerin Nr. 6 1906–1918* (Vienna: Rudolf M. Rohrer, 1933), p. 153.

41 A. V. Slivinsky, *Konnyi boi 10-i Kavaleriiskoi divizii generala grafa Kellera 8/21 avgusta 1914 goda u d. Iaroslavitse* (Belgrade: n.p., 1921), p. 21.

42 Schindler, *Fall of the Double Eagle*, pp. 167–8.

43 Danilov, *Rußland im Weltkriege*, p. 176.

44 *Strategicheskii ocherk voiny 1914–1918 g.g.* (7 vols., Moscow: Vysshii voennyi redaktsionnyi sovet, 1920–23), I, p. 47.

45 D. R. Stone, *The Russian Army in the Great War. The Eastern Front, 1914–1917* (Lawrence, KS: University Press of Kansas, 2015), p. 86.

46 L. von Pastor, *Generaloberst Viktor Dankl der Sieger von Krasnik und Verteidiger Tirols* (Vienna: B. Herder, 1916), pp. 13–14.

47 Rothenberg, *The Army of Francis Joseph*, p. 174.

48 Golovine, *The Russian Campaign of 1914*, pp. 27–8.

49 M. von Auffenberg-Komarów, *Aus Österreich-Ungarns Teilnahme am Weltkriege* (Berlin and Vienna: Verleft bei Ullstein & Co., 1920), pp. 160–61.

50 E. Wißhaupt, *Die 52. Landwehr-Infanteriebrigade (Landwehrinfanterieregimenter 9 und 10) im Weltkriege 1914–1918* (Reichenberg: Der Heimat söhne im Weltkrieg, 1928), p. 34.

51 V. Schemfil, *Das K.u.K. 3. Regiment der Tiroler Kaiserjäger im Weltkrieg 1914–1918* (Bregenz: J. N. Teutsch, 1926), p. 34; and Airapetov, *Uchastie Rossiiskoi imperii v Pervoi mirovoi voine (1914–1917). 1914 god*, p. 194.

52 Auffenberg-Komarów, *Aus Österreich-Ungarns Teilnahme am Weltkriege*, p. 248; and Stone, *The Eastern Front*, p. 87.

53 Auffenberg-Komarów, *Aus Österreich-Ungarns Teilnahme am Weltkriege*, p. 151.

54 'Glänzender Sieg an der ganzen Nordfront', *Voralberger Volksfreund*, 8 September 1914.

2. *'A new and difficult task'*

1 Reichsarchiv, *Der Weltkrieg 1914 bis 1918*. II. *Die Befreiung Ostpreußens* (Berlin: E. S. Mittler & Sohn, 1925), pp. 40–41.

2 A. A. Uspenskii, *Na voine: vostochnaia Prussiia-Litva, 1914–1915* (Kaunas, Lithuania: n.p., 1932), p. 47.

3 N. N. Golovine, *The Russian Campaign of 1914. The Beginning of the War and Operations in East Prussia*, trans. A. G. S. Muntz (Fort Leavenworth, KS: Command & General Staff School Press, 1933), p. 127; and Reichsarchiv, *Der Weltkrieg*, II, p. 93.

4 Rennenkampf to Yanushkevich, 21 August 1914, in *Vostochno-Prusskaia operatsiia. Sbornik dokumentov mirovoi imperialisticheskoi voiny na russkom fronte (1914–1917)* (Moscow: Voenizdat, 1939), pp. 204–5.

5 W. Elze, *Tannenberg. Das Deutsche Heer von 1914, seine Grundzüge und deren Auswirkung im Sieg an der Ostfront* (Breslau: Ferdinand Hirt, 1928), pp. 241, 243.

6 D. J. Hughes (ed.), *Moltke on the Art of War. Selected Writings*, trans. D. J. Hughes and H. Bell (New York: Presidio, 1993), p. viii.

7 E. Ludendorff, *My War Memories 1914–1918* (2 vols., London: Hutchinson & Co., 1919), I, p. 41.

8 D. E. Showalter, *Tannenberg. Clash of Empires, 1914* (Washington DC: Potomac Books, 2004; first publ. 1991), pp. 214–17; and Golovine, *The Russian Campaign of 1914*, p. 170.

9 Golovine, *The Russian Campaign of 1914*, pp. 195, 203–4.

10 Showalter, *Tannenberg*, pp. 229–30.

11 P. von Hindenburg, *Out of My Life*, trans. F. A. Holt (2 vols., New York and London: Harper & Brothers, 1921), I, p. 109.

12 T. von Schäfer, *Tannenberg* (Berlin: Gerhard Stalling, 1927), p. 53.

13 Showalter, *Tannenberg*, pp. 240–42.

14 Golovine, *The Russian Campaign of 1914*, pp. 254–5.

15 Showalter, *Tannenberg*, p. 118; D. R. Stone, *The Russian Army in the Great War. The Eastern Front, 1914–1917* (Lawrence, KS: University Press of Kansas, 2015), p. 52; and Golovine, *The Russian Campaign of 1914*, p. 21.

16 Showalter, *Tannenberg*, p. 323.

17 Golovine, *The Russian Campaign of 1914*, p. 325.

18 Ibid., p. 164.

19 Rennenkampf to Zhilinsky, 25 and 26 August 1914, in *Vostochno-Prusskaia operatsiia*, pp. 219, 221–2.

20 P. Robinson, *Grand Duke Nikolai Nikolaevich. Supreme Commander of the Russian Army* (DeKalb, IL: Northern Illinois University Press, 2014), p. 164.

21 P. K. Kondzerovskii, *V stavke verkhovnogo. 1914–1917* (Paris: n.p., 1967), p. 37.

22 Zhilinsky to Grand Duke Nikolai, 31 August 1914, in *Vostochno-Prusskaia operatsiia*, pp. 313–16.

23 J. N. Danilov, *Rußland im Weltkriege 1914–1915*, trans. R. Freiherr von Campenhausen (Jena: Walter Biedermann, 1925), p. 238.

24 'Proclamation of the Supreme Commander-in-Chief', 14 August 1914, in F. A. Golder (ed.), *Documents of Russian History 1914–1917* (Stanford, CA: The Century Co., 1927), pp. 37–8.

25 N. Stone, *The Eastern Front 1914–1917* (London: Penguin, 1998; first publ. 1975), p. 88.

26 N. Golovin[e], 'The Great Battle in Galicia (1914): A Study in Strategy', *The Slavonic Review*, Vol. 5, No. 13 (June 1926), p. 40.

27 J. R. Schindler, *Fall of the Double Eagle. The Battle for Galicia and the Demise of Austria–Hungary* (Lincoln, NE: Potomac Books, 2015), p. 163; and E. Glaise-Horstenau, *Österreich-Ungarns Letzter Krieg 1914–1918*, I, *Das Kriegsjahr 1914* (Vienna: Verlag der Militärwissenschaftlichen Mitteilungen, 1931), p. 206.

28 G. W. Kühne-Hellmessen, *Kaiserjäger – Ausharren! Vom Heldensterben des 2. Regiments der Tiroler Kaiserjäger in den Septembertagen 1914* (Berlin: Gerhard Stalling, 1936), pp. 174–5.

29 R. Pfeffer, *Zum 10. Jahrestage der Schlachten von Zloczow und Przemyślany 26–30 August 1914* (Vienna: self-published, 1924), pp. 46–7.

30 F. Conrad von Hötzendorf, *Aus Meiner Dienstzeit 1906–1918* (5 vols., Vienna: Rikola Verlag, 1921–5), IV, pp. 540, 603–4.

31 Bruderman cited in G. Wawro, *A Mad Catastrophe. The Outbreak of World War I and the Collapse of the Habsburg Empire* (New York: Basic Books, 2015; first publ. 2014), p. 228.

32 C. Mick, *Lemberg, Lwów, L'viv, 1914–1947. Violence and Ethnicity in a Contested City* (West Lafayette, IN: Purdue University Press, 2016), pp. 25–6.

33 Danilov, *Rußland im Weltkriege*, p. 246.

34 *Strategicheskii ocherk voiny 1914–1918 g.g.* (7 vols., Moscow: Vysshii voennyi redaktsionnyi sovet, 1920–23), I, pp. 182–3.

35 Stone, *The Russian Army in the Great War*, p. 95.

36 *Strategicheskii ocherk voiny 1914–1918 g.g.*, I, p. 184.

37 Cited in M. von Auffenberg-Komarów, *Aus Österreich-Ungarns Teilnahme am Weltkriege* (Berlin and Vienna: Verleft bei Ullstein & Co., 1920), p. 313.

38 HIA: Golovine Papers, Box 16, Memoirs of General Shkinsky, pp. 116–17.

39 *Strategicheskii ocherk voiny 1914–1918 g.g.*, I, p. 207.

40 Conrad von Hötzendorf, *Aus Meiner Dienstzeit*, IV, pp. 690–91.

41 Ibid., pp. 701–2.

42 Glaise-Horstenau, *Österreich-Ungarns Letzter Krieg 1914–1918*, I, p. 319.

43 R. Thomas, *Infanterie-Regiment 94 im Weltkriege* (Reichenberg: self-published, 1933), p. 31.

44 Glaise-Horstenau, *Österreich-Ungarns Letzter Krieg 1914–1918*, I, p. 273.

45 J. Stürgkh, *Im Deutschen Großen Hauptquartier* (Leipzig: Paul List, 1921), pp. 158–9.

46 L. Cecil, *Wilhelm II. Volume 2. Emperor and Exile, 1900–1941* (Chapel Hill, NC: University of North Carolina Press, 1996), p. 216.

47 E. von Falkenhayn, *General Headquarters 1914–1916 and Its Critical Decisions* (London: Hutchinson & Co., 1919), p. 20.

48 Hindenburg, *Out of My Life*, I, pp. 123–4.

49 Reichsarchiv, *Der Weltkrieg*, II, p. 280.

50 O. R. Airapetov, *Uchastie Rossiiskoi imperii v Pervoi mirovoi voine (1914–1917). 1914 god* (Moscow: Kuchkovo Pole, 2014), pp. 247–8.

51 Reichsarchiv, *Der Weltkrieg*, II, pp. 316–17.

52 Reichsarchiv, *Der Weltkrieg 1914 bis 1918*. V. *Der Herbst-Feldzyg 1914. Im Westen bis zum Stellungskrieg. Im Osten bis zum Rückzüg* (Berlin: E. S. Mittler & Sohn, 1929), pp. 407–9.

53 Robinson, *Grand Duke Nikolai Nikolaevich*, pp. 167–8; and Reichsarchiv, *Der Weltkrieg*, II, p. 314.

3. 'Our brave army deserved a better fate'

1 G. A. Tunstall, *Written in Blood. The Battles for Fortress Przemyśl in WW1* (Bloomington, IN: Indiana University Press, 2016), pp. 1, 17; and A. Watson, *The Fortress. The Great Siege of Przemyśl* (London: Allen Lane, 2019), p. 48.

2 F. Conrad von Hötzendorf, *Aus Meiner Dienstzeit 1906–1918* (5 vols., Vienna: Rikola Verlag, 1921–5), IV, p. 805.

3 M. Rauchensteiner, *The First World War and the End of the Habsburg Monarchy, 1914–1918*, trans. A. J. Kay and A. Güttel-Bellert (Vienna: Böhlau Verlag, 2014; first publ. 1993), pp. 233, 237.

4 Conrad von Hötzendorf, *Aus Meiner Dienstzeit*, IV, pp. 769–70.

5 J. Lyon, *Serbia and the Balkan Front, 1914. The Outbreak of the Great War* (London: Bloomsbury, 2015), p. 160.

6 J. R. Schindler, 'Disaster on the Drina: The Austro-Hungarian Army in Serbia, 1914', *War in History*, Vol. 9, No. 2 (2002), pp. 182–3.

7 E. Glaise-Horstenau, *Österreich-Ungarns Letzter Krieg 1914–1918*, I, *Das Kriegsjahr 1914* (Vienna: Verlag der Militärwissenschaftlichen Mitteilungen, 1931), p. 643.

8 A. Krauss, *Die Ursachen unserer Niederlage. Erinnerungen und Urteile aus dem Weltkrieg* (Munich: J. F. Lehmanns, 1921), pp. 152–3.

9 Conrad von Hötzendorf, *Aus Meiner Dienstzeit*, IV, pp. 795–6; and E. Ludendorff, *My War Memories 1914–1918* (2 vols., London: Hutchinson & Co., 1919), I, p. 75.

10 Conrad von Hötzendorf, *Aus Meiner Dienstzeit*, IV, p. 797.

11 Ibid., p. 799.

12 Glaise-Horstenau, *Österreich-Ungarns Letzter Krieg 1914–1918*, I, pp. 379–80.

13 P. Robinson, *Grand Duke Nikolai Nikolaevich. Supreme Commander of the Russian Army* (DeKalb, IL: Northern Illinois University Press, 2014), p. 171.

14 J. N. Danilov, *Rußland im Weltkriege 1914–1915*, trans. R. Freiherr von Campenhausen (Jena: Walter Biedermann, 1925), p. 304; and Robinson, *Grand Duke Nikolai Nikolaevich*, pp. 171–2.

15 D. R. Stone, *The Russian Army in the Great War. The Eastern Front, 1914–1917* (Lawrence, KS: University Press of Kansas, 2015), p. 106.

16 Danilov, *Rußland im Weltkriege*, pp. 305–7.

17 M. Paléologue, *An Ambassador's Memoirs*, trans. F. A. Holt (3 vols., London: Hutchinson & Co., 1925), I, pp. 129–30.

18 N. Stone, *The Eastern Front 1914-1917* (London: Penguin, 1998; first publ. 1975), p. 95.

19 Ivanov to Yanushkevich, 21 September 1914, in *Varshavsko-Ivangorodskaia operatsiia. Sbornik dokumentov mirovoi imperialisticheskoi voiny na russkom fronte (1914–1917)* (Moscow: Voenizdat, 1938), p. 24.

20 O. R. Airapetov, *Uchastie Rossiiskoi imperii v Pervoi mirovoi voine (1914–1917). 1914 god* (Moscow: Kuchkovo Pole, 2014), p. 275.

21 A. M. Zaionchkovskii, *Mirovaia voina 1914–1918 g.g.* (2 vols., Moscow: Voenizdat, 1938), I, p. 227.

22 Sir A. Knox, *With the Russian Army 1914–1917* (2 vols., London: Hutchinson & Co., 1921), I, p. 146.

23 Ludendorff, *My War Memories*, I, p. 82.

24 Conrad von Hötzendorf, *Aus Meiner Dienstzeit*, V, p. 51.

25 E. von Falkenhayn, *General Headquarters 1914–1916 and Its Critical Decisions* (London: Hutchinson & Co., 1919), p. 14.

26 P. von Hindenburg, *Out of My Life*, trans. F. A. Holt (2 vols., New York and London: Harper & Brothers, 1921), I, pp. 146–7.

27 Airapetov, *Uchastie Rossiiskoi imperii v Pervoi mirovoi voine 1914*, p. 264.

28 Yanushkevich to Alekseev, 29 September 1914, in *Varshavsko-Ivangorodskaia operatsiia*, p. 37.

29 Watson, *The Fortress*, p. 90; and Tunstall, *Written in Blood*, p. 92.

30 W. Foerster (ed.), *Mackensen. Briefe und Aufzeichnungen des Generalfeldmarschalls aus Krieg und Frieden* (Leipzig: Bibliographisches Institut, 1938), p. 75.

31 M. Hoffmann, *War Diaries and Other Papers*, trans. E. Sutton (2 vols., London: Martin Secker, 1929), I, p. 46.

32 Reichsarchiv, *Der Weltkrieg 1914 bis 1918. V. Der Herbst-Feldzug 1914. Im Westen bis zum Stellungskrieg, im Osten bis zum Rückzüg* (Berlin: E. S. Mittler & Sohn, 1929), p. 454.

33 Reichsarchiv, *Der Weltkrieg*, V, p. 467; and Conrad von Hötzendorf, *Aus Meiner Dienstzeit*, V, p. 181.

34 Yanushkevich to Ruzski and Ivanov, 22 October 1914, in *Lodzinskaia operatsiia. Sbornik dokumentov mirovoi imperialisticheskoi voiny na russkom fronte (1914–1917)* (Moscow: Voenizdat, 1936), pp. 25–6.

35 Danilov, *Rußland im Weltkriege*, p. 321.

36 Ludendorff, *My War Memories*, I, p. 93.

37 Reichsarchiv, *Der Weltkrieg 1914 bis 1918. VI. Der Herbst-Feldzug 1914. Der Abschluß der Operationen im Westen und Osten* (Berlin: E. S. Mittler & Sohn, 1929), p. 37; and R. T. Foley, *German Strategy and the Path to Verdun. Erich von Falkenhayn and the Development of Attrition, 1870–1916* (Cambridge: Cambridge University Press, 2005), p. 110, n. 5.

38 Reichsarchiv, *Der Weltkrieg*, VI, pp. 54, 56.

39 Glaise-Horstenau, *Österreich-Ungarns Letzter Krieg 1914–1918*, I, p. 470.

40 Conrad von Hötzendorf, *Aus Meiner Dienstzeit*, V, p. 364; and Watson, *The Fortress*, pp. 130–31.

41 Airapetov, *Uchastie Rossiiskoi imperii v Pervoi mirovoi voine (1914–1917). 1914 god*, p. 282.

42 Yanushkevich to Ivanov and Ruzski, 2 November 1914, in *Lodzinskaia operatsiia*, pp. 57–9. Original emphasis.

43 Knox, *With the Russian Army*, I, p. 213.

44 Foerster (ed.), *Mackensen*, p. 94.

45 A. V. Oleinikov, *Uspeshnye generaly zabytoi voiny* (Moscow: Veche, 2014), pp. 71–2.

46 Hoffmann, *War Diaries and Other Papers*, I, p. 50.

47 J. N. Danilov, *Velikii kniaz' Nikolai Nikolaevich* (Paris: Imprimerie de Navarre, 1930), p. 156.

48 Foerster (ed.), *Mackensen*, p. 115.

49 Airapetov, *Uchastie Rossiiskoi imperii v Pervoi mirovoi voine (1914–1917). 1914 god*, p. 302.

50 'German Repulse Near Lodz', *The Times*, 3 December 1914.

51 Reichsarchiv, *Der Weltkrieg*, VI, pp. 254–5.

52 H. H. Herwig, *The First World War. Germany and Austria–Hungary 1914–1918* (London: Arnold, 1997), p. 114.

53 Reichsarchiv, *Der Weltkrieg*, VI, pp. 255–6.

54 H. Afflerbach, *Falkenhayn. Politisches Denken und Handeln im Kaiserreich* (Munich: R. Oldenbourg, 1994), p. 222.

4. *'Not a battle but a slaughter!'*

1 S. Washburn, *Field Notes from the Russian Front* (London: Andrew Melrose, 1915), pp. 41–7.

2 J. N. Danilov, *Rußland im Weltkriege 1914–1915*, trans. R. Freiherr von Campenhausen (Jena: Walter Biedermann, 1925), pp. 358–61.

3 Ibid., pp. 369–72; and N. N. Golovine, *The Russian Army in the World War* (New Haven: Yale University Press, 1931), pp. 126–7.

4 Cited in S. McMeekin, *The Russian Origins of the First World War* (Cambridge, MA: Harvard University Press, 2011), p. 114.

5 Danilov, *Rußland im Weltkriege*, pp. 379–80.

6 Grand Duke Nikolai Nikolaevich to Tsar Nicholas II, 30 November 1914, in *Lodzinskaia operatsiia. Sbornik dokumentov mirovoi imperialisticheskoi voiny na russkom fronte (1914–1917)* (Moscow: Voenizdat, 1936), pp. 328–9.

7 'Minutes of the Meeting Held in Brest, 30 November (13 December) 1914', in *Lodzinskaia operatsiia*, pp. 417–19.

8 W. Foerster (ed.), *Mackensen. Briefe und Aufzeichnungen des Generalfeldmarschalls aus Krieg und Frieden* (Leipzig: Bibliographisches Institut, 1938), pp. 118–19, 120.

9 L. Sondhaus, *Franz Conrad von Hötzendorf. Architect of the Apocalypse* (Boston: Humanities Press, 2000), pp. 108–13.

10 G. Gräfin Conrad von Hötzendorf, *Mein Leben mit Conrad von Hötzendorf. Sein geistiges Vermächtnis* (Leipzig: Greithlein & Co., 1935), pp. 127–8.

11 Ibid., p. 131.

12 O. R. Airapetov, *Uchastie Rossiiskoi imperii v Pervoi mirovoi voine (1914–1917). 1915 god* (Moscow: Kuchkovo Pole, 2014), p. 11.

13 F. Conrad von Hötzendorf, *Aus Meiner Dienstzeit 1906–1918* (5 vols., Vienna: Rikola Verlag, 1921–5), V, p. 685.

14 E. Glaise-Horstenau, *Österreich-Ungarns Letzter Krieg 1914–1918*, I, *Das Kriegsjahr 1914* (Vienna: Verlag der Militärwissenschaftlichen Mitteilungen, 1931), p. 686.

15 R. Jeřábek, *Potiorek. General im Schatten von Sarajevo* (Vienna: Verlag Styria, 1991), p. 173.

16 J. Lyon, *Serbia and the Balkan Front, 1914. The Outbreak of the Great War* (London: Bloomsbury, 2015), p. 199.

17 M. Hoen, J. Waldstätten-Zipperer and J. Seifert, *Die Deutschmeister. Taten und Schicksale des Infanterieregiments Hoch- und Deutschmeister Nr. 4 Insbesondere im Weltkriege* (Vienna: Druck und Verlag der Österreichischen Staatsdruckerei, 1929), p. 347.

18 Lyon, *Serbia and the Balkan Front, 1914*, p. 181; D. Djordjevic, 'Vojvoda Putnik, the Serbian High Command, and Strategy in 1914', in B. K. Király and N. F. Dreisziger (eds.), *War and Society in East Central Europe. Vol. XIX. East Central European Society in World War I* (Boulder, CO: Social Science Monographs, 1985), p. 581; and *Veliki rat Srbije za oslobođenje i ujedinjenje Srba, Hrvata i Slovenaca* (28 vols., Belgrade: Glavni đeneralštab, 1924–37), III, p. 146.

19 Lyon, *Serbia and the Balkan Front, 1914*, p. 216.

20 Ibid., p. 202.

21 R. Chambry, *Pierre Ier Roi de Serbie* (Paris: Bloud et Gay, 1917), pp. 6–7.

22 *Veliki rat Srbije*, V, p. 385.

23 Kalser cited in Jeřábek, *Potiorek*, pp. 182–3.

24 E. Zanantoni, *Geschichte der 29. Infanterie Division im Weltkrieg 1914–1918. Bd. 1* (Brunnengasse: Heimatsöhne im Weltkrieg, 1929), p. 153.

25 Potiorek to Bolfras, 10 December 1914, in Jeřábek, *Potiorek*, p. 187.

26 M. Rauchensteiner, *The First World War and the End of the Habsburg Monarchy, 1914–1918*, trans. A. J. Kay and A. Güttel-Bellert (Vienna: Böhlau Verlag, 2014; first publ. 1993), p. 280.

27 Glaise-Horstenau, *Österreich-Ungarns Letzter Krieg 1914–1918*, I, p. 759.

28 E. Glaise-Horstenau, *Österreich-Ungarns Letzter Krieg 1914–1918*, II, *Das Kriegsjahr 1915. Erster Teil* (Vienna: Verlag der Militärwissenschaftlichen Mitteilungen, 1931), p. 9.

29 BA-MA: RH 61/933, Plessen diary, 2 December 1914.

30 Glaise-Horstenau, *Österreich-Ungarns Letzter Krieg 1914–1918*, II, p. 55.

31 G. E. Silberstein, *The Troubled Alliance. German–Austrian Relations 1914 to 1917* (Lexington, KY: University Press of Kentucky, 1970), p. 267.

32 Reichsarchiv, *Der Weltkrieg 1914 bis 1918.* VI. *Der Herbst-Feldzug 1914. Der Abschluß der Operationen im Westen und Osten* (Berlin: E. S. Mittler & Sohn, 1929), p. 361.

33 Glaise-Horstenau, *Österreich-Ungarns Letzter Krieg 1914–1918*, II, pp. 91–3.

34 Sondhaus, *Franz Conrad von Hötzendorf*, p. 167.

35 G. A. Tunstall, *Blood on the Snow. The Carpathian Winter War of 1915* (Lawrence, KS: University Press of Kansas, 2010), pp. 4–7.

36 Ibid., p. 37; and Glaise-Horstenau, *Österreich-Ungarns Letzter Krieg 1914–1918*, II, p. 125.

37 Zanantoni, *Geschichte der 29. Infanterie Division im Weltkrieg*, p. 177.

38 Reichsarchiv, *Der Weltkrieg 1914 bis 1918.* VII. *Die Operationen des Jahres 1915. Die Ereignisse im Winter und Frühjahr* (Berlin: E. S. Mittler & Sohn, 1931), p. 91.

39 *Strategicheskii ocherk voiny 1914–1918 g.g.* (7 vols., Moscow: Vysshii voennyi redaktsionnyi sovet, 1920–23), III, pp. 48–9.

40 Ibid., p. 50; I. I. Rostunov, *Russkii front pervoi mirovoi voiny* (Moscow: Nauka, 1976), p. 225; and Danilov, *Rußland im Weltkriege*, p. 420.

41 Danilov, *Rußland im Weltkriege*, pp. 409, 422; and P. Robinson, 'A Study of Grand Duke Nikolai Nikolaevich as Supreme Commander of the Russian Army, 1914–1915', *The Historian*, Vol. 75, No. 3 (Fall 2013), pp. 485–6.

42 Glaise-Horstenau, *Österreich-Ungarns Letzter Krieg 1914–1918*, II, pp. 141–2.

43 Ibid., p. 165.

5. 'The agony of defence'

1 Reichsarchiv, *Der Weltkrieg 1914 bis 1918.* VII. *Die Operationen des Jahres 1915. Die Ereignisse im Winter und Frühjahr* (Berlin: E. S. Mittler & Sohn, 1931), p. 175.

2 Ibid., p. 178.

3 E. Ludendorff, *My War Memories 1914–1918* (2 vols., London: Hutchinson & Co., 1919), I, p. 118.

4 Ludendorff to Moltke, 27 January 1915, in E. Zechlin, 'Ludendorff im Jahre 1915. Unveröffentlichte Briefe', *Historische Zeitschrift*, Vol. 211 (1970), p. 330.

5 R. T. Foley, *German Strategy and the Path to Verdun. Erich von Falkenhayn and the Development of Attrition, 1870–1916* (Cambridge: Cambridge University Press, 2005), pp. 122–3.

6 Reichsarchiv, *Der Weltkrieg*, VII, p. 17.

7 S. J. Main, 'Gas on the Eastern Front During the First World War (1915–1917)', *Journal of Slavic Military Studies*, Vol. 28, No. 1 (2015), pp. 101–2; and M. Hoffmann, *War Diaries and Other Papers*, trans. E. Sutton (2 vols., London: Martin Secker, 1929), II, pp. 87, 88.

8 O. R. Airapetov, *Uchastie Rossiiskoi imperii v Pervoi mirovoi voine (1914–1917) 1915 god* (Moscow: Kuchkovo Pole, 2014), pp. 15–16.

9 M. P. Kamenskii, *Gibel' XX korpusa 8/21 fevralia 1915 goda (Po arkhivnym materialam Shtaba 10 armii)* (Petrograd: Gosudarstvennoe Izdatel'stvo, 1921), p. 17.

10 N. Stone, *The Eastern Front 1914–1917* (London: Penguin Books, 1998; first publ. 1975), p. 116.

11 Reichsarchiv, *Der Weltkrieg*, VII, p. 181.

12 Kamenskii, *Gibel' XX korpusa 8/21 fevralia 1915 goda*, p. 49.

13 I. I. Rostunov, *Russkii front pervoi mirovoi voiny* (Moscow: Nauka, 1976), p. 213.

14 A. P. Budberg, *Iz vospominanii o voine 1914–1917 g.g.: Tret'ya Vostochno-Prusskaia katastrofa 25 yanvarya–8 fevralya 1915 g.* (San Francisco, CA: n.p., 1930), p. 41.

15 H. Henning von Grote, *Unvergleichliche Deutsche Infanterie* (Hamburg: Hanseatische Verlagsanstalt, 1938), p. 214.

16 I. A. Khol'msen, *Mirovaia voina. Nashi operatsii na vostochno-Prusskom fronte zimoiu 1915 g.* (Paris: V. Beilinson, 1935), p. 203.

17 Hoffmann, *War Diaries and Other Papers*, II, p. 92.

18 Airapetov, *Uchastie Rossiiskoi imperii v Pervoi mirovoi voine (1914–1917). 1915 god*, pp. 52–3.

19 *Strategicheskii ocherk voiny 1914–1918 g.g.* (7 vols., Moscow: Vysshii voennyi redaktsionnyi sovet, 1920–23), III, p. 84.

20 E. Glaise-Horstenau, *Österreich-Ungarns Letzter Krieg 1914–1918*, II, *Das Kriegsjahr 1915. Erster Teil* (Vienna: Verlag der Militärwissenschaftlichen Mitteilungen, 1931), p. 180.

21 Ibid., pp. 17–18.

22 Ibid., p. 196; and G. A. Tunstall, *Blood on the Snow. The Carpathian Winter War of 1915* (Lawrence, KS: University Press of Kansas, 2010), pp. 125–7.

23 Glaise-Horstenau, Österreich-Ungarns Letzter Krieg 1914–1918, II, p. 203.

24 S. Dobiasch, Kaiserjäger im Osten. Karpathen-Tarnow-Gorlice (Graz: Leykam-Verlag, 1934), pp. 85–6.

25 A. Watson, The Fortress. The Great Siege of Przemyśl (London: Allen Lane, 2019), pp. 188–90; and Glaise-Horstenau, Österreich-Ungarns Letzter Krieg 1914–1918, II, p. 214.

26 F. Stuckheil, 'Die Zweite Einschließung der Festung Przemyśl. III. Das Ende', Militärwissenschaftliche und Technische Mitteilungen, Vol. 57 (1926), p. 534.

27 G. A. Tunstall, Written in Blood. The Battles for Fortress Przemyśl in WW1 (Bloomington, IN: Indiana University Press, 2016), p. 285.

28 Airapetov, Uchastie Rossiiskoi imperii v Pervoi mirovoi voine (1914–1917). 1915 god, p. 75.

29 KA: Conrad Papers, AOK Op.-Abteilung 490, Falkenhayn to Conrad, 22 March 1915.

30 Ibid., Conrad to Falkenhayn, 22 March 1915.

31 Glaise-Horstenau, Österreich-Ungarns Letzter Krieg 1914–1918, II, p. 270.

32 Ibid., p. 217.

33 'Surrender of Przemysl' and 'The Fall of Przemysl', The Times, 23 March 1915.

34 Nicholas to Alexandra, 9 March 1915 [OS], in C. E. Vulliamy (ed.), The Nicky–Sunny Letters. Correspondence of the Tsar and Tsaritsa 1914–1917, trans. A. L. Hynes (Hattiesburg, MS: Academic International, 1970), p. 38.

35 Agreement Between France, Russia, Great Britain and Italy, Signed at London, April 26, 1915 (London: HMSO, 1920).

36 Rostunov, Russkii front pervoi mirovoi voiny, pp. 229–30.

37 J. N. Danilov, Rußland im Weltkriege 1914–1915, trans. R. Freiherr von Campenhausen (Jena: Walter Biedermann, 1925), p. 456.

38 Tunstall, Blood on the Snow, p. 185.

39 Glaise-Horstenau, Österreich-Ungarns Letzter Krieg 1914–1918, II, p. 240.

40 A. A. Brussilov, A Soldier's Note-Book 1914–1918 (London: Macmillan & Co., 1930), p. 126; and Brusilov to Ivanov, 9 April 1915, in Gorlitskaia operatsiia. Sbornik dokumentov mirovoi imperialisticheskoi voiny na russkom fronte (1914–1917) (Moscow: Voenizdat, 1941), p. 32.

41 Danilov, Rußland im Weltkriege, pp. 463–4.

42 Airapetov, Uchastie Rossiiskoi imperii v Pervoi mirovoi voine (1914–1917). 1915 god, p. 85.

43 J. R. Schindler, 'A Hopeless Struggle: The Austro-Hungarian Army and Total War, 1914–1918' (PhD diss., McMaster University, 1995), pp. 104–6; and M. Rauchensteiner, *The First World War and the End of the Habsburg Monarchy, 1914–1918*, trans. A. J. Kay and A. Güttel-Bellert (Vienna: Böhlau Verlag, 2014; first publ. 1993), pp. 347–9.

44 Rauchensteiner, *The First World War and the End of the Habsburg Monarchy*, pp. 326–41.

45 N. Stone, 'Army and Society in the Habsburg Monarchy, 1900–1914', *Past & Present*, No. 33 (April 1966), p. 100.

46 G. Wawro, *A Mad Catastrophe. The Outbreak of World War I and the Collapse of the Habsburg Empire* (New York: Basic Books, 2015; first publ. 2014), pp. 34–5.

47 F. Conrad von Hötzendorf, *Aus Meiner Dienstzeit 1906–1918* (5 vols., Vienna: Rikola Verlag, 1921–5), V, pp. 852–3.

48 G. Gräfin Conrad von Hötzendorf, *Mein Leben mit Conrad von Hötzendorf. Sein geistiges Vermächtnis* (Leipzig: Greithlein & Co., 1935), p. 37. See also L. Sondhaus, *Franz Conrad von Hötzendorf. Architect of the Apocalypse* (Boston: Humanities Press, 2000), p. 172.

49 Rauchensteiner, *The First World War and the End of the Habsburg Monarchy*, p. 368; and Glaise-Horstenau, *Österreich-Ungarns Letzter Krieg 1914–1918*, II, p. 283.

50 Sondhaus, *Franz Conrad von Hötzendorf*, pp. 64–71; and G. E. Silberstein, *The Troubled Alliance. German–Austrian Relations 1914 to 1917* (Lexington, KY: University Press of Kentucky, 1970), p. 282.

51 Ministère de la Guerre, *Les Armées Françaises dans la Grande Guerre* (Paris: Imprimerie Nationale, 1922–39), Tome 2, p. 481.

52 H. H. Herwig, *The First World War. Germany and Austria–Hungary 1914–1918* (London: Arnold, 1997), pp. 140–41.

53 Reichsarchiv, *Der Weltkrieg*, VII, p. 353.

6. 'The forerunner of a catastrophe'

1 Nicholas to Alexandra, 12 April 1915 [OS], in C. E. Vulliamy (ed.), *The Nicky–Sunny Letters. Correspondence of the Tsar and Tsaritsa 1914–1917*, trans. A. L. Hynes (Hattiesburg, MS: Academic International, 1970), pp. 46–8.

2 C. Mick, *Lemberg, Lwów, L'viv, 1914–1947. Violence and Ethnicity in a Contested City* (West Lafayette, IN: Purdue University Press, 2016), p. 29.

3 A. Watson, *The Fortress. The Great Siege of Przemyśl* (London: Allen Lane, 2019), pp. 224–5.

4 A. A. Brussilov, *A Soldier's Note-Book 1914–1918* (London: Macmillan & Co., 1930), p. 130.

5 P. Robinson, *Grand Duke Nikolai Nikolaevich. Supreme Commander of the Russian Army* (DeKalb, IL: Northern Illinois University Press, 2014), pp. 226–7.

6 *Strategicheskii ocherk voiny 1914–1918 g.g.* (7 vols., Moscow: Vysshii voennyi redaktsionnyi sovet, 1920–23), IV, pp. 12–13. Original emphasis.

7 O. R. Airapetov, *Uchastie Rossiiskoi imperii v Pervoi mirovoi voine (1914–1917). 1915 god* (Moscow: Kuchkovo Pole, 2014), p. 82.

8 *Strategicheskii ocherk voiny 1914–1918 g.g.*, IV, p. 23.

9 Brusilov to Dragomirov, 26 April 1915, in *Gorlitskaia operatsiia. Sbornik dokumentov mirovoi imperialisticheskoi voiny na russkom fronte (1914–1917)* (Moscow: Voenizdat, 1941), p. 55.

10 I. I. Rostunov, *Russkii front pervoi mirovoi voiny* (Moscow: Nauka, 1976), pp. 235–6.

11 Radko-Dmitriev to Ivanov, 28 April 1915, in *Gorlitskaia operatsiia*, p. 44.

12 Falkenhayn to Conrad, 13 April 1915, in E. von Falkenhayn, *General Headquarters 1914–1916 and Its Critical Decisions* (London: Hutchinson & Co., 1919), p. 83.

13 Rostunov, *Russkii front pervoi mirovoi voiny*, p. 236.

14 J. N. Danilov, *Rußland im Weltkriege 1914–1915*, trans. R. Freiherr von Campenhausen (Jena: Walter Biedermann, 1925), p. 487.

15 Falkenhayn, *General Headquarters 1914–1916*, pp. 80–81.

16 W. Foerster (ed.), *Mackensen. Briefe und Aufzeichnungen des Generalfeldmarschalls aus Krieg und Frieden* (Leipzig: Bibliographisches Institut, 1938), p. 146.

17 U. Trumpener, 'The Road to Ypres: The Beginnings of Gas Warfare in World War I', *Journal of Modern History*, Vol. 47, No. 3 (September 1975), p. 468.

18 H. von François, *Gorlice 1915. Der Karpathendurchbruch und die Befreiung von Galizien* (Leipzig: K. F. Koehler, 1922), pp. 47–8.

19 O. T. von Kalm, *Schlachten des Weltkrieges. Gorlice* (Berlin: Gerhard Stalling, 1930), pp. 69, 71.

20 G. Gräfin Conrad von Hötzendorf, *Mein Leben mit Conrad von Hötzendorf. Sein geistiges Vermächtnis* (Leipzig: Greithlein & Co., 1935), p. 134.

21 Radko-Dmitriev to Ivanov, 2 May 1915, in *Gorlitskaia operatsiia*, pp. 108–9.

22 Foerster (ed.), *Mackensen*, pp. 150, 153.

23 *Strategicheskii ocherk voiny 1914–1918 g.g.*, IV, pp. 30–31.

24 Robinson, *Grand Duke Nikolai Nikolaevich*, p. 232.

25 Danilov, *Rußland im Weltkriege*, p. 489.

26 E. Glaise-Horstenau, *Österreich-Ungarns Letzter Krieg 1914–1918*, II, *Das Kriegsjahr 1915. Erster Teil* (Vienna: Verlag der Militärwissenschaftlichen Mitteilungen, 1931), p. 328; 61st Division Report, 4 May 1915, in *Gorlitskaia operatsiia*, p. 140; and Danilov, *Rußland im Weltkriege*, p. 494.

27 Dragomirov to army commanders, 6 May 1915, in *Gorlitskaia operatsiia*, p. 173.

28 *Gorlitskaia operatsiia*, p. 23.

29 Brussilov, *A Soldier's Note-Book*, p. 141; and Danilov, *Rußland im Weltkriege*, p. 494.

30 J. H. Cockfield, *Russia's Iron General. The Life of Aleksei A. Brusilov, 1853–1926* (Lanham, MD: Lexington Books, 2019), pp. 94–5; and *Strategicheskii ocherk voiny 1914–1918 g.g.*, IV, pp. 43–4.

31 François, *Gorlice 1915*, p. 174.

32 *Strategicheskii ocherk voiny 1914–1918 g.g.*, IV, p. 56. Original emphasis.

33 Robinson, *Grand Duke Nikolai Nikolaevich*, p. 241.

34 Reichsarchiv, *Der Weltkrieg 1914 bis 1918. VIII. Die Operationen des Jahres 1915. Die Ereignisse im Westen im Frühjahr und Sommer, im Osten von Frühjahr bis zum Jahresschluß* (Berlin: E. S. Mittler & Sohn, 1932), p. 5.

35 Ibid., p. 7; and Glaise-Horstenau, *Österreich-Ungarns Letzter Krieg 1914–1918*, II, pp. 412–13.

36 Falkenhayn, *General Headquarters 1914–1916*, pp. 94, 101; and R. T. Foley, *German Strategy and the Path to Verdun. Erich von Falkenhayn and the Development of Attrition, 1870–1916* (Cambridge: Cambridge University Press, 2005), p. 143.

37 'Italy Joins the Allies', in C. F. Horne (ed.), *Source Records of the Great War* (7 vols., USA: National Alumni, 1923), III, pp. 216, 221–8.

38 M. Thompson, *The White War. Life and Death on the Italian Front, 1915–1919* (London: Faber & Faber, 2008), pp. 22–3.

39 Lord Northcliffe, *At the War* (London: Hodder & Stoughton, 1916), p. 73.

40 F. Cappellano, 'The Evolution of Tactical Regulations in the Italian Army in the Great War', in V. Wilcox (ed.), *Italy in the Era of the Great War* (Leiden and Boston: Brill, 2019), pp. 30–31.

41 J. Gooch, *The Italian Army and the First World War* (Cambridge: Cambridge University Press, 2014), p. 46.

42 D. G. Hermann, 'The Paralysis of Italian Strategy in the Italian–Turkish War, 1911–1912', *English Historical Review*, Vol. 104, No. 411 (April 1989), p. 341; and Ministero della Guerra, *L'Esercito Italiano nella Grande Guerra (1915–1918)* (7 vols., Rome: Provveditorato Generale dello Stato Libreria, 1927–88), I, p. 58.

43 Gooch, *The Italian Army*, p. 50; Ministero della Guerra, *L'Esercito Italiano nella Grande Guerra*, I, pp. 67–8; and L. Cadorna, *La Guerra alla Fronte Italiana* (2 vols., Milani: Fratelli Treves, 1921), I, pp. 13–19.

44 Ministero della Guerra, *L'Esercito Italiano nella Grande Guerra*, I, pp. 68; and Gooch, *The Italian Army*, pp. 51, 142.

45 Cadorna, *La Guerra alla Fronte Italiana*, I, pp. 111–12.

46 Ministero della Guerra, *L'Esercito Italiano nella Grande Guerra*, II, pp. 9–10.

47 Thompson, *The White War*, p. 64; and Cadorna, *La Guerra alla Fronte Italiana*, I, p. 126.

48 R. Corselli, *Cadorna* (Milan: Edizioni Corbaccio, 1937), pp. 318–19.

49 Ministero della Guerra, *L'Esercito Italiano nella Grande Guerra*, II, p. 168.

50 Ibid., p. 225.

51 Corselli, *Cadorna*, p. 319.

7. 'I will save Russia'

1 W. Foerster (ed.), *Mackensen. Briefe und Aufzeichnungen des Generalfeldmarschalls aus Krieg und Frieden* (Leipzig: Bibliographisches Institut, 1938), p. 172.

2 H. von François, *Gorlice 1915. Der Karpathendurchbruch und die Befreiung von Galizien* (Leipzig: K. F. Koehler, 1922), p. 195.

3 N. N. Golovine, *The Russian Army in the World War* (New Haven: Yale University Press, 1931), pp. 220–21.

4 J. H. Morrow Jr., *The Great War in the Air. Military Aviation from 1909 to 1921* (Tuscaloosa, AL: University of Alabama Press, 2009), pp. 81, 107,

123–5; and R. L. DiNardo, *Breakthrough. The Gorlice–Tarnow Campaign, 1915* (Santa Barbara, CA: Praeger, 2010), pp. 89–90.

5 E. Glaise-Horstenau, *Österreich-Ungarns Letzter Krieg 1914–1918*, II, *Das Kriegsjahr 1915. Erster Teil* (Vienna: Verlag der Militärwissenschaftlichen Mitteilungen, 1931), p. 470.

6 J. H. Cockfield, *Russia's Iron General. The Life of Aleksei A. Brusilov, 1853–1926* (Lanham, MD: Lexington Books, 2019), p. 100.

7 J. N. Danilov, *Rußland im Weltkriege 1914–1915*, trans. R. Freiherr von Campenhausen (Jena: Walter Biedermann, 1925), p. 517.

8 François, *Gorlice 1915*, pp. 218, 228, 229.

9 Foerster (ed.), *Mackensen*, pp. 177–8.

10 Reichsarchiv, *Der Weltkrieg 1914 bis 1918. VIII. Die Operationen des Jahres 1915. Die Ereignisse im Westen im Frühjahr und Sommer, im Osten von Frühjahr bis zum Jahresschluß* (Berlin: E. S. Mittler & Sohn, 1932), p. 243.

11 M. Hoffmann, *War Diaries and Other Papers*, trans. E. Sutton (2 vols., London: Martin Secker, 1929), II, pp. 107–8.

12 Reichsarchiv, *Der Weltkrieg*, VIII, p. 236.

13 E. von Falkenhayn, *General Headquarters 1914–1916 and Its Critical Decisions* (London: Hutchinson & Co., 1919), pp. 115–16; and Hoffmann, *War Diaries and Other Papers*, II, p. 109.

14 F. von Lossberg, *Lossberg's War. The World War I Memoirs of a German Chief of Staff*, ed. and trans. D. T. Zabecki (Lexington, KY: University Press of Kentucky, 2017), pp. 123, 155–6.

15 Danilov, *Rußland im Weltkriege*, p. 521.

16 N. Stone, *The Eastern Front 1914–1917* (London: Penguin, 1998; first publ. 1975), pp. 145, 147.

17 D. R. Jones, 'Imperial Russia's Forces at War', in W. Murray and A. R. Millett (eds.), *Military Effectiveness. Volume I: The First World War* (Winchester, MA: Allen & Unwin, 1988), pp. 266–7, 270; and Stone, *The Eastern Front*, pp. 196–7.

18 W. C. Fuller, Jr., *The Foe Within. Fantasies of Treason and the End of Imperial Russia* (Ithaca and London: Cornell University Press, 2006), pp. 192, 215.

19 O. R. Airapetov, *Uchastie Rossiiskoi imperii v Pervoi mirovoi voine (1914–1917). 1915 god* (Moscow: Kuchkovo Pole, 2014), p. 269.

20 Denikin cited in Golovine, *The Russian Army in the World War*, p. 145.

21 Airapetov, *Uchastie Rossiiskoi imperii v Pervoi mirovoi voine 1915*, p. 235; Danilov, *Rußland im Weltkriege*, p. 522; and I. I. Rostunov, *Russkii front pervoi mirovoi voiny* (Moscow: Nauka, 1976), p. 255.

22 P. Robinson, *Grand Duke Nikolai Nikolaevich. Supreme Commander of the Russian Army* (DeKalb, IL: Northern Illinois University Press, 2014), p. 249.

23 Airapetov, *Uchastie Rossiiskoi imperii v Pervoi mirovoi voine 1915*, p. 237.

24 Nicholas to Alexandra, 23 June 1915 [OS], in C. E. Vulliamy (ed.), *The Nicky–Sunny Letters. Correspondence of the Tsar and Tsaritsa 1914–1917*, trans. A. L. Hynes (Hattiesburg, MS: Academic International, 1970), p. 66.

25 R. K. Massie, *Nicholas and Alexandra* (London: Victor Gollancz, 1968), pp. 188–9.

26 Ibid., pp. 300–301; and Alexandra to Nicholas II, 16 June 1915 [OS], in Vulliamy (ed.), *The Nicky–Sunny Letters*, pp. 97–8. Original emphasis.

27 M. V. Rodzianko, *The Reign of Rasputin. An Empire's Collapse*, trans. C. Zvegintzoff (London: A. M. Philpot, 1927), pp. 110–11.

28 E. Lohr, 'Patriotic Violence and the State. The Moscow Riots of May 1915', *Kritika. Explorations in Russian and Eurasian History*, Vol. 4, No. 3 (Summer 2003), p. 607.

29 M. Paléologue, *An Ambassador's Memoirs*, trans. F. A. Holt (3 vols., London: Hutchinson & Co., 1925), II, p. 23.

30 G. E. Silberstein, *The Troubled Alliance. German–Austrian Relations 1914 to 1917* (Lexington, KY: University Press of Kentucky, 1970), pp. 291–2.

31 Reichsarchiv, *Der Weltkrieg 1914 bis 1918. IX. Die Operationen des Jahres 1915. Die Ereignisse im Westen und auf dem Balkan vom Sommer bis zum Jahresschluß* (Berlin: E. S. Mittler & Sohn, 1933), p. 159.

32 M. Rauchensteiner, *The First World War and the End of the Habsburg Monarchy, 1914–1918*, trans. A. J. Kay and A. Güttel-Bellert (Vienna: Böhlau Verlag, 2014; first publ. 1993), p. 465.

33 E. Bauer, *Der Löwe vom Isonzo. Feldmarschall Svetozar Boroević de Bojna* (Graz: Styria, 1985), pp. 8–9; and F. Weber, *Isonzo 1915* (Klagenfurt and Vienna: Artur Kollitisch, 1933), p. 27.

34 J. R. Schindler, *Isonzo. The Forgotten Sacrifice of the Great War* (Westport, CT: Praeger, 2001), p. 66.

35 TNA: WO 106/758, 'Notes of a Conversation with General Cadorna: 15th July'.

36 M. Brunner, 'Der Stellungsbau im Karst', *Militärwissenschaftliche und Technische Mitteilungen*, Vol. 53 (1922), p. 340.

37 A. Omodeo, *Momenti della Vita di Guerra. Dai Diari e dalle Lettere dei Caduti 1915–1918* (Torino: Einaudi, 1968), p. 429.

38 Schindler, *Isonzo*, p. 70.

39 Glaise-Horstenau, *Österreich-Ungarns Letzter Krieg 1914–1918*, II, pp. 749, 758.

40 Boroević to Tisza, 10 August 1915, in Rauchensteiner, *The First World War and the End of the Habsburg Monarchy*, p. 410.

41 Ministero della Guerra, *L'Esercito Italiano nella Grande Guerra (1915–1918)* (7 vols., Rome: Provveditorato Generale dello Stato Libreria, 1927–88), II, p. 287.

42 L. Cadorna, *La Guerra alla Fronte Italiana* (2 vols., Milan: Fratelli Treves, 1921), I, pp. 143–5.

43 Reichsarchiv, *Der Weltkrieg*, VIII, p. 284.

44 Rostunov, *Russkii front pervoi mirovoi voiny*, p. 258.

45 K. Gabriel, *Die 4. Garde-Infanterie-Division. Der Ruhmesweg einer bewährten Kampftruppe durch den Weltkrieg* (Berlin: Klasing & Co., 1921), p. 19.

46 Reichsarchiv, *Der Weltkrieg*, VIII, p. 288; and Airapetov, *Uchastie Rossiiskoi imperii v Pervoi mirovoi voine (1914–1917). 1915 god*, pp. 238, 240, 243.

47 J. A. Sanborn, *Imperial Apocalypse. The Great War and the Destruction of the Russian Empire* (Oxford: Oxford University Press, 2015; first publ. 2014), pp. 73, 77–8.

48 P. K. Kondzerovskii, *V stavke verkhovnogo. 1914–1917* (Paris: n.p., 1967), p. 63.

49 Sanborn, *Imperial Apocalypse*, p. 79.

50 'The Eve of the Retreat', *The Times*, 9 August 1915.

51 HIA: Stavka Verkhovnogo Glavnokomanduiushchego, Box 1, Grand Duke Nikolai to Ruzski and Alekseev, 17 August 1915.

52 Robinson, *Grand Duke Nikolai Nikolaevich*, p. 256.

53 Rodzianko, *The Reign of Rasputin*, p. 150.

8. 'The European war is nearing its end'

1 G. E. Silberstein, *The Troubled Alliance. German–Austrian Relations 1914 to 1917* (Lexington, KY: University Press of Kentucky, 1970), pp. 173–4.

2 S. Constant, *Foxy Ferdinand 1868–1948. Tsar of Bulgaria* (London: Sidgwick & Jackson, 1979), pp. 303–4.

3 'Ferdinand of Bulgaria', *The Times*, 11 September 1948.

4 Reichsarchiv, *Der Weltkrieg 1914 bis 1918*. VIII. *Die Operationen des Jahres 1915. Die Ereignisse im Westen im Frühjahr und Sommer, im Osten von Frühjahr bis zum Jahresschluß* (Berlin: E. S. Mittler & Sohn, 1932), pp. 368–9, 420.

5 Ibid., pp. 364–6.

6 Ludendorff to Moltke, 15 August 1915, in E. Zechlin, 'Ludendorff im Jahre 1915. Unveröffentlichte Briefe', *Historische Zeitschrift*, Vol. 211 (1970), p. 346.

7 Hindenburg to Falkenhayn, 13 August 1915, in E. von Falkenhayn, *General Headquarters 1914–1916 and Its Critical Decisions* (London: Hutchinson & Co., 1919), p. 127.

8 Ibid., p. 115.

9 W. Foerster (ed.), *Mackensen. Briefe und Aufzeichnungen des Generalfeldmarschalls aus Krieg und Frieden* (Leipzig: Bibliographisches Institut, 1938), p. 210.

10 Ibid., p. 212.

11 Conrad to Bolfras, 4 October 1915, in M. Rauchensteiner, *The First World War and the End of the Habsburg Monarchy, 1914–1918*, trans. A. J. Kay and A. Güttel-Bellert (Vienna: Böhlau Verlag, 2014; first publ. 1993), pp. 460–61.

12 E. Glaise-Horstenau, *Österreich-Ungarns Letzter Krieg 1914–1918*, III, *Das Kriegsjahr 1915. Zweiter Teil* (Vienna: Verlag der Militärwissenschaftlichen Mitteilungen, 1932), pp. 52, 61.

13 Ibid., pp. 139, n. 1, 180; and H. Kerchnawe, 'Der Feldzug von Rowno', *Militärwissenschaftliche Mitteilungen*, Vol. 63 (1932), p. 230.

14 Glaise-Horstenau, *Österreich-Ungarns Letzter Krieg 1914–1918*, III, pp. 133, 181.

15 KA: Conrad Papers, AOK Op.-Abteilung 490, Falkenhayn to Conrad, 12 September 1915.

16 Ibid., Conrad to Falkenhayn, 13 September 1915.

17 H. H. Herwig, *The First World War. Germany and Austria–Hungary 1914–1918* (London: Arnold, 1997), p. 147.

18 Falkenhayn, *General Headquarters 1914–1916*, p. 150.

19 Alexandra to Nicholas, 22 August 1915, and reply, 25 August 1915 [OS], in C. E. Vulliamy (ed.), *The Nicky–Sunny Letters. Correspondence of the Tsar and Tsaritsa 1914–1917*, trans. A. L. Hynes (Hattiesburg, MS: Academic International, 1970), pp. 70–71, 114. Original emphasis.

20 'Progressive Bloc', 7 September 1915, in F. A. Golder (ed.), *Documents of Russian History 1914–1917* (Stanford, CA: The Century Co., 1927), pp. 134–6.

21 R. S. Wortman, *Scenarios of Power. Myth and Ceremony in Russian Monarchy from Peter the Great to the Abdication of Nicholas II* (Princeton, NJ, and Oxford: Princeton University Press, 2006), p. 404.

22 P. Gilliard, *Thirteen Years at the Russian Court* (New York: George H. Doran & Co., 1921), p. 137.

23 'Meeting of the Council of Ministers', 8 and 15 September 1915, in Golder (ed.), *Documents of Russian History 1914–1917*, pp. 136–44.

24 A. A. Polivanov, *Iz dnevnikov i vospominanii po dolzhnosti voennogo ministra i ego pomoshchnika 1907–1916 g.,* ed. A. M. Zaionchkovskii (2 vols., Moscow: Vysshii voennyi redaktsionnyi sovet, 1924), I, p. 211.

25 M. K. Lemke, *250 dnei v tsarskoi stavke (25 sentiabria 1915–2 iiulia 1916)* (Petrograd: Gosudarstvennoe Izdatel'stvo, 1920), p. 32.

26 S. Washburn, *Victory in Defeat. The Agony of Warsaw and the Russian Retreat* (London: Constable & Co., 1916), p. 173; and O. R. Airapetov, *Uchastie Rossiiskoi imperii v Pervoi mirovoi voine (1914–1917). 1915 god* (Moscow: Kuchkovo Pole, 2014), pp. 246–7.

27 N. N. Golovine, *The Russian Army in the World War* (New Haven: Yale University Press, 1931), p. 222.

28 J. N. Danilov, *Rußland im Weltkriege 1914–1915*, trans. R. Freiherr von Campenhausen (Jena: Walter Biedermann, 1925), p. 516.

29 'Procès-verbal de la conférence des représentants des différentes armées alliées tenue à Chantilly, le 7 juillet 1915', in Ministère de la Guerre, *Les Armées Françaises dans la Grande Guerre* (Paris: Imprimerie Nationale, 1922–39) [hereafter *AFGG*], Book 3 – *Annexes*, Vol. 2, No. 860, pp. 75–84.

30 D. Lloyd George, *War Memoirs of David Lloyd George* (2 vols., London: Odhams Press, 1933–6), I, p. 223.

31 A. Mitrović, *Serbia's Great War 1914–1918* (London: Hurst, 2007), pp. 118, 142–3.

32　J. C. King, *Generals and Politicians. Conflict Between France's High Command, Parliament and Government, 1914–1918* (Berkeley and Los Angeles: University of California Press, 1951), p. 67.

33　S. B. Chester, *Life of Venizelos* (London: Constable and Company, 1921), p. 255.

34　*AFGG*, Book 8/1, p. 145.

35　D. Dutton, *The Politics of Diplomacy. Britain and France in the Balkans in the First World War* (London and New York: I. B. Tauris, 1998), pp. 44–7.

36　Reichsarchiv, *Der Weltkrieg 1914 bis 1918. IX. Die Operationen des Jahres 1915. Die Ereignisse im Westen und auf dem Balkan vom Sommer bis zum Jahresschluß* (Berlin: E. S. Mittler & Sohn, 1933), p. 202.

37　Foerster (ed.), *Mackensen*, pp. 216–17.

38　Glaise-Horstenau, *Österreich-Ungarns Letzter Krieg 1914–1918*, III, p. 200.

39　R.L. DiNardo, *Invasion. The Conquest of Serbia, 1915* (Santa Barbara, CA: Praeger, 2015), p. 62.

40　Foerster (ed.), *Mackensen*, p. 221.

41　*Veliki rat Srbije za oslobođenje i ujedinjenje Srba, Hrvata i Slovenaca* (28 vols., Belgrade: Glavni đeneralštab, 1924–37), IX, p. 102.

42　Glaise-Horstenau, *Österreich-Ungarns Letzter Krieg 1914–1918*, III, p. 213.

43　Foerster (ed.), *Mackensen*, pp. 223–4.

44　H. Stegemann, *Hermann Stegemann's Geschichte des Krieges. Dritter Band* (Stuttgart and Berlin: Deutsche Verlags, 1919), p. 461.

45　Reichsarchiv, *Der Weltkrieg*, IX, p. 232.

46　S. Skoko, *Vojvoda Radomir Putnik* (2 vols., Belgrade: Beogradski izdavačko-grafički zavod, 1984), II, p. 260.

47　R. L. DiNardo, 'The Limits of Envelopment: The Invasion of Serbia, 1915', *The Historian*, Vol. 78, No. 3 (2016), pp. 495–6.

48　Mitrović, *Serbia's Great War*, p. 149.

49　Reichsarchiv, *Der Weltkrieg*, IX, pp. 286–7.

9. 'Even victorious wars leave wounds'

1　J. K. Tanenbaum, *General Maurice Sarrail 1856–1929. The French Army and Left-Wing Politics* (Chapel Hill, NC: University of North Carolina Press, 1974), p. 9.

2 D. Dutton, *The Politics of Diplomacy. Britain and France in the Balkans in the First World War* (London and New York: I. B. Tauris, 1998), p. 47; and M. Sarrail, 'La Grèce Venizéliste', *La Revue de Paris*, 15 December 1919, p. 685.

3 A. Bernède, '"The Gardeners of Salonika": The Lines of Communication and the Logistics of the French Army of the East, October 1915–November 1918', *War & Society*, Vol. 16, No. 1 (1998), p. 46; and Ministère de la Guerre, *Les Armées Françaises dans la Grande Guerre* (Paris: Imprimerie Nationale, 1922–39) [hereafter *AFGG*], Book 8/1, p. 180.

4 Sarrail to Millerand, 19 October 1915, in *AFGG*, Book 8/1 – *Annexes*, Vol. 2, No. 210, p. 230.

5 'Ordre d'opérations no. 1 de la 156 division', 20 October 1915, in *AFGG*, Book 8/1 – *Annexes*, Vol. 2, No. 220, pp. 238–40.

6 G. F. Abbott, *Greece and the Allies 1914–1922* (London: Methuen & Co., 1922), pp. 56–61; and S. B. Chester, *Life of Venizelos* (London: Constable and Company, 1921), pp. 258–9.

7 'Attitude of Greece', *The Times*, 7 December 1915.

8 Ibid.

9 S. P. P. Cosmetatos, *The Tragedy of Greece*, trans. E. W. & A. Dickes (London: Kegan Paul, Trench, Trubner & Co., 1929), p. 94.

10 Tanenbaum, *General Maurice Sarrail 1856–1929*, pp. 78–80.

11 'Plan of Action Proposed by France to the Coalition', Appendix 1, in *Military Operations. France and Belgium, 1916. Appendices* (London: Macmillan & Co., 1932), pp. 1–5.

12 Sir J. Edmonds, *Military Operations. France and Belgium, 1916* (2 vols., London: Macmillan & Co., 1933), I, pp. 5–9.

13 TNA: CAB 28/1, 'Summary of the Conference Held at Calais on December 5, 1915, between British and French Governments'.

14 'Rapport sur les travaux de la conférence tenue à Chantilly les 6, 7 et 8 décembre 1915', in *AFGG*, Book 4/1 – *Annexes*, Vol. 1, No. 56, p. 137.

15 D. French, *British Strategy and War Aims 1914–1916* (London: Allen & Unwin, 1986), p. 151.

16 'Ordine di Operazione No. 14', 1 October 1915, in Ministero della Guerra, *L'Esercito Italiano nella Grande Guerra (1915–1918)* (7 vols., Rome: Provveditorato Generale dello Stato Libreria, 1927–88), II, bis, p. 378;

J. R. Schindler, *Isonzo. The Forgotten Sacrifice of the Great War* (Westport, CT: Praeger, 2001), p. 92; J. Gooch, *The Italian Army and the First World War* (Cambridge: Cambridge University Press, 2014), p. 115; and L. Cadorna, *La Guerra alla Fronte Italiana* (2 vols., Milan: Fratelli Treves, 1921), I, pp. 153–4.

17 E. Glaise-Horstenau, *Österreich-Ungarns Letzter Krieg 1914–1918*, III, *Das Kriegsjahr 1915. Zweiter Teil* (Vienna: Verlag der Militärwissenschaftlichen Mitteilungen, 1932), p. 391.

18 *La Guerra d'Italia* (6 vols., Milan: Fratelli Treves, 1916–24), III, p. 72.

19 Ministero della Guerra, *L'Esercito Italiano nella Grande Guerra*, II, pp. 444, 447.

20 Cadorna, *La Guerra alla Fronte Italiana*, I, p. 154.

21 M. Isnenghi and G. Rochat, *La Grande Guerra 1914–1918* (Milan: Sansoni, 2004; first publ. 2000), p. 167.

22 ADN: MG/99, F. Bucci diary, 1 November 1915.

23 Capello to Frugoni, 15 November 1915, and Frugoni to Cadorna, 16 November 1915, in Ministero della Guerra, *L'Esercito Italiano nella Grande Guerra*, II, bis, pp. 424–8.

24 Cadorna, *La Guerra alla Fronte Italiana*, I, p. 158.

25 M. Mondini, *Il Capo. La Grande Guerra del Generale Luigi Cadorna* (Bologna: Società Editrice il Mulino, 2017), p. 184.

26 KA: Conrad Papers, AOK Op.-Abteiling 525, Fifth Army to AOK, 14 November 1915.

27 Glaise-Horstenau, *Österreich-Ungarns Letzter Krieg 1914–1918*, III, pp. 510, 514.

28 *La Guerra d'Italia*, III, pp. 73–4.

29 *Strategicheskii ocherk voiny 1914–1918 g.g.* (7 vols., Moscow: Vysshii voennyi redaktsionnyi sovet, 1920–23), V, pp. 7–9.

30 A. Arz von Straussenburg, *Zur Geschichte des Grossen Krieges 1914–1918* (Vienna, Munich and Leipzig: Rikola, 1924), p. 97.

31 E. Glaise-Horstenau, *Österreich-Ungarns Letzter Krieg 1914–1918*, IV, *Das Kriegsjahr 1916. Erster Teil* (Vienna: Verlag der Militärwissenschaftlichen Mitteilungen, 1933), pp. 27–30.

32 *Strategicheskii ocherk voiny 1914–1918 g.g.*, V, p. 13; and O. R. Airapetov, *Uchastie Rossiiskoi imperii v Pervoi mirovoi voine 1915* (Moscow: Kuchkovo Pole, 2014), p. 433.

33 *Strategicheskii ocherk voiny 1914–1918 g.g.*, V, pp. 14–15.

34 Airapetov, *Uchastie Rossiiskoi imperii v Pervoi mirovoi voine (1914–1917). 1915 god*, p. 433.

35 M. K. Lemke, *250 dnei v tsarskoi stavke (25 sentiabria 1915–2 iiulia 1916)* (Petersburg: Gosudarstvennoe Izdatel'stvo, 1920), pp. 347–8.

36 KA: Conrad Papers, AOK Op.-Abteilung 520, Conrad to Falkenhayn, 9 October 1915.

37 Ibid., Falkenhayn to Conrad, 10 October 1915.

38 M. Rauchensteiner, *The First World War and the End of the Habsburg Monarchy, 1914–1918*, trans. A. J. Kay and A. Güttel-Bellert (Vienna: Böhlau Verlag, 2014; first publ. 1993), pp. 471–3.

39 Glaise-Horstenau, *Österreich-Ungarns Letzter Krieg 1914–1918*, III, pp. 590–91.

40 H. Afflerbach, *Falkenhayn. Politisches Denken und Handeln im Kaiserreich* (Munich: Oldenbourg, 1994), p. 355.

41 E. von Falkenhayn, *General Headquarters 1914–1916 and Its Critical Decisions* (London: Hutchinson & Co., 1919), pp. 195–9.

42 Reichsarchiv, *Der Weltkrieg 1914 bis 1918. X. Die Operationen des Jahres 1916 bis zum Wechsel in der Obersten Heeresleitung* (Berlin: E. S. Mittler & Sohn, 1936), pp. 5–6; and R. T. Foley, *German Strategy and the Path to Verdun. Erich von Falkenhayn and the Development of Attrition, 1870–1916* (Cambridge: Cambridge University Press, 2005), p. 189.

43 Reichsarchiv, *Der Weltkrieg*, X, pp. 1–2.

44 Afflerbach, *Falkenhayn*, p. 358.

45 A. Urbanski von Ostrymiecz, *Conrad von Hötzendorf. Soldat und Mensch* (Graz: Ulrich Mosers, 1939), p. 345.

46 'The Attacks on Montenegro', *The Times*, 11 January 1916.

47 S. Pavlović, *Balkan Anschluss. The Annexation of Montenegro and the Creation of the Common South Slavic State* (West Lafayette, IN: Purdue University Press, 2008), p. 77.

48 'Die Unterwerfung Montenegros', *Innsbrucker Nachrichten*, 18 January 1916.

49 R. J. Kerner, 'Austro-Hungarian War-Aims in the Winter of 1915–1916 as Revealed by Secret Documents', *Journal of International Relations*, Vol. 10, No. 4 (April 1920), pp. 460–64.

50 Ibid., pp. 464–70.

51 'Vienna, 7 January 1916', in M. Komjáthy (ed.), *Protokolle des Gemeinsamen Ministerrates der Österreichisch-Ungarischen Monarchie (1914–1918)* (Budapest: Akadémiai Kiadó, 1966), pp. 352–74.

52 Conrad to Bolfras, 11 January 1916, in Rauchensteiner, *The First World War and the End of the Habsburg Monarchy*, pp. 488–9.

10. *'Outstanding men are needed everywhere'*

1 P. Gilliard, *Thirteen Years at the Russian Court* (New York: George H. Doran & Co., 1921), pp. 162–3.

2 R. K. Massie, *Nicholas and Alexandra* (London: Victor Gollancz, 1968), pp. 327–8.

3 O. Figes, *A People's Tragedy. The Russian Revolution 1891–1924* (London: Jonathan Cape, 1996), p. 278.

4 J. T. Fuhrmann, *Rasputin. The Untold Story* (New York: John Wiley & Sons, 2013), p. 11.

5 Figes, *A People's Tragedy*, p. 284; and D. Smith, *Rasputin* (London: Macmillan, 2016), pp. 492–3.

6 Fuhrmann, *Rasputin*, pp. 165–6; and Smith, *Rasputin*, p. 505.

7 M. V. Rodzianko, *The Reign of Rasputin. An Empire's Collapse*, trans. C. Zvegintzoff (London: A. M. Philpot, 1927), pp. 181–2.

8 M. Paléologue, *An Ambassador's Memoirs*, trans. F. A. Holt (3 vols., London: Hutchinson & Co., 1925), II, p. 166.

9 N. Stone, *The Eastern Front 1914–1917* (London: Penguin, 1998; first publ. 1975), p. 211.

10 'Mémorandum pour la réunion des commandants en chef des armées alliées', 15 February 1916, in Ministère de la Guerre, *Les Armées Françaises dans la Grande Guerre* (Paris: Imprimerie Nationale, 1922–39) [hereafter *AFGG*], Book 4/1 – *Annexes*, Vol. 1, No. 237, pp. 438–50.

11 I. I. Rostunov, *Russkii front pervoi mirovoi voiny* (Moscow: Nauka, 1976), p. 283.

12 *Strategicheskii ocherk voiny 1914–1918 g.g.* (7 vols., Moscow: Vysshii voennyi redaktsionnyi sovet, 1920–23), V, pp. 15–17, and VI, p. 12.

13 Nicholas to Alexandra, 12 February 1916 [OS], in C. E. Vulliamy (ed.), *The Nicky–Sunny Letters. Correspondence of the Tsar and Tsaritsa 1914–1917*, trans. A. L. Hynes (Hattiesburg, MS: Academic International, 1970), pp. 146–7.

14 Sir A. Knox, *With the Russian Army 1914–1917* (2 vols., London: Hutchinson & Co., 1921), II, pp. 402–3.

15 M. K. Lemke, *250 dnei v tsarskoi stavke (25 sentiabria 1915–2 iiulia 1916)* (Petersburg: Gosudarstvennoe Izdatel'stvo, 1920), pp. 538, 564.

16 D. Šarenac, 'Golgotha: The Retreat of the Serbian Army and Civilians in 1915–16', in P. Gatrell and L. Zhvanko (eds.), *Europe on the Move. Refugees in the Era of the Great War* (Manchester: Manchester University Press, 2017), p. 246.

17 'Compte rendu des opérations de la mission du lt-colonel Broussaud du 17 au 18 janvier 1916', in *AFGG*, Book 8/1 – *Annexes*, Vol. 3, No. 1128, pp. 353–5.

18 A. Mitrović, *Serbia's Great War 1914–1918* (London: Hurst, 2007), pp. 159–60.

19 A. Palmer, *The Gardeners of Salonika* (London: Andre Deutsch, 1965), pp. 52–3.

20 'On Our Salonika Front', *The Times*, 30 December 1915.

21 R. C. Hall, *Balkan Breakthrough. The Battle of Dobro Pole 1918* (Bloomington, IN: Indiana University Press, 2010), p. 52. Original emphasis.

22 E. von Falkenhayn, *General Headquarters 1914–1916 and Its Critical Decisions* (London: Hutchinson & Co., 1919), pp. 188–90; and Hall, *Balkan Breakthrough*, pp. 58–9.

23 Joffre to Sarrail, 17 January 1916, in *AFGG*, Book 8/1 – *Annexes*, Vol. 3, No. 1123, pp. 349–50; and J. K. Tanenbaum, *General Maurice Sarrail 1856–1929. The French Army and Left-Wing Politics* (Chapel Hill, NC: University of North Carolina Press, 1974), pp. 86–7.

24 'Conversation tenue entre le général Joffre et le général Robertson', 14 February 1916, in *AFGG*, Book 8/1 – *Annexes*, Vol. 3, No. 1187, pp. 426–30.

25 *AFGG*, Book 8/1, pp. 424–6.

26 C. Falls, *Military Operations Macedonia* [Vol. I]. *From the Outbreak of War to the Spring of 1917* (London: HMSO, 1933), pp. 110–11.

27 TNA: CAB 42/11/9, 'Note by the Chief of the Imperial General Staff on the Situation at Salonika', 22 March 1916, and 'War Committee', 23 March 1916.

28 F. von Lossberg, *Lossberg's War. The World War I Memoirs of a German Chief of Staff*, ed. and trans. D. T. Zabecki (Lexington, KY: University Press of Kentucky, 2017), pp. 195–6.

29 K.-H. Janßen, *Der Kanzler und der General. Die Führungskrise um Beth-mann Hollweg und Falkenhayn (1914–1916)* (Göttingen: Musterschmidt, 1967), p. 191.

30 Ibid., p. 195.

31 KA: Conrad Papers, AOK Op.-Abteilung 520, Conrad to Falkenhayn, 19 January 1916.

32 Ibid., Falkenhayn to Conrad, 25 January 1916.

33 W. Flex, *Die Russische Frühjahroffensive 1916* (Oldenburg: Gerhard Stall-ing, 1919), p. 17.

34 E. Ludendorff, *My War Memories 1914–1918* (2 vols., London: Hutchin-son & Co., 1919), I, p. 210; and M. Hoffmann, *War Diaries and Other Papers*, trans. E. Sutton (2 vols., London: Martin Secker, 1929), I, p. 113.

35 Flex, *Die Russische Frühjahroffensive 1916*, p. 20; and Stone, *The Eastern Front*, p. 227.

36 R. G. Robbins Jr., *Overtaken by the Night. One Russian's Journey Through Peace, War, Revolution, and Terror* (Pittsburgh, PA: University of Pitts-burgh Press, 2017), p. 337.

37 Flex, *Die Russische Frühjahroffensive 1916*, p. 36.

38 N. E. Podorozhnyi, *Narochskaia operatsiia v marte 1916 g. na russkom fronte mirovoi voiny* (Moscow: Gosudarstvennoye Voyennoye Izdatel'stvo narkomata oborony Soyuza SSR, 1938), pp. 23–4.

39 Ibid., p. 93.

40 Reichsarchiv, *Der Weltkrieg 1914 bis 1918. X. Die Operationen des Jahres 1916 bis zum Wechsel in der Obersten Heeresleitung* (Berlin: E. S. Mittler & Sohn, 1936), p. 434.

41 Podorozhnyi, *Narochskaia operatsiia v marte 1916 g.*, pp. 80–81.

42 O. R. Airapetov, *Uchastie Rossiiskoi imperii v Pervoi mirovoi voine (1914–1917). 1916 god* (Moscow: Kuchkovo Pole, 2015), p. 73.

43 *Strategicheskii ocherk voiny 1914–1918 g.g.*, V, p. 26.

44 Lemke, *250 dnei v tsarskoi stavke*, p. 617.

45 Falkenhayn, *General Headquarters 1914–1916*, p. 240.

46 A. V. Oleinikov, *Uspeshnye generaly zabytoi voiny* (Moscow: Veche, 2014), p. 224; Podorozhnyi, *Narochskaia operatsiia v marte 1916 g.*, pp. 150–51; and D. R. Stone, *The Russian Army in the Great War. The Eastern Front, 1914–1917* (Lawrence, KS: University Press of Kansas, 2015), p. 236.

47 O. R. Airapetov, 'The Naroch Offensive and the Dismissal of A. A. Polivanov', *Russian Studies in History*, Vol. 51, No. 4 (Spring 2013), p. 26.

48 Lemke, *250 dnei v tsarskoi stavke*, p. 643.

11. 'A moment of utmost gravity'

1 'Télégramme adressé le 3 mars 1916 par le général commandant en chef au chef de la mission militaire française attachée à l'armée italienne', in Ministère de la Guerre, *Les Armées Françaises dans la Grande Guerre* (Paris: Imprimerie Nationale, 1922–39) [hereafter *AFGG*], Book 4/1 – *Annexes*, Vol. 2, No. 962, pp. 62–3.

2 'Télégramme adressé au général en chef par la mission militaire française attachée à l'armée italienne, le 3 mars 1916', in *AFGG*, Book 4/1 – *Annexes*, Vol. 2, No. 963, pp. 63-4.

3 Ministero della Guerra, *L'Esercito Italiano nella Grande Guerra (1915–1918)* (7 vols., Rome: Provveditorato Generale dello Stato Libreria, 1927–88), III, Tomo 1, p. 179.

4 'The Battle-Fronts of the Isonzo', *Manchester Guardian*, 10 January 1916.

5 L. Cadorna, *La Guerra alla Fronte Italiana* (2 vols., Milan: Fratelli Treves, 1921), I, p. 172.

6 M. Isnenghi and G. Rochat, *La Grande Guerra 1914–1918* (Milan: Sansoni, 2004; first publ. 2000), p. 177.

7 V. Wilcox, *Morale and the Italian Army during the First World War* (Cambridge: Cambridge University Press, 2018; first publ. 2016), pp. 77, 82.

8 M. Mondini, *Il Capo. La Grande Guerra del Generale Luigi Cadorna* (Bologna: Società editrice il Mulino, 2017), pp. 261–3.

9 L. Cadorna, *Lettere Famigliari*, ed. R. Cadorna (Milan; Arnoldo Mondadori, 1967), p. 138 (letter, 2 February 1916).

10 J. R. Schindler, *Isonzo. The Forgotten Sacrifice of the Great War* (Westport, CT: Praeger, 2001), pp. 48–9.

11 Ministero della Guerra, *L'Esercito Italiano nella Grande Guerra*, III, Tomo 1, pp. 184–8.

12 Ibid., pp. 189–93.

13 R. Corselli, *Cadorna* (Milan: Edizioni Corbaccio, 1937), pp. 368–9.

14 B. Pares, *The Fall of the Russian Monarchy* (London: Phoenix Press, 2001; first publ. 1939), p. 327.

15 W. Gleason, 'Alexander Guchkov and the End of the Russian Empire', *Transactions of the American Philosophical Society*, Vol. 73, No. 3 (1983), p. 63.

16 O. R. Airapetov, *Uchastie Rossiiskoi imperii v Pervoi mirovoi voine (1914–1917). 1916 god* (Moscow: Kuchkovo Pole, 2015), p. 80; and N. N. Golovine, *The Russian Army in the World War* (New Haven: Yale University Press, 1931), p. 156.

17 M. V. Rodzianko, *The Reign of Rasputin. An Empire's Collapse*, trans. C. Zvegintzoff (London: A. M. Philpot, 1927), p. 184.

18 M. Paléologue, *An Ambassador's Memoirs*, trans. F. A. Holt (3 vols., London: Hutchinson & Co., 1925), II, p. 223.

19 T. Hasegawa, *The February Revolution, Petrograd, 1917. The End of the Tsarist Regime and the Birth of Dual Power* (Leiden and Boston: Brill, 2017; first publ. 1981), pp. 94–6.

20 R. K. Massie, *Nicholas and Alexandra* (London: Victor Gollancz, 1968), pp. 282–92.

21 Sir J. Hanbury-Williams, *The Emperor Nicholas II. As I Knew Him* (London: Arthur L. Humphreys, 1922), p. 83.

22 Nicholas to Alexandra, 14 March 1916 [OS], in C. E. Vulliamy (ed.), *The Nicky–Sunny Letters. Correspondence of the Tsar and Tsaritsa 1914–1917*, trans. A. L. Hynes (Hattiesburg, MS: Academic International, 1970), pp. 157–8.

23 I. I. Rostunov, *Russkii front pervoi mirovoi voiny* (Moscow: Nauka, 1976), pp. 290–91.

24 A. Knox, 'General Kuropatkin', *The Slavonic Review*, Vol. 4, No. 10 (June 1925), pp. 164–8; B. W. Menning, *Bayonets Before Bullets. The Imperial Russian Army, 1861–1914* (Bloomington and Indianapolis, IN: Indiana University Press, 1992), p. 197; and A. Kuropatkin, *The Russian Army and the Japanese War*, trans. A. B. Lindsay (2 vols., New York: E. P. Dutton, 1909), I, pp. 199–309, and II, pp. 1–97.

25 J. H. Cockfield, *Russia's Iron General. The Life of Aleksei A. Brusilov, 1853–1926* (Lanham, MD: Lexington Books, 2019), p. 3; and A. A. Brussilov, *A Soldier's Note-Book 1914–1918* (London: Macmillan & Co., 1930), p. 22.

26 *Strategicheskii ocherk voiny 1914–1918 g.g.* (7 vols., Moscow: Vysshii voennyi redaktsionnyi sovet, 1920–23), V, p. 27.

27 Ibid., p. 28.

28 S. Washburn, *The Russian Offensive* (London: Constable, 1917), p. 5.

29 Brussilov, *A Soldier's Note-Book*, pp. 213–16.

30 Ibid., pp. 216–18; and P. Buttar, *Russia's Last Gasp. The Eastern Front 1916–17* (Oxford: Osprey, 2017; first publ. 2016), p. 125.

31 M. K. Lemke, *250 dnei v tsarskoi stavke (25 sentiabria 1915–2 iiulia 1916)* (Petersburg: Gosudarstvennoe Izdatel'stvo, 1920), p. 702.

32 E. Glaise-Horstenau, *Österreich-Ungarns Letzter Krieg 1914–1918*, IV, *Das Kriegsjahr 1916. Erster Teil* (Vienna: Verlag der Militärwissenschaftlichen Mitteilungen, 1933), pp. 173–4.

33 M. Rauchensteiner, *The First World War and the End of the Habsburg Monarchy, 1914–1918*, trans. A. J. Kay and A. Güttel-Bellert (Vienna: Böhlau Verlag, 2014; first publ. 1993), p. 504.

34 Glaise-Horstenau, *Österreich-Ungarns Letzter Krieg 1914–1918*, IV, p. 175.

35 Ibid., p. 195.

36 Ibid., p. 229; and A. Krauss, *Die Ursachen unserer Niederlage. Erinnerungen und Urteile aus dem Weltkrieg* (Munich: J. F. Lehmanns, 1921), pp. 189–90.

37 L. Sondhaus, *Franz Conrad von Hötzendorf. Architect of the Apocalypse* (Boston: Humanities Press, 2000), p. 185; and Rauchensteiner, *The First World War and the End of the Habsburg Monarchy*, pp. 510–11.

38 Conrad cited in Corselli, *Cadorna*, p. 371.

39 Brusati to Cadorna, 22 March 1916, and reply, 6 April 1916, in Ministero della Guerra, *L'Esercito Italiano nella Grande Guerra*, III, Tomo 2, bis, pp. 43, 55.

40 J. Gooch, *The Italian Army and the First World War* (Cambridge: Cambridge University Press, 2014), p. 153.

41 Sondhaus, *Franz Conrad von Hötzendorf*, pp. 184–5.

42 *IR 14. Ein Buch der Erinnerung an Große Zeiten 1914–1918* (Linz: J. Feichtingers Erben, 1919), p. 73.

43 Glaise-Horstenau, *Österreich-Ungarns Letzter Krieg 1914–1918*, IV, pp. 258–9.

44 Ibid., p. 266.

45 A. von Cramon, *Unser Österreichisch-Ungarischer Bundesgenosse im Weltkriege* (Berlin: E. S. Mittler & Sohn, 1922), p. 57.

46 Mondini, *Il Capo*, p. 219.

47 Salandra to Cadorna, 24 May 1916, in Ministero della Guerra, *L'Esercito Italiano nella Grande Guerra*, III, Tomo 2, bis, p. 132.

48 Gooch, *The Italian Army and the First World War*, pp. 157–8; and Cadorna, *La Guerra alla Fronte Italiana*, I, p. 229.

49 Gooch, *The Italian Army*, p. 157.

50 Rauchensteiner, *The First World War and the End of the Habsburg Monarchy*, pp. 516–17; and Glaise-Horstenau, *Österreich-Ungarns Letzter Krieg 1914–1918*, IV, p. 300.

51 Sondhaus, *Franz Conrad von Hötzendorf*, p. 187; Rauchensteiner, *The First World War and the End of the Habsburg Monarchy*, pp. 517–18; G. E. Rothenberg, *The Army of Francis Joseph* (West Lafayette, IN: Purdue University Press, 1976), p. 195; and Glaise-Horstenau, *Österreich-Ungarns Letzter Krieg 1914–1918*, IV, pp. 348, 354.

52 Mondini, *Il capo*, p. 220.

12. 'The greatest crisis of the world war'

1 E. Steinitz, 'Aus den Tagen von Luck im Spätfrühling 1916. Erlebnisse eines Brigadekommandos', *Militärwissenschaftliche Mitteilungen*, Vol. 65 (1934), p. 12; and E. Glaise-Horstenau, *Österreich-Ungarns Letzter Krieg 1914–1918*, IV, *Das Kriegsjahr 1916. Erster Teil* (Vienna: Verlag der Militärwissenschaftlichen Mitteilungen, 1933), p. 374.

2 *Nastuplenie iugo-zapadnogo fronta v mae-iiune 1916 goda. Sbornik dokumentov mirovoi imperialisticheskoi voiny na russkom fronte (1914–1917)* (Moscow: Voenizdat, 1940), p. 17.

3 Brusilov to Alekseev, 19 April 1916, in *Nastuplenie iugo-zapadnogo fronta v mae-iiune 1916 goda*, pp. 118–22.

4 N. Stone, *The Eastern Front 1914–1917* (London: Penguin, 1998; first publ. 1975), p. 239.

5 A. A. Brussilov, *A Soldier's Note-Book 1914–1918* (London: Macmillan & Co., 1930), pp. 236–7.

6 S. Washburn, *The Russian Offensive* (London: Constable, 1917), pp. 6–7.

7 M. Schönowsky-Schönwies and A. Augenetter, *Luck. Der Russische Durchbruch im Juni 1916* (Vienna and Leipzig: Wilhelm Braumüller, 1919), p. 58.

8 Glaise-Horstenau, *Österreich-Ungarns Letzter Krieg 1914–1918*, IV, p. 378; and M. Rauchensteiner, *The First World War and the End of the Habsburg*

Monarchy, 1914–1918, trans. A. J. Kay and A. Güttel-Bellert (Vienna: Böhlau Verlag, 2014; first publ. 1993), p. 526.

9 O. R. Airapetov, *Uchastie Rossiiskoi imperii v Pervoi mirovoi voine (1914–1917). 1916 god* (Moscow: Kuchkovo Pole, 2015), p. 133.

10 Glaise-Horstenau, *Österreich-Ungarns Letzter Krieg 1914–1918*, IV, p. 387; and Schönowsky-Schönwies and Augenetter, *Luck*, p. 72.

11 Airapetov, *Uchastie Rossiiskoi imperii v Pervoi mirovoi voine (1914–1917). 1916 god*, p. 132.

12 I. I. Rostunov, *Russkii front pervoi mirovoi voiny* (Moscow: Nauka, 1976), p. 312.

13 J. Schindler, 'Steamrollered in Galicia: The Austro-Hungarian Army and the Brusilov Offensive, 1916', *War in History*, Vol. 10, No. 1 (2003), p. 43; and Glaise-Horstenau, *Österreich-Ungarns Letzter Krieg 1914–1918*, IV, p. 410.

14 Reichsarchiv, *Der Weltkrieg 1914 bis 1918. X. Die Operationen des Jahres 1916 bis zum Wechsel in der Obersten Heeresleitung* (Berlin: E. S. Mittler & Sohn, 1936), p. 486.

15 G. Gräfin Conrad von Hötzendorf, *Mein Leben mit Conrad von Hötzendorf. Sein geistiges Vermächtnis* (Leipzig: Greithlein & Co., 1935), pp. 151–2.

16 Rauchensteiner, *The First World War and the End of the Habsburg Monarchy*, p. 529.

17 E. von Falkenhayn, *General Headquarters 1914–1916 and Its Critical Decisions* (London: Hutchinson & Co., 1919), pp. 250–52.

18 Glaise-Horstenau, *Österreich-Ungarns Letzter Krieg 1914–1918*, IV, p. 464.

19 G. E. Silberstein, *The Troubled Alliance. German–Austrian Relations 1914 to 1917* (Lexington, KY: University Press of Kentucky, 1970), p. 303; Glaise-Horstenau, *Österreich-Ungarns Letzter Krieg 1914–1918*, IV, pp. 484–5; and Reichsarchiv, *Der Weltkrieg*, X, pp. 484–5.

20 H. von Seeckt, *Aus Meinem Leben 1866–1917* (Leipzig: V. Hase & Koehler, 1941), p. 384.

21 Reichsarchiv, *Der Weltkrieg*, X, p. 474.

22 G. von der Marwitz, *Weltkriegsbriefe*, ed. E. von Tschischwitz (Berlin: Steiniger-Verlage, 1940), p. 171.

23 *Strategicheskii ocherk voiny 1914–1918 g.g.* (7 vols., Moscow: Vysshii voennyi redaktsionnyi sovet, 1920–23), V, p. 56.

24 Stone, *The Eastern Front*, pp. 256–7; and *Strategicheskii ocherk voiny 1914–1918 g.g.*, VI, p. 32.

25 *Strategicheskii ocherk voiny 1914–1918 g.g.*, VI, pp. 32–4.

26 Brusilov to Alekseev, 18 June 1916, in *Nastuplenie iugo-zapadnogo fronta v mae-iiune 1916 goda*, p. 345.

27 Alekseev to Brusilov, 22 June 1916, in *Nastuplenie iugo-zapadnogo fronta v mae-iiune 1916 goda*, p. 387.

28 Brussilov, *A Soldier's Note-Book*, p. 246.

29 W. Vogel, *Schlachten des Weltkrieges. Die Kämpfe um Baranowitschi* (Berlin: Gerhard Stalling, 1926), p. 44.

30 Sir A. Knox, *With the Russian Army 1914–1917* (2 vols., London: Hutchinson & Co., 1921), II, pp. 453–4; and *Strategicheskii ocherk voiny 1914–1918 g.g.*, V, p. 62.

31 Glaise-Horstenau, *Österreich-Ungarns Letzter Krieg 1914–1918*, IV, pp. 341, 348.

32 Silberstein, *The Troubled Alliance*, pp. 314–16.

33 A. Watson, *Ring of Steel. Germany and Austria–Hungary, 1914–1918* (London: Allen Lane, 2015; first publ. 2014), p. 324.

34 Sir J. Edmonds, *Military Operations. France and Belgium, 1916* (2 vols., London: Macmillan & Co., 1933), I, pp. 45–6.

35 K.-H. Janßen, *Der Kanzler und der General. Die Führungskrise um Bethmann Hollweg und Falkenhayn (1914–1916)* (Göttingen: Musterschmidt, 1967), p. 230.

36 R. B. Asprey, *The German High Command at War. Hindenburg and Ludendorff and the First World War* (London: Warner Books, 1994; first publ. 1991), p. 248; M. Kitchen, *The Silent Dictatorship. The Politics of the German High Command under Hindenburg and Ludendorff, 1916–1918* (London: Routledge, 2020; first publ. 1976), pp. 34–5; and Reichsarchiv, *Der Weltkrieg*, X, pp. 532–3.

37 M. Hoffmann, *War Diaries and Other Papers*, trans. E. Sutton (2 vols., London: Martin Secker, 1929), II, p. 143.

38 E. Ludendorff, *My War Memories 1914–1918* (2 vols., London: Hutchinson & Co., 1919), I, p. 227.

39 V. M. Bezobrazov, *Diary of the Commander of the Russian Imperial Guard 1914–1917*, ed. M. Lyons (Boynton Beach, FL: Dramco, 1994), p. 106.

40 Airapetov, *Uchastie Rossiiskoi imperii v Pervoi mirovoi voine (1914–1917). 1916 god*, p. 160.

41 Stone, *The Eastern Front*, p. 262; and Airapetov, *Uchastie Rossiiskoi imperii v Pervoi mirovoi voine (1914–1917). 1916 god*, p. 161.

42 Bezobrazov, *Diary of the Commander of the Russian Imperial Guard*, pp. 106–8.

43 Brussilov, *A Soldier's Note-Book*, p. 267; and Knox, *With the Russian Army*, II, p. 476.

44 Bezobrazov, *Diary of the Commander of the Russian Imperial Guard*, p. 112.

45 G. A. Goshtovt, *Kirasiry yego velichestva v velikuyu voynu 1916, 1917 goda* (Paris: Renaissance, 1944), p. 64.

13. 'This means the end of the war!'

1 Ministero della Guerra, *L'Esercito Italiano nella Grande Guerra (1915–1918)* (7 vols., Rome: Provveditorato Generale dello Stato Libreria, 1927–88), III, Tomo 3, pp. 17–18.

2 R. Corselli, *Cadorna* (Milan: Edizioni Corbaccio, 1937), pp. 165–7.

3 F. Cappellano, 'The Evolution of Tactical Regulations in the Italian Army in the Great War', in V. Wilcox (ed.), *Italy in the Era of the Great War* (Leiden and Boston: Brill, 2019), pp. 38–9.

4 Ministero della Guerra, *L'Esercito Italiano nella Grande Guerra*, III, Tomo 3, p. 24; and E. Glaise-Horstenau, *Österreich-Ungarns Letzter Krieg 1914–1918*, V, *Das Kriegsjahr 1916. Zweiter Teil* (Vienna: Verlag der Militärwissenschaftlichen Mitteilungen, 1934), p. 40.

5 M. Thompson, *The White War. Life and Death on the Italian Front, 1915–1919* (London: Faber & Faber, 2008), p. 172; Glaise-Horstenau, *Österreich-Ungarns Letzter Krieg 1914–1918*, V, p. 41; and M. Isnenghi and G. Rochat, *La Grande Guerra 1914–1918* (Milan: Sansoni, 2004; first publ. 2000), p. 188.

6 'How Gorizia was Taken', *The Times*, 12 August 1916.

7 L. Cadorna, *La Guerra alla Fronte Italiana* (2 vols., Milan: Fratelli Treves, 1921), I, pp. 289–90.

8 Glaise-Horstenau, *Österreich-Ungarns Letzter Krieg 1914–1918*, V, pp. 68–9.

9 E. Glaise-Horstenau, *Österreich-Ungarns Letzter Krieg 1914–1918*, IV, *Das Kriegsjahr 1916. Erster Teil* (Vienna: Verlag der Militärwissenschaftlichen Mitteilungen, 1933), p. 663.

10 T. C. Dowling, *The Brusilov Offensive* (Bloomington, IN: Indiana University Press, 2008), pp. 121, 123; and M. Hoffmann, *War Diaries and*

Other Papers, trans. E. Sutton (2 vols., London: Martin Secker, 1929), I, p. 143.

11 Reichsarchiv, *Der Weltkrieg 1914 bis 1918. X. Die Operationen des Jahres 1916 bis zum Wechsel in der Obersten Heeresleitung* (Berlin: E. S. Mittler & Sohn, 1936), p. 535; and J. Schindler, 'Steamrollered in Galicia: The Austro-Hungarian Army and the Brusilov Offensive, 1916', *War in History*, Vol. 10, No. 1 (2003), p. 37, n. 26.

12 Hoffmann, *War Diaries and Other Papers*, I, p. 141.

13 K.-H. Janßen, *Der Kanzler und der General. Die Führungskrise um Bethmann Hollweg und Falkenhayn (1914–1916)* (Göttingen: Musterschmidt, 1967), pp. 239–40.

14 Ibid., p. 244.

15 J. K. Tanenbaum, *General Maurice Sarrail 1856–1929. The French Army and Left-Wing Politics* (Chapel Hill, NC: University of North Carolina Press, 1974), pp. 104–5; and C. Falls, *Military Operations Macedonia* [Vol. I]. *From the Outbreak of War to the Spring of 1917* (London: HMSO, 1933), p. 121.

16 Briand to Sarrail, 1 June 1916, in M. Sarrail, *Mon Commandement en Orient* (Paris: Ernest Flammarion, 1920), p. 354.

17 S. B. Chester, *Life of Venizelos* (London: Constable and Company, 1921), pp. 282–3; and G. F. Abbott, *Greece and the Allies 1914–1922* (London: Methuen & Co., 1922), p. 102.

18 Sarrail, *Mon Commandement en Orient*, p. 132.

19 Falls, *Military Operations Macedonia* [Vol. I], pp. 119–20.

20 TNA: WO 106/1350, 'Report on the Efficiency of the Serbian Army', 30 June 1916.

21 Falls, *Military Operations Macedonia* [Vol. I], pp. 115, 150.

22 Tanenbaum, *General Maurice Sarrail 1856–1929*, p. 106.

23 TNA: WO 106/1345, Milne to Robertson, 30 October 1916.

24 K. Hitchins, *Ionel Bratianu* (London: Haus Publishing, 2011), p. 66.

25 Ibid., p. 82. Original emphasis.

26 G. E. Torrey, *The Romanian Battlefront in World War I* (Lawrence, KS: University Press of Kansas, 2011), pp. 14, 23.

27 V. N. Vinogradov, 'Romania in the First World War: The Years of Neutrality, 1914–1916', *The International History Review*, Vol. 14, No. 3 (August 1992), pp. 454–9; Torrey, *The Romanian Battlefront in World War I*,

p. 64; and O. R. Airapetov, *Uchastie Rossiiskoi imperii v Pervoi mirovoi voine (1914–1917). 1916 god* (Moscow: Kuchkovo Pole, 2015), p. 231.

28 'Proclamation of August 28, 1916', in C. F. Horne (ed.), *Source Records of the Great War* (7 vols., USA: National Alumni, 1923), IV, pp. 326–7.

29 Torrey, *The Romanian Battlefront in World War I*, p. 46.

30 Glaise-Horstenau, *Österreich-Ungarns Letzter Krieg 1914–1918*, V, pp. 244, 246; and A. Arz von Straussenburg, *Zur Geschichte des Grossen Krieges 1914–1918* (Vienna, Munich and Leipzig: Rikola, 1924), p. 102.

31 M. B. Barrett, *Prelude to Blitzkrieg. The 1916 Austro-German Campaign in Romania* (Bloomington, IN: Indiana University Press, 2013), pp. 51–3.

32 W. Görlitz (ed.), *The Kaiser and His Court. The Diaries, Note Books and Letters of Admiral Georg Alexander von Müller, Chief of the Naval Cabinet, 1914–1918* (London: Macdonald & Co., 1961; first publ. 1959), p. 198 (entry, 27 August 1916).

33 G. E. Silberstein, *The Troubled Alliance. German–Austrian Relations 1914 to 1917* (Lexington, KY: University Press of Kentucky, 1970), p. 324.

34 E. Ludendorff, *My War Memories 1914–1918* (2 vols., London: Hutchinson & Co., 1919), I, p. 239.

35 Reichsarchiv, *Der Weltkrieg*, X, p. 645.

36 H. H. Herwig, *The First World War. Germany and Austria–Hungary 1914–1918* (London: Arnold, 1997), p. 217.

37 Glaise-Horstenau, *Österreich-Ungarns Letzter Krieg 1914–1918*, V, pp. 267–8.

38 M. Rauchensteiner, *The First World War and the End of the Habsburg Monarchy, 1914–1918*, trans. A. J. Kay and A. Güttel-Bellert (Vienna: Böhlau Verlag, 2014; first publ. 1993), p. 552; and Glaise-Horstenau, *Österreich-Ungarns Letzter Krieg 1914–1918*, V, p. 269.

39 *România in Timpul Razboiului 1916–1918* (June 1919), p. 45; and Reichsarchiv, *Der Weltkrieg 1914 bis 1918. XI. Die Kriegführung im Herbst 1916 und im Winter 1916/17* (Berlin: E. S. Mittler & Sohn, 1938), p. 204.

40 I. G. Duca, *Memorii Volumul III. Războiul Partea I (1916–1917)*, ed. S. Neagoe (Bucharest: Machiavelli, 1994), p. 38.

41 A. Averescu, *Operaţiile dela Flămânda* (Bucharest: Cultura Nationala, n.d.), pp. 119–23.

42 Torrey, *The Romanian Battlefront in World War I*, p. 91; and Janßen, *Der Kanzler und der General*, p. 251.

43 E. von Falkenhayn, *Der Feldzug der 9. Armee gegen die Rumänen und Russen 1916/17* (2 vols., Berlin: E.S. Mittler & Sohn, 1921), I, pp. 11, 14.

44 Reichsarchiv, *Der Weltkrieg*, XI, p. 225.

45 Barrett, *Prelude to Blitzkrieg*, p. 109.

46 Falkenhayn, *Der Feldzug der 9. Armee*, I, p. 53.

47 Ibid., p. 54; Reichsarchiv, *Der Weltkrieg*, XI, p. 229; Torrey, *The Romanian Battlefront in World War I*, p. 18; and G. A. Dabija, *Armata Română in Răsboiul Mondial (1916–1918)* (4 vols., Bucharest: I. G. Hertz, 1928–37), II, pp. 109–10.

48 Dabija, *Armata Română in Răsboiul Mondial*, II, p. 117.

49 A. Averescu, *Notiţe Zilnice din Războiu (1916–1918)* (Bucharest: Cultura Nationala, 1935), p. 50 (entry 26 September 1916 [OS]).

14. 'Falkenhayn is here!'

1 A. A. Brussilov, *A Soldier's Note-Book 1914–1918* (London: Macmillan & Co., 1930), p. 258.

2 T. C. Dowling, *The Brusilov Offensive* (Bloomington, IN: Indiana University Press, 2008), pp. 149, 160.

3 D. R. Stone, *The Russian Army in the Great War. The Eastern Front, 1914–1917* (Lawrence, KS: University Press of Kansas, 2015), p. 255.

4 *Strategicheskii ocherk voiny 1914–1918 g.g.* (7 vols., Moscow: Vysshii voennyi redaktsionnyi sovet, 1920–23), VI, p. 82.

5 B. V. Gerua, *Vospominaniya o moyey zhizni* (2 vols. Paris: Voenno-istoricheskoe, 'Tanais', 1969), II, pp. 160–61.

6 Guchkov to Alekseev, 15 August 1916, in N. N. Golovine, *The Russian Army in the World War* (New Haven: Yale University Press, 1931), pp. 245–6.

7 S. McMeekin, *The Russian Revolution. A New History* (New York: Basic Books, 2017), p. 77.

8 M. V. Rodzianko, *The Reign of Rasputin: An Empire's Collapse*, trans. C. Zvegintzoff (London: A. M. Philpot, 1927), p. 219; and Alexandra to Nicholas, 22 September 1916 [OS], in C. E. Vulliamy (ed.), *The Nicky–Sunny Letters. Correspondence of the Tsar and Tsaritsa 1914–1917*, trans. A. L. Hynes (Hattiesburg, MS: Academic International, 1970), p. 410. Original emphasis.

9 'Miliukov's Speech in the Duma', 14 November 1916, in F. A. Golder (ed.), *Documents of Russian History 1914–1917* (Stanford, CA: The Century Co., 1927), pp. 154–66.

10 O. R. Airapetov, *Uchastie Rossiiskoi imperii v Pervoi mirovoi voine (1914–1917). 1916 god* (Moscow: Kuchkovo Pole, 2015), pp. 282–4; and Alexandra to Nicholas, 18 September 1916 [OS], in Vulliamy (ed.), *The Nicky–Sunny Letters*, p. 402. Original emphasis.

11 Airapetov, *Uchastie Rossiiskoi imperii v Pervoi mirovoi voine (1914–1917). 1916 god*, p. 285.

12 Ibid., p. 239.

13 N. Stone, *The Eastern Front 1914–1917* (London: Penguin, 1998; first publ. 1975), p. 278; and M. B. Barrett, *Prelude to Blitzkrieg. The 1916 Austro-German Campaign in Romania* (Bloomington, IN: Indiana University Press, 2013), p. 150.

14 G. E. Torrey (ed.), *General Henri Berthelot and Romania: Mémoires et Correspondance, 1916–1919* (Boulder, CO: East European Monographs, 1987), p. 8.

15 L. Cadorna, *La Guerra alla Fronte Italiana* (2 vols., Milan: Fratelli Treves, 1921), II, pp. 10–11.

16 E. Glaise-Horstenau, *Österreich-Ungarns Letzter Krieg 1914–1918*, V, *Das Kriegsjahr 1916. Zweiter Teil* (Vienna: Verlag der Militärwissenschaftlichen Mitteilungen, 1934), pp. 652–3, 657.

17 A. Wakefield, 'A Most Cosmopolitan Front. Defining Features of the Salonika Campaign 1915–1918', in A. Shapland and E. Stefani (eds.), *Archaeology Behind the Battle Lines. The Macedonian Campaign (1915–19) and Its Legacy* (Oxford: Routledge, 2017), pp. 11–13; and C. Falls, *Military Operations Macedonia* [Vol. I]. *From the Outbreak of War to the Spring of 1917* (London: HMSO, 1933), p. 185.

18 Ministère de la Guerre, *Les Armées Françaises dans la Grande Guerre* (Paris: Imprimerie Nationale, 1922–39) [hereafter *AFGG*], Book 8/2, p. 41.

19 Sarrail to Cordonnier, 15 September 1916, in *AFGG*, Book 8/2 – *Annexes*, Vol. 1, No. 254, p. 238.

20 E. Cordonnier, *Ai-je trahi Sarrail?* (Paris: Les Étincelles, 1930), p. 156.

21 G. Ward Price, *The Story of the Salonica Army* (London: Hodder & Stoughton, 1918), pp. 156–7.

22 Reichsarchiv, *Der Weltkrieg 1914 bis 1918. XI. Die Kriegführung im Herbst 1916 und im Winter 1916/17* (Berlin: E. S. Mittler & Sohn, 1938), p. 340.

23 A. Palmer, *The Gardeners of Salonika* (London: Andre Deutsch, 1965), p. 83; and Cordonnier to Sarrail, 29 September 1916, in *AFGG*, Book 8/2 – *Annexes*, Vol. 1, No. 436, pp. 407–9.

24 *AFGG*, Book 8/2, p. 126, n. 2; and Cordonnier, *Ai-je trahi Sarrail?*, pp. 324–5.

25 'Mud in Macedonia', *The Times*, 31 October 1916.

26 Derougemont to GQG, 21 November 1916, in *AFGG*, Book 8/2 – *Annexes*, Vol. 2, No. 972, p. 167.

27 E. Ludendorff, *My War Memories 1914–1918* (2 vols., London: Hutchinson & Co., 1919), I, p. 250.

28 S. Noikov, *Zashto ne pobedikhme 1915–1918* (Sofia: Army Military Publishing, 1922), p. 78; and Reichsarchiv, *Der Weltkrieg*, XI, p. 342, n. 1.

29 Ludendorff, *My War Memories*, I, p. 253.

30 Reichsarchiv, *Der Weltkrieg*, XI, pp. 340–41.

31 *AFGG*, Book 8/2, pp. 131, 213.

32 Ibid., p. 205.

33 Derougemont to GQG, 21 November 1916, in *AFGG*, Book 8/2 – *Annexes*, Vol. 2, No. 972, p. 167.

34 Ward Price, *The Story of the Salonica Army*, pp. 173, 175.

35 M. Sarrail, *Mon Commandement en Orient* (Paris: Ernest Flammarion, 1920), pp. 181–2.

36 E. von Falkenhayn, *Der Feldzug der 9. Armee gegen die Rumänen und Russen 1916/17* (2 vols., Berlin: E. S. Mittler & Sohn, 1921), II, pp. 42–3.

37 G. E. Torrey, *The Romanian Battlefront in World War I* (Lawrence, KS: University Press of Kansas, 2011), pp. 116, 131.

38 Falkenhayn, *Der Feldzug der 9. Armee*, II, p. 35.

39 Ministerul de Razboi, *România în Războiul Mondial 1916–1919* (4 vols., Bucharest: Imprimeria Nationala, 1934–46), III, *Documente-Anexe*, p. 236.

40 Torrey, *The Romanian Battlefront in World War I*, pp. 135–7; and W. Foerster (ed.), *Mackensen. Briefe und Aufzeichnungen des Generalfeldmarschalls aus Krieg und Frieden* (Leipzig: Bibliographisches Institut, 1938), p. 300.

41 A. Averescu, *Notițe Zilnice din Războiu (1916–1918)* (Bucharest: Cultura Nationala, 1935), pp. 95–6, 99 (entries 6 and 10 November 1916 [OS]).

42 Torrey (ed.), *General Henri Berthelot and Romania*, p. 22.

43 Barrett, *Prelude to Blitzkrieg*, pp. 263–5; and G. A. Dabija, *Armata Română in Răsboiul Mondial (1916–1918)* (4 vols., Bucharest: I. G. Hertz, 1928–37), III, p. 107.

44 P. Buttar, *Russia's Last Gasp. The Eastern Front 1916–17* (Oxford: Osprey, 2017; first publ. 2016), p. 384.

45 E. Kabisch, *Der Rumänien Krieg 1916* (Berlin: Otto Schlegel, 1938), pp. 142–3.

46 M. Sturdza, *Avec l'armée Roumaine (1916–1918)* (Paris: Hachette, 1918), p. 141.

47 Foerster (ed.), *Mackensen*, p. 315.

48 Reichsarchiv, *Der Weltkrieg*, XI, p. 306; and Averescu, *Notițe Zilnice din Război*, p. 111 (entry 27 November 1916 [OS]).

15. 'Born for misfortune'

1 'Purishkevich's Speech in the Duma', 2 December 1916, in F. A. Golder (ed.), *Documents of Russian History 1914–1917* (Stanford, CA: The Century Co., 1927), pp. 166–75.

2 J. T. Fuhrmann, *Rasputin. The Untold Story* (New York: John Wiley & Sons, 2013), pp. 208–13.

3 R. K. Massie, *Nicholas and Alexandra* (London: Victor Gollancz, 1968), pp. 360–61; and Alexandra to Nicholas, 17 December 1916 [OS], in C. E. Vulliamy (ed.), *The Nicky–Sunny Letters. Correspondence of the Tsar and Tsaritsa 1914–1917*, trans. A. L. Hynes (Hattiesburg, MS: Academic International, 1970), pp. 461–2. Original emphasis.

4 A. Viroubova, *Memories of the Russian Court* (London: Macmillan & Co., 1923), p. 183.

5 'Rasputin's Death', *The Times*, 4 January 1917.

6 M. Paléologue, *An Ambassador's Memoirs*, trans. F. A. Holt (3 vols., London: Hutchinson & Co., 1925), III, p. 170. Original emphasis.

7 TNA: CAB 28/1, 'Proceedings of a Conference Held at Paris on Wednesday, November 15, 1916, at 3 p.m.'

8 Nivelle to Sir D. Haig, 21 December 1916, Appendix 2, in *Military Operations. France and Belgium, 1917. Appendices* (London: Macmillan & Co., 1940), pp. 4–6. Original emphasis.

9 'Prime Minister's Statement', in House of Commons Debates, 19 December 1916, Vol. 88, cc. 1333–94.

10 D. Lloyd George, *War Memoirs of David Lloyd George* (2 vols., London: Odhams Press, 1933–6), I, p. 838.

11 TNA: CAB 28/2, 'The Conference of the Allies at Rome on January 5, 6, and 7, 1917'.

12 TNA: CAB 28/2, 'Secretary's Notes of Allied Conferences Held at the Consulta, Rome, on January 5, 6, and 7, 1917'.

13 Robertson to Lloyd George, 6 January 1917, cited in D. R. Woodward, *Lloyd George and the Generals* (London and Toronto: Associated University Presses, 1983), p. 141.

14 TNA: POWE 33/2664, 'Report on the Destruction of Roumanian Oilfields', 22 January 1917.

15 W. Foerster (ed.), *Mackensen. Briefe und Aufzeichnungen des Generalfeldmarschalls aus Krieg und Frieden* (Leipzig: Bibliographisches Institut, 1938), p. 321.

16 E. von Falkenhayn, *Der Feldzug der 9. Armee gegen die Rumänen und Russen 1916/17* (2 vols., Berlin: E. S. Mittler & Sohn, 1921), II, p. 115; and M. B. Barrett, *Prelude to Blitzkrieg. The 1916 Austro-German Campaign in Romania* (Bloomington, IN: Indiana University Press, 2013), pp. 298–9.

17 Reichsarchiv, *Der Weltkrieg 1914 bis 1918. XII. Die Kriegführung im Frühjahr 1917* (Berlin: E. S. Mittler & Sohn, 1939), p. 1.

18 'Proposals for Peace Negotiations Made by Germany', 12 December 1916, in J. B. Scott (ed.), *Official Statements of War Aims and Peace Proposals. December 1916 to November 1918* (Washington DC: Carnegie Endowment for International Peace, 1921), pp. 2–3.

19 Hindenburg to Bethmann Hollweg, 23 December 1916, and reply, 24 December 1916, in E. Ludendorff, *The General Staff and Its Problems*, trans. F. A. Holt (2 vols., London: Hutchinson & Co., 1920), I, pp. 293–7.

20 Reichsarchiv, *Der Weltkrieg 1914 bis 1918. XI. Die Kriegführung im Herbst 1916 und im Winter 1916/17* (Berlin: E. S. Mittler & Sohn, 1938), p. 471.

21 H. H. Herwig, *The First World War. Germany and Austria–Hungary 1914–1918* (London: Arnold, 1997), pp. 275–7; and E. Langthaler, 'Dissolution Before Dissolution. The Wartime Food Regime in Austria–Hungary', in R. P. Tucker, T. Keller, J. R. McNeill and M. Schmid (eds.), *Environmental Histories of the First World War* (Cambridge: Cambridge University Press, 2018), pp. 51–2.

22 E. Demmerle, *Kaiser Karl I. 'Selig, die Frieden stiften . . .' Die Biographie* (Vienna: Amalthea Signum Verlag, 2004), pp. 95, 97.

23 G. E. Rothenberg, *The Army of Francis Joseph* (West Lafayette, IN: Purdue University Press, 1976), p. 202; L. Sondhaus, *Franz Conrad von Hötzendorf. Architect of the Apocalypse* (Boston: Humanities Press, 2000), pp. 185–6; and G. Gräfin Conrad von Hötzendorf, *Mein Leben mit Conrad von Hötzendorf. Sein geistiges Vermächtnis* (Leipzig: Greithlein & Co., 1935), p. 160.

24 Sondhaus, *Franz Conrad von Hötzendorf*, p. 199; and A. Urbanski von Ostrymiecz, *Conrad von Hötzendorf. Soldat und Mensch* (Graz: Ulrich Mosers, 1939), pp. 349–50.

25 A. Arz von Straussenburg, *Zur Geschichte des Grossen Krieges 1914–1918* (Vienna, Munich and Leipzig: Rikola, 1924), p. 124.

26 M. Rauchensteiner, *The First World War and the End of the Habsburg Monarchy, 1914–1918*, trans. A. J. Kay and A. Güttel-Bellert (Vienna: Böhlau Verlag, 2014; first publ. 1993), pp. 649–50.

27 O. Czernin, *In the World War* (London: Cassell & Co., 1919), pp. 123–5.

28 Rauchensteiner, *The First World War and the End of the Habsburg Monarchy*, pp. 677–8.

29 'Entente Reply to German Proposals', 29 December 1916, in Scott (ed.), *Official Statements of War Aims and Peace Proposals*, pp. 26–8.

30 G. de Manteyer (ed.), *Austria's Peace Offer, 1916–1917* (London: Constable & Co., 1921), p. 37.

31 Ibid., pp. 37, 47–9.

32 K. Urbach, *Go-Betweens for Hitler* (Oxford: Oxford University Press, 2015), p. 78.

33 Manteyer (ed.), *Austria's Peace Offer*, pp. 51–4.

34 Ibid., pp. 57, 64–5.

35 R. Pipes, *The Russian Revolution 1899–1919* (London: Collins Harvill, 1990), p. 272; and T. Hasegawa, *The February Revolution, Petrograd, 1917. The End of the Tsarist Regime and the Birth of Dual Power* (Leiden and Boston: Brill, 2017; first publ. 1981), pp. 186–7.

36 Paléologue, *An Ambassador's Memoirs*, III, p. 215, original emphasis; and Pipes, *The Russian Revolution*, p. 275.

37 Rodzianko to Tsar Nicholas II, 11 and 12 March 1917, in Golder (ed.), *Documents of Russian History 1914–1917*, p. 278.

38 Massie, *Nicholas and Alexandra*, p. 381.

39 E. I. Martynov, *Tsarskaia armiia v fevral'skom perevorote* (Leningrad: Voyennaia tipografiia Upr. Delami Narkomvoyenmor I RVS SSR, 1927), pp. 114–15.

40 Hasegawa, *The February Revolution, Petrograd, 1917*, p. 287.

41 Nicholas to Alexandra, 27 February 1917 [OS], in Vulliamy (ed.), *The Nicky–Sunny Letters*, p. 317.

42 Alekseev to Ivanov, 28 February 1917 [OS], in G. Katkov, *Russia 1917. The February Revolution* (New York: Harper & Row, 1967), pp. 302–3.

43 Pipes, *The Russian Revolution*, p. 310.

44 Katkov, *Russia 1917*, pp. 327–30.

45 Alekseev to Commanders-in-Chief of all fronts, 15 March 1917, in ibid., p. 331.

46 Katkov, *Russia 1917*, pp. 332–3.

47 O. Figes, *A People's Tragedy. The Russian Revolution 1891–1924* (London: Jonathan Cape, 1996), p. 342.

48 'Manifesto of Nicholas II', 15 March 1917, and 'Abdication of Grand Duke Michael Alexandrovich', in Golder (ed.), *Documents of Russian History 1914–1917*, pp. 297–9; and Figes, *A People's Tragedy*, p. 344.

49 N. de Basily, *The Abdication of Emperor Nicholas II of Russia* (Princeton, NJ: Kingston Press, 1984), p. 145.

16. 'Neither peace nor war'

1 O. R. Airapetov, *Uchastie Rossiiskoi imperii v Pervoi mirovoi voine (1914–1917). 1917 god* (Moscow: Kuchkovo Pole, 2015), p. 164; and Grand Duke Alexander, *Once a Grand Duke* (London: Cassell & Co., 1932), p. 322.

2 'Formation and Program of Provisional Government' and 'Socialistic Support of the Provisional Government', in F. A. Golder (ed.), *Documents of Russian History 1914–1917* (Stanford, CA: The Century Co., 1927), pp. 308–10.

3 Guchkov to Alekseev, 22 March 1917, in D. R. Stone, *The Russian Army in the Great War. The Eastern Front, 1914–1917* (Lawrence, KS: University Press of Kansas, 2015), p. 280.

4 V. D. Medlin and R. P. Browder (eds.), *V. D. Nabokov and the Russian Provisional Government, 1917* (New Haven and London: Yale University Press, 1976), pp. 82–5.

5 P. Robinson, *Grand Duke Nikolai Nikolaevich. Supreme Commander of the Russian Army* (DeKalb, IL: Northern Illinois University Press, 2014), p. 302; and Airapetov, *Uchastie Rossiiskoi imperii v Pervoi mirovoi voine (1914–1917). 1917 god*, p. 171.

6 'Order No. 1', in R. P. Browder and A. F. Kerensky (eds.), *The Russian Provisional Government 1917. Documents* (3 vols., Stanford, CA: Stanford University Press, 1961), II, pp. 848–9.

7 *Strategicheskii ocherk voiny 1914–1918 g.g.* (7 vols., Moscow: Vysshii voennyi redaktsionnyi sovet, 1920–23), VII, pp. 41–2.

8 Airapetov, *Uchastie Rossiiskoi imperii v Pervoi mirovoi voine (1914–1917). 1917 god*, pp. 172–3.

9 Alekseev to Lvov, 14 March 1917 [OS], in Browder and Kerensky (eds.), *The Russian Provisional Government 1917. Documents*, II, pp. 862–5.

10 'The Soviet Decision to Appoint Commissars to Military Commands, March 19, 1917 [OS]', in ibid., p. 865.

11 'Order of Guchkov on Elective Military Organizations and Disciplinary Courts', 16 April 1917 [OS], in ibid., pp. 876–7; and Airapetov, *Uchastie Rossiiskoi imperii v Pervoi mirovoi voine (1914–1917). 1917 god*, p. 181.

12 G. Katkov, *Russia 1917. The Kornilov Affair. Kerensky and the Break-up of the Russian Army* (London and New York: Longman, 1980), pp. 16–17.

13 E. Ludendorff, *My War Memories 1914–1918* (2 vols., London: Hutchinson & Co., 1919), II, p. 413.

14 W. Görlitz (ed.), *The Kaiser and His Court. The Diaries, Note Books and Letters of Admiral Georg Alexander von Müller, Chief of the Naval Cabinet, 1914–1918* (London: Macdonald & Co., 1961; first publ. 1959), pp. 247–8 (entries, 14 and 16 March 1917); and Reichsarchiv, *Der Weltkrieg 1914 bis 1918. XII. Die Kriegführung im Frühjahr 1917* (Berlin: E. S. Mittler & Sohn, 1939), pp. 483–4.

15 H. H. Herwig, *The First World War. Germany and Austria–Hungary 1914–1918* (London: Arnold, 1997), p. 325.

16 Ludendorff, *My War Memories*, II, p. 418.

17 Reichsarchiv, *Der Weltkrieg*, XII, pp. 479, 520.

18 M. Hoffmann, *War Diaries and Other Papers*, trans. E. Sutton (2 vols., London: Martin Secker, 1929), I, pp. 174–5.

19 V. Sebestyen, *Lenin the Dictator* (London: Weidenfeld & Nicolson, 2017), p. 271.

20 N. N. Sukhanov, *The Russian Revolution 1917*, ed. and trans. J. Carmichael (Princeton, NJ: Princeton University Press, 1984; first publ. 1955), p. 270; and O. Figes, *A People's Tragedy. The Russian Revolution 1891–1924* (London: Jonathan Cape, 1996), p. 387.

21 'The Provisional Government's Declaration of March 27 on War Aims', in Browder and Kerensky (eds.), *The Russian Provisional Government 1917. Documents*, II, pp. 1045–6.

22 'The Tasks of the Proletariat in the Present Revolution', in V. I. Lenin, *Collected Works* (45 vols., Moscow: Progress Publishers, 1960–70), XXIV, pp. 22–3.

23 S. McMeekin, *The Russian Revolution. A New History* (New York: Basic Books, 2017), pp. 132–6.

24 R. Pipes, *The Russian Revolution 1899–1919* (London: Collins Harvill, 1990), p. 410. Original emphasis.

25 'State Secretary to the Foreign Ministry Liaison Officer at General Headquarters', 3 December 1917, in Z. A. B. Zeman (ed.), *Germany and the Revolution in Russia 1915–1918. Documents from the Archives of the German Foreign Ministry* (London: Oxford University Press, 1958), p. 94.

26 O. Czernin, *In the World War* (London: Cassell & Co., 1919), pp. 146–50; and Emperor Karl to Kaiser Wilhelm II, 14 April 1917, in H. Michaelis, E. Schraepler and G. Scheel (eds.), *Ursachen und Folgen. Vom deutschen Zusammenbruch 1918 und 1945 bis zur staatlichen Neuordnung Deutschlands in der Gegenwart. Die Wende des ersten Weltkrieges und der Beginn der innerpolitischen Wandlung 1916/1917* (Berlin: Herbert Wendler & Co., 1958), pp. 378–9.

27 G. Brook-Shepherd, *The Last Habsburg* (London: Weidenfeld & Nicolson, 1968), p. 78.

28 Kaiser Wilhelm II to Emperor Karl, May 1917, in Michaelis, Schraepler and Scheel (eds.), *Ursachen und Folgen*, pp. 382–3.

29 E. Demmerle, *Kaiser Karl I. 'Selig, die Frieden stiften . . .' Die Biographie* (Vienna: Amalthea Signum Verlag, 2004), p. 123.

30 G. de Manteyer (ed.), *Austria's Peace Offer, 1916–1917* (London: Constable & Co., 1921), pp. 83–4.

31 D. Lloyd George, *War Memoirs of David Lloyd George* (2 vols., London: Odhams Press, 1933–6), II, pp. 1187–8.

32 Manteyer (ed.), *Austria's Peace Offer*, pp. 119, 130, 145–7.

33 Ibid., pp. 158–67.

34 Sir G. Buchanan, *My Mission to Russia and Other Diplomatic Memories* (2 vols., London: Cassell & Co., 1923), II, p. 114.

35 P. G. Halpern, *A Naval History of World War I* (London: UCL Press, 1994), p. 341.

36 TNA: CAB 28/2, 'Summary of the Proceedings of the Anglo-French Conference Held at Paris on May 4 and 5'.

37 'M. Venizelos's Arrival at Salonika', *The Times*, 11 October 1916; and J. K. Tanenbaum, *General Maurice Sarrail 1856–1929. The French Army and Left-Wing Politics* (Chapel Hill, NC: University of North Carolina Press, 1974), pp. 121–3.

38 M. Sarrail, *Mon Commandement en Orient* (Paris: Ernest Flammarion, 1920), pp. 399–401; and C. Falls, *Military Operations Macedonia* [Vol. I]. *From the Outbreak of War to the Spring of 1917* (London: HMSO, 1933), pp. 294–5, 339.

39 Falls, *Military Operations Macedonia* [Vol. I], p. 307.

40 IWM: LBY 33019, Major Nedeff, 'Operations on the Dorian [*sic*] Front, Macedonia 1915–1918', pp. 86, 106.

41 TNA: CAB 28/2, 'Summary of the Proceedings of the Anglo-French Conference Held at Paris on May 4 and 5'.

42 Robertson to Lord Stamfordham, 7 May 1917, in D. R. Woodward (ed.), *The Military Correspondence of Field-Marshal Sir William Robertson, Chief of the Imperial General Staff, December 1915–February 1918* (London: Bodley Head for the Army Records Society, 1989), pp. 182–3.

43 Ministère de la Guerre, *Les Armées Françaises dans la Grande Guerre* (Paris: Imprimerie Nationale, 1922–39) [hereafter *AFGG*], Book 8/2, pp. 460, 467.

44 'Capitaine Montagne à M. le général commandant en chef des armées alliées', 12 May 1917, in *AFGG*, Book 8/2 – *Annexes*, Vol. 3, No. 1892, pp. 770–71; and ibid., p. 472.

45 D. T. Bataković, 'The Salonica Trial 1917: Black Hand vs. Democracy (The Serbian Army from Internal Strife to Military Success)', in *The Salonica Theatre of Operations and the Outcome of the Great War* (Thessaloniki: Institute for Balkan Studies, 2005), p. 284; and A. Palmer, *The Gardeners of Salonika* (London: Andre Deutsch, 1965), pp. 132–3.

46 'Serbian Treason Society', *The Times*, 11 July 1917.

47 D. MacKenzie, *The 'Black Hand' on Trial. Salonika, 1917* (Boulder, CO: East European Monographs, 1995), p. 396.

48 Sarrail to Painlevé, 23 May 1917, in *AFGG*, Book 8/2 – *Annexes*, Vol. 3, No. 1982, p. 874.

17. *'Days of imperishable glory'*

1 L. Cadorna, *La Guerra alla Fronte Italiana* (2 vols., Milan: Fratelli Treves, 1921), II, pp. 36–8.

2 Nivelle to Cadorna, 9 February 1917, in Ministère de la Guerre, *Les Armées Françaises dans la Grande Guerre* (Paris: Imprimerie Nationale, 1922–39) [hereafter *AFGG*], Book 5/1 – *Annexes*, Vol. 2, No. 640, pp. 1140–42.

3 Cadorna to Nivelle, 21 February 1917, in *AFGG*, Book 5/1 – *Annexes*, Vol. 2, No. 721, pp. 1316–18.

4 Cadorna to Raffaele Cadorna, 24 March 1917, cited in J. Gooch, *The Italian Army and the First World War* (Cambridge: Cambridge University Press, 2014), pp. 206–7.

5 E. Greenhalgh, *Foch in Command. The Forging of a First World War General* (Cambridge: Cambridge University Press, 2011), pp. 217, 222; 'Note rédigée par le général Foch en vue de la réunion du comité de Guerre, le 5 avril 1917', in *AFGG*, Book 5/1 – *Annexes*, Vol. 3, No. 1189, pp. 584–5; and Gooch, *The Italian Army and the First World War*, p. 207.

6 Ministero della Guerra, *L'Esercito Italiano nella Grande Guerra (1915–1918)* (7 vols., Rome: Provveditorato Generale dello Stato Libreria, 1927–88), IV, Tomo I, pp. 172–3.

7 Ibid., pp. 197–9; Gooch, *The Italian Army and the First World War*, pp. 209–10; and R. Corselli, *Cadorna* (Milan: Edizioni Corbaccio, 1937), p. 509.

8 J. R. Schindler, *Isonzo. The Forgotten Sacrifice of the Great War* (Westport, CT: Praeger, 2001), p. 204.

9 Ministero della Guerra, *L'Esercito Italiano nella Grande Guerra*, IV, Tomo I, p. 203; and Cadorna, *La Guerra alla Fronte Italiana*, II, p. 58.

10 Capello to Cadorna, 17 May 1917, in Ministero della Guerra, *L'Esercito Italiano nella Grande Guerra*, IV, Tomo I, bis, p. 634.

11 A. Baldini, *Il Libro dei Buoni Incontri di Guerra e di Pace* (Florence: Sansoni, 1953), p. 147.

12 D. Bragatto and R. Massetti (eds.), *Vodice 1917. Enrico Torazzi. 261 Reggimento Fanteria Brigata Elba* (Ferrara: Historical Documentation Centre, 2005), p. 15.

13 TNA: WO 106/772, Delme-Radcliffe report, 21 May 1917.

14 Schindler, *Isonzo*, p. 213; and E. Glaise-Horstenau, *Österreich-Ungarns Letzter Krieg 1914–1918*, VI, *Das Kriegsjahr 1917* (Vienna: Verlag der Militärwissenschaftlichen Mitteilungen, 1936), p. 171.

15 *Lettere di Guerra di un Ufficiale del Genio dal 29 Agosto 1915 al 17 Agosto 1918* (Perugia: Unione Tipografica Cooperativa, 1919), p. 295.

16 Gooch, *The Italian Army*, p. 211.

17 TNA: WO 106/762, Delme-Radcliffe report, 31 July 1917.

18 Gooch, *The Italian Army*, pp. 211–12; and Corselli, *Cadorna*, p. 515.

19 Glaise-Horstenau, *Österreich-Ungarns Letzter Krieg 1914–1918*, VI, p. 181.

20 'Der Kaiserpaar an der Isonzofront', *Wiener Bilder*, 10 June 1917.

21 'Press Interview with Miliukov', 23 March 1917 [OS], in R. P. Browder and A. F. Kerensky (eds.), *The Russian Provisional Government 1917. Documents* (3 vols., Stanford, CA: Stanford University Press, 1961), II, pp. 1044–5.

22 'The Provisional Government's Declaration of March 27 on War Aims' and 'The Note of April 18', in ibid., pp. 1045–6, 1098.

23 'The Note of the Provisional Government', in A. Trachtenberg (ed.), *Collected Works of V. I. Lenin, Vol. XX* (New York: International Publishers, 1929), p. 235.

24 N. N. Sukhanov, *The Russian Revolution 1917*, ed. and trans. J. Carmichael (Princeton, NJ: Princeton University Press, 1984; first publ. 1955), p. 330.

25 M. Paléologue, *An Ambassador's Memoirs*, trans. F. A. Holt (3 vols., London: Hutchinson & Co., 1925), III, pp. 269–70; and A. F. Kerensky, *The Catastrophe. Kerensky's Own Story of the Russian Revolution* (London and New York: D. Appleton & Co., 1927), p. 184.

26 'Kerensky's Order to the Army and Navy after Assuming Office as Minister of War', 12 May 1917 [OS], in Browder and Kerensky (eds.), *The Russian Provisional Government 1917. Documents*, II, p. 936.

27 Alekseev to Guchkov, 12 March 1917 [OS], in ibid., pp. 923–4.

28 Kerensky, *The Catastrophe*, pp. 196–7.

29 L. Trotsky, *The History of the Russian Revolution*, trans. M. Eastman (London: Victor Gollancz, 1965), p. 387.

30 'Speech of General Alexeev at the Congress of Officers of the Army and Navy', 20 May 1917, in F. A. Golder (ed.), *Documents of Russian History 1914–1917* (Stanford, CA: The Century Co., 1927), p. 406.

31 Sir J. Hanbury-Williams, *The Emperor Nicholas II. As I Knew Him* (London: Arthur L. Humphreys, 1922), pp. 263–4.

32 O. Figes, *A People's Tragedy. The Russian Revolution 1891–1924* (London: Jonathan Cape, 1996), p. 415.

33 J. H. Cockfield, *Russia's Iron General. The Life of Aleksei A. Brusilov, 1853–1926* (Lanham, MD: Lexington Books, 2019), pp. 250–51.

34 'Report of General Denikin', 11 June 1917 [OS], in Browder and Kerensky (eds.), *The Russian Provisional Government 1917. Documents*, II, pp. 940–41.

35 *Strategicheskii ocherk voiny 1914–1918 g.g.* (7 vols., Moscow: Vysshii voennyi redaktsionnyi sovet, 1920–23), VII, p. 66.

36 I. I. Rostunov, *Russkii front pervoi mirovoi voiny* (Moscow: Nauka, 1976), pp. 358–9.

37 *Strategicheskii ocherk voiny 1914–1918 g.g.*, VII, p. 66.

38 A. K. Wildman, *The End of the Russian Imperial Army, Volume II. The Road to Soviet Power and Peace* (Princeton, NJ: Princeton University Press, 1987), pp. 73–7.

39 'Kerensky's Order for the Offensive', 16 June 1917 [OS], in Browder and Kerensky (eds.), *The Russian Provisional Government 1917. Documents*, II, p. 942. Original emphasis.

40 A. A. Brussilov, *A Soldier's Note-Book 1914–1918* (London: Macmillan & Co., 1930), p. 313.

41 Wildman, *The End of the Russian Imperial Army, Volume II*, p. 78.

42 R. S. Feldman, 'The Russian General Staff and the June 1917 Offensive', *Soviet Studies*, Vol. 19, No. 4 (April 1968), p. 538; and Glaise-Horstenau, *Österreich-Ungarns Letzter Krieg 1914–1918*, VI, p. 252.

43 HIA: Konstantin Konstantinovich Akintievskii Memoirs, Box 1, pp. 123–4.

44 *Strategicheskii ocherk voiny 1914–1918 g.g.*, VII, pp. 70–71.

45 Reichsarchiv, *Der Weltkrieg 1914 bis 1918. XIII. Die Kriegführung im Sommer und Herbst 1917. Die Ereignisse außerhalb der Westfront bis November 1918* (Berlin: E. S. Mittler & Sohn, 1942), p. 160.

46 O. R. Airapetov, *Uchastie Rossiiskoi imperii v Pervoi mirovoi voine (1914–1917). 1917 god* (Moscow: Kuchkovo Pole, 2015), p. 262.

47 Reichsarchiv, *Der Weltkrieg*, XIII, p. 165.

48 'The Attack on the Southwestern Front: The 11th Army', 9 July 1917 [OS], in Browder and Kerensky (eds.), *The Russian Provisional Government 1917. Documents*, II, pp. 967–8.

49 A. I. Denikin, *The Russian Turmoil. Memoirs: Military, Social, and Political* (London: Hutchinson & Co., 1922), pp. 287–8.

50 M. Botchkareva, *Yashka. My Life as Peasant, Exile and Soldier* (London: Constable, 1919), pp. 211–16.

51 'Kerensky Requests Honors for the Regiments Leading the Offensive', 20 June 1917 [OS], in Browder and Kerensky (eds.), *The Russian Provisional Government 1917. Documents*, II, p. 943.

52 V. D. Medlin and R. P. Browder (eds.), *V. D. Nabokov and the Russian Provisional Government, 1917* (New Haven and London: Yale University Press, 1976), p. 148.

53 G. Katkov, *Russia 1917. The Kornilov Affair* (London and New York: Longman, 1980), p. 35.

54 Kerensky's Order to the Army and Navy, No. 28', 8 July 1917 [OS], and 'Report of the Commander of the 11th Army to Stavka', 12 July 1917 [OS], in Browder and Kerensky (eds.), *The Russian Provisional Government 1917. Documents*, II, pp. 968–9.

18. 'Time is running out'

1 C. Falls, *Military Operations Macedonia* [Vol. I]. *From the Outbreak of War to the Spring of 1917* (London: HMSO, 1933), p. 351; and Ministère de la Guerre, *Les Armées Françaises dans la Grande Guerre* (Paris: Imprimerie Nationale, 1922–39) [hereafter *AFGG*], Book 8/2, p. 485.

2 TNA: CAB 23/2/66, 'War Cabinet, 148', 28 May 1917.

3 H. A. Gibbons, *Venizelos* (Boston and New York: Houghton Mifflin Company, 1920), p. 312.

4 TNA: CAB 23/3/2, 'War Cabinet, 155', 5 June 1917.

5 D. Dutton, *The Politics of Diplomacy. Britain and France in the Balkans in the First World War* (London and New York: I. B. Tauris, 1998), pp. 131–2.

6 TNA: WO 106/1345, Milne to Robertson, 30 October 1916.

7 IWM: Documents 12313, Private Papers of W. D. Mather, 'Life with the British Salonika Forces 1917–1919', p. 87.

8 G. E. Torrey, *The Romanian Battlefront in World War I* (Lawrence, KS: University Press of Kansas, 2011), pp. 170, 183–4.

9 M. Sturdza, *Avec l'armée Roumaine (1916–1918)* (Paris; Hachette, 1918), p. 179.

10 G. A. Dabija, *Armata Romînă in Răsboiul Mondial (1916–1918)* (4 vols., Bucharest: I. G. Hertz, 1928–37), IV, p. 42; and Torrey, *The Romanian Battlefront in World War I*, pp. 190–91, 200.

11 A. Averescu, *Notițe Zilnice din Războiu (1916–1918)* (Bucharest: Cultura Nationala, 1935), pp. 170, 173 (entries 9 and 11 July 1917 [OS]).

12 Reichsarchiv, *Der Weltkrieg 1914 bis 1918. XIII. Die Kriegführung im Sommer und Herbst 1917. Die Ereignisse außerhalb der Westfront bis November 1918* (Berlin: E. S. Mittler & Sohn, 1942), p. 180; and Torrey, *The Romanian Battlefront in World War I*, pp. 202–3, 209.

13 Reichsarchiv, *Der Weltkrieg*, XIII, p. 183.

14 Ibid., p. 184.

15 W. Foerster (ed.), *Mackensen. Briefe und Aufzeichnungen des Generalfeldmarschalls aus Krieg und Frieden* (Leipzig: Bibliographisches Institut, 1938), pp. 335–6; and Reichsarchiv, *Der Weltkrieg*, XIII, p. 185.

16 L. Cadorna, *La Guerra alla Fronte Italiana* (2 vols., Milan: Fratelli Treves, 1921), II, pp. 76–7, 83; J. R. Schindler, *Isonzo. The Forgotten Sacrifice of the Great War* (Westport, CT: Praeger, 2001), pp. 223–4; and 'Bei der Isonzoarmee', *Neue Freie Presse*, 4 April 1916.

17 F. Cappellano, 'The Evolution of Tactical Regulations in the Italian Army in the Great War', in V. Wilcox (ed.), *Italy in the Era of the Great War* (Leiden and Boston: Brill, 2019), pp. 40–42; and M. Isnenghi and G. Rochat, *La Grande Guerra 1914–1918* (Milan: Sansoni, 2004; first publ. 2000), p. 207.

18 Ministero della Guerra, *L'Esercito Italiano nella Grande Guerra (1915–1918)* (7 vols., Rome: Provveditorato Generale dello Stato Libreria, 1927–88), IV, Tomo 2, p. 246, n. 1.

19 E. Glaise-Horstenau, *Österreich-Ungarns Letzter Krieg 1914–1918*, VI, *Das Kriegsjahr 1917* (Vienna: Verlag der Militärwissenschaftlichen Mitteilungen, 1936), p. 442.

20 'Kaiser Karl an der Isonzofront', *Neue Freie Presse*, 24 August 1917.

21 Glaise-Horstenau, *Österreich-Ungarns Letzter Krieg 1914–1918*, VI, pp. 454, 456–7.

22 *IR 14. Ein Buch der Erinnerung an Große Zeiten 1914–1918* (Linz: Feichtingers Erben, 1919), p. 273.

23 Cadorna, *La Guerra alla Fronte Italiana*, II, p. 101; and Glaise-Horstenau, *Österreich-Ungarns Letzter Krieg 1914–1918*, VI, p. 484.

24 Ministero della Guerra, *L'Esercito Italiano nella Grande Guerra*, IV, Tomo 2, p. 397.

25 Glaise-Horstenau, *Österreich-Ungarns Letzter Krieg 1914–1918*, VI, pp. 483–5.

26 Emperor Karl to Kaiser Wilhelm II, 26 August 1917, in A. Arz von Straussenburg, *Zur Geschichte des Grossen Krieges 1914–1918* (Vienna, Munich and Leipzig: Rikola, 1924), p. 171.

27 Glaise-Horstenau, *Österreich-Ungarns Letzter Krieg 1914–1918*, VI, p. 496–7.

28 Reichsarchiv, *Der Weltkrieg*, XIII, p. 194; and D. T. Zabecki, *Steel Wind. Colonel Georg Bruchmüller and the Birth of Modern Artillery* (Westport, CT: Praeger, 1994), p. 24.

29 O. R. Airapetov, *Uchastie Rossiiskoi imperii v Pervoi mirovoi voine (1914–1917). 1917 god* (Moscow: Kuchkovo Pole, 2015), pp. 300–301.

30 KA: Conrad Papers, B/1450:198, Ludendorff to Conrad, 12 September 1917.

31 E. Ludendorff, *My War Memories 1914–1918* (2 vols., London: Hutchinson & Co., 1919), II, p. 482.

32 Reichsarchiv, *Der Weltkrieg*, XIII, pp. 216–18.

33 'Gen. Korniloff's Career', *The Times*, 6 August 1917.

34 G. Katkov, *Russia 1917. The Kornilov Affair. Kerensky and the Break-up of the Russian Army* (London and New York: Longman, 1980), p. 42.

35 A. F. Kerensky, *The Prelude to Bolshevism. The Kornilov Rebellion* (London: T. Fisher Unwin, 1919), pp. 53–7. Original emphasis.

36 'Letter of the Cadets to Kerenski', 28 July 1917, in F. A. Golder (ed.), *Documents of Russian History 1914–1917* (Stanford, CA: The Century Co., 1927), pp. 472–3.

37 'Kerenski's Speech Before the Executive Committees', in ibid., p. 482.

38 'Kornilov's Speech', in R. P. Browder and A. F. Kerensky (eds.), *The Russian Provisional Government 1917. Documents* (3 vols., Stanford, CA: Stanford University Press, 1961), III, pp. 1474–8.

39 Miliukov cited in L. Trotsky, *The History of the Russian Revolution*, trans. M. Eastman (London: Victor Gollancz, 1965), p. 692.

40 '*Novoe Vremia* on Kornilov's Speech', in Browder and Kerensky (eds.), *The Russian Provisional Government 1917. Documents*, III, pp. 1515–16.

41 O. Figes, *A People's Tragedy. The Russian Revolution 1891–1924* (London: Jonathan Cape, 1996), p. 447.

42 A. F. Kerensky, *The Catastrophe. Kerensky's Own Story of the Russian Revolution* (London and New York: D. Appleton & Co., 1927), p. 280.

43 'General Lukomski's Account of the Kornilov Affair', in Golder (ed.), *Documents of Russian History 1914–1917*, pp. 528–9.

44 'Kerenski's Explanation of the Kornilov Affair', in ibid., pp. 520–21.

45 'Proclamations of General Kornilov', in ibid., pp. 521–2.

46 'From the Memoirs of V. N. L'vov', in Browder and Kerensky (eds.), *The Russian Provisional Government 1917. Documents*, III, pp. 1563, 1567.

47 Kerensky, *The Prelude to Bolshevism*, p. 166.

48 'Appeal from the All-Russian Soviet Executive Committees' and 'The Arming of the Workers', in Browder and Kerensky (eds.), *The Russian Provisional Government 1917. Documents*, III, pp. 1589–91; and R. Pipes, *The Russian Revolution 1899–1919* (London: Collins Harvill, 1990), pp. 466–7.

49 A. K. Wildman, *The End of the Russian Imperial Army, Volume II. The Road to Soviet Power and Peace* (Princeton, NJ: Princeton University Press, 1987), pp. 195–6.

50 Airapetov, *Uchastie Rossiiskoi imperii v Pervoi mirovoi voine (1914–1917). 1917 god*, pp. 309–10.

51 A. I. Denikin, *The Russian Turmoil. Memoirs: Military, Social, and Political* (London: Hutchinson & Co., 1922), p. 319.

52 R. Abraham, *Alexander Kerensky. The First Love of the Revolution* (New York: Columbia University Press, 1987), pp. 101, 278.

19. 'The troops do not fight'

1 Reichsarchiv, *Der Weltkrieg 1914 bis 1918. XIII. Die Kriegführung im Sommer und Herbst 1917. Die Ereignisse außerhalb der Westfront bis November 1918* (Berlin: E. S. Mittler & Sohn, 1942), pp. 222–3.

2 E. Glaise-Horstenau, *Österreich-Ungarns Letzter Krieg 1914–1918*, VI, *Das Kriegsjahr 1917* (Vienna: Verlag der Militärwissenschaftlichen Mitteilungen, 1936), p. 502.

3 Ibid., pp. 502–3; and A. Krauss, *Das 'Wunder von Karfreit' im besonderen der Durchbruch bei Flitsch und die Bezwingung des Tagliamento* (Munich: J. F. Lehmanns, 1926), pp. 17–18, 23.

4 M. Rauchensteiner, *The First World War and the End of the Habsburg Monarchy, 1914–1918*, trans. A. J. Kay and A. Güttel-Bellert (Vienna: Böhlau Verlag, 2014; first publ. 1993), p. 788.

5 B. I. Gudmundsson, *Stormtroop Tactics. Innovation in the German Army, 1914–1918* (Westport, CT: Praeger, 1989), p. 130.

6 Cadorna to Capello, 19 September 1917, and reply, 22 September 1917, in Ministero della Guerra, *L'Esercito Italiano nella Grande Guerra (1915–1918)* (7 vols., Rome: Provveditorato Generale dello Stato Libreria, 1927–88), IV, Tomo 3, bis, pp. 56–60.

7 J. R. Schindler, *Isonzo. The Forgotten Sacrifice of the Great War* (Westport, CT: Praeger, 2001), p. 251; and Ministero della Guerra, *L'Esercito Italiano nella Grande Guerra*, IV, Tomo 3, pp. 114, 205.

8 Cadorna to Capello, 20 October 1917, in Ministero della Guerra, *L'Esercito Italiano nella Grande Guerra*, IV, Tomo 3, p. 114.

9 Krauss, *das 'Wunder von Karfreit'*, p. 34.

10 Relazione della Commissione d'Inchiesta, *Dall'Isonzo al Piave. 24 Ottobre–9 Novembre 1917* (3 vols., Rome: Stabilimento Poligrafico per l'Amministrazione della Guerra, 1919), II, p. 114.

11 V. Wilcox, 'Generalship and Mass Surrender during the Italian Defeat at Caporetto', in I. F. W. Beckett (ed.), *1917. Beyond the Western Front* (Leiden: Brill, 2009), p. 35.

12 Glaise-Horstenau, *Österreich-Ungarns Letzter Krieg 1914–1918*, VI, p. 529; and K. Krafft von Dellmensingen, *Schlachten des Weltkrieges. Der Durchbruch am Isonzo* (2 vols., Berlin: Gerhard Stalling, 1926), I, p. 59.

13 Relazione della Commissione d'Inchiesta, *Dall'Isonzo al Piave*, II, p. 127, n. 1.

14 M. Mondini, *Il Capo. La Grande Guerra del Generale Luigi Cadorna* (Bologna: Società Editrice il Mulino, 2017), p. 281.

15 A. Gatti, *Caporetto. Dal Diario di Guerra Inedito (Maggio–Dicembre 1917)*, (Bologna: Società Editrice il Mulino, 1964), pp. 263–4.

16 Relazione della Commissione d'Inchiesta, *Dall'Isonzo al Piave*, II, pp. 552–5.

17 ADN: DG/90, Account of Mario Bosisio.

18 Reichsarchiv, *Der Weltkrieg*, XIII, p. 260.

19 M. Isnenghi and G. Rochat, *La Grande Guerra 1914–1918* (Milan: Sansoni, 2004; first publ. 2000), pp. 386–7.

20 Reichsarchiv, *Der Weltkrieg*, XIII, pp. 276–80.

21 Rauchensteiner, *The First World War and the End of the Habsburg Monarchy*, pp. 792–3.

22 Mondini, *Il Capo*, p. 295.

23 J. Gooch, *The Italian Army and the First World War* (Cambridge: Cambridge University Press, 2014), p. 248.

24 A. Baldini, *Diaz*, trans. W. J. Monson (London: Humphrey Toulmin, 1935), p. 22.

25 'Order to the Army and Navy from the Provisional Government', 10 September 1917 [OS], and 'Military Intelligence Report from the Commander of the 6th Siberian Corps and of the 3rd Siberian Division', in R. P. Browder and A. F. Kerensky (eds.), *The Russian Provisional Government 1917. Documents* (3 vols., Stanford, CA: Stanford University Press, 1961), III, pp. 1617, 1619.

26 R. Pipes, *The Russian Revolution 1899–1919* (London: Collins Harvill, 1990), pp. 465–6.

27 Lenin to the Bolshevik Central Committee, 30 August 1917 [OS], in Browder and Kerensky (eds.), *The Russian Provisional Government 1917. Documents*, III, p. 1695.

28 V. Sebestyen, *Lenin the Dictator* (London: Weidenfeld & Nicolson, 2017), pp. 336–7.

29 N. N. Sukhanov, *The Russian Revolution 1917*, ed. and trans. J. Carmichael (Princeton, NJ: Princeton University Press, 1984; first publ. 1955), p. 620.

30 Pipes, *The Russian Revolution*, pp. 488–9, 493.

31 R. Abraham, *Alexander Kerensky. The First Love of the Revolution* (New York: Columbia University Press, 1987), pp. 318, 323.

32 'Lenin's Speech Before the Soviet at about 3:00 p.m.', in Browder and Kerensky (eds.), *The Russian Provisional Government 1917. Documents*, III, p. 1793.

33 'Decree of Peace Passed Unanimously by the All-Russian Congress of Soviets of Workers', Soldiers', and Peasants' Deputies on November 8th, 1917', and 'The Land Decree', 8 November 1917, in F. A. Golder (ed.), *Documents of Russian History 1914–1917* (Stanford, CA: The Century Co., 1927), pp. 620–23.

34 A. K. Wildman, *The End of the Russian Imperial Army, Volume II. The Road to Soviet Power and Peace* (Princeton, NJ: Princeton University Press, 1987), pp. 380–81.

35 S. McMeekin, *The Russian Revolution. A New History* (New York: Basic Books, 2017), p. 228.

36 Wildman, *The End of the Russian Imperial Army, Volume II*, pp. 400–401.

37 G. A. Hill, *Go Spy the Land. Being the Adventures of I.K.8 of the British Secret Service* (London: Cassell & Co., 1932), p. 110.

38 TNA: CAB 28/3, 'Meeting of Representatives of the British and French Governments, Held at the "New Casino Hotel", Rapallo, Italy, on Monday, November 5, 1917, at 8 p.m.'

39 TNA: CAB 28/3, 'Procès-Verbal of a Conference of the British, French, and Italian Governments, Held at the "New Casino Hotel", Rapallo, on Tuesday, November 6, 1917, at 6.50 p.m.'

40 D. Lloyd George, *War Memoirs of David Lloyd George* (2 vols., London: Odhams Press, 1933–6), II, pp. 1442–4.

41 TNA: CAB 28/3, 'Procès-Verbal of the Second Session of the Supreme War Council, Held at the Trianon Palace, Versailles, on Saturday, December 1, 1917, at 11 a.m.'

42 Robertson to Milne, 23 November 1917, in G. H. Cassar, *The Forgotten Front. The British Campaign in Italy 1917–1918* (London: Hambledon, 1998), p. 91.

43 Robertson to Plumer, 26 November 1917, in D. R. Woodward (ed.), *The Military Correspondence of Field-Marshal Sir William Robertson, Chief of the Imperial General Staff, December 1915–February 1918* (London: Bodley Head for the Army Records Society, 1989), p. 259.

44 Ministero della Guerra, *L'Esercito Italiano nella Grande Guerra*, IV, Tomo 3, pp. 521–2; Isnenghi and Rochat, *La Grande Guerra 1914–1918*, p. 444; and M. A. Morselli, *Caporetto 1917. Victory or Defeat?* (Abingdon: Routledge, 2001), p. 105.

45 Fayolle to Foch, 23 December 1917, in Ministère de la Guerre, *Les Armées Françaises dans la Grande Guerre* (Paris: Imprimerie Nationale, 1922–39) [hereafter *AFGG*], Book 6/1, p. 117.

46 Isnenghi and Rochat, *La Grande Guerra 1914–1918*, pp. 452–3.

47 Baldini, *Diaz*, pp. 51–2; and Gooch, *The Italian Army*, p. 252.

48 *AFGG*, Book 6/1, pp. 122–3.

49 A. Barbero, *Caporetto* (Bari: Editori GLF Laterza, 2017), p. 512.

20. 'We are going out of the war'

1 I. I. Rostunov, *Russkii front pervoi mirovoi voiny* (Moscow: Nauka, 1976), p. 373.

2 M. Hoffmann, *War Diaries and Other Papers*, trans. E. Sutton (2 vols., London: Martin Secker, 1929), II, p. 190

3 Czernin to Hertling, 10 November 1917, in Z. A. B. Zeman (ed.), *Germany and the Revolution in Russia 1915–1918. Documents from the Archives of the German Foreign Ministry* (London: Oxford University Press, 1958), pp. 76–8.

4 G. E. Torrey, *The Romanian Battlefront in World War I* (Lawrence, KS: University Press of Kansas, 2011), p. 263.

5 G. E. Torrey, 'Romania Leaves the War: The Decision to Sign an Armistice, December 1917', *East European Quarterly*, Vol. 23, No. 3 (September 1989), pp. 285, 288; and 'Official Roumanian Announcement of an Armistice with the Central Powers', 6 December 1917, in J. B. Scott (ed.), *Official Statements of War Aims and Peace Proposals. December 1916 to November 1918* (Washington DC: Carnegie Endowment for International Peace, 1921), p. 203.

6 'Rumania a Victim of Circumstances', *The Times*, 18 December 1917.

7 J. W. Wheeler-Bennett, *Brest-Litovsk. The Forgotten Peace, March 1918* (London: Macmillan, 1963), pp. 85–7; and Hoffmann, *War Diaries and Other Papers*, II, p. 195.

8 B. Chernev, *Twilight of Empire. The Brest-Litovsk Conference and the Remaking of East-Central Europe, 1917–1918* (Toronto: University of Toronto Press, 2017), p. 25; *Proceedings of the Brest-Litovsk Peace Conference. The Peace Negotiations Between Russia and the Central Powers, 21*

November, 1917–3 March, 1918 (Washington DC: Government Printing Office, 1918), pp. 14–15; and O. Czernin, *In the World War* (London: Cassell & Co., 1919), p. 221.

9 *Proceedings of the Brest-Litovsk Peace Conference*, pp. 17–22; and Chernev, *Twilight of Empire*, p. 27.

10 'The Armistice Terms with Russia of December 15, 1917', in E. Ludendorff, *The General Staff and Its Problems*, trans. F. A. Holt (2 vols., London: Hutchinson & Co., 1920), II, pp. 517–23.

11 J. Bunyan and H. H. Fisher (eds.), *The Bolshevik Revolution 1917–1918. Documents and Materials* (Stanford, CA: Stanford University Press, 1961; first publ. 1934), p. 274; and 'Fear of the Collapse of the Old and the Fight for the New', 24–27 December 1917 [OS], in V. I. Lenin, *Collected Works* (45 vols., Moscow: Progress Publishers, 1960–70), XXVI, p. 400.

12 'Hindenburg und Ludendorff über Krieg und Frieden', *Neue Freie Presse*, 2 December 1917.

13 Diaz to Orlando, 19 January 1918, in Ministero della Guerra, *L'Esercito Italiano nella Grande Guerra (1915–1918)* (7 vols., Rome: Provveditorato Generale dello Stato Libreria, 1927–88), V, Tomo 1, bis, pp. 1–2.

14 M. Sarrail, *Mon Commandement en Orient* (Paris: Ernest Flammarion, 1920), p. 293.

15 D. Dutton, *The Politics of Diplomacy. Britain and France in the Balkans in the First World War* (London and New York: I. B. Tauris, 1998), p. 168.

16 'Directives pour le général commandant en chef des armées alliées d'Orient', 16 December 1917, in Ministère de la Guerre, *Les Armées Françaises dans la Grande Guerre* (Paris: Imprimerie Nationale, 1922–39) [hereafter *AFGG*], Book 8/2 – *Annexes*, Vol. 4, No. 2314, pp. 440–41.

17 TNA: CAB 28/3, 'Procès-Verbal of the Second Session of the Supreme War Council, Held at the Trianon Palace, Versailles, on Saturday, December 1, 1917, at 11 a.m.'

18 *AFGG*, Book 8/2, p. 550.

19 'Rapport du général Guillaumat, commandant en chef des armées alliées d'Orient sur la situation d'ensemble des armées d'Orient au 1er fevrier 1918', in *AFGG*, Book 8/2 – *Annexes*, Vol. 4, No. 2390, p. 563.

20 TNA: CAB 25/27, 'Weekly Report from General Guillaumat, January 15th'.

21 TNA: CAB 25/27, Milne to Robertson, 17 January 1918; and *AFGG*, Book 8/3, pp. 8–9.

22 *AFGG*, Book 8/2, p. 552.

23 R. C. Hall, *Balkan Breakthrough. The Battle of Dobro Pole 1918* (Blooming-ton, IN: Indiana University Press, 2010), p. 94.

24 Reichsarchiv, *Der Weltkrieg 1914 bis 1918*. XIII. *Die Kriegführung im Sommer und Herbst 1917. Die Ereignisse außerhalb der Westfront bis November 1918* (Berlin: E. S. Mittler & Sohn, 1942), pp. 403–4.

25 Chernev, *Twilight of Empire*, pp. 165–6.

26 *Proceedings of the Brest-Litovsk Peace Conference*, pp. 38–40.

27 Czernin, *In the World War*, p. 228.

28 'Liaison Officer at General Headquarters to the Foreign Ministry', 16 December 1917, in Zeman (ed.), *Germany and the Revolution in Russia 1915–1918*, pp. 106–7.

29 Hindenburg to Kaiser Wilhelm II, 7 January 1918, in Ludendorff, *The General Staff and Its Problems*, II, pp. 524–8.

30 'Enclosure' in Kaiser Wilhelm II to Hindenburg, undated [January 1918], in ibid., pp. 532–8.

31 Hoffmann, *War Diaries and Other Papers*, II, pp. 202–3.

32 *Proceedings of the Brest-Litovsk Peace Conference*, pp. 53–4.

33 Ibid., p. 55.

34 Czernin, *In the World War*, p. 234.

35 G. Swain, *The Origins of the Russian Civil War* (London: Routledge, 1996), pp. 76–7.

36 'Thesis on the Constituent Assembly', in Lenin, *Collected Works*, XXVI, pp. 379–83.

37 'Theses on the Question of the Immediate Conclusion of a Separate and Annexationist Peace', in ibid., pp. 442–50. Original emphasis.

38 'Hoffmann's Reply', 12 January 1918, and 'Extract from Trotsky's State-ment', 18 January 1918, in Bunyan and Fisher (eds.), *The Bolshevik Revolution 1917–1918*, pp. 495–8.

39 Emperor Karl to Count Czernin, 17 January 1918, in C. A. Wargelin, 'A High Price for Bread: The First Treaty of Brest-Litovsk and the Break-Up of Austria–Hungary, 1917–1918', *International History Review*, Vol. 19, No. 4 (November 1997), p. 778.

40 Chernev, *Twilight of Empire*, p. 130; and M. Rauchensteiner, *The First World War and the End of the Habsburg Monarchy, 1914–1918*, trans. A. J. Kay and A. Güttel-Bellert (Vienna: Böhlau Verlag, 2014; first publ. 1993), pp. 876–7.

41 *Proceedings of the Brest-Litovsk Peace Conference*, pp. 171–4; and Wheeler-Bennett, *Brest-Litovsk*, p. 227.

42 Reichsarchiv, *Der Weltkrieg*, XIII, p. 366.

43 'Germany's New Peace Terms', 21 February 1918, in Bunyan and Fisher (eds.), *The Bolshevik Revolution 1917–1918*, pp. 517–19.

44 E. A. Vertsinsky, *God revoliutsii. Vospominaniia ofitsera generalnago shtaba za 1917–1918 goda* (Tallinn: n.p., 1929), pp. 57–8.

45 A. Rabinowitch, *The Bolsheviks in Power. The First Year of Soviet Rule in Petrograd* (Bloomington, IN: Indiana University Press, 2007), pp. 182–4; and Wheeler-Bennett, *Brest-Litovsk*, pp. 258–9.

46 Bunyan and Fisher (eds.), *The Bolshevik Revolution 1917–1918*, pp. 522–3.

47 Ibid., pp. 523–4.

21. 'Gambler's throw'

1 TNA: CAB 23/4/68, 'War Cabinet, 294', 7 December 1917.

2 E. Greenhalgh, *Foch in Command. The Forging of a First World War General* (Cambridge: Cambridge University Press, 2011), pp. 270–71, 273.

3 R. Luckett, *The White Generals. An Account of the White Movement and the Russian Civil War* (London: Routledge & Kegan Paul, 1987; first publ. 1971), p. 100.

4 O. Figes, *A People's Tragedy. The Russian Revolution 1891–1924* (London: Jonathan Cape, 1996), p. 563; and P. Kenez, *Civil War in South Russia, 1918. The First Year of the Volunteer Army* (Berkeley: University of California Press, 1971), p. 115.

5 M. Kettle, *The Allies and the Russian Collapse. March 1917–March 1918* (London: Andre Deutsch, 1981), pp. 153, 230.

6 G. F. Kennan, *The Decision to Intervene. Soviet–American Relations, 1917–1920* (Princeton, NJ: Princeton University Press, 1958), pp. 140–42.

7 G. Becvar, *The Lost Legion. A Czechoslovakian Epic* (London: Stanley Paul & Co., 1939), pp. 71–2.

8 D. Lloyd George, *War Memoirs of David Lloyd George* (2 vols., London: Odhams Press, 1933–6), II, p. 1901.

9 I. Somin, *Stillborn Crusade. The Tragic Failure of Western Intervention in the Russian Civil War 1918–1920* (New Brunswick, NJ: Transaction Publishers, 1996), p. 34.

10 C. Kinvig, *Churchill's Crusade. The British Invasion of Russia, 1918–1920* (London: Hambledon Continuum, 1996), p. 18.

11 M. Kettle, *The Road to Intervention. March–November 1918* (London: Routledge, 1988), p. 4.

12 TNA: CAB 28/3, 'Notes of the Meeting Held on 15th March, 1918, at 3.15 p.m., in London'.

13 J. F. N. Bradley, 'The Allies and the Czech Revolt Against the Bolsheviks in 1918', *The Slavonic and East European Review*, Vol. 43, No. 101 (June 1965), pp. 285–6; and TNA: CAB 28/3, 'Procès-Verbal of the Second Meeting of the Fifth Session of the Supreme War Council, Held in the Chambre des Notaires, at Abbeville, on Thursday, the 2nd May, 1918 at 11.35 a.m.'

14 Lloyd George, *War Memoirs*, II, p. 1904.

15 R. Poincaré, *Au Service de la France. Vol. 10. Victoire et Armistice 1918* (Paris: Librairie Plon, 1933), pp. 265–6.

16 Sir J. Edmonds, *Military Operations. France and Belgium, 1918* (5 vols., London: Macmillan & Co., 1937), II, pp. 9, 115.

17 Reichsarchiv, *Der Weltkrieg 1914 bis 1918. XIV. Die Kriegführung an der Westfront im Jahre 1918* (Berlin: E. S. Mittler & Sohn, 1944), pp. 254–5.

18 KA: Arz von Straussenburg Papers, B/63:10, Hindenburg to Arz von Straussenburg, 25 March 1918.

19 E. Glaise-Horstenau, *Österreich-Ungarns Letzter Krieg 1914–1918*, VII, *Das Kriegsjahr 1918* (Vienna: Verlag der Militärwissenschaftlichen Mitteilungen, 1938), pp. 41–4.

20 Ibid., pp. 186–7.

21 E. Bauer, *Der Löwe vom Isonzo. Feldmarschall Svetozar Boroević de Bojna* (Graz: Styria, 1985), p. 80.

22 Ibid., p. 79.

23 M. Rauchensteiner, *The First World War and the End of the Habsburg Monarchy, 1914–1918*, trans. A. J. Kay and A. Güttel-Bellert (Vienna: Böhlau Verlag, 2014; first publ. 1993), p. 911.

24 A. Arz von Straussenburg, *Zur Geschichte des Grossen Krieges 1914–1918* (Vienna, Munich and Leipzig: Rikola, 1924), p. 263.

25 Glaise-Horstenau, *Österreich-Ungarns Letzter Krieg 1914–1918*, VII, pp. 189–90.

26 Bauer, *Der Löwe vom Isonzo*, pp. 81–2.

27 Glaise-Horstenau, *Österreich-Ungarns Letzter Krieg 1914–1918*, VII, p. 193.

28 A. Krauss, *Die Ursachen unserer Niederlage. Erinnerungen und Urteile aus dem Weltkrieg* (Munich: J. F. Lehmanns, 1921), p. 250.

29 G. Brook-Shepherd, *The Last Habsburg* (London: Weidenfeld & Nicolson, 1968), pp. 142–3.

30 E. Demmerle, *Kaiser Karl I. 'Selig, die Frieden stiften . . .' Die Biographie* (Vienna: Amalthea Signum Verlag, 2004), pp. 155–6.

31 Reichsarchiv, *Der Weltkrieg*, XIV, p. 727.

32 Demmerle, *Kaiser Karl I*, p. 155.

33 Brook-Shepherd, *The Last Habsburg*, p. 116.

34 'Address to Congress Stating the Peace Terms of the United States', 8 January 1918, in *America Joins the World. Selections From the Speeches and State Papers of President Wilson, 1914–1918* (New York: Association Press, 1919), pp. 70–79.

35 TNA: CAB 28/3, 'Notes of an Anglo-French Conference Held at 10, Downing St, S.W., on Tuesday, May 28, 1918, at 4 p.m., with Conclusions'.

36 TNA: WO 106/814, C. Delme-Radcliffe to Director of Military Operations, War Office, 11 April 1918.

37 M. Isnenghi and G. Rochat, *La Grande Guerra 1914–1918* (Milan: Sansoni, 2004; first publ. 2000), p. 452.

38 Ministero della Guerra, *L'Esercito Italiano nella Grande Guerra (1915–1918)* (7 vols., Rome: Provveditorato Generale Dello Stato Libreria, 1927–88), V, Tomo 1, p. 87, n. 3, p. 97.

39 J. Gooch, *The Italian Army and the First World War* (Cambridge: Cambridge University Press, 2014), p. 270; and TNA: CAB 28/3, 'Procès-Verbal of the Third Meeting of the Fifth Session of the Supreme War Council, Held in the Chambre des Notaires, at Abbeville, on Thursday, the 2nd May, 1918 at 2.45 p.m.'

40 Ministère de la Guerre, *Les Armées Françaises dans la Grande Guerre* (Paris: Imprimerie Nationale, 1922–39) [hereafter *AFGG*], Book 6/2, pp. 18–20.

41 Foch to Diaz, 12 June 1918, in *AFGG*, Book 6/2 – *Annexes*, Vol. 2, No. 1484, p. 672.

42 Isnenghi and Rochat, *La Grande Guerra 1914–1918*, pp. 462–3; and Rauchensteiner, *The First World War and the End of the Habsburg Monarchy*, p. 921.

43 Ministero della Guerra, *L'Esercito Italiano nella Grande Guerra*, V, Tomo I, p. 428, n. 2.

44 A. Mangone, *Diaz. Da Caporetto al Piave a Vittorio Veneto* (Milan: Frassinelli, 1987), p. 110.

45 Glaise-Horstenau, *Österreich-Ungarns Letzter Krieg 1914–1918*, VII, p. 241.

46 *Geschichte des Steirischen k.u.k. Infanterie-Regimentes Nr. 27 für den Zeitraum des Weltkrieges 1914–1918* (2 vols., Innsbruck: Wagner'sche Universitäts-Buchdruckerei, 1937), II, p. 350; and Glaise-Horstenau, *Österreich-Ungarns Letzter Krieg 1914–1918*, VII, p. 259.

47 Glaise-Horstenau, *Österreich-Ungarns Letzter Krieg 1914–1918*, VII, pp. 266, 275.

48 Rauchensteiner, *The First World War and the End of the Habsburg Monarchy*, pp. 919–20.

49 IWM: Documents 9970, Private Papers of E. Kunisch, 'The Diary of a Soldier of the Austro-Hungarian Empire', p. 30.

50 Glaise-Horstenau, *Österreich-Ungarns Letzter Krieg 1914–1918*, VII, p. 359; and F. Weber, *Sturm an der Piave* (Berlin: Steyrermühl, 1932), p. 38.

51 Mangone, *Diaz*, p. 116.

52 Glaise-Horstenau, *Österreich-Ungarns Letzter Krieg 1914–1918*, VII, pp. 285–6.

53 Jan Tríska cited in J. Hutečka, *Men Under Fire. Motivation, Morale and Masculinity among Czech Soldiers in the Great War, 1914–1918* (New York and Oxford: Berghahn, 2020), p. 220.

54 Glaise-Horstenau, *Österreich-Ungarns Letzter Krieg 1914–1918*, VII, pp. 298, 359; and C. Schiaparelli, *La Battaglia del Piave (15–25 Giugno 1918)* (Torino: Istituto Nazionale per le Biblioteche dei Soldati, 1922), p. 211.

55 Arz von Straussenburg, *Zur Geschichte des Grossen Krieges 1914–1918*, p. 271.

56 Glaise-Horstenau, *Österreich-Ungarns Letzter Krieg 1914–1918*, VII, pp. 319–20.

22. 'The off-chance of something good'

1 P. Azan, *Franchet d'Espèrey* (Paris: Flammarion, 1949), p. 281.

2 D. Dutton, *The Politics of Diplomacy. Britain and France in the Balkans in the First World War* (London and New York: I. B. Tauris, 1998), p. 170.

3 Clemenceau to Franchet d'Espèrey, 23 June 1918, Appendix 6, in C. Falls, *Military Operations Macedonia* [Vol. II]. *From the Spring of 1917 to the End of the War* (London: HMSO, 1935), pp. 321–2.

4 Ministère de la Guerre, *Les Armées Françaises dans la Grande Guerre* (Paris: Imprimerie Nationale, 1922–39) [hereafter *AFGG*], Book 8/3, p. 71.

5 L. Franchet d'Espèrey, 'Les Armées Alliées en Orient: Du 18 Juin au 30 Septembre 1918: I', *Revue des Deux Mondes*, Vol. 47, No. 1 (September 1938), pp. 6, 10.

6 Azan, *Franchet d'Espèrey*, pp. 187–8.

7 Falls, *Military Operations Macedonia* [Vol. II], p. 90.

8 'Examen des possibilités d'une opération offensive sur le front du Dobro Polje', 5 June 1918, in *AFGG*, Book 8/3 – *Annexes*, Vol. 1, No. 228, pp. 408–14.

9 A. Palmer, *The Gardeners of Salonika* (London: Andre Deutsch, 1965), p. 185.

10 Franchet d'Espèrey to Mišić, 6 July 1918, and 'Étude sommaire d'une action offensive d'ensemble sur le front macédonien, avec opération principale sur le Dobropolie', in *AFGG*, Book 8/3 – *Annexes*, Vol. 1, Nos. 376, 377, pp. 661–6; and Franchet d'Espèrey, 'Les Armées Alliées en Orient: Du 18 Juin au 30 Septembre 1918: I', pp. 17–18.

11 TNA: CAB 28/4, 'Procès-Verbal of the Second Meeting of the Seventh Session of the Supreme War Council, Held at the Trianon Palace, Versailles, on Wednesday, 3rd July, 1918, at 3 p.m.'

12 'Plan d'offensive sur le théâtre des Balkans', in *AFGG*, Book 8/3 – *Annexes*, Vol. 1, No. 430, p. 730.

13 'Note sur le projet d'offensive des armées alliées en Orient', 19 July 1918, in *AFGG*, Book 8/3 – *Annexes*, Vol. 1, No. 452, pp. 759–62.

14 TNA: CAB 25/26, Milne to War Office, 22 July 1918.

15 Franchet d'Espèrey to Milne, 24 July 1918, Appendix 7, in Falls, *Military Operations Macedonia* [Vol. II], pp. 323–4.

16 TNA: CAB 25/26, Milne to War Office and reply, 25 and 27 July 1918.

17 Falls, *Military Operations Macedonia* [Vol. II], p. 110.

18 D. Lloyd George, *War Memoirs of David Lloyd George* (2 vols., London: Odhams Press, 1933–6), II, pp. 1918–19.

19 Ministero della Guerra, *L'Esercito Italiano nella Grande Guerra (1915–1918)* (7 vols., Rome: Provveditorato Generale dello Stato Libreria, 1927–88), V, Tomo 2, pp. 72, 128; and A. Baldini, *Diaz*, trans. W. J. Monson (London: Humphrey Toulmin, 1935), p. 133.

20 Sir J. Edmonds and H. R. Davies, *Military Operations. Italy, 1915–1919* (London: HMSO, 1949), p. 243; and Foch to Diaz, 17 July 1918, in *AFGG*, Book 7/1 – *Annexes*, Vol. 1, No. 77, pp. 118–19.

21 Diaz to Foch, 30 July 1918, in Ministero della Guerra, *L'Esercito Italiano nella Grande Guerra*, V, Tomo 2, bis, pp. 198–202.

22 Ibid., p. 73.

23 A. Barbero, *Caporetto* (Bari: Editori GLF Laterza, 2017), p. 513.

24 'Promemoria', 16 August 1918, in Ministero della Guerra, *L'Esercito Italiano nella Grande Guerra*, V, Tomo 2, bis, pp. 238–41.

25 'Memori', n.d., in ibid., pp. 252–60.

26 Wilson diary, 24–7 June 1918, in G. H. Cassar, *The Forgotten Front. The British Campaign in Italy 1917–1918* (London: Hambledon, 1998), p. 168.

27 A. Mangone, *Diaz. Da Caporetto al Piave a Vittorio Veneto* (Milan: Frassinelli, 1987), p. 123.

28 V. G. Liulevicius, *War Land on the Eastern Front. Culture, National Identity, and German Occupation in World War I* (Cambridge: Cambridge University Press, 2004), p. 213.

29 Ludendorff to Hertling, 9 June 1918, in E. Ludendorff, *The General Staff and Its Problems*, trans. F. A. Holt (2 vols., London: Hutchinson & Co., 1920), II, pp. 571–5.

30 M. Hoffmann, *War Diaries and Other Papers*, trans. E. Sutton (2 vols., London: Martin Secker, 1929), II, p. 228.

31 'The Minister in Moscow to the State Secretary', 25 June 1918, in Z. A. B. Zeman (ed.), *Germany and the Revolution in Russia 1915–1918. Documents from the Archives of the German Foreign Ministry* (London: Oxford University Press, 1958), pp. 137–9. Original emphasis.

32 H. Rappaport, *The Last Days of the Romanovs. Tragedy at Ekaterinburg* (New York: St Martin's Griffin, 2008), p. 141.

33 J. Ryan, *Lenin's Terror. The Ideological Origins of Early Soviet State Violence* (Abingdon: Routledge, 2012), p. 107.

34 A. Rabinowitch, *The Bolsheviks in Power. The First Year of Soviet Rule in Petrograd* (Bloomington, IN: Indiana University Press, 2007), p. 313; and R. Service, *Lenin. A Biography* (London: Macmillan, 2000), p. 365. Original emphasis.

35 Liulevicius, *War Land on the Eastern Front*, p. 212; and J. W. Wheeler-Bennett, *Hindenburg. The Wooden Titan* (London: Macmillan, 1967; first publ. 1936), p. 127.

36 W. Dornik and P. Lieb, 'Misconceived Realpolitik in a Failing State: The Political and Economical Fiasco of the Central Powers in the Ukraine, 1918', *First World War Studies*, Vol. 4, No. 1 (2013), pp. 117–18.

37 'Antwort des österreichisch-ungarischen Botschafters in Kiew, Forgach, an das Ministerium des Aeußern', 20 August 1918, in *Die Deutsche Okkupation der Ukraine. Geheimdokumente* (Strasbourg: Prométhée, 1937), p. 204.

38 R. B. Asprey, *The German High Command at War. Hindenburg and Ludendorff and the First World War* (London: Little, Brown & Company, 1993; first publ. 1991), pp. 442–3.

39 E. Glaise-Horstenau, *Österreich-Ungarns Letzter Krieg 1914–1918*, VII, *Das Kriegsjahr 1918* (Vienna: Verlag der Militärwissenschaftlichen Mitteilungen, 1938), pp. 438, 445–6.

40 G. A. Tunstall, *The Austro-Hungarian Army and the First World War* (Cambridge: Cambridge University Press, 2021), p. 342; and L. Sondhaus, *Franz Conrad von Hötzendorf. Architect of the Apocalypse* (Boston: Humanities Press, 2000), pp. 210–11.

41 Glaise-Horstenau, *Österreich-Ungarns Letzter Krieg 1914–1918*, VII, pp. 447–8.

42 P. S. Wandycz, *France and Her Eastern Allies 1919–1925. French–Czechoslovak–Polish Relations from the Paris Peace Conference to Locarno* (Minneapolis, MN: University of Minnesota Press, 1962), p. 14.

43 G. Brook-Shepherd, *The Last Habsburg* (London: Weidenfeld & Nicolson, 1968), pp. 106–7.

44 Count A. Polzer-Hoditz, *The Emperor Karl* (London and New York: Putnam, 1930), p. 291.

45 A. Watson, *Ring of Steel. Germany and Austria–Hungary, 1914–1918* (London: Allen Lane, 2015; first publ. 2014), pp. 538–9.

46 E. Demmerle, *Kaiser Karl I. 'Selig, die Frieden stiften . . .' Die Biographie* (Vienna: Amalthea Signum Verlag, 2004), pp. 157–8; and Polzer-Hoditz, *The Emperor Karl*, p. 208.

47 S. Burián, *Austria in Dissolution. Being the Personal Recollections of Stephan, Count Burián*, trans. B. Lunn (New York: George H. Doran, n.d.), p. 380.

48 A. Arz von Straussenburg, *Zur Geschichte des Grossen Krieges 1914–1918* (Vienna, Munich and Leipzig: Rikola, 1924), p. 284.

49 L. Cecil, *Wilhelm II. Volume 2. Emperor and Exile, 1900–1941* (Chapel Hill, NC: University of North Carolina Press, 1996), p. 275; and A. Niemann, *Kaiser und Revolution. Die eintscheidenden Ereignnisse im Großen Hauptquartier* (Berlin: August Scherl, 1922), p. 61.

50 Arz von Straussenburg, *Zur Geschichte des Grossen Krieges 1914–1918*, p. 284.

23. 'The honour of the army'

1 P. Azan, *Franchet d'Espèrey* (Paris: Flammarion, 1949), p. 192.

2 R. C. Hall, *Balkan Breakthrough. The Battle of Dobro Pole 1918* (Bloomington, IN: Indiana University Press, 2010), p. 135.

3 HIA: Tsar Ferdinand Papers, Box 74/6, 'Heeresgruppe von Scholtz an den Kaiserlich deutschen Militärbevollmächtigten für Bulgarien,', 15 June 1918.

4 Ibid., 'Bemerkungen über bulgarischen OHL', 15 June 1918; and Hall, *Balkan Breakthrough*, pp. 136–7.

5 S. Noikov, *Zashto ne pobedikhme 1915–1918* (Sofia: Army Military Publishing, 1922), pp. 172, 178.

6 Ministère de la Guerre, *Les Armées Françaises dans la Grande Guerre* (Paris: Imprimerie Nationale, 1922–39) [hereafter *AFGG*], Book 8/3, p. 309.

7 *Veliki rat Srbije za oslobođenje i ujedinjenje Srba, Hrvata i Slovenaca* (28 vols., Belgrade: Glavni đeneralštab, 1924–37), XXVII, p. 101.

8 *AFGG*, Book 8/3, pp. 315–17.

9 Franchet d'Espèrey to War Ministry, 16 September 1918, and Mišić to Franchet d'Espèrey, 17 September 1918, in *AFGG*, Book 8/3 – *Annexes*, Vol. 2, Nos. 994, 1013, pp. 726–7, 752–3.

10 B. R. Mullaly, *The South Lancashire Regiment. The Prince of Wales's Volunteers* (Bristol: The White Swan Press, 1955), pp. 332–3.

11 C. Falls, *Military Operations Macedonia* [Vol. II]. *From the Spring of 1917 to the End of the War* (London: HMSO, 1935), pp. 113–16, 186.

12 OHL to Bulgarian GHQ, 19 September 1918, Appendix 16, in Falls, *Military Operations Macedonia* [Vol. II], p. 348.

13 A. Dieterich, *Weltkriegsende an der Mazedonischen Front* (Berlin: Gerhard Stalling, 1925), pp. 48–9.

14 H. A. Jones, *The War in the Air. Being the Story of the Part Played in the Great War by the Royal Air Force* (6 vols., Oxford: Clarendon Press, 1922–37), VI, pp. 307–8; and IWM: Documents 17806, Private Papers of H. J. Arnold, p. 11.

15 'Bulgarian Announcement of the Request for an Armistice', 24 September 1918, and 'Reply of General Franchet d'Espèrey to the Bulgarian Request for an Armistice', 26 September 1918, in J. B. Scott (ed.), *Official Statements of War Aims and Peace Proposals. December 1916 to November 1918* (Washington DC: Carnegie Endowment for International Peace, 1921), p. 398.

16 Azan, *Franchet d'Espèrey*, p. 197.

17 L. Franchet d'Espèrey, 'Les Armées Alliées en Orient: Du 18 Juin au 30 Septembre 1918: II', *Revue des Deux Mondes*, Vol. 47, No. 2 (September 1938), pp. 263–4; and 'Bulgaria Armistice Convention, September 29, 1918', in Scott (ed.), *Official Statements of War Aims and Peace Proposals*, pp. 405–6.

18 'German Request for an Armistice', in Scott (ed.), *Official Statements of War Aims and Peace Proposals*, p. 415.

19 'Inquiry from President Wilson Concerning the German Proposal', in ibid., pp. 418–19.

20 'Austrian Request for an Armistice', in ibid., pp. 417–18.

21 G. Brook-Shepherd, *The Last Habsburg* (London: Weidenfeld & Nicolson, 1968), pp. 175–6; and J. Leonhard, *Pandora's Box. A History of the First World War*, trans. P. Camiller (Cambridge, MA: Harvard University Press, 2018), pp. 804–5.

22 'Reply of President Wilson to the Austrian Proposal', in Scott (ed.), *Official Statements of War Aims and Peace Proposals*, pp. 428–9.

23 S. Burián, *Austria in Dissolution. Being the Personal Recollections of Stephan, Count Burián*, trans. B. Lunn (New York: George H. Doran, n.d.), p. 410.

24 'Tisza Now Admits the War is Lost', *New York Times*, 20 October 1918.

25 A. Baldini, *Diaz*, trans. W. J. Monson (London: Humphrey Toulmin, 1935), pp. 143–4; E. Greenhalgh, *Foch in Command. The Forging of a First World War General* (Cambridge: Cambridge University Press, 2011), p. 449; and R. Poincaré, *Au Service de la France*. Vol. 10. *Victoire et Armistice 1918* (Paris: Librairie Plon, 1933), p. 330.

26 Foch to Orlando, 28 September 1918, in *AFGG*, Book 7/2 – *Annexes*, No. 38, pp. 71–2; and Greenhalgh, *Foch in Command*, p. 417.

27 S. M. Di Scala, *Vittorio Emanuele Orlando* (London: Haus, 2010), p. 127.

28 A. Mangone, *Diaz. Da Caporetto al Piave a Vittorio Veneto* (Milan: Frassinelli, 1987), p. 126.

29 Orlando to Diaz, and reply, 14 October 1918, in Ministero della Guerra, *L'Esercito Italiano nella Grande Guerra (1915–1918)* (7 vols., Rome: Provveditorato Generale Dello Stato Libreria, 1927–88), V, Tomo 2, bis, pp. 700–701.

30 Sir J. Edmonds and H. R. Davies, *Military Operations. Italy, 1915–1919* (London: HMSO, 1949), pp. 265–6; and Ministero della Guerra, *L'Esercito Italiano nella Grande Guerra*, V, Tomo 2, pp. 312–13.

31 E. Glaise-Horstenau, *Österreich-Ungarns Letzter Krieg 1914–1918*, VII, *Das Kriegsjahr 1918* (Vienna: Verlag der Militärwissenschaftlichen Mitteilungen, 1938), pp. 571–6.

32 Ministero della Guerra, *L'Esercito Italiano nella Grande Guerra*, V, Tomo 2, pp. 440–53.

33 G. H. Cassar, *The Forgotten Front. The British Campaign in Italy 1917–1918* (London: Hambledon, 1998), p. 249, n. 5.

34 IWM: Documents 4328, Private Papers of H. Wright, 'A Diary of Italy', pp. 52–4.

35 E. Caviglia, *Le Tre Battaglie del Piave* (Milan: A. Mondadori, 1935), p. 177.

36 Glaise-Horstenau, *Österreich-Ungarns Letzter Krieg 1914–1918*, VII, pp. 617–19.

37 Ibid., p. 632.

38 Karl I to Wilhelm II, and reply, 27 October 1918, in H. Michaelis, E. Schraepler and G. Scheel (eds.), *Ursachen und Folgen. Vom deutschen*

Zusammenbruch 1918 und 1945 bis zur staatlichen Neuordnung Deutschlands in der Gegenwart. Die Wende des ersten Weltkrieges und der Beginn der innerpolitischen Wandlung 1916/1917 (Berlin: Herbert Wendler & Co., 1958), pp. 438–40.

39 M. Rauchensteiner, *The First World War and the End of the Habsburg Monarchy, 1914–1918*, trans. A. J. Kay and A. Güttel-Bellert (Vienna: Böhlau Verlag, 2014; first publ. 1993), pp. 1002–3.

40 Arz von Straußenburg to Hindenburg, 28 October 1918, cited in Rauchensteiner, *The First World War and the End of the Habsburg Monarchy*, p. 1001.

41 *La Guerra d'Italia* (6 vols., Milan: Fratelli Treves, 1916–24), VI, p. 295.

42 Glaise-Horstenau, *Österreich-Ungarns Letzter Krieg 1914–1918*, VII, p. 644.

43 Mangone, *Diaz*, p. 147.

44 P. Formiconi, 'Diaz, il Generale della Vittoria', in *L'Italia e la Grande Guerra – il 1918. La Vittoria e il Sacrificio* (Rome: Ufficio Storica della Difesa, 2019), pp. 194–5.

45 'Protocol of the Conditions of an Armistice Between the Allied and Associated Powers and Austria–Hungary', in Scott (ed.), *Official Statements of War Aims and Peace Proposals*, pp. 446–8.

46 Edmonds and Davies, *Military Operations. Italy, 1915–1919*, p. 371; and Glaise-Horstenau, *Österreich-Ungarns Letzter Krieg 1914–1918*, VII, p. 714.

47 A. Arz von Straussenburg, *Zur Geschichte des Grossen Krieges 1914–1918* (Vienna, Munich and Leipzig: Rikola, 1924), p. 364; and Brook-Shepherd, *The Last Habsburg*, pp. 196–8.

48 IWM: Documents 27390, Private Papers of B. Hoffmann, 'I was a Prisoner of War', p. 3.

49 'By General Armando Diaz', 4 November 1918, in C. F. Horne (ed.), *Source Records of the Great War* (7 vols., USA: National Alumni, 1923), VI, p. 374.

Epilogue

1 G. Brook-Shepherd, *The Last Habsburg* (London: Weidenfeld & Nicolson, 1968), p. 214.

2 H. Vivian, *The Life of the Emperor Charles of Austria* (London: Grayson & Grayson, 1932), p. 181.

3 'Preliminary Peace Conference, Protocol No. 1, Session of January 18, 1919', in J. V. Fuller (ed.), *Papers Relating to the Foreign Relations of the United States, The Paris Peace Conference, 1919, Volume III* (Washington: Government Printing Office, 1943), Document 3.

4 J. A. S. Grenville and B. Wasserstein (eds.), *The Major International Treaties of the Twentieth Century. A History and Guide with Texts* (2 vols., London: Routledge, 2001), I, pp. 94, 110.

5 J. Claude Roberts, 'The Austrian Reaction to the Treaty of St. Germain', *Southwestern Social Science Quarterly*, Vol. 40 (1959), pp. 88–9.

6 T. Sakmyster, *Hungary's Admiral on Horseback. Miklós Horthy, 1918–1944* (Boulder, CO: East European Monographs, 1994), p. 50.

7 Grenville and Wasserstein (eds.), *The Major International Treaties of the Twentieth Century*, p. 94; N. Horthy, *Memoirs* (Westport, CT: Greenwood Press, 1957), pp. 114–15; and F. Deák, *Hungary at the Paris Peace Conference. The Diplomatic History of the Treaty of Trianon* (New York: Columbia University Press, 1942), p. 555.

8 Horthy, *Memoirs*, pp. 124–5.

9 E. Demmerle, *Kaiser Karl I. 'Selig, die Frieden stiften . . .' Die Biographie* (Vienna: Amalthea Signum Verlag, 2004), p. 218.

10 R. Gerwarth, *The Vanquished. Why the First World War Failed to End, 1917– 1923* (London: Penguin Books, 2017; first publ. 2016), pp. 223–4.

11 'Notes of a Meeting Held at Mr. Lloyd George's Residence, 23 Rue Nitot, Paris, on Thursday, April 24, 1919', in J. V. Fuller (ed.), *Papers Relating to the Foreign Relations of the United States, The Paris Peace Conference, 1919, Volume V* (Washington: Government Printing Office, 1946), Document 19.

12 M. A. Ledeen, *The First Duce. D'Annunzio at Fiume* (London: Johns Hopkins Press, 1977; first publ. 1975), p. 69.

13 'Italy's Foreign Policy Regarding German Reparations, Hungary, Bulgaria, Austria, Yugoslavia, Turkey, Russia, Poland and Other Countries', 8 June 1923, in B. B. Quaranta di San Severino (ed. and trans.), *Mussolini as Revealed in his Political Speeches* (London: J. M. Dent & Sons, 1923), pp. 293–4.

14 R. Service, *Lenin. A Biography* (London: Macmillan, 2000), p. 385.

15 'Report on the International Situation and the Fundamental Tasks of the Communist International', in V. I. Lenin, *Collected Works* (45 vols., Moscow: Progress Publishers, 1960–70), XXXI, p. 234.

16 Piłsudski cited in N. Davies, *White Eagle, Red Star. The Polish–Soviet War 1919–1920 and 'The Miracle on the Vistula'* (London: Pimlico, 2003; first publ. 1972), p. 264.

17 R. Luckett, *The White Generals. An Account of the White Movement and the Russian Civil War* (London: Routledge & Kegan Paul, 1987; first publ. 1971), p. 383; and E. Mawdsley, *The Russian Civil War* (New York: Pegasus Books, 2007; first publ. 2005), pp. 285–6.

18 J. H. Cockfield, *Russia's Iron General. The Life of Aleksei A. Brusilov, 1853–1926* (Lanham, MD: Lexington Books, 2019), p. 329. Original emphasis.

19 HIA: Alekseev Papers, Box 1, General Denikin, memorandum on General Alekseev's death, 25 September 1918 [OS].

20 L. Sondhaus, *Franz Conrad von Hötzendorf. Architect of the Apocalypse* (Boston: Humanities Press, 2000), pp. 214–15. Original emphasis.

Select Bibliography

Abbott, G. F., *Greece and the Allies 1914–1922* (London: Methuen & Co., 1922)

Abraham, R., *Alexander Kerensky. The First Love of the Revolution* (New York: Columbia University Press, 1987)

Afflerbach, H., *Falkenhayn. Politisches Denken und Handeln im Kaiserreich* (Munich: Oldenbourg, 1994)

Airapetov, O. R., 'The Naroch Offensive and the Dismissal of A. A. Polivanov', *Russian Studies in History*, Vol. 51, No. 4 (Spring 2013), pp. 7–30.

——, *Uchastie Rossiiskoi imperii v Pervoi mirovoi voine (1914–1917). 1914 god* (Moscow: Kuchkovo Pole, 2014)

——, *Uchastie Rossiiskoi imperii v Pervoi mirovoi voine (1914–1917). 1915 god* (Moscow: Kuchkovo Pole, 2014)

——, *Uchastie Rossiiskoi imperii v Pervoi mirovoi voine (1914–1917). 1916 god* (Moscow: Kuchkovo Pole, 2015)

——, *Uchastie Rossiiskoi imperii v Pervoi mirovoi voine (1914–1917). 1917 god* (Moscow: Kuchkovo Pole, 2015)

Arz von Straussenburg, A., *Zur Geschichte des Grossen Krieges 1914–1918* (Vienna, Munich and Leipzig: Rikola, 1924)

Averescu, A., *Operațiile dela Flămânda* (Bucharest: Cultura Nationala, n.d.)

——, *Notițe Zilnice din Războiu (1916–1918)* (Bucharest: Cultura Nationala, 1935)

Azan, P., *Franchet d'Espèrey* (Paris: Flammarion, 1949)

Baldini, A., *Diaz*, trans. W. J. Monson (London: Humphrey Toulmin, 1935)

Barbero, A., *Caporetto* (Bari: Editori GLF Laterza, 2017)

Barrett, M. B., *Prelude to Blitzkrieg. The 1916 Austro-German Campaign in Romania* (Bloomington, IN: Indiana University Press, 2013)

Bauer, E., *Der Löwe vom Isonzo. Feldmarschall Svetozar Boroević de Bojna* (Graz: Styria, 1985)

Bernède, A., '"The Gardeners of Salonika": The Lines of Communication and the Logistics of the French Army of the East, October 1915–November 1918', *War & Society*, Vol. 16, No. 1 (1998), pp. 43–59.

Bezobrazov, V. M., *Diary of the Commander of the Russian Imperial Guard 1914–1917*, ed. M. Lyons (Boynton Beach, FL: Dramco, 1994)

Brook-Shepherd, G., *The Last Habsburg* (London: Weidenfeld & Nicolson, 1968)

Browder, R. P. and A. F. Kerensky (eds.), *The Russian Provisional Government 1917. Documents* (3 vols., Stanford, CA: Stanford University Press, 1961)

Brussilov, A. A., *A Soldier's Note-Book 1914–1918* (London: Macmillan & Co., 1930)

Bunyan, J. and H. H. Fisher (eds.), *The Bolshevik Revolution 1917–1918. Documents and Materials* (Stanford, CA: Stanford University Press, 1961; first publ. 1934)

Burián, S., *Austria in Dissolution. Being the Personal Recollections of Stephan, Count Burián*, trans. B. Lunn (New York: George H. Doran, n.d.)

Buttar, P., *Russia's Last Gasp. The Eastern Front 1916–17* (Oxford: Osprey, 2017; first publ. 2016)

Cadorna, L., *La Guerra alla Fronte Italiana* (2 vols., Milan: Fratelli Treves, 1921)

——, *Lettere Famigliari*, ed. R. Cadorna (Milan; Arnoldo Mondadori, 1967)

Cassar, G. H., *The Forgotten Front. The British Campaign in Italy 1917–1918* (London: Hambledon, 1998)

Caviglia, E., *Le Tre Battaglie del Piave* (Milan: A. Mondadori, 1935)

Cecil, L., *Wilhelm II. Volume 2. Emperor and Exile, 1900–1941* (Chapel Hill, NC: University of North Carolina Press, 1996)

Chernev, B., *Twilight of Empire. The Brest-Litovsk Conference and the Remaking of East-Central Europe, 1917–1918* (Toronto: University of Toronto Press, 2017)

Chester, S. B., *Life of Venizelos* (London: Constable and Company, 1921)

Churchill, W. S., *The World Crisis. The Eastern Front* (London: Thornton Butterworth, 1931)

Clark, C., *The Sleepwalkers. How Europe Went to War in 1914* (London: Penguin, 2013; first publ. 2012)

Cockfield, J. H., *Russia's Iron General. The Life of Aleksei A. Brusilov, 1853–1926* (Lanham, MD: Lexington Books, 2019)

Conrad von Hötzendorf, F., *Aus Meiner Dienstzeit 1906–1918* (5 vols., Vienna: Rikola Verlag, 1921–5)

Conrad von Hötzendorf, G. Grafin, *Mein Leben mit Conrad von Hötzendorf. Sein geistiges Vermächtnis* (Leipzig: Greithlein & Co., 1935)

Constant, S., *Foxy Ferdinand 1868–1948. Tsar of Bulgaria* (London: Sidgwick & Jackson, 1979)

Corselli, R., *Cadorna* (Milan: Edizioni Corbaccio, 1937)

Cramon, A. von, *Unser Osterreichisch-Ungarischer Bundesgenosse im Weltkriege* (Berlin: E. S. Mittler & Sohn, 1922)

Czernin, O., *In the World War* (London: Cassell & Co., 1919)

Dabija, G. A., *Armata Română in Răsboiul Mondial (1916–1918)* (4 vols., Bucharest: I. G. Hertz, 1928–37)

Danilov, J. N., *Rußland im Weltkriege 1914–1915*, trans. R. Freiherr von Campenhausen (Jena: Walter Biedermann, 1925)

——, *Velikii kniaz' Nikolai Nikolaevich* (Paris: Imprimerie de Navarre, 1930)

Dedijer, V., *The Road to Sarajevo* (London: MacGibbon & Kee, 1966)

Demmerle, E., *Kaiser Karl I. 'Selig, die Frieden stiften . . .' Die Biographie* (Vienna: Amalthea Signum Verlag, 2004)

Denikin, A. I., *The Russian Turmoil. Memoirs: Military, Social, and Political* (London: Hutchinson & Co., 1922)

Dieterich, A., *Weltkriegsende an der Mazedonischen Front* (Berlin: Gerhard Stalling, 1925)

DiNardo, R. L., *Breakthrough. The Gorlice–Tarnów Campaign, 1915* (Santa Barbara, CA: Praeger, 2010)

——, *Invasion. The Conquest of Serbia, 1915* (Santa Barbara, CA: Praeger, 2015)

——, 'The Limits of Envelopment: The Invasion of Serbia, 1915', *The Historian*, Vol. 78, No. 3 (2016), pp. 486–503.

Dowling, T. C., *The Brusilov Offensive* (Bloomington, IN: Indiana University Press, 2008)

Dutton, D., *The Politics of Diplomacy. Britain and France in the Balkans in the First World War* (London and New York: I. B. Tauris, 1998)

Edmonds, Sir J. E. and H. R. Davies, *Military Operations. Italy, 1915–1919* (London: HMSO, 1949)

Falkenhayn, E. von, *General Headquarters 1914–1916 and Its Critical Decisions* (London: Hutchinson & Co., 1919)

——, *Der Feldzug der 9. Armee gegen die Rumänen und Russen 1916/17* (2 vols., Berlin: E. S. Mittler & Sohn, 1921)

Falls, C., *Military Operations Macedonia* [Vol. I]. *From the Outbreak of War to the Spring of 1917* (London: HMSO, 1933)

———, *Military Operations Macedonia* [Vol. II]. *From the Spring of 1917 to the End of the War* (London: HMSO, 1935)

Figes, O., *A People's Tragedy. The Russian Revolution 1891–1924* (London: Jonathan Cape, 1996)

Flex, W., *Die Russische Frühjahroffensive 1916* (Oldenburg: Gerhard Stalling, 1919)

Foerster, W. (ed.), *Mackensen. Briefe und Aufzeichnungen des Generalfeldmarschalls aus Krieg und Frieden* (Leipzig: Bibliographisches Institut, 1938)

Franchet d'Espèrey, L., 'Les Armées Alliées en Orient: Du 18 Juin au 30 Septembre 1918: I', *Revue des Deux Mondes*, Vol. 47, No. 1 (September 1938), pp. 5–33.

———, 'Les Armées Alliées en Orient: Du 18 Juin au 30 Septembre 1918: II', *Revue des Deux Mondes*, Vol. 47, No. 2 (September 1938), pp. 241–65.

François, H. von, *Gorlice 1915. Der Karpathendurchbruch und die Befreiung von Galizien* (Leipzig: K. F. Koehler, 1922)

French, D., *British Strategy and War Aims 1914–1916* (London: Allen & Unwin, 1986)

Fuhrmann, J. T., *Rasputin. The Untold Story* (New York: John Wiley & Sons, 2013)

Fuller, Jr., W. C., *The Foe Within. Fantasies of Treason and the End of Imperial Russia* (Ithaca & London: Cornell University Press, 2006)

Gatti, A., *Caporetto. Dal Diario di Guerra Inedito (Maggio–Dicembre 1917)* (Bologna: Società Editrice il Mulino 1964)

Gerwarth, R. *The Vanquished. Why the First World War Failed to End, 1917–1923* (London: Penguin Books, 2017; first publ. 2016)

Glaise-Horstenau, E. *Österreich-Ungarns Letzter Krieg 1914–1918* (7 vols., Vienna: Verlag der Militärwissenschaftlichen Mitteilungen, 1931–8)

Golder, F. A. (ed.), *Documents of Russian History 1914–1917* (Stanford, CA: The Century Co., 1927)

Golovine, N. N., 'The Great Battle in Galicia (1914): A Study in Strategy', *The Slavonic Review*, Vol. 5, No. 13 (June 1926), pp. 25–47.

———, *The Russian Army in the World War* (New Haven: Yale University Press, 1931)

———, *The Russian Campaign of 1914. The Beginning of the War and Operations in East Prussia*, trans. A. G. S. Muntz (Fort Leavenworth, KS: Command & General Staff School Press, 1933)

Gooch, J., *The Italian Army and the First World War* (Cambridge: Cambridge University Press, 2014)

Gorlitskaia operatsiia. Sbornik dokumentov mirovoi imperialisticheskoi voiny na russkom fronte (1914–1917) (Moscow: Voenizdat, 1941)

Görlitz, W. (ed.), *The Kaiser and His Court. The Diaries, Note Books and Letters of Admiral Georg Alexander von Müller, Chief of the Naval Cabinet, 1914–1918* (London: Macdonald & Co., 1961; first publ. 1959)

Greenhalgh, E., *Victory Through Coalition. Britain and France During the First World War* (Cambridge: Cambridge University Press, 2005)

———, *Foch in Command. The Forging of a First World War General* (Cambridge: Cambridge University Press, 2011)

———, *The French Army and the First World War* (Cambridge: Cambridge University Press, 2014)

Gudmundsson, B. I., *Stormtroop Tactics. Innovation in the German Army, 1914–1918* (Westport, CT: Praeger, 1989)

Gumz, J. E., *The Resurrection and Collapse of Empire in Habsburg Serbia, 1914–1918* (Cambridge: Cambridge University Press, 2013; first publ. 2009)

Hall, R. C., *Balkan Breakthrough. The Battle of Dobro Pole 1918* (Bloomington, IN: Indiana University Press, 2010)

Hamilton, R. F. and H. H. Herwig (eds.), *War Planning 1914* (Cambridge: Cambridge University Press, 2013; first publ. 2010)

Hasegawa, T., *The February Revolution, Petrograd, 1917. The End of the Tsarist Regime and the Birth of Dual Power* (Leiden and Boston: Brill, 2017; first publ. 1981)

Hastings, M., *Catastrophe. Europe Goes to War 1914* (London: William Collins, 2013)

Herwig, H. H., *The First World War. Germany and Austria–Hungary 1914–1918* (London: Arnold, 1997)

Hindenburg, P. von, *Out of My Life*, trans. F. A. Holt (London: Cassell and Company, 1920)

Hoffmann, M., *War Diaries and Other Papers*, trans. E. Sutton (2 vols., London: Martin Secker, 1929)

Hutečka, J., *Men Under Fire. Motivation, Morale and Masculinity among Czech Soldiers in the Great War, 1914–1918* (New York and Oxford: Berghahn, 2020)

Isnenghi, M. and G. Rochat, *La Grande Guerra 1914–1918* (Milan: Sansoni, 2004; first publ. 2000)

Janßen, K.-H., *Der Kanzler und der General. Die Führungskrise um Bethmann Hollweg und Falkenhayn (1914–1916)* (Göttingen: Musterschmidt, 1967)

Jeřábek, R., *Potiorek. General im Schatten von Sarajevo* (Vienna: Verlag Styria, 1991)

Kabisch, E., *Der Rumänien Krieg 1916* (Berlin: Otto Schlegel, 1938)

Kamenskii, M. P., *Gibel' XX korpusa 8/21 fevralia 1915 goda (Po arkhivnym materialam Shtaba 10 armii)* (Petrograd: Gosudarstvennoe Izdatel'stvo, 1921)

Katkov, G., *Russia 1917. The February Revolution* (New York: Harper & Row, 1967)

——, *Russia 1917. The Kornilov Affair. Kerensky and the Break-up of the Russian Army* (London and New York: Longman, 1980)

Kerensky, A. F., *The Prelude to Bolshevism. The Kornilov Rebellion* (London: T. Fisher Unwin, 1919)

——, *The Catastrophe. Kerensky's Own Story of the Russian Revolution* (London and New York: D. Appleton & Co., 1927)

Kerner, R. J., 'Austro-Hungarian War-Aims in the Winter of 1915–1916 as Revealed by Secret Documents', *Journal of International Relations*, Vol. 10, No. 4 (April 1920), pp. 444–70.

Kettle, M., *The Allies and the Russian Collapse. March 1917–March 1918* (London: Andre Deutsch, 1981)

——, *The Road to Intervention. March–November 1918* (London: Routledge, 1988)

Khol'msen, I. A., *Mirovaia voina. Nashi operatsii na vostochno-Prusskom fronte zimoiu 1915 g.* (Paris: V. Beilinson, 1935)

Knox, Sir A., *With the Russian Army 1914–1917* (2 vols., London: Hutchinson & Co., 1921)

Kondzerovskii, P. K., *V stavke verkhovnogo. 1914–1917* (Paris: n.p., 1967)

Krauss, A., *Die Ursachen unserer Niederlage. Erinnerungen und Urteile aus dem Weltkrieg* (Munich: J. F. Lehmanns, 1921)

——, *Das 'Wunder von Karfreit' im besonderen der Durchbruch bei Flitsch und die Bezwingung des Tagliamento* (Munich: J. F. Lehmanns, 1926)

Lemke, M. K., *250 dnei v tsarskoi stavke (25 sentiabria 1915–2 iiulia 1916)* (Petersburg: Gosudarstvennoe Izdatel'stvo, 1920)

Lenin, V. I., *Collected Works* (45 vols. Moscow: Progress Publishers, 1960–70)

Leonhard, J., *Pandora's Box. A History of the First World War*, trans. P. Camiller (Cambridge, MA: Harvard University Press, 2018)

Lieven, D., *The End of Tsarist Russia: The March to World War I and Revolution* (London: Viking, 2015)

Liulevicius, V. G., *War Land on the Eastern Front. Culture, National Identity, and German Occupation in World War I* (Cambridge: Cambridge University Press, 2004)

Lloyd, N., *Hundred Days. The End of the Great War* (London: Viking, 2013)

——, *Passchendaele. A New History* (London: Viking, 2017)

——, *The Western Front. A History of the Great War, 1914–1918* (New York: W. W. Norton, 2021)

Lloyd George, D., *War Memoirs of David Lloyd George* (2 vols., London: Odhams Press, 1933–6)

Lodzinskaia operatsiia. Sbornik dokumentov mirovoi imperialisticheskoi voiny na russkom fronte (1914–1917) (Moscow: Voenizdat, 1936)

Luckett, R., *The White Generals. An Account of the White Movement and the Russian Civil War* (London: Routledge & Kegan Paul, 1987; first publ. 1971)

Ludendorff, E., *My War Memories 1914–1918* (2 vols., London: Hutchinson & Co., 1919)

——, *The General Staff and Its Problems*, trans. F. A. Holt (2 vols., London: Hutchinson & Co., 1920)

Lyon, J. M. B., ' "A Peasant Mob": The Serbian Army on the Eve of the Great War', *The Journal of Military History*, Vol. 61, No. 3 (July 1997), pp. 481–502.

——, *Serbia and the Balkan Front, 1914. The Outbreak of the Great War* (London: Bloomsbury, 2015)

Main, S. J., 'Gas on the Eastern Front during the First World War (1915–1917)', *Journal of Slavic Military Studies*, Vol. 28, No. 1 (2015), pp. 99–132.

Mangone, A., *Diaz: Da Caporetto al Piave a Vittorio Veneto* (Milan: Frassinelli, 1987)

Manteyer, G. de (ed.), *Austria's Peace Offer, 1916–1917* (London: Constable & Co., 1921)

Martynov, E. I., *Tsarskaia armiia v fevral'skom perevorote* (Leningrad: Voyennaia tipografiia Upr. Delami Narkomvoyenmor I RVS SSR, 1927)

Marwitz, G. von der, *Weltkriegsbriefe*, ed. E. von Tschischwitz (Berlin: Steiniger-Verlage, 1940)

Massie, R. K., *Nicholas and Alexandra* (London: Victor Gollancz, 1968)

McMeekin, S., *The Russian Origins of the First World War* (Cambridge, MA: Harvard University Press, 2011)

——, *July 1914. Countdown to War* (London: Icon Books, 2013)

——, *The Russian Revolution. A New History* (New York: Basic Books, 2017)

Medlin, V. D. and R. P. Browder (eds.), *V. D. Nabokov and the Russian Provisional Government, 1917* (New Haven and London: Yale University Press, 1976)

Menning, B. W., *Bayonets Before Bullets. The Imperial Russian Army, 1861–1914* (Bloomington and Indianapolis, IN: Indiana University Press, 1992)

Michaelis, H., E. Schraepler and G. Scheel (eds.), *Ursachen und Folgen. Vom deutschen Zusammenbruch 1918 und 1945 bis zur staatlichen Neuordnung Deutschlands in der Gegenwart. Die Wende des ersten Weltkrieges und der Beginn der innerpolitischen Wandlung 1916/1917* (Berlin: Herbert Wendler & Co., 1958)

——, *Ursachen und Folgen. Vom deutschen Zusammenbruch 1918 und 1945 bis zur staatlichen Neuordnung Deutschlands in der Gegenwart. Der Militärische Zusammenbruch und das Ende des Kaiserreichs* (Berlin: Herbert Wendler & Co., n.d.)

Ministère de la Guerre, *Les Armées Françaises dans la Grande Guerre* (Paris: Imprimerie Nationale, 1922–39)

Ministero della Guerra, *L'Esercito Italiano nella Grande Guerra (1915–1918)* (7 vols., Rome: Provveditorato Generale dello Stato Libreria, 1927–88)

Ministerul de Razboi, *România în Războiul Mondial 1916–1919* (4 vols., Bucharest: Imprimeria Nationala, 1934–46)

Mitrović, A., *Serbia's Great War 1914–1918* (London: Hurst, 2007)

Mombauer, A. (ed. and trans.), *The Origins of the First World War. Diplomatic and Military Documents* (Manchester: Manchester University Press, 2013)

Mondini, M., *Il Capo. La Grande Guerra del Generale Luigi Cadorna* (Bologna: Società Editrice il Mulino, 2017)

Murray, W. and A. R. Millett (eds.), *Military Effectiveness. Volume I: The First World War* (Winchester, MA: Allen & Unwin, 1988)

Nastuplenie iugo-zapadnogo fronta v mae-iiune 1916 goda. Sbornik dokumentov mirovoi imperialisticheskoi voiny na russkom fronte (1914–1917) (Moscow: Voenizdat, 1940)

Noikov, S., *Zashto ne pobedikhme 1915–1918* (Sofia: Army Military Publishing, 1922)

Oleinikov, A. V., *Uspeshnye generaly zabytoi voiny* (Moscow: Veche, 2014)

Paléologue, M., *An Ambassador's Memoirs*, trans. F. A. Holt (3 vols., London: Hutchinson & Co., 1925)

Palmer, A., *The Gardeners of Salonika* (London: Andre Deutsch, 1965)

Pipes, R., *The Russian Revolution 1899–1919* (London: Collins Harvill, 1990)

Podorozhnyi, N. E., *Narochskaia operatsiia v marte 1916 g. na russkom fronte mirovoi voiny* (Moscow: Gosudarstvennoye Voyennoye Izdatel'stvo Narkomata Oborony Soyuza SSR, 1938)

Polzer-Hoditz, Count A., *The Emperor Karl* (London and New York: Putnam, 1930)

Rauchensteiner, M., *The First World War and the End of the Habsburg Monarchy, 1914–1918*, trans. A. J. Kay and A. Güttel-Bellert (Vienna: Böhlau Verlag, 2014; first publ. 1993)

Redlich, J., *Emperor Francis Joseph of Austria. A Biography* (London: Macmillan & Co., 1929)

Reichsarchiv, *Der Weltkrieg 1914 bis 1918* (15 vols., Berlin: E. S. Mittler & Sohn, 1925–44)

Robbins, R. G. Jr, *Overtaken by the Night. One Russian's Journey Through Peace, War, Revolution, & Terror* (Pittsburgh, PA: University of Pittsburgh Press, 2017)

Robinson, P., 'A Study of Grand Duke Nikolai Nikolaevich as Supreme Commander of the Russian Army, 1914–1915', *The Historian*, Vol. 75, No. 3 (Fall 2013), pp. 475–498.

——, *Grand Duke Nikolai Nikolaevich. Supreme Commander of the Russian Army* (DeKalb, IL: Northern Illinois University Press, 2014)

Rodzianko, M. V., *The Reign of Rasputin. An Empire's Collapse*, trans. C. Zvegintzoff (London: A. M. Philpot, 1927)

Romeo di Colloredo, P., *Luigi Cadorna. Una Biografia Militare* (Agosta: Soldiershop Publishing, 2018)

Rostunov, I. I., *Russkii front pervoi mirovoi voiny* (Moscow: Nauka, 1976)

Rothenberg, G. E., *The Army of Francis Joseph* (West Lafayette, IN: Purdue University Press, 1976)

Sanborn, J. A., *Imperial Apocalypse. The Great War and the Destruction of the Russian Empire* (Oxford: Oxford University Press, 2015; first publ. 2014)

Sarrail, M., *Mon Commandement en Orient* (Paris: Ernest Flammarion, 1920)

Schiaparelli, A., *La Battaglia del Piave (15–25 Giugno 1918)* (Torino: Istituto Nazionale per le Biblioteche dei Soldati, 1922)

Schindler, J. R., *Isonzo. The Forgotten Sacrifice of the Great War* (Westport, CT: Praeger, 2001)

——, 'Disaster on the Drina: The Austro-Hungarian Army in Serbia, 1914', *War in History*, Vol. 9, No. 2 (2002), pp. 159–95.

——, 'Steamrollered in Galicia: The Austro-Hungarian Army and the Brusilov Offensive, 1916', *War in History*, Vol. 10, No. 1 (2003), pp. 27–59.

——, *Fall of the Double Eagle. The Battle for Galicia and the Demise of Austria–Hungary* (Lincoln, NE: Potomac Books, 2015)

Scott J. B. (ed.), *Official Statements of War Aims and Peace Proposals. December 1916 to November 1918* (Washington DC: Carnegie Endowment for International Peace, 1921)

Sebestyen, V., *Lenin the Dictator* (London: Weidenfeld & Nicolson, 2017)

Seeckt, H. von, *Aus Meinem Leben 1866–1917* (Leipzig: V. Hase & Koehler, 1941)

Shapland, A. and E. Stefani (eds.), *Archaeology Behind the Battle Lines. The Macedonian Campaign (1915–19) and Its Legacy* (Oxford: Routledge, 2017)

Showalter, D. E., *Tannenberg. Clash of Empires, 1914* (Washington DC: Potomac Books, 2004; first publ. 1991)

Silberstein, G. E., *The Troubled Alliance. German–Austrian Relations 1914 to 1917* (Lexington, KY: University Press of Kentucky, 1970)

Skoko, S., *Vojvoda Radomir Putnik* (2 vols., Belgrade: Beogradski izdavačko-grafički zavod, 1984)

Smith, D., *Rasputin* (London: Macmillan, 2016)

Sondhaus, L., *Franz Conrad von Hötzendorf. Architect of the Apocalypse* (Boston: Humanities Press, 2000)

Stevenson, D., *1914–1918. The History of the First World War* (London: Penguin, 2005; first publ. 2004)

——, *With Our Backs to the Wall. Victory and Defeat in 1918* (London: Penguin, 2012; first publ. 2011)

——, *1917. War, Peace, and Revolution* (Oxford: Oxford University Press, 2017)

Stone, D. R., *The Russian Army in the Great War. The Eastern Front, 1914–1917* (Lawrence, KS: University Press of Kansas, 2015)

Stone, N., 'Army and Society in the Habsburg Monarchy, 1900–1914', *Past & Present*, No. 33 (April 1966), pp. 95–111.

——, 'Hungary and the Crisis of July 1914', *Journal of Contemporary History*, Vol. 1, No. 3 (July 1966), pp. 153–70.

——, 'Moltke–Conrad: Relations Between the Austro-Hungarian and German General Staffs, 1909–14', *The Historical Journal*, Vol. IX, No. 2 (1966), pp. 201–28.

——, *The Eastern Front 1914–1917* (London: Penguin Books, 1998; first publ. 1975)

Strachan, H., *The First World War. Volume I, To Arms* (Oxford: Oxford University Press, 2001)

Strategicheskii ocherk voiny 1914–1918 g.g. (7 vols., Moscow: Vysshii voennyi redaktsionnyi sovet, 1920–23)

Sturdza, M., *Avec l'armée Roumaine (1916–1918)* (Paris: Hachette, 1918)

Sukhanov, N. N., *The Russian Revolution 1917*, ed. and trans. J. Carmichael (Princeton, NJ: Princeton University Press, 1984; first publ. 1955)

Tanenbaum, J. K., *General Maurice Sarrail 1856–1929. The French Army and Left-Wing Politics* (Chapel Hill, NC: University of North Carolina Press, 1974)

Thompson, M., *The White War. Life and Death on the Italian Front, 1915–1919* (London: Faber & Faber, 2008)

Torrey, G. E., *The Romanian Battlefront in World War I* (Lawrence, KS: University Press of Kansas, 2011)

—— (ed.), *General Henri Berthelot and Romania: Mémoires et Correspondance, 1916–1919* (Boulder, CO: East European Monographs, 1987)

Tunstall, G. A., *Blood on the Snow. The Carpathian Winter War of 1915* (Lawrence, KS: University Press of Kansas, 2010)

——, *Written in Blood. The Battles for Fortress Przemyśl in WW1* (Bloomington, IN: Indiana University Press, 2016)

——, *The Austro-Hungarian Army and the First World War* (Cambridge: Cambridge University Press, 2021)

Urbanski von Ostrymiecz, A., *Conrad von Hötzendorf. Soldat und Mensch* (Graz: Ulrich Mosers, 1939)

Uspenskii, A. A., *Na voine: vostochnaia Prussiia-Litva, 1914–1915* (Kaunas, Lithuania: n.p., 1932)

Varshavsko-Ivangorodskaia operatsiia. Sbornik dokumentov mirovoi imperialisticheskoi voiny na russkom fronte (1914–1917) (Moscow: Voenizdat, 1938)

Veliki rat Srbije za oslobođenje i ujedinjenje Srba, Hrvata i Slovenaca (28 vols., Belgrade: Glavni đeneralštab, 1924–37)

Vinogradov, V. N., 'Romania in the First World War: The Years of Neutrality, 1914–1916', *The International History Review*, Vol. 14, No. 3 (August 1992), pp. 452–61.

Vostochno-Prusskaia operatsiia. Sbornik dokumentov mirovoi imperialisticheskoi voiny na russkom fronte (1914–1917) (Moscow: Voenizdat, 1939)

Vulliamy, C. E. (ed.), *The Nicky–Sunny Letters. Correspondence of the Tsar and Tsaritsa 1914–1917*, trans. A. L. Hynes (Hattiesburg, MS: Academic International, 1970)

Ward Price, G., *The Story of the Salonica Army* (London: Hodder & Stoughton, 1918)

Watson, A., *Ring of Steel. Germany and Austria–Hungary at War, 1914–1918* (London: Penguin Books, 2014)

——, *The Fortress. The Great Siege of Przemyśl* (London: Allen Lane, 2019)

Wawro, G., *A Mad Catastrophe. The Outbreak of World War I and the Collapse of the Habsburg Empire* (New York: Basic Books, 2015; first publ. 2014)

Weber, F., *Menschenmauer am Isonzo* (Berlin: Steyrermühl, 1932)

——, *Sturm an der Piave* (Berlin: Steyrermühl, 1932)

Wheeler-Bennett, J. W., *Brest-Litovsk. The Forgotten Peace. March 1918* (London: Macmillan, 1963)

Wilcox, V., *Morale and the Italian Army during the First World War* (Cambridge: Cambridge University Press, 2018; first publ. 2016)

——(ed.), *Italy in the Era of the Great War* (Leiden and Boston: Brill, 2019)

Wildman, A. K., *The End of the Russian Imperial Army, Volume II. The Road to Soviet Power and Peace* (Princeton, NJ: Princeton University Press, 1987)

Woodward, D. R., *Lloyd George and the Generals* (London and Toronto: Associated University Presses, 1983)

——(ed.), *The Military Correspondence of Field-Marshal Sir William Robertson, Chief of the Imperial General Staff, December 1915–February 1918* (London: Bodley Head for the Army Records Society, 1989)

Zaionchkovskii, A. M., *Mirovaia voina 1914–1918 gg.* (2 vols., Moscow: Voenizdat, 1938)

Zeman, Z. A. B. (ed.), *Germany and the Revolution in Russia 1915–1918. Documents from the Archives of the German Foreign Ministry* (London: Oxford University Press, 1958)

Index

Adler, Victor, 496
air power: German
   reconnaissance, 66, 143, 177,
   368; Russian inferiority, 143;
   German response to Brusilov
   Offensive, 266; increases in
   Hindenburg Programme, 315;
   increase in Italy, 448; at Battle
   of the Piave, 453; at Battle of
   Dobro Pole, 482; Allied
   advantage, 488
Albania, 175, 182, 321, 471, 485
Alekseev, General Mikhail:
   overview, 507; Galician offensive,
   62–3; command of Northwest
   Front, 121–2; appointed Tsar's
   Chief of Staff, 172–3; command
   of new Western Front, 161;
   withdraws troops from Poland,
   150–51, 160–61; failure of New
   Year offensive, 198–201;
   disappointment with Tsar,
   201; plans Lake Naroch
   offensive, 213–14; reaction to
   failure of Lake Naroch offensive,
   227; advises Tsar on importance
   of further attacks, 235–6;
   conference at *Stavka*, 237; doubts
   over Brusilov Offensive, 250–51;
   cancels attack on Vilnius, 258–9;

reassures Brusilov, 259–60;
   sceptical of Romania's entry into
   war, 278–80; warns Tsar of lack
   of army morale, 291; fails to
   warn Tsar against Rasputin,
   292–3; ill-health, 292–3; orders
   Ivanov to restore order in
   Petrograd, 324–5; encourages
   Tsar's abdication, 326–8; informs
   Tsar he is under arrest, 331;
   becomes Commander-in-Chief,
   333; warns of degradation of
   Russian Army, 334–6; relieved of
   command, 362–3; Kerensky's
   Chief of Staff, 391; resigns as
   Chief of Staff, 406; joins
   Volunteer Army, 435; death with
   Volunteer Army, 504–5;
   achievements, 506
Alexander, Crown Prince of
   Serbia, 6, 217, 459, 511–12
Alexander, King of Greece, 372
Alexander Mikhailovich, Grand
   Duke, 331
Alexandra, Tsarina of Russia:
   under Rasputin's influence,
   152–3; persuades Tsar to take
   command of army, 169–70;
   influence on Russian politics,
   210–11, 233; warns Tsar